The Wiley Book
of Business Quotations

The Wiley Book
of Business Quotations

Henry Ehrlich

John Wiley & Sons, Inc.

New York • Chichester • Weinheim • Brisbane • Singapore • Toronto

For Margie

Published by John Wiley & Sons, Inc.
Published simultaneously in Canada

Library of Congress Cataloging-in-Publication Data:

The Wiley book of business quotations / [compiled by] Henry Ehrlich.
    p. cm.
   Includes index.
   ISBN 0-471-18207-9 (cloth : alk. paper)
   1. Business—Quotations, maxims, etc. I. Ehrlich, Henry.
PN6084.B87W55 1998
650—dc21   98-13845

Printed in the United States of America

10 9 8 7 6 5 4 3 2 1

CONTENTS

ACKNOWLEDGMENTS

Several people were extremely helpful in putting this book together. First, for research, I owe a great deal to Bethany Tarbell, without whom this book would not be a mile wide, and Joan L. Silverman, without whom it would not be a full inch deep. Nina Rodriguez and my sons, Mickey and Sam, also were kind enough to spend some of their time off from school at various levels going through magazines at the Brooklyn Public Library.

I would also like to thank my wife, Tamara Glenny, for preliminary copyediting, which brought order out of chaos, and my father, Eugene Ehrlich, author of many dictionaries and other reference books, for his help in finding an accessible format and for reading the galleys.

In addition, I am grateful to three people at John Wiley & Sons: editor Judith McCarthy, who adopted the project enthusiastically, worked with me for a year, and, most important, told me how entertaining she found the selection; Elaine O'Neal, editorial assistant, who always cheerfully kept the process going; and PJ Dempsey, formerly of Wiley, who thought of me when the idea of a new business quote book came up, embraced my vision of the book, and steered it through the acquisition process.

Finally, I would like to thank the Business Library of the New York Public Library at Cadman Plaza in Brooklyn. I can say categorically that going through real newspapers and magazines is infinitely preferable to reading them online.

INTRODUCTION

Business has plenty of drama, but it sometimes seems to need better dialogue. I hope that this volume shows that the dialogue isn't that bad after all. While most of it isn't up to Oscar Wilde's standard—except for Oscar Wilde himself—there are wit, insight, conviction, and authority from the best-known figures in world business, as well as from some of the most obscure. There are also examples of pomposity, myopia, and mendacity.

This book tries as much as possible to really be about business and is compiled largely of statements from the mouths and pens of people who have been shaping the modern business world on scales both large and small. As a corporate speechwriter for nearly 20 years, I have found most such volumes are full of material about many things but not particularly about the themes that have been developing over the past generation—for example, the computer revolution; the impact of deregulation on finance; the demise of the paternalistic, middle-management heavy corporation; globalization; the rise of the diverse workforce; and the embrace of market economics in countries around the world.

The material is drawn preponderantly from the business press. That is where the live public voice of business is found. Even such widely collected, trenchant thinkers as Peter Drucker seem to speak in fresher terms when talking to reporters than in their own published work. That's why I've only included Drucker items that have appeared in the press, such as his 1994 pronouncement in *Fortune* on one of the shibboleths of modern management:

> Leadership is all hype. We've had three great leaders in this century—Hitler, Stalin, and Mao.

Many of the entries in this book haven't been read since the magazines disappeared from your dentist's waiting room. Other sources include public speeches, journals, radio and television, and books.

The hierarchy of sources is headed by people directly engaged in manufacturing, managing, buying and selling, and other moneymaking activities, followed by supporting fields such as economics, consulting, accounting, and law, and by interested parties such as regulators, politicians, journalists, and customers.

It's not that I don't like books of "great" quotations—they belong in any reference library, and there's no shortage of them—it's just that I find most to be irrelevant to the run-of-the-mill sphere of business rhetoric. The words of German poets or philosophers sound disingenuous in the mouths of most executives. Military officers are more convincing, provided we look at them in their role as managers of large organizations rather than as combat commanders.

It takes a titan like Jack Welch, CEO of GE, interviewed in the *Harvard Business Review* in 1989, to cut through some of the trappings and put the subject into perspective:

> People always overestimate how complex business is. This isn't rocket science; we've chosen one of the world's more simple professions.

The Real Issues

Most business writing doesn't deal with life-or-death issues anyway. It deals with a relatively small number of subjects with immediate implications for relatively few people. In such cases, we are better served by knowing what other people have said about that subject instead of what Sun-Tzu said about the art of war. Even in extreme cases, jobs lost in a corporate reorganization are not the same as lives lost in combat.

I haven't gone out of my way to balance any particular section with opposing points of view—the selection reflects what's out there in nonspecialist publications. Generally, the bias is toward advancing the dominant business argument on any subject, such as free trade (pro) or expansive use of tort law (con).

I have done my best to bring non-American, non-Western voices into this book, reflecting the inevitable further globalization of the world economy. In addition, I have included a number of idiosyncratic subjects, such as the influence of Yogi Berra on contemporary business rhetoric, from which readers can draw their own conclusions.

A Broad Definition of Quotation

In some cases, the definition of what constitutes a quotation is stretched. The quote may contain an idea that is more important than the words used to express it. It may consist of a factoid or piece of information that can readily shed useful light on a subject. For example, there's this item from a 1995 column by Laura Pedersen in the *New York Times*:

> Nynex, the [then] phone company in New York, actively recruits Hispanic, Asian, and other minority workers. The benefits are not just theoretical. A South Korean employee, for example, told his bosses that the number 4 could be considered unlucky back home; Nynex took that into account when assigning phone numbers to Korean customers.

As a speechwriter with a general practice, I frequently wish that I had ready access to such nuggets.

In other instances, the quote may consist of statistics, such as the numbers of computers in different countries or the proportion of corporate sponsorship for the arts compared to those for sports. Statistics do become dated, but they don't date all that fast. I have chosen ones that provide revealing snapshots of business at a particular time and that with updating could provide the basis for a compelling point.

Certain items, while well written, shouldn't be quoted verbatim. They appear here because they may serve as a useful reference point for a tempered discussion of the subject at hand—notably, the John Le Carré entry in the section on the defense industry.

Context

The words by themselves may not be enough, so I have provided notes where necessary to explain the context of a quotation as well as something about the person who said it. Using a quotation without regard to the larger context may be setting yourself up for embarrassment.

Professor Jerry Tarver of the University of Richmond, one of the foremost speech-writing teachers in the United States, tells a story about a hot faculty argument in which a teacher rose and gave an eloquent call to action, finishing with the peroration, "As Shakespeare said, 'There is a tide in the affairs of men, / Which, taken at the flood, leads on to fortune . . .'" The head of the English department rose and thanked him for his stirring rendering of Brutus's speech, "Just before he made the biggest mistake of his life." In the next scene, Brutus and his confederates march on Philippi, lose, Brutus kills himself, and the rest, as they say, is history.

Business writing offers similar opportunities for embarrassment. I came across a rather sensible speech about that most difficult of business subjects—ethics. For me, its credibility—carefully built in the first 19 minutes—was undone by the conclusion:

> When Oliver Cromwell reorganized his army, he said he wanted honest leaders. "When leaders are honest," he said, "honest men follow." And I bet every one of them could probably look themselves in the mirror and smile.

Oliver Cromwell? History does not relate whether they looked in the mirror before they beheaded King Charles I or massacred all those Irish landowners. But at least they did it honestly.

In certain cases, the quote may be very lengthy, with only a sentence or two that might qualify as a quotation in the traditional pithy, epigrammatic sense. I have supplied the larger quotation so that the reader can understand what it really means. For example, Warren Buffett wrote to his shareholders in his 1994 annual report:

> Many CEOs attain their positions in part because they possess an abundance of animal spirits and ego. If an executive is heavily endowed with these qualities—which, it should be acknowledged, sometimes have their advantages—they won't disappear when he reaches the top. When a CEO is encouraged by his advisers to make deals, he responds much as would a teenage boy who is encouraged by his father to have a normal sex life. It's not a push that he needs.

The first two sentences help tell the full story, but anyone could have written them. It's the last two sentences that really make it worth quoting Warren Buffett.

The Pace of Change

The blistering pace of change is a dominant characteristic of the contemporary business environment. One of the weaknesses of any anthology that attempts to be contemporary is that a line must be drawn somewhere while events continue to unfold. In the month before this volume went into production, for example, fear of deflation began to take hold after generations of more or less steady concern about inflation. The economies of South Korea and Indonesia were threatening to collapse. And the U.S. Justice Department was mounting a serious antitrust assault on Microsoft.

There was no way for me, as the compiler, to keep up with these developments in any comprehensive way. But I'd like to think that there was no compelling need to do so, because in the preceding 12 months, my helpers and I had done our best to chronicle the beginnings of these stories. The headlines on a given day are part of an ongoing story. If one must write a speech in 2001 on the plight of the Japanese financial system, it might help to know that in April of 1997, Goro Tatsumi, founder and president of the financial firm Kosei, said:

> There can be no soft landing, because there is nowhere to land. We have to adapt or prepare for death.

Contrast that with the August 1987 hubris of Kaneshisa Nishida of the Long-Term Credit Bank of Japan:

> We learned the bond market in a couple of years. Once we start to really buy stocks, we will move quickly.

Taken together, you've got the basis of a compelling perspective on the protracted decline of Japan as an economic power—which may, after all, rise again. If there is another edition of this book a few years down the road, the selection will reflect that next wave of change.

How to Use This Book

The table of contents contains 44 separate sections, arranged alphabetically, and hundreds more subsections under those umbrellas, also arranged alphabetically. The index is by the person quoted and by the subject.

Within the hundreds of sections, the quotes are mostly arranged chronologically and sometimes on the basis of some connection between entries. Where available, the first quotations will provide some historical perspective. For example, the section on free trade begins with figures such as Benjamin Franklin and Ralph Waldo Emerson; clearly, certain subjects have been with us for a long time and the combination of the venerable with the contemporary makes for a more interesting discussion. In other cases, such as computer-related entries, the selection doesn't go back that far.

1.1 ADVERTISING

Half my advertising is wasted, and the trouble is I don't know which half.

> LORD LEVERHULME, founder of the pharmaceutical firm Unilever, quoted in David Ogilvy, *Confessions of an Advertising Man* (Atheneum, 1963)

The question is not whether advertising works but how much it works. It is not whether advertising will achieve a sales blip, but whether it will achieve a sufficiently big blip to pay for itself and more.

> WINSTON FLETCHER, chairman of the British advertising agency Delaney Fletcher Bozell, quoted in the *Financial Times,* May 5, 1997

We [the advertising industry] do things in much the same way as we did 50, 60, or even 70 years ago. The answers may not be wrong, but we haven't experimented to see whether they are or not.

> MARTIN SORRELL, CEO of the advertising and public relations conglomerate WPP, quoted in the *Financial Times,* March 14, 1997

The advertising business used to be almost entirely a business of middle-aged white guys from the suburbs. Today, it's almost entirely a business of young white guys who live in both the city and the suburbs.

> MARK ROBINSON, head of Spike/DDB, movie director Spike Lee's partnership with DDB Needham, quoted in *Fortune,* April 14, 1997

When business is good, it pays to advertise; when business is bad, you've got to advertise.

> ANONYMOUS

If I were starting life over again, I am inclined to think that I would go into the advertising business in preference to almost any other. . . . The general raising of the standards of modern civilization among all groups of people during the past half century would have been impossible without the spreading of the knowledge of higher standards by means of advertising.

> U.S. PRESIDENT FRANKLIN D. ROOSEVELT, quoted in David Ogilvy, *Confessions of an Advertising Man* (Atheneum, 1963)

Advertising nourishes the consuming power of men. It sets up before a man the goal of a better home, better clothing, better food for himself and his family. It spurs individual exertion and greater production.

> WINSTON CHURCHILL, quoted in David Ogilvy, *Confessions of an Advertising Man* (Atheneum, 1963)

Much advertising—indeed all of the most conspicuous and costly advertising—is neither informative nor persuasive.

> JOHN KEY, director of the School of Management Studies, Oxford, quoted in the *Financial Times,* March 14, 1997

Nothing reflects a country and its age better than its advertising.

> JEAN-MARIE DRU, chairman of the French agency BDDP, quoted in the *New Yorker,* April 28 and May 5, 1997

There's no way I can sell the product without selling sex. [The company's ad theme in 1985 was "A hard man is good to find."]

> JERRY WILSON, founder of the exercise equipment company Soloflex, quoted in *Time,* October 21, 1985

The consumer isn't a moron; she is your wife.

> DAVID OGILVY, *Confessions of an Advertising Man* (Atheneum, 1963)

Unless your campaign has a big idea, it will pass like a ship in the night.

> DAVID OGILVY, *Confessions of an Advertising Man* (Atheneum, 1963)

Good advertising can make people buy your product even if it sucks.

> SCOTT ADAMS, *The Dilbert Principle* (HarperBusiness, 1996)

All detergents clean clothes, so you have to go a little bit deeper.

> JANE FITZGIBBON of the advertising agency Ogilvy & Mather, on the use of psychology to distinguish brands, quoted in *Newsweek,* February 13, 1989

You can tell the ideals of a nation by its advertisements.

> NORMAN DOUGLAS (1868–1952), British novelist
> and essayist

The most successful advertisements are usually outside your comfort zone.

> JAMES LOWTHER of the advertising agency M&C
> Saatchi, quoted in *Forbes*, January 13, 1997

I have never met anyone so idiotic as an American adman. Or so smart. Or both. There is more hope and vision in American advertising than in European. In Europe we are more narrow-minded, more local, more national. I'm really inspired by America.

> OLIVIERO TOSCANI of the clothing firm Benetton,
> quoted in the *New York Times Magazine*, June 8,
> 1997

Everything in American advertising is pretty good. It looks the same. It looks American—overfed, oversexed, overpaid.

> OLIVIERO TOSCANI of the clothing firm Benetton,
> quoted in the *New York Times Magazine*, June 8, 1997

If you have to scream louder or whatever, then so what? No one's really worrying about what it's teaching impressionable youth. Hey, I'm in the business of convincing people to buy things they don't need.

> WILLIAM OBERLANDER of the advertising agency Kirshenbaum Bond & Partners, quoted in *Business Week*, August 11, 1997

We'll all be jockeying for position in *Playboy* and *Penthouse*.

> R.J. Reynolds employee, on the new restrictions on
> where tobacco can be advertised, quoted in *Time*,
> June 30, 1997

It's like reaching through someone's TV screen when they're hungry and giving them popcorn.

> NANCY FRIEDMAN of the clothing company Levi
> Strauss & Co., on advertising directly to business
> desktops through PointCast, quoted in the *Wall
> Street Journal*, December 13, 1996

Advertising is a craft, and it has to be learned. It's not something that consumers can do successfully.

> ELLIS VERDI, president of the advertising agency
> DeVito/Verdi, New York agency, on using unsolicited

ideas, quoted in the *New York Times*, October 16, 1997

The greatest risk of all is the risk of going unnoticed.

> Created by the late BILL BERNBACH, cofounder of
> DDB, and used as screensaver at DDB Needham
> worldwide, quoted in the *Wall Street Journal*,
> March 11, 1996

Properly practiced creativity can make one ad do the work of 10.

> Created by the late BILL BERNBACH, cofounder of
> DDB, and used as screensaver at DDB Needham
> worldwide, quoted in the *Wall Street Journal*,
> March 11, 1996

Prohibiting antipathetic advertising [for products like tobacco and alcohol] is a nice, easy, and seemingly cheap way for well-meaning politicians to earn brownie points. But the costs to society—though they may be hidden—are exceptionally high, and the effectiveness of such bans . . . is highly questionable.

> WINSTON FLETCHER, chairman of the British advertising agency Delaney Fletcher Bozell, quoted in the *Financial Times*, May 26, 1997

At cocktail parties, people in the advertising business wince when asked what they do for a living.

> STEPHEN FOX, *The Mirror Makers: A History of American Advertising and Its Creators* (William Morrow, 1984)

1.1.1 Product Placement

If you're noticing the products on the screen, you're probably not grabbed by the story. I doubt that a can of Coke ever sold because it appeared in a movie.

> HAROLD VOGEL of the investment firm Merrill
> Lynch, quoted in *New York*, November 29, 1993

This is just the tip of the iceberg—it's a fraction of the whole but it's very visible. It makes our whole staff feel good.

> DAVID MURREL of the accounting and consulting
> firm KPMG, on the fact that the firm's logo would be
> appearing in movies, a form of placement common
> for tobacco and candy companies, quoted in the
> *Financial Times*, September 22, 1997

1.1.2 The Super Bowl

You get to talk to more people on that program than on any other program you can buy on any other day of the year.

> WILLIAM D. FAUDE of the advertising agency Cramer-Krasselt, quoted in the *New York Times*, January 6, 1991

The game is not a typical football event that caters to male viewers. It really is the convening of American men, women, and children, who gather around the sets to participate in an American ritual.

> THOMAS R. ELROD of Walt Disney Attractions, which operates Walt Disney Company's theme parks, quoted in the *New York Times*, January 6, 1991

A typical 30-second spot on the January 25 football game will cost a record $1.3 million, up from about $1.2 million last year and more than four times the average price of a non–Super Bowl commercial, ad-industry executives say.

> *Wall Street Journal*, January 5, 1998

1.2 CHANGING DEMOGRAPHICS

When the death rate starts increasing, we don't have to do anything but be a recipient of the windfall.

> ROBERT WALTRIP, CEO of the funeral directors Service Corporation International, November 16, 1996

1.3 CORPORATE IDENTITY AND DESIGN

Identity is absolutely worth spending money on. If I were a start-up company, I'd put everything in my business card, even if it was all I had.

> DAVID HERTZ, founder and CEO of Syndesis, which makes Syndecrete, a lightweight concrete used as a decorative surface (his first business card was made out of it), quoted in *Inc.*, January 1993

Watching the television coverage of the Los Angeles riots, Carl Jones and T. J. Walker were struck by how many of the rioters and cleanup volunteers wore red, green, black, and gold sportswear made by their apparel company Cross Colours Inc. . . . Cross Colours makes shirts, jeans, hats, and jackets emblazoned with slogans like "Stop the Violence," "Love Sees No Color," and "Education Is the Key."

> VICKI CONSTAVESPI, *Forbes*, July 20, 1996

Lucent! You're joking! What the heck is that? What does it mean? That name is going to be used for a lot of jokes around the world.

> BO HEDFUS of the Swedish telecommunications equipment manufacturer L. M. Ericsson, responding to the name given to the AT&T equipment spinoff, quoted in *Fortune*, April 29, 1996

When we handled the switch from General Electric to GE, we thought we'd get rid of "the meatball"—the GE logo. But it became clear that people all over the world recognized it.

> HAYES ROTH of the corporate identity firm Landor Associates, quoted in *Strategy & Business*, published by Booz Allen & Hamilton, 1997

Diageo [new name for the conglomerate formed from Guinness and Grand Metropolitan, which owns Burger King, Guinness, Johnny Walker scotch, and Pillsbury, among other brands]. Based on the Latin word for "day" and the Greek word for "world," Diageo captures what this business is all about—bringing pleasure to consumers every day, around the world. The vitality of the name echoes the enjoyment which our brands give to consumers wherever they are.

> Rationale for new name offered by the company, quoted in the *Wall Street Journal*, October 30, 1997

1.4 MARKETING

Every time I reduce the charge for our car by one dollar, I get a thousand new buyers.

> HENRY FORD

There is a commodity in human experience. If it's happened to one person, it has happened to thousands of others.

> Talk show host OPRAH WINFREY, quoted in *Time*, August 8, 1988

Commercial society regards people as bundles of appetites, a conception that turns human beings inside out, leaving nothing to be regarded as inherently private.

> GEORGE F. WILL, *The Pursuit of Happiness and Other Sobering Thoughts* (Harper & Row, 1978)

Good packaging creates companies.

> ELINOR SELANE, principal of BrandEquity International, quoted in *Worth*, May 1995

Our research showed that almost everyone has a can or two of Campbell's soup in the cupboard. The problem was to get them to eat the soup.

> DEL MACAULAY, former package design chief of Campbell's, quoted in *Worth*, May 1995

We overestimated how often people shave.

> STEW LEONARD JR., son of legendary Connecticut supermarket owner (and convicted tax evader) on a 1985 purchase of 80,000 cans of shaving cream offered at $1.29 when they cost $2 elsewhere, quoted in *New York*, October 25, 1993

You can't sell successfully to the black consumer without me.

> JOHN H. JOHNSON, publisher of *Ebony*, quoted in Robert Sobel and David B. Sicilia, *The Entrepreneurs—An American Adventure* (Houghton Mifflin, 1986)

Tide tests as Sylvester Stallone. It doesn't beg the question. It gets your clothes clean.

> Psychological researcher, quoted in *Worth*, May 1995

The things that people take home from the store become a part of their identities.

> DAVID MASTEN of the market research firm Cheskin-Masten, quoted in *Worth*, May 1995

It's hard to get people to relate potato chips to any positive nutritional thought.

> LINDA McCASHION of the National Potato Promotion Board, quoted in the *Wall Street Journal*, September 5, 1996

People do not need snack foods. Our jobs as marketers is to entertain and bring happiness to people.

> DAVID J. GUSTON of the snack-food firm Frito-Lay, quoted in *Fortune*, May 19, 1991

We sell sex. It is never going to go out of style.

> BOB GUCCIONE, publisher, *Penthouse*, quoted in the *Wall Street Journal*, March 22, 1996

The last thing we wanted to do was tell the customer these are better but you'll have to pay more.

> KIRSTEN HEGBERG-PURCEL of the fast-food chain Jack in the Box, on decision to swallow the extra costs of potato starch coating for extra crispness of french fries, quoted in the *Wall Street Journal*, October 24, 1996.

The essence of a megabrand [The Gap] is leveraging your brand into other product categories.

> ADELLE B. KIRK of the consulting firm Kurt Salmon Associates, quoted in *Business Week*, January 27, 1997

I'm not as concerned about communicating a squeaky-clean image for milk as making milk cool and contemporary.

> KURT GRAETZER of the National Fluid Milk Processor Promotion Board, on 1990 ad campaign featuring milk mustaches on celebrities

We found out that not having milk or rice in Hispanic households is not funny; running out of milk means you failed your family.

> JEFF MANNING of the California Milk Processor Board (their "Got Milk?" campaign failed in the Hispanic market because the slogan roughly translates as "Are You Lactating?"), quoted in the *Wall Street Journal*, March 6, 1996

I look in my closet, and if I need it, I design it. If it works for me, it works for the customer.

> DONNA KARAN, fashion designer, quoted in *Fortune*, Autumn/Winter 1993 special issue

There are kinds of things that just don't have any good explanation. I suppose you could say that if it had been a really nice animal, something sympathetic, then maybe nothing would have happened. Suppose I had picked a rooster. Well, that's French, but it doesn't have the same impact.

> RENÉ LACOSTE, in 1973 interview, on choice of alligator as trademark for his shirts, quoted in his obituary, the *New York Times*, October 14, 1996

This Week's Sign That the Apocalypse Is Upon Us. Arby's Beef-of-the-Game advertising spot on Pittsburgh Penguins telecasts features a replay of the most action-packed fight during that evening's game.

> *Sports Illustrated*, October 28, 1996

I'm training kids to fool their friends and neighbors. Money is made from customer inattention, not indifference.

> Movie theater manager, on practice of offering extra toppings to popcorn buyers without telling them that each topping costs more, quoted by Ellen Cohen, *Premiere,* cited in *Forbes,* June 22, 1992

Huge numbers of baby boomers have sophisticated tastes. They want less of the cheap fattening foods at places like McDonald's. As soon as their kids are old enough, they go elsewhere.

> CHERYL RUSSELL, demographer and editor of the newsletter *Boomer Report,* quoted in *Fortune,* November 4, 1996

The Arch Deluxe burger tastes like (ouch!) a Burger King Whopper only with more "glop."

> Consensus of informal marketing survey taken by *Fortune,* November 4, 1996

No one makes bad cars anymore, so you must sell cars on the emotions and the lifestyles they represent.

> Marketing director of the automobile company Volkswagen, on sponsoring a European tour of the rock group Genesis, quoted in the *Economist,* October 17, 1992

We don't know how to sell products based on performance. Everything we sell, we sell on image.

> The late ROBERTO GOIZUETA, CEO of the beverage firm Coca-Cola, on the failure of New Coke, which had been developed after blind taste tests showed that most people liked Pepsi better than Coke, quoted in the *Wall Street Journal,* February 3, 1997

A sweet, brown, fizzy beverage that at once represents the best and worst of American business enterprise . . . Coca-Cola is one of the world's truly nonessential products brilliantly marketed.

> Anonymous commentator, quoted in the *Wall Street Journal,* February 3, 1997

I'm sorry, we're not in the rainbow colors.

> Regional dealer for Coke, after being asked by Ray Kroc to sell him orange soda and root beer as well as Coke, quoted in David Halberstam, *The Fifties* (Villard, 1993)

The world is first a cola world, then an orange world, then a lemon-lime world.

> The late ROBERTO GOIZUETA, CEO of Coca-Cola, quoted in the *Wall Street Journal,* February 3, 1997

Ego is a treacherous and debilitating force. Nowhere is that more true than in marketing and product design.

> ARNOLD HIATT, then-chairman of the shoe company Stride-Rite, interviewed in *Harvard Business Review,* March–April 1992

In the past, if we were trying to sell sushi, we would market it as cold, dead fish.

> BOJANA FAZARINC of the computer firm Hewlett-Packard, quoted in *Fortune,* March 4, 1996

Will the introduction by Carolina Herrera of 212, a fragrance named for Manhattan's [telephone] area code, inspire other perfume makers to bring out brands like 516, evocative of the scent of new money wafting through the Hamptons, in Long Island, or Brooklyn's 718, blended with essences of Lundy's chowder, Vassilaros coffee, Junior's cheesecake, Old London Melba toast, and Nathan's frankfurters?

> STUART ELLIOTT, *New York Times,* September 2, 1997

For all the money we spend on marketing, we know very little about our customers.

> ROBERT THOMAS, president of the automobile firm Nissan Motor Corporation USA, quoted in the *Wall Street Journal,* December 9, 1996

I watch where the cosmetics industry is going and then walk in the opposite direction.

> ANITA RODDICK, founder of the cosmetic firm The Body Shop, quoted in *Harvard Business Review,* July-August 1996

Black people know more about white consumers than white people understand about black consumers.

> THOMAS BURRELL, CEO of the black-owned advertising agency Burrell Communications, quoted in *Fortune,* April 14, 1997

1.4.1 Alcohol

The object [of a nineteenth-century marketing campaign] is to make the whole population use cold drinks instead of warm or tepid, and it will be effected in the course of three years. A single conspicuous barkeeper . . . selling steadily his liquors all cold without an increase in price [would] render it absolutely necessary that the others come into it or lose their customers— they are compelled to do what they could in no other way be induced to undertake.

> RICHARD O. CUMMINGS, *The American Ice Harvests: A Historical Study in Technology, 1800–1849* (Berkeley, 1949)

The brandies are looking at A & E Networks, Crown Royal, and the mass brown goods are looking at ESPN, all the scotches are looking at golf on broadcast and cable. And premium white spirits, gins and vodkas, will look at tennis and the Academy Awards.

> Media executive at agency with a good deal of liquor business, quoted in the *Wall Street Journal*, June 12, 1996

We've come to the conclusion that people drink to get buzzed.

> A brewer's director of brand management, on mediocre sales of nonalcoholic beer, cited in Philip Van Munching, *Beer Blast: The Inside Story of the Brewing Industry's Bizarre Battles for Your Money* (Times Books, 1997)

Beer has been the beverage of male bonding for thousands of years.

> STEVE BROWN of the advertising agency J. Walter Thompson, quoted in the *Wall Street Journal*, February 11, 1985

70,000.

> Number of members in the Frank Bartles and Ed Jaymes fan club in 1987 (Bartles and Jaymes were fictional TV characters created to promote a new brand of wine coolers), cited in *Business Week*, January 12, 1987

For over 70 years, Soviet policies included no advertising or limited availability of alcohol [while managing to maintain one of the highest rates of alcoholism in the world].

> WARREN DUNN, CEO of Miller Brewing, in a speech July 15, 1993

We are the tenth largest brewer in the United States. Do you know what that means? We have one two-hundredth of the beer market. That's minuscule. Twelve years of busting my ass, and we've gone from nothing to infinitesimal. If I'm lucky, I'll go another 12 years and get to be small.

> JIM KOCH, founder and CEO of the Boston Beer Company, maker of Samuel Adams beer, in a speech quoted in *Inc.*, September 1996

There's a strong index of beer drinkers with hunters and people that fish and enjoy the great outdoors.

> AUGUST BUSCH IV of the beer company Anheuser Busch, quoted in the *Wall Street Journal*, November 19, 1996

The only thing better than cold beer is cheap beer.

> DAVID BATULA, 29-year-old landscaper who bought a case of Miller Lite in Texas during price war with Bud, quoted in the *Wall Street Journal*, December 5, 1996

The perfect toast to the beginning of a new chapter in Hong Kong history.

> Slogan for Red Dawn Beer, which was colored red, brewed in Hong Kong by a subsidiary of American Craft Brewing International, and sold all 10,000 cases in spite of apprehension about China's takeover, quoted in the *Wall Street Journal*, April 30, 1997

You know you're a redneck if: You think a cow says moo, a sheep says baa, and a frog says Bud.

> Plaque for sale at Houston gift shop, quoted in the *Wall Street Journal*, December 5, 1997

The students aren't upset about the suites themselves, but they resent the fact that they'll be the only places in the new building where alcohol will be permitted.

> KAREN KERSTING of the student paper *The Daily Cardinal*, on the inclusion of 36 luxury suites, to be leased for $35,000 per year, in the University of Wisconsin's new basketball and hockey arena, quoted in the *Wall Street Journal*, August 22, 1997

Gallo was slow to get into premium wine, but that's their style. They watch, they wait, then they jump in and take over. They have no stockholders and they put everything back in the business. They take advantage of their massive economies of scale, and they are very, very aggressive.

> JON FREDRICKSEN of the wine consulting firm Gomberg Fredriksen, quoted in the *New York Times*, September 4, 1997

The gay affinity [for Black Sheep beer, brewed by a gay-owned company] will make a difference only if people like the product and think it's equal to what they've been drinking. They won't support a product just because the company that makes it is gay-owned.

> BILL SWETZ of Fritz, a Boston gay bar, quoted in *Inc.*, March 1996

1.4.2 Automobiles

[I]f you really want to understand our customers, you have to understand the phrase, "If I were going to be a car, I'd be a Porsche."

> PETER SCHUTZ, chief executive of Porsche AG, quoted in *Harvard Business Review,* March–April, 1986

This is an emotional business. If you're not emotional there's something wrong with you.

> LEW VERALDI, "Father of the Ford Taurus," quoted in Mary Walton, *Car* (Norton, 1997)

Automobiles are not a mass market in the traditional sense. We have to sell millions of vehicles one at a time.

> PHILIP GUARESCO of General Motors, quoted in *Fortune,* April 4, 1994

The sports utility vehicle is at one end of the spectrum. It comes across as a rugged, tough vehicle that gives you freedom. The mini-van is at the other end of the spectrum, which would be imprisonment—with kids and family and responsibility.

> CHRISTOPHER W. CEDERGREN of the research group Nextrend, quoted in the *New York Times,* May 12, 1997

Every American thinks he's alone on the continent.

> PHILIP SLATER, *The Pursuit of Loneliness: American Culture at the Breaking Point* (Beacon Press, 1976)

The Ford Edsel, that legendary 1950s flop, was based on accurate analysis of changing consumer tastes. It was just a crummy car.

> PETER MARTIN, *Financial Times,* May 15, 1997

1.4.3 Brands

[C]onsumers are right to believe that branded products are of good quality, not because the manufacturer says

they are—mostly they do not—but because there is little point in branding products that are not.

> JOHN KEY, British director of the School of Management Studies, Oxford, quoted in the *Financial Times,* March 14, 1997

I'm a brand.

> MARTHA STEWART, quoted in *People,* October 1995

The third part is the irreplaceable part. If I get hit by a truck, we just won't have that. We get business that we wouldn't get if I were an inanimate object. Mr. Reuters is dead. Mr. Dow is dead. We don't have 'em anymore.

> MICHAEL BLOOMBERG, CEO of the financial news firm Bloomberg, referring to the third of what he considers to be his three jobs—CEO, risk taker, and living brand, quoted in the *Financial Times Weekend,* May 24–25, 1997

Simon [Fuller, manager of the Spice Girls] is very aware the Spice Girls are a brand.

> JAMES FREEDMAN of the entertainment firm Zone, quoted in *Forbes,* September 22, 1997

The brand is the engine that will drive the business. If we cannot use the brand, we won't be in the business.

> GEORGE FARR of the financial services firm American Express, quoted in *Fortune,* October 30, 1995

To make a brand pervasive in the consumer's mind, you need to use all channels of communication, not just TV.

> KEN ROBBINS, head of the advertising agency Lintas, quoted in the *Economist,* February 1, 1992

Anybody who said that brands were irrelevant in the 1980s will be singing the blues in the next millennium.

> MICHAEL OVITZ, former head of the talent agency CAA and briefly president of Disney, quoted in *Fortune,* March 4, 1996

It continually amazes me, but when we go into a new community or a new country, when we open the first day, we time and again set new sales records, new customer records. We open up with the Golden Arches: the sales team looks great in their uniforms. It is a huge event. It is a happening.

> MICHAEL QUINLAN, CEO of the fast-food chain McDonald's, quoted in *Fortune,* March 4, 1996

There is a limit to how many times you can zig and zag without really doing damage to the brand. We don't think it's reached that point.

> KEITH REINHARD, CEO of the advertising agency DDB Needham, after recapturing the McDonald's account, quoted in the *Wall Street Journal*, July 30, 1997

The central element of brand stewardship . . . is recognizing that the brand is a relationship.

> CATHLEEN BLACK, president of Hearst Magazines, in a speech, March 4, 1997

Sometimes a bad brand name is better than no brand name at all.

> BRIAN KLENE of the computer firm Micron Electronics, quoted in *Fortune*, June 9, 1997

A successful brand has a personality and a conversation with consumers. But if you keep changing the voice of the person talking, it's very hard for consumers to trust a brand.

> STEVE GOLDSTEIN of the clothing company Levi Strauss, quoted in *Time*, June 16, 1997

Brands will be the shortcut . . . with a trusted brand, the consumer can cut through the clutter.

> CARL F. PASCARELLA, CEO of the credit-card firm Visa U.S.A., quoted in the *New York Times*, October 21, 1997

This is a violation of the brand, and we're not doing it.

> LOUIS V. GERSTNER, then head of American Express's card business, on gimmicks such as discounting, cited by Shelley Lazarus, CEO of the advertising firm Ogilvy & Mather, quoted in *Fortune*, April 14, 1997

Once upon a time, it was okay to make good shows and put them on the air. You can't do that anymore. You have to have a strategy of who you want to be as a network.

> WARREN LITTLEFIELD, president of the TV network division NBC Entertainment, quoted in the *Wall Street Journal*, April 2, 1997

You could sell Pepsi or Coke out of an old tub inside a dusty garage, but consumers will think your private brand cola is horrible if it's sold in a crummy store.

> PROFESSOR ARUN JAIN of the University of Buffalo, quoted in *Business Week*, October 16, 1996

No matter how powerful a brand is, if you stop advertising, there will be a decay in equity.

> BOB LEPRE of the New England Consulting Group, quoted in the *Wall Street Journal*, January 5, 1998

1.4.4 To Children

The toys that sell are those of traditional sexual values; the macho big toy or tank for boys and the cuddly warm stuff for girls.

> Senior toy buyer for a big national chain, quoted in the *Wall Street Journal*, February 7, 1985

It's a copycat industry.

> ELENA DIAZ, senior toy buyer for the retail chain Marshall Field, quoted in the *Wall Street Journal*, February 7, 1985

We have to be able to stop on a dime if we think there's trouble. Once you have brought the product to market, all emotion should go away. You have to face reality as quickly as possible.

> ALAN HASSENFELD, president of the toy firm Hasbro, quoted in *Forbes*, August 24, 1987

Being a manager in the toy business is to be a poker player forever attempting to draw to an inside straight. Grown men and women wager millions in the hope that they have figured out what eight-year-olds will kill for two years down the road.

> BILL SAPORIA, *Fortune*, October 8, 1990

Radio is a drive-time phenomenon. Mommy spends more and more time in the car. If you give kids something to listen to and they shut up, it can work.

> BISHOP CHEEN of the investment firm Paul Kagan & Associates, quoted in the *New York Times*, May 20, 1990

There is nothing subtle about American mall retailing.

> JOHN LEE of Early Learning Center, quoted in the *New York Times*, January 5, 1992

We grew up on *Sesame Street*; you know "*habla español*" and racial harmony on the playground.

> Duke University student, quoted originally in the *Washington Post* and cited in the *Economist*, January 18, 1992

It is not about attracting kids, it is about making Las Vegas not unattractive to people with kids.

> Casino executive, on family friendly casino development, quoted in the *Economist*, December 26, 1992

[T]he reborn Captain America could end up as a financial hero if his new fight against self-doubt and neo-Nazis grabs the attention of the preteen to twenty-something audience.

> DEBORAH SHAPELY on comic books, quoted in the *New York Times*, September 30, 1996

The insert cards are what everyone's after. When you buy a $3 pack, you are looking for the value that's hidden inside the pack. You might get nothing or you might get a $125 card. [Children sit outside stores tearing packs open looking for them.]

> KEVIN HAAKE, 16 years old, of Overland Park, Kansas, on the gimmick of putting limited-run cards inside trading-card packs, quoted in the *Wall Street Journal*, October 25, 1996

Comic strips pay the bills for syndication companies, because comic strips can be developed into other properties. Nobody ever bought a lunch box with a Bill Buckley column on it.

> LEE SALEM of Universal Press Syndicate, distributor for the comic strips *Doonesbury* and *Garfield*, quoted in the *New York Times*, October 28, 1996

The three R's don't include retailing.

> MELINDA ANDERSON of the National Education Association, quoted in the *Wall Street Journal*, October 28, 1996

I have more stuff than anybody.

> Eight-year-old TOM BUZBEE who usually spends his $3 weekly allowance on books in the *Goosebumps* series by R. L. Stine, quoted in *Business Week*, November 4, 1996. (He also has the full line of *Goosebumps* accessories such as sheets and pillowcases, a backpack, a flashlight, and T-shirts.)

It's easy to make fun of playing the cello. The message is, if I play the cello I'm not going to have any fun. If I eat a Whopper, then of course I'm going to see the light.

> LAWRENCE HURST, chairman of Indiana University's string department, on Burger King commercial in which a nerd-cellist is transformed into cool electric-

guitar wizard after eating a burger, quoted in the *Wall Street Journal*, December 16, 1996

R.J. Reynolds Tobacco Co. believes firmly in its long-held position that "Kids should not smoke." We stand behind our position by offering programs that supplement other youth nonsmoking efforts in schools, at retail [outlets] and in the home. These programs . . . reflect the many studies that show the key factors affecting youth smoking to be the influences of peers and family.

> R.J. Reynolds company statement in November 1995, quoted in *Governing*, December 1, 1995

Are you kidding? We reserve that right for the poor, the young, the black, and the stupid.

> One of a group of R.J. Reynolds executives in answer to model David Goerlitz's question, "Do any of you smoke?" at a Winston ad photo shoot, quoted by Bob Herbert, the *New York Times*, October 21, 1996

We sell an enormous amount into the market knowing full well what we are doing—it's real negative PR, but it's a fact of this business, and if we didn't do it someone else would.

> MARTY HYMAN of the tobacco distributor Bonanza Trading Associates on the industry's knowledge of "blunting" (removing tobacco from the cigars and stuffing them full of marijuana), quoted in the *Wall Street Journal*, April 8, 1996

We think girls are interested in music and sports and computers and careers and family relationships and friendships. You don't have to exploit them with, "If I had my hair this way or I shaved my legs this way, life would be better."

> ALISON AMOROSO, editor of *Teen Voices*, quoted in the *New York Times*, November 4, 1996

For the past 10 years, we've made football look too dangerous and complicated. We've forgotten that all the flag [football] game needs is four boys or girls with a football and a couple of T-shirts.

> PAUL KAYAIAN, director of the National Football League European sales, on the challenge of increasing sales of NFL clothes and other products in Europe, quoted in the *Wall Street Journal*, November 29, 1996

Kids' No. 1 desire is to be up on new stuff all the time and know things that their parents don't.

> EDWARD VOLKWEIN of the electronic game firm Sega of America, quoted in *Fortune,* Autumn/Winter 1993 special issue

Videogames will never again be a child-only business because we've finally crossed the threshold where kids who played Pong are now the parents of kids who play Sonic.

> TOM KALINSKI, CEO of the electronic game firm Sega of America, quoted in *Fortune,* Autumn/Winter, 1993 special issue

Kids can't buy guns, you say? Well, yes and no. . . . Schools can be a huge asset. They collect, in one place, a large number of minds and bodies that are important to your well-being. What can you do to take advantage of this opportunity? Get to know the principals and coaches at schools in your area. Get them on your side. Impress on them that you'd like to help with the education of children and teachers in the outdoor fields.

> GRITS GRESHAM, shooting editor of *Sports Afield,* on techniques to create a new generation of shooting enthusiasts, originally published in September-October 1995 issue of *SHOT Business,* and cited in *Harper's* in 1995

We know our biggest challenge is to win over mom and dad.

> ERIC ROLLMAN, executive producer of the new version of the children's TV program *Captain Kangaroo,* on the challenge of finding someone to replace Bob Keeshan, the original Captain Kangaroo, quoted in the *Wall Street Journal,* March 5, 1997

In 1991, the Motion Picture Association of America rated only 16 percent of American movies as fit for kids under thirteen. Yet a PG film is more than three times as likely as an R-rated film to gross over a hundred million dollars at the domestic box office.

> KEN AULETTA, "What Won't You Do?" *New Yorker,* May 17, 1993

We would never do violence such as you see in a Nintendo game. When I see kids playing Nintendo, and they're able to actually get their character on the screen to bite his opponent in the face, that's pretty sick violence.

> RUPERT MURDOCH, chairman of the media conglomerate News Corporation, which owns Fox movie and television companies, in response to the question, What won't you do? quoted in Ken Auletta, "What Won't You Do?" *New Yorker,* May 17, 1993

Their shows [Fox Kids Network] teach kids it's okay to be violent if you're the good guy. They are corrupting American youth.

> BOB KEESHAN, television's original Captain Kangaroo, who declined to be on Fox Kids' *The All New Captain Kangaroo,* quoted in the *Wall Street Journal,* October 1, 1997

We're not into the fluffy-bunny shows. Fluffy bunny, no.

> HAIM SABAN, 50 percent shareholder with News Corporation of Fox Kids Network, quoted in the *Wall Street Journal,* October 1, 1997

Now we're watching kids, whereas we used to watch designers.

> RUTH A. DAVIS of the sports clothing firm Reebok International, quoted in the *Wall Street Journal,* July 11, 1996

You go into a shoe store. The kid picks up the shoe and says, "Ah, man, this is nice." He turns the shoe around and around. He looks at it underneath. He looks at the side and he goes, "Ah, this is Reebok," and says, "I ain't buying this," and puts the shoe down and walks out.

> E. SCOTT MORRIS of the sports clothing firm Reebok, quoted in the *New Yorker,* March 17, 1997

Many of these kids would rather have a Rolex than a home.

> Fashion designer TOMMY HILFIGER on his customers, quoted in *Forbes,* April 21, 1997

Leave It to Beaver. Bucky O'Hare [rabbit in space]. *The Jetsons. The Flintstones. GI Joe. Superboy. Super Mario Bros. Chip 'n Dale Rescue Rangers. Teenage Mutant Ninja Turtles* (nutrition and physical fitness).

> TV programs that various stations claimed were educational for compliance with 1990 Children's Television Act, cited in William Lutz, *The New Doublespeak* (HarperCollins, 1996)

What kind of cultural void has given rise to our society's readiness to view our children as "the most pure consumers you could have"? If 200 years of a free-market economy has led to this, I'm ready to consider socialism.

> HELEN VAN RYZIN, letter to the editor in response to a recent cover article, *Business Week,* July 21, 1997

A toy company's stock rose 20 percent when it won the license to distribute Spice Girl action figures. A clothing store's stock fell 40 percent when it underestimated the demand for Spice Girl–style outfits.

> DAVID PLOTZ, *Slate,* November 15, 1997

Young people want to alter their moods in a safe and acceptable way, and caffeine has covertly been recognized as a safe stimulant. With the effect of sugar, some of these drinks are hand-made for the young teen audience.

> TOM PIRKO, president of the consulting firm Bevmark, quoted in the *Wall Street Journal,* December 17, 1996

[C]affeine is the new-millennium drug of choice.

> GERALD CELENTE, publisher, *Trends Journal,* on the boom in soft drinks targeting children and teenagers and charged with megadoses of caffeine and "natural stimulants," quoted in the *New York Times,* August 22, 1997 (Some have names like XTC and Krank20, suggesting the names of illegal drugs "ecstasy" and "crank.")

Teens are looking for a turn-on that doesn't put them in jail.

> TOM PIRKO, president of Bevmark LLC, a beverage consultant, quoted in the *New York Times,* August 22, 1997

The Spice Girls seem to be the very first group ever that have got four-, five-, and six-year-old girls and boys to own music.

> ROY COOPER of Virgin Records, quoted in *Forbes,* September 22, 1997

Daddy, when I grow up I want to be a man. I want to drive fast cars and smoke cigarettes.

> Dr. Paul Fischer's two-year-old son, whose remark prompted Fischer to study children's familiarity with

Joe Camel, quoted in the *Wall Street Journal,* February 21, 1997

Parents give teens what teens think of as necessities—a car, computer, video games—that we could call luxuries.

> LESTER ROND, president of Rond Youth Poll, quoted in *Business Week,* April 11, 1994

A preschooler in Mongolia, or one in Los Angeles, or one in Sydney or wherever, all have basically the same concerns about life, about learning to behave and all that sort of stuff.

> MARK BERNARD of the TV show *Bananas in Pajamas,* which started in Australia in 1991 and has spread to 36 countries, quoted in the *Wall Street Journal,* March 4, 1996

The key for any toy is the play value. If kids don't enjoy playing it, it just won't sell well.

> MICHAEL GOLDSTEIN, CEO of Toys "R" Us, quoted in the *New York Times,* December 7, 1997

1.4.5 Clothing

Women want women's clothing, and men want women who want women's clothes.

> RICHARD M. LYONS, president of the clothing chain The Gap, on decision to add more high-margin fashions and fewer jeans and T-shirts, quoted in *Business Week,* March 21, 1994

It's a hormone-driven business.

> ALAN MILLSTEIN, retail consultant, quoted in *Business Week,* September 5, 1994

Today's brands are built emotionally. You have to get a message across and show what the brand ideology means to her life.

> STACY LASTRINA of the shoe firm Nine West, quoted in the *New York Times,* October 9, 1997

Translation: You too may have three gorgeous men gaze lovingly at your sandal-clad ankles while you hang loose in a really hip North African–themed bar, if only you shop at Nine West.

> JENNIFER STEINHAUER, journalist responding to Lastrina's statement (above), the *New York Times,* October 9, 1997

1.4.6 Food

[Market research is a] waste of time.

> JOSEPH A. UNANUE, CEO of the privately held Goya Foods, quoted in the *New York Times,* February 24, 1991

Crunchy foods may provide stress-relief, like hitting a racquetball after a hectic day at the office. There are theories that people who tend to be aggressive enjoy foods that require more aggression to destroy.

> GAIL VANCE CIVILLE, president of the food flavor and texture firm Sensory Spectrum, quoted in the *Wall Street Journal,* April 2, 1997

During the early 1990s, Frito-Lay researchers found that most people preferred a chip that broke under about four pounds of pressure per square inch. And consumers demand consistency: They would complain . . . if chips were just eight one-thousandths of an inch too thick or thin.

> MICHAEL J. McCARTHY, the *Wall Street Journal,* April 2, 1997

1.4.7 To Generation X

Please let this come between us.

> Cocktail napkin with picture of condom, to be given with drinks to couples on dates, cited in *Fortune,* November 16, 1992

If you doubt that coffee means business, consider: A latte and scone per day is a $1,400-a-year habit.

> JENNIFER REESE, "Starbucks: Inside the Coffee Cult," *Fortune,* December 9, 1996

We specifically target cafés in low-income areas. We're trying to get the have-nots on computer.

> WAYNE GREGORI, founder of SF Net, which installs computers and Internet connections in cafés, quoted in *Fortune,* October 18, 1993

Gen X is committed. Gen X is connected. Gen X craves success American style.

> J. WALKER SMITH of the polling firm Yankelovich Partners, quoted in *Time,* June 9, 1997

The soul of Gen X is amorphous, intangible, exclusive. That's why I like the term X: fill in the blanks.

> RICHARD THAU, 32, head of the civic group Third Millennium, quoted in *Time,* June 9, 1997

If you go out with the idea that you're not going to offend anybody, you probably won't make much of an impression.

> JAMIE BARRETT of the advertising agency Wieden & Kennedy, quoted in *Business Week,* August 11, 1997

It's time to shut up and drink some beer.

> Tag line for Miller Genuine Draft, created by Wieden & Kennedy, quoted in *Business Week,* August 11, 1997

1.4.8 Health Care

I felt we could brand health care in 50 states, and no matter what city you were in, you could have consistent treatment.

> RICHARD SCRUSHY, chairman of the health care firm Healthsource, which uses athletes such as Michael Jordan, Emmitt Smith, and Kristi Yamaguchi to attract the attention of consumers, quoted in the *Wall Street Journal,* December 4, 1996

We hope to be right up there with the Cokes and Nikes.

> VINCE THOMPSON, of the health care firm Healthsource, quoted in the *Wall Street Journal,* December 4, 1996

There are wars all over the world, bombs all over the world.

> JOHN HUTCHINS of Johns Hopkins Medical Center, which was cultivating foreign governments for limb replacement on wounded soldiers at $35,000 per, quoted in the *Wall Street Journal,* October 7, 1996

We are a business, and hospitals are like Switzerland—neutral territory.

> MAUREEN RYAN, who opened Johns Hopkins Medical Center's marketing office on Embassy Row in Washington, D.C., quoted in the *Wall Street Journal,* October 7, 1996

They come to us with money in a suitcase.

> JOSE NUÑEZ of Methodist Hospital in Houston, Texas, on the hospital's marketing efforts, quoted in the *Wall Street Journal,* October 7, 1996

We call this health tourism.

> BOB JIMENEZ of a travel agency in Orlando, Florida, that packages physical examinations for parents with trips to Disney World for the kids, quoted in the *Wall Street Journal,* October 7, 1996

1.4.9 Interactive TV

I spent 20 years marketing products the traditional way with big advertising bucks. The amount you need is staggering. This is a very clean way of doing business.

> FRANK MONTEMURRO, manufacturers' agent on the advantages of launching products through the TV shopping network QVC, quoted in *Inc.,* June 1994

It was the ultimate Nielsen rating. The phones light up. You don't wait till you come into the office tomorrow to find out how you did.

> BRIAN ROBERTS, president of the cable TV company Comcast, quoted in Ken Auletta, "Diller Peeks into the Future," *New Yorker,* February 22, 1993

1.4.10 Late Celebrities (Elvis and Princess Diana)

How is a fading star transformed into a perpetual money machine? A few hints:

* Premature death. Essential. Aging icons don't sell (see Marlon Brando) but youngish dead ones do (see Marilyn Monroe and James Dean).
* Control the brand. "Elvis" and "Elvis Presley" are registered trademarks, which Elvis Presley Enterprises protects with a ferocity Disney would appreciate. . . .
* Tackiness sells. . . .
* Keep the music coming.

> *The Economist,* August 16, 1997

[W]e went into full memorial mode.

> HOWARD CHUA-EOAN, senior editor at *Time,* which assembled 21 pages of articles and pictures about Princess Diana's life and death in about 12 hours, quoted in the *Wall Street Journal,* September 1, 1997

You see yourself as a good product that sits on a shelf and sells well, and people make a lot of money out of you.

> PRINCESS DIANA, answering a question about her celebrity, in a 1995 interview with the BBC, which was licensed to broadcasters in 30 countries, quoted in the *Wall Street Journal,* September 1, 1997

Diana souvenirs make up 80 percent of my sales.

> GAUTAM PATEL, souvenir shop cashier on Buckingham Palace Road, which had its busiest day in six years the day of Diana's death, with £1,000 ($1,619) in sales of items, mostly embossed with Princess

Diana's image, quoted in the *Wall Street Journal,* September 1, 1997

Graceland effect.

> Name given by DOUGLAS McWILLIAMS, chief executive of London's Centre for Economics and Business Research, to a projected rise in economic activity from Princess Diana–related business, cited in the *Financial Times,* September 8, 1997 (Graceland is the name of Elvis Presley's home in Memphis, Tennessee.)

I do believe it [Princess Diana's death] did have an effect on the business. This [September 1997] is one of the weaker months that we've seen in quite a while.

> PETER SCHAEFFER of the investment firm SBC Warburg Dillon Read, quoted in the *Wall Street Journal,* October 10, 1997

First of all, I'm still devastated by Diana's death. I was one of her confidantes, along with Lucia Flecha de Lima [wife of Britain's ambassador in Washington]. Lucia and I were her two best friends in the U.S. If you look at some of the last pictures of Diana with Dodi, you'll notice the bags and belts I designed for her . . . It's my way of trying to do what I can to help, and to deal with my own sense of loss. The Princess's projects were very important to me.

> LANA MARKS, who was selling "The Princess Diana Handbag," as yet unlicensed by the estate, for $6,000 at her Madison Avenue store less than three weeks after Princess Diana's death, quoted in the *New York Post,* September 19, 1997

1.4.11 Old Age

The elderly are still an untapped market in housing, clothing, tours, and investment advice.

> ERIC PFEIFFER, director of the Suncoast Gerontology Center at the University of South Florida, quoted in *Business Week,* September 12, 1994

People over 60 shouldn't be allowed to design cars.

> Former Chrysler executive on Lee Iacocca's intrusion into styling decisions for Chrysler cars, quoted in *Fortune,* November 16, 1996

When baby boomers are 70, they'll still eat pizza and listen to the [Rolling] Stones. The popular view that the old are behaving younger is really misplaced. It's rather that the young are becoming older, and those habits are sticking with them.

> BILL WHITEHEAD, CEO of the advertising agency Bates North America, quoted in the *Wall Street Journal,* August 13, 1996

One baby boomer turns 50 every 7.6 seconds.

> J. KEITH GREEN, founder of the (failed) health information video company Time Life Medical, quoted in the *Wall Street Journal,* February 13, 1997

I sometimes wonder whether a 30-year-old account manager really has an understanding of what boomers have gone through.

> JANE GWILLIAN, author of *Connecting with Baby Boomers,* quoted in the *Financial Times,* May 26, 1997 (Apparently, baby boomer consumers are less wedded to brands, among other things, than are younger people.)

1.4.12 Sports and Athletic Equipment

How can it be the great American game if blacks can't play? Hell, we sell beer to everyone.

> GUSSIE BUSCH, new owner of the St. Louis Cardinals baseball team in the early 1950s, when he learned that the team had no black players, quoted in David Halberstam, *October 1964* (Villard, 1994)

We're sold on sports because sports sells beer.

> STEVEN SHAFER of the beer firm Adolph Coors Company, quoted in *U.S. News & World Report,* August 13, 1984

Hertz had a huge investment in O.J. [Simpson] and now all that equity is gone.

> JED PEARSALL, president of the market research firm Performance Research, on pitfalls of celebrity endorsement, quoted in *Worth,* May 1995

There was nothing to prevent Shaq[uille O'Neal, basketball player] from pulling out a Pepsi in the locker room during an on-camera interview.

> Spokesperson for Coca-Cola, which withdrew as a sponsor of the Los Angeles Lakers after O'Neal signed with the team because he had a separate contract with Pepsi, quoted in the *Wall Street Journal,* September 4, 1997

We took our money and put it into soccer.

> CHRIS BEVILACQUA of Nike after Major League baseball owners turned down combined offers of $325 million over 10 years from Nike and Reebok, quoted in the *Wall Street Journal,* November 15, 1996

The product baseball players wear [compared to basketball players] is very narrow. There is no street appeal at all.

> JOHN MORGAN of the sports apparel firm Reebok, quoted in the *New York Times,* April 4, 1993

You have to be very naive to see all those soccer fields and not think that's a lot of shoes.

> ROB PRAZMARK of the sports marketing firm International Management Group, quoted in the *Wall Street Journal,* October 22, 1997

Figure skating sponsorship dollars are coming out of sports like tennis and golf, which are now more vulnerable to losing backers than football, basketball, and baseball, which have a more locked-in audience.

> STEPHEN DISSON, president of D&F Consulting, quoted in *New York,* December 13, 1993

Figure skating is athletic and suggests a wellness—which dovetails with our product and philosophy. Sudafed is a daytime nondrowsy cold medicine that lets you get on with life even when you've got a cold.

> RICK GLEBER, of Sudafed, which sponsors Sudafed Skate America, quoted in *New York,* December 13, 1993

We play for more prize money in a month now on the Senior PGA tour than we played for in a year 25 years ago on the PGA tour.

> Golfer GARY PLAYER, quoted in *Business Week,* February 7, 1994

Marketers who support events like these are rewarded with an immense sense of loyalty from the gay and lesbian community. I think we've laid to rest the myth of backlash.

> HAROLD LEVINE of the Gay Games in New York City, whose sponsors included AT&T and Miller Brewing Company, quoted in *Business Week,* July 4, 1994

Companies aren't hiring these players to win games but to sell products.

> DAVID FALK, agent for Michael Jordan, quoted in the *Wall Street Journal,* February 9, 1996

With players having endorsements before they even put on a [pro] jersey, they have to grow up extremely fast. Some go great. And some fall on their face.

> ANDREA KIRBY, media coach to professional athletes, quoted in the *Wall Street Journal,* February 9, 1996

When Michael [Jordan] was a rookie, I would approach companies and they would say, "David, what on earth are we going to do with a black basketball player?" And I said, "Don't black people use your product?"

> DAVID FALK, sports agent, quoted in the *New York Times,* November 17, 1996

[*Estimated financial impact of Tiger Woods on golf industry—in millions*]

$ 4.1	Winnings and appearance money for Woods
150.0	1 percent increase in course fees and merchandise sales
1.1	Rise in tour ticket, concession, and souvenir sales
60.0	10 percent rise in sales of Nike golf footwear and apparel
95.2	Value of Woods's endorsement deals
343.0	100 percent increase in value of TV deals for golf

$653.4 million

> *Sports Illustrated,* September 8, 1997

The difference is you don't serve as well as Arthur.

> DONALD DELL, founder of the sports management firm ProServ, to an executive of AMF Head who balked at renewing Arthur Ashe's $400,000-a-year racquet endorsement because it was more than his salary, quoted in the *Wall Street Journal,* September 5, 1997

The real challenge for these teams is not how to expand their fan base, but how to reach them as customers . . . These aren't sports clubs. They're leisure businesses.

> MAX ALEXANDER of the London sports advisory firm Oliver & Ohlbaum, quoted in the *New York Times,* September 10, 1997

Retailers estimate that the Nike Inc. line of shoes with Michael Jordan's name rings up more than $100 million per year.

> *Wall Street Journal,* September 23, 1997

The Olympics are one of the marquee properties that have not only retained value but improved over the years. The American public is pretty much wedded to the concept of being glued to the Olympics.

> NEAL PILSON, television industry consultant and former president of CBS Sports, quoted in the *New York Times,* July 28, 1997

My marketers tell me that bird-watching is the single biggest spectator sport in America.

> RICHARD THALHEIMER, founder and chairman of the catalogue firm Sharper Image, quoted in the *Wall Street Journal,* September 30, 1996

By getting to know athletes in their early teens, I can tell if they are the types of people who would work well with Nike over the long term. Are they committed to the sport? Do they have a sense of humor? Do they have an attitude the public will embrace?

> IAN HAMILTON of Nike, who started working with Andre Agassi when Agassi was 15 and grew his hair long on one side and shaved on the other, quoted in *Harvard Business Review,* July–August 1992

Being provocative is ultimately more important than being pleasant. But you have to know what you're doing when you walk into the room with broadswords.

> DAN WIEDEN of the advertising agency Wieden & Kennedy, which created the "just do it" campaign for Nike, quoted in *Harvard Business Review,* July–August 1992

You can't create an emotional tie to a bad product because it's not honest.

> PHILIP KNIGHT, CEO of Nike, quoted in *Harvard Business Review,* July–August 1992

I'm not going to let them [Nike] take over the world. When competition is eliminated they can do anything they want. What's going to happen when they own everything? No more incentive to make the bread better and the milk pure.

> SONNY VACCARO, formerly of Nike, now working for Adidas to do the same thing, quoted in the *New York Times,* July 6, 1997

140. Dollars charged by Nike for a pair of CWEBB sneakers, a price so high it was denounced by Washington

Bullets forward Chris Webber, for whom the shoe is named.

Sports Illustrated, November 18, 1996

1.4.13 Unpleasant Products

It is a difficult marketing chore for a firm to convey to the public that it would like to serve their funeral needs.

JOHN MURROW JR. of the funeral directors Service Corporation International, quoted in *Fortune,* November 16, 1992

This way the girlfriend can go through the drive-through and pay her respects in whatever way she chooses, while the wife is inside with the deceased. It happens all the time.

LAFAYETTE GATLING, whose Chicago funeral home has drive-through service during which bodies can be viewed on closed-circuit TV, quoted in *Newsweek,* March 6, 1989

It ain't the dead who give you trouble, it's the living.

Favorite saying among funeral directors, cited in *Harper's,* November 1997

You see, there is usually only one thought going through the mind of a bereaved family when they walk through the doors of a funeral home . . . get me *out* of *here.* Of course, every funeral director knows this. Which is why the most expensive merchandise is always brought to their attention first—and why, for example, the less expensive caskets are always shown in the ugliest possible colors.

JIM ST. GEORGE, CEO of the coffin maker Consumer-Casket USA, quoted in *Harper's,* November 1997

It's becoming cooler to be a funeral director than it once was. . . . This is still a very clip-on-tie-and-polyester crowd, though.

Young funeral director at a funeral directors convention, quoted in *Harper's,* November 1997

We're Number 1 in the Number 2 business.

Slogan of Blow Brothers, a New Hampshire and Maine portable toilet company, on a New Hampshire billboard

1.5 TELEMARKETING

We're turning the hold button into the sold button.

RON KIRKPATRICK, CEO of Accurate Communications, who says that 20 percent of those who hear on-hold commercials make a purchase or decision based on what they hear, quoted in the *Financial Times,* September 22, 1997

First, you have to tell me what kind of underwear you're wearing.

Shhh. Wait a minute. I'm here robbing the house. Whoa! I think the owners just got home. Can you hold?

You want to sell me insurance? I've been trying to get insurance for years, but nobody will sell me any!

To a phone company solicitor: That sounds GREAT! Wait, can you hold for a minute? (Leave the phone off the hook until he hangs up.)

Responses to annoying telemarketing calls, compiled by the Anti-Telemarketing Source, quoted in the *New York Times,* June 22, 1997

Telemarketing is sociopathic behavior.

ROBERT S. BULMASH, head of the consumer group Private Citizen, quoted in the *New York Times,* June 22, 1997

6-5-4-5 6-6-6; 5-5-5-; 6-6-6. 6-5-4-5 6-6-6-6 5-5-6-5-444444444444444.

Numbers for playing "Mary Had a Little Lamb," one of the songs that can be played on a telephone to annoy unwanted callers, quoted in the *New York Times,* June 22, 1997

2.1 LATIN AMERICA

By combining better economic policies with a greater educational effort, per capita income in Latin America could be 20 percent higher within a decade and in two decades 50 percent higher than it would be without such strategies.

> Inter-American Development Bank report, cited in the *Financial Times,* September 15, 1997

The financial services industry in the region [Latin America] has been in turmoil: dozens of family-owned banks have no future.

> GIOVANNI ORLANDO of the investment bank SBC Warburg, quoted in the *Financial Times,* January 17, 1997

2.1.1 Argentina

Argentina began the century as the ninth richest country on earth but is now number 49.

> ALLAN R. TAYLOR, CEO of the Royal Bank of Canada, in a speech, January 23, 1992

Argentineans are always in trouble about their currency. Either it is too good for home use, or as frequently happens, it is too bad for foreign exchange. Generally they have too much of it, but their own idea is that they do not have enough. The Argentineans alter their currency almost as frequently as they change their finance ministers. No people on earth has a keener interest in currency experimentation than the Argentineans.

> *Bankers* magazine, 1889; reprinted in the *Wall Street Journal,* February 28, 1997

Argentina is saying: "We are now a responsible economy which investors can trust."

> New York bond dealer, on Argentina's retirement of $1 billion of debt through issuance of 30-year bonds, further casting off the stigma of its credit problems in the '80s, quoted in the *Financial Times,* September 3, 1997

Less than a decade after the Falklands War, British merchant banks are drawing fees from a Peronist government for advising on privatizations to stop Argentine industries being mismanaged by Peronist colonels.

> NORMAN MACRAE, *The Economist,* December 21, 1991 (Five years later, the Peronist government is gone.)

The people who used to discuss Karl Marx now want to talk about sewers and parking.

> RICARDO PUGA, host of a popular radio talk show in Mendoza, Argentina, quoted in the *Wall Street Journal,* August 28, 1997

2.1.2 Bolivia

Their attitude has never changed. They [Chileans] live to take advantage of us.

> GERMÁN BARRIAGA, veteran union leader and former congressman, expressing the regional resentment of Chile, quoted in the *Wall Street Journal,* October 3, 1997

Politicians who manage well at the municipal level will be the new leaders. That's a huge change, and it's a positive sign for the future.

> Former Bolivian president GONZALO SÁNCHEZ DE LOZADA, commenting on a general ascendancy in Latin America of local politicians who are accountable for delivery of services supplanting *caudillos* (traditional power brokers), *Wall Street Journal,* August 28, 1997

2.1.3 Brazil

The twenty-first century may well be the century of Brazil.

> PROFESSOR RICHARD COPPER of Harvard University, quoted in *Forbes,* May 5, 1986

We have to do away with this inferiority complex, especially strong in the Brazilian left, that the presence of foreign investment in the economy means the presence of the colonizer oppressing the colonized.

> FERNANDO COLLOR DE MELLO, then president-elect of Brazil, quoted in the *New York Times,* January 1, 1990 (Collor was impeached for corruption in 1992.)

Russia in one year moved one quarter of the public sector into private hands; Mexico in four years has done over 1,000 privatizations. Brazil's program is timid. It isn't major. It isn't impressive.

> PROFESSOR RUDIGER DORNBUSCH of MIT, quoted in the *New York Times,* October 31, 1993

Brazil today can function despite the screwups, sometimes criminal, perpetrated in Brasilia [the nation's capital].

> *Exame,* Brazil's leading business magazine, reported in the *New York Times,* October 31, 1993

I don't have any scruples.

> Brazilian Finance Minister, conceding on national television that he hides bad economic news from the public, quoted in the *Financial Times,* September 19, 1997

People complaining about Brazil's economy today don't have any perspective on how much better things have gotten.

> LUIS CEZAR FERNANDES, president of the Brazilian investment bank Banco Pactual SA, quoted in the *Wall Street Journal,* May 17, 1996

If the Malaysians don't leave our forests in peace, we don't leave the Malaysians in peace. If they come to Brazil acting as if it is a banana republic, they are going to have a very rough time of it.

> GUSTAVO KRAUSE, Environment Minister, on ambitions of Asian logging companies in the Amazon, quoted in the *Wall Street Journal,* November 11, 1996

Of course, you're not going to lose your virginity. . . . That will happen in a much more romantic way.

> Culturally sensitive Tambrands tampon commercial on Brazilian television, cited in the *Wall Street Journal,* March 17, 1997

It used to be most corruption was petty stuff like paying off a tax inspector or offering a bribe to get a paper stamped. Nowadays it's more opportunistic, institutionalized, and very close to the style of organized crime. It's very, very large because the stakes are very large.

> JAMES WYGAND, managing director of the Brazilian office of the business security firm Kroll Associates, quoted in the *Wall Street Journal,* July 1, 1996

In Brazil some of the most corrupt politicians are the ones screaming bloody murder. They are opposed to economic reform and want to have a big money state back. There's more money to spend.

> HENRIQUE DE CAMPOS MEIRELLES, president of the Bank of Boston, São Paulo, quoted in the *Wall Street Journal,* July 1, 1996

The advantage of not being a giant is that you have to be more humble, you have to play with other skills. If I have to fight Mike Tyson, I should use a gun, not my hands. They are much stronger and bigger than us. We can't fight them in a price war.

> LUIZ ANTONIO VIANA, chief executive of Grupo Pao de Acucar SA, Brazil's largest locally owned supermarket chain, about competition from Wal-Mart and Carrefour SA of France, quoted in the *Wall Street Journal,* October 13, 1997

2.1.4 Chile

We may not be a tiger yet [referring to the East Asian economies known as tigers] but we are already a jaguar.

> Chilean businessman, quoted in *Worth,* August 1995

It's easier for a Chilean to buy a company in Argentina than it is to buy duty free.

> One Chilean executive to another during flight after closing big deal in Buenos Aires, quoted in the *New York Times,* November 17, 1996

Chileans have always been kind, humble, hardworking people. But now they've earned a few pennies and learned how to dress, and now they think they rule the world.

> RICARDO FERNANDEZ, Argentine businessman sitting behind the two executives mentioned in the previous quote, quoted in the *New York Times,* November 17, 1996

No long-term world-class performer saves only 26 percent of GDP.

> SEBASTIAN EDWARDS, economist, UCLA, on deficiencies in the vaunted Chilean economy, quoted in the *Wall Street Journal,* December 4, 1996

One of Santiago's most thriving new industries nowadays is international economic consulting. Its brightest talents: [former dictator August] Pinochet's retired bureaucrats.

> MICHAEL HIRSH, *Newsweek*, July 24, 1995

2.1.5 Colombia

If you're taken [kidnapped] in Bogotá, you'll probably spend six to nine months in a box the size of a refrigerator. If you're taken here [in Casanare] then you face nine months up in the mountains.

> PHIL MEAD, head of operations for BP in Casanare, Colombia, quoted in the *Financial Times*, January 7, 1997

As long as things [armed crime rate and competition from contraband dealers] remain as they are, no one is going to invest here.

I came here with nothing and now have my own company. In Japan I would be just another employee in a huge corporation, a cog in a machine. This society has allowed me to be creative and I feel I have a responsibility to it.

> MACHIDA SAKAE, Japanese-born electrical goods distributor in Cali, Colombia, quoted in *Asia, Inc.*, March 1997

2.1.6 Cuba

If Cuba were to somehow sink tomorrow and disappear from the map, it would hardly make a ripple in the hemisphere's economy. It would just not be felt.

> World Bank official, quoted in the *New York Times*, April 19, 1992

Like any big company in the United States, we are keeping an eye on the situation there. As soon as things change, we will be taking a hard look at the opportunities there.

> GEORGE JAMISON of GE, quoted in the *New York Times*, April 19, 1992

What they're buying is a population of 11 million people who can't communicate [by phone].

> TOM WELLS, president of Intercom Corporation, consultants on a deal between a Mexican company

and Cuba's antiquated state phone system, quoted in *Business Week*, June 27, 1994

What good is revolutionary theory if I have to buy everything in dollars?

> EDUARDO, Havana mechanic, on Cuba since Castro legalized holding of dollars and other hard currencies, quoted in *Harper's*, March 1995

We're not repressing the *paladares* [self-employed street vendors and private restaurants], we're repressing thieves.

> CUBAN VICE PRESIDENT CARLOS LAGA, on crackdown against certain kinds of private business activity, quoted in the *Financial Times*, May 1, 1997

We [(ITT) are] not an eleemosynary institution. Why should we share this with some Cuban claimants? Fidel Castro might have a claim. [ITT recovered money from its pre-revolutionary investment in the Cuban Telephone Company because Telecom Italia paid up rather than contest litigation under the Burton-Helms law, but ITT refused to try to track down Cuban investors who might also have claims.]

> DICK WARD, general counsel of ITT, quoted in the *New York Times*, December 7, 1997

2.1.7 Dominican Republic

We [cigar smokers] do not inhale. The cigar smoker is a slave of his pleasure. The cigar smoker is not an addict. Cigar smoking is a hobby.

> Dominican cigar producer, quoted in *Financial Times Weekend*, January 11–12, 1997 (The Dominican Republic has overtaken Cuba as the world's leading exporter of cigars.)

2.1.8 Ecuador

We came back from [Ecuador in 1969] and we were writing our recommendation. We thought Ecuador was a very stable country. There hadn't been a revolution in 40 years . . . an Ecuadorian friend called to inform us a revolution had just broken out.

> MELVYN KLEIN, founding partner of the investment partnership GKH, quoted in *Financial World*, October 21, 1996

2.1.9 Guatemala

Guatemala cannot remain outside the economic revolutions circling the world.

> GUSTAVO SARAVIA, state modernization commissioner, quoted in the *Financial Times,* February 26, 1997

It is very important not to frighten tourists with too visible a display of armaments.

> ROBERTO ROBLES, head of Guatemala's national tourist board, quoted in the *Financial Times,* September 19, 1997

2.1.10 Mexico

[A study in San Diego County, California] showed that more than 120,000 Mexicans legally cross the border into San Diego County every day—to work, to socialize, and to shop—spending an average of $75 per family per visit. A higher standard of living in Mexico would certainly increase the number of people who visit and spend in this country.

> AUGUSTINE P. GALLEGO, chancellor of San Diego Community College District, in a speech, October 8, 1992

The Mexican central bank calculates that dollar remittances to Mexico [from the 9 to 10 million Mexicans who live in the United States] top $2 billion annually; independent studies indicate that the figure is actually higher. The remittances are now the third largest source of hard currency for Mexico after oil and tourism.

> DOUGLAS W. PAYNE, "Letter from Mexico," *Harper's,* April 1995

If there were no American cartoon characters, there would be no piñata business.

> LORENZO GARCÍA, manager of a piñata store in Mexico City, quoted in the *Wall Street Journal,* September 13, 1996 (Almost all the piñatas he sold depicted U.S. cartoon characters. The only "Mexican" design bore the face of former president Carlos Salinas de Gortari.)

Capital flight is as old as Mexican history. Even the Spaniards took their silver out of Mexico.

> JOSÉ MANTECÓN, former Mexican securities regulator, quoted in the *Wall Street Journal,* August 8, 1996

A U.S. [factory] manager, hoping to show his democratic spirit, habitually wore jeans and rumpled sports shirts, insisted that everyone call him by his first name, and addressed the Mexican managers by theirs. He was amazed to hear through the grapevine that supervisors and workers alike consider him a boor.

> MARIAH E. DE FOREST, Chicago management consultant, quoted in the *Financial Times,* October 17, 1996

We can't fight all the bulls at once. We have to take them one, maybe two, at a time.

> GUILLERMO ORTIZ, Mexican Finance Minister, on half-hearted economic reforms in Mexico, quoted in the *Economist,* November 28, 1995

Multinationals are no longer immune [from violence in Mexico]. I personally know of seven American chief executives that have looked at the wrong end of a weapon in Mexico.

> MORTON PALMER, head of Palmer Associates security consultants, quoted in the *Wall Street Journal,* October 29, 1996.

Mexico has no tax on capital gains and no tax on dividends. If the U.S. doesn't get serious about capital formation, you may soon see American millionaires swimming across the Rio Grande to the land of plenty.

> JAMES MYERS, North Carolina investment manager, quoted in *Fortune,* November 16, 1992

NAFTA has forced the Mexican business community to think more globally. With these new linkages, Mexican companies will be tougher competitors and more global competitors.

> WILLIAM R. RHODES, vice chairman of Citibank, quoted in the *Wall Street Journal,* September 30, 1997

The economy has lost its national meaning. Wealth and economic strength and the existence of well-established firms are just being siphoned off to globalization.

> RICARDO PASCOE, "director of international affairs for Mexico's largest left-wing political party," quoted in the *Wall Street Journal,* September 30, 1997

2.1.11 Peru

We've gotten into a kind of vicious cycle here. Everyone expects, no one believes, and no one explains.

> MIGUEL PALOMINO of Merrill Lynch in Peru, quoted in the *Wall Street Journal,* December 13, 1996

2.1.12 Uruguay

The inefficiency is brutal.

> RAMÓN DÍAZ, former Central Bank president, on the overstaffing of the civil service, quoted in the *Economist,* March 23, 1996

The hot money is the difference between living hand-to-mouth and doing substantially better than that.

> ROBERT DWYER, American private investigator, on the fiscal luxury allowed to Uruguayan envoys because of its Swiss-like bank-secrecy environment, which attracts huge amounts of off-shore cash, quoted in the *Wall Street Journal,* February, 13, 1997

Socialism is beautiful when it's right next door to capitalism.

> GILBERTO SCARPA, Brazilian industrialist charged with tax evasion at home who spends several months in Uruguay each year, quoted in the *Wall Street Journal,* February 13, 1997

2.1.13 Venezuela

What's the chance that I'd want to own this [Venezuelan] company for a long time because I have confidence in the company and the country? Very, very small.

> West Coast emerging markets fund manager, quoted in the *Wall Street Journal,* November 21, 1996

Sixty years ago we thought we had oil left for another 10 years; now for all practical purposes, our reserves are infinite.

> RAMÓN ESPINOSA, chief economist of the state-owned Petroleos de Venezuela, quoted in the *Financial Times,* October 21, 1997

2.2 CANADA

Never again will there be any doubt that Canada can manufacture anything that can be manufactured elsewhere.

> C. D. HOWE, minister of munitions and supply, Canada, who had helped turn Canada from a depressed, agricultural society into an industrial country during World War II

Geography has made us [United States and Canada] neighbors. History has made us friends. Economics has made us partners. And necessity has made us allies.

Those whom nature hath so joined together, let no man pull asunder.

> PRESIDENT JOHN F. KENNEDY, address to the Canadian Parliament, Ottawa, May 17, 1961

When times get tough, we [Canadians] get terribly pro-American and cost-conscious. When times get better, we get a little more uppity with the U.S.

> PROFESSOR MORTON (first name not given), University of Toronto, quoted in *Forbes,* May 16, 1986

Unfortunately, I often feel we've become a society where sex education is commonplace, and it's the economic facts of life that have become our street-corner mysteries.

> ROBERT A. FERCHAT, president of Northern Telecom Canada, in a speech, February 23, 1987

[I]n today's economy, comparative advantage has evolved from endowment to creation, from natural resource advantages to advantages that are man-made, or mind-made.

In the past, the "have" economies of the world, like Canada, had all the advantages; the "have-not" economies of the world were disadvantaged.

In the future, it will be the know-nots of the world who will be disadvantaged. Ignorant economies will be broken economies.

> JOHN MANLEY, Canadian Minister of Industry, in a speech, June 11, 1996

Toronto, Canada—Canada's largest pizza chain, threatened by competition, established a policy of giving customers their pizza free if the delivery driver fails to smile, and then firing the driver, according to the *Globe and Mail.* "That's corporate policy. It's not cutthroat. It's getting back to basics. It's service," the chain's executive director told the newspaper.

> JUDITH MARTIN, *Miss Manners Rescues Civilization* (Crown, 1994)

Welcome to Canada, the only country in the world that jails its farmers for selling their own grain.

> Billboard message in Minton, Saskatchewan, and in Coutts, Alberta, protesting the requirement that farmers must sell their grain to the Canadian Wheat Board at approximately half the price that they could get across the border in the United States. Cited in the *Wall Street Journal,* November 15, 1996

It's really hard for us to meet those salaries. . . . Some of the brightest ones take the money and run. It's very difficult to woo back someone who has already left.

> KAREN KOSTASZEK, president of Imaginia, a Canadian network engineering company, on brain drain to U.S. companies, quoted in the *Financial Times,* May 5, 1997

It makes a lot of sense to have the senior part of the group where the greatest volume of mining companies, mining finance, new issues, etc., is located.

> TYE BURT, head of Deutsche Morgan Grenfell's mining finance operations in Toronto (which has become the world's most important center for mining finance), quoted in the *Wall Street Journal,* October 3, 1997

2.3   FALKLAND ISLANDS

The only scenario for rapid growth will be if we discover oil. Then our problem will be controlling what's going on, not deciding what's going on. [The economy is trying to diversify beyond sheep farming.]

> ANDREW GURR, governor and chief executive, Falkland Islands; quoted in the *Financial Times,* April 1, 1997

2.4   ANTARCTICA

[*Note:* The compiler is fully aware that Antarctica is not in the Americas, but there was no convenient place to put it.]

There's a small PX-like store for souvenirs, alcohol, and toiletries, [there are] a few bars, and you can always order from Lands' End or L.L. Bean. Just don't ask for overnight delivery.

> ROB HOLMES, meteorologist, McMurdo Station (where there is also an ATM), quoted in the *New York Times,* September 14, 1997

3.1 ASIA

The feeling I have when I travel to the cities of Asia now is what people must have felt when they went to New York 100 years ago. The energy pulls you in like a conveyor belt. There's a sense that anything is possible.

KENNETH COURTIS of Deutsche Bank Capital Markets, quoted in *Forbes,* July 15, 1996

[Starting in the late 1960s or early 1970s] politicians in Asia decided to give economic efficiency priority over everything else because they were scared. South Korea was scared of the North, Hong Kong and Taiwan were scared of China, Thailand of Vietnam. And Singapore was scared of everybody.

WILLIAM OVERHOLT, managing director of Bankers Trust Asia, quoted in *Forbes,* July 15, 1996

The Asian mentality is everyone has to fend for himself, failing which you have the family to fall back on. The political pressure is not there for governments to tax the rich to pay the poor.

C. Y. LEUNG, who runs a Hong Kong real estate firm, quoted in *Forbes,* July 15, 1996

Why is it that people don't question the limits of productivity growth in Japan—or other Asian countries? They accept it because they understand that the source of that growth is *cultural*—not cutting, combining, or all the things that it's come to be associated with in this country.

JOHN F. WELCH JR., CEO of GE, in a speech, November 1989

Given the economic growth and blossoming of billionaires in the region, Asia is likely to produce the world's first trillionaire.

Asia, Inc., September 1996

These guys really want cutting-edge modern design, things that people haven't seen before. They want to be in the top echelon of global players.

JEFFREY McCARTHY of the architectural firm Skidmore, Owings & Merrill, on Asian building projects, quoted in the *Wall Street Journal,* March 21, 1996

Britain's GDP today is almost twice the size of China's, and larger than those of Hong Kong, Thailand, Malaysia, Indonesia, Singapore, the Philippines, and India put together. China's GDP is about the same as those of Belgium, the Netherlands, and Luxembourg combined.

CHRISTOPHER PATTEN, the last British governor of Hong Kong, quoted in the *Economist,* January 4, 1997

In the American-style model the basic reason for having an economy is to raise the consumer's standard of living. In the Asian model it is to increase the collective national strength.

The view of surprise and unpredictability. The Anglo-American model views surprise as the key to economic life. We believe that it is precisely because markets are fluid and unpredictable that they work. The Asian-style system deeply mistrusts markets.

JAMES FALLOWS, "What Is an Economy For?" *Atlantic Monthly,* January 1994

- Avoid the Yankee getting-down-to-business attitude in initial business encounters with Koreans, Chinese, and other Asians.
- Sit down only when invited to do so.
- Establish a cordial, friendly relationship, which can be improved by giving small gifts.
- Do not be either too casual or overly friendly.
- Listen more; speak less.

NORINE DRESSER, *Multicultural Manners: New Rules of Etiquette for a Changing Society* (Wiley, 1996)

The rules and regulations [for marketing liquor in Asia] are rather vague and confusing. You don't know whether you're breaking any laws until you are told you are doing it.

RUBY TANG of the liquor firm Moët Hennessey Asia-Pacific, quoted in the *Wall Street Journal,* June 16, 1996

Those [Asian countries] perceived to be least corrupt were also the richest. Singapore, the best-scoring Asian country, was the seventh cleanest of the 54 with a per-capita GNP of $23,360, second highest in Asia, and

10th highest in the world. China was among those seen as most corrupt (50th cleanest out of 54), and it was also among the poorest (per capita GNP of $530, second to last among the Asian countries and 48th out of the 54).

> Study by Germany's Göttingen University and Transparency International, a Berlin-based nonprofit group dedicated to fighting corruption, cited by Urban C. Lehner, Asian edition of the *Wall Street Journal,* October 22, 1996

Even if you emptied the Bay Area of engineers, you would have a hard time staffing all the wafer fabs [silicon chip factories] going up in Asia.

> RON JONES, Taiwan-based semiconductor consultant, quoted in *Business Week,* December 2, 1996

There is a widening consensus in East Asia that those who liberalize [their economies] first and fastest gain the most.

> HEATHER J. SMITH, guest scholar at the Brookings Institution, a liberal think tank, quoted in the *Journal of Commerce,* November 21, 1996

So far, most Asian theme parks owe more to Disney World than to Confucius.

> *The Economist,* December 21, 1996

It is incredible how much nonsense is talked about East Asia. On the one hand there are the miracle believers, who are still looking for some magical explanation—something unique, something mystical that explains the region's amazing economic results. On the other hand there are the skeptics who think the region is finished.

> NOORDIN SOPIEE, *Asia, Inc.*, December 1996–January 1997

In China, [a Taiwanese national] told [Philip Morris] the cowboy is considered a lower-class worker, little better than a farmhand, and certainly nothing to aspire to. The solution he suggested was to focus the advertisements on the horses, a symbol of aristocracy.

> CATHLEEN BLACK, president of Hearst Magazines, on why the Marlboro Man was a bust in Taiwan, in a speech, March 4, 1997

Although Asian women have always been accorded a low status by their societies, it is intriguing that so many of them should occupy top official positions.

> PROFESSOR DIPANKAR GUPTA, center for the Study of Social Systems, Delhi, India, quoted in *Asia, Inc.,* April 1997

I've been going through ups and downs for 40 years in this business and Asian ups and downs seem to be quicker. You seem to hit puddles and just keep on going. For us, Asia is a long-term play.

> J. WILLARD MARRIOTT JR., CEO of the hotel firm Marriott International, quoted in the *Wall Street Journal,* October 3, 1997

There was a great deal of mythmaking throughout Asia about the real sources of prosperity. They believed their own spin, and we believed it too, because who could argue with success?

> PROFESSOR JOHN DOWER of MIT, quoted in the *New York Times,* November 23, 1997

It is now dawning on Asian policy makers that the old ways of doing business—"the government-business nexus"—can't be done anymore.

> MANU BHASKARAN, of SocGen Crosby Securities in Singapore, quoted in the *Wall Street Journal,* November 28, 1997

The elites [in East Asian countries] will lower their profile, but they won't change. Rule of law is a Western concept. You'll hear a lot of lip service paid to it, but everything will just move underground.

> Asian diplomat stationed in Bangkok, quoted in the *Wall Street Journal,* November 28, 1997

3.2 ASIAN CAPITAL MARKETS

Today mergers and acquisitions may seem like a fraction of the figures in the United States. But five years from now, the Asian figures will be bigger.

> GARY STEAD of the investment firm Merrill Lynch Singapore, quoted in *Asia, Inc.,* April 1997

Four or five years ago, intra-Asian mergers and acquisitions were virtually nonexistent. Basically you didn't sell assets; you passed them on to the next generation.

If you think you can waste your time [before you start] getting into this market, you're wrong.

> DANIEL SCHWARTZ of AVCJ Holdings, publishers of the *Asian M&A Reporter,* quoted in *Asia, Inc.,* April 1997

We get these family-owned banks run by people who are also in other businesses. They just aren't trained to be bankers; they are entrepreneurs. There's a matter of conflict of interest in a region where there has been so much opportunity for the taking.

> WASHINGTON SYCIP, founder of Manila's SGV Group, dean of Philippine financial industry, quoted in the *Wall Street Journal,* October 6, 1997

3.3 AUSTRALIA

In Sydney, you're in Asia, but not of Asia. Basing your Asian operations in Sydney is like basing your operations for the Americas in Rio de Janeiro.

> DONALD SAUNDERS of Platinum Technology in Singapore, quoted in *Asia, Inc.,* December 1996–January 1997

It's often the wife of the CEO who influences the choice [of where to locate regional headquarters for operations in Asia]. And if she finds she can't afford to be a member of two golf clubs, or can't afford a car, she will vote for Sydney.

> Official of Australia's New South Wales administration, quoted in *Asia, Inc.,* December 1996–January 1997

One of our big problems is that we went through a period where we could export anything we picked off the ground, and a job was whatever you decided to do. Trade was taking a mountain and shipping it off to Japan.

> RICHARD HUMPHRY, managing director of Australian Stock Exchange, quoted in the *National Times,* July–August 1996

Seinfeld is the number-one television program in Australia, and the Chicago Bulls are on more often in Australia than in New York.

> TOM SCOTNICKI, New York correspondent, *New Limited of Australia,* speaking on New York Public Radio, November 20, 1996

Look at what happened in Australia under Bob Hawke. A country with a triple-A credit rating. It's now economically pretty sad. In the newspaper, these problems were looked upon as a lot of bumbling and incompetence. But, in fact, they were quite well conceived and carried off. It took, you know, 20 or 30 years for a country with the highest credit rating in the world, with 98 percent of all known natural resources, and only a population of 15 million to be ruined. So, I mean, it couldn't have been done better if it was more purposeful.

> Actor MEL GIBSON, quoted in *Vanity Fair,* August 1997

The Australian economy has averaged 3.5 percent annual growth over the last six years, with inflation at 2.3 percent. . . . The economy is now more profitable than it ever was.

> IAN MacFARLANE, governor of Australian Reserve Bank, quoted in the *Financial Times,* September 19, 1997

3.4 BHUTAN

We will succeed through customer support. We offer a one-year warranty with 24-hour on-site service. Foreign companies can't do this. Their volume is too small.

> KARMA SINGAY, founder of Peljorkhang Infotech Pvt. Ltd., which assembles foreign-made parts into a proprietary line of PCs, quoted in *Asia, Inc.,* April 1997

3.5 BURMA

There are a lot of Burmese yuppies.

> JAN STANDAERT, research adviser to Nielsen SRG Myanmar Project, which conducted Burma's first economic surveys, quoted in the *Wall Street Journal,* August 1, 1996

We're trading geological risk for political risk. If you're in early and establish strong relationships [with the government], they don't forget you.

> ROBERT BEECH, chairman of the oil firm Unocal, on decision to continue oil-field development in Burma in spite of pressure on Burma's president by its Congress to ban new investment, quoted in the *Wall Street Journal,* November 20, 1996

3.6 CHINA

When China wakes it will shake the world.

> NAPOLEON, who advised that China be allowed to
> sleep

[The] 1990s is a decade of crucial importance for our modernization construction. Our main target in the decade is to realize the second phase strategy objective for modern development, doubling our GNP over again and bringing people's living standards up to a well-off level by the end of the century. With accomplished second-step strategy objectives, we shall be assured of coming to the third-step objective to promote average per capita GNP to the level of medium-developed countries and realize the modernization of our national economy between the 30s and the 50s of the next century. [The phrasing reflects the official translation.]

The central task for accelerating reform is to change the highly centralized planned economic structure in the past, to illuminate obstacles to the development of productivity, and establish new socialist economic structure as early as possible, so as to further liberate the social productivity. [The phrasing reflects the official translation.]

> GAN ZIU, vice chairman, State Planning Commission,
> People's Republic of China, in a speech, July 28,
> 1992

It's no longer a question of what the leaders want. If the leaders don't [promote] progress and prosperity to replace backwardness and poverty, there will be a revolution in China, a real one in which armies will change sides and shoot ministers. That's part of the Chinese tradition.

The people know that it's the system that is at fault. They see the Taiwanese. . . . They look at Hong Kong. If people in Singapore and Taiwan can make it and people in China cannot, then it has to be because of the stupidity of the Soviet system that Mao adopted.

> LEE KUAN YEW, former Prime Minister of Singapore,
> quoted in the Economist, November 28, 1992

In 1978 one in 300 Chinese owned a television set and one in 10,000 a washing machine. Now there are roughly 13 televisions and seven washing machines for every 100 people.

> The Economist, June 6, 1992

. . . China is in uncharted waters. No country has tried to accomplish so much in so short a time. China's unique attempt to complete two transitions at once—from a command economy to a market economy and from a rural to an urban society—is without historical precedent.

> China 2020: Development Challenges in the New Century (The World Bank, 1997)

3.6.1 Banks

Any transitional economy is going to have banking sector problems. The question is not whether this is the tip of the iceberg but how big is the iceberg.

> Representative of an international lending institution in Beijing, on the collapse of China Agribusiness Development Trust and Investment Corporation, quoted in the Financial Times, January 15, 1997

3.6.2 Capitalism

Money worship is so much in vogue that it has caused concern, for this is intolerable under socialism.

> Peking Review, an official Chinese journal, quoted in U.S. News & World Report, August 25, 1985

China doesn't seem to have the same intellectual fetters as the Soviet Union. It is, to a laudable extent, imitating capitalistic development paths that the Japanese took after the Meiji restoration in the last century. They sent students all over to learn Western technology so they could create their own educational capital for a new generation to carry on the development of capital, which was the basis for their industrial progress.

> PROFESSOR ROBERT MUNDELL of Columbia University, quoted in Forbes, May 5, 1986

You can't really govern a billion people with one doctrine. The more they try to control centrally, the more trouble they have. On the other hand, if you leave these regions to prosper and go their own way, i.e., the "Commonwealth of China" approach, there will be "20 Singapores" in China and they will prosper.

> KENICHI OHMAE of the consulting firm McKinsey & Co., in a speech, February 7, 1992

I thought the factory had an obligation to take care of me. The managers sit in their Mercedes-Benzes, and we are hardly getting a thing.

> Thirty-eight-year-old mother fired after 12 years working at a state-run Shanghai firm, quoted in Business Week, January 31, 1994

If you have money, then you can buy human rights.

> FUZHOU, taxi driver, on the privileges of wealth, including winning court cases against government officials, quoted in *Business Week,* June 6, 1994

State companies are just getting swamped. Private or basically private companies are flourishing. I think the socialist sector will just fade away.

> EIICHI WATANABE of the Asian Development Bank, quoted in the *Wall Street Journal,* July 20, 1995

To get rich is glorious.

> THE LATE PRESIDENT DENG XIAOPING, quoted in the *New York Times Magazine,* February 18, 1996

Giving credit is like taking drugs. . . . Distributors get hooked and demand ever larger amounts.

> DANIEL WONG, Chinese manager for the computer firm AST Research, quoted in the *Wall Street Journal,* April 8, 1996

Here, a lot more companies die of indigestion than of starvation.

> STEPHAN CHAN of Digital Equipment Corporation in China, on the problem of uncollectable commercial loans, quoted in the *Wall Street Journal,* April 8, 1996

We mostly talk about how to make more money.

> PETER ZHAO, former Red Guard, on reunions with old comrades, quoted in the *Wall Street Journal,* April 21, 1996

Under capitalism, you have to pinch people to make them move, like frogs.

> WANG HONGBIN, Communist Party chief in Najie Village, China (which is being subsidized to prove that Communism is still viable), quoted in the *Wall Street Journal,* October 7, 1996

This is China's Gilded Age. These Chinese Carnegies and Rockefellers are more successful than their American counterparts—they made more money within a shorter time.

> Chinese academic quoted in Xiao-huang Yin, "China's Gilded Age," *Atlantic Monthly,* April 1994

Iron rice bowl.

> Term for Chinese system of guaranteed employment and minimum living standards, cited in the *New York Times,* September 18, 1997

[W]e're not eating from the big iron rice bowl anymore.

> Chinese insurance customer, quoted in *Asia Times,* January 22, 1996

China has emphasized the spirit and culture throughout history, but now in Shenzhen and other parts of China, money is most important. You earn respect if you're rich.

> KITTY, 27, former university language student, on why she has become a *mamasan* at a hostess bar instead of a tour guide (the normal career path for her field), quoted in *Asia, Inc.,* March 1997

It's easy to become a factory official if you're a woman, and you're willing to pay a price.

> HONG XIAOHUIA, who assembles Barbie dolls for Mattel in Changan, quoted in the *Wall Street Journal,* October 29, 1996 (She declined her manager's offer to promote her if she would become his girlfriend.)

3.6.3 Changing Management Practice

We chose the strong points of Japanese and U.S. management styles. Japan is very successful at building group spirit. U.S. companies emphasize individual abilities. We designed a system to let people show off their own talents.

> ZHANG RUIMIN, president of the consumer electronics firm Haier Group Company, quoted in the *Wall Street Journal,* September 17, 1997

3.6.4 Consumers

Consumers' limited experience with modern marketing makes them depend on reputable brands and track records.

As one indicator of brand importance, Chinese consumers usually leave the makers' tags on the sleeves of their suits and the brand stickers on their sunglasses.

> RICH YAN, vice president of the Hong Kong office of the consulting firm Bain & Co., quoted in the *Harvard Business Review,* September–October 1994

There's no infrastructure there [in China]. People can't afford cars. They buy appliances first.

> WALLY TSUKA, founder and chairman of Saturn Electronics & Engineering, quoted in *Inc. 500,* 1996

People in the cities have a TV, stereo, fridge and washing machine. Now they want a PC. It's a symbol of modernity.

China could be number three in the world [in new PC sales, after the United States and Japan] by the year 2000.

> RICHMOND LO of Personal Computer Company, part of IBM's Greater China Group, quoted in *Forbes*, October 6, 1997

The assumption, usually correct, is that foreign goods are better than China's own goods—and in any case they have the sub appeal of the exotic. This appeal can take surprising forms: one bathhouse in Beijing offers a reviving soak in the instant coffee of Nescafé and Maxwell House.

> *The Economist,* June 6, 1992

We [my husband and I] spend all our money without thinking much about the future.

> CHEN XIOLI, Chinese consumer, quoted in the *Wall Street Journal,* July 15, 1996

The couple [Chen Xioli and her husband] earn a combined monthly income of 4,500 yuan ($542) . . . Marlboro cigarettes—which cost the equivalent of $1.80 a pack . . . 50 percent more than local brands . . . imported appliances, including two Sony televisions, Mitsubishi air conditioner . . . Eat regularly at McDonald's. [Some of the things Chen Xioli and her husband spend their money on.]

> Cited in the *Wall Street Journal,* July 15, 1996

The philosophy [of Chinese tourists] is spend less money, see more places.

> SONG CHAOGI, general manager of China International Travel Service, Shanghai, quoted in the *Financial Times,* May 26, 1997

3.6.5 Democracy

[W]e must not assume that a free market in goods can produce or protect a free market in ideas. Nor can we abandon our responsibility to support human rights around the world. . . . The American people would have it no other way.

> FORMER U.S. SECRETARY OF STATE WARREN CHRISTOPHER, quoted in the *Washington Post,* March 22, 1994

The best lessons that China will learn about the dignity and treatment of workers, education and training, fair practice free of corruption, environmental consciousness and ethical conduct are being learned from American enterprises.

> LYN W. EDINGER, chairman of the American Chamber of Commerce in Hong Kong, testifying at a House of Representatives subcommittee hearing, February 24, 1994

China will never accept the U.S. human rights concept. History has already proven that it is futile to apply pressure on China.

> PRIME MINISTER LI PENG, quoted in *Congressional Quarterly,* April 15, 1996

Management training is the most sought-after commodity in China today. . . . Within the next five years, foreign companies will be relying much less on imported Chinese as local training grows and supplies more local managers.

> JOHN DOLFIN of Hong Kong–based executive search firm Amrop International

One of the reasons for optimism about China. . . . is that communism is finished, having been replaced by nationalism. High-speed economic growth is now the legitimating factor behind the government.

The greatest weakness of the Chinese military is the possibility of its cutting off China's greatest asset—the 62 million overseas Chinese, some of the most highly educated and richest people anywhere. Without them, China will not be able to develop.

> CHALMERS JOHNSON, president of the Japan Policy Research Institute, *Asia, Inc.,* June 1996

I don't pay personal income taxes. Everything belongs to my companies, nothing to me.

> LIU XIAOQING, millionaire movie actress, quoted in the *Wall Street Journal,* June 11, 1997

3.6.6 Doing Business

You just have to do things the way you think they should be done and see what happens sometimes. If you ask outright the answer is always no.

> MELVIN SONG, head of Dentsu, Young & Rubicam Advertising in Beijing, quoted in the *New York Times,* October 11, 1992

First, you must sell yourself. Then, you can sell the product.

> EDMUND WANG HUA, salesman for the insurance company American International Group, quoted in the *Asia Times,* January 22, 1996

I have no interest in dealing with China because their mentality and system of working is not up to international standards.

> Manager of Chinese-run company in Thailand, quoted in *Asia, Inc.,* May 1996

China has too many rules to be comprehensible to people not familiar with the Chinese way of doing things. On the face of it, the system is rigid, but the people operating the system aren't rigid. They can bend. If you can establish a good relationship with them, things can be easier.

> PAUL WONG, associate director of China project development for K. Wah Management Services, Ltd., Hong Kong, quoted in the *New York Times Magazine,* February 18, 1996

We don't want to resolve issues through wining and dining but through the law.

> ZHOU YONGPING, Overseas Chinese Affairs official, quoted in the *New York Times Magazine,* February 18, 1996

Five Rules for Doing Business in China:

1. Think small—focus on one region at a time.
2. Skip the manager, talk to the clerk.
3. Study the side streets.
4. Get the goods to market.
5. Above all be flexible.

> MICHAEL McCUNE, American management consultant, cited in the *New York Times Magazine,* February 18, 1996

When you're in China, you should do as the Chinese. Drink alcohol. Sing karaoke.

> Former Guangzhou TV news reporter, quoted in *Asia Online,* September 1996

3.6.7 Economic Policy

China's need for a lot of foreign exchange may be just psychological.

> PAULINE LOONG of the investment firm Jardine Fleming Securities Ltd., commenting on China's

amassing of more hard currency reserves than any country except Japan, quoted in the *Wall Street Journal,* February 16, 1997

If China can intervene to prop up the currency [of Hong Kong], what's to stop it from manipulating the currency to less virtuous ends?

> DWIGHT PERKINS of the Harvard Institute for International Development, on the possibility that China's vast reserves may be used to stop a run on the Hong Kong dollar, quoted in the *New York Times,* October 30, 1997

Having an economy which is half planned and half free is like driving fast with a foot on the brake and the accelerator at the same time.

> DAVID ROCHE of the London forecasting firm Independent Strategy, quoted in *Forbes,* December 29, 1997

3.6.8 The Environment

. . . China in the next 10 to 15 years plans to produce 100 million new refrigerators—using CFCs as the refrigerant—and to install 100 gigawatts of coal-burning power plants, vastly increasing its output of greenhouse gases.

> FRED KRUPP, executive director of the Environmental Defense Fund, in a speech, August 1, 1992

3.6.9 *Feng Shui*

Feng Shui—the two Chinese characters stand for "wind" and "water"—is a 4,000-year-old technique for improving your chances in life by arranging furniture, travel dates, choice of mistress, and so on in a way that takes best advantage of luck and natural forces.

In late 1991, as a lark the Hong Kong office of Credit Lyonnais Securities ask the *feng shui* men to deliver their thoughts about the 1992 stock market. . . . [It proved "remarkably accurate"] . . . [A]n Elliott wave analysis of the chart found an eerie number of near-perfect Fibonacci ratios between the chart movements.

> *The Economist,* January 23, 1993

[When he tried to get me to accept a license plate with the number 2958, he (a car dealer)] obviously thought I was an ignorant foreigner, but I knew that the plate meant "continuous improvement with no money." I would have been a laughingstock. I told him to find something better, and he got 782 meaning "always prospering in business"—which, I am happy to say, has proved true.

> STEPHEN CODRON, businessman, quoted in *Harvard Business Review,* May–June 1991

When people walk into a place and there's a good feeling, it registers on the subconscious, and they're more relaxed, more effective. This is what I engineer.

> PUN YIN of Tin Sun Metaphysics in New York, who has consulted with executives at Kleinwort Benson, Morgan Stanley, Smith Barney, and clothing designer Elie Tahari at fees starting at $400 per site visit, quoted in *Fortune,* September 29, 1997

3.6.10 Foreign Companies

With the largest population on earth, traders for 150 years have dreamed of tapping the China market. Businessmen in nineteenth-century Britain dreamed of adding an inch to the shirt of every Chinese. Today, we dream of putting a cellular phone in the hands of every Chinese.

> AMBASSADOR CHARLENE BARSHEFSKY, U.S. trade representative, in a speech, May 21, 1996

I have always been amazed at the ignorance of cosmetics companies which fill Asian markets with foundations and colors that look perfect on Caucasians and ridiculous on us.

> YUE-SAI KAN, founder of Yue-Sai Kan Cosmetics Ltd. in China, quoted in *Asia, Inc.,* November 1996

Some years ago, after we'd introduced Tang into China, a number of look-alike knock-offs appeared, including one fairly good effort named "Tong," which was manufactured, coincidentally enough, by the General Foods Company of China—apparently they'd even copied our company's name.

But before we could mount a counterattack, consumers solved the problem for us. Even though our advertising was very modest, *Tang's* reputation had been established among the local "influentials" abroad. The result was that Tong and its fellow counterfeits failed, while *Tang* became a major brand in the emerging Chinese market.

> JOHN RUFF of Kraft Foods International, in a speech, April 22, 1996

The decision [by a foreign company] on whether to make an investment is dependent on advice they get from a foreign law firm. This will be another barrier they will have to hurdle.

> "Western diplomat," referring to restrictions on certification of foreign lawyers practicing in China to protect local jobs, quoted in the *Wall Street Journal,* December 13, 1996

3.6.11 Foreign Managers

It's a dirty secret among the human resources community as to the number of times executives fail to fulfill the terms of their overseas contracts. The cost it implies, in terms of dispensing cash and losing clients, is enormous.

> ROBIN V. SEARS of the executive recruiting firm Korn/ Ferry International China-Hong Kong Ltd., quoted in the Asian edition of the *Wall Street Journal,* September 27, 1997

Many experts estimate 25–40 percent of ex-pats assigned to China fail to complete their contracts.

> HAL LIPPER, quoted in the Asian edition of the *Wall Street Journal,* September 27, 1997

Nine out of 10 failures are family related.

> RICHARD BAHNER, former head of human relations for Citibank's North Asian division, quoted in the Asian edition of the *Wall Street Journal,* September 27, 1997

3.6.12 Greater China

Chinese businesses—many of which are located outside the People's Republic itself—make up the world's fourth economic power.

. . . Chinese-owned businesses in East Asia, the United States, Canada, and even further afield are increasingly becoming part of what I call the *Chinese Commonwealth.*

> JOHN KAO of Harvard Business School, *Harvard Business Review,* March–April 1993

The more people of Chinese descent are successful in business the more others are envious of their success.

> WANG GUNGWU, chancellor of the University of Hong Kong, quoted in *Asia, Inc.,* May 1996

The influence of U.S. values and business practices on Chinese communities around the world is most obvious where the connection is weakest. As experienced victims of racial persecution, the Chinese of the Pacific Basin have good reason to welcome big friends like the United States. Especially in Southeast Asia, Chinese have been victimized by people who envy their success. The vivid images of ancestors slaughtered in racial massacres do not fade easily—all the more reason for overseas Chinese to appreciate America's continued political and military presence in the region.

America has become the educator for the Pacific Rim. Unlike the exclusionist universities of Japan, where foreigners will not have an easy time finding teaching jobs at Tokyo University, American education is determinedly internationalist. No one has benefited more from U.S. higher education and technological training than the overseas Chinese.

> FRANK B. GIBNEY, president of the think tank Pacific Basin Institute, *Harvard Business Review*, March–April 1993

Many of our forebears came to this country as laborers. They built the railroads and harvested the pineapple and other crops. But then they did something no one expected. Like other immigrants, freed from the constraints of the old country, they reinvented themselves.

They became entrepreneurs, inventors, scientists.

> GARETH C. C. CHANG, of Hughes Electronics Corporation, in a speech, March 15, 1997

Over the years, the overseas Chinese have flourished as entrepreneurs, bankers, traders, and investors. . . . By harnessing the talents of the overseas Chinese to an accelerated program of financial market liberalization, China's leaders can overcome the problems that threaten privatization.

> KLAUS FRIEDERICH, chief economist for Germany's Dresdner Bank, quoted in the *New York Times*, September 28, 1997

Chinese in general are not . . . comfortable [having] others advise them on their money. They like to keep their net worth within the family.

> DOMINIC NG, president of East-West Bank in Los Angeles, explaining why he and other bankers have

been slow to offer a broad menu of financial services to Chinese clients, quoted in the *Financial Times*, January 15, 1997

Chinese buyers are bottom feeders.

> BILL McMORROW, CEO of Kennedy Wilson International, Santa Monica real estate brokers with links to Asia, quoted in the *Financial Times*, January 15, 1997

3.6.13 *Guo quing*

[*Note: Guo quing* connotes consistency with Chinese ways of doing things. Examples of acceptable marketing are items that cater to the single "emperor" child each family is allowed to have and foreign autos purchased on government expense accounts in such arms of the state as the military, ministries, and schools.]

Western cultures and ideas should be adopted only if they fit *guo quing*. Good ideas applicable in China should be promoted; corrupted and inapplicable ideas should be discarded.

> THE LATE PRESIDENT DENG XIAOPING, Communist Party directive 1984, cited by Rich Yan of the consulting firm Bain & Co., quoted in the *Harvard Business Review*, September–October 1994

Never make a purchase until you have compared three shops. [Chinese wisdom that reflects standards of *guo quing*. This precludes impulse buying; retailers should expect a great deal of browsing.]

> Cited by Rich Yan of the consulting firm Bain & Co., quoted in the *Harvard Business Review*, September–October 1994

3.6.14 The Internet

Don't expect home access to the Internet to be a factor in China for another five years. Most of the growth will be in corporate use. That's where the market is today and that's where the market is going to be five years from now.

The lack of local content is the No. 1 inhibitor for the Internet in China.

> SIMON BAKER, chairman of the Hong Kong information-technology research firm New Century Group, quoted in *Asia, Inc.*, September 1997

3.6.15   Life Insurance

In China under the welfare benefits system in the past, everything was provided by the country. Only with the reforms do people think they need the type of security of insurance.

> KAREN X. Q. HU of the Shanghai office of the insurance firm American International Group (AIG), quoted in the *Washington Post,* February 15, 1995

Let's get the boss to sign up. If the boss buys, the rest of them [the sales staff] will be easy.

I go for the women. You sell a policy to a man and the next day he may come back and ask for a refund because his wife objected. That never happens when I sell to a woman.

> LILY HUA, door-to-door life insurance salesperson for American International Group (AIG) in Shanghai, on the key to selling policies at a department store, quoted in the *New York Times,* April 4, 1995

3.6.16   The Military and Business

China isn't like the West. Even the military is in business. Everyone is in business.

> YUKUO TAHENAKA, consultant for trans-Pacific investment, on flight of Chinese government capital to the United States, quoted in the *Wall Street Journal,* July 21, 1996

At the end of the day, this is an army that is more interested in making money than it is in being the guardian of the national interest. [Military commanders have opened coal mines, karaoke bars, real estate, bean curd, livestock, and other businesses, as well as peddled surplus arms.]

> JONATHAN D. POLLACK, China specialist for the think tank Rand Corporation, quoted in the *New York Times,* December 3, 1996

They [the military] have to come up with a third of their own budget so they cannot afford to get rid of these businesses.

> American military official who served in Beijing Corporation, quoted in the *New York Times,* December 3, 1996

Key supporters [of the post–Deng Xiaoping regime] are the military, whose budget grew 12.7 percent this year, and impoverished inland provinces, where the government has set the costly goal of eradicating poverty in 2 ½ years.

> *Wall Street Journal,* June 11, 1997

In China, corruption is so disorganized, you don't know how to calculate your costs. You build a highway, every time the highway goes through a village, somebody will ask for money. You can't just go to the leader and solve the problem; you really don't know who you should pay.

> MAN-LUI LAU, Hong Kong economist at the University of San Francisco, quoted in the Asian edition of the *Wall Street Journal,* October 22, 1996

All of us working in China realize we are probably working ourselves out of future opportunities as the Chinese obtain the experience.

> DON HACKL, Chicago architect designing high-rises in Shenzhen, quoted in *Business Week,* November 28, 1994

3.6.17   Post–Deng Xiaoping

People need to buy moisturizer. They couldn't care much if Deng Xiaoping has passed away.

> MISS WANG, working at the cosmetics counter of a Shanghai department store the day after Deng Xiaoping died, quoted in the *Financial Times Weekend,* February 22–23, 1997

Why should we be sad? He might have been good for the economy, but he butchered the students in Beijing.

> "One young graduate," quoted in the *Financial Times Weekend,* February 22–23, 1997

The challenge for Deng's successors is whether they can create a new legitimacy that will be the basis for completing China's transition into a functioning modern nation-state.

> PROFESSOR EMERITUS LUCIAN PYE of MIT, quoted in the *Financial Times,* February 21, 1997

Leninism and consumerism are not an easy mix.

> ROSS TERRILL, author of *China in Our Time,* quoted in the *New York Times,* February 20, 1997

They've reached the conclusion that state ownership won't work; China is now committed to free markets.

> JEFFREY SACHS, director of the Harvard Institute for International Development, quoted in the *New York Times,* September 18, 1997

With the economy booming, they can afford the hard decisions.

> HARRY BROADMAN, senior economist at the World Bank, quoted in the *New York Times,* September 18, 1997

Communism has lost every sort of bearing. In China, it is essentially a mafia offering rising prosperity in exchange for political submission. In the West, it has given up all talk of seizing the commanding heights of the economy in exchange for a rearguard action against the sweeping advance of market forces.

> JONATHAN EYAL, director of studies at London's Royal United Services Institute, reacting to President Jiang Zemin's announcement that 10,000 state-owned companies would be sold to shareholders, quoted in the *New York Times,* September 21, 1997

We absolutely condemn the latest Chinese decisions. They illustrate the way in which the Chinese have become one of the bulwarks of American-driven globalization, the very force that is threatening European workers.

> RAMON MANTOVANI, Italian Communist and Member of Parliament, quoted in the *New York Times,* September 21, 1997

3.6.18 Privatization

The West privatized industries, China is privatizing cities.

> PHILIP TOSE, chairman of Peregrine Investments, quoted in the *Financial Times,* June 16, 1997

Although on the one hand they are saying assets are being sold cheaply to foreign investors, on the other hand what is the alternative? There are no alternatives. They need money to expand the economy.

> LOUIS KOO, head of corporate finance (Hong Kong and China) for ABN Amro Hoare Govett, quoted in the *Financial Times,* June 16, 1997

China's political philosophy is, you cannot be a great power if you are heavily indebted to the rest of the world, as it was in the early twentieth century. Its whole philosophy is to limit dependence on foreign debt.

> STEPHEN TARAN of the investment bank Lehman Brothers in Hong Kong, quoted in the *Financial Times,* June 16, 1997

Everybody's calling it "privatization," which may not be the case. All we really know is that Jiang made it politically correct to sell shares.

> ROBERT DERNBERGER, director of the Center for Chinese Studies at the University of Michigan, quoted in the *New York Times,* September 18, 1997

3.6.19 Profits

What the researchers found surprising was that although Hong Kong and Taiwanese investments represented more than 80 percent of foreign enterprises at the time, U.S. and Japanese investments had greater overall profits: As many as 21.82 percent of Japanese and 18.03 percent of U.S. companies made profits of more than 15 percent of revenues, compared to 7.65 percent of Hong Kong companies and 1.86 percent of Taiwanese.

[T]he findings suggest that companies manufacturing in China for Chinese consumers are more profitable than companies that manufacture to export . . .

> From research of PROFESSOR PETER S. K. CHI of Cornell, YIGANG PAN of DePaul University, and CHARNG KAO of First Institute of Ching-Hua Institute for Economic Research, Taipei, cited in the *Harvard Business Review,* January–February 1996

3.6.20 Role of Politics

We [senior Communist Party officials] have our role. We provide the vision that managers are too busy for.

> LI WEIDONG, vice director of the Communist Party Affairs Department, on the contribution that senior Party officials make in upper management of Chinese companies, quoted in the *New York Times,* November 23, 1996

Government control, that's what's keeping us back. We want to be international, but the central government is afraid we'll grow too fast. They want to tighten control.

> WANG HUIZHONG, Shanghai stock analyst, quoted in the *New York Times,* November 23, 1996

Talking politics in China is dangerous.

I need billions of dollars. In China, you can only find millions. China is too small for me.

> MOU QIZHONG, "China's most popular capitalist," quoted in the *Wall Street Journal,* August 28, 1996

In China, it's important that you can prove to the leaders that you do not abandon them when they are in trouble.

> ADRIAN FU, chairman of Hong Kong's Furama Hotel Enterprises Ltd., quoted in *Forbes,* July 28, 1997

3.6.21 Size of Market

If we can get a 10 percent share, we'll sell more toothbrushes there than we do in the United States.

> ALFRED ZIEN, CEO of Gillette on the introduction of Oral-B at $.90 to compete with the local brand, which costs $.19, quoted in *Fortune,* August 23, 1993

Everything kind of pales next to China.

> ROBERT E. ALLEN, CEO of AT&T, quoted in *Business Week,*, March 27, 1995

Not many people in China can afford a Porsche but they all buy toothpaste.

> ADRIAN BENDALL-CHARLES, corporate security adviser, noting the volume of corporate espionage in mass-market consumer companies, quoted in *Asia, Inc.,* March 1997

I go to Mount Sinai Hospital, and I have got to get down on my knees to sell one CAT scan. I go to China, a guy comes to lunch and orders 100.

> JOHN F. WELCH JR., CEO of GE, quoted in *Fortune,* February 21, 1994

China is such a potentially huge market that if 1 percent of Chinese people could afford cars, that would be 12 million. That's roughly our market size of Europe.

> MICHAEL G. MEYERAND of General Motors, quoted in the *New York Times Magazine,* February 18, 1996

There are 809 million television homes in the world; 250 million of them are in China.

> MARK HERSHHORN, CEO of National Media Corporation, quoted in the *New York Times,* November 17, 1996

3.6.22 Stock Market

After the rush of the past 10 years, Chinese companies realize that Hong Kong is not a gold mine. Our experience tells us we can earn most of our money from China.

> FRANK NING of the mainland investment firm China Resources, quoted in the *Financial Times,* January 21, 1997

I think they [red chip companies] will play by the rules to the same degree they feel the local tycoons have played by the rules. But their interpretation of the rules in Hong Kong is that you use whatever clout you can bring to bear.

> JOHN MULCAHY of the Hong Kong investment firm W.I. Carr, quoted in the *Financial Times,* February 24, 1997

Flogging off the state silver, particularly to foreigners, is obviously a bit touchy. There is also the fact that some of these "red chip" manufacturers are becoming instant millionaires through allocation of share options when they come to market. That may well spark some resentment back home.

> Honk Kong investment banker, quoted in the *Financial Times Weekend,* May 24–25, 1997

A mile-long queue of thousands of people twisted along the south end of Jiangning Road. They wished to become stockholders.

> *China Daily,* Beijing, reporting that the first public stock offering in China in 36 years—100,000 shares of a Shanghai photocopying firm—sold out in less than eight hours. Quoted in *U.S. News & World Report,* February 19, 1985

There are bull markets and there are bear markets, but Shanghai is a money market, because it jumps up and down.

> Professor at Fudan University, Shanghai, quoted in *Fortune,* July 22, 1996

3.6.23 Tycoons

He [the kind of entrepreneur we like to invest in] has a very simple objective. He's not interested in cleaning up the environment, or in saving the people in Guangdong, or in affirmative action. He's interested in making money.

> ROBERT THELEEN, chairman of the investment firm ChinaVest Ltd., quoted in *Forbes,* August 3, 1992

I am not in the job of trying to get idiots to understand. I tell them to go to hell.

> Hong Kong businessman GORDON WU, developer of the Guangzhou-Shenzhen Superhighway from Hong Kong to Guangzhou, quoted in *Asia, Inc.,* September 1996

When I was young, I envied the democratic freedom of the West, their sexual liberty. Now I envy their horses.

> GAO HUAN, Chinese entrepreneur who owns both a factory that makes electronic components for the credit-card industry and a stud farm, quoted in the *New York Times Magazine,* February 18, 1996

In China, the boundaries between legality and illegality are often unclear. Western companies have been penalized when their employees have crossed a boundary line they did not know existed.

> *Outlook '97,* publication of the Control Risk Group, U.K., cited in the *Financial Times,* February 17, 1997

3.6.24 U.S. Policy

What is America's agenda in China? Most important, it should promote young, reform-minded Chinese—not party hacks trained during the excesses of the past 40 years—as the successors to the current generation of leaders. A key goal: Encourage these new leaders to see economic growth and widening prosperity as the dominant political direction for China in the years ahead.

> PROFESSOR RUDI DORNBUSCH of MIT, quoted in *Business Week,* September 30, 1996

Let me start with a simple proposition: We will never achieve China's full integration into the international community by building walls that divide us. The most repressive periods in modern Chinese history did not occur in times of open exchange—they occurred in times of isolation.

> U.S. TRADE REPRESENTATIVE MICKEY KANTOR, in a speech, January 31, 1996

Looking ahead, in terms of the policy environment, the U.S. has to realize that we are sending the Chinese mixed messages. On the one hand, our corporate community is telling them that business is the priority between our countries and we want closer ties. On the other hand, our government policy is telling them that the Cold War is still alive and what we merely deplore in other countries we condemn in China.

> GARETH C. C. CHANG of Hughes Electronics Corporation, in a speech, September 20, 1996

The United States has no interest in containing China. What the United States wants is to sustain commercial engagement with China . . . in a way that will include the chances that there will be more liberty and more prosperity.

> U.S. PRESIDENT BILL CLINTON, in a speech, quoted in the *Wall Street Journal,* November 21, 1996

We've been told that if we keep our months shut about human rights and [arms] proliferation there would be a big economic payoff. Except for airplanes and a number of low-value commodities like oil seeds and textile fibers, our exports to China have been pathetic.

> ALAN TONELSON, senior researcher for the U.S. Business and Industrial Council, quoted in the *Wall Street Journal,* February 21, 1997

We can properly be faulted for vastly underinvesting in our relationships with Chinese officials up and down the line.

> U.S. TREASURY SECRETARY ROBERT RUBIN, quoted in the *New York Times,* September 28, 1997

3.6.25 The United States and China by the Numbers

Each Chinese consumer buys an average of less than $10 worth of U.S.-made goods each year, compared with $1,000 for every Taiwanese, around $550 for every Japanese and South Korean, $80 for every Brazilian, and even $20 for each Indonesian.

> THOMAS J. DUESTERBERG of the think tank Hudson Institute and former assistant Secretary of Commerce, quoted in the *Wall Street Journal,* April 23, 1997

3.7 HONG KONG

What was once a barren rock has been transformed into a twenty-first-century international metropolis. This is thanks largely to a British financial government that was just unimaginative enough to let the once penniless refugee population alone to pursue millions of dreams of how to get rich quickly.

> KEVIN RAFFERTY, former Asian editor for *Financial Times,* quoted in the *Harvard Business Review,* May–June 1991

There's nowhere in the world people can derive as much income and pay as little tax as Hong Kong.

> Anonymous investment analyst, quoted in *Asia, Inc.,* September 1996

People said the Chinese didn't eat cheese. Rubbish.

> MUNGO GILCHRIST III, business development manager for Hong Kong franchise of Pizza Hut, quoted in the *Economist,* March 5, 1988 (Hong Kong has the world's biggest Pizza Hut, and the company's franchises there were its biggest earners.)

Hong Kong (which means "fragrant harbor") dumps two million metric tons of raw sewage into Victoria Harbor every day.

> LINDA G. STUNTZ, Acting Deputy Secretary of Energy, in a speech, April 30, 1992

For a lot of big U.S. companies, it doesn't matter how much they pay the landlord as along as they can get close to the Chinese border.

> LYALL ALEXANDER-WEBBER, Hong Kong property agent, on skyrocketing rents in Hong Kong, quoted in *Business Week,* March 14, 1994

The people who are still here have to be optimistic or else they would have left by now.

> ALAN WONG, associate director at brokerage house W.I. Carr (Far East), quoted in the *Wall Street Journal,* October 28, 1996

[W]e can safely say that China will continue to make progress in the years to come. Hong Kong's way of life will remain. There is nothing to worry about.

> JAMES CAI, Jinghua, executive director of Guangdong Investment, quoted in *Asia, Inc.,* November 1996

If Hong Kong stands firm and fights then we will have a strong chance of autonomy. If we let [the mainland Chinese] run Hong Kong, no matter how sincere they are, they wouldn't know how to run it. All we have to do is to try to uphold the freedoms we have—to really love them.

> JIMMY LAI CHEE YING, Hong Kong garment and publishing magnate, quoted in *Asia, Inc.,* February 1996

[After handing over of Hong Kong] the Chinese will not suddenly behave as though they are graduates of the Wharton Business School. When you tell the Chinese they are in danger of killing the goose that laid the golden egg, they will look you right in the eye and tell you that Chinese history is littered with dead geese.

> CHALMERS JOHNSON, president of the Japan Policy Research Institute, quoted in *Asia, Inc.,* June 1996

Hong Kong will be the melting pot of Western and Chinese business.

> ANTONY K. LEUNG, managing director of Chase Manhattan Bank in Hong Kong and member of the future cabinet of Hong Kong, quoted in *Business Week,* June 9, 1997

Chinese leaders are control freaks. If, as some have suggested, economic growth numbers are state secrets, who among us will have the courage to make predictions?

> MEET LEE, Hong Kong fund manager known for being outspoken, quoted in *Business Week,* June 9, 1997

I like to see myself as the McDonald's of small power stations.

> SAM LEUNG, owner of Hong Kong-based Powerhouse Electric Ltd., developer of small, diesel-driven power plants on the mainland, quoted in *Asia, Inc.,* March 1997

3.8 INDIA

Please understand, to have success traditionally [in India], you require education or money or family background. I didn't have education, I didn't have money, and I didn't have family background. So people say: "Where did this [jerk] come from?"

> DHIRUBHAI AMBANI, chairman of the textile manufacturer Reliance Industries, quoted in *Forbes,* April 7, 1986

India has screwed multinationals for decades. There is no Aladdin's lamp to wish the past away.

> S. K. KHANNA of the accounting firm Arthur Andersen's India operations, quoted in *Fortune,* November 16, 1992

Will it work this time? This government means business, not only because it is ideologically committed to liberalization but also because there is absolutely no option.

> TITOO AHLUWALIA, chairman of the Marketing and Research Group, Bombay, quoted in *Fortune,* November 16, 1992

The problem of socialism is one of performance, not of vision. If it worked, we would all be socialists. Ironically, the legacy of the collectivist bias in Indian thinking has been the perpetuation of poverty. We created an overregulated private sector and an inefficient public sector.

> GURCHARAN DAS of Procter & Gamble, *Harvard Business Review,* March–April 1993

In most sectors, the labor force doesn't see technology as a means for upgrading careers, but as the death of their careers.

> L. V. SUBRAMANIAM, editor of India's *Labour Herald,* quoted in *Business Week,* October 17, 1994

The conventional wisdom is that it [the Indian insurance market] will open [to foreign competition] some time next year. But it's like seeing water in the desert; it keeps moving away from you.

> GORDON CLONEY, International Insurance Council, quoted in the *Economist,* June 17, 1995

Every big American corporation is trying to turn professional managers into entrepreneurs. At least we are going the other way around.

> ANIL AMBANI of Reliance Oil, India's biggest company (which was built by Ambani's father, a former service-station attendant, on a license granted by the government), quoted in the *Economist,* March 9, 1997

The foremost task for any new government will be to set credible rules of the game for attracting private investment into infrastructure.

> MANMOHAN SINGH, Indian finance minister, quoted in *Business Week,* April 29, 1996

There is a big fear that the country is being sold too cheaply.

> MRITYUNJAY ATHREYA, New Delhi consultant, quoted in *Business Week,* April 29, 1996

India's financial boom is being pushed along by Indian expatriates working on Wall Street.

> KAREN TREHON of the investment firm Alliance Capital, quoted in *Business Week,* July 11, 1994

We are telling [foreign companies] that the disincentives are gone. For the rest, we don't have to tell them what India offers because they know it already. In fact, many people told us that but for these restrictions, India would have been much higher in industrialization than it is.

> PRIME MINISTER P. V. NARASHIMHA RAO, quoted in *Forbes,* July 20, 1996

The best way to enter the Indian market is with Indian partners, and the best Indian partners get taken quickly. Coming in late with a partner who is not as strong is a serious double whammy.

> PAOLO FRESCO, GE's head of international operations, quoted in *Forbes,* July 20, 1996

A company sponsoring the upcoming Miss World pageant in Bangalore was recently attacked by women wielding cakes of dried cow dung soaked in kerosene. . . . [N]obody has yet asked the real question: Why was India chosen by the organizers in the first place? It is a little bizarre that the Miss World is being held in a country which cannot even come to grips with the current spread of malaria, dengue, and yellow fever, and in a city which has up to six hours of power cuts daily, no municipal water on alternate days, and not even enough hotel rooms to accommodate all the visitors for this event.

> SUBHASH AGRAWAL, Asian edition of the *Wall Street Journal,* November 14, 1996

India's army of small shareholders face a glum time after the government announced a crackdown on corporate gifts. The move will disappoint the thousands of small investors who turn up at annual general meetings—usually mind-numbingly boring even by international standards—hoping to get a cup of tea, a couple of biscuits, and perhaps nothing more.

> *Financial Times,* March 11, 1997

[P]olitics matters less than it once did. The government's agenda is increasingly set by the middle class, which is aware of how the old statist policies stifled opportunities and depressed their living standards.

> GAURAV DALMIA, member of the conglomerate Dalmia Group, advising potential foreign investors on how to succeed in India, quoted in *Forbes,* August 25, 1997

Hint: Avoid a high profile because it attracts the wrath of vested interest groups. Enron and Kentucky Fried Chicken had to put up with unending hurdles because they got lots of publicity. GVK Power and Domino's Pizza were silent—and successful.

> *Forbes,* August 25, 1997

Negotiating terms in Bombay is a problem. There are no norms and there is a sense of difficulty in concluding deals.

> IAN GOSLING, managing director of Ford Credit India, quoted in *Asia, Inc.,* August 1997

India has an old civilization with ingrained attitudes. For foreigners looking to succeed here, it is crucial to make an effort to understand local culture. Look to integrate, or you will never succeed.

> RUNJIT DUA of the consulting firm Dua & Associates, quoted in the *Financial Times,* April 14, 1997

Foreign investors sometimes rely on their Indian partners too much.

> O. P. VAISH of the consulting firm Vaish Associates, quoted in the *Financial Times,* April 14, 1997

3.9 INDONESIA

[S]ince business arrangements are too often based on connections and not on ability, Indonesia isn't building an entrepreneurial class. And it's difficult for any except the well-connected to accumulate enough capital for investment.

> RAYMOND BONNER, *New Yorker,* June 13, 1988

We haven't reached a consensus about value systems.

> CHRISTIANTO WIBISONO, Indonesian Business Information Center, on the absence of conflict-of-interest laws, quoted in the *New Yorker,* June 13, 1988

Deregulation and debureaucratization certainly do not mean setting up a liberal economic system that allows free competition.

> PRESIDENT SUHARTO, quoted in *Asia, Inc.,* March 1995

Members of the first family do not run real businesses. They are franchise operators. In five years, they won't exist.

> Hong Kong–based American banker with extensive experience in Jakarta, quoted in the *Far Eastern Economic Review,* September 5, 1996

When you talk about economic institutions, Indonesia is going global. When you talk about political institutions, Indonesia is Jurassic Park.

> SJAHRIR, Harvard University–educated economist who runs the Econit consultancy in Jakarta, quoted in *Business Week,* June 16, 1997

Intellectually, I know it would be better for Indonesia if Suharto stepped aside. But . . . as a businessman, I want to postpone the day of reckoning for as long as possible.

> American executive, quoted in *Foreign Affairs,* July–August 1997

There is no good ethic of land management in Indonesia. An underlying view is that this is a developing country; they feel they need to develop with nothing getting in the way.

> Senior environmental official with the World Bank, on Indonesian forest fires (set to clear land) that blanketed Southeast Asia with smoke, quoted in the *Wall Street Journal,* September 30, 1997

My cousin works in the agriculture department.

> RAHMAWATI, orange farmer, who plans to set more fires in spite of a ban, quoted in the *Wall Street Journal,* September 30, 1997

3.10 JAPAN

My predecessor, Irwin Miller, always says, "Facts are friendly." Well, the fact is that the Japanese have established a new world price for our product. Face that fact. Don't pretend that it's not there. Operate in the world the way it is, not the way you wish it were.

> HENRY R. SCHACHT, CEO of Cummins Engine, quoted in *Forbes*, July 14, 1986

In modern times, Japan has been faced with a stark choice: export or die. Japan had a necessity placed upon it by geography and demography. It has lived with the sort of predicament that America has up until recently had the luxury of avoiding.

Unlike nations such as Brazil and Mexico, Japan refused the option of heavy foreign borrowing. Unlike many third world nations, Japan also refused the policy option of allowing extensive direct foreign investment by multinational corporations. Finally, Japan spurned the industrialized path—à la Sweden and France—and emphasized state capitalism.

> DR. PETER CANNON, then of the aerospace firm Rockwell International, in a speech, March 5, 1987

Tokyo makes everything possible—except living.

> JUNKO YOSHIDA of the Victor Company, noting that 30 million people live within a 31-mile radius of the Imperial Palace, quoted in *Forbes*, August 10, 1987

Japan will be the last country to share in a global economic recession if it happens.

> Japan strategist from the investment bank First Boston, quoted in *Fortune*, September 24, 1990

The message [of Nintendo], which is alien to Japanese culture, is that one can take active control of one's situation and change one's fate.

> KENICHI OHMAE, formerly of McKinsey & Company's Tokyo office, quoted in *Harvard Business Review*, May–June 1995

As Japan grew larger and its export share in key industries—such as VCRs, TVs, and automobiles—increased, it ran up against a basic but bitter truth: No country can grow faster than its markets forever.

> WALTER RUSSELL MEAD, presidential fellow at the World Policy Institute at the New School, quoted in *Worth* magazine, August 1996

What we are left with is an overmanipulated economy that can't function normally. It has never been good for

Japan's consumers, and now it isn't working for the producers either.

> KENICHI OHMAE of the consulting firm McKinsey & Co. in Tokyo, quoted in *Fortune*, November 1, 1993

For too long we have been soldiers fighting for the economy, but more and more of us are beginning to think that life is not supposed to always be a war.

> MITSUKO SHIMOMURA, columnist for the Japanese newspaper *Asahi Shimbun*, quoted in *Fortune*, November 1, 1993

Uh oh. People are too worried about job security and falling household incomes to go shopping.

> CARL B. WEINBERG, chief economist at High Frequency Economics, quoted in *Fortune*, October 30, 1995

Japan is the Italy of Asia.

> JESPER KOLL, economist for the bank JP Morgan, quoted in the *Economist*, March 2, 1996

Japan has gone from a Marilyn Monroe economy, which looked better than it really was, to the Elephant Man.

> PAUL SUMMERVILLE of the investment firm Jardine Fleming Securities, quoted in *Fortune*, December 28, 1992.

Japan's macroeconomic policy is the worst anywhere since the Great Depression.

> JOHN MAKIN of the American Enterprise Institute, quoted in the *New York Times*, September 19, 1996

Although still among the younger of the OECD [Organization for Economic Cooperation and Development] countries, with only 14 percent of its population aged 65 or over, some 26 percent are likely to fit that description by 2025. Japan will then have a higher proportion of elderly people than any other country in the world, including Germany and Sweden.

> *The Economist*, March 2, 1996

[T]he Japanese have a rule that if you finished high school you can't be a blue-collar worker, you have to be a clerk. And if you finish college, you have to be a professional or a manager. Since everybody in Japan now at least finishes high school, there is an incredible surplus of clerks and would-be managers.

> PETER DRUCKER, management guru, interviewed in *HotWired 1.3.,* 1996

Manipulating the so-called fundamentals seems to come naturally to them [the Japanese], while we [the United States] put our faith in the invisible hand. Now we are trying to imitate them, just as they are getting caught up in a web of their own weaving.

> GEORGE SOROS, international investor, 1995

In the past, Japan solved all its political problems by fast economic growth. That's why our political life is so primitive.

> NOBORU KAWAI, of the investment bank Morgan Stanley in Japan, quoted in *Forbes,* May 25, 1996

Japanese constituents view politicians not as policy makers but as favor givers.

> ROBERT ORR, director at the Kyoto Center for Japanese studies, quoted in *Forbes,* July 20, 1992

I worry that in our effort to become a "lifestyle superpower," Japan will become too consumption oriented, like the United States, without meaning to.

> MASARU YOSHITOMI, Japanese former chief government economist, quoted in *Fortune,* December 28, 1992

The Westerner is like the hunter. He shoots and retreats. The Japanese is like the farmer. He endures.

> LOUIS HUGHES of General Motors in Europe, quoted in *Fortune,* January 11, 1993.

Direct investment in Europe and America was to stop trade friction. Investment in Asia is done for cost reasons.

> YUKO IWASAKI of the Bank of Tokyo, quoted in the *Far Eastern Economic Review,* February 1, 1996

Japanese workers work harder, they have a stronger loyalty to the company, and they tend to stay in the company for a long time. They don't often have bright creativity, but they work very hard to make continuous improvements.

> MASHAYOSHI SON, Japanese-born-of-Korean-heritage, American-educated founder and CEO, Softbank

Corp. of Tokyo, interviewed in *Harvard Business Review,* January–February 1992

Japan is notoriously consensus oriented, and companies have a strong tendency to mediate differences among individuals rather than accentuate them. Strategy, on the other hand, requires hard choices.

> PROFESSOR MICHAEL PORTER of Harvard Business School, quoted in *Harvard Business Review,* November–December 1996

3.10.1 Accounting

Most auditors in Japan don't understand how today's markets work.

> TOMONICHI TOMIE of Andersen Consulting, quoted in the *Wall Street Journal,* July 12, 1996

The word for an auditor in Japanese is "kansa-yaku." But people here jokingly call them "kansan-yaku," meaning a do-nothing job.

> ANDREW POLLACK, *New York Times,* August 5, 1997

One of the most important conditions is transparency. Without that, whatever deregulation occurs, it will not create an efficient market.

> KOYO OZEKI, director of Tokyo office of the British credit-rating agency IBCA Ltd., quoted in the *New York Times,* August 5, 1997

When I go to a bank and the person there is one of my seniors, it is difficult for me to say bad things to him.

> A Bank of Japan regulator on the practice known as *amakudari* ("descent from heaven"), under which retired bureaucrats take senior jobs at private firms, quoted in the *Wall Street Journal,* January 19, 1996

3.10.2 Aging Population

According to Japan's Ministry of Health and Welfare, in less than five years the country's demographic trends will give it a population like Florida's.

> MILTON EZRATI of the investment firm Nomura Capital Management, quoted in *Foreign Affairs,* May–June 1997

Over the next 30 years the elderly population is expected to almost double again, so that by 2025 one-quarter of the Japanese population will be senior citizens.

> PROFESSOR HASHIMOTO AKIKO, of the University of Pittsburgh, quoted in *Asia, Inc.,* March 1997

3.10.3　Auto Safety

The Japanese base their safety on the tests the United States gives. . . . It's not based on a philosophy. It's for advertising purposes.

> AKIO TAKOAKA, former engineer for Honda Motor Company who now works as an expert witness in American lawsuits against Honda, quoted in the *New York Times,* November 22, 1996

If we make the car bodies stronger today, it would probably mean more damage to pedestrians and people riding bicycles.

> NOBUHIKO KAWAMOTO, president of Honda, noting that pedestrians represent a higher proportion of those injured in traffic accidents in Japan than in the United States, quoted in the *New York Times,* November 22, 1996

3.10.4　Business and the English Language

Using English gives products a stylish image.

> Japanese coffee company Doutor, cited in the *New York Times,* May 20, 1992 ("Ease your bosoms," Japanese translation of "take a load off your chest" by City Original Coffee.)

3.10.5　The Computer

Managers in Japan don't know what PCs can do. Banks still don't know what a spreadsheet is.

> MAKOTO NARUKE, president of Microsoft Japan, quoted in *Forbes,* June 8, 1992

People don't type in Japan.

> JAMES FALLOWS, journalist, on why Japan has been slow in establishing an Internet, *Atlantic Monthly,* September 11, 1994

For many Japanese, using a keyboard is kind of like experiencing magic.

> YOSHI TAKAYAMA of the PC division of the computer firm NEC, quoted in *Fortune,* July 12, 1993

In 1993 . . . only 10 percent of Japanese office workers had personal computers on their desks, 9 percent of these were plugged into local networks, there was just over one Internet per 1,000 people (a tenth the U.S. rate) and only 8 percent of top managers thought computers were critical to their jobs.

> Figures from the *Economist,* August 12, 1995

The Information Highway is so tied to American culture that we can't even understand what we're getting into.

> TAKASHI KIUCHI, chairman of Mitsubishi Electric America, quoted in *Business Week,* March 28, 1994

After they looked at the Internet, and they realized how huge it was, one of them came to me and said, "Japan's toast." The people in my office were just blown away by the medium. The fact that everything was in English also didn't escape them.

> Anonymous American expatriate businessman in Tokyo on reaction of his Japanese employees to the Internet, quoted in the *Wall Street Journal,* October 22, 1996

3.10.6　Economic Adjustment

Japan took its success for granted. Now it does not really want to face, and it does not know how to face, the empty charade of subsidy and protection. High unemployment, declining tax income, extensive corporate restructuring—that is not the kind of environment to which the Japanese system can easily adapt.

> KENICHI OHMAE, formerly of McKinsey & Company's Tokyo office, quoted in *Harvard Business Review,* May–June 1995

You can't have a self-sustaining recovery when only leading manufacturers are experiencing a big improvement. We cannot expect the top leading elite companies to pull the rest of the economy out.

> MINEKO SASAKI-SMITH of the investment bank Credit Suisse First Boston, on the adjustment problems in the two-tiered economy of Japan, in which a state-of-the-art laptop that takes hours to manufacture can take three months to arrive in stores, quoted in the *New York Times,* September 16, 1997

3.10.7 Entrepreneurship

In general, it's harder to be an entrepreneur [in Japan] than in the United States. Japanese banks will not loan money to you because they are more conservative. And because of the culture, it's harder to attract the best employees.

> MASHAYOSHI SON, Japanese-born-of-Korean heritage, American-educated founder and CEO of the software firm Softbank, interviewed in *Harvard Business Review,* January-February 1992

Most Japanese venture capitalists are on salary, so there's a disincentive to take risks. If you make a decision that goes wrong, it's trouble. If you make one that goes right, there's no upside.

> YASUMASA ISHIZAKA of China Capital Holdings, quoted in the *Wall Street Journal,* November 8, 1996

Young entrepreneurs in Japan don't have much capital, and the rules are severe as well. If they can't start a business, Japan will no longer be able to compete internationally.

> HIDEO SAWADA, travel broker who started Skymark Airlines, discount carrier, and poster boy for Transport Ministry's declared new determination to encourage more competition, quoted in the *Wall Street Journal,* February 4, 1997

3.10.8 Financial Markets

We learned the bond market in a couple of years. Once we start to really buy stocks, we will move quickly.

> KANESHISA NISHIDA of the Long-Term Credit Bank of Japan, quoted in *Forbes,* August 10, 1987

It's shocking how fast Japanese banks have come up to dominate the banking industry.

> WILLIAM M. ISAAC, former chairman of the U.S. Federal Deposit Insurance Corporation, quoted in the *New York Times,* July 20, 1988

Over the past few years, we may have overemphasized the positive side of all the changes taking place. There was a relatively small amount of discussion of the negative side, the limits that we would face.

> YOSHIHISA TABUCHI, chief executive of Nomura Securities, quoted in the *New York Times,* March 10, 1991

During the course of deregulation and financial innovation, people tended to forget about the ethics of the market.

> *New York Times,* March 10, 1991

Japanese banks believed we were almighty, that we had enough capital to compete in every business.

> KANEO MUROMACHI of the bank Sanwa, quoted in *Business Week,* October 2, 1995

[A]s I understand it, the Ministry of Finance and the Bank of Japan have a combined examination staff of considerably less than 1,000 employees. Based on my experience, a workforce of this size is not even remotely adequate to the task at hand.

> E. GERALD CORRIGAN of the investment bank Goldman, Sachs and former president of the Federal Reserve Bank of New York, in a speech, September 24, 1995

Until now, deregulation has meant that everyone spends more money and makes less profit, because [profit margins] fall.

> JIM McGINNIS of Kleinwort Benson Securities, quoted in the *Wall Street Journal,* November 21, 1996

Japanese policy with respect to the resolution of distressed institutions is shifting from one of protection and forbearance to one of resolution via liquidation, which may expose creditors to risk.

> MOODY'S, international credit-rating agency on dire state of Japanese banks, quoted in the *Financial Times,* January 28, 1997

I think we are much closer to a meltdown in Japanese financial assets now than we have ever been.

> JEFF USCHER, editor *Grant's Asia Observer,* quoted in the *New York Times,* January 12, 1997

We've had a global stock market frenzy. Cheap money in Tokyo has been at the center of it.

> KENNETH S. COURTIS, Tokyo-based chief economist at Deutsche Bank Group Asia Pacific, *Wall Street Journal,* September 30, 1996

When Japanese companies start accepting the need for full disclosure, the system will really change.

> Adviser to big securities broker, reacting to arrest of three former Nomura executives for payoffs to

sokaiya (extortionists), quoted in the *Financial Times Weekend*, May 11–18, 1997

Japanese judges don't know very much about the stock market. Of course, thanks to the recent spate of stock market scandals, the judges are being given plenty of opportunity to learn.

> TANAKA SEIJI, lawyer for Japanese scholar who lost money on risky investments that had been sold as bonds, quoted in *Asia, Inc.*, August 1997

Everybody is afraid of the Big Bang.

> MASAHIKO TSUYUZAKI of Tachibana Securities, quoted in the *Wall Street Journal*, January 10, 1997

Unless reforms include provisions for more transparency in financial dealings, and a properly staffed watchdog body to prosecute wrongdoers, Tokyo's Big Bang may amount to little more than a whimper.

> ANDREW HORVAT, *Wall Street Journal*, January 10, 1997

There can be no soft landing, because there is nowhere to land. We have to adapt or prepare for death.

> GORO TATSUMI, founder and president of Kosei, on preparing for Big Bang, quoted in the *Financial Times*, April 3, 1997

What's happened in the last 25 years is that enormous risk has been added to the financial markets. There's liquidity risk, interest-rate risk, exchange-rate risk, portfolio-composition risk. The U.S. and European banks have geared themselves up. In Japan, because of the closeted nature of the system, there hasn't been the same focus on the changing world.

> KENT PRICE, former banker and head of global securities and capital markets business for IBM, quoted in the *Wall Street Journal*, September 16, 1997

Japan will probably reform policy just enough to skirt disaster.

> ROSANNE M. CAHN of the investment bank Credit Suisse First Boston, quoted in the *New York Times*, October 5, 1997

These guys at the Ministry of Finance will fool, lie, do anything until they are proven wrong, and then they just say "Sorry."

> RICHARD KOO of the Nomura Research Institute, quoted in *Fortune*, October 13, 1997

They had nothing left to defend.

> Japanese finance ministry official on the ministry's foreign exchange committee decision to drop remaining exchange controls, quoted in the *Financial Times*, February 24, 1997

They [Japanese bankers] have the information. Yet, they continue extending loans easily, just to expand their profits.

> *Financial Times Weekend*, February 15–16, 1997

My salary comes from banks, my bonus comes from stockbroking firms.

> Gangster quoted by retired Japanese police officer, *The Economist*, December 9, 1995

There's been a fundamental change in the way the Japanese market works: It's based more on fundamental research, quality, and price, rather than on relationships.

> MARK O'FRIEL of the investment bank Morgan Stanley, quoted in the *Wall Street Journal*, October 8, 1997

3.10.9 Foreign Business

In the past, all Western companies were places to avoid. Now it's a gray area rather than all black.

> TAKASHI KURISAKA of the executive recruiting firm Egon Zehnder International, quoted in the *Wall Street Journal*, January 2, 1985

They [Japanese telecoms companies] like selling equipment, but they are not so keen on helping other people to run a system, which is what a lot of these countries need.

> Western rival explaining why Japanese companies have failed to dominate the Asian market, quoted in the *Economist*, January 18, 1992

I think doing business in Japan as being like a game of football. But first you have to know which game of football you are playing. Is it the American gridiron sport—or what the rest of the world calls football, which we call soccer?

American football is a bruising battle. The players are huge and strong. They have nicknames like "Refrigerator." And the game is played in short bursts of intense energy.

In soccer football the players are shorter and faster. Play is continuous, and a soccer fullback weighs less than lunch for a gridiron fullback.

> M. GEORGE ALLEN of the 3M Company, in a speech, February 17, 1994

Mergers and acquisitions are becoming an acceptable solution [to company problems], whereas before, the last thing a company wanted to do was to be sold to a foreigner.

> COLIN STUART of the accounting and consulting firm KPMG, quoted in the *Financial Times*, January 23, 1997

Companies that come over to Japan to negotiate a deal might divulge some important business information. The Japanese are very good at asking a lot of questions. Then at the last minute the deal does not go through, but the Japanese have the information they want.

> DEBBIE HOWARD, president of Japan Market Resource Network, Tokyo, quoted in *Asia, Inc.,* March 1997

I can't tell you how many times I've been told, "You don't understand Japanese business practices." It just means they don't want to change.

> HENRY D. G. WALLACE, president of the auto company Mazda, which is partly owned by Ford, quoted in the *Wall Street Journal*, April 15, 1996 (Wallace is the first non-Japanese president of a Japanese auto company.)

[T]o be honest, at the bottom of my heart, I would naturally feel like I would do anything I can for him. But if the president is a foreigner, I wonder if I would feel the same way.

> SYOHACHIRO TAKAHASHI, former Mazda executive and now president of Delta Corp., a supplier of car seats to Mazda, quoted in the *Wall Street Journal,* April 15, 1996

You can't come to talk instead of listen. The Japanese don't take well to that. Oh, they will listen to you politely and take notes, but they won't pay attention. We have to realize that in some areas, like process technology, they are the innovators.

> JAMES MORGAN, CEO of the chip manufacturing equipment firm Applied Materials, quoted in the *New York Times,* April 28, 1991

3.10.10 Hollywood

Hollywood is a person-to-person, free-wheeling business with great creativity and dreams. The Japanese are conservative and hierarchical. A marriage is difficult.

> SHIGERU MASUDA, president of the venture-capital group Zeron, quoted in *Newsweek,* March 20, 1989

Quite simply, Hollywood still scares the Japanese.

> Entertainment lawyer, quoted in *Newsweek,* March 20, 1989

Until the Japanese came through, I was going around with a begging bowl.

> JEREMY THOMAS, producer of the movie *The Last Emperor,* quoted in *Newsweek,* March 20, 1989

3.10.11 Industrial Policy

[During] the Meiji period of 1868 . . . Meiji leaders put in place a rule that has governed Japan since. Because of its late start in the industrial revolution, Japan had to catch up to the West in manufacturing. If you understand this philosophy, you understand how Japan policy-making of the past 130 years has been aimed at learning how to make things, make more of them, and continually make them better.

The government bureaucracy that nourished and protected business since the Meiji period began—and especially during the past 50 years—has outlived its usefulness—and indeed became a burden.

> TAKASHI KITAOKA, CEO of Mitsubishi Electric, in a speech, April 16, 1997

Someone in Japan told me with a straight face this year that the Ministry of International Trade and Industry's newest industrial policy was to promote entrepreneurship and venture capital.

> MICHAEL GONZALEZ, deputy editorial page editor of the Asian edition of the *Wall Street Journal,* September 13, 1996

3.10.12 Investment Strategy

Our president read that the current record price for a single building, as listed in the *Guinness Book of World Records,* is $600 million. He wants to beat the record.

> Representative of Mitsui Corporation on reason his company was willing to pay $610 million in 1986 for

the Exxon Building in Manhattan, on the market for $375 million, cited by Ted Rall, who worked at New York branch of the Industrial Bank of Japan, quoted in *Harper's*, August 1995

3.10.13 Management

Japanese companies are still using more than double the percentage of expatriates in their foreign affiliates than are typical Western multinationals.

> PROFESSOR SCHON BEECHLER, Columbia Business School, quoted in *Harvard Business Review*, September–October 1994

I wanted to simplify management. I hate taking a long time to study things. I want to condense things, American style.

> YOICHI MORISHITA of Matsushita Electric, quoted in *Business Week*, October 31, 1994

Many of the brightest local people do not want to join Japanese companies because they know they will not get to the top.

> CHI KWAN, economist at Nomura Research Institute, on problem confronting Japanese operations in Asia, quoted in the *Economist*, March 16, 1996

My daughter was bullied at work. Whenever she made a mistake, it was pointed out in front of everybody . . . she resigned but the company refused to accept it, so she committed suicide.

> Woman who called a bullying hotline, sponsored by Tokyo Manager's Union, quoted in the *Financial Times*, January 30, 1997 (Management abuse of workers is rising.)

We as a society are on the threshold of appreciating diversity and difference . . . For the first time, we are beginning to accept that individuals have different needs and abilities.

> SUSUMU TAKITOMI of Industrial Bank of Japan, quoted in the *Financial Times*, February 17, 1997

The proliferation of these scandals and disclosure of them are part of a general shift from the traditional system to more global standards. It is inevitable because many companies still carry with them old attitudes.

> MASAYA MIYOSHI, president of Keidanren economic federation in Japan, quoted in the *Financial Times*, March 13, 1997

[M]anagement inbreeding makes it very hard to deal with these problems. Western companies bring in outside management when they want real change.

> CRAIG CHUDLER of the investment bank Salomon Brothers, quoted in the *Financial Times*, March 13, 1997

Major Japanese companies think that in order for them to develop into the next century, they need to let the ideas buried within the company bloom on an individual basis rather than in an organized effort.

> YOSHIHITO IWAMA of Keidanren economic federation in Japan, quoted in the *New York Times*, October 9, 1997

3.10.14 Marketing

The easiest way to transmit the Western style of life was to use foreign personalities.

> AKIO NAKAMURA of the advertising agency Dentsu, on the proliferation of celebrity endorsements, quoted in *Forbes*, July 14, 1986

It's cheaper to spend money on a major talent than on additional TV exposure . . . In this country, if you have unknown people marketing your product, you're going to lose.

> BARRINGTON HILL of the advertising agency McCann-Erickson Worldwide, quoted in *Forbes*, July 14, 1986

The word *marketing* literally does not exist in Japanese.

> Executive quoted in Bain & Co. research on Japan, cited by Katherine J. Sweetman, *Harvard Business Review*, September–October 1996

3.10.15 Retailing

Executives tell me that when Japanese consumers placed an order with Neiman Marcus Direct Catalogue, they would receive it within five business days; the next nearest Japanese competitors would take three times as long.

> PAULA STERN, president of Stern Group, a trade consulting firm, in a speech, December 9, 1996

There is a huge window of opportunity for U.S. retailers here.

> TAKUYA OKADE, head of Jusco Co., Japanese mall developer, who has been trying to woo reluctant

American retail companies, quoted in the *Wall Street Journal,* July 30, 1997

You've got to make them [American retailers] dream the American dream.

> EIJI AKIYAMA, of the Japanese mall developer Jusco, quoted in the *Wall Street Journal,* July 30, 1997

3.10.16 Trade Surplus

I call on you, the Japanese people, to buy as many imported goods as possible.

> YASUHIRO NAKASONE, Japanese Prime Minister, trying to alleviate Japan's chronic trade surplus, quoted in *U.S. News & World Report,* April 22, 1985

Japan is not a closed market. You just have to understand it.

> LOUIS HUGHES, president of General Motors' international operations, quoted in the *Wall Street Journal,* October 24, 1997

3.10.17 The United States and Japan

Many people have pointed out there are no business schools in Japan; no one seems to have pointed out that there are also very few law firms in Japan. The Japanese seem to work things out themselves better than anyone. [This quote is clearly dated in its assumptions about the success of the Japanese economy, compared to the United States.]

> MARK H. McCORMACK, *What They Don't Teach You at Harvard Business School* (Bantam Doubleday Dell, 1984)

Wanted: Japanese who can swear in English.

> Ad for Sony Corporation, cited in *U.S. News & World Report,* February 18, 1985

Once the walls come down in Japan, the game has only begun. You think you're home free, but really you've been dropped in a maze.

> Western diplomat in Tokyo on doing business in Japan, quoted in *Newsweek,* February 13, 1989

It was equivalent to flogging beachfront property to someone for nine years and having them turn around and say, "I'll take 200 grains of sand."

> Semiconductor analyst on the experience of Intel Japan KK, which spent nine years trying to sell computer chips to the auto firm Nissan, which signed up for 200 chips a month after Tokyo signed an agreement to increase U.S. semiconductor sales, quoted in *Newsweek,* February 13, 1989

The U.S. government tends to listen to those who fail in Japan rather than those who succeed.

> TAKESHI ISAYAMA, director of the Americas division of MITI (a.k.a. Japan Inc.), quoted in *Time,* June 5, 1989

[W]e must admit that no matter how good the English-Japanese interpreters are in the English language, the word *agreement* used in the U.S.-Japanese context has lost its meaning and no longer connotes "resolution."

> PAULA STERN, president of the Stern Group, a trade consulting firm, in a speech, December 9, 1996

I believe in many ways Japan and the United States were born to misunderstand each other.

> WILLIAM E. FRANKLIN, president of the manufacturing company Weyerhouser Far East Ltd., in a speech, September 14, 1995

Technically the Japan market is open . . . it is just that sometimes the door is so small it is hard for a foreigner to get in.

> AKIO MORITA, chairman of SONY, quoted by William E. Franklin, president of Weyerhouser Far East Ltd., September 14, 1995

The Americans wore jackets and ties, figuring the Japanese would dress up for drinks. But the Japanese, noting that the affair was to be held in the "Aloha Room," all showed up in brightly colored aloha shirts.

> Refers to a Honolulu cocktail party hosted by U.S. State Department negotiators, transportation officials, and airline representatives for their Japanese counterparts, in an article on different negotiating styles of the two sides, cited by Bernard Wysocki Jr., staff reporter, the *Wall Street Journal,* January 22, 1985

The Japanese aren't nimble. They are like a slow glacier advancing towards you.

> NATHANIEL WILSON of the Air Transport Association of America, quoted in the *Wall Street Journal,* January 22, 1985

Hell, I didn't go to Japan to help open the rice market. The last time I looked, we don't grow any rice in Detroit.

[T]he Japanese would have to be stupid *not* to keep breaking our laws—and the Japanese are not stupid.

The Japanese are masters at making you peel the onion. You get through one layer and you're looking at another one just like it. One year we negotiated on oranges, the next beef, the next tomato puree, and even ravioli, yet! And in the end we're further and further behind.

> LEE IACOCCA, former chairman of Chrysler, in a speech, January 10, 1992

With what we pay, if they wear shoes we'll hire them.

> Manager of a Japanese-owned California factory, cited in a study by Professor Ruth Milkman of UCLA, which found that most such plants are sweatshops and almost none use quality circles or other vaunted Japanese management methods, quoted in the *Economist*, February 15, 1992

Perhaps the best sign of Honda's success at establishing Japanese standards in Ohio is that BMW has poached two of Honda's top American executives, including the man responsible for quality control, to run its South Carolina plant.

> *The Economist,* November 28, 1992

The bureaucrats tell us they're looking for direction from the politicians, and the politicians tell us they can't budge the bureaucrats.

> Senior U.S. official, expressing frustration over trade, quoted in *Business Week,* April 18, 1994

If you're willing to work enough, you can do business here and you shouldn't have to go running to the American embassy for help.

> BRAD BARTZ, who went to Tokyo to teach English and ended up founding Internet Access Center KK with second-hand computers, quoted in the *Wall Street Journal,* November 8, 1996

Japanese presidents don't talk to janitors.

> Personnel director, Apple Computer, Japan, to Seiji "Frank" Sanda, then president, after Sanda greeted a cleaning woman, quoted in the *Wall Street Journal,* June 3, 1996

Americans view things in minutes, the Japanese think in centuries.

> JOHN BOLLOCK of Canon USA, quoted in the *Wall Street Journal,* June 4, 1996

If you learn one or two sentences [of Japanese], people will start communicating to you in paragraphs, assuming you understand everything.

> BILL GSAND of Hitachi America, quoted in the *Wall Street Journal,* June 4, 1996

[Japanese bosses] don't like to say no. So you have to look for key phrases. If you hear the phrase, "very difficult," that probably means no.

> GERRY SHANHOLT, CEO of the high-tech start-up SRX, quoted in the *Wall Street Journal,* June 4, 1996

The jury will see that you have black eyes and yellow skin. It's easy to see what side a jury will be on.

> YUKIO SADAMORI, head of Mitsui & Co. international personnel division, who trains Japanese managers on sexual harassment, discrimination, and labor law before assignment to the United States, quoted in the *Wall Street Journal,* July 9, 1996

[M]ost Japanese would wince at the idea of doing business in such a competitive society [as the United States].

> SHINTARO KUBO, business editor, *Yomiuri Shimbum,* largest daily paper in Japan, quoted in the *Financial Times,* February 17, 1997

Do we sit back like we did with the transistor and let Japan take the technology and feed it back to us?

> ROBERT STEMPEL, retired chairman of General Motors, now of Energy Conversion Devices, which makes batteries for electrical cars, quoted in the *Wall Street Journal,* October 22, 1997

3.10.18 The United States and Japan by the Numbers

. . . United States and Japan, together they account for 20 percent of that $3 trillion in global trade, 40 percent of the world's $20 trillion in gross national products, and 35 percent of all foreign aid.

> WILLIAM C. STEERE JR., CEO of the pharmaceutical firm Pfizer, in a speech, September 18, 1992

It is said that the maximum share non-American cars can have in the United States is 30 percent—more than that would lead to friction.

> HIROSHI OKUDA, president of Toyota, quoted in the *Wall Street Journal,* November 22, 1996

The ratio of consumer finance loans to disposable income in Japan has surpassed that in the United States since 1990.

> *Financial Times,* January 28, 1997

3.11 NORTH KOREA

That's how you treat criminals who normally don't pay their bills.

> Businessman commenting on a German consortium's refusal to start work on a North Korean modern cement factory until the government deposited over $300 million in gold into a Swiss Bank account, quoted in *Asia, Inc.,* October 1994

[Why North Koreans are the toughest negotiators in the world.] They're the most relentless, the most dogmatic. They can't make any decisions on the spot. They always have to check with their superiors, but you don't know who the superiors are.

> U.S. REPRESENTATIVE BILL RICHARDSON (Democrat, New Mexico), quoted in *Fortune,* May 27, 1996

North Korean real estate is untouched, unspoiled. It's like an egg yolk.

Reunification is far off. But investment and trade can help us coexist. As a Korean, I have an obligation to work towards coexistence.

> PARK KYUNG TOUHNE, Korean-born California real estate developer, with plans to build a resort in North Korea, quoted in the *Wall Street Journal,* July 15, 1996

In many ways North Korea is not ready for investment, but for certain types of companies it's beginning to make business sense. They need everything. You just have to find a way to get the money.

> MICHAEL BREEN of Seoul-based Breen and Gustaveson Consultants, quoted in *Asia, Inc.,* July 1996

There are so many horror stories that you can't ignore them. These are uncharted waters.

> NIGEL COWIE of Peregrine Investment Holdings Ltd.'s joint-venture bank in Pyongyang, quoted in *Asia, Inc.,* July 1996

3.12 SOUTH KOREA

They're into ceramics, computer chips, advanced electronics, biotech; these are technologies that can ripple across whole families of industries and products. Korea has gone from having virtually no electronics industry to the point now that they are producing 256K advanced semiconductors.

> PAT CHOATE, TRW economist and later prominent anti-NAFTA propagandist who was Ross Perot's 1996 running mate, quoted in *Forbes,* May 5, 1986

If the United States overlooks the peculiarities of the Korean economy and only emphasizes world trade across the board, they would in no way guarantee profitability for the United States and at the same time it could considerably weaken Korea's economic foundation. The reason for this is simple, Japan.

> KIM WOO CHOONG, chairman of the industrial Daewoo Group, articulating the geographical constraints on Korean policy, in a speech, July 25, 1992

We never plan industrial projects here looking at the domestic market. The scale is too small.

> PARK UNG SOH, president of Samsung's petrochemical subsidiary, quoted in the *Economist,* March 14, 1992

Knowing yourself and your enemies is the first prerequisite to becoming a warrior.

> KEE KUN-HEE, chairman of the industrial group Samsung, paraphrasing Sun Tzu, Chinese military theorist much admired by management almost everywhere, quoted in *Business Week,* February 28, 1994

The [sales volume] at our restaurant in Seoul is double the volume of our average restaurant in America.

> JÜRGEN BARTELS of the restaurant chain Carlson Companies, quoted in *Business Week,* January 10, 1994

The government would never allow [hostile acquisitions]. It is culturally unacceptable.

> STEPHEN E. MARVIN of SsangYong Investment & Securities, quoted in the *Wall Street Journal,* February 21, 1996

We see globalization as a survival strategy.

> KANG HYO JIN, an executive director, Samsung Corp., South Korea's largest conglomerate, quoted in the *Wall Street Journal,* May 14, 1996

My five-year-old son spent nearly three hours a day commuting to and from the school, and on most days he came back with tears as a result of the use of tear gas.

> Foreign journalist on life in Seoul, quoted in *Asia, Inc.*, September 1996

Housewives just love foreign products.

> BAE BO YOUNG, Seoul housewife, sorting through Estée Lauder lipsticks, quoted in the *Wall Street Journal*, September 11, 1996

Only organizations which contribute to mankind will last; those organizations which lack humanism and morality can never become premier companies and will not endure.

> Chairman of Samsung Group, quoted without identification by Daniel Tully, chairman and CEO, Merrill Lynch, in a speech, October 19, 1994

Someday foreigners will say it is easy to do business in Korea.

> PRESIDENT KIM YOUNG SAM, quoted in *Time*, March 28, 1994

Once Samsung and Hyundai get into petrochemicals, they will overbuild like they do in autos. They're going to crash the world market.

> STEVE TAGTMEIER, chemical consultant at McKinsey & Co., quoted in *Business Week*, December 2, 1996

On the one hand, they have the entrepreneurialism and drive. But they've gone too far too fast and haven't really invested in management systems required to understand those businesses.

> TREVOR MACMURRAY, of McKinsey & Co., Hong Kong, quoted in *Business Week*, December 2, 1996

The cigarette for the successful man.

> Tag line for Virginia Slims, which are marketed to men—not women—in Korea, quoted in the *Wall Street Journal*, January 14, 1997

It's totally irrelevant. It doesn't hurt my pride as a man.

> OH SONG RYONG, Seoul radio broadcaster, on the feminine associations of smoking Virginia Slims, quoted in the *Wall Street Journal*, January 14, 1997

Without massive restructuring, Korea will be the most vulnerable Asian economy to the global deflationary trend of the 1990s.

> RHEE NAMUH of the investment firm Dongbang Peregrine Securities, quoted in the *Wall Street Journal*, January 27, 1997

As long as the red tape remains, corruption will persist. The kickbacks that some bureaucrats demand have only gone up.

> Manager of a small Korean venture-capital firm, quoted in the *Wall Street Journal*, January 27, 1997

Change everything but your wives and children.

> LEE KUM HEE, chairman of Samsung, exhorting his huge, inefficient workforce to the measures needed to become competitive, quoted in *Fortune*, April 18, 1994

Korea's industrial structure has an Arnold Schwarzenegger upper body on Woody Allen legs.

> STEPHEN E. MARVIN of SsangYong Investment and Securities, meaning that the Korean economy is dominated by large corporations and that smaller, innovative companies don't develop. Quoted in the *New York Times*, February 4, 1997

After the dinosaurs, smaller, smarter mammals took over. I'm one of those small mammals.

I'm an idea man. The big companies don't accept new ideas.

> YOON SUK MIN, who dropped out of graduate engineering school to start his own software company, quoted in the *Wall Street Journal*, June 11, 1997

3.13 MALAYSIA

We are small at present. But we have our fair share of the capital outflow from Hong Kong, and it will increase as 1997 approaches. At the touch of a button, the money can be transferred here instantly.

> NATHANIEL SAVARIMUTHI, general manager of off-shore banking on island of Labuan for Malaysia's Public Bank, which is trying to attract money fleeing Hong Kong, quoted in *Asia Online* 1995

We want to create the right ambiance for multinationals to operate in the region. You can't beat an address like Petronas Towers. People will return your calls.

> AZIZIAN ZAINUL ABIDIN, chairman of Petronas, on business wisdom of building the world's tallest building in Kuala Lumpur, quoted in *Asia, Inc.,* November 1996

When it is complete, Kuala Lumpur will have the world's tallest building, Asia's highest communications tower, and now the longest building in the world.

> DAVID CHEW, managing director of Linear City, 10-story, 2 km (about 1.2 miles), tubelike mall to be built on stilts overlooking Klang River, quoted in the *Economist,* December 21, 1996

The ideology and logic of materialism have all too easily influenced human society. This is a direct result of the input of Western thought, which fanatically focuses on the material as the basis of life.

> Statement by MAHATHIR MOHAMAD, Prime Minister of Malaysia, in 1986, quoted in the *Economist,* October 17, 1992

What you should do is find projects that they like and then propose them. Then you have to complete them ahead of schedule and make them serve a social purpose. That is the way you win favor.

> Managing director of a large Malaysian corporation of "Malaysia Inc.," the informal federation of private and government interests, quoted in the *Financial Times,* March 11, 1997

We are not going to allow these people to manipulate our economy as if they have a right to have a free ride on us. My view is that this level of manipulation must be made illegal.

> PRIME MINISTER MAHATHIR MOHAMAD, attacking "speculators" during currency crisis, quoted in the *Wall Street Journal,* August 29, 1997

As in the case of [Princess] Diana where strenuous attempts are being made to exonerate the paparazzi and put the blame on the dead driver . . . The Western press, and even the International Monetary Fund, are trying to

blame everything on the governments of the Asian countries.

> DR. MAHATHIR BIN MOHAMAD, Malaysia Prime Minister, quoted in the *Financial Times,* October 2, 1997

3.14 MONGOLIA

Whatever the market is going to pay, the government will accept. Some people say this is a crazy way to do reform, but this is such a small country. Either they do this, or the assets rot forever. [Assets include 20 percent of the world's cashmere production.]

> OLEG GORELIK, adviser to Mongolia's state privatization committee, quoted in the *Financial Times,* September 17, 1997

3.15 PAKISTAN

People are worried India will dominate. I say let them dominate. If we don't import from India, we will import from China and Australia and they will dominate us. This is not a tug-of-war—if we continue to pull too hard, the rope will break.

> RASHID SOORTY, leading Karachi manufacturer, quoted in *Asia, Inc.,* August 1997

American and Israeli agents go home.

> Placard greeting IFC (International Finance Corporation, private sector arm of World Bank) representatives during visit to sell a Pakistani state power-distribution company, cited in the *Wall Street Journal,* October 3, 1997

3.16 REPUBLIC OF PALAU

Because of the accumulation of wealth, people are resorting to court rather than tradition.

> MOSES ULUDONG, head of the Palau Bar Association and editor of Palau's weekly newspaper *Tia Belau,* quoted in the *Wall Street Journal,* August 1, 1997

3.17 PAPUA NEW GUINEA

One for flushing, one for washing.

> FRED RICH, a partner at Sullivan & Cromwell, referring to the two buckets of seawater brought

every morning to his Port Moresby hotel room, after local guerrillas blew up the town's water supply, quoted in the *Wall Street Journal,* October 30, 1996

3.18 THE PHILIPPINES

You have got to be prepared to make the necessary changes to adapt to local market conditions.

> TONY KITCHENER, Australian head of international operations for Jollibee, the Philippine-based fast-food chain, on the strategy that has supplanted McDonald's as the number-one chain in the Philippines and both McDonald's and Kentucky Fried Chicken in Vietnam, quoted in the *Economist,* September 28, 1996

The root causes of our problems were never in the jungles.

> GENERAL JOSÉ ALMONTE, national security adviser to President Fidel Ramos, referring to the obsession with decades-long Communist insurgency that was used as an excuse for avoiding market reforms by the Marcos government, quoted in the *Wall Street Journal,* October 7, 1996

He (a conference organizer) asked if they could bring firearms. The first delegate arrived with a bazooka on his shoulder.

> OLIVER TRINQUAND, manager at Insular Century Hotel, South Philippines island of Mindanao, quoted in *Asia, Inc.,* April 1997

If you look at turnover, it's way down here. It leaves a lot to be desired, considering the size of the companies in the Philippines. The exchange is not encouraging people to participate in the market. Filipinos in the exchange have carried on in the old tradition of the Spanish aristocracy.

> MARK MOBIUS, president of Templeton Emerging Market Funds, on the Philippine stock market, quoted in *Asia, Inc.,* August 1997

Some of my friends are getting out of textiles and into property.

> PROFESSOR BEN DIOKNO of the University of the Philippines, on signs that the economic transformation may not be as profound as had been thought, quoted in the *Financial Times,* February 28, 1997

3.19 SINGAPORE

Simply smile and be gracious. After all, our smiles have reaped S$12 billion (US$8.5 billion) in tourism earnings last year.

> Poster and TV campaign, cited in the *Wall Street Journal,* October 7, 1996

They take enough already. They can tax my money, but they can't tax my smile.

> ALVIN WONG, quoted in the *Wall Street Journal,* October 7, 1996

When it comes to money from your pocket, you see how fast those traditional Asian values can dissipate.

> ANAMAH TAN, family lawyer, on rash of lawsuits by aged parents against their affluent children for support, being heard before the Tribune for the Maintenance of Parents, quoted in the *Wall Street Journal,* September 17, 1996

I've been out here six years and heard the argument about the savings culture and Confucianism. It doesn't wash. CNN is the great leveler. Younger people [in Asia] identify with Western culture.

> JAMES CASSIN, president of Asia-Pacific division of the credit-card company MasterCard International, based in Singapore, quoted in *Forbes,* May 6, 1996

When we started [the onetime British colony became self-governing in 1959 and broke off from Malaysia to become an independent state in 1965], we started with British punitive rates of personal income tax. We were stupid! It was the influence of British education.

> LEE KUAN YEW, former prime minister of Singapore, quoted in *Forbes,* August 12, 1996

As long as there are restrictions in Singapore on the free flow of information, Singapore can't expect to be a major fund-management and stockbroking center.

> WILLIAM OVERHOLT of Bankers Trust in Hong Kong, quoted in *Asia, Inc.,* February 1996

Entrepreneurs are a very rare phenomenon in Singapore. It's a managerial rather than an entrepreneurial economy.

> DAVID DODWELL, co-author of *The Hong Kong Advantage,* quoted in *Asia, Inc.,* November 1996

We're comfortable wherever they sell the Singapore way of doing business.

> HARTMUT LUECK, managing director, Siemens Group, Singapore, referring to arrangements with Singapore's government creating "mini-Singapores" in other Asian countries, free of local work rules and regulations, substituting those of Singapore instead (Singapore gets a piece of the action, and the investor shortcuts a lot of bureaucratic headaches), quoted in *Fortune,* March 4, 1997

Chinese officials are asking themselves: what does a city-state of not even 3 million people have to teach to China, it is the size of one of the suburbs of Shanghai.

> Diplomat on the declining influence of Singapore in China, quoted in the *Financial Times,* May 27, 1997 (The China-Singapore Industrial Park in Suzhow—one of the zones described above—was not as successful as had been hoped and is unlikely to be replicated.)

Historically, people have had a mental block to having an herbal tea or some medicinal product in ready-to-drink form. The belief has been that these things are good for you, but only if you make them yourself.

> KENNETH TAN of Acorn Marketing and Research Consultants Pte. Ltd., Singapore, on roadblocks to acceptance of mass-produced traditional drinks, quoted in the *Wall Street Journal,* February 21, 1997

We can become the first developed country in the tropics if we do not let up.

> PRIME MINISTER GOH CHOK TONG, quoted in the *Financial Times,* February, 18, 1997

A drop of sweat is the precious gift for your guts.

> English tag line on a Japanese sports bag, cited in the *New York Times,* May 20, 1992

3.20 TAIWAN

[In the 1950s] we didn't even know about toilet paper—we used bamboo sticks.

> One of Taiwan's "biggest businessmen," quoted in the *Economist,* March 5, 1988

Better to be in front of a chicken than behind a pig.

> Taiwanese proverb, used in the context of Taiwan's reliance on family fortunes as a source of start-up

capital for new businesses instead of the big industrial model of Japan's *keiretsu* and South Korea's *chaebol,* quoted in the *Economist,* January, 4, 1992

In Chinese culture, you have to respect your mother and father. This respect kills creativity. If you have to respect what your father says, then you tend to kill your own thinking.

> JAMES YEN, president of Advanced Microelectronics Products, quoted in the *Harvard Business Review,* March–April 1993

Doing business is like driving a car. In the United States, everybody has rules and regulations, and you just follow the rules, and it's easy. In Taiwan, even if the light is red, somebody can get through it. If it's green, there still aren't rules to tell you how to go.

> P. T. DE, of San Sun Hats, quoted in the *Harvard Business Review,* March–April 1993

I'll be honest with you. I haven't paid taxes in 10 years.

> STAN SHIH, founder of Acer Inc., Taiwan's largest PC company, when asked the secret of his success, quoted by Yeh Wan-an, a longtime economic policy maker, cited in the Asian edition of the *Wall Street Journal,* October 22, 1996

We are extremely efficient manufacturers; and we are becoming good developers. But we are not yet researchers. [Apparently, 85 percent of scientific graduates stay in academia instead of going into industry.]

> STEVE HSIEH, director-general of Hsinchu Companies, quoted in the *Economist,* March 9, 1997

Many Taiwan companies have staked their future on the mainland, and that can't be changed all of a sudden.

> YANK DA ZHENG, president of the Taiwan Chamber of Commerce in Shanghai, quoted in the *Wall Street Journal,* March 13, 1996

The more the Taiwanese have economic interests in the mainland, the more they will assume political ties with the mainland. The Chinese have seen this play out in Hong Kong—the major supporters of the Chinese position in Hong Kong have substantial investments in mainland China.

> Diplomat quoted in the *Financial Times,* May 1, 1997

[T]he murder rate in Taiwan is 8.5 per 100,000, compared with 8.2 in the United States in 1995.

> *New York Times,* July 14, 1997

Mr. Chen? It's time you bought coffins for yourself, your wife, and your children. We offer the best coffins in Taiwan. Would you like to see them?

> Two A.M. phone call to REGIS CHEN, chairman of Taiwan's state-owned BES Engineering Corp., which was bidding to build a $4 billion freeway against a company affiliated with the United Bamboo triad, one of Taiwan's top organized crime families, quoted in *Asia, Inc.,* April 1997

We can't enjoy success forever if we are just a good, fast follower. The next stage is to develop our own technology through research.

> STEVE HSIEH, former director-general of Hsinchu Science-based Industrial Park, quoted in *Business Week,*, August 25, 1997

3.21 THAILAND

Number of licensed taxis in Bangkok:

> 12,000 in 1990   54,000 in 1996

Number of licensed *tuk-tuks* (traditional 3-wheelers, fixed by law)

> 7,406 in 1990   7,406 in 1996

> Thai Department of Transportation, cited in *Asia, Inc.,* September 18, 1996

A study . . . by a top Thai university [Political Economy Centre, Chulalongkorn University, Bangkok] says six categories of major illegal activities accounted for $24 billion to $32 billion in economic activity a year between 1993 and 1995. That equals 14 percent to 19 percent of Thailand's official gross domestic product in 1995 . . . nearly the size of Thailand's government budget and well above the volume of its agricultural output.

> PAUL M. SHARER, *Wall Street Journal,* December 3, 1996

The efficiency of a system and public access to one matter just as much as its size. Where are all the telephones in Eastern Europe and Russia? They're on the desks of people who do very little in ministries. Here [Thailand]

there may not be enough of them, but they are used to make money.

> PHILIPPE ANMEZ, World Bank representative in Bangkok, quoted in the *Economist,* January 18, 1992

The Japanese don't mind even if you pair up with their competitors. But with Americans it's either you love me or you hate me.

> PRAMON SUTIVONG of Siam Cement, on joint venturing with foreign companies, quoted in *Fortune,* November 1, 1993

Look at Thailand. They are raising the minimum wage, and that has decimated their textile sector. The production is moving to China, to Indonesia, to Vietnam. Something that started out as well-meaning is costing jobs. In five years, Thailand won't have a textile sector.

> RODNEY JONEY of George Soros's firm Quantum Fund, quoted in William Greider, *One World, Ready or Not: The Manic Logic of Global Capitalism* (Simon & Schuster, 1997)

The national symbol of Thailand, one could say, is the traffic jam.

> WILLIAM GREIDER, *One World, Ready or Not: The Manic Logic of Global Capitalism* (Simon & Schuster, 1997)

It is . . . a striking commentary on the power of financial contagion today that recent stock market volatility resulted from a chain of financial linkages that began with the collapse of a speculative real estate bubble in Bangkok.

> DAVID HALE, *Financial Times,* November 7, 1997

3.22 VIETNAM

The old Communists who run Vietnam actually believe they defeated decadent Western capitalism. So where did the little girl in Hoan Kiem Park, in the middle of downtown Hanoi, get a hula hoop?

> P. J. O'ROURKE, *All the Trouble in the World* (Atlantic Monthly Press, 1994)

The Vietnamese know that investors want to make prudent investments. But there is a paranoia about being exploited by Western capitalism, which can lead them to mess up a bit in negotiations and be too tough.

> EUGENE MATTHEWS, quoted in the *New York Times*, February, 17, 1991 (In 1991, Matthews was the only American businessman living in Hanoi.)

There is a driven and determined middle class that remembers what it's like to be prosperous.

> JOHN ENGLEHART of the Bangkok office of Ogilvy & Mather, on American consumer companies' prospects in Vietnam, quoted in *Business Week*, May 23, 1994

They just say they're busy. Every day busy.

> JOO SUNG KIM, regional representative of South Korea's Daewoo Group, on the help he never receives from the Vietnamese government on the $600 million in investment projects he oversees in Vietnam, quoted in the *Wall Street Journal*, June 10, 1996

I'd like the citizens of Canada to know the trade show is being used as a tool by certain members of the Communist elite in Vietnam for propaganda and financial purposes.

> HOANG MINH, Vietnamese delegate to a Canadian trade show who defected, quoted in *Asia, Inc.*, August 1996

If you want growth, you have to allow the private sector to grow. But if you get a strong private sector, it will seek political control.

> Unnamed diplomat in Hanoi on slow progress and regressive reform policies, quoted in *Business Week*, July 1, 1996.

This is a controlled economy trying to operate as a market economy. At some point you run into a political agenda.

> Head of Vietnamese operations for an American multinational corporation, quoted in the *Economist*, December 9, 1995

They get mad. They tell the tour guide: "You are lying. This is Asia: You must have massage." [Reaction of many visitors when told that massage parlors have been closed recently by the government.]

> SU JIAMN YUAN, vice general manager, Vung Tau Paradise Golf & Country Club, quoted in *Asia, Inc.*, November 1996

A six-foot pothole on the way to Nirvana.

> American executive on the short-term pitfalls of trading with Vietnam, quoted in *Business Week*, February 14, 1994

Don't feel awkward bringing a laptop and a printer to a [contract] signing ceremony. There are almost always last-minute changes.

> Advice from KATHY CHARLTON, businesswoman with four years of experience in Hanoi, quoted in the *Financial Times*, January 20, 1997

James Bond has finally met his match: the Vietnamese authorities. [Permission to film a new movie was withdrawn a week before shooting was supposed to start.]

> *Financial Times*, March 11, 1997

Twenty-five years ago, Bangkok was a country village. Vietnam has a lot of the same factors Bangkok had then.

> SIMON MILLARD of Thailand-based Harmony Property, quoted in *Asia, Inc.*, May 1997

4.1 BANKING AND ISLAM

Those who benefit from interest shall be like those driven mad by the touch of the devil.

The Koran

According to Islamic law, usury is lending money that results in compensation for the lender. Bank interest looks like usury because it is compensation. But bank interest also can be considered as a means of profit-sharing, because the bank has to sustain defaults, and also has to pay the cost of credit guarantees, insurance, and the changing value of foreign exchange.

ABDURRAHMAN WAHID, Muslim cleric in Indonesia, quoted in *Asia, Inc.,* December 1995

The motive of the bank was to lead Moslems away from Islam and promote shamelessness among women.

MULLAH MOHAMED HASSAN, governor of Kandahar in southern Afghanistan, after fundamentalist Taliban militia forced the Bangladesh-based Grameen Bank to fold, quoted in the *Financial Times,* September 16, 1997

4.2 BANKERS AND JUDGMENT

Is not commercial credit based primarily upon money or property?

No sir. The first thing is character.

Before money or property?

Before money or anything else. Money cannot buy it . . . Because a man I do not trust could not get money from me on all the bonds in Christendom.

Exchange between Samuel Untermyer, Pujo Committee counsel, investigating the money trust, and J. P. Morgan Sr., 1912, quoted in Ron Chernow, *The House of Morgan* (Atlantic Monthly Press, 1990)

Deregulation gave the banks enough rope to kill themselves, and they almost have.

ALBERT WOJNILOWER, chief economist at the investment banking firm First Boston, quoted in *Time,* December 3, 1984

Fear of personal exposure to liability often leads bankers to say no to creditworthy borrowers seeking to finance creditworthy projects. The age-old character loan is a thing of the past.

TIMOTHY RYAN, former director of Resolution Trust Corporation, quoted in the *Wall Street Journal,* in November 1992, cited in the *New Republic,* January 4, 1993

In our business, it's dangerous to embrace very aggressive return targets because the markets interpret that as an appetite for risk.

JOHN S. REED, CEO of Citicorp, quoted in *Fortune,* April 29, 1996

When it comes to getting into trouble, commercial bankers are hard to beat.

The Economist, November 30, 1996

We firmly believe that banks get into the most trouble when they aggressively lend on an asset class they believe is virtually risk free.

LAWRENCE COHEN, Paine Webber analyst, referring to banks' enthusiastic lending on home equity and used cars to less creditworthy consumers, quoted in the *Wall Street Journal,* March 5, 1997

Banks should be conservative about taking care of people's money. In all other matters they should be innovative and aggressive.

ESQUIEL NASSAR, chairman of Brazil's Banco Excele Economico, quoted in the *Financial Times,* March 4, 1997

Bankers are always the same. When there's an upswing they fall over each other to attract new borrowers without asking too many questions.

OSCAR GARCIA MENDOZA, president of Venezuela's Banco Venezolano de Credito, quoted in the *Financial Times,* October 21, 1997

I grew up naive, believing that banks know what they're doing. After all, they're banks. But the potential for incompetency in a bank is as large as any other business. It's higher because banks don't pay much [for talent].

RONALD RUS, lawyer who helped expose a leasing scam that forced a California bank into receivership, quoted in *Forbes,* September 8, 1997

[O]verreliance on advanced statistical techniques could breed what some call a "Zen banker"—one who lies back and trusts the model rather than using his own judgment.

GEORGE GRAHAM, *Financial Times,* April 4, 1997

This week's sign that the apocalypse is upon us: The First State Bank of Brownsville, Tenn., is offering customers a certificate of deposit with an interest rate that is based on the local high school football team's margin of victory.

Sports Illustrated, September 15, 1997

We keep blaming this crisis [the South Korean banking crisis] on corruption and bad banking practices. But this all happened in the private marketplace. It was so often a case of big foreign lenders pushing their money on the Koreans and the Korean banks enthusiastically taking it in.

PROFESSOR JEFFREY SACHS of Harvard University, quoted in the *New York Times,* December 4, 1997

4.3 CARD-BASED PAYMENT SYSTEMS

Ultimately, every transaction will be triggered by some kind of multifunctional plastic card.

PATRICK THOMAS, CEO of financial data processing firm First Financial Management, quoted in *Forbes,* May 25, 1992.

Ultimately, a consumer would have a single card that supports all the kinds of purchasing they do today. You would have the equivalent of a PC in your pocket.

RONALD BRACO of Chemical Bank, quoted in *Fortune,* February 14, 1994

It was a way you could tell who was rich. And with the cards, we will not be able to see how much money we have spent.

French regular at the Club Med resorts, lamenting the replacement of bead necklaces as the Club currency for buying alcoholic drinks by smart cards, quoted in the *Financial Times,* February 25, 1997

4.4 COMMERCIAL AND RETAIL BANKING

A bank is a place that will lend you money if you can prove that you don't need it.

The comedian BOB HOPE, quoted in Allan Harrington's *Life in the Crystal Palace* (Knopf, 1959)

If you're not actually stupid or dishonest, it's hard not to make money in banking.

GEORGE S. MOORE, former chairman of Citibank, in *The Banker's Life* (Norton, 1987)

Bankers are no longer bankers. They are a whole lot of different things, and above all they are managers who can handle a group of disparate enterprises.

DONALD WAITE of management consultants McKinsey & Co., quoted in *Time,* December 3, 1984

A modern run on a bank doesn't show up in lines at the teller windows, but in an increasing erosion of its capacity to purchase large blocks of funds in money markets.

WILLIAM OGDEN, chairman of Continental Illinois, quoted in *Time,* December 3, 1984 (Ogden was installed as chairman of Continental after it became insolvent because of heavy investment in bad oil loans through Penn Square Bank in Oklahoma.)

Selling financial services is no different from selling hats or making ball bearings. If you've got the customers, you've got a huge advantage over the guy who doesn't have the customers.

THOMAS C. THEOBALD, chairman of Continental Illinois Bank, quoted in *Forbes,* November 30, 1987

This industry [banking] has one foot in the grave and the other on a banana peel.

JAMES SIDELL, president of UST Corp, a bank holding company, quoted in *Fortune,* October 8, 1990

Many pundits have looked at the range of financial innovations in the 1980s and pronounced banks "obsolete." This is nonsense.

LOWELL L. BRYAN of McKinsey & Co., "Blueprint for Financial Reconstruction," *Harvard Busi-ness Review,* May–June 1993

[D]espite all the consolidation of the last decade, there still are more [banks] in First Union's eight-state market than in Canada, Japan, Germany, France, and Great Britain combined.

EDWARD E. CRUTCHFIELD JR., CEO of the banking firm First Union, in a speech, April 28, 1994

I've come to the belief that banks are not in the business of banking. They're in the business of collecting fees.

> PATRICK C. KELLY, CEO, Physicians Sales and Service, an entrepreneurial medical services company, quoted in *Inc.,* October 1995

Our financial services consulting business is very strong because banks have downsized so much that they don't have the human resources to do the things they need to do to compete.

> BUD WARD, national director of financial services at the accounting firm Ernst and Young, quoted in *Fortune,* October 30, 1995

Everybody in this industry ought to be planning for career changes.

> JOHN RUSSELL, chief communications officer at the banking firm Banc One, quoted in *Fortune,* October 30, 1995

The banking industry is dead, and we ought to just bury it.

> RICHARD KOVACEVICH, CEO of the banking firm Norwest, quoted in *Fortune,* November 27, 1995

Bankers seem schizophrenic.

> DAVID PARTRIDGE, director of Towers Perrin Financial Institutions Practice, referring to a study showing that only 10 percent of bank CEOs were prepared to commit to bringing about changes they recognized as necessary, quoted in *Fortune,* November 27, 1995

Dear Nancy,

Why do banks buy each other? If they keep on buying each other there will be no more banks except one? If there's only one bank company, then everyone will have to go to the same bank and there will be too big of lines. Then there will be one bank company that will get all the money for being the bank. There should be more of one kind of company of banks. Then this one bank company would have to be huge. Tons of problems, there would be tons of problems. Tons of people would have to work for this one bank.

> Letter from a child to banking industry analyst, quoted by Hugh McColl, CEO of NationsBank, in a speech, February 26, 1996

As every school child knows, the dinosaur didn't survive the ice age. His world underwent sudden, unfore-seeable, cataclysmic change. It's not that he lacked the capacity to evolve. He just didn't have time. Unlike the dinosaur, bankers can see the changes ahead. We have a choice in the matter the dinosaur never did.

> HUGH McCOLL JR., CEO of NationsBank, responding to Bill Gates's pronouncement that banks were dinosaurs, in a speech, December 4, 1995

Banking is essential to the modern economy, but banks are not.

> J. RICHARD FREDERICKS of the investment firm Montgomery Securities, quoted in *Business Week,* June 12, 1995

[T]o anyone who thinks banking is a dinosaur, "Welcome to Jurassic Park."

> DAVE COULTER, CEO of Bank of America, in a speech, February 22, 1996

Once you open up someone's eyes to the possibility of restructuring their debt, there's no reason for them to think they can't do it themselves.

> Anonymous American banker on South Korea's efforts to restructure its debt by selling bonds in the international capital markets with help from investment banks instead of relying on commercial banks as developing countries had in the 1980s, quoted in the *New York Times,* January 5, 1998

It used to be that you'd get a good loan officer, establish a relationship, and then he'd disappear. Nowadays you get a good bank, establish a relationship, and the bank disappears.

> JEFFREY McKEEVER, cofounder MicroAge Inc., reseller of computer equipment and systems, quoted in *Inc.,* September 1996

In a virtual banking world, what is the value of your brand when I can page through my PC and see every financial institution that I want to deal with?

> ROBERT M. HOWE, IBM financial services expert, quoted in *Fortune,* April 29, 1996

Bankers are torn between the knowledge that their branch infrastructure is largely irrelevant to their future business model and customers' insistence on convenient locations for the few transactions they undertake. Supermarket banking is the obvious solution.

> PETER MARTIN, *Financial Times,* September 18, 1997

In the world of financial services branding, the word "bank" doesn't cut it . . . Nirvana is when people know us as a financial services firm that happens also to be a bank.

> STEPHEN CONE of the banking firm Key Corp, quoted in the *Wall Street Journal,* November 15, 1996

Essentially, banking is very close to a commodity business. Bank manufacturing has to be less about financial wizardry and more about courtesy and professionalism.

> TRACY BRITTON, of Home Savings, quoted in the *Wall Street Journal,* March 20, 1995

Unfortunately, bankers aren't marketers, and we hate to think of ourselves as sales units.

> SUE P. PERROTY of Meridien Bank, a Pennsylvania regional bank, quoted in the *Wall Street Journal,* March 20, 1995

Banking is a business of caution. If it's done properly there should be no upside potential.

> JOHN KEEFE, New York banking analyst, quoted in the *New York Times,* July 5, 1997

To be a banker today is to be a beggar.

> DOMINIC NG, president of East-West Bank in Los Angeles, which relies on its connections with China-linked businesses to compete, quoted in the *Financial Times,* January 15, 1997

One day, I couldn't spell bank, and the next day I was the president of one.

> GERALD J. FORD, former Dallas tax lawyer, entrepreneurial banker, and partner of financier Ronald Perelman, quoted in *Business Week,* December 9, 1996

Being in American banking today is a very strong advantage because the American banking and financial system have gone through a great deal of the adjustments attendant to deregulation and restructuring, a challenge still ahead for many countries around the world

> GEORGE VOJTA, vice chairman of Bankers Trust, interviewed in *ABA Banking Journal,* June 1997

4.5 CREDIT CARDS

You want 21 percent [return on investment] risk free? Pay off your credit cards.

> ANDREW TOBIAS, financial writer, quoted in *American Way,* November 1982

Only about 6 percent of premium-card holders actually use the extra services.

> SPENCER NILSON, publisher of the Consumer Credit Card Rating Service, quoted in *U.S. News & World Report,* March 23, 1987

It's getting harder and harder to impress the waiter.

> ELGIE HOLSTEIN, executive director of the consumer group BankCard Holders of America, on proliferation of gold cards, quoted in *U.S. News & World Report,* March 23, 1987

Anyone who can't make a profit by borrowing money at 5.8 percent and lending at 13.8 percent should find another line of work.

> U.S. REPRESENTATIVE FRANK ANNUNZIO (Democrat, Illinois) on banking-industry protests against limiting credit-card interest rates, quoted in *U.S. News & World Report,* March 30, 1987

When my dog came down with lymphoma, I maxed out two credit cards on chemotherapy trying to save her.

> JEANNE HILL, former legal secretary, quoted in the *New York Times,* December 26, 1995

Biggest government spenders on travel and entertainment: Department of Defense—440,000 employees charged more than $750 million.

> Why American Express outbid Diners Club to become the official charge card of the U.S. government, cited in *Fortune,* November 1, 1993

I wanted to keep a high balance so I wouldn't be tempted to run up my card again.

> A Westchester County, New York, woman on why she paid off only $1,000 of a $4,000 Visa balance when she had the cash to pay it all, quoted in *Fortune,* October 30, 1995

What a retailer has to do is get as many people through his door as possible and sell them as much as possible. What a credit-card issuer has to do is turn down probably more than half the people who want to buy his product.

RICHARD REAY-SMITH of Barclay's, quoted in the *Financial Times,* February 21, 1997

Easy credit, the way it's been offered in this country, is like a drug. It was offered to everyone on easy terms and once people got hooked, now all of a sudden they change the rules and add these fees.

EARL LUI of the Consumer's Union, quoted in the *Wall Street Journal,* June 11, 1997

Tiger Woods probably gets his meals gratis at the All Star Cafe, the chain of theme restaurants in which he is a celebrity owner. But if not, he'd better bring cash. The credit card Tiger endorses, American Express, is not welcome there.

Sports Illustrated, June 16, 1997

The credit-card industry is in the same position as the airline industry was three or four years ago. The players have come to the conclusion that too often they are giving away the goods for far less than their costs.

SEAMUS P. McMAHON of First Manhattan Consulting Group, on the movement among credit-card companies to tighten standards because of record losses, quoted in the *New York Times,* July 6, 1997

Some banks thought that any co-branded deal would make money. They didn't know what they were doing and they got hammered.

JOSEPH SAUNDERS, president of credit-card division of Household International, quoted in the *New York Times,* July 6, 1997

The customers on whom card companies make money are getting better and better terms. But the ones on whom they don't make money are getting terrible terms.

PROFESSOR ERIC K. CLEMONS of Wharton, quoted in the *New York Times,* July 6, 1997

[F]or the average account, every day a payment is delayed adds about four cents to the following month's interest fee. Though barely noticeable to individual cardholders, a one-day delay in the deposit of every payment . . . would mean an annual windfall of well over $150 million for the credit-card industry.

From research by SUSAN ROTH of the investment firm Donaldson, Lufkin & Jenrette, on the cost to

consumers of late mail deliveries, cited in the *Wall Street Journal,* August 22, 1997

I was a freshman and there was this guy giving out free T-shirts, so I just went over. "Want a free T-shirt, just sign up here for a Discover card." So I did. And I've been signing and paying ever since.

LATOYA DAILEY, who had accumulated an $8,000 credit-card balance by her sophomore year of college, quoted in the *New York Times,* August 24, 1997

Who's hurt by someone opening an envelope because they think they're going to get a bigger credit line than they're actually going to get?

MOSHE ORENBUCH of the investment firm Sanford Bernstein, quoted in the *Wall Street Journal,* September 18, 1997

Our biggest competitors are cash and checks. That's where the biggest opportunity is.

When I can go out of a hotel and tip the porter using a Visa card and he'll accept it, that's when we will have succeeded.

ED JENSEN, CEO of the credit-card firm Visa International, quoted in the *Financial Times,* September 15, 1997

Friend: My wife had her credit card stolen.

Dagwood: That's terrible!

Friend: It's not so terrible—the thief's been spending less than she did!

DEAN YOUNG and JIM RAYMOND, *Blondie* cartoon

Through their convenience and the stimulus that the banks are giving them, credit cards will eventually bring American-type levels of consumer debt [to Europe].

UDO REIFNER, head of Hamburg's Institute for Financial Services, quoted in the *New York Times,* April 13, 1991

About one in nine high school students has a credit card—cosigned by parents.

MasterCard survey, cited in *Business Week,* April 11, 1994

It's costing us over $100,000 a year [letting students pay tuition by credit card because of 2 percent fee].

MARJORIE M. POYCK of Mary Washington College, quoted in the *New York Times,* October 12, 1997

4.6 ELECTRONIC MONEY

Nowadays, half a trillion dollars changes hands every day—although no hands are involved, and, in a sense, no dollars either, and it's not even numbers really. It's just binary sequences of pulses racing between computers.

> ROBERT KRULWICH, economics correspondent for National Public Radio and CBS, quoted in the *New Yorker,* February 18, 1988

Over the long haul, this is going to lead to the separation of economy and state.

> BILL A. FREZZA, president of Wireless Computing Associates, quoted in *Business Week,* June 12, 1995

People expect it [electronic banking] to be faster and more accurate, but it's put together with chewing gum and baling wire behind the scenes.

> JIM BRUENE, editor, *Online Banking Report,* quoted in the *Wall Street Journal,* February 7, 1996

This [Internet] thing is like a tidal wave. If you fail in the game, you're going to be dead.

> HUGH McCOLL JR., CEO of NationsBank, quoted in the *Wall Street Journal,* July 25, 1996

We'd deliver everything electronically if we could. But it's really a chicken-and-egg game. To really move the merchants, you need to show them volume.

> MARK A. JONSON of the online bill payment company Checkfree, quoted in the *Wall Street Journal,* February 7, 1996

Money represents not merely our property—that is, our past—but also our wishes for the future . . . Should it be reduced to an electrical impulse, it would seem little more than the quantitative expression of our mental impulses, more action and capacity, nothing special.

> JAMES BUCHAN, author of *Frozen Desire: The Meaning of Money* (Farrar Straus & Giroux, 1997), quoted in the *New York Times,* October 13, 1997

4.7 INSURANCE

Nobody has endurance like the man who sells insurance.

> 1930s vaudeville lyric, quoted in the *Economist,* April 19, 1997

Roots of the insurance industry's inefficiency are manifold. The fire insurance business grew up as a massive exercise in price fixing. The life insurance business is dominated by giant mutual insurers whose managements have no one to answer to but themselves. They are motivated toward growing larger, not leaner.

> ANDREW TOBIAS, *The Invisible Bankers* (Linden Press/Simon & Schuster, 1982)

In the U.S. insurance business, the regulatory bureaucracy is repeated 50 times, because we are subject to the individual regulatory system in each state where we do business. Does this make us stronger? Does it make us better able to provide security, which is what our customers pay us to do? Ask the policyholders of the seven insurers in Florida that went belly-up in the wake of Hurricane Andrew in 1993.

> DEAN O'HARE, CEO of the insurance company Chubb, in a speech, October 20, 1995

Gamblers may think they are betting on red or seven or four-of-a-kind, but *in reality they are betting on the clock.* The loser wants a short run to look like a long run, so that the odds will prevail. The winner wants a long run to look like a short run, so that the odds will be suspended. Far away from the gaming tables, the managers of insurance companies conduct their affairs in the same fashion. They set their premiums to cover the losses they will sustain in the long run; but when earthquakes and fires and hurricanes all happen at about the same time, the short run can be very painful. Unlike gamblers, insurance companies carry capital and put away reserves to tide them over during the inevitable sequences of short runs of bad luck.

> PETER L. BERNSTEIN, *Against the Gods* (Wiley, 1996)

If you're not rich, we're not really interested.

> DEAN O'HARE, CEO of the insurance firm Chubb, on his company's decision to concentrate on high-net-worth clients and profitable specialty underwriting, quoted in *Fortune,* August 23, 1993

Turning around an insurance company is like parallel parking a battleship.

> MICHAEL A. SMITH of the investment bank Lehman Brothers, quoted in the *Wall Street Journal,* March 25, 1995

I don't think the banks and the investment bankers are going to be a significant threat or factor in this business [insurance brokerage] because they don't have the expertise. And I don't think they can build that expertise—any more than you'll see good brokers becoming investment bankers. It's just too hard, too complicated.

> DENNIS CHOOKASZIAN, CEO of CNA Insurance
> Companies, *Marsh & McLennan Companies—*
> *Viewpoint,* Winter 1996.

You learn the art of having dinner for three hours and never saying anything.

> DAN LOGAN, formerly of the insurance company The
> New England, on adapting to the culture of the insurance industry, quoted in *Inc.,* November 1995

Insurance companies traditionally have selected CEOs from the ranks of actuaries and underwriters. . . . Their practitioners are risk-averse, most at home in the world of numbers. When they rise to the top, they treat fellow technicians as more important than sales and marketing professionals.

> ERNEST AUERBACH of the insurance firm United
> Companies, quoted in the *Wall Street Journal,* July 8,
> 1996

We either get the assets and capital into the hands of managers who know what to do with it, or we'll all be subsidiaries of banks one day.

> STEVEN HILBERT, head of the insurance holding
> company Conesco, quoted in the *Wall Street Journal,*
> February 14, 1997

Reinsurers are above all risk takers and insurers are essentially distribution companies. The natural partner of a reinsurer is an investment bank which provides advice on financial management.

> WALTER KIELHOLZ, chief executive of the reinsurance firm Swiss Re, quoted in the *Financial Times,*
> September 5, 1997

Insurance companies and buyers have not yet fully come to terms with the new reality of megacatastrophes in the 1990s, and nowhere in the United States is this issue seen more dramatically than in Florida.

> SEAN MOONEY of the Insurance Information Institute, quoted in the *Wall Street Journal,* July 12, 1996

I become very religious [when Florida's hurricane season starts].

> BILL NELSON, Florida Insurance commissioner,
> quoted in the *Wall Street Journal,* July 12, 1996

Personal pensions, life and health insurance, mortgage protection policies, unemployment and long-term care insurance—you name it and the industry will write you a policy.

And it will. But only if you are fit, able, or affluent. The poor, the sick, and the unemployed need not apply.

> PHILIP STEPHENS, *Financial Times,* February 28, 1997

If God hadn't meant them to be sheared, he wouldn't have made them sheep.

> ROBERT HISCOX of the insurance organization Lloyd's
> of London, on "names" who complained about $13
> billion of underwriting losses and their unlimited liability, quoted in Elizabeth Luessenhop and Martin
> Mayer, *Risky Business* (Scribner, 1995)

I've never understood why people regard insurance as a conservative business. Really, it's bookmaking.

> ROBERT HISCOX of the insurance organization Lloyd's
> of London, quoted in Elizabeth Luessenhop and
> Martin Mayer, *Risky Business* (Scribner, 1995)

The American Names may make the legal costs of collecting from them greater than the recovery of their debts to Lloyd's. And for the Americans who declare bankruptcy and move to Florida, well, that's the end of it. The Americans are giving Yeltsin only one year to turn around the entire Russian economy. We should be given five years to make Lloyd's profitable. And the Americans should remember it took them ten years to write their Constitution. And the Americans after that, one hundred years later, they had a Civil War.

> PETER MIDDLETON, chief executive and deputy
> chairman of Lloyd's, quoted in Elizabeth Luessenhop
> and Martin Mayer, *Risky Business* (Scribner, 1995)

The available English remedies are not adequate substitutes for the firm shields and finely honed swords provided by American securities law.

> Opinion by federal Court of Appeals in California
> saying that U.S. names can sue the British insurance
> organization Lloyd's under securities fraud and
> racketeering statutes, quoted in the *Financial Times,*
> March 10, 1997

The same reasoning could provide protection for Americans who lost money betting on chicken fights in Mexico.

> Summary of dissenting opinion for Judge Alfred Goodwin, quoted in the *Financial Times,* March 10, 1997

5.1 CALIFORNIA

From time to time the continent shifts, and everything that isn't fastened down slides into southern California.

> FRANK LLOYD WRIGHT, in a TV interview.

All things start in California and spread to New York, then to London, and then throughout Europe.

> STELIOS HAJI-IOANNOU, owner of easyJet, European discount airline, quoted in the *Wall Street Journal*, December 9, 1996

Hollywood is now a bigger empire than the whole of California's defense sector—and with an average wage of $39,000, moviemaking pays almost as well.

> *The Economist*, December 2, 1995

The entertainment industry now employs more people than the aerospace industry.

> *The Economist*, March 30, 1996

The GDP of Silicon Valley's 2 million inhabitants comes to around $65 billion—around the same as Chile.

> Information from STEPHEN LEVY, Center for the Continuing Study of the Californian Economy, cited in the *Economist*, March 9, 1997

More people are working in California today than when the recession began in 1990, more than making up for the 525,000 jobs that were lost in the recession.

> DAVE COULTER, CEO of Bank of America, in a speech, February 22, 1997

If it's worth doing, California will do it to excess.

> Comment on National Public Radio, occasioned by an announcement that a bank would share space with a drugstore chain, fall 1996

If some of you know where there is still a fast lane left in Los Angeles, look out: it will soon vanish. By 2010, 9 million more people, with 8 million more cars, will move to California. Without new roads, the average commuting time will hit two hours by 2010, up from 45 minutes now. In 20 years average travel speeds will slow from today's 35 mph to 19 mph More than half of daily travel time will be spent at a dead stop.

> THOMAS J. DONAHUE, CEO of American Trucking Associates, in a speech, July 7, 1989.

[T]he old adage is that people in L.A. want buses and mass transit so all these other guys will get off the freeway.

> ROBERT HARNAR of Ford Motor Company, quoted in *Time*, March 27, 1989

If you're an Indian, or Korean or Taiwanese with money to invest in the United States and you've got relatives in L.A., you're not going to invest in Topeka.

> KEVIN McCARTHY of the think tank Rand Corporation, on the economic benefits of immigration on Los Angeles, quoted in the *Wall Street Journal*, January 15, 1985

The California "Phase II" gasoline standards will reduce emissions an extra 39 tons per day, at a cost of $130,000 per ton . . . Studies project that a high-tech automobile inspection and maintenance program could remove 240 tons of pollutants per day for only $7,000 a ton. And a statewide effort to scrap older high-polluting vehicles could remove 170 tons a day for only $3,500 a ton.

> KENNETH T. DERR, CEO of the oil company Chevron, in a speech, August 7, 1992

The California lifestyle is a product that is exported all over the world. Beach volleyball is a part of that.

> JERRY SOLOMON, chief executive, the Association of Volleyball Professionals, quoted in *Forbes*, September 8, 1997

Immigration has always been a mix of benefits and costs. For California, more than for any other state, the balance is shifting to the cost side.

> Rand Corporation report, cited in the *Financial Times*, September 16, 1997

You will face difficulty in California: workers there know everything about their rights and study them in school.

> YUKIO SADAMORI, head of the Japanese manufacturing firm Mitsui & Co., who trains Japanese managers

before assignment to the United States, quoted in the *Wall Street Journal*, July 9, 1996

When you come to a four-way stop in Beverly Hills, between Santa Monica and Sunset, you defer to whoever has the snazziest car. If they see any marks on your car, they're going first.

> FLOYD BYARS, screenwriter, quoted in the *New York Times,* April 12, 1992

Los Angeles acts as a window on Japan, and San Francisco acts as a window on China.

> Senior San Francisco lawyer, quoted in the *Financial Times,* October 21, 1997

5.2 FLORIDA

Miami's single most important economic development agent turned out to be Fidel Castro.

> ROSABETH MOSS KANTER, *World Class: Thriving Locally in the Global Economy* (Simon & Schuster, 1995)

Miami has the infrastructure of North America and the comfort level of South America. You can't beat it.

> PETER REEAVELY of Miami International Airport, quoted in Rosabeth Moss Kanter, *World Class: Thriving Locally in the Global Economy* (Simon & Schuster, 1995)

Between 1991 and late last year, nearly 100,000 new jobs were created in the [Ft. Lauderdale] area, almost one in 100 of all new U.S. jobs in the period.

> GERARD BAKER, *Financial Times,* January 30, 1997

5.3 LAS VEGAS

Las Vegas has always represented the tremendous freedom to do nutty things.

> STEVE WYNN, chairman of the hotel and casino firm Mirage Resorts, quoted in the *Economist,* January 20, 1996

Will we overbuild? The answer is yes. We don't know when to stop. That's the free market working.

> R. KEITH SCHWER, director of the Center for Business and Economic Research, University of Nevada,

Las Vegas, quoted in the *Wall Street Journal,* November 15, 1996

5.4 TEXAS

Lenders jumped in here on a scale and proportion that is unknown in the annals of real estate. Anybody who could spell "office buildings" thought he ought to build one.

> JOE RUSSO, Houston developer, quoted in the *Wall Street Journal,* January 17, 1985

The thing about Texas is that everything is based on money. If you lose your money, you become a nonperson.

> A. C. GREENE, Dallas historian, quoted in *U.S. News & World Report,* September 15, 1986

Increasingly, it's appearing the easiest way to become a millionaire in Texas is to start as a billionaire.

> HAROLD GROSS of Southern Methodist University quoted in *U.S. News & World Report,* September 15, 1986

We went from riches to rags. We're not going to go from rags to riches.

> T. R. FEHRENBACH, Texas state historian, quoted in *Newsweek,* January 23, 1989

Good thing we've still got politics in Texas—finest form of free entertainment ever invented.

> MOLLY IVINS, *Molly Ivins Can't Say That, Can She?* (Random House, 1991)

Texans believe it's a whole different country down here. They don't want you to just slap an armadillo in a TV spot.

> MIKE JOHNSON of the beer company Miller Lite, which has paid dearly to be the "official beer" of the Dallas Cowboys and Houston Rockets, quoted in the *Wall Street Journal,* December 5, 1996

6.1 BRAINS

When I was in my late 30s, I was invited to join other CEOs from much larger corporations at social and sporting events. I soon came to think, "these guys really aren't that smart."

I was surprised at how he [James E. Lee, the No. 2 man at Gulf] agonized over each discard [in a card game]. I couldn't help but wonder if he made decisions at Gulf with the same painful deliberation.

> T. BOONE PICKENS, CEO of Mesa Petroleum and corporate raider, quoted in *Fortune*, February 16, 1987

People always overestimate how complex business is. This isn't rocket science; we've chosen one of the world's more simple professions.

> JOHN F. WELCH, CEO of GE, interviewed in *Harvard Business Review*, September–October 1989

You don't need a rocket scientist. Investing is not a game where the guy with the 160 IQ beats the guy with 130 IQ.

> WARREN BUFFETT, CEO of investment firm Berkshire Hathaway, quoted in *Fortune, 1990 Investors' Guide*

Finding intelligent people is harder than finding people who have money.

> ED ORPINA, founder of software firm Hitech Information, quoted in *Asia, Inc.*, September 1996

America's richest man was Bill Gates, a college dropout who did not need a lot of formal education to build the world's most powerful information technology company.

> PAUL KRUGMAN, professor of economics at MIT, looking back 100 years from 2096, quoted in the *New York Times Magazine*, September 30, 1996

Nothing in the world can take the place of persistence. Genius will not. Unrewarded genius is almost a problem. Talent will not. The world is filled with unsuccessful men of talent. Education alone will not. The world is filled with educated derelicts.

> RAY KROC, McDonalds, quoted in David Halberstam, *The Fifties* (Villard, 1993)

No amount of genius will make up for a true reversal in the market as a whole.

> AUSTIN M. LONG III of University of Texas Investment Management, quoted in *Business Week*, May 6, 1996

[Y]ou're going to find that 95 percent of all the decisions you'll ever make in your career could be made by any reasonably intelligent high school sophomore.
>
> But they'll pay you for the other 5 percent.

> MARION FOLSOM of Eastman Kodak, quoted in a speech by Willard Butcher, former CEO of the banking firm Chase Manhattan, May 15, 1987

All you need [in Silicon Valley] is a computer and a brain and you can get really rich.

> JAYSON ADAMS, age 29, after selling his fourth Silicon Valley start-up since graduating from Stanford to Netscape, quoted in the *Wall Street Journal*, October 8, 1996

My experience is that people who are really, really bright find it very difficult to delegate, because they literally could do the job better themselves. For them, it's kind of unnatural to delegate and do all the things you have to do to go to a big organization. But for people like me, who are average, it's different. Oh, I've got an ego and all that, but I know I need help. So I go and get the very best people. Then you've got to motivate 'em, create a good environment, and so on.

> H. ROSS PEROT, CEO of the data processing firm EDS, quoted in *Inc.*, January 1989

It always amazes me that you can take people who are equally bright, sharp, focused, and so forth and get such different results from them. The only thing I have ever figured out is that some have the ability to shed the past, others do not.

> ROBERT H. BOHAUMON, CEO of Travellers Express, quoted in Charles B. Wendel, *The New Financiers: Profiles of the Leaders Who Are Reshaping the Financial Services Industry* (Irwin Professional Publishers, 1996)

There was no evidence that [Sir Isaac Newton] had ever led any group of people in a successful enterprise; on the contrary, he was . . . the kind of researcher who is only really happy in his laboratory but who needs approbation and admiration lavished on him by the chairman to keep him within the corporation. All too many corporations would assume that the only way was to pay him more money, and the system would then force them to take him away from actual research and appoint him head of the research division, which would be a disaster for him, for the corporation, and for science.

> ANTONY JAY, on Newton's potential as a corporate executive, *Corporate Man* (Random House, 1971)

People don't do business with you because you're a geek and can do regressions in your head. They come to do business with you because they like you.

> JAMES LEE, of Chase Manhattan Bank, quoted in Martin Mayer, *The Bankers* (E. P. Dutton, 1997)

What I'm always astounded by is that just because I have had some business success, people assume I do not have intellectual interests and intellectual capabilities.

> MORTIMER ZUCKERMAN, real estate developer and publisher of the *Atlantic Monthly, U.S. News & World Report,* and the *New York Daily News,* quoted in *Fortune,* November 29, 1993

The profile that correlates with high-quant/low-verbal scores is appalling.

> PROFESSOR MICHAEL DRIVER of the University of Southern California, on results of a personality profile he administered to MBA students, quoted in *Fortune,* January 24, 1994 (The profile showed them to be intolerant of uncertainty, surprisingly unanalytical, uncomfortable with complex data, unsocial, unartistic, and unenterprising.)

Smartness isn't by itself especially attractive (which may account for the poor newsstand sales of *Playboy's* November 1995 cover "The Women of MENSA").

> ALAN FARNHAM, *Fortune,* January 15, 1996

You think you're a smart businessman, but you must realize that many people are smarter than you. If there are smarter people—stronger, better horses running—then why aren't you putting some of your money on them and not all of it on yourself.

> ROBERT KUOK, Chinese businessman, quoted in *Forbes,* July 28, 1997

It takes a smart man to make dumb TV.

> CHRIS SMITH, writer, on Harvard-educated Latin scholar Stephen Chao, who conceived such TV shows as *America's Most Wanted, Cops,* and *Studs,* quoted in *New York,* October 18, 1993

By photographing every meal he has had for 25 years [Yoshiro Nakamats, Japanese inventor] claims to have discovered which foods are good for the brain and which are not. Yogurt, chicken livers, and seaweed are in. Alcohol and coffee are not. Snacks containing all the most cerebrally correct ingredients are available from Dr. Nakamats High-Tech Innovation Corporation at 500 yen ($5) a packet. [Nakamats holds 3,000 patents, including floppy-disk technology licensed to IBM.]

> *The Economist,* November 28, 1995

6.2 BROADWAY

It's a good depiction of industrial America [the play *Other People's Money,* which drew record crowds from Wall Street]. It's a reminder to us that there are people out there in those companies, all working in jobs.

> Bond salesman, Merrill Lynch, quoted in the *New York Times,* February 25, 1990

Carl [Icahn, the corporate raider] has an idea to do a story about a raider who wears a white hat instead of a black hat. He said we'd make it into a film.

> JERRY STERNER, author of the play *Other People's Money,* quoted in the *New York Times,* February 25, 1990

6.3 CIVILIZATION

Industry without art is barbarism.

> HERBERT READ, quoted in the *Economist,* October 24, 1987

6.4 THE INTANGIBLES

I don't want people whose livelihood depends on fulfilling a certain function.

CHARLES WANG, founder and CEO Computer Associates International, quoted in *Inc.,* September 1994

[T]here are the intangibles that don't show up on a résumé—things like intelligence, judgment, a sense of humor, and energy level. Those are the qualities I use to pick my own team.

Twenty years ago, it was simple to select people. You just looked at the results. Anybody who could bring home the bacon was, by definition, a terrific person. Today we go through an elaborate selection process that goes well beyond bottom-line numbers.

JAN LESHLY, CEO of the pharmaceutical firm SmithKline Beecham, interviewed in *Harvard Business Review,* September–October 1995

6.5 LANGUAGE—ENGLISH

[T]he contributions of business to the health of the language have not been outstanding. Spelling has been assaulted by Duz, and E-Z Off, and Fantastik, and Kool and Arrid and Kleen, and the tiny containers of milk and cream catchily called Pour Shun, and by products that make you briter, so that you will not be left hi and dri at a parti, but made welkom.

EDWIN NEWMAN, *Strictly Speaking: Will America Be the Death of English* (Warner, 1975)

Plain English is like pornography. It's hard to define, but you know it when you see it. If companies do not submit documents that comply, we will send them back and tell them to try again.

NANCY M. SMITH, director of the Securities and Exchange Commission Office of Investor Education and Assistance, quoted in the *New York Times,* August 25, 1996

Perhaps more than anyone else in the world, Americans are devoted to hyperbole.

FRED WASHOFSKY, *The Chip Wars* (Scribner, 1989)

What is a hack? It suggests the second rate, the mediocre, the inferior. Unions and governments seem to have lots of hacks. One hardly ever seems to find them

in the for-profit sector. Are there CEO hacks, Chairman of the Board hacks? Is a hack always relegated to middle management?

EMILY MICHAEL, graduate student, New York University, 1996

If it is a support job, it is not a job we need. We do not have any job description that says a person supports or contributes. We want a job description that says a person will drive—that stresses an action verb.

ROBERT H. BOHAUMON, CEO of the consumer financial services firm Travellers Express, interviewed in Charles B. Wendel, *The New Financiers: Profiles of the Leaders Who Are Reshaping the Financial Services Industry* (Irwin Professional Publishers, 1996)

Every adjective used to scorn Los Angeles has an opposite term of praise. Instead of chaos, think adversity. Instead of ferment, think energy. Instead of recession, think transition.

PAUL ALVAREZ, chairman of the PR firm Ketchum Communications, on changing pessimistic discussion of Los Angeles in the wake of Rodney King–verdict riots, quoted in *Fortune,* November 15, 1993

I have a rule of thumb that I will cancel subscriptions to economic journals if I go a whole year without being able to understand at least one article.

Unnamed economist, quoted in the *Los Angeles Times,* January 8, 1993

Even as the experts you must get a little bewildered sometimes at the mess of acronyms we've created—ECCHO, PSN, and NACHA—ECP, BIPS, FSTC—I-NET, A-P-I, and OFC—ANSI-X9, ISO and NISTPFS, ISC, NYCE and PAX—on and on. Maybe we need to create a new Berlitz school for cyberspeak!

JIM CAMPBELL of the banking firm Norwest, in a speech, September 25, 1996

And then there is the *level playing field* that businessmen endlessly plead for. Has no one told them that a sloping field slopes equally for both sides?

Johnson column, ridiculing sports-based metaphors that are imprecise, *The Economist,* June 14, 1997

Dress for power, and you're usually in gray. Gray labels us solid, cautious, conservatively dependable, responsible, nonfrivolous, trustworthy. Money should be gray. After all, you keep score with it in business.

Call it jargon, corporatese, bureaucratese, journalese, bafflegab, gobbledygook, double speak, or whatever critics label bloated, sluggish writing these days.

> LIONEL L. FISHER, communications consultant, in a speech, September 23, 1992

Executives at every level are prisoners of the notion that a simple style reflects a simple mind.

> WILLIAM ZINSSER, writing guru, cited by Lionel L. Fisher, communications consultant, in a speech, September 23, 1992

In every private conversation I've had with Larry [Ellison, CEO of Oracle software] over the past 15 or 20 years, the metaphors are always violent. He'll say, "This is the quarter we put a knife in their chest," or "The life will be choked out of them." The metaphors don't come from chess, and they don't come from the Bible. He sees this as personal combat.

> Industry figure, quoted in *Time*, May 12, 1997

We haven't been using the word "real" before. Maybe that sounds like a technicality, but there's a distinction between "buttery taste" and "*real* buttery taste."

> JOHN BARROWS of the food company Nabisco, on Parkay margarine, which had long used the slogan "The flavor says 'Butter,'" quoted in *Fortune*, October 13, 1997

Purists may turn in their graves as the Czechs and Japanese murder the English language—and get their [business] deal[s]. Most purists actually are in their graves. What happens to this language is no longer our prerogative. English is no longer our possession. It's not a monolith. It's in an incredible state of flux.

> ALAN FIRTH, linguist, quoted in the *Wall Street Journal*, March 22, 1995

Professor Firth [a linguist] has an idea of what makes foreigners so good at getting points across in English. They don't joke. They ignore gaffes. They don't mind pauses. They don't care if two people speak at once. They aim for normality, and live with confusion.

> BARRY NEWMAN, *Wall Street Journal*, March 22, 1995

There are new Englishes in Asia and the tiger [rapidly developing Asian] economies. If economic power passes to the tiger economies, they will be telling us what to do.

> GERRY KNOWLES, author of *A Cultural History of the English Language* (Edward Arnold, 1997), quoted in the *Financial Times*, January 6, 1997

Our designers can talk on the phone and swap ideas using computer-aided design, but they get together twice a year in Taiwan to review their work. The common language we use is English.

> ANTONY LO, CEO of the bicycle firm Giant, which has 65 designers in different countries, quoted in the *Financial Times*, October 24, 1997

It is a standard paradox of management that those who write best about it could seldom run a fruit stall. The converse is equally true. Most real managers lack the gift of abstraction, and cannot write from experience without being ambushed by detail.

> TONY JACKSON, reviewing Arie de Geus, *The Living Company* (Harvard Business School Press, 1997), in the *Financial Times*, May 15, 1997

If some tortured souls of journalism had their way, newspaper and magazine articles could come to resemble a stock prospectus, in which half the space is taken up with warnings about why you shouldn't make this investment.

> *Washington Monthly*, April 1984

George Orwell once blamed the demise of the English language on politics. It's quite possible he never read a prospectus.

> ARTHUR LEVITT JR., chairman of the U.S. Securities and Exchange Commission, quoted in the *New York Times*, August 25, 1996

While prospectuses are legal documents, and their legal function must be preserved, they are not sacred texts. Since the plain-language movement began in 1975, the courts and most lawyers have recognized that even complex documents like prospectuses can be made simple and accessible without losing their legal vitality. Not one has ever been held liable for communicating clearly and plainly.

> KENNETH MORRIS, president of the communications firm Siegal & Gale, which helped develop the SEC's *Plain English Handbook*, quoted in the *New York Times*, September 20, 1997

Please read these materials so that you'll know what we plan to do at the meeting.

> Ford Motor Company proxy statement, which won the Clarity Award for Legal Writing from the Plain English Committee of the State Bar of Michigan, cited in the *Wall Street Journal,* April 29, 1997

The windbag postulate: The chairman's verbosity increases in direct proportion to the severity of the company's problems.

> JASON ZWEIG and JOHN CHAMBERLAIN, *Forbes,* August 3, 1992

[*Translation of common annual report phrases by someone who writes them.*]

The company is downsizing. We're closing a couple of plants and laying off a few hundred workers. The cutbacks do not apply to executive salaries or bonuses, which, deservedly, are being upsized.

We have a global thrust. We don't have a prayer of increasing sales at home.

We have increased our productivity. We're determined to get more for our buck, even if it means paying Honduran children 31 cents an hour.

The company has a commitment to quality. We didn't say high quality.

> J. H. COHEN, *New York Times,* August 18, 1996

It is possible that no document on earth has committed as many sins against the language as the prospectus. The prose trips off the tongue like peanut butter. Poetry seems to be reserved for claims about performance, and conciseness for discussions about fees.

> ARTHUR LEVITT, chairman of the U. S. Securities and Exchange Commission, quoted in the *Financial Times Weekend,* March 1–2, 1997

6.6 LANGUAGE—FRENCH

Whenever you receive a letter from a creditor, write fifty lines upon some extraterrestrial subject, and you will be served.

> CHARLES BAUDELAIRE (1821–1867)

The French language is very constrictive in a world—especially in business—which wants to speak English.

> MICHAEL JOHNSON, journalist turned corporate manager, and author of *French Resistance* (Cassell, 1997), quoted in the *Financial Times,* April 11, 1997

6.7 LANGUAGE—GERMAN

Germany's stodgy stock market has never offered the same easy exit for venture investors that start-ups have access to in America. A linguistic difficulty reflects the problem: "Venture capital" translates badly as *Risikokapital,* which sounds risky rather than appealing. An alternative, *Chancenkapital,* has caught on.

> *The Economist,* June 28, 1997

6.8 LANGUAGE—SPANISH

Those who made this dictionary of synonyms are imbeciles and cretins.

> Historian FERNANDO BENITEZ on Microsoft's Spanish-language thesaurus (which used monster, cannibal, and barbarian as synonyms for *negro* [Spanish word for black person], bastard for people of mixed race, and vicious and pervert for lesbian), quoted in the *Wall Street Journal,* July 8, 1996

6.9 POSTERITY

Who the hell cares? The day you retire, you're finished. The day you die, you're dead.

> WILLIAM JOVANOVICH, CEO of publishers Harcourt Brace Jovanovich, when asked by reporter how he'd like to go down in history, quoted in *Forbes,* April 22, 1997

6.10 RELIGION

A well-run company is a sign of God's grace.

> ROBERT G. PEARSON of the computer firm Sun Microsystems, quoted in the *New York Times,* November 28, 1993

I've often wondered if it isn't easier to practice one's faith in a large corporation than to practice it in church—because what is right is always so much clearer when it stands in contrast to that which is equivocal.

> VIRGINIA WELDON, M.D., executive of the chemical company Monsanto, in a speech, January 24, 1996

Many executives ask themselves if Sunday has anything to do with Monday through Friday.

> WILLIAM GLAVIN, president of Babson College, a business school in Boston, on rising interest among

business people in religion, quoted in the *Financial Times,* January 19, 1997

6.11 SCIENCE

You can build a computer in a garage. You can have a great idea for a drug. But to get the ultimate molecule takes enormous effort, and it's not going to be done in a garage.

> P. ROY VAGELOS, CEO of the pharmaceutical firm Merck & Co., quoted in *Fortune,* January 19, 1987

Science can amuse and fascinate us all—but it is engineering that changes the world.

> ISAAC ASIMOV, writer and science popularizer, quoted by Robert G. McVicker Sr. of Kraft General Foods, in a speech April 3, 1992

Science permeates every aspect of our daily lives—the way we work, the way we travel, the way we communicate, the way we live. Yet Americans tend to distrust science and may not fully appreciate the connection between research and development and our economy. That's especially ironic, given that they are increasingly anxious about their future.

> DR. AUGUST M. WATANABE of the pharmaceutical firm Eli Lilly, in a speech, August 21, 1996

R&D trends are . . . disconcerting—not only underscoring an ominous downtrend in publicly sponsored research commitments but also suggesting that corporate fixation on cost control may now be having a discernible impact on the commitment of businesses to the technological discovery process.

> STEPHEN S. ROACH, chief economist of Morgan Stanley, "A New Competitive Dilemma," *Wall Street Journal,* June 20, 1996.

The majority of the things we do fail. The fact that anything comes out the door is a tribute to the tremendous tenacity of hundreds of people.

> DR. P. ROY VAGELOS, CEO of the pharmaceutical firm Merck & Co., quoted in *Business Week,* October 12, 1987

6.12 SOCIAL RESPONSIBILITY

I have never known much good done by those who affected to trade for the public good.

> ADAM SMITH, *The Wealth of Nations*

When an executive decides to take action for reasons of social responsibility, he is taking money from someone else—from the stockholders in the form of lower earnings; or from the consumer in the form of higher prices.

> Nobel Prize–winning economist MILTON FRIEDMAN, interviewed in *Playboy,* February 1973

Plain and simple, banks tend not to respond to negative pressure. . . . You don't have to love us. But I will never understand those who attack us and then expect us to love them.

> HUGH L. McCOLL JR., CEO of NationsBank, in a speech, September 15, 1995

Business is the most important engine for social change in our society . . . And you're not going to transform society until you transform business. But you're not going to transform business by pretending it's not a business. Business means profit. You've got to earn your cost of capital. They didn't do it in the former Soviet Union, and that's why it's former.

> LAWRENCE PERLMAN, CEO of the information and defense electronics firm Ceridian Corporation, quoted in *Twin Cities Business Monthly,* November 1994

Chrysler, Ford, and General Motors have been generous to this community for decades. . . . But our real contribution has been staying in business. That's our role, and when we're successful, the whole community benefits.

> ROBERT J. EATON, CEO of the car company Chrysler, March 18, 1996

Selling 60 million doses of our [hepatitis B] vaccine every year for 20 years would represent a huge market, but the Chinese government could not afford to buy our vaccine, and the epidemic was running wild. So in 1989 we made a strategic and humanitarian decision to sell the Chinese the technology to make the vaccine and then teach them how to make it.

> P. ROY VAGELOS, CEO of the pharmaceutical firm Merck, in an interview, *Harvard Business Review,* November–December 1994

In the foundation and development of a successful enterprise there must be a single-minded pursuit of financial profit. Bring in some other motive, admirable though it may be in itself—the desire to produce employment, the wish to bring prosperity to a poor district, the gaining of prestige for one's country, the urge even to provide evidence to support one's favorite religious, political, or economic dogma—and our whole effort has from the outset a probably fatal defect.

> PROFESSOR C. NORTHCOTE PARKINSON, introduction to *Famous Financial Fiascoes* by John Train (Fraser Publications, 1995)

[W]e have not laid off or furloughed a single employee for lack of work for more than 25 years . . . Most of our plants are located in small towns and rural areas . . . We cannot just lay people off, because they have no place to go. So, if we have a slow economic period, everybody works four days a week instead of five, or five days instead of six. But everybody still has a job. You do not get good people if you lay off half of your workforce just because one year the economy isn't very good and then you hire them back.

> F. KENNETH IVERSON, CEO of the steel company Nucor, in a speech, February 5, 1996

Our strength lies in building on classics, on knowing who we are. That is how we succeeded as a company. And that same quality lies behind the social programs and policies we've introduced over the years. They are conservative in the best sense of the word because they restore something that was in danger of being lost—extended families, a healthy work environment.

> ARNOLD HIATT, CEO of the shoe company Stride Rite, interviewed in *Harvard Business Review*, March–April 1992

Companies have to be socially responsible or the shareholders pay eventually.

> WARREN SHAW, CEO of Chancellor LGT Asset Management, quoted in *Fortune*, August 4, 1997

6.13 TALENT

Being good in business is the most fascinating kind of art. Making money is art, and working is art, and good business is art.

> ANDY WARHOL, quoted in *U.S. News & World Report*, March 9, 1987

I was an average kid; I was an average student . . . I doubted I could be a terrific lawyer or a doctor, but I realized I could make a lot of money.

> NEIL HIRSCH, founder of the financial information firm Telerate Systems, quoted in *Time*, January 23, 1984

6.14 TIME

Several years ago I invited the Dalai Lama to participate in a gathering of leaders at the University of Southern California. The living embodiment of thousands of years of Tibetan spiritual wisdom graciously declined—by fax. [As of September 1996, the Dalai Lama's web site was http://emma.manymedia.com/tibet/DalaiLama.html]

> WARREN BENNIS, in a preface to *Leaders on Leadership: Interviews with Top Executives* (Harvard Business Review, 1991)

Yesterday's lifesaving, fireproof building material is today's carcinogen.

> DEAN O'HARE, CEO of the insurance firm Chubb, in a speech, October 20, 1997

At the turn of the century, one of the largest employers in America was the U.S. Ice Trust, which cut, stored, and delivered ice for people's "iceboxes." That industry doesn't employ many people now, although it's not because people have forsaken the need to cool fresh food. Rather, a product born of new technology, the refrigerator, entered American homes and all but eliminated the need for ice cutters. Another prominent firm in the early part of the century, the Fisher Company, produced carriages and buggies. This firm is still in business, making the automotive bodies for Chevrolet.

> JERRY L. JORDAN, president of the Federal Reserve Bank of Cleveland, in a speech, October 1, 1996

I'll bet a lot of you can still sing the Pepsodent jingle, "You'll wonder where the yellow went, when you brush your teeth with Pepsodent." But you'll have a hard time finding it [Pepsodent] in the store.

> CATHLEEN BLACK, president of Hearst Magazines, in a speech, March 4, 1997

6.15 TRAVEL

Business people don't like to travel on buses.

> MITCH ROUSE, founder of the airport taxi service SuperShuttle International, quoted in *Forbes*, August 11, 1986

For most executives, a trip on an airplane tends to be a quiet period rather than a period of work.

> GEORGE COLONY of the research firm Forrester Research, quoted in the *New York Times*, April 28, 1991

For a lot of guys it's just another place to have an office. You get on the plane with a satchel full of work and write memos and get in the car and get to the hotel and get back on the phone.

> Disney executive on first-class travel, quoted in the *New York Times*, October 18, 1992

Just sitting there in the waiting room at the airport and giving the serial number of the plane you are waiting for is enough to set you apart from the rest of the world and make you feel special.

> LOIS WYSE, *Company Manners* (McGraw-Hill, 1987)

If you get on a flight—God forbid—15 hours to Singapore, eventually you'll take out your credit card and play a couple of rounds of blackjack. It's the boredom factor.

> JOE BRANCATELLI, an editor of *Travel Holiday* magazine, quoted in the *Wall Street Journal*, May 24, 1996

People have asked me time and again, "Why do you spend all that time traveling?" And the answer to that is really kind of simple. I travel because that is where the people are.

> AL ZEIEN, CEO of the razor company Gillette, quoted in *Harvard Business Review*, May–June 1996

We've found that the needs of business travelers differ depending on whether they are going to or coming from a meeting.

> Airline executive, quoted in *Harvard Business Review*, January–February 1997

The idea of working on board [an airplane] is a myth. In the first hour or two of a flight everyone is busy on their laptops, but then they settle down to a soporific state. There is 25 percent less oxygen on board an aircraft than on the ground and the most sensitive organ to lack of oxygen is the brain. Some people are surprised when they look at the notes they have written while in the air and compare them with what they would normally achieve on the ground.

I advise people to relax or do something creative, such as preparing a speech or dreaming up new ideas. It is in that state between consciousness and sleeping that we can be at our most inspired.

> FARROL KAHN, director of the British Aviation Health Institute, quoted in the *Financial Times*, April 1, 1997

GBT syndrome—get the boss there. [Contributor to the accident rate for corporate jets, which is substantially higher than for commercial airlines.]

Scud running. [Name given to visual navigation through clouds instead of waiting for an approved instrument flight plan, under influence of GBT.]

> Cited in the *Wall Street Journal*, April 18, 1997

[Executive pilots] are like chauffeurs, waiting around all day while the boss attends his meeting. And when the boss comes out saying, "Let's go to London," the pilots may have to fly [six or seven hours].

> STUART MATHEWS, chairman of the Flight Safety Association, cited in the *Wall Street Journal*, April 18, 1997

Fatigue is the No. 1 factor that detrimentally impacts the ability of pilots.

> JIM HALL, chairman of the National Transportation Safety Board, quoted in the *Wall Street Journal*, July 1, 1996

I was on a flight recently coming home from Japan when a man came up to me and asked which Game Boy game I was playing. He then asked me if I'd heard about the newest one yet. It was kind of like "my car's bigger than your car."

> ROBERT HOLMES, president of Acclaim Entertainment, which distributes Game Boy, quoted in the *New York Times*, May 6, 1990

Airline executives go to bed every night praying corporate America isn't going to wake up and decide they just won't take it [high business airfares] anymore.

> SAM BUTTRICK of the investment firm Paine Webber, quoted in the *Wall Street Journal*, December 3, 1997

The frequent-flier plan is the only marketing program that has ensured brand loyalty.

> JOHN PINCAVAGE of the investment firm Paine Webber, quoted in *Time*, March 7, 1988

Cash is not what consumers want anymore. The whole lure of something for nothing is very powerful. Miles are almost a second national currency.

> STEVEN GROSVALD, consultant to frequent-flier programs, quoted in the *Wall Street Journal*, April 15, 1996

A lot of people probably think twice before eating somewhere they wouldn't get miles.

> GARY SNYDER of the Seattle restaurant Coastal Kitchen, which pays a percentage of customer checks to a firm that brokers miles to restaurants, quoted in the *Wall Street Journal*, April 15, 1996

Every secretary in L.A. spends 20 percent of her time organizing her boss's frequent-flier miles.

> ZINA KLAPPER, Los Angeles freelance writer.

6.16 YOGI BERRA—BUSINESS PHILOSOPHER

As Yogi Berra says, "It's never over till it's over," and that's true of negotiations as well.

> OWEN BIEBER, president of the United Auto Workers, during strike between UAW and General Motors, September 24, 1984

As I listened to the President's speech, I couldn't help but think of Yogi Berra, who once said, apropos of something, it was déjà vu all over again. I have a terrible sense of déjà vu. I heard that speech in 1979, when Carter gave it. I heard it in 1982—President Reagan gave it. I heard it in 1984—President Reagan gave it again. I heard it in 1988—Ambassador Yeutter gave it. And now I've heard it in 1992—President Bush gave it.

> CLYDE PRESTOWITZ, founder and president of Economic Strategy Institute and former U.S. Trade Representative, in a speech, April 27, 1992

If their company "gets competitive" [workers] may surely be out of a job. Ultimately, their jobs are at risk either way. They are left with little but Yogi Berra's line about hard choices. "When you're at a fork in the road, take it."

> JOE NEUBAUER, CEO of the food service firm ARA Services, in a speech, June 4, 1993

When faced with the enormity and complexity of the transition some retreat to the view best enunciated by Yogi Berra when he said, "What we have here is an insurmountable opportunity."

> U.S. VICE PRESIDENT AL GORE, in a speech, January 11, 1994

When you come to a fork in the road, take it.

> NORMAN R. AUGUSTINE, president of Lockheed Martin, quoted in *Harvard Business Review*, November–December 1995

Which of you will be the pioneers of the new interactive medium? You'd better decide quick, because it won't be "new" very long. The leaders will establish themselves very fast. The rest will have trouble ever catching up. Yogi Berra once said, "When you come to a crossroads—take it!" I couldn't have said it better myself.

> RAYMOND W. SMITH, CEO of the telecommunications firm Bell Atlantic, in a speech, February 1, 1995

A wise man, probably Yogi Berra, once said, "Prediction is very difficult, especially about the future."

> A. MAURICE MYERS, CEO of Yellow Corporation, in a speech, November 18, 1996

Looking ahead, I think it was Yogi Berra who said, "You know, the trouble with the future is it ain't what it used to be."

> PHILIP G. SATRE, CEO of the casino company Harrah's Enterprises, in a speech, December 5, 1996

It's been three years since I've spoken here, and to say something that Yogi Berra probably should have said: "The future's changed a lot in the past three years."

> DOUGLAS E. OLESON, CEO of Batelle, in a speech, January 12, 1997

7.1 COMPETITION

Of all human powers operating on the affairs of mankind, none is greater than that of competition.

> U.S. SENATOR HENRY CLAY, in a speech, February 2, 1832

The growth of a large business is merely a survival of the fittest . . . The American beauty rose can be produced in the splendor and fragrance which bring cheer to its beholder only by sacrificing the early buds which grow up around it.

> JOHN D. ROCKEFELLER, oil magnate, quoted in W. J. Ghent, *Our Benevolent Feudalism,* 1902

I found that competition was supposed to be a menace and that a good manager circumvented his competitors by getting a monopoly by artificial means.

> HENRY FORD, *My Life and Work* (Doubleday, 1922)

We have seen what better-quality competition can do to you. We are building cars now that we wouldn't even have thought about building 10 years ago.

> ROBERT STEMPEL, president of the auto firm, General Motors, quoted in *Time,* November 13, 1989

We realize that we are in a race without a finish line. As we improve, so does our competition.

> DAVID KEARNS, chairman of the high-tech electronics firm Xerox, quoted in *Time,* November 13, 1989

If you are a fierce competitor, you want to beat the brains out of the other guy, because that's what you love doing.

> AL TELLER, president of the music firm CBS Records U.S., quoted in Fredric Dannen, *Hit Men* (Times Books, 1990)

We sold [the tile firm Color Tile] because our chairman went to a Home Depot [superstore] and got scared to death.

> Former executive, Knoll International, quoted in *Business Week,* August 29, 1994

What do you do when your competitor's drowning? Get a live hose and stick it in his mouth.

> RAY KROC, driving force behind McDonald's, quoted in the *Wall Street Journal,* October 20, 1997

Back in the 1960s, busybodies from the Ministry of International Trade and Industry [in Japan] tried to make the 11 motor manufacturers of the day band together to form three mega-firms—all the better, they were told, for competing against Detroit. Fortunately for motorists everywhere, the car makers would have none of it.

> *The Economist,* December 21, 1991

In the software industry, one player has thermonuclear weapons, and the other guys have bows and arrows.

> PHILIPPE KAHN, CEO of Starfish Software and founder and former CEO of the software firm Borland International, quoted in *Fortune,* June 10, 1996

I've been to China and the former Soviet Union, and I've seen what controlled economies are like. They suck. If Microsoft dominates the computer business the way Bill [Gates] would like to, our industry would suck too.

> SCOTT McNEALY, CEO of the computer firm Sun Microsystems, quoted in *Fortune,* February 19, 1996

Microsoft's alleged sins are like all "predatory" behavior: They are indistinguishable from dynamic competition. Every price cut, quality improvement, and innovation in distribution challenges firms to compete more energetically for consumers' dollars.

> PROFESSOR DONALD J. BOUDREAUX of Clemson University, quoted in the *Wall Street Journal,* October 7, 1996.

You either eat someone for lunch, or you can be lunch.

> SCOTT McNEALY, CEO of the computer firm Sun Microsystems, in a speech, 1992

This is the future. If you're just a milkman making home deliveries, one day a drive-through store puts you out of business.

> ROGER AILES, former Republican campaign consultant, and formerly head of NBC's cable division CNBC, quoted in *New York,* September 13, 1993

I don't like my competitors. I don't eat with them, don't do anything with them except try to waste them.

> HUGH L. McCOLL JR., CEO of NationsBank, quoted in the *Wall Street Journal,* July 25, 1996

[*Ken Auletta, writer*] **Q.** . . . Is the future business model for communications companies predicated on more warfare or more competition?

[*Andrew Grove, CEO Intel*] **A.** What's the difference? Competition *is* warfare. Mostly it is played by prescribed rules—there is sort of a Geneva Convention for competition—but it's thorough and often brutal.

So, yes, the future of business being based on technology (which changes rapidly and gives new opportunity for renewed attacks) and being global in form (those attacks can come from any corner of the world) is going to be warlike.

> E-mail exchange, quoted in "Only the Fast Survive," *New Yorker,* October 20 & 27, 1997

The goal of competitors is to prevail, not to preserve competition in the markets.

> GEORGE SOROS, founder of the Quantum Fund, quoted in the *Atlantic Monthly,* January 1998

7.2 COMPETITIVENESS AND THE CORPORATION

Again and again in business history, an unknown company has come from nowhere and in a few short years overtaken the established leaders without apparently even breathing hard . . . The reason is always the same: the new company knows and manages the costs of the entire economic chain rather than its costs alone.

> PETER F. DRUCKER, "The Information Executives," *Harvard Business Review,* January–February 1995

We became uncompetitive by not being tolerant of mistakes. The moment you let avoiding failure become your motivator, you're down the path of inactivity. You can stumble only if you're moving.

> The late ROBERTO GOIZUETA, CEO of Coca-Cola, quoted in *Fortune,* May 1, 1995

Competition is a way of life. If you don't have a really tough competitor, you ought to invent one.

> BILL SMITHBURG, CEO of Quaker Oats, quoted in *Fortune,* July 10, 1996

Only the paranoid survive.

> ANDREW GROVE, cofounder and CEO of the computer chip firm Intel, quoted in *Fortune,* July 10, 1995

To succeed, I believe an organization has to change and adjust before it is forced to do so by external forces. It must reinvent itself and become the very company that could put it out of business before someone else does.

> HARVEY GOLUB, CEO of American Express, quoted in *Fortune,* October 30, 1995

I think we need to be paranoid optimists.

> ROBERT J. EATON, CEO of Chrysler, in a speech, February 26, 1997

Either we obsolete ourselves, or the competition will. [Popular saying in Silicon Valley.]

> Quoted in the *Economist,* March 29, 1997

If a dominant company responds to a competitor's price cut by cutting its prices, is that a normal commercial response or abuse of market power?

> GRAHAM MASON, director of Confederation of British Industry, quoted in the *Financial Times,* May 15, 1997

We have a philosophy that we will eat our own young before someone else does.

> JOHN CHAMBERS, president and chief executive of computer firm Cisco Systems, quoted in *Strategy& Business,* Spring 1997, quarterly journal of Booz Allen & Hamilton

U.S. management will find its greatest security by maintaining an environment of insecurity.

> FRED G. STEINGRABER, CEO of the consulting firm A. T. Kearney, in a speech, July 21, 1987

It's counter to human nature, but you have to kill your business while it's still working.

> LEWIS PLATT, CEO of Hewlett-Packard, quoted in *Fortune,* May 2, 1994

It's [running a high-tech firm] like being the pilot of a fighter plane flying at Mach 3 while you're redesigning the plane to fly at Mach 6.

> GARY EICHORN, CEO of high-tech firm Open Market, quoted in the *Wall Street Journal,* August 30, 1996

Almost anyone who has worked for GM could get every organ in his body replaced and it would not cost him a dime.

> MARYANN KELLER, analyst at Furman Selz, on health benefits at General Motors, quoted in the *Economist*, December 5, 1992

It's very difficult in this business, and I suppose in a lot of businesses, to try to be the best. Because to be the best means you have to spend more, you have to work harder, and you have to have some vision. And those things are not in abundance in any company as far as I can see.

> DICK LANDGRAFF of the Ford Motor Company, quoted in Mary Walton, *Car* (Norton, 1997)

Corporate culture: The defining ethic of a company, expressed in the speech, dress, and behavior deemed proper at the firm, which are carefully designed to ward off the incursion of dangerous new ideas.

> DAVID OLIVE, *Business Babble* (Wiley, 1991)

Every company has its own language, its own version of its own history (its myths), and its own heroes and villains (its legends), both historical and contemporary. The whole flourishing tangle serves to confirm old-timers and to induct newcomers in the corporation's distinctive identity and its particular norms of behavior. In myriad ways, formal and informal, it tells them what is okay—and what is not.

> DR. MICHAEL HAMMER, *Beyond Reengineering* (HarperCollins, 1996)

Companies 20, 30, 50 years ago never worried about culture. Culture wasn't in a manager's vocabulary. People needed jobs; they came to work; they worked 8 to 5; they got paid for overtime; they went home.

> SAMUEL L. EICHENFELD, chairman and CEO of the FINOVA Group, Inc., interviewed in Charles B. Wendel, *The New Financiers: Profiles of the Leaders Who Are Reshaping the Financial Services Industry* (Irwin, 1996)

Someone once wrote that "Culture is what your people do when you're not around."

> JAMES A. UNRUH of the computer firm Burroughs Corporation, in a speech, January 16, 1997

In a dying company, the steady hand of the old culture will not save it. Part of my strategy in such a situation is to paint a bleak picture of the status quo and make sure that everybody knows the old culture wasn't successful.

> ALBERT "CHAINSAW AL" DUNLAP, *Mean Business* (Times Books, 1996)

Unlike a more communal environment, where eccentricities can be tolerated, because trust is based on deep personal knowledge, those who run the bureaucratic corporation often rely on outward manifestations to determine the "right sort of person."

> PROFESSOR ROSABETH MOSS KANTER of the Harvard Business School, from a 1977 study of "Indsco," a pseudonymous industrial conglomerate, quoted in *The Economist*, March 28, 1992

We don't have a culture, we have an attitude. Our attitude is every customer gets satisfied.

> CHARLES M. CAWLEY, CEO of the banking company MBNA, quoted in the *New York Times,* October 22, 1997

All those Big Steel companies are the same. They are a culture, it's a bureaucratic culture, and there isn't a nickel's worth of difference between 'em.

> KEITH EARL BUSSE of the steel company Nucor, quoted in the *New Yorker*, February 25, 1991

One of those chairs cost more than the four in my office and I'm the executive vice president of a $500 million company.

> RICHARD HOCHHAUSER of the publisher Harte-Hanks, to a 27-year-old head of a web site developer that his company had invested in, and on whose board he served, quoted in the *Wall Street Journal*, September 30, 1996 (The web site developer had just bought $15,000 worth of ergonomic chairs for his staff.)

8.1 CULTURE—INDIVIDUAL COMPANIES

8.1.1 Apple

Nobody here cares which washroom you use.

> DEBI COLEMAN, 34-year old CFO, commenting on how well women were treated at Apple, quoted in *U.S. News & World Report*, September 14, 1987

I don't think anyone can manage Apple.

> JOHN SCULLEY, former Apple CEO, quoted in *Fortune*, February 19, 1996

Apple doesn't need to be reengineered. It needs to be engineered.

> GUY KAWASAKI, *Fortune*, February 19, 1996

Thank God there's finally some adult supervision around here.

> Reaction at Apple when Gilbert F. Amelio was appointed chairman, quoted in the *New York Times*, September 9, 1996

I saw Gil Amelio making a speech at Apple. He was dressed in a coat and tie. During the speech somebody asked him to take it off. For his answer he made a little quip but said something like, "I won't take it off because I like to wear a tie around the office because it makes me want to get down to business."

> KEVIN HAUS of the computer industry research firm International Data, quoted in *Management Review*, September 1, 1996

Apple has to be more pragmatic and less religious. And the only one who can really do that is the person who created the religion in the first place [Steven Jobs].

> JOHN SCULLEY, former CEO of Apple, quoted in *Newsweek*, August 18, 1997

8.1.2 Boeing

In the old Boeing, you could walk out the door and touch 90 percent of your executives. They were within a fairly short radius. I personally know 95 percent of them. All of a sudden, 60 percent of our executives are going to be non-Seattle.

Experience away from Seattle did not help your career. If you disappeared for a while, people would say "where have you been?" Now I think we can make it a valuable thing.

> PHILIP CONDIT, CEO of the aerospace firm Boeing, interviewed in *Financial Times*, March 12, 1997

8.1.3 Boston Celtics

We're still the only NBA team without a dance team or cheerleaders. That is indicative of what our fan base believes the Celtics are about.

> STUART LAYNE of the basketball team, the Boston Celtics, quoted in *Strategy&Business*, published by Booz Allen & Hamilton, 1997

8.1.4 Coca-Cola

The company has never disclosed the secret formula for its products, and that policy will not change.

> Coca-Cola spokesman after a federal judge ordered its 99-year-old secret recipe for Coke unveiled to 40 bottlers, which were suing the company, quoted in *U.S. News & World Report*, September 2, 1985

I'm sorry, we're not in the rainbow flavors.

> WADDY PLATT, regional Coca-Cola dealer, to Ray Kroc when Kroc asked him to supply root beer and orange soda to his first franchise in Des Plaines, Illinois, quoted in David Halberstam, *The Fifties* (Villard, 1993)

Don't wrap the flag of Coca-Cola around you to prevent change from taking place. It is extremely important that you show some insensitivity to your past in order to show the proper respect for the future.

> The late ROBERTO C. GOIZUETA, CEO of Coca-Cola, to a group of the corporation's quality-assurance personnel, quoted in *Fortune*, December 11, 1995

8.1.5 Compaq

When we formed the company in 1982, we viewed it as a major in its formative stages, rather than a small company with big plans.

> Compaq's first annual report

8.1.6 Disney

You see guys like [Michael] Eisner as a little crazy . . . but every great studio in this business has been run by crazies. What do you think Walt Disney was? The guy was goddamned off the wall. This is a creative institution. It needs to be run by crazies again.

> STANLEY GOLD, Eisner's lawyer, quoted in *Time*, April 25, 1988

Humbling is something at Disney we encourage.

> It reminds me of an experience one of our young American Disney executives had when he was opening a new office for us in London and wanted to impress his new British secretary. When she entered his office, he was speaking on the telephone and said, "Why, of course, Your Majesty. Think nothing of it. You can call me any time. See you soon. Regards to Prince Philip."

Then he hung up and said, "Oh hello, Miss Brown. Did you want to see me?"

"I just wanted to tell you, sir," says the secretary, "that the men are here to hook up your telephone."

> MICHAEL EISNER, CEO of Walt Disney, on how humbled he is to receive an award as an outstanding international executive, in a speech, April 19, 1996

The term, synergy, may be the object of ridicule throughout the world, but not in Burbank, California.

I have always felt that Walt's unerring instinct for what would please and capture an American audience grew from his roots and sense of values.

Mickey Mouse, his most famous character, embodies traits—like honesty, courage, virtue, enthusiasm, optimism—that I believe most Americans still value today.

[A] man named Walt Disney was born in Chicago in 1901 . . . The name, Disney, is one of the world's most powerful brands . . . and just think, it all started here in Chicago, which is also the birthplace of our new President, Michael Ovitz.

> MICHAEL EISNER, CEO of Walt Disney, in a speech, April 19, 1996

8.1.7 Ford

To me, Mr. Ford is still sitting in that chair sometimes. In many ways I still think this is his office.

> ALEX TROTMAN, CEO of Ford Motor Company, recalling his meetings with Henry Ford II, who ran the company for 35 years and died in 1987, quoted in *Fortune,* September 18, 1995

It was civil war at the top. The question was never "Are we winning against the Japanese?" but rather "Are we winning against each other?"

> Ford manager quoted in Mary Walton, *Car* (Norton, 1997)

8.1.8 E. & J. Gallo

First would have been better. Second is O.K., too. But just being in the top 10 is unacceptable.

> GINA GALLO, marketing executive, on news that a new premium wine had rated in the top 10 in a taste test for a new premium wine, quoted in the *New York Times,* September 4, 1997

We don't want most of the business; we want it all.

> ERNEST GALLO, family patriarch, quoted in the *New York Times,* September 4, 1997

8.1.9 General Motors

Chevrolet is such a big monster that you twist its tail and nothing happens at the other end for months and months. It is so gigantic that there isn't any way to really run it. You just sort of keep track of it.

> ELLIOT M. ESTES, former president of General Motors, quoted by Professor Walter Adams of Michigan State University, in a speech, December 14, 1991

I come from an environment where, if you see a snake, you kill it. At GM, if you see a snake, the first thing you do is go hire a consultant on snakes. Then you get a committee on snakes, and then you discuss it for a couple of years. The most likely course of action is—nothing. You figure, the snake hasn't bitten anybody yet, so you just let him crawl around on the factory floor. We need to build an environment where the first guy who sees the snake kills it.

> H. ROSS PEROT, then director of General Motors, 1988, quoted by Professor Walter Adams of Michigan State University, in a speech, December 14, 1991

They didn't sell; they took orders.

> Former GM Chairman ROGER B. SMITH, talking about the automotive industry in the post–World War II era, quoted in Earl Shorris, *A Nation of Salesmen* (Norton, 1994)

8.1.10 Goldman, Sachs

Morgan will show up with 20 people for a three-hour presentation to a client. Goldman, Sachs will just send two people to sketch out a deal on a napkin at the golf club bar.

> "Former executive" quoted in article on JP Morgan, the investment bank, *New York Times,* August 10, 1997

[T]here's always the Goldman, Sachs solution: Some buttoned-down bosses of this New York City investment bank have left group voice-mail messages codifying precisely what to wear on casual days. Now that's empowerment.

> WILLIAM NABES, "The New Corporate Uniforms," *Fortune,* November 13, 1995

Dear Diary:

Overheard on the elevator at Goldman, Sachs on a recent "dress-down Friday," a conversation between a longtime partner and a smartly attired young analyst.

Partner (sternly): "It's Friday. You're not supposed to be wearing a tie."

Analyst (crestfallen): "But it's not silk."

> THERESA M. POTTER, Metropolitan Diary column, *New York Times*, November 13, 1996

8.1.11 Hewlett-Packard

Over the years we have had a number of people leave because opportunities seemed greater elsewhere. We've always taken the view that as long as they have not worked for a direct competitor, and if they have a good work record, they are welcomed back. They know the company, need no retraining, and usually are happier and better motivated for having had the additional experience.

> DAVID PACKARD, cofounder of Hewlett-Packard, *The HP Way* (HarperCollins, 1995)

8.1.12 Hustler Clubs

Gradually I developed what amounted to an indoctrination program. I ran a tight ship. There was more hanky-panky in a church pew than in my clubs. I only sold the *hope* of hanky-panky. I developed a program that seemed like a combination of the Naval Academy's honor code, the rules of conduct for a nunnery, and the regulations for the Miss America Pageant. I lectured the girls on how to handle amorous customers, ward off pimps, behave like ladies, and not offend customers. I admonished them to tell the truth about their work, never complain about the club, and not discuss their personal lives or other girls. They weren't allowed to accept tips, eat in the club, sit with each other, or discuss their pay. I instructed them to clap for other girls after each dance, help the waitresses clear tables if they got behind, and take their jobs seriously. [Rules for dancers at Hustler Clubs]

> LARRY FLYNT, *An Unseemly Man* (Dove, 1996)

8.1.13 IBM

I don't really give a damn about a white shirt but, if I wear a nice looking blue shirt, the next fellow down is going to wear a purple shirt, and then. . . . we're going to have an aloha shirt down at the salesman level.

> THOMAS J. WATSON JR., former chairman of IBM

If you have a $7 billion company, it's a real company right off the bat. You can't populate it with new people, so they all come from the same gene pool.

> PROFESSOR DAVID B. JEMISON of the University of Texas, quoted in the *New York Times*, September 6, 1992

I'm almost *not* trying to understand IBM's culture.

> LOUIS V. GERSTNER JR., CEO of IBM, quoted in *Fortune*, May 31, 1993

Armonk, N.Y.—IBM, renowned in corporate America for its rigid dress code of white shirts and dark suits, has adopted a policy of allowing headquarters employees to wear casual dress. The *Wall Street Journal* reported that IBM employees at other, already casual, locations seemed to have adopted a chinos-and-loafers dress code just as rigid as the old one.

> JUDITH MARTIN, *Miss Manners Rescues Civilization* (Crown, 1996)

At its [IBM] Somer's (New York) PC headquarters there are so many sweaters the place looks like a ski lodge.

> SERGE BLUES, *Business Week*, February 7, 1994

Our culture was very congenial, so congenial you never knew where you stood. Meetings would always go fine. You'd go in, and everyone would be very proper and well-dressed, and a bunch of people would sit around and have a nice chat. The results might be good, and people would say, "Thank you very much." Or the results might be awful, and it would still be, "Thank you very much; we know you did your best."

> SAMUEL J. PALMISANO of IBM Personal Computer Company, describing the company before Gerstner took over, quoted in *Fortune*, April 14, 1997

If IBM is getting out [of basic research], who's going to do it?

> Official of the U.S. National Science Foundation in 1993 when IBM chairman Louis Gerstner announced a $1 billion cut in its research budget, quoted in the *Wall Street Journal*, October 6, 1997

The long-term outlook went very sour. Almost everything became short-term directed: solutions and applications.

> RICHARD WEBB, a physicist who left IBM in 1993, quoted in the *Wall Street Journal,* October 6, 1997

This used to be a country-club atmosphere. I really enjoy solving real-world problems, having the feeling that I'm really needed and appreciated.

> HANS COUFAL of IBM's Almaden Research Center, quoted in the *Wall Street Journal,* October 6, 1997

The people who are willing to change their heroes, they do very well.

> ROBERT H. KOCH, manager of superconducting science and technology for IBM, on his ability to pursue research after having it rejected several years previously, quoted in *Business Week,* May 16, 1994

8.1.14 Intel

You could tell when it was noon at Intel, because at noon men in white aprons arrived at the front entrance gasping from the weight of the trays they were carrying. The trays were loaded down with deli sandwiches and waxed cups full of drinks with clear plastic tops, and globules of Sprite or Diet Shasta sliding around the tops on the inside . . . You ate some sandwiches made of roast beef or chicken sliced into translucent rectangles by a machine in a processing plant and then reassembled on the bread in layers that gave off dank whiffs of hormones and chemicals.

> TOM WOLFE, "new journalist," novelist, essayist, in *Esquire,* 1983. Reprinted in *Forbes ASAP,* August 25, 1997

8.1.15 McDonald's

I had pictured in my mind this long imposing table in some wood-paneled room where everyone had assigned seats. [The boardroom turned out to be a circular room with a giant "hamburger-shaped" table.]

> TERRY SAVAGE, first woman elected director of McDonald's board, quoted in the *New York Times,* February 2, 1992

We have found out, as you have, that we cannot trust some people who are nonconformists. We will make conformists out of them in a hurry.

The organization cannot trust the individual; the individual must trust the organization [or] he shouldn't go into this kind of business.

> RAY KROC, driving force behind McDonald's, in 1958, quoted in David Halberstam, *The Fifties* (Villard, 1993)

McDonald's isn't a job. It's a life. Our employees have ketchup in their veins.

> PAUL PRESTON, president of McDonald's U.K., quoted in *Strategy&Business,* published by Booz Allen & Hamilton, 1997.

8.1.16 McKinsey & Co.

[W]e look to hire people who are, first, very smart; second, insecure and thus driven by their insecurity; and third, competitive. Put together 3,000 of these egocentric, talk-oriented, achievement-oriented people and it produces an atmosphere of something less than humility. Yes, it's elitist. But don't you think that there has to be room somewhere in this politically correct world for something like this?

> RON DANIEL, formerly of McKinsey & Co., quoted in *Fortune,* November 1, 1993

8.1.17 Merrill Lynch

We are trying to change the culture of Merrill [Lynch & Company]. We are trying to get the firm's employees to treat the money they spend as if it were their own.

> Executive at Merrill Lynch, quoted in the *New York Times,* February 4, 1990

Until the last few months, it seemed like you could spend money on almost anything if you could find a way to say it would help business.

> "One Merrill Lynch executive," quoted in the *New York Times,* February 4, 1990

8.1.18 Microsoft

It's amusing to think that this youthful co-ed landscape is to the 1990s approximately what the image of middle-aged men in dark suits and white shirts getting in and out of elevators in the General Motors Building was to the 1950s. Remember *The Man in the Gray Flannel Suit?* Today it would have to be called *The Person in the Plaid Flannel Shirt.*

> MICHAEL KINSLEY, on what it's like to work at Microsoft, *New Republic,* September 2, 1996

Oh, our eyes have seen the glory of the coming of the Net

We are ramping up our market share, objectives will be met.

Soon our browser will be everywhere,

You ain't seen nothin' yet,

We embrace and we extend.

Our competitors were laughing, said our network was a fake,

Saw the Internet economy as simply theirs to take.

They'll regret the fateful day

The sleeping giant did awake,

We embrace and we extend!

> "Battle Hymn of the Reorg" by an anonymous Microsoft employee, in *MicroNews,* the in-house newsletter, quoted in *Business Week,* July 15, 1996

The only trouble with Microsoft is that they just have no taste. They don't think of original ideas, and they don't bring much culture into their products.

> STEVEN JOBS, Apple cofounder, 1996 PBS documentary "Triumph of the Nerds." Quoted in coverage of Microsoft's $150 million investment in Apple, the *New York Times,* August 7, 1997

We use his [CEO Bill Gates] celebrity shamelessly.

> PAUL MARITZ, head of Microsoft's development division, quoted in the *Wall Street Journal,* September 3, 1997

8.1.19 JP Morgan

Morgan executives talk so much about culture that it sometimes sounds as if they're in the yogurt business. The rules—unspoken of course—frown on flamboyance, boasting, loud ties, and strong language. Other banks may have star systems; at Morgan, hotshots are simply not tolerated.

> SAUL HANSELL, *New York Times,* August 10, 1997

8.1.20 Netscape

[At Netscape] A couple of dogs roam the aisles of work cubicles, which are separated by shoulder-high partitions. A few programmers have tossed a military camouflage net over their work areas, while another has shrouded her cubicle in black mesh. On one wall hangs

a satirical shrine to William H. Gates, complete with a gilt-framed picture of Microsoft's chairman.

> *New York Times,* September 9, 1996

8.1.21 Nomura

If you look over our history, you'll see that we have succeeded in everything we have tried. We haven't had a failure. To me that is a weakness. I think Nomura needs a failure. [Nomura is one of many Japanese financial institutions that became mired in scandal.]

Past success can be as much a trap as a failure.

> YOSHIHISA TABUCHI, president and CEO of Nomura Securities Co. Ltd., quoted in *Harvard Business Review,* July–August 1989

8.1.22 Starbucks

The biggest defense against pilferage is a strong culture.

> ORIN SMITH, CFO of the coffee bar chain Starbucks, quoted in *Inc.,* January 1993

We're not in the business of undercutting the price of commonly available merchandise and putting existing retailers out of business. We're elevating the coffee experience.

> SCOTT BEDBURY of Starbucks, quoted in *Fortune,* December 9, 1996

8.1.23 3M

Our company has, indeed, stumbled onto some of its new products. But never forget that you can only stumble if you're moving.

> RICHARD P. CARLTON, former CEO of the 3M Corporation, cited in James C. Collins and Jerry I. Porras, *Built to Last* (HarperCollins, 1994)

Since the 1920s, when the company's fortunes were turned around by the development of waterproof sandpaper and adhesive tape, 3M management has valued the enormous potential of the entrepreneurs in its midst . . . For example, the 15 percent rule allows employees to spend up to 15 percent of their time on bootleg projects that they believe have potential for the company.

> PROFESSOR CHRISTOPHER A. BARTLETT of Harvard Business School, and Professor Sumantra Ghoshal of

London Business School, quoted in *Harvard Business Review,* November–December 1994

Because [3M] was founded in the Midwest, many of our early researchers had farming backgrounds. They had studied science and engineering, but they grew up knowing that if the tractor broke in the field, you figured out how to fix it . . . They were independent, they knew how to tinker, and they understood the importance of making something grow.

L. D. DeSIMONE, CEO of 3M, quoted in *Harvard Business Review,* November–December 1995

8.1.24 Toyota

We have a saying at Toyota, slow decision, quick action.

SHOICHIRO TOYODA, CEO and son of founder of the auto company Toyota, quoted in *Fortune,* August 3, 1987

8.1.25 *Wired*

You can only become cool once. So I think we're going into a postcool period and we're going to be as radical as we can without being cool.

It sounds kind of grandiose for a magazine to attempt to be building a civilization.

KEVIN KELLY, executive editor of *Wired* magazine, after a shake-up that included the announced plan of a cofounder to resign, quoted in the *New York Times,* August 4, 1997

Corporation, *n.* An ingenious device for obtaining profit without individual responsibility.

> AMBROSE BIERCE, *The Devil's Dictionary*, 1906

A man is known by the company he organizes.

> AMBROSE BIERCE, quoted in John A. Byrne, *The Whiz Kids* (Doubleday, 1993)

The biggest corporation, like the humblest private citizen, must be held to strict compliance with the will of the people.

> THEODORE ROOSEVELT, in a speech, 1902

The healthy corporation, like the healthy human organism, has an inner drive to strengthen itself and to create new cells in a compulsion to continue its growth.

> ROY LARSEN, Henry Luce's successor as president of Time Inc., quoted in *The World of Time Inc.* (Curtis Prendergast, 1986)

When asked what they do for a living, most people describe the tasks they perform every day, not the purpose of the greater enterprise in which they take part. Most see themselves within a "system" over which they have little or no influence. They do their jobs, put in their time, and try to cope with forces outside their control.

> PETER SENGE, *The Fifth Discipline* (Doubleday, 1990)

We didn't come to the table with a clean sheet of paper. We came with the business that we have.

> JOHN AKERS, on his years as CEO of IBM (he resigned soon after announcing a $4.7 billion loss), quoted in the *Economist*, January 16, 1993

9.1 THE CHANGING CORPORATION

It [1960–1980] was a wonderful age. If you were managing a public company, you didn't have to explain anything to anybody. People from that time have no idea what it is like today.

> NICHOLAS NICHOLAS, president of Time, Inc., quoted in the *New Yorker,* January 8, 1990

It's like a whale trying to crawl up on the beach, shed some weight, and walk like a man.

> WILLIAM M. BLUESTEIN of the research firm Forrester, on IBM's spin-off of its personal computer operations into a separate unit called the IBM Computer Company, quoted in the *New York Times,* September 6, 1992

Fully one third of our more than $13 billion in worldwide revenues comes from products that simply did not exist five years ago.

> RALPH S. LARSEN, CEO of the pharmaceutical company Johnson & Johnson, in a speech, October 22, 1992

One of our people was telling me that about five years ago he asked this question of one of our senior executives in manufacturing. "In one word, what is the single most important thing about manufacturing?" That executive's answer was "repeatability" [i.e., the ability to get the same result again and again]. Two years ago, this fellow asked the same question . . . this time it was a supervisor in charge of making gears. He said, "Control." Two months ago, he put the question to a "module leader"—that's what supervisors are now called at the John Deere Harvester works . . . and his answer was "flexibility."

> JOHN KLAWSON of the Lawn and Grounds Care Division of Deere & Co., in a speech, February 24, 1994

If anyone left the company, there were five guys behind him, waiting to take the job. I don't know of any company today that has that luxury.

> GARY KNISELY, formerly of Time Inc., later with John Smith & Knisely Accord, quoted in *Business Week,* April 4, 1994

Instead of being a castle, a home for life for its defenders, an organization will be more like an apartment block, an association of temporary residents gathered together for mutual convenience.

We were not destined to be empty raincoats, nameless numbers on a payroll. . . . If that is to be its price, economic progress is an empty promise.

> CHARLES HANDY, business philosopher, quoted in *Business Week,* April 4, 1994

The Bell System I went to work for—which then approximated the institutional stability and authority of the Catholic Church—has long been broken apart. The assumptions on which my whole generation of management built our careers—[basically, that the future would look much like the past, except with nicer carpeting]—have been blown to bits by global competition.

> RAYMOND W. SMITH, CEO of the telecommunications company Bell Atlantic, in a speech, November 1, 1995

Traditional management structures were devised when information was a scarce commodity, so that knowledge about how to run the business could be communicated layer by layer, over time, by means of an elaborate supervisory structure designed to control, filter, and edit the flow of information to the troops. But today's information technology not only makes that kind of controlled information flow unproductive—it also makes it impossible.

> RAYMOND W. SMITH, CEO of the telecommunications company Bell Atlantic, in a speech, October 17, 1995

There's a widespread popular perception that during recessions, large firms shed employees and small companies struggle valiantly to take up the slack. We found large firms create jobs year in and year out, regardless of recession.

> PROFESSOR STEVEN DAVIS of the Graduate School of Business, University of Chicago, quoted in *Inc.*, March 1994

There can be real value in having a throwaway executive, who can come in and do unpleasant, nasty things, like kill off a few sacred cows.

> MATTHEW HARRISON of the executive temp firm Imcor, quoted in *Fortune*, January 24, 1994

Nobody gave a hoot about corporate governance 15 years ago because a large part of what a company did to grow also increased shareholder value. In the same way, Japanese companies could pursue a market-share strategy as long as their cost of capital was low.

> PROFESSOR JOHN POUND of Harvard University's Kennedy School of Government, quoted in *Fortune*, January 11, 1993

More and more CEOs have become conscious that they are the CEO of marketing. You're selling trust.

> PROFESSOR PHILIP KOTLER of the J. L. Kellogg School of Management, Northwestern University, quoted in *Business Week*, December 9, 1996

There are just two people between me and a salesman—information technology replaced the rest.

> JOHN OPIE of GE Lighting, quoted in *Fortune*, December 13, 1993

When I came to Goodyear in 1958, my chances of promotion were one in eight. For a young person today, they are one in 30, and it's going to be one in 50.

> FREDERICK KOVAC of Goodyear Tire and Rubber, quoted in *Fortune*, December 13, 1993

Executives who were granted status because they were related to, or kissed up to, the right people have always been known as frauds. The difference is that two decades ago, the glacial slowness with which markets changed afforded those pampered pets the luxury of dying on the job.

> STEVEN BERGLAS, "The Death of Status," *Inc.*, October 1996

What were once believed to be real tradeoffs—between defects and costs, for example—turned out to be illusions created by poor operational effectiveness. Managers have learned to reject such false tradeoffs.

> PROFESSOR MICHAEL PORTER of Harvard Business School, *Harvard Business Review*, November–December 1996

A lot of corporations lost their bench strength when they downsized for a weak economy in the early '90s. Then along came 1994—a gangbuster year—and companies lacked the managers to go after the markets.

> MAURY HARRIGAN, human resources consultant, on surge in recruiting, quoted in *Fortune*, April 14, 1997

Size is not a deterrent to success. I've never seen a small company that didn't want to be a big one. The challenge is being big without being slow.

> LOUIS V. GERSTNER JR., CEO of IBM, in a speech, October 9, 1996

Horror stories abound [from the relaxation of corporate dress codes]. IBM tells of Japanese visitors deeply offended when their hosts were not wearing business suits. Aetna Insurance says male employees have arrived at work in stained T-shirts and ripped jeans. Charles Schwab, the San Francisco–based discount broker, says some of its female workers came in sporting scanty tops and bare midriffs shortly after its casual-dress policy went into effect.

Financial Times, January 22, 1997

9.2 CORE COMPETENCIES

People say that I could run any other business. They used to put in the paper that I should take over the Red Sox or manage the Patriots. But that doesn't make sense. My knowledge of the product isn't there.

RED AUERBACH, legendary basketball coach, quoted in *Harvard Business Review,* March–April, 1987.

There has to be a fairly simple identity that drives a company, and when you get too far away from it, you begin to have problems.

GERALD LEVIN, CEO of the publishing and media firm Time Warner, to a *New York Times* reporter in the early 1980s. Quoted in an article about Time Warner's problems managing its size and diversity of business, *The Economist,* December 5, 1992

Core competence is a strategic concept that captures your organization's capabilities—what you are particularly good at—whereas core ideology captures what you stand for and why you exist.

JAMES C. COLLINS and JERRY I. PORRAS, *Built to Last* (HarperCollins, 1994)

Anyone who says you should stick to your knitting is wrong. And anyone who says do or die, create something for the sake of being different, is wrong too.

NATHAN MYHRVOLD of the software firm Microsoft, quoted in *Business Week,* March 21, 1994

We never set out to be a chess-playing company.

IBM executive, on why Big Blue turned down chess genius Garry Kasparov's request for a rematch, quoted in *Newsweek,* October 6, 1997

Companies that compete effectively on time—speeding new products to market, manufacturing just in time, or

responding promptly to customer complaints—tend to be good at other things as well.

GEORGE STALK, PHILIP EVANS, and LAWRENCE E. SHULMAN of Boston Consulting Group, *Harvard Business Review,* March–April 1992

9.3 CORPORATE ARCHITECTURE

The elevator made it possible to build structures that increased the numbers of people who lived or worked in proximity but did not know one another. People became neighbors in the geographic but not in the personal sense; social contacts became more superficial. And now as people live and work surrounded by strangers, they feel more alienated and distanced from each other than they did before the advent of the skyscraper.

PROFESSOR SARA KIESLER of Carnegie-Mellon University, *Harvard Business Review,* January–February 1986

[W]hile employers ranging from telecommunications companies and catalog retailers to credit-card companies and airline reservations departments are figuring how to make do with less floor space per employee, they haven't devised a way to squeeze more cars into the same parking lot.

CHARLES GOLDSMITH, *Wall Street Journal,* October 25, 1996

Most companies are out of the business of creating monuments. They want their building to look financially responsible, in case their shareholders drive by.

BOB HEDRICK, architect, quoted in the *Wall Street Journal,* May 7, 1997

9.4 CORPORATE ESPIONAGE

This is not warfare. I don't consider our competitors as Communists or Hitler.

EMMANUEL A. KAMPOURIS, CEO of the bathroom fixture firm American Standard, on businesses that practice high-powered intelligence gathering, quoted in *Business Week,* October 26, 1996

The whole idea of military intelligence was to know your enemy. With business intelligence, the idea is for a company to know both its competitors and its partners as it knows itself.

> ROBERT GUILLAUMOT, president of Paris-based business intelligence firm, Inforama, quoted in *Asia, Inc.,* March 1997

Much of this activity works on the principle that it's cheaper and quicker to obtain someone else's R&D through bribery or theft, than to spend years and large sums of money on trying to achieve something similar.

> Corporate intelligence analyst, quoted in *Asia, Inc.,* March 1997

You must find the balance between maximizing profits and being fair and honest. A lot of the time, companies forget they are dealing with human beings.

> TONY McSTRAVIDE of the security consulting firm Control Risk Group, and former acting head of London's Metropolitan Police Fraud Squad, quoted in the *Financial Times,* April 12–13, 1997

A survey by the Society of Competitive Intelligence Professionals finds salaries [in the field] average $69,000, up 21 percent during the past two years.

> *Wall Street Journal*, September 30, 1997

A good spy always looks for the path of least resistance before trying anything fancy or high tech.

> IRA WINKLER, private detective, quoted in *Corporate Espionage* (Prima Publications, 1997)

9.5 CORPORATE FAILURES

Business men go down with their businesses because they like the old way so well they cannot bring themselves to change. One sees them all about—men who do not know that yesterday is past, and who woke up this morning with their last year's ideas. It could almost be written down as a formula that when a man begins to think that he has at last found his method he had better begin a most searching examination of himself to see whether some part of his brain has gone to sleep.

> HENRY FORD, *My Life and Work* (Doubleday, 1922)

Many corporate failures occur because the team of decision makers is tired . . . The founders who were once innovators run out of ideas.

> LAWRENCE A. BOSSIDY, CEO of the industrial firm Allied-Signal, quoted in *Harvard Business Review,* March–April 1995

Asking why a company has failed is somewhat like asking why the *Titanic* sank. Was it the iceberg? The captain's navigational incompetence? The ship's faulty construction? The lookout crew's negligence? The arrogance of thinking the ship was unsinkable? Or was it all of them combined? Failure is complicated.

> CHARLES M. FARKAS and PHILIPPE DE BACKER, *Fortune,* January 15, 1996

Either you replace the strategy or the strategist.

> JIM SEVERANCE, portfolio manager, State of Wisconsin Investment Board, quoted in *Business Week,* June 20, 1994

When a business goes wrong, look only to the people who are running it.

> MICHAEL DELL, CEO of Dell Computer, interviewed in Rama Dev Jager, *In the Company of Giants* (McGraw-Hill, 1997)

First of these [reasons for business failure] is confusion of purpose.

. . . [Second] overgenerous investment, the overcapitalization of ventures which may be sound in themselves.

. . . . [Third] results in a mistake in timing. A good idea can be put forward 50 years too late. A still better idea can be advocated some 20 years too soon. Even 5 years either way can be fatal.

> C. NORTHCOTE PARKINSON, introduction to John Train, *Famous Financial Fiascoes* (Fraser Publications, 1995)

It doesn't take very long to screw up a company. Two, three months should do it. All it takes is some excess inventory, some negligence in collecting, and some ignorance about where you are.

> MARY BAECHLER, of the stroller manufacturer Racing Strollers, quoted in *Inc.,* October 1994

When the rate of change outside exceeds the rate of change inside, the end is in sight.

> JOHN F. WELCH, CEO of GE, quoted in *Inc.,* March 1995

9.6 CORPORATE JARGON

Criticizing those who wanted more time to consider whether to hire personal assistants, she said: "Those who don't have the balls to go ahead and do what they need to do, and bite whatever bullet or whatever they need to bite, then they ought to allow some of us to bite it."

> Unnamed executive, quoted in the Jacksonville, Florida, *Times-Union,* cited in the *New Yorker,* April 1, 1996

Put in some pathetic drivel from the company plan about how they were going to be an employee-friendly company, blah, blah.

> White House staff notation (cited in draft of House GOP report on the White House travel office) recommending quoting corporate literature of a travel firm owned by a friend of President Clinton to buttress support for giving the firm a role in White House travel, quoted in the *Wall Street Journal,* September 13, 1996

The problem started small: a word sprinkled here or there in managers' conversations. Someone felt "empowered"; someone else was breaking free of "paradigms." Then it spread. Managers started speaking in tongues. You'd round a corner and you'd hear a manager say, "through virtual leadership, I took the cultural determinants and broke through."

> PAUL THEIBERT, speechwriter for a utility in the Midwest, quoted in the *Wall Street Journal,* August 1, 1996

Team Player
An employee who substitutes the thinking of the herd for his/her own good judgment.

Reengineering
The principal slogan of the Nineties, used to describe any and all corporate strategies.

Vision
Top management's heroic guess about the future, easily printed on mugs, T-shirts, posters, and calendar cards.

Paradigm Shift
A euphemism companies use when they realize the rest of their industry has expanded into Guangdong while they were investing in Orange County.

Restructuring
A simple plan instituted from above in which workers are right-sized, downsized, surplused, lateralized, or in the business jargon of the days of yore, fired.

Empowerment
A magic wand management waves to help traumatized survivors of restructuring suddenly feel engaged, self-managed, and in control of their futures and their jobs.

> *Fortune,* February 15, 1995

"Synergy," the most screwball buzzword of the past decade. It has a phony sound to it, as though it were made up. Say it out loud. Don't you feel a little embarrassed?

> HAROLD GENEEN, former chairman of the conglomerate ITT, with Brent Bowers, *The Synergy Myth* (St. Martins, 1997)

9.7 CORPORATE PHILANTHROPY

Corporate philanthropy is stealing from your shareholders. A corporation should maximize profit.

> Unnamed Hong Kong billionaire, quoted by Barnett Baron, chairman of the Asia Pacific Philanthropy Consortium, in *Asia, Inc.,* April 1997

Business now shares in much of the responsibility for our global quality of life. Successful companies will handle this heightened sense of responsibility quite naturally, if not always immediately. I say this not because successful business leaders are altruistic at heart. I can assure you, many are not. I say it because, again, they will demand their companies remain intensely focused on the needs of their customers and consumers.

> The late ROBERTO C. GOIZUETA, CEO of Coca-Cola, in a speech, October 27, 1992, cited in the *Wall Street Journal,* October 20, 1997

We based our product gifts on wholesale prices, a more realistic value of what a company is giving. But if a comparison is going to be made, we argued that you should compare apples with apples, not with oranges. [IBM recalculated its product gifts based on retail, rather than wholesale, pricing, to bring its total up to $92.7 million, from $72.2 million.]

> STANLEY LITOW, IBM's vice president of corporate-community relations, commenting on Microsoft's record gift to libraries of software, quoted in the *Wall Street Journal,* September 9, 1997

Percentage of all U.S. corporate sponsorship that goes to the arts: 6.

Percentage of all U.S. corporate sponsorship that goes to sports: 65.

> *Harper's* Index, April 1995

9.8 CORPORATE PRODUCTIVITY

When the organization is overstaffed, the problem is not one of work being done twice but of work wholly neglected, everyone having left everything to everyone else.

> PROFESSOR C. NORTHCOTE PARKINSON, introduction to John Train, *Famous Financial Fiascoes* (Fraser Publications, 1995)

Law Number V: One-tenth of the participants produce over one-third of the output. Increasing the number of participants merely reduces the average output.

> NORMAN R. AUGUSTINE, CEO of the aerospace firm Lockheed Martin, *Augustine's Laws* (Viking, 1986)

9.9 CORPORATE RELOCATION

It [Denver] was like living in a loaf of Wonder Bread. There's no culture, no diversity, no research university, no vitality or resiliency to the job market.

> JAMES FINUCANE, formerly of the telecommunications company MCI, who ended up taking a job back East with a competitor after relocating with the company to Denver, quoted in the *Wall Street Journal,* June 25, 1996

This whole notion of having a balanced life is something the Colorado people didn't just give lip service to. I began to buy into that myself. If no one's there to work with, there's no point in being there.

> JOHN W. HARDING of MCI, who estimates that his average work week declined by 15 hours after relocation, quoted in the *Wall Street Journal,* June 25, 1996

9.10 CORPORATE STRATEGY

When I came here 12 years ago, we were worshiping at the shrine of strategic planning. The whole exercise was irrelevant. It was a popular way to control a company, but the plan became an end instead of a means.

> ROBERT J. BUCKLEY, CEO of Allegheny International, quoted in *U.S. New & World Report,* February 6, 1984

The sure path to oblivion is to stay where you are.

> BERNARD FAUBER, CEO of the retail chain Kmart, quoted in *Forbes,* May 5, 1986

A strategy is no good if people don't fundamentally believe in it.

> ROBERT HAAS, CEO of the jeans manufacturer Levi Strauss, quoted in *Harvard Business Review,* September–October 1990

Companies don't have strategies. They have ongoing strategic conversations by a body of people. Out of these ongoing conversations, decisions are made.

> STEWART BRAND, cofounder of the Global Business Network, author of the original *Whole Earth Catalogue,* member of the hippie adventurers the Merry Pranksters, and business guru, quoted in *Fortune,* October 16, 1995

Strategy is easy, implementation is hard. . . . [O]nly the superb companies actually find a way to do what they say they're going to do.

> RAYMOND W. SMITH, chairman of the telecommunications firm Bell Atlantic, in a speech, November 1, 1995

There's no rocket science to strategy. . . . you're supposed to know where you are, where your competition is, what your cost position is, and where you want to go.

Strategies are intellectually simple; their execution is not.

> LAWRENCE A. BOSSIDY, CEO of the heavy industrial firm Allied-Signal, interviewed in *Harvard Business Review,* March–April 1995

We'd rather be a small carrier with a high profit rate than a big carrier with a low profit rate.

> LEWIS JORDAN, president of the discount airline ValuJet, quoted in *Fortune,* November 27, 1995

Strategy has to be subversive. If it's not challenging internal company rules or industry rules, it's not strategy.

> GARY HAMEL of the consulting firm Strategos, quoted in *Business Week,* August 26, 1996

Strategy is the domain of the business units because the people running them are closest to the markets.

> PETER GEORGE, CEO of the British gaming and hotel company Ladbroke Group, quoted in *Harvard Business Review,* May–June 1996

All in all, top management's efforts to provide strategic leadership often had the opposite effect.

The problem is not the CEO but rather the assumption that the CEO *should* be the corporation's chief strategist, assuming full control of setting the company's objectives and determining its priorities. In an environment where the fast-changing knowledge and expertise required to make such decisions are usually found on the front lines, this assumption is untenable.

> "Changing the Role of Management: Beyond Strategy to Purpose," *Harvard Business Review,* November–December 1994

Competitive strategy is about being different. It means deliberately choosing a different set of activities to deliver a unique mix of values.

> PROFESSOR MICHAEL PORTER, Harvard Business School, *Harvard Business Review,* November–December 1996

How often has strategy planning produced true strategic innovation? No wonder that in many organizations, corporate planning departments are being disbanded.

> GARY HAMEL, visiting professor of strategy and international management at London Business School, chairman of the consulting firm Strategos, *Harvard Business Review,* July–August 1996

9.11 CORPORATE SUCCESS

Here we were in the boondocks. We didn't have distributors falling over themselves to serve us like our competitors did in larger towns. Our only alternative was to build our own warehouse so we could buy in volume at attractive prices and store the merchandise.

> SAM WALTON, founder of the department store chain Wal-Mart, describing the 1970 decision that lay at the heart of his success, quoted in *Forbes,* October 10, 1987

With all due respect to Microsoft and Intel, there is no substitute for being in the right place at the right time.

> ANDREW GROVE, CEO of the computer chip firm Intel, quoted in *Fortune,* June 14, 1993

9.12 FINANCIAL CONTROL

Knowledge is power. And in this chaos, we're going to be the only people with knowledge. Everyone else will be guessing.

> CHARLES "TEX" THORNTON, founder of Ford's Whiz Kids after World War II, quoted in John A. Byrne, *The Whiz Kids* (Doubleday, 1993)

Watch the costs and the profits will take care of themselves.

> ANDREW CARNEGIE, steel magnate, quoted in Robert Sobel and David B. Sicilia, *The Entrepreneurs— An American Adventure* (Houghton Mifflin, 1986)

The easiest way to do a snow job on investors (or on yourself) is to change one factor in the accounting each month. Then you can say, "It's not comparable with last month or last year. And we can't really draw any conclusions from the figures."

> ROBERT TOWNSEND, *Up the Organization* (Knopf, 1970)

Expense reports are like a truth serum.

> MARK H. McCORMACK, *What They Don't Teach You at Harvard Business School* (Bantam Doubleday Dell, 1988)

If the CFO understands the businesses, he can go toe-to-toe with the other managers and win.

> CHRISTOPHER STEFFEN of Citicorp, former CFO at Kodak, quoted in *Fortune,* November 13, 1995 (A month after making this statement, Steffen was asked to resign.)

The secret isn't counting the beans, it's growing more beans.

> The late ROBERT GOIZUETA, CEO of Coca-Cola, quoted in *Fortune,* November 13, 1995

In the past you had a subsidiary make a decision on how they were going to accumulate their financial data and information. They reported back to the parent company in some standard reporting format, and then the parent consolidated all these bits and pieces.

Today, the parent company can reach right in and extract that data.

> JIM SCHIRO, then prospective chief executive of the firm resulting from the merger of Price Waterhouse and Coopers & Lybrand, quoted in the *Financial Times*, October 3, 1997

Making a budget is an exercise in minimalization. You're trying to get the lowest out of people, because everyone is out to get a lower number.

> JOHN F. WELCH JR., CEO of GE, quoted in *Fortune*, May 29, 1995

People spend what's in a budget, whether they need it or not.

> GEORGE W. SZTYKIEL, CEO of Sparta Motors, quoted in *Fortune*, December 28, 1992

The budget is God.

> Slogan at the Japanese optical company Topcom, cited in the *Economist*, January 13, 1996

9.13   LOYALTY TO A CORPORATE EMPLOYER

Around here you're either expense or you're revenue.

> DONNA VAILLANCOURT of the software firm Spectrum Associates, quoted in *Inc.*, March 1994

Forget loyalty. Or at least loyalty to one's corporation. Try loyalty to your Rolodex—your network—instead.

> TOM PETERS, management guru, quoted in the *Economist*, January 6, 1996

I wasn't on their radar screen [for first big promotion] even though I'd already done so much work. It took a lot for me to raise my hand, and I'm glad I did. I will remain committed to this company as long as I have the opportunity to grow.

> IRENE ROSENFELD of the food company Kraft Canada, quoted in the *Wall Street Journal*, February 4, 1997

The false security of a company
Will never control my life
I have faith in myself
That I will continue to provide
A comfortable upper middle class life
For my dogs, my cats,
My kids, and my wife.

> DICK FERRINGTON, former employee of Crocker Bank, who went on to make a living as an executive temp, putting together project teams from a network of other corporate refugees, quoted in *Fortune*, July 12, 1993

The emotional contract with the employer has changed because people no longer see a job as being for life. Their loyalty now is not loyalty to the employer but to themselves, plus a desire to be professional in their work. We certainly tend not to go for people who are motivated only by money.

> DR. PAUL DOREY of Britain's Barclay's Bank, quoted in the *Financial Times*, April 2, 1997

9.14   PEOPLE—THE MOST IMPORTANT RESOURCE

The secret of success of Standard Oil was that there had come together a body of men who from the beginning to end worked in single-minded cooperation.

> JOHN D. ROCKEFELLER, quoted in Robert Sobel and David B. Sicilia, *The Entrepreneurs—An American Adventure* (Houghton Mifflin, 1986)

These men are smarter than I am a great deal [sic]. They are very enterprising and smart men. I never came into contact with any class of men so smart and able as they are in their business.

> WILLIAM H. VANDERBILT, head of the New York Central railroad, speaking of Standard Oil, quoted in Robert Sobel and David B. Sicilia, *The Entrepreneurs—An American Adventure* (Houghton Mifflin, 1986)

Look, you can take away anything from IBM. You can take away our technology. You can take away our plants. You can take away our labs. You can take away any facility. You can take away our headquarters, but leave our people and this business will re-create itself over-night.

> THOMAS J. WATSON JR., former chairman of IBM

Take our 20 best people away, and I will tell you that Microsoft would become an unimportant company.

> BILL GATES, CEO of software firm Microsoft, 1992 statement quoted in *Fortune,* November 25, 1996

One of the worst things we do in corporate America is not tell people what we think of them.

> LAWRENCE A. BOSSIDY, CEO of the heavy industrial firm Allied-Signal, interviewed in *Harvard Business Review,* March–April 1995

You issue this values statement that says you treasure and trust your people, and then you say, "Oh, by the way, we're laying off 900 of you." It creates a tremendous clash.

> ROBERT SALDICH, CEO of the chemical company Raychem, quoted in *Fortune,* January 10, 1994

It would be hard to find a corporate annual report in my country that does not state "Our most important asset is our people"—yet our accounting rules make it literally impossible to reflect this on the balance sheet, and we have just completed a decade in which business after business in the United States has flagrantly ignored its reality in part because that is not the way we "keep score."

> JOHN DIEBOLD, chairman of the consulting firm Diebold Group, Inc., in a speech, August 24, 1991

10.1 CUSTOMER SERVICE

The most surprising feature of business as it was conducted was the large attention given to finance and the small attention to service. That seemed to me the reversing of the natural process, which is that money should come as the result of work and not before the work.

A dissatisfied customer was regarded not as a man whose trust had been violated, but either as a nuisance or a possible source of more money in fixing up the work which ought to have been done correctly in the first place.

A manufacturer is not through with his customer when a sale is completed. He has then only started with his customer.

> HENRY FORD, *My Life and Work* (Doubleday, 1922)

Service is not a kind of blackmail paid to representatives of social morality; it is the way money is made. Service is what the typical American businessman would do his best to render even if there weren't a cop or a preacher in sight. The businessman makes money in America, typically by serving his fellow man in ways his fellow man wants to be served.

> HENRY R. LUCE, "The Reformation of the World's Economics," *Fortune,* February 1950, quoted in Richard M. Huber, *The American Idea of Success* (McGraw-Hill, 1971)

People are so unaccustomed to very good service that when they see it they are dazzled by it.

> JAMES BARKSDALE, then of the overnight delivery firm Federal Express, quoted in *U.S. News & World Report,* October 22, 1984

They [baby boomer customer service representatives] seem to demand that customers should be nice to them rather than the other way around.

> CAROL SAPIN GOLD, consultant, quoted in *U.S. News & World Report,* November 5, 1984

When the Russians make a sale [in the arms industry], they come in with 600 technicians, build a base and start to meddle with the country. Brazil makes a straight commercial deal, and we even give a year's guarantee.

> JOSE LUIZ WHITAKER RIBEIRO, Brazilian arms dealer, quoted in the *Wall Street Journal,* January 4, 1985

Never cheat a customer, even if you can.

> A. T. STEWART, "America's first department store magnate," quoted by Edward C. Hambrecht, chairman of Hambrecht Terrell International, interior designers, in a speech, 1989

As long as one customer exists, we [Fujitsu] will never abandon him. Even if it is unprofitable, we would never do that. [This apparently admirable policy encourages customers to use Fujitsu's proprietary systems and precludes taking advantage of marketplace developments.]

> MICHIO NARUBO of Fujitsu's computer division, quoted in the *Economist,* January 4, 1992

The customer isn't king anymore. The customer is dictator.

> Retailer, quoted in *Fortune,* Autumn–Winter 1993 special issue

Clients have different opinions. We try not to have an opinion because it's dangerous to do so. We just listen to the client.

> ROBERT WORKMAN, principal of BSW International, architects for Wal-Mart, Sam's Club, and other big companies, quoted in *Fortune,* December 27, 1993

Recently, a long-time Brooks Brothers customer returned three 42-long suits he'd special ordered a year before; the trouser knees, he said, were already wearing through. The haberdashery issued him a $3,000 credit and then quickly had the pants inspected. Brooks experts were stumped—until a date was found in the back pocket showing that the suit had been made 22 years earlier; the embarrassed complainant had simply confused a few older wardrobe pieces with the new additions.

> BERNICE KANNER, *New York,* January 3, 1994

We're taking customer service from the must-have necessary evil it was in the past and turning it into a competitive advantage.

> SALLY PRICE of PepsiCo, quoted in *Business Week,* March 21, 1994

Customers are an economic asset. They are not on the balance sheet but they should be.

> PROFESSOR CLAESS FORNELL of the University of Michigan, quoted in *Business Week,* August 8, 1994

Some customers are more right than others.

> GEORGE RIGGS, president of Embroidery Services, who says that 20 percent of his customers account for 85 percent of his sales, quoted in *Inc.,* October 1994

The customer doesn't expect everything will go right all the time; the big test is what you do when things go wrong.

> SIR COLIN MARSHALL, chairman of British Airways, quoted in *Harvard Business Review,* November–December 1995

Everybody says they provide great service these days, and except for Nordstrom and Ritz-Carlton and a few others, they are all full of shit. Self-service, when provided properly, is the best kind of service there is.

> JIM SENEGAL, CEO of the discount retailer Price/Costco, quoted in *Fortune,* May 29, 1995

The customer is supposed to be king, and you as the manufacturer are supposed to produce whatever he wants. But it turns out most customers actually care more about price than about selection.

> TAKAICHI MABUCHI, president of Mabuchi Motors in Japan, in a speech, November 27, 1995

We have hundreds of thousands of salespeople. They are our customers.

> SCOTT COOK, founder of financial software company Intuit, quoted in the *Economist,* January 6, 1996

The core of my comfort is in percentages. Everyone uses the free service the first year they have the bike, but I saw only 20 to 30 percent come back the second year.

I figured my liability for free lifetime service would be minuscule.

> CHRIS ZANE of the independent bicycle dealer Zane's Cycles, quoted in *Inc.,* February 1996

I came with the mind-set of a customer.

> LOU V. GERSTNER, CEO of IBM, explaining why he was able to run the corporation successfully despite the lack of a technology background, quoted in the *Economist,* June 6, 1998

The customer comes first, IBM comes second, and the business unit comes third.

> "Mr. Gerstner's mantra" for company priorities in solving customer problems and avoiding conflicts of interest, from the *Economist,* June 6, 1998

[W]e surveyed thousands of old Walt Disney World guests to find out what impressed them most about their visit. They told us the most memorable part of their Disney experience was the way they were treated by our cast members.

> JUDSON GREEN, president of Walt Disney Attractions, in a speech, reprinted in *Speechwriter's Newsletter,* December 1, 1996

Rules are great, programs are great, but the bottom line is to do the right thing [on a pilot's decision to return to a gate to pick up a passenger who arrived late].

> HERB KELLEHER, CEO of Southwest Airlines, quoted in *Fortune,* February 21, 1994

If customers think you have a high level of expertise and it can help them, you're worth more to them.

> MARK LANDIAK, sales trainer, quoted in *Inc.,* February 1996

Customer service is a true profession now. In years gone by . . . it was a dumping ground for many things in the company.

> WILMA BREWER, president-elect of International Customer Service Association, quoted in the *New York Times,* March 30, 1997

I think customer service is a really brilliant system designed to keep customers from ever getting service. My theory is that the most hated group in any company is the customers.

> DAVE BARRY, interviewed in *Fortune,* July 7, 1997

My people constantly get asked, "Well, have you been there?" It might be a little difficult to give sage travel advice when you cannot travel.

> MIKE PINGREY, of the travel agency ACT Travel, reacting to news of founding of a corporate travel reservations center in a prison, quoted in the *Wall Street Journal*, September 16, 1997

Nowhere do we find Jesus telling someone to wait. He never put anyone on hold.

> BOB BRINER, *The Management Method of Jesus* (Thomas Nelson, 1996)

[S]peaking as a Christian, I have to say that Jesus himself would have made a terrible CEO. For one thing, he never grasped the concept of sales; he insisted on giving everything away. He was lousy at dealing with the capital markets. And he refused to do anything until he checked with a higher authority. On the other hand, he could never be accused of short-term thinking.

> GEORGE GENDRON, editor in chief, *Inc.*, April 1996

I never let hookers in my club and only hired wholesome looking girls. I wanted to serve the solitary businessman who would otherwise be sitting in a hotel room, staring at four walls and watching Johnny Carson. . . . I carefully instructed my hostesses to pay attention to the guy who was getting a little older and fatter, the one who smelled of cigar smoke. . . . This kind of guy had money, maybe even an expense account. I told the girls that, when talking to a customer, they must never complain and absolutely never nag. These guys got enough at home.

> LARRY FLYNT, publisher of *Hustler* magazine, *An Unseemly Man* (Dove, 1996)

Web site queries:

Kellogg: Has the company discontinued its low-fat plain granola? Why do local stores only carry the raisin version?

Twenty days later: Distribution may be limited in your area . . . may we suggest you discuss this matter with your store manager.

Reebok: Is it dangerous to wear running shoes to play basketball?

Four weeks later: Sorry for the delay . . . running shoes are oftentimes lighter with not as much lateral support. Hope this helps!

Sony: For a malfunctioning television set, is there anything Sony recommends trying before calling a repair technician?

Six days later: Try leaving the TV unplugged for a while. Sony also offered to track down the nearest service center.

> *Wall Street Journal,* October 21, 1996

10.2 CONSUMER BEHAVIOR

[You are reluctant to spend when] the toaster you buy next year will be cheaper than the one you buy this year.

> Economist JOHN MAKIN of the conservative think tank the American Enterprise Institute, quoted in the *New York Times,* September 19, 1996

Until a year ago, my middle name was Pay Full Retail. Six months ago I'd have said this [shopping at discount stores] was a temporary change in our spending habits. But not now. It's become a game we play.

> ROGER ANDERSON, former CEO of a company that went bankrupt in 1991, quoted in *Fortune,* December 28, 1992

[Consumers are] no longer children of the '60s and they're no longer behaving like spoiled children of the '70s and '80s. They're tough, hardened adults—with kids and friends out of work.

> JOHN O'SHEA, CEO of the catalogue company Spiegel, in a speech, April 9, 1992

If I go to the mall alone, I'm in and out in half an hour. If I go with my wife and kids, it's much more drawn out.

> LAURENCE C. SIEGEL, CEO of the mall developer Mills Corporation (which produced Ontario Mills, a $189 million, 1.7-million-square-foot mall in San Bernardino, California, with 30 movie screens, virtual-reality arcade, man-made wildlife preserve, two ice-skating rinks and 214 stores that is on track to become a bigger tourist attraction in California than Disneyland), quoted in the *Wall Street Journal,* June 11, 1997

I just think that many stores put themselves at the whim of the consumer. And over time that is not a bet I want to make. There are better places money can be put to use right now.

> PETER KUPFERBERG, portfolio manager at the investment firm Gofen & Glossberg, quoted in the *New York Times,* June 6, 1997

I sat through a hundred hours of focus groups where people were asked, "Why do you choose one store over another?" In appliances, or any commodity, it's always the same answer: price.

> R. CARTER PATE of the accounting firm Price Waterhouse, trying to turn around a money-losing Ohio chain appliance store, quoted in *Fortune,* July 7, 1997

Most lay people and even intelligent business people are more swayed by a good marketing pitch than by a research program they don't really understand.

> DR. JOHN KAMP, industrial psychologist, quoted in the *New York Times,* November 28, 1997

11.1 DIRECTORS AND CORPORATE GOVERNANCE

I know when we talk, they [corporate senior managers] now listen.

CAROL O'CLEIREANCAIN, New York City Finance Commissioner, trustee of four pension funds, quoted in the *Economist*, December 5, 1992

When you own one million shares of stock, you don't have to picket.

CARL McCALL, New York State Financial Controller and sole trustee of employee pension funds, on suggestion that he join a picket line to protest racial discrimination at Texaco, quoted in *Fortune*, August 4, 1997

Now diversity has become a bottom-line issue. Before Texaco it was not.

ROBERT J. BROWN, board member of Duke Power Company, First Union Corporation, and others, quoted in the *Wall Street Journal*, November 22, 1996

In the years that I've spent on various boards I've never heard a single suggestion from a director (made as a director at a board meeting) that produced any result at all.

ROBERT TOWNSEND, *Up the Organization* (Knopf, 1970)

People have two false notions [about the corporate board]: one is that it is an elite society and doesn't do anything; the other is that it's kind of a subdivision of religion—that there's somebody up there who knows and solves everything. Neither one of them is valid.

[O]ne of the psychic rewards of being on a directorate—to sit on the board with somebody who's distinguished. You don't get overpaid in fees, you certainly get the liabilities, but you get to know some interesting people pretty well.

ROBERT K. MUELLER, chairman of the consulting firm Arthur D. Little, quoted in *U.S. News & World Report*, January 28, 1985

There's almost an implicit contract when an individual brings in a board member. They're saying, "You're a friend of mine and we don't want any trouble and if there's a problem, we'll handle it between us."

GERARD R. ROCHE, chairman of the executive search firm Heidrick & Struggles, quoted in the *New York Times*, July 12, 1992

No one in his right mind would take the job [a bank directorship].

DAVE THOMAS, founder of the hamburger chain Wendy's, quoted in *New Republic*, January 4, 1993

It's a question of where you stand and where you sit. And we want these people to sit a little farther apart.

NELL MINOW, shareholder of activist investment firm LENS, referring to directors of corporations with professional links to the companies, quoted in *Business Week*, May 2, 1994

A company should never put its investment banker, commercial banker, or attorney on its board.

JOHN M. NASH, president of the National Association of Corporate Directors, quoted in *Business Week*, May 2, 1994

A CEO who doesn't want to be monitored closely wants a director with lots of board seats.

PROFESSOR CHARLES ELSON, Stetson Law School, quoted in the *New York Times*, November 17, 1996

[O]verpayment [of directors and executives increases] . . . when two or more trophy directors adorn a board, which is the case at 64 companies including Time Warner, Kmart, Xerox, American Express, Allied-Signal, Sara Lee, Dow Jones, Fluor, and Avon. These 64 companies, as a class, overpay their chief executives by more than 13 percent, compared with their peers in size and performance, and overpay their outside directors by nearly 20 percent by the same measures.

GRAEF CRYSTAL, corporate compensation expert, quoted in the *New York Times*, November 17, 1996

I would say that [the Disney board of directors] is living in the Dark Ages of good corporate governance practices.

> JOHN NASH, president of the National Association of Corporate Directors, quoted in the *Wall Street Journal*, February 24, 1997

[C]hairman's Christmas card list. [Where British companies apparently find their outside directors.]

> ANN SIMPSON of the corporate governance watchdog group PIRC, in the *Financial Times*, May 6, 1997

The typical board member of a large Canadian corporation earns about $30,000 a year. The CEO of the same company has total cash compensation of between $500,000 and $1,500,000 with a few outsiders above and below. I believe that the two tasks should be valued per unit of time. Making this assumption, how much of the director's time can a corporation fairly lay claim to for $30,000?

> WILLIAM A. DIMMA, chairman of the chemical company Monsanto Canada, in a speech, October 11, 1995

[B]oards should have active executives with proven performance records.

The ideal board should also include a brilliant investment banker and a skilled lawyer, preferably one who understands securities. You want individuals with global experience, particularly in Europe and Asia. And you must have people with real marketing skills. These are the kinds of people who will be valuable resources to a chief executive, the company, and its shareholders.

> ALBERT J. DUNLAP, former CEO of the consumer appliance firm Sunbeam, quoted in the *New York Times*, August 10, 1997

Look what happened to IBM. Four or five of those directors didn't ever use a personal computer.

> JOHN M. NASH, president of the National Association of Corporate Directors, quoted in *Business Week*, November 25, 1996

Go to any big mutual fund, and it's like the dog that didn't bark. Their emphasis has been on bringing money in the door. There is no recognition that being an active owner can benefit the funds.

> Corporate governance expert, quoted in *Business Week*, November 25, 1996

You can make clear to directors that they are the fiduciaries of shareholders, not of management. They are not there to be management's friends.

> JANIE HESTER-AMEY, Corporate Governance Officer, Calpers (California Public Employees Retirement System), quoted in *Fortune*, March 8, 1993

Should Calpers [California Public Employees Retirement System] wait until companies are in the dumper before asking them to have decent corporate governance?

> PATRICIA K. MACHT, spokeswoman for Calpers, quoted in the *New York Times*, August 3, 1997

Any age is arbitrary. The point, if you do some historical research, is that a lot of corporate boards didn't replace their members, and their members got older. It wasn't their age that was the problem, but that they had been talking to themselves for a very long time.

> WILLIAM D. CRIST, president of Calpers, quoted in the *New York Times*, August 3, 1997

If you look at the power meter, it's still 99 percent in management hands.

> SARA TESLIK, of the Council of Institutional Investors, on the stalling of Calpers's initiative to reform corporate board practices, quoted in the *Financial Times*, September 3, 1997

How much time do I want to spend doing somebody else's work? Eight to 10 days a year is a lot. I could go fishing [instead] and get more returns doing something I'd rather do.

> GORDON BETHUNE, CEO of Continental Airlines, quoted in the *Wall Street Journal*, October 28, 1997

If you can't mind your own store, why should you mind someone else's?

> PROFESSOR CHARLES ELSON, Stetson University Law School, quoted in the *Wall Street Journal*, October 28, 1997

The pleasant but vacuous director need never worry about job security.

> WARREN BUFFETT, CEO of the investment firm Berkshire Hathaway, quoted in *Fortune*, April 4, 1994

11.2 DIRECTOR AND SHAREHOLDER ACTIVISM

Don't be in a hurry. A good coup takes time. [Advice to directors thinking about ousting management]

ALAN FARNHAM, *Fortune,* January 11, 1993

[Eight rules for strengthening corporate boards]

1. There should clearly be a majority of outside directors.
2. The individual members of a board should select a lead director.
3. The individual directors should meet alone in executive session on a regularly scheduled basis.
4. The individual directors should take responsibility for all board procedures.
5. The board should have the basic responsibility for selection of its own members.
6. The board should conduct regularly scheduled performance reviews of the CEO and key executives.
7. The board must understand and fully endorse the company's long-term strategies.
8. The board must give an adequate amount of attention to its most important responsibility, the selection of the CEO.

JOHN SMALE, retired CEO of the detergent company Procter & Gamble, cited in *Fortune,* November 29, 1993

I've harassed guys all my life.

DARLA MOORE, CEO of the investment firm Rainwater Inc., and former banker who has been instrumental in shaking up the management of several corporations, quoted in *Fortune,* September 8, 1997

11.3 WOMEN IN THE BOARDROOM

Of the 500 companies on *Fortune's* list, 404 (or 81 percent) had at least one woman on the board (up from 69 percent in 1993) . . . All told, women had 600 (or 9.5 percent) of the 6,274 *Fortune* 500 board seats in 1995.

Figures from 1995 Census of Female Board of Directors of the *Fortune* 500, quoted in *Harvard Business Review,* January–February 1996

The pool of women with the capability and experience to serve on boards is larger than generally believed. Availability is no longer an excuse.

JOHN H. BRYAN, CEO of the food and underwear company Sara Lee, and chairman of the board of Catalyst (organization that studies corporate women's interests), quoted in *Harvard Business Review,* January– February 1996

Sixty percent of all purchases in this country are made by women, having women on the board just makes good sense.

JAMES PRESTON, CEO of Avon Products, quoted in *Harvard Business Review,* January–February 1996

We expect our next set of numbers to show little or no increase in the number of women on *Fortune* 500 boards. Many already have one token woman, and see no need to add another.

SHEILA WELLINGTON, president of the corporate women's organization Catalyst, quoted in the *Financial Times,* September 15, 1997

Bluntly stated, a "woman's view" on how to run our semiconductor company does not help us, unless that woman has an advanced technical degree and experience as a CEO . . . You ought to get down from your moral high horse.

T. J. RODGERS, CEO of Cypress Semiconductor, responding to urgings that he make his board more diverse, quoted in the *Wall Street Journal,* July 15, 1996

The assumption is that CEOs are bad guys and in acting on their own without prodding from politically correct types, they wouldn't make the right decision. And that assumption is just flat a—[sic] wrong.

T. J. RODGERS, CEO of Cypress Semiconductor, in an interview after making the previous remark, quoted in the *Wall Street Journal,* July 15, 1996

I began to feel that you were perhaps a person who enjoys finding spiders on the sidewalk so that he can squish them. You were using a sledgehammer to put a thumbtack in place. Restated in terms that a graduate engineer can understand—I think you acted like a bully.

Cypress shareholder replying to Rodgers, quoted in the *Wall Street Journal,* July 15, 1996

12.1 DIVERSITY

If you don't have a workforce that reflects your customers, you are not going to be competitive.

> YVONNE ALVERIO of the insurance company Aetna, quoted in Michael F. Kastre, Nydia Rodriguez Kastre, and Alfred G. Edwards, *The Minority Career Guide* (Peterson's, 1993)

Diversity isn't a slogan—it's a reality when you're hiring people everywhere.

> ROBERT M. TEETER, Republican pollster and board member of UPS, quoted in *Fortune,* November 13, 1995

Nynex [now Bell Atlantic], the [then] phone company in New York, actively recruits Hispanic, Asian, and other minority workers. The benefits are not just theoretical. A South Korean employee, for example, told his bosses that the number 4 could be considered unlucky back home; Nynex took that into account when assigning phone numbers to Korean customers.

> LAURA PEDERSEN, *New York Times,* December 31, 1995

We're finding that Hispanics do best in those companies that do a lot of business with governments and are under pressure for diversity in hiring.

> HECTOR CONTU, editor of the magazine *Hispanic Business,* quoted in the *New York Times,* December 31, 1995

It is no accident that the companies that practice affirmative action most conspicuously . . . are precisely those companies selling a product to consumers in the retail marketplace. Corporations are not inherently ideological; they are inherently greedy: if you will buy a product or service more readily from a minority, they will hire minorities to pitch or sell their products.

> MICHAEL LEWIS, *New York Times,* December 8, 1996

Every time I hear it (diversity) described as a marketplace issue—as in, we have 20 percent minority customers so we need minorities in marketing—I just sigh. It's bigger than marketshare.

> LOUIS W. HOYES, of the mortgage agency Fannie Mae, quoted in *Harvard Business Review,* September–October 1997

Hiring alone doesn't give equal opportunity. Studies have shown that many of us carry a burden of subjective baggage about women and minorities in the workplace. For women and minorities striving to move up the corporate ladder, this can pose an enormous barrier.

> RICHARD J. MAHONEY, CEO of the chemical company Monsanto, quoted by Virginia V. Weldon of Monsanto, in a speech at a women-in-leadership conference, November 9, 1993

Hiring large numbers of women and members of minorities, only to see them leave after a brief stint on the job, does little to diversify a company's workforce. Affirmative action has had only a modest impact on the American corporate culture and on the personal comfort levels of workers in that environment.

> PROFESSOR WALTER C. FARRELL JR. of the University of Wisconsin at Milwaukee and PROFESSOR JAMES H. JOHNSON JR. of the University of North Carolina, *New York Times,* January 12, 1997

There was a strong emphasis in the seventies for getting the right numbers of black managers. But now we're stagnating, as if the motivation was to get numbers, not create opportunity.

> A high-level black executive, quoted by Edward W. Jones Jr., founder of Corporate Organization Dynamics Inc., cited in *Harvard Business Review,* May–June 1986

Group members of different cultural backgrounds are talking right past each other. But given the current lack of training in cross-cultural communication, the result isn't surprising. Representatives from marketing and manufacturing have difficulty communicating, and their perspectives are probably a lot closer than those of people from different cultures.

> PROFESSOR JOSEPH DI STEFANO, of Western Business School, Ontario, *Harvard Business Review,* September–October 1993

We're good at sending people to diversity training, using politically correct language, and making sure we have people of color in our Annual Report photos. But when it comes to the hard work of encouraging diversity—including new ways of thinking, implementing more flexible work schedules, or examining deep-rooted prejudices—we're much more reluctant. So while the surface problems get better and our workplace has all the outer trappings of diversity, the deep-seated issues of intolerance and exclusivity go unexamined.

> RAYMOND W. SMITH, chairman of the telecommunications firm Bell Atlantic, in a speech, November 1, 1995

Affirmative action [alone] was divisive in some ways. [Allstate's approach is] not based on what you *think,* it's based on what you *observe.* That gives you feedback that you can use.

> JERRY CHOATE, CEO of the insurance firm Allstate, quoted in the *Wall Street Journal,* October 1, 1997

I have yet to see a diversity-training program that's led to the promotion or hiring of a woman or minority.

> CLIFFORD L. ALEXANDER, formerly Secretary of the Army and chairman of the Equal Employment Opportunity Commission, later hired as a consultant to assess diversity-training program, quoted in the *Wall Street Journal,* January 30, 1997

Paul [Brown, the first National Football League owner to hire black players] was a top business person who was driven to setting up an organization that would be the best in the world, utilizing the best personnel, developing the best devices to win. Color never came into his philosophy—neither positive nor negative. The way he carried his organization was that everybody was afraid of him, so you didn't have any dissension.

> JIM BROWN, all-time football great for the Cleveland Browns, quoted in the *New York Times,* September 25, 1997

I feel very strongly that race has not been a factor in my career at American Express. I didn't have to go through the trials and tribulations of Jackie Robinson. I've had a straightforwardly fair chance to get where I did on merit.

> KEN CHENAULT, new president of the financial services firm American Express, and at the time, the most senior black executive in American business, quoted in the *Financial Times,* February 28, 1997

It wasn't fair or efficient to have him fix the problem. My priority was a flood, his was God.

> VICTOR ARAGONA, manager of a New York City hotel, on finding a Muslim room attendant bowing toward Mecca when pipes needed to be repaired, quoted in the *Wall Street Journal,* November 20, 1996

As minorities we are so used to not having a full range of favorable choices that we tend to seize either the first or the wrong opportunity. Whatever turns up too often decides the direction of our professional lives.

> Anonymous Hispanic businessman, quoted in Michael F. Kastre, Nydia Rodriguez Kastre, and Alfred G. Edwards, *The Minority Career Guide* (Peterson's, 1993)

Any colour you want as long as it's not black. [Echoes Henry Ford's remark about the Model T—"any color you want as long as it's black."]

> Joke about Ford paint options after it was discovered that ads depicting its workforce were different in Poland than in the U.K. (the agency inadvertently used the Polish photo of white faces in an English ad, which should have shown black and Indian faces), *The Economist,* February 24, 1996

The two jobs which still discriminate against [stammerers] are news reading and air-traffic control.

> KELVIN MACKENZIE, British TV magnate on his plans to hire a stutterer to read evening news to fulfill a regulatory obligation to hire minorities, quoted in the *Economist,* February 24, 1996

Should I spend $100,000 doing a search for a Hispanic chemist when I know a [white] chemist who can do the job perfectly?

> ROBERT SALTER, president of the high-tech firm Osmotek, quoted in the *Wall Street Journal,* September 5, 1996

Sometimes I knock on doors to get business, and people look at me like I am a savage because I don't speak English right. My daughter, she will speak better. Nobody will call her savage. And her children, they won't have to work this hard.

> DANNY RHEE, immigrant from Korea, quoted in *Forbes,* October 6, 1986

[W]e challenged [the predominantly minority women] to come up with a solution in their own way. We worked with them to organize them into teams. They then took over. They used a lot of common sense. They found ways to streamline the assembly process. They reduced scrap costs. They asked for and got training so they could maintain and calibrate equipment. They even shopped the malls on weekends to get a better price on Q-Tips than the one corporate purchasing department got. They solved problems, they charted their progress, they raised the bar whenever they reached a goal.

> LAWRENCE PERLMAN, CEO of the information and defense electronics firm Ceridian Corporation, on giving employees a chance to save their jobs from being sent overseas, in a speech, April 28, 1992

I am a realist. The chances of any executive being asked to join as chief executive are slim, and for a black executive odds may be slimmer still.

> WILLIAM NORMAN, then second in command at the railroad company Amtrak, quoted in *Forbes*, August 24, 1987

The fact is that minorities always have to adapt to majority culture. And adapting to American corporate culture is easy compared with what most blacks have had to adapt to in the past.

Corporations, even progressive ones, with supposedly flat structures, are still pretty hierarchical, and hierarchy is not popular with people whose racial or ethnic identity has long defined the bottom of the ladder.

> REGINALD D. DICKSON, CEO of Inroads, which trains and develops minority professionals in business and technology, quoted in *Harvard Business Review*, January–February 1992

Every time you see one of us [successful black people], we are singing, blowing a horn, or dribbling a ball, but we're not portrayed as business people. So when we are working as managers in real life, it makes people uncomfortable. They can't believe it.

> KEN BACON of the mortgage agency Fannie Mae, "A Question of Color: A Debate on Race in the Workplace," *Harvard Business Review*, September–October 1997

Ninety-nine point nine percent of the white men I send out get hired.

> MARC WHITEHEAD, corporate recruiter, quoted in the *Wall Street Journal*, September 5, 1996

When the requirement is for an executive with a "diverse background," a search often necessitates 500 con-

testants or more, compared with about 150 for a typical search.

> Information supplied by JEFFREY CHRISTIAN, of executive search firm Christian & Timbers, *Wall Street Journal*, February 18, 1997

The Supreme Court is going their way, the dire predictions about an invasion of nonwhite males into the workplace have not materialized, and there has been no landing of strange people to take their jobs. White men can catch their breath again.

> HARRIS SUSSMAN, diversity consultant, *Wall Street Journal*, February 18, 1997

[M]iddle-class white women are the chief beneficiaries of affirmative action. And one-fourth of the contracts awarded by the Small Business Administration as set-asides in 1994 went to 1 percent of the "minority" firms.

> TONY BROWN, *Black Lies, White Lies* (William Morrow, 1995)

Eight (8) vacancies are anticipated to be filled in the Staff Services Occupational Grouping [the entry-level civil service position for college graduates]. Four (4) vacancies will be filled by whites; four (4) will be filled by men. It is anticipated that it will take four (4) years to reach parity for whites; four (4) to reach parity with men.

> LISA FEIN of the California Department of Alcohol and Drug Programs; in an affirmative action memo, quoted in the *Wall Street Journal*, October 3, 1996

Karl Marx insisted that for any sort of class consciousness to arise, there must be communication of a common sense of oppression. With the mass media and the social sciences rarely recognizing the phenomenon, much less portraying it sympathetically, white males have been easily and silently victimized one by one.

> FREDERICK LYNCH, sociologist at Claremont McKenna College, quoted in *Forbes*, May 25, 1996

The "angry white men" that we hear so much about in the political debate are in fact the very people who've been at the losing end in this two-decade-long trend (rising income inequality). The current fine state of the macroeconomy has muted their complaints; but when the next recession comes, who doubts they'll be back louder and angrier than ever?

> ALAN MURRAY, bureau chief at the *Wall Street Journal,* quoted in *Slate* magazine, September 9, 1996

This diversity thing, you know how all the black jelly beans agree.

> ROBERT ULRICH, retired treasurer for the oil company Texaco, secretly taped in discussion of a bias suit by black employees, quoted in the *New York Times,* November 4, 1996

That's funny. All the black jelly beans seem to be glued to the bottom of the bag.

> RICHARD A. LUNDWALL of Texaco's finance department who taped the conversation, responding to Ulrich, quoted in the *New York Times,* November 4, 1996

I'm still struggling with Hanukkah, and now we have Kwanzaa. Poor St. Nicholas, they shitted all over his beard.

> ROBERT ULRICH, on agitation by blacks for company recognition of Kwanzaa as seasonal holiday, from same tapes, quoted in the *New Republic,* December 9, 1996

I work as a service adviser at an auto dealership. In this industry, there are few black managers, service advisers, or technicians. Why? Because the owners and managers don't even bother to look at the employment applications of blacks. How did I get the job? Because one white man saw me as a person—not a black person.

> JOHN HAWKINS, Union City, California, letter to editor, responding to article about problems at Texaco, *Business Week,* December 9, 1996

It's hard to get inside people's heads and manage their attitudes.

> PATSY A. RANDELL of the computer firm Honeywell, *Business Week,* November 25, 1996

"The social event as an extension of business, politics, or work is essentially a white phenomenon," one African-American social theorist told the [New York] *Times.*

> JUDITH MARTIN, *Miss Manners Rescues Civilization* (Crown, 1996)

In the 1976 Santa Fe decision, the Supreme Court held that Federal law prohibits race discrimination against men. White men have as much protection from discrimination as anyone else. They bring fewer race and sex discrimination cases than other groups. But in the area of age discrimination, white men file more cases than any other group. Not surprisingly, it is in this area that damage awards, from juries and judges alike, are the highest.

> DAVID B. OPPENHEIMER, associate law professor at Golden Gate University, letter to editor, the *New York Times,* January 19, 1997

What you learn is that you can't start a biotechnology company by hiring a bunch of white men from New Jersey. . . .

This isn't about designing an approach for every group and every issue. It's about listening to people—their problems and their aspirations. It's amazing how unaware you can be of the impact you have on people different from you . . .

> DENNIS LONGSTREET, president of the biotechnology firm Ortho Biotech, quoted in *Fortune,* February 21, 1994

My job as a black woman is to put you at ease at work. I'm not saying it's fair, I'm saying it is.

I can't get mad every time you ask about the O. J. trial or the Million Man March. If I get mad every day, they're going to fire me and say I'm confrontational and difficult to work with.

> ANCELLA LIVERS, director of the Leadership for African-Americans program, Center for Creative Leadership, quoted in the *Wall Street Journal,* March 4, 1997

Hispanic magazine says it found only 75 companies worthy of being named . . . to its eighth annual corporate 100 list of the best firms for Hispanics.

> *Wall Street Journal,* March 5, 1997

Only 2.4 percent of lawyers in the country's 250 biggest firms are black, up from 1.5 percent in 1985, according to the *National Law Journal.*

> *Wall Street Journal,* July 8, 1997

I think the word "diversity" is divisive.

> JANET HILL, African American management consultant on "inclusiveness," quoted in *Fortune,* August 4, 1997

They've gotten into the system and figured out how to use it.

> THOMAS BETTRIDGE, regional administrator of the SBA's office in New York City, on success of Asian Americans in getting Small Business Administration loans, quoted in the *New York Times*, September 9, 1997

During the past decade, Asian-American–owned businesses have more than doubled their share of contracts awarded under the Small Business Administration's so-called 8a program, getting 23.7 percent of the contracts in 1996, compared with 10.5 percent in 1986. By contrast, black contractors have seen their share of the total number of contracts drop by more than one-quarter, to 36.7 percent in 1996 from 50.5 percent in 1986. Hispanics' portion has hovered around 30 percent throughout the period.

> ROCHELLE SHARPE, *New York Times*, September 9, 1997 (Figures obtained through a Freedom of Information Act request)

How am I going to get on with the airlines? Wrong pigment, wrong plumbing.

> White male applicant for baggage-handler job, quoted in *Business Week*, January 31, 1994

The arrival of multicultural companies means that people can no longer rely on shared backgrounds and tacit understanding to bind them together.

> JOHN MICKLETHWAITE and ADRIAN WOODRIDGE of the *Economist*, in *The Witch Doctors* (Times Books, 1996)

You can judge the sentiments of the country by who you can make fun of. Nowadays, the ultimate villain, I suppose, would be a fat white male terrorist who ran a Fortune 500 company on the side.

> TERRY RUSSIO, screenwriter for Disney's "Pocahontas," quoted in *Fortune*, July 10, 1995

12.2 GAY ISSUES

The higher up you go, the deeper the closets get.

> ED MICKENS, editor of *Working It Out*, a New York–based newsletter about gay and lesbian issues, quoted in the *New York Times*, June 27, 1993

We regret that some people have taken offense at a health issue regarding our employees [extending health benefits to domestic partners of gay employees], but we aren't going to change it.

> JOHN DREYER of Walt Disney, quoted in *Fortune*, December 25, 1995

Gay people don't lie; they dissemble. "What did you do this past weekend?" people will ask. "Well, I did a few things, and gee, I was busy and wasn't it hot and the Tigers won?" or something. You give, if you will, a little answer. Not the wrong answer, but a partial answer.

When people asked me about my marital status, I had begun using the response, "I married Ford Motor Company."

> ALLAN GILMOUR, former CFO, Ford Motor Company, on the pressures of being gay in a corporation, quoted in *Fortune*, September 8, 1997

12.3 THE GLASS CEILING

When the day comes that American Express Company has to hire a female employee, it will close its doors.

> JAMES CONGDELL FARGO, president of American Express, 1881–1914

I look forward to the day when we don't think in terms of a woman executive at all, but just an executive.

> ELLEN GORDON, president of the candy manufacturer Tootsie Roll Industries, quoted in *Fortune*, August 31, 1987

There are people in the [movie] industry who cannot imagine a woman in the director's chair being in charge of the crew. There's a certain Boys' Club reality to all business, not just film.

> MARTHA COOLIDGE, quoted in *Film Yearbook*, 1987

Top jobs are designed for people with wives.

> LUCY HELLER of the British food company Booker, quoted in the *Economist*, March 28, 1992

Our managers are all white, middle-aged men, and they promote in their own image.

> "One woman" in financial services industry, quoted in the *Economist*, March 28, 1992

The consensus was that if you can get three women to the top level of management, change can occur. One can't do it. Two can't do it, but three can.

> KATHERINE M. HUDSON of the Eastman Kodak Company, quoted in the *New York Times,* September 27, 1992

The same things make women successful that make men successful. The main thing is desire.

> MYELLE ("MILLIE") BELL, president of the telecommunications company BellSouth International, quoted in *Fortune,* August 31, 1987

[N]ot many of us would relish being described as a "screamer who's not above swearing like a trooper" or "the queen of impatience"—but one of the men so honored was called the "pompadoured bully." If I were forced to choose, I think I would take the screamer. [Referring to *Fortune*'s list of America's toughest bosses, only one of whom was a woman—Linda Wachner, of Warnaco.]

> VIRGINIA V. WELDON of chemical company Monsanto, in a speech, November 9, 1993

There's an economic cost to gender inequality. Paying attention to women is central to growth.

> MINH CHAN NGUYEN of the World Bank, quoted in *Business Week,* August 29, 1994

You can't touch it, or quantify it, but it's there. You know it. You feel it. Being both a woman and an Asian, I have to work twice as hard.

> KIJA KIM, Korean-born founder of the Harvard Design and Mapping Company (HDM), quoted in *Asia, Inc.,* April 1997

I think women today are tired of waiting for organizations to deliver. They don't want to act just like men and hope for the best.

> DEBORAH SWISS, consultant and author, quoted in *Harvard Business Review,* July–August 1996

At a party I attended last weekend, a bunch of women deconstructed the physique in a Levi's advertisement. Men aren't supposed to talk like that.

No wonder sperm counts are dropping.

> "N.M." quoted in *Forbes,* August 11, 1997

[A] census of women at the top of corporate America delivers the somber news that women hold just about 2 percent of the power positions no matter how they are defined—by title, by paycheck, or by responsibility for the bottom line. Of the nation's 500 largest companies, only 61 can count a woman among their five top earners or can say that a quarter or more of their officers are women. Just 13 of the 61 can do both.

> *New York Times,* November 5, 1996. Results of a study by Catalyst, a nonprofit women's research group

[W]omen are less likely than men to have learned to blow their own horn. And they are more likely than men to believe that if they do so, they won't be liked.

> PROFESSOR DEBORAH TANNEN, of Georgetown University, quoted in *Harvard Business Review,* September–October 1995

There is no additional risk entailed in doing business and extending credit to women-owned firms.

> Attributed to DAVID KRESGE, senior vice president of Dun & Bradstreet, by Susan Maltby, of the bank Key Corp, in a speech, October 11, 1995

Some companies with a good reputation for policies on paper are not so good in practice. It can be perceived as a negative if you take advantage of these policies. It may mean what we always thought it meant, that family-friendly policies are a way to keep women in their place and not let them rise too far, that the policies that allow for advancement may also limit advancement.

> ROBIN ELY, associate professor at Columbia University, who specializes in gender and race relations, quoted by Susan Maltby, of the bank Key Corp, in a speech, October 11, 1995

[While I was in labor in hospital] he continued the conversation for 20 minutes even though I alerted him each time a new contraction was beginning. My daughter was born an hour later. First thing the next morning, guess who called my hospital room to discuss business again?

> Woman who nominated her boss as worst boss in the country, quoted in *Fortune,* October 18, 1993

You're [to a group of male executives] eunuchs. How can your wives stand you? You've got nothing between your legs.

> LINDA WACHNER, CEO of the intimate apparel company Warnaco, quoted in *Fortune,* October 18, 1993.

We need women designing vehicles for the simple reason that they use them.

> MIMI VANDERMOLEN, principal designer of the Ford Probe, and auto industry's highest-ranked female designer, quoted in *Fortune,* October 18, 1993

A car that lets you drive in high heels. [The biggest challenge to car designers]

> According to KAREN KUZINKOSKI, Chrysler, quoted in *Fortune,* October 18, 1993

There was a time when working women's shoulders had to be as broad as the man's. . . . But women in modern times can safely wear almost anything they want. Women can look like women.

> CYNTHIA STEFFE, designer, quoted in the *Wall Street Journal,* October 8, 1997

I can't think of anybody in my professional life that wears stiletto heels. In the workplace, you're not there to seduce people.

> JILL TOTENBERG of the management consulting firm, CSC Index, quoted in the *Wall Street Journal,* October 8, 1997

All things being equal, I like to give business to women—and sometimes even when they're not. There's a general comfort level with women. I don't have to start from scratch, I can start in midsentence—especially if we're the same age.

> PATRICIA DIAZ DENNIS, associated general counsel of SBC Communications, quoted in the *Wall Street Journal,* March 4, 1997

I don't play golf. I don't go to the men's room. I didn't have the ability to network the way men do. But I made myself visible.

> JILL BARAD, CEO of the toy company Mattel, quoted in the *Wall Street Journal,* March 5, 1997

We've all had the experience of a man we worked for say, "I went out of my way for you, I ignored all my peers who said you couldn't do it, I even gave you a flexible schedule—and now you're leaving me?" What's implied is "you were supposed to take care of me forever."

> PAT COOK, an executive recruiter at Heidrick & Struggles, quoted in the *Wall Street Journal,* November 11, 1997

Women who are excitable and emotional may be dismissed as temperamentally unsuited for management. Yet men who vent their emotions by slamming the door and pounding the desk may be considered "aggressive."

When I tell people I work for a bank, they almost always assume that I am a teller.

> JANET MARTIN of the Canadian Imperial Bank of Commerce, in a speech December 4, 1991

People come up to you at a party and say, "Aren't you bright?" It isn't a compliment.

> Female director of a London investment bank, quoted in the *Economist,* March 28, 1992

It is a comfort level thing. Most of the male managers are in their mid-40s to 60s, which is about half a generation ahead of us. Their real concern is, "Can I tell this joke? Can I go golfing with her? What about business trips?"

> DIANA KREITLING, a marketing executive, quoted in the *New York Times,* May 5, 1991

Only 30 percent of the men [who work for Hewlett-Packard] have a working spouse—compared to fully 86 percent of the women. That means that 70 percent of our men simply have never experienced the challenge of trying to complete the business plan and still have time to pick up the dry cleaning on the way home.

Both professional men and women average about 50 hours in the office weekly. But women spend an average of 33 hours weekly on household chores or child care—compared to 19 for men. Said differently, men have an extra two hours a day of leisure time.

> LEWIS E. PLATT, CEO of Hewlett-Packard, in a speech, October 18, 1995

[W]omen who get ahead fit in. They're smart enough to get into a corporate culture which takes advantage of their strengths and doesn't highlight their weakness. Someone might do very well at Coca-Cola but be fired at Pepsi-Cola. Those are very different corporate cultures. If you're in the wrong corporate culture, look for a better fit.

> MARILYN CARLSON NELSON of the restaurant firm Carlson, in a speech, April 17, 1996

One of the biggest mistakes women make in business is that they aren't friendly enough.

> CHARLOTTE BEERS, CEO of the advertising firm Ogilvy & Mather, quoted in *Fortune,* August 5, 1996

When people see something unusual like a woman who is No. 1, rumors provide a rationale. Defensiveness causes more. You know. "The lady doth protest too much."

> PROFESSOR KATHLEEN REARDON of the University of Southern California, *Fortune,* August 5, 1996

Yeah, I'll get you coffee if you'll Xerox these papers for me.

> DIANA "DEDE" BROOKS, CEO of the auction house Sotheby's, recalling her first response to owner Alfred Taubman when she worked in the finance department and he asked her to get coffee, quoted in *Fortune,* August 5, 1996

In order to lead in a man's world, you can't be plain vanilla.

> LINDA MARCELLI of the investment bank Merrill Lynch, *Fortune,* August 5, 1996

Even if that's [staying home to raise a family] a consideration for some women, it's at most a question of a temporary break until their kids reach school age.

> PROFESSOR ROSABETH MOSS KANTER, of Harvard Business School, quoted in the *Financial Times,* September 15, 1997

Women's networks do women zero good professionally. My advice is to find a niche and then become the best there is in that field.

> DARLA MOORE, CEO of the investment firm Rainwater, Inc., quoted in *Fortune,* August 5, 1996

You run into subtle sexism every day [in Silicon Valley companies]. It's like water torture. It wears you down.

> ANITA BORG, senior researcher at Digital Equipment Corp. in Palo Alto, quoted in *Business Week,* August 25, 1997

The difficulty that women face in tapping into informal networks at a corporation is very subtle. They are not officially shut out. But a lot of the conversations about what's going on in a company happen in places women are not likely to frequent, like the bar next door to the office or at a friendly game of golf over the weekend.

> ELLEN KNAPP of the accounting firm Coopers & Lybrand, quoted in the *Financial Times,* September 15, 1997

I remember the first day [as a manuscript girl] I wore a pants suit to the office. I was shaking because I was afraid I would get fired. Everyone was staring at me. The next day, everyone showed up in pants.

> JONI EVANS, editor in chief of Turtle Bay Books, quoted in the *New York Times,* March 17, 1991

If you really want to shoot to the top you probably have to start your own business.

> KIM POLESE, formerly of the computer firm Sun Microsystems Inc., founder of Web start-up firm Marimba Inc., and member of Babes in Boyland, an organization of female technology executives, quoted in the *New York Times,* March 17, 1991

The need for risk-taking that was instilled early on made me better suited to start my own business. And my feeling of being shut out gave me the will to do it.

> ANDI GRAY, consultant, formerly of Xerox, quoted in the *Financial Times,* September 15, 1997

Remember the guy who wouldn't dream of his wife working? He's the same guy who now wakes up in the middle of the night to suggest that she ask her boss for a raise.

> JOHN L. ADAMS, CEO of Texas Commerce Bank, in a speech to the National Council of Jewish Women, September 9, 1993

A majority of men (71 percent) emphasize logic over intuition, while the women are more evenly split (47 percent emphasize logic, 53 percent intuition), leading the authors to conclude that "women business owners, on average, can thus be said to be more "whole brain" in their thinking." Which is like saying that since half the survey respondents are male and half female, on average, they're hermaphrodites. [In a report by the National Association of Women Business Owners]

> *Inc.,* October 1994

Women, for the most part, tend to be more collaborative and less individually competitive.

> PAULA CHRONISTER of the accounting firm Price Waterhouse, quoted in the *Wall Street Journal,* September 24, 1996

Many women are working mothers, and I think in order to survive on a daily basis, they have to be extremely organized and productive.

> SUSAN LIEBSON, senior counsel, Atlantic Richfield, *Wall Street Journal,* September 24, 1996

I negotiate with people as if they are peers. If you believe it, then they will believe it.

> KAY KOPLOVITZ, president and chief executive of the USA Network, quoted in the *New York Times*, September 15, 1991

"Career commitment" is a euphemism for "what if she has a baby?" Well, what if she [a female employee] has a baby?

If companies want stronger career commitment from women, they should hasten to correct pay inequities and create equal opportunities for promotion.

> LAWRENCE PERLMAN, president and CEO of Ceridian Corporation, in a speech, April 28, 1992

It is now possible for a flight attendant to get a pilot pregnant.

> RICHARD J. FERRIS, president of United Airlines

12.4 IMMIGRATION

All of the economists, all of the academics, all of the people who wring their hands over America's decline forget that coming off the boat down at the docks this morning were 25 Koreans, 150 Mexicans, 3 Hungarians, and many more.

> WALTER WRISTON, *Harvard Business Review*, January–February, 1990

The challenge is not to restrict the number of foreign nationals in the country. The trouble is to turn them into Americans.

> PETER CANNON of Rockwell International, in *Physics Today*, 1988

Fifty percent of our Santa Clara technical staff is Asian.

> ANDREW GROVE, cofounder and CEO of computer chip firm Intel, interviewed in Rama Dev Jager, *In the Company of Giants* (McGraw-Hill, 1997)

We remain a fiercely merit-oriented, anti-xenophobic community, but the current situation knows no precedent.

> Mathematician ERIC WEINSTEIN and 20 other scholars in an appeal to Congress to restrict increased quotas for admitting immigrants with extraordinary

skills, quoted in the *Wall Street Journal*, September 4, 1996

Fabio gets his green card, but other aspiring U.S. immigrants must wait.

> *Wall Street Journal*, September 3, 1996

Immigration is income redistribution, and the people who are 100 percent for immigration often downplay that aspect.

> RICHARD B. FREEMAN, economist at Harvard, quoted in the *Wall Street Journal*, September 4, 1996

12.5 MANAGING A LOW-SKILL, ENTRY-LEVEL WORKFORCE

There is an average response time for each question. It usually takes longer to tell a lie than to tell the truth. If there is a longer response time to questions about bias, drugs, or theft, we will follow up with face-to-face interviews.

> NORMAN HILL of the fast-food chain Denny's, on its automated phone recruiting interviews with questions like "Have you ever used drugs?" and "Do you like dealing with people of different races?" quoted in *Fortune*, May 13, 1996

We cannot create enough public-service jobs to hire these folks; so they have to be hired in the private sector, and I ask you to help. This has basically got to be a private-sector show.

> PRESIDENT BILL CLINTON in a speech to business leaders, October 1996

It is getting harder to find anyone who can add, talk, and run a cash register for $6 an hour.

> Dallas district retailer quoted in labor market survey, cited in the *Wall Street Journal*, June 19, 1997

The best way to relieve a critical recruiting situation is to raise pay. You can say we're going to give you a pension plan or 20 cents more an hour, and it's the 20 cents that's going to grab them.

> MITCHELL FROMSTEIN, CEO of the employment firm Manpower, quoted in the *Wall Street Journal*, November 8, 1996

Many managers spend 15 percent of their time doing social work. That's time not spent dealing with customer issues.

> CLIFFORD J. EHRLICH of the hotel firm Marriott International, referring to Marriott's low-wage workforce, quoted in *Business Week,* November 11, 1996

People at the lower [wage] levels beg for the intangibles—the pat on the back, the verbal "thank yous." Self-esteem is a little lower, and they want to know they're OK.

> ROSALIND JEFFRIES, president of the human resources consulting firm Performance Enhancement Group, quoted in *Nation's Business,* May 1997

Supply and demand matter more than what the minimum-wage mandate is.

> HUGH SCHMIDT, McDonald's franchisee in Vail, Colorado, who paid wages well above the minimum because of competition with tourism employers, quoted in the *Wall Street Journal,* November 20, 1996

These [jobs at McDonald's] are breeding grounds for robots working for yesterday's assembly lines, not tomorrow's high-tech posts.

> PROFESSOR AMITAI ETZIONI of George Washington University, quoted in *Business Week,* October 13, 1986

[Y]ou don't have to pay them [prisoners] benefits.

> DANIEL P. BOHAN of Travel Wholesalers International in Fairfax, Virginia, on an advantage of setting up the first corporate travel reservations center inside a prison, quoted in the *Wall Street Journal,* September 16, 1997

12.6   SEXUAL HARASSMENT

If a man makes a pass at a female colleague, it isn't sexual harassment. If he continues, it is.

> LETITIA BALDRIGE, PR consultant and expert on corporate etiquette, quoted in *U.S. News & World Report,* 1985

If you're gonna screw someone these days, you'd better watch who you do it to.

> PETER HARRISON, of the recruiting firm Access Management, quoted in the *New York Times,* April 4, 1993

Within a year [of the amendment of Title VII of the Civil Rights Act to allow jury trials and compensatory and punitive damages in harassment cases] EEOC harassment complaints rose 53 percent, topping 10,000, and have been rising since. From 1991 to 1995, the number of plaintiff's attorneys roughly tripled, to 3,000.

> *Forbes,* May 6, 1996

The relationship's gone sour—there's nothing uglier. It's in these cases that you hear the outrageous—and sometimes fictitious—claims.

> MARGARET STRANGE, Connecticut attorney, quoted in *Forbes,* May 6, 1996

As case law demonstrates, words like "stupid," "useless," "worthless," and "incompetent" constitute non-actionable, protected opinions. These words fall into the category of rhetorical hyperbole and vigorous epithets that courts have held state opinions rather than facts.

> ATTORNEY CAROLYN T. ELLIS, from a motion to dismiss a sexual harassment suit against an advertising executive, quoted in the *New York Times,* March 27, 1997

I'm treating an executive now who's been sued for calling a secretary "honey." He's become functionally paranoid, afraid to talk to people—especially women at work—at all.

> STEVEN BERGLAS, clinical psychologist, quoted in *Fortune,* September 8, 1997

Victim after victim reports a workplace saturated with sexuality, most of it demeaning to women. Sexual graffiti were placed on the cars as they came down the line. . . . The men's bathrooms were virtually papered with sexual graffiti, including insulting pictures and names and phone numbers of individual female employees.

> Equal Employment Opportunity Commission report on Mitsubishi Motors, quoted in the *Financial Times,* September 17, 1997

12.7   SEX IN THE WORKPLACE

Sexual accusations are serious ones. They can ruin personal lives and they can ruin careers. And with more and more women rising up the corporate leader [sic], the weapon of sexual accusations will be used again.

> MARY CUNNINGHAM, wife of former Bendix CEO William Agee, in her book *Powerplay* (Simon & Schuster, 1984)

"What you need now is to be mentored," said William Agee to Mary Cunningham. Then he lifted her gently in his strong, pinstriped arms, carried her to his executive desk, and mentored her till dawn.

> MICHAEL KINSLEY *Fortune,* June 25, 1984

12.8 SKILLS FOR WORK

There is no question that the half-life of most job skills is dropping all the time.

> EDWARD LAWLER, professor of management at the University of South Carolina, *Time,* April 24, 1989

When you explain the German system [of apprenticeship] to American businessmen, they say, "Wow, it looks great." But when you ask them to adopt it, they complain that their company can't afford it.

> OLIVIER BERTRAND of the think tank CEREQ Institute, Paris, quoted in *Fortune,* December 14, 1992

I needed a temporary a couple of months ago, and they sent me a black man. And I dictated a letter to him. He took shorthand, which was good. Something like "Dear Mr. So-and-So, I am writing to ask about how your business is doing." And then he typed the letter, and I read the letter, and it's "I am writing to ax about your business." Now you hear about them speaking a different language and all that, and they say "ax" for "ask." Well, I don't care about that, but I didn't say "ax," I said ask.

> Anonymous "president of an inner-city advertising agency," quoted by William Julius Wilson in the *New York Times Magazine,* August 18, 1996

12.9 TOKENISM

If you feel people are there because you had to have them then you work around them not with them. Then they feel underutilized, because they probably are.

> NANCY GHEEN of the chemical company Monsanto, quoted in the *Economist,* March 28, 1992

13.1 BUDGET DEFICITS

During the reign of France's Louis XVI, Marie Antoinette supposedly once asked the royal finance minister, "What will you do about the deficit, Monsieur le Ministre?" His reply: "Nothing, Madame. It is too serious."

CHARLES P. ALEXANDER, *Time*, March 5, 1984

It seems that nearly every American either has a share of federal spending or has a close relative who does.

U.S. REPRESENTATIVE TRENT LOTT (Republican, Miss.), on why it's so hard to cut the federal budget, quoted in *U.S. News & World Report*, March 7, 1983

The real harm done by deficits is the negative impacts on long-run growth and future living standards. The process is gradual, with no easily identifiable, traumatic event that clearly illustrates the effects of deficits.

RUDOLPH PENNER, Congressional Budget Office Director, quoted in *Time*, March 5, 1984

The budget's like an ugly baby. You have to tie a pork chop around its neck to get the dog to play with it.

REPRESENTATIVE W. G. HEFNER (Democrat, North Carolina), quoted in *Time*, April 16, 1984

If I confess to you why I was so far behind you [junior high school students] in these examples, you'd know why we have a budget deficit.

PRESIDENT RONALD REAGAN, watching a math class, quoted in *U.S. News & World Report*, September 10, 1984

Peacetime deficits of that magnitude [5 to 6 percent of gross domestic product] are unknown in the United States.

MARTIN FELDSTEIN, President Reagan's chief economic adviser, forecasting deficits during a second Reagan term, quoted in *U.S. News & World Report*, February 7, 1983

If someone had told you four years ago that the national debt would be doubled in the next four years, you would have insisted on a saliva test for that person.

U.S. SENATOR DALE BUMPERS (Democrat, Arkansas), quoted in *U.S. News & World Report*, May 28, 1984

I don't know what they're on down there in Washington, but we ain't gonna have 5 percent interest rates. It's wack time, believe me.

LEE IACOCCA, chairman of the auto company Chrysler, on White House forecasts that low interest rates would help cut the budget deficit, quoted in *U.S. News & World Report*, March 5, 1984

At the rate we're borrowing from abroad, in the space of three years we will have wiped out all of the holdings we've built up overseas since the Second World War and become a debtor nation.

PAUL VOLCKER, chairman of the U.S. Federal Reserve Board, quoted in *U.S. News & World Report*, March 12, 1984

The president [Reagan] wants to take from farms and give to arms.

U.S. SENATOR CHARLES E. GRASSLEY (Republican, Iowa), on President Reagan's budget priorities, quoted in the *Wall Street Journal*, February 1, 1985

If the effects of years of unnecessary military spending could somehow be subtracted, our federal budget today [fiscal 1995] would show an $11 billion surplus as opposed to a deficit of almost $164 billion.

WALTER RUSSELL MEAD, *Worth*, February 1996

Christmas is a time when kids tell Santa Claus what they want and adults pay for it. Deficits are when adults tell the government what they want—and their kids pay for it.

RICHARD LAMM, then governor of Colorado, quoted in *U.S. News & World Report*, December 23, 1985

Whatever we do on trade is a sham, a complete waste of time, unless we begin to tackle the budget deficit.

FELIX ROHATYN of the investment bank Lazard Frères, quoted in *Time*, May 9, 1988

The president [Reagan] who campaigned on a promise that we would balance the budget by the end of his first term is now finishing his second term with that goal nowhere in sight.

Time, February 29, 1988

Things continue in government unless you feel a crisis. In fact, we didn't have a crisis, so the deficit persisted.

> PAUL VOLCKER, former chairman of the U.S. Federal Reserve Board, quoted in *Time,* January 23, 1989

One third of Medicare benefits, nearly two fifths of Social Security benefits, and more than two thirds of federal pension benefits now go to households with incomes above the U.S. median. Back in the early 1960s the typical 70-year-old consumed about 30 percent less (in dollars) than the typical 30-year-old; today the typical 70-year-old consumes nearly 20 percent more.

> PETER G. PETERSON, chairman of the investment firm The Blackstone Group, *Atlantic Monthly,* May 1996

If we were to do no more than declare that henceforth the cost of living adjustment will be CPI minus one percentage point, we would save $634 billion over the next 10 years. . . . Now here is a bipartisan agreement worth having.

> U.S. SENATOR DANIEL PATRICK MOYNIHAN (Democrat, New York), *Washington Post,* September 26, 1995

I recently came across an interesting statement. "Let us be happy and live within our means . . . even if we have to borrow to do it." The American humorist Artemus Ward wrote that line in 1872. Evidently, deficit spending is a long-standing American tradition.

> LAWRENCE A. BOSSIDY, CEO of the industrial company Allied-Signal, in a speech, June 21, 1995

A balanced budget amendment can work if the economy stays on a steady-state path of stable growth and low inflation. As soon as the economy deviates from that path and the Fed takes a shot at controlling the economy and we have a recession, which is obviously going to happen in the next few years, the path gets altered permanently.

> STEPHEN S. ROACH, chief economist of the investment bank Morgan Stanley, quoted in the *New York Times,* November 24, 1996

We've become too obsessed with 2002. Our objective is not simply to balance the budget for a nanosecond in 2002. Our objective is to gain control of fiscal policy— to balance the budget in the year 2002 and to stay in balance in the years that follow.

> U.S. SENATOR PETE DOMENICI (Republican, New Mexico), chairman of the Senate Budget Committee, quoted in the *Wall Street Journal,* February 3, 1997

The balanced budget holds an important lesson for conservatives: beware of what you wish for—you may get it. They will soon discover that it's easier to limit government when deficits are high, while a balanced budget is conducive to activist government.

The old fiscal formula of tax and spend held sway from the 1950s to the 1970s. Then came tax and cut, which ruled from 1982 to this year. Now a new model is emerging: Keep cutting obsolete programs and shift the money to public investment in areas like education, science, and health. That's the formula for activist government under a balanced budget.

> ROBERT J. SHAPIRO, former Clinton administration economic adviser and a founder of the think tank Progressive Policy Institute, quoted in the *New York Times,* August 12, 1997

13.2 THE BUSINESS CYCLE

What we used to say was bring on the recession. Recession drove people to church, and they realized they were missing their Bible.

> HARGIS THOMAS of Oxford University Press, which publishes Bibles, quoted in the *Economist,* October 28, 1996

13.3 THE BUSINESS CYCLE— DEAD OR NOT?

The biggest single myth is that the economy could easily expand far faster if we made a few simple policy changes. This myth achieved a kind of Olympian apogee in the vice presidential debate, when Jack Kemp blithely asserted that we should double our recent 2.5 percent average growth rate to 5 percent. Economists and others who share Kemp's supply-side politics swear loudly that GDP could effortlessly grow at 4 percent-plus. Listening to that kind of talk is like listening to small children talk about sex: It's alternately charming and unsettling—but you know they're talking about something they don't understand.

ROB NORTON, "Exploding the Myths About Growth," *Fortune,* November 25, 1996

Myth. . . . Recessions are inevitable.

Downturns remain possible—no use denying that—but as chance, not imperative, events. The economy no longer needs nationwide recessions to correct imbalances. Corrections instead are made locally.

THOMAS PETZINGER JR., *Wall Street Journal,* May 9, 1997

The impressive new concept underlying the greatest boom in history appears to be no more than a thinly disguised version of the old cynical epigram: "Investment is successful speculation."

BENJAMIN GRAHAM and DAVID DODD, *Security Analysis* (McGraw-Hill, 1934)

There is no natural law that says we have to have a recession.

ARTHUR C. MARTINEZ, chairman of the department store chain Sears, Roebuck, quoted in the *Wall Street Journal,* November 15, 1996

I am deeply suspicious of the seemingly smug attitude that we have tamed the once-ominous business cycle, that inflation is dead, and that it is onward and upward for the economy, the markets, and for Washington's ability to fix anything and everything that ails America.

STEPHEN S. ROACH, chief economist of the investment bank Morgan Stanley, quoted in the *New York Times,* November 24, 1996

Whatever one calls it, this new view of the economy has spread with a rapidity rare in the annals of economic thought. There is only one problem: when you think about it carefully, you realize that the new paradigm simply does not make sense.

PROFESSOR PAUL KRUGMAN of MIT, *Harvard Business Review,* July 1997

It's reasonable to think better inventory management will reduce volatility in the business cycle, but the evidence so far isn't convincing.

VICTOR ZARNOWITZ of Columbia University, quoted in the *New York Times,* August 29, 1997

It is indeed a "New World." And it is not just a cyclical phenomenon, but the result of radical change.

ALLEN SINAI of Pimark Decision Economics Company, quoted in the *Financial Times,* September 9, 1997

Regrettably, history is strewn with the visions of such "new eras" that, in the end, have proven to be a mirage. In short, history counsels caution.

ALAN GREENSPAN, chairman of the Federal Reserve Board, testifying to Congress, cited in the *Financial Times,* September 9, 1997

There are limits. They may not be the old limits that disciplined policy in the past. But even if the limits are new, they must be respected. Overheating is a natural product of expansions that overtax these limits. Recessions typically follow overheating. Good policy must therefore balance regularities and possibilities.

LAURENCE H. MEYER, Federal Reserve Board Governor, quoted in the *New York Times,* September 18, 1997

It's easy to be sucked into the "new era thinking" of something special going on with corporate profitability.

MARTIN BARNES of the Canadian firm Bank Credit Analyst Research Group, quoted in the *Wall Street Journal,* September 23, 1997

There is no evidence that the business cycle has been repealed.

ALAN GREENSPAN, chairman of the Federal Reserve Board, quoted in the *Wall Street Journal,* February 27, 1997

The law of supply and demand has not been repealed. If labor demand continues to outpace sustainable increases in supply, the question is surely when, not whether, labor costs will rise rapidly.

ALAN GREENSPAN, chairman of the Federal Reserve Board, before Congress, October 8, 1997, cited in the *Financial Times,* October 9, 1997

Profits cannot rise relative to GDP forever.

DAVID WYSS, of DRI, a unit of the rating firm Standard & Poors, quoted in the *Wall Street Journal,* October 9, 1997

Too many economists want to put a wall around the economy and believe that the productive elements are locked within those limits.

> WILLIAM HUDSON, president of the electronics company AMP, vice chairman of the National Association of Manufacturers, quoted by Reuters, October 23, 1997

When you have overcapacity, you have low inflation. I don't believe that that will last forever and that therefore recessions are a thing of the past.

> LAWRENCE BOSSIDY, CEO of the industrial company Allied-Signal and chairman of the Business Council, quoted by Reuters, October 23, 1997

13.4 DEMOGRAPHERS

The only professional group with a worse record [than demographers] are the economists.

> CALVIN BEALE, U.S. Agriculture Department demographer, quoted in the *Wall Street Journal*, January 29, 1985

We're just more honest than the economists in admitting how badly we do.

> PETER MORRISON of the policy analysis firm Rand Corporation, quoted in the *Wall Street Journal*, January 29, 1985

Pity those who must extrapolate for a living. The electricity industry is a compulsive extrapolator. Because power stations take so long to build, it must forecast demand a decade or more ahead. Twice in recent years it has proved spectacularly bad at this . . . The rising price of energy, slow economic growth, and the rise in importance of low-energy industries meant that energy demand leveled off . . .

Three things devil extrapolations: politics, technology, and self-correction.

> *The Economist*, December 21, 1991

13.5 ECONOMISTS AND ECONOMICS

Practical men, who believe themselves to be quite exempt from any intellectual influences, are usually the slaves of some defunct economist.

> The late JOHN MAYNARD KEYNES, economist often considered defunct

If all economists were laid end to end, they would not reach a conclusion.

> GEORGE BERNARD SHAW, playwright and Fabian thinker

I was in search of a one-armed economist so that the guy could never make a statement and then say: "On the other hand . . ."

> PRESIDENT HARRY S. TRUMAN, repeated in *Time,* January 30, 1989

I learned more about economics from one South Dakota dust storm than I did in all my years in college.

> VICE PRESIDENT HUBERT HUMPHREY

1. "Economics is the dismal science." This was a favorite line of President Nixon's early in his administration, perhaps because that was the only thing his speechwriter, William Safire, knew about the subject. As time passed, both the president and his speechwriter learned more and gave up the cliché.

2. "As President Truman said, 'I wish I had a one-armed economist, so that he wouldn't say on the one hand and on the other hand.'" If that was what Truman wanted, he was wrong. . . . It is the president's role to decide what to do when no one "knows" what to do. It is the role of the president"s economic advisers to tell him of the options and of the *possible* consequences of his decision. It is their role to tell him that on the one hand this might happen and on the other hand that might happen.

3. "Economists never agree." This is sometimes buttressed with a quotation attributed to George Bernard Shaw, that if all economists were laid end to end, they would not reach a conclusion.

> HERBERT STEIN, economist, on the clichés used by noneconomists in introducing economists to an audience, *Fortune,* reprinted in Henry Ehrlich, *Writing Effective Speeches* (Paragon House, 1992)

In economics, hope and faith coexist with great scientific pretension and also a deep desire for respectability.

> JOHN KENNETH GALBRAITH, economist, *New York Times Magazine,* June 7, 1970

Like Maynard Keynes, [economist] Friedrich von Hayek achieved far less for what he wrote than for what others said he wrote.

> Obituary of Hayek, in the *Economist,* March 28, 1992

My father started me milking cows while I was still a small boy. I learned the relationship between hard work and a quart of milk. All else in economics is an embellishment of this primary lesson.

> LEONARD E. READ, quoted in Richard M. Huber, *The American Idea of Success* (McGraw-Hill, 1971)

In the mid-1980s monetarism was reported dead and buried. In 1991 the vampire clambered out of its grave.

> *The Economist,* December 21, 1991

[D]espite our years of learning and our efforts at education, we [doctors and central bankers] still find our patients and clients longing for relief, turning with distressing frequency to today's equivalent of snake oil and witchcraft.

> PAUL VOLCKER, chairman of the U.S. Federal Reserve Board, speaking to an audience of doctors, quoted in the *Wall Street Journal,* January 2, 1985

We have learned that the various schools of thought all have important elements of truth in them. But none of them is by itself a sufficient explanation of what goes on in the economy.

> MICHAEL BOSKIN, chairman of the President's Council of Economic Advisors, quoted in *Time,* January 30, 1989

The economics profession is the only one in which a man can rise to preeminence and never be right.

> GEORGE MEANY, former head of the labor union AFL-CIO, quoted by Colby Chandler, former CEO of Eastman Kodak, in a speech, April 6, 1989

An economist without his numbers is like [O. J. Simpson's lawyer] Johnnie Cochran without his rhyming couplets.

> Heard on National Public Radio during partial shutdown of U.S. government when the government couldn't issue economic statistics, January 5, 1996

When an economist looks at an economy, it's something like a physician examining a patient. It's a very serious business. A good doctor doesn't tell you what you want to hear.

> MURRAY WEIDENBAUM, director of the Center for the Study of American Business, Washington University, in a speech, September 16, 1992

[C]onflict between what the public wants and what economists can deliver explains why economists continue to face ridicule at the same time they are courted by government, business, and the media.

> GARY S. BECKER of the University of Chicago, *Business Week,* February 2, 1987

At Chicago, they do revolution.

> PROFESSOR RUDIGER DORNBUSCH of MIT, economist, on the University of Chicago economics department, which has produced 10 Nobel Prize winners since 1974

I think the essence of being an economist, especially a Chicago economist, has to do with learning to turn off all your emotions and say, "Let's think abstractly about adoption or crime." We have a name for people who are innately really good at this. They're psychopaths, people who are incapable of feeling guilt, or remorse, or any emotional reaction.

> PAUL M. ROMER, senior fellow of the Hoover Institution, *Worth,* September 1996

Economists tend to attribute some condition to changes in technology (or taxes) when they don't have a good explanation.

> WILLIAM NISKANEN, chairman of the Cato Institute, libertarian think tank, quoted in *Slate,* September 12, 1996

Our best hope is probably to make the self-interested part of our economic system as smooth running as possible, so that more and more of our conscious effort can be directed toward the solution of those problems that cannot be resolved without explicit ethical considerations.

> PROFESSOR WILLIAM VICKREY of Columbia University in 1950, a 1996 Nobel Prize winner who died three days after his award was announced, quoted in the *Boston Globe,* October 13, 1996

Now we know that he [Vickrey] is an obsolete socialist, representing all the values that collapsed with the Berlin Wall.

> SPEAKER OF THE U.S. HOUSE OF REPRESENTATIVES NEWT GINGRICH, after Vickrey won the Nobel Prize but before he died, quoted in the *Boston Globe,* October 13, 1996

Most corporate executives don't listen to economists, in part because the professionals get it wrong. Instead, they make their decisions based on gut feeling.

NOEL PERRY, former corporate economist, November 30, 1987

Neoclassical economics . . . has uncovered important truths about the nature of money and markets because its fundamental model of rational self-interested human behavior is correct about 80 percent of the time. But there is a missing 20 percent of human behavior about which neoclassical economics can give only a poor account.

FRANCIS FUKUYAMA, *Trust: The Social Virtues and the Creation of Prosperity* (The Free Press, 1995)

[E]conomists are very biased people. They tend to believe numbers that support their outlook, and to question statistics that suggest they are wrong.

DR. EDWARD YARDEMI, chief economist of the investment firm C. J. Lawrence, quoted in *Forbes,* June 22, 1992

Economists love preaching about policy. The trouble is, not many of them know much about it.

HOWARD PARAMETER, Lucky Goldstar Fellow in economics at the Chaotic Strategy Institute of Deadwood, Kansas, in a spoof dialogue between an economist and a management scientist, quoted in the *Economist,* December 21, 1991

The "market basket" of goods and services is updated only once a decade, based on a huge survey of people's spending. But buying patterns regularly change, in part because consumers buy more of things that become cheaper. If renting videocassettes costs less than going to movies, people will rent more. The CPI understates such changes, because the "market basket" is revised only periodically. Similar gaps arise from new products. In the early years, their prices tend to drop rapidly. The CPI often misses these, because the products aren't yet in the "market basket." Microwave ovens were included only in 1978, VCRs and personal computers only in 1987. Worse, quality improvements in all products are usually ignored, because they're hard to gauge in relation to price. New drugs may replace costly surgery; the CPI misses that. New refrigerators may use less electricity than the old; the CPI misses that.

ROBERT J. SAMUELSON, *Newsweek,* October 23, 1996

I have a good suggestion on how you can reduce the cost of burials—sell your dying parents . . . for dog meat. You'll save $5,000—you might even get a few hundred dollars for their cadavers . . . We don't do it and it's not because it wouldn't be economically efficient—we don't do it because the thought revolts us. There is such thing as morality and morality is higher than economics [applause].

ROBERT FOGEL of the University of Chicago, 1993 Nobel Prize winner, on National Public Radio's *All Things Considered,* October 12, 1993

Slavery was a highly efficient system of production. It was very immoral and one of the things that I did was to point out that this was a system that market forces, by themselves, would not have brought to an end.

ROBERT FOGEL of the University of Chicago, 1993 Nobel Prize winner, on National Public Radio's *All Things Considered,* October 12, 1993

John Maynard Keynes showed that full employment is not the natural outcome of a market equilibrium. To bring about full employment, an economy needs government policies specifically designed for the purpose. Some of these may not be sustainable in the long run. Keynes' favorite prescription, fiscal stimulation through increased government spending, no longer works, since financial markets have developed an allergic reaction to such increases. If he were alive today Keynes would prescribe a different remedy, but he would understand that the invisible hand will not get us to a happy equilibrium.

GEORGE SOROS, "Can Europe Work?" *Foreign Affairs,* September–October 1996.

There are three kinds of economists: those who can count and those who can't.

Old joke

We insist on at least a three-to-four year cleansing experience [of work after graduate school] to neutralize the brainwashing that takes place in these graduate programs.

STEPHEN ROACH, chief economist the investment bank Morgan Stanley, quoted in the *New Yorker,* December 2, 1996

With the blinds closed, it's hard to see anything.

LAURENCE MEYER, Federal Reserve Board Governor and former head of a forecasting firm, criticizing approach of neoclassical economists, quoted in the *New Yorker*, December 2, 1996

Economists are like dairy farmers. We think we deserve every penny we get.

> PROFESSOR GREG MANKIW of Harvard University, quoted in the *New Yorker*, December 2, 1996

Our results indicate that rational decision theory cannot explain contestant behavior on *The Price is Right*.

> *American Economic Review*, journal devoted heavily to game theory, quoted in the *New Yorker*, December 2, 1996

Our data are weakest in precisely those areas where economic change has been most dynamic, such as technological innovation, the service sector, and trade.

> ZVI GRILICHES of Harvard University, quoted in *Fortune*, March 8, 1996

Market economics enshrines individual choice and lionizes the individual. Carried to its extreme, it all but suggests that anything the individual really feels like doing can't be wrong. It is a branch of 1960s ideology in formal dress.

> ALAN EHRENHALT, executive editor of *Governing*, quoted in the *New York Times*, February 23, 1997

Economics is giving elegant answers to questions that may or may not matter.

> *Wall Street Journal*, November 21, 1994

Economists, when they seek to be profound, often succeed only in being wrong.

> JOHN KENNETH GALBRAITH, *The Great Crash* (Houghton Mifflin, 1955)

Most financial models assume that people are relentlessly logical maximizers of their financial wealth. Well, I have been in this business for 34 years and I have yet to meet the famous Rational Economic Man theorists describe. Real people have always done inexplicable things from time to time, and they show no sign of stopping.

> CHARLES S. SANFORD JR., former CEO of Bankers Trust, in a speech, October 1994

Fortunately . . . nobody has yet suggested that economists actually be allowed to manage anything.

> *The Economist*, on the misuse of economists by industrialists, who look to them as fortune-tellers instead of business analysts, June 14, 1997

If your job is forecasting recessions, you've got a pretty sleepy job.

> PAUL BLOTZ, of the mutual fund firm T. Rowe Price Associates, quoted in the *New York Times,* September 18, 1997

Ten Principles of Economics

1. People face tradeoffs.
2. The cost of something is what you give up to get it.
3. Rational people think at the margin.
4. People respond to incentives.
5. Trade can make everyone better off.
6. Markets are usually a good way to organize economic activity.
7. Governments can sometimes improve market outcomes.
8. A country's standard of living depends on its ability to produce goods and services.
9. Prices rise when the government prints too much money.
10. Society faces a short-run tradeoff between inflation and unemployment.

> GREGORY MANKIW of Harvard University, *Principles of Economics* (Dryden Press, 1997) predicted to become the staple economic textbook of the future, cited in *Fortune*, October 13, 1997

A depression is either a 12 percent unemployment rate for nine months or more, or a 15 percent unemployment rate for three to nine months.

> ALAN GREENSPAN, 1982, quoted by William Safire, *New York Times Magazine*, November 23, 1997

[A depression is] unemployment above 10 percent with two quarters of consecutive decline in real G.N.P.

> PROFESSOR ALFRED KAHN of Cornell University, and former economist in the Carter administration, 1982, cited by William Safire, *New York Times Magazine*, November 23, 1997

13.6 THE ECONOMY, STUPID

I think this may be the best economy in U.S. history and probably the world.

> ALLEN SINAI, Wall Street economist, quoted in *Fortune*, June 9, 1997

13.7 EMPLOYMENT TRENDS

It is now clear that if present trends continue, by the turn of the century workforces in the United States, Australia, indeed throughout the industrial world, will increasingly stratify into two separate blocs. Fundamentally, people with high skills will earn high wages and people with low skills will earn low wages or no wages at all.

> LAWRENCE PERLMAN, CEO of the information and defense electronics firm Ceridian Corporation, in a speech, March 24, 1995

It [working in a variety of jobs] is wonderful, exhilarating, rewarding, and challenging. And it is also horrible, demeaning, thankless, and boring.

> KAREN MENDENHALL, *Making the Most Out of the Temporary Employment Market* (Betterway, 1993), quoted in *Fortune,* January 24, 1994

13.8 THE FEDERAL RESERVE AND CENTRAL BANKING

There have been three great inventions since the beginning of time: fire, the wheel, and central banking.

> The humorist WILL ROGERS

You've got all the cards when you trade for the Fed.

> PAUL VOLCKER, former chairman of the Federal Reserve Board, quoted in *Time,* January 23, 1989

When a system of national currencies run by central banks is transformed into a global electronic marketplace driven by currency traders, power changes hands.

> WALTER B. WRISTON, former chairman of Citicorp, in a speech, January 25, 1993

Once again, Chairman Greenspan and the Federal Reserve have mugged America.

> U.S. REPRESENTATIVE HENRY GONZALES (Democrat, Texas) then head of the House Banking Committee, after an interest-rate hike, quoted in *Business Week,* August 29, 1994

It's a tempting suggestion [to shut up], but I'm trying to resist it.

> ALAN BLINDER, then vice chairman of the U.S. Federal Reserve Board, quoted in *Business Week,* September 26, 1994

The advantage of having credibility is that it lets you cheat when you want to.

> LOUIS CRANDALL of the investment firm R. H. Wrightson & Associates, on Fed's decision not to raise interest rates during 1996 presidential campaign, quoted in the *New York Times,* October 3, 1996

People are always searching for the Holy Grail, the magic statistic that swings the Fed.

> ALAN BLINDER, former vice chairman of the U.S. Federal Reserve Board, on life after the Fed, quoted in the *Wall Street Journal,* October 22, 1996

Cyclical conditions in the U.S. economy are more favorable than at any time in the past 25 years, a combination for which the Federal Reserve is primarily responsible. President Clinton's main contribution has been his uncharacteristic reluctance to nag the Fed.

> WILLIAM NISKANEN, chairman of the libertarian think tank Cato Institute, quoted in *Slate,* September 11, 1996

Relative values of national currencies are increasingly set by the market rather than by government policy. More and more private institutions are moving to create new forms of money, such as stored-value cards, that are beyond the control of governments.

So one has to wonder if it will be possible for governments to have effective monetary policies in the future.

> WILLIAM DAVIDOW, "Does Money Exist?" quoted in *Forbes,* June 3, 1996

It's very hard to surgically prick a balloon. You may let out a lot more air than you bargained for.

> ALAN BLINDER, former vice chairman of the U.S. Federal Reserve Board, quoted in the *Wall Street Journal,* November 25, 1996

How do we know when irrational exuberance has unduly escalated asset values, which then become subject to unexpected and prolonged contractions as they have in Japan over the past decade?

> ALAN GREENSPAN, chairman of the U.S. Federal Reserve Board, in a speech, December 5, 1996

The current world monetary system assigns no special role to gold; indeed, the Federal Reserve is not obliged to tie the dollar to anything. It can print as much or as little money as it deems appropriate. There are powerful advantages to such an unconstrained system. Above all, the Fed is free to respond to actual or threatened recessions by pumping in money. To take only one example, that flexibility is the reason the stock market crash of 1987—which started out every bit as frightening as that of 1929—did not cause a slump in the real economy.

PROFESSOR PAUL KRUGMAN of MIT, *Slate,* November 22, 1996

A central banker cannot be exempted from one very basic fact: In the long run inflation is essentially a monetary phenomenon. . . . Accordingly, the best approach is to maintain a steady course with an appropriate level of restraint. Countries whose currencies are widely used internationally, like the United States, have a special responsibility to provide an anchor of stability for themselves and the world at large.

ALAN GREENSPAN, chairman of the Federal Reserve Board, in a speech, quoted in the *New York Times,* January 14, 1997

I spend a substantial amount of my time endeavoring to fend off questions, and worry terribly that I might end up being too clear. [Case in point: "We should endeavor to gain long-term sustainable growth at its maximum level, and that we should be continuously observing the internal structure of the economy—the financial aspects of it, the inflationary aspects of it—to make judgments as to whether we are straining the system. The question isn't, is a certain amount of growth a ceiling which we should not endeavor to go beyond; but more importantly, try to evaluate as we look at the economy whether it is moving forward in a reasonably solid, non-destabilizing sense, in which case what we're saying is that's good growth—or whether we're looking at imbalances which are creating the seeds of some major structural change which would contract the economy and raise the unemployment rate."—January 31, 1994]

ALAN GREENSPAN, chairman of the Federal Reserve Board, June 20, 1995, quoted in the *New York Times,* January 4, 1996

The reasons why central bankers have certain currencies in reserve is because these are the currencies they intervene with.

AVINASH PERSAUD of the banking firm JP Morgan, quoted in the *Financial Times,* September 9, 1997

Preparing the speech is a joy. Giving the speech is fun. Dealing with the aftermath of the speech is the only thing where there's stress.

LAURENCE H. MEYER, Federal Reserve Board Governor, quoted in the *Wall Street Journal,* April 25, 1997

All of a sudden, your platitudes are quoted all over the wires. I could get up there and read Samuelson [introductory economics textbook] and it'd be on Reuters and Bloomberg and it might move the markets.

ALICE RIVLIN, vice chairman of the Federal Reserve, quoted in the *Wall Street Journal,* April 25, 1997

The Federal Reserve has an extremely strong culture of its own, like any central bank. If you really want to have any influence over policy you have to subscribe to the norm.

PROFESSOR ALLAN MELTZER of Carnegie-Mellon University, quoted in the *Financial Times,* January 16, 1997

A strong chairman really has the opportunity to be the dominant voice on the board. It is very hard for another board member to oppose his line.

GEORGE PERRY, former president of the Council of Economic Advisors, quoted in the *Financial Times,* January 16, 1997

[R]ecent research strongly indicates that central banks which are much more independent from the political process are associated with lower inflation rates over longer periods.

GAVYN DAVIES, chief economist of the investment bank Goldman, Sachs, quoted in the *Financial Times,* October 22, 1997

What I say to people who now say we went too far in late 1987 is "You should have been there! We could have had a complete deflationary disaster on our hands. You just can't take those kinds of risks."

MANUEL JOHNSON, deputy to Fed chairman Alan Greenspan in 1987, on the Fed's actions following the October 19 crash, quoted in the *Financial Times,* October 16, 1997

You have to remember, the last 18 years are probably the first 18 years in history where the Federal Reserve was intent on killing inflation. And nothing kills the value of financial assets more vehemently than inflation.

> RICHARD BERNSTEIN of the investment firm Merrill Lynch, quoted in the *New York Times*, January 6, 1998

13.9 THE FEDERAL RESERVE AND DIVERSITY

The place is just permeated with white maleness.

> Ex-Fed staff member, quoted in *Business Week*, January 10, 1994

We've got good women and minorities coming up the pipeline, but it takes 20 years [for them] to get to the top.

> THEODORE E. ALLISON, coordinator of regional Federal Reserve banks, quoted in *Business Week*, January 10, 1994

13.10 THE FEDERAL RESERVE BY THE NUMBERS

The Fed has 25,000 employees, runs its own air force of 47 Learjets and small cargo planes, and has fleets of vehicles, including personal cars for 59 Fed bank managers.

> JOHN R. WILKE, *Wall Street Journal*, September 12, 1996

13.11 FORECASTING

We've seen a lot of banks and corporations that assume the world is stable and predictable. They also assume that factors outside their control will never be harmful to them, that markets will always be there for them and for everyone else. They also assume that they can predict interest rates.

> EUGENE ROTBERG, then head of the World Bank, quoted in *Forbes*, May 19, 1986

While Albert Einstein is queuing to enter heaven, he meets three men. He asks about their IQs. The first replies, 190. "Wonderful," exclaims Einstein. "We can discuss my theory of relativity." The second answers 150. "Good," says Einstein. "I look forward to discussing the prospects for world peace." The third mumbles

50. Einstein pauses. "So what is your forecast for GDP growth next year?"

> *The Economist*, June 13, 1992

Economists are about as useful as astrologers in predicting the future (and, like astrologers, they never let failure on one occasion diminish certitude on the next).

> ARTHUR SCHLESINGER JR., quoted in the *New York Times*, April 15, 1993

There is nothing in classical economic theory that will lead you to believe you can predict the future.

> KARL BRUNNER of the University of Rochester, quoted in *Fortune*, June 12, 1995

The further ahead you forecast, the less well you do.

> C.W. J. GRANGER of the University of California, San Diego, quoted in *Fortune*, January 25, 1996

Historically, every year gold prices go up relative to the year before, interest rates tend to move up the following year.

> MICHAEL COSGROVE, who writes the economic newsletter *The Econoclast*, who made the most accurate interest rate forecast for the first half of 1996, quoted in the *Wall Street Journal*, July 1, 1996

Over the past 25 years, economic forecasters have missed four of the past five recessions.

> *Business Week*, September 30, 1996

The commercial forecasters would simply do better if they could discard their own forecasts and use the Fed's.

> CHRISTINA and DAVID ROMER, in a study for the U.S. National Bureau of Economic Research, cited in the *Financial Times*, April 1, 1997

What lies ahead? I always taught my students that here was an answer that worked remarkably well most of the time to interesting questions in economics: It depends.

> LAURENCE MEYER, quoted in the *Wall Street Journal*, April 25, 1997

We were in nirvana as economists in the early '80s. . . . Forecasting is not what we do best.

> BERNARD M. MARKSTEIN, a consultant who used to work for a bank, quoted in the *New York Times*, September 18, 1997

13.12 INFLATION AND DEFLATION

I am an advocate of paper money, but that paper money must represent what it professes on its face. I do not wish to hold in my hands the printed lies of government.

FORMER U.S. PRESIDENT JAMES A. GARFIELD, then a congressman, speaking in Congress, 1866

Patriotism is no substitute for a sound currency.

FORMER U.S. PRESIDENT GROVER CLEVELAND, 1892

There are plenty of good five-cent cigars in the country. The trouble is they cost a quarter. What this country really needs is a good five-cent nickel.

FRANKLIN P. ADAMS, quoted in Robert E. Drennan, *The Algonquin Wits* (Citadel Press, 1989)

Inflation is the one form of taxation that can be imposed without legislation.

Technically, inflation isn't terribly hard to stop. The real problem is that the favorable effects of inflation come early, the bad effects late. In a way, it's like drink. The first few months or years of inflation, like the first few drinks, seem just fine.

When you start to take some action against inflation, the bad effects are felt right away.

MILTON FRIEDMAN, Nobel Prize–winning economist, interviewed in *Playboy*, February 1973

How to hedge against inflation.

Eat right, get plenty of sleep, and see your doctor for an annual checkup. The chemicals in your body, which sold for just 98 cents in 1936, are now worth $5.60.

PETER PASSELL, in an essay written in the mid-1970s, cited in *Fortune*, July 8, 1996

Since 1933 consumer prices have risen by 950 percent in America and by 4,000 percent in Britain. To put this another way, the dollar today is worth only 10 cents in 1933 money, and the pound worth a paltry 2 1/2 pence.

So far as economic growth is concerned, the volatility of inflation matters as much as its level. An inflation rate that averages zero percent, but which swings from plus to minus 10 percent, is as damaging as one that swings between 10 percent and 30 percent—the more volatile inflation is, the more uncertainty it creates, and this discourages investment.

"A Short History of Inflation," *The Economist*, February 22, 1992

We found that the economy doesn't work properly with zero inflation, if productivity growth is also low.

If you get there on purpose, or you stumble there as they did in Japan, you create serious inefficiencies in the labor market.

GEORGE PERRY of the liberal think tank Brookings Institution, quoted in the *Wall Street Journal*, August 13, 1996

Whether higher growth leads to more inflation or less inflation depends on what produces the higher growth. If the higher growth comes from easy monetary policy, it will indeed tend to lead to more inflation. On the other hand, if, in the context of a stable monetary policy, the higher growth is produced by greater capital investment, technological improvements, deregulation, increasing flexibility of prices, increased competition or a host of other real changes, such growth will lead to lower inflation or even deflation. Why? Because such growth would mean that the same amount of purchasing power was competing for more goods, which would tend to drive prices lower.

MILTON FRIEDMAN, Nobel Prize-winning economist, *Wall Street Journal*, September 24, 1996

Inflation will work as a lubricant only if it fools people into believing that they are better off than they really are.

GORDON THIESSEN, head of Canada's central bank, quoted in the *New York Times*, November 9, 1996

Technology is not the answer there [to lack of inflationary pressures], unless the fear of being made obsolete by technology restrains people from demanding higher wages. And that's the dark side of technology, not the positive side.

PROFESSOR PAUL KRUGMAN of MIT, quoted in the *New York Times*, October 5, 1997

Adjusted for inflation . . . *Cleopatra* cost 219 million 1995 dollars, a solid 25 percent more than the reported high-end estimate of $175 million for *Waterworld. E.T.*'s gross revenues were 632 million 1995 dollars, vs. $2.11 billion for *Gone with the Wind*.

DAVID HENDERSON, *Fortune*, March 18, 1996

This deflation thing could be big, if it really gets going.

PROFESSOR RUDI DORNBUSCH of MIT, quoted in the *New York Times*, December 4, 1997

Even a moderate rate of inflation can hamper economic performance. Moderate rates of deflation would most probably lead to similar problems.

> ALAN GREENSPAN, chairman of the Federal Reserve Board, quoted in the *New York Times,* January 4, 1998

Deflation is the easiest thing in the world to avoid; you just print more money.

You can have mild depression, but it needn't be depression. From 1879 to 1896 prices in the United States fell by an average of 3 percent a year. From 1896 to 1914 they rose by an average of 3 percent a year. The economic rate of growth was identical in the two periods. So it's pretty clear that deflation doesn't mean depression.

> MILTON FRIEDMAN, Nobel Prize–winning economist, interviewed in *Forbes,* December 29, 1997

3.13 MONETARY POLICY

The implementation of monetary policy actions has much in common with sailing. Just as watching the crew adjust the sails provides little information about the boat's destination, the techniques surrounding the monetary policy process provide little information about the outcome.

> JERRY L. JORDAN, president of the Federal Reserve Board of Cleveland, in a speech, May 4, 1992

13.14 THE NATIONAL DEBT

A national debt if it is not excessive will be to us a national blessing; it will be powerful cement of our union. It will also create a necessity for keeping up taxation to a degree which without being oppressive, will be a spur to industry.

> ALEXANDER HAMILTON (who later became Treasury Secretary), 1781

I sincerely believe . . . that banking establishments are more dangerous than standing armies, and that the principle of spending money to be paid by posterity, under the name of funding, is but swindling futurity on a large scale.

> THOMAS JEFFERSON, in a letter, May 28, 1816

It is incumbent on every generation to pay its own debts as it goes. A principle which, if acted on, would save one-half the wars of the world.

> THOMAS JEFFERSON, 1820

There are but two ways of paying debt: increase of industry in raising income, increase of thrift in laying out.

> THOMAS CARLYLE, *Past and Present* (1843)

Blessed are the young, for they shall inherit the national debt.

> PRESIDENT HERBERT HOOVER

The debt is like a crazy aunt we keep down in the basement. All the neighbors know she's there, but nobody wants to talk about her.

> H. ROSS PEROT, *United We Stand: How We Can Take Back Our Country* (Hyperion, 1992)

3.15 PRODUCTIVITY

[E]very new method which leads by a shorter road to wealth, every machine which spares labor, every instrument which diminishes the cost of production, every discovery which facilitates pleasures or augments them seems to be the grandest effort of the human intellect.

> ALEXIS DE TOCQUEVILLE, *Democracy in America,* 1835–1840

Productivity is misunderstood by many in the financial and media communities. They don't question its importance intellectually, but they see it as a function of, as they put it, squeezing the grape, taking out people, restructuring, rationalizing, things that have defined limits. But the greatest productivity growth in our company's history will come in 1989—a year of stable employment levels and relatively low volume growth.

> JOHN F. WELCH JR., CEO of GE, in a speech, November 1989

How does a government measure capital formation, when much new capital is intellectual? How does it measure the productivity of knowledge workers whose product cannot be counted on your fingers? If it cannot do that, how can it track productivity growth? How does it track or control the money supply when the financial markets create new financial instruments faster than the regulators can keep track of them? And if it cannot do these things with the relative precision of simpler times, what becomes of the great mission of modern governments: controlling and manipulating the national economy?

> WALTER B. WRISTON, former CEO of Citicorp, in a speech, January 25, 1993

If 2 percent of the population can grow all the food we eat, what if another 2 percent can manufacture all the refrigerators and other things we need?

> GEORGE BENNETT of consulting firm Symmetrix, quoted in *Fortune,* December 13, 1993

Government statistics treat spending on the intellectual capabilities of the workforce no differently than spending on candy bars. The data suggests that a company is deemed to be investing if it purchases a new machine, but not if it pays for the employee training needed to use that machine efficiently.

> HENRY KELLY and ANDREW WYCKOFF of the government Office of Technology Assessment, *Atlantic Monthly,* March 1994

It undercounts the number of workers on the factory floor and overcounts those in the service sector.

> STEPHEN ROACH, chief economist of Morgan Stanley, on the flaws in the method of counting and categorizing jobs, *Wall Street Journal,* September 20, 1996 (The same jobs labeled "manufacturing" on a company payroll are called "service" when outsourced.)

There is a big debate whether productivity growth in manufacturing is okay and whether that in nonmanufacturing is not okay.

> PROFESSOR JOHN HALTIWANGER of the University of Maryland, quoted in the *Wall Street Journal*, September 20, 1996

Productivity is not a household term, but it should be. Many workers think productivity means "the boss wants me to work harder." But actually productivity— the value of goods or services produced per hour of work—grows mainly through time-saving innovations, more and better equipment, greater knowledge, advanced skills, and more efficient organizations.

> PROFESSOR JOHN B. TAYLOR of Stanford University, quoted in the *Wall Street Journal,* October 18, 1996

Bill Gates probably has more to do, for good or ill, with the growth of productivity than Bill Clinton. Anyone who has spent time sitting in front of a computer screen, as we are doing, must frequently have thought that the new technology is a drag on productivity.

> HERBERT STEIN, economist, *Slate,* September 11, 1996

[G]enerating more output by working longer hours fails the test of meaningful production gains.

> "Technology and the 24-hour Day," *Harvard Business Review,* September–October 1996

Knowledge applied to existing processes, services, and products is productivity; knowledge applied to the new is innovation.

> PETER DRUCKER, in an interview, *HotWired 1.3,* 1996

A couple hundred years ago, bureaucracy seemed like a good idea. . . . Nowadays when a CEO of a company can look at a computer screen and realize what the sales per square foot, per employee, per unit, per minute for every robot or whatever it is across the company across the world, then all of a sudden we don't need all those middle-manager bureaucrat types in between.

> JAMES P. PINKERTON, journalist, in a speech, New York City, February 7, 1996

Conventional wisdom has long held that there are few opportunities for leverage in professional activities.
[A]dding professionals at the very least multiplies costs at the same rate as benefits. In the past, growth most often brought diseconomies of scale as the bureaucracies coordinating, monitoring, or supporting the professionals expanded faster than the professional base. Universities, hospitals, research firms, accounting groups, and consultancies all seemed to pay the price.

> PROFESSORS JAMES BRIAN QUINN, PHILIP ANDERSON, and SYDNEY FINKELSTEIN, of Amos Tuck School of Business, Dartmouth, *Harvard Business Review,* March–April 1996

Gaining productivity is not like squeezing a lemon. You have to find a new way of gaining productivity every time.

> UWE WASCHER of GE Plastics in Europe, quoted in *Fortune,* September 9, 1996

The numbers must be wrong; they must be understated. There is no way we could have had the outstanding economic performance this country has had over the last couple of years if those numbers were remotely accurate.

> BRUCE STEINBERG, chief economist of Merrill Lynch, reacting to U.S. Labor Department measurement of productivity growth of six-tenths of one percent in the second quarter of 1997, quoted in the *New York Times* August 13, 1997

In a random survey of 500 small-business employees, 37 percent identified Norm Peterson, the barfly from the sitcom *Cheers,* as the most unproductive worker on television. Thirty-one percent picked Homer Simpson of *The Simpsons,* and 23 percent chose George Costanza of *Seinfeld.*

> *Wall Street Journal,* September 9, 1997

The main reason the service sector has not reached its total potential output is management. If managers were focused energetically and intelligently on putting the existing technologies, labor force, and capital stock to work, rapid productivity growth would follow.

> MICHAEL VAN BIEMA and BRUCE GREENWALD, Columbia Business School, *Harvard Business Review,* July–August 1997

Martin Luther got all his best ideas on the toilet; is that work? Work is less structured today than it was 30 years ago, when time clocks were more prevalent, but government data is still based on the structure of work in the old days.

> DANIEL HAMERMESH of the University of Texas, Austin, *New York Times,* October 5, 1997

There is no question that a raise is a better deal than more hours on the job, when you consider that a 5 percent raise is the equivalent of two and one-half extra weeks of work.

> STEVEN ROSE, senior economist of Educational Testing Service, quoted in the *New York Times,* October 5, 1997

They should make profits, but not like weasels stomping in a field of gold.

> DAVID YATTAW, president of union local at Buick, on GM's plans to build too many cars with too few people, quoted in *Business Week,* October 10, 1994

It takes less labor to display a four-pack than to set out one tube at a time. And a cashier can ring up four tubes in the same time it would take to ring up one. We pass along those savings on to the customer.

> CRAIG JELINEK of the discount retail chain Price/Costco, quoted in *Fortune,* May 29, 1995

13.16 RECESSION AND DEPRESSION

Innovating economies expand and develop. Economies that do not add new kinds of goods and services, but continue only to repeat old work, do not expand much nor do they, by definition, develop.

> JANE JACOBS, *The Economy of Cities* (Random House, 1969)

Busts are not only preceded by booms; fundamentally they are caused by them.

> JAMES GRANT, editor of *Grant's Interest Rate Observer,* quoted in the *Wall Street Journal,* January 5, 1998

13.17 STATISTICS

Far from being objective and trustworthy, statistics are often based on flimsy data and shaped by the prejudices of those who collect them.

> JOHN MICKLETHWAIT and ADRIAN WOOLDRIDGE, *The Witch Doctors* (Times Books, 1996)

[T]here's a problem with just statistics; one captured in capsule form on a university T-shirt I recently saw that read, "Torture the statistics long enough, and they'll confess to anything."

> C. MICHAEL ARMSTRONG, CEO of the high-tech firm Hughes Electronics Corporation, in a speech, February 11, 1997

13.18   THE TRANSFORMED ECONOMY

In the five years just past 143 companies have disappeared from the *Fortune* 500.

It took corporate raiders, activist public pension funds, advocacy groups of every stripe—and competition from every corner of the globe—to shake American business out of its lethargy.

> RALPH S. LARSEN, CEO of the pharmaceutical firm Johnson & Johnson, in a speech, October 22, 1992

Every major industry was once a growth industry.

They [railroads] let others take customers away from them because they assumed themselves to be in the railroad business rather than in the transportation business. The reason they defined their industry wrong was because they were railroad-oriented instead of transportation-oriented; they were product-oriented instead of customer-oriented.

> THEODORE LEVITT, of Harvard Business School, from "Marketing Myopia," *Harvard Business Review,* September–October 1975

In 1992, according to the Statistical Abstract of the United States, manufacturing output was 39 percent higher than in 1980 and 95 percent higher than in 1970.

> JOHN KLAWSON of the agricultural machinery manufacturer John Deere, in a speech, February 24, 1994

It happened to farmers 100 years ago. It happened to sweatshop workers at the early part of this century. Now it's us.

> STEPHEN ROACH, chief economist of the investment bank Morgan Stanley, on the Group of 7 jobs summit convened to address workplace changes that afflict modern workers, quoted in *Business Week,* March 21, 1994

White-collar workers think unions don't matter, but they're not on a separate boat from blue-collar ones.

> LAWRENCE MISHEL of the think tank Economic Policy Institute, quoted in *Business Week,* May 23, 1994

It used to be I'd go to parties and meet my friends' friends and we'd start sleeping together . . . Now my friends introduce their friends to each other's and we go into business together.

> STEFANIE SYMAN, co-editor of webzine *feed,* quoted in "The Great American Geek Rush," *New York,* November 3, 1995

There are some 550,000 computer programmers in America, according to the Labor Department's Bureau of Labor Statistics, about the same number as bus drivers, real estate agents, or house painters. [The number has increased 25 percent in 12 years and is likely to surpass 600,000 by 2005.]

> *New York Times,* September 9, 1996

It's hard to overstate the extent to which American manufacturing has become more competitive.

> JERRY JASINOWSKI, president of the National Association of Manufacturers, quoted in *Fortune,* February 19, 1996

Venture capitalists will tell you that it takes about $400,000 to create a job. If you take the nearly $30 billion raised by IPOs [initial public offerings] last year, that's the equivalent of 750,000 new jobs.

> MARK LACKRITZ, president of the Securities Industries Association, quoted in *Fortune,* May 27, 1996

As a nation, we already know enough about huge dysfunctional corporations—the kind whose managers seem to care more about what Wall Street thinks than about the long-term interests of their companies. Let's start paying more attention to what works in our economy: the small privately held growth companies.

> MARTHA E. MANGELSDORF, senior editor of *Inc.,* July 1996

Never has the world been more hospitable to industry revolutionaries and more hostile to industry incumbents.

> GARY HAMEL, chairman of the consulting firm Strategos, international consulting firm in California, quoted in *Harvard Business Review,* July–August 1996

[P]eople might be doing better than 20 years ago but they're being told they're worse off. A report by Michael Cox and Richard Allen of the Federal Reserve Bank of Dallas puts some perspective on this paradox.

Comparing 1970 and 1990, Cox and Allen found the following:

The average size of a new house went from 1,500 to 2,100 square feet.

People using computers rose from 100,000 to 76 million.

Households with VCRs went from zero to 67 million.

Attendance at symphonies and concerts rose from 13 million to 44 million.

The amount of time worked to buy gas for a 100-mile trip fell from 49 to 31 minutes.

People finishing high school [rose from] 52 percent to 78 percent.

People finishing college went from 14 percent to 24 percent.

And life expectancy: 71 to 75 years.

> DANA G. MEAD, CEO of the automotive and energy company Tenneco, in a speech, May 15, 1995

The motion picture industry has created more jobs since 1990 than all of America's motor vehicles and parts manufacturers, pharmaceutical companies, and hotel industry combined.

> JAMES ALEY, staff writer, quoted in *Fortune*, September 18, 1997

These [high-knowledge industries such as software] are industries that haven't just seen the future, they are the future.

> NUALA BECK, economic consultant, quoted in *Fortune*, September 18, 1995

Today, nearly 60 percent of all American workers are "knowledge workers"—and 8 out of 10 new jobs are in the information sectors of our economy.

> ROBERT F. GAULT, *Management Review*, October 1, 1996

The idea that "temp" workers are only low-wage people doing routine clerical work is a myth. Fact: each day more than 125,000 professionals go to work [as] part-time or "leased" employees—including contract attorneys, accountants, physicians, and environmental scientists.

> PHILLIP M. BURGESS, president of the think tank Center for the New West, in a speech, June 11, 1994

The best thing about being a temp is that it's the ultimate meritocracy. You don't have to worry about office politics. You don't have to worry about how long you have worked for a company. And you don't have to kiss up the boss.

> Employee, cited by John Chuang, CEO of the temporary employment agency Mac Temps, quoted in *Inc.*, November 1994

The new dominance of this technology-based, entrepreneurial economy harks back to 1979—a moment that will someday be recalled in the way we speak of the dawn of the industrial revolution. That was the year the payrolls of the largest *Fortune* 500 industrial companies peaked. Since then those payrolls have dropped by over 25 percent to less than 25 million jobs. At the same time an ostensibly invisible and unmeasured realm of the economy occupied by the high-growth, knowledge-based or technology-based ventures of entrepreneurs has accounted for over 24 million new jobs.

> WILLIAM WETZEL of the University of New Hampshire, quoted in *Worth*, December–January 1996

In one fell swoop [the 1986 tax code changes], we made real estate, the second largest investment pool in the world, a lousy investment.

> FRANK CAPPIELLO, president of McCullough, Andrews & Cappiello, *Worth on-line forum*

There's a lingering notion that somehow we have to bring back the buffalo. You do an elaborate rain dance and somehow you drag in a manufacturing plant.

> GARY GAPPERT of the University of Akron, quoted in the *Wall Street Journal*, February 1, 1985

Homes have tended to be very good collateral. But, of course, so at one time was the oil industry, so at one time was farming.

> ALLEN SINAI, of the investment firm Shearson-Lehman, quoted in *Forbes*, August 25, 1986

We have, since World War II, eliminated more than 1 million railroad jobs, yet we move 20 percent more freight on the rails. We have eliminated 300,000 jobs in mining, yet produce 50 percent more coal. We have cut textile mill jobs by 550,000 but are producing just as much cloth. Is our country the worse for it?

> PROFESSOR RICHARD B. MCKENZIE of Clemson University, quoted in *Forbes*, July 13, 1987

It's easier to waltz with a cow than to get a bank loan for a project that isn't pre-leased to a strong tenant.

> Real estate developer, quoted in *Fortune*, January 10, 1994

A key but undramatic crossover occurred in the 1980s. For the first time in over half a century, the magnitude of company-sponsored R&D exceeded the total of government-financed R&D.

The basic initiative in the global marketplace has shifted to private enterprise [since the end of the cold war].

> PROFESSOR MURRAY WEIDENBAUM of Washington University, in a speech, November 13, 1995

In the global economy created by a worldwide communications network, advantages that once were primary— geography, size, natural resources—become secondary, revealing the true competitive advantages: speed, service, innovation, and intelligence.

> JAMES G. CULLEN of the telecommunications firm Bell-Atlantic, in a speech, December 11, 1995

Rewards in the past decade have tilted dramatically toward providers of capital. We're kidding ourselves if we believe the free-market system works this way forever. I am a firm believer in the notion that extreme trends are breeding grounds for equally powerful countertrends. To prevent the pendulum from tipping dangerously into the populist realm, a critical reexamination of restructuring strategies takes on a new urgency for Corporate America.

> STEPHEN S. ROACH, chief economist of the investment bank Morgan Stanley, "A New Competitive Dilemma," *Wall Street Journal,* June 20, 1996

[O]ur balance sheets are meaningless. Our accounting system is still based on the assumption that 80 percent of our costs are manual labor. Even GM operates with only 28 percent manual labor. And the figure for the factory that's now on the drawing boards at Ford will be down to 11 percent. Not because it will be automated, but because they finally went to work and redesigned the process around information.

> PETER DRUCKER, in an interview in *HotWired 1.3,* 1996

We [the state of Connecticut] were exceptionally vulnerable to swings in federal funding for defense. If anything, by diversifying into tourism we may have exposed ourselves to downturns in other areas, but you would hope they wouldn't all go south at the same time.

> PROFESSOR EDWARD DEAK of Fairfield University, Connecticut, quoted in the *Wall Street Journal,* October 7, 1996

We're moving into an era when people will say what's good for Intel and Microsoft is good for the American economy.

> G. DAN HUTCHESON, of the research firm VLSI Research, quoted in the *Wall Street Journal,* September 30, 1996

It may come as a surprise to you but manufacturing is not in decline. Since World War II, manufacturing's base in the economy has remained remarkably stable, ranging from 20 percent to 23 percent of the GDP. Many goods are produced at the intermediate level for use in making other products. If you factor in this intermediate activity, manufacturing's share of the total economic activity in the United States rises to 31 percent.

> F. KENNETH IVERSON, CEO of the steel company Nucor, in a speech, February 5, 1996

If housing starts are 3.6 percent of GDP and the medical sector is 13 percent, why do we emphasize housing?

> NUALA BECK, *Shifting Gears: Thriving in the New Economy* (HarperCollins, 1992)

Adjustment is the dismal part of the dismal science.

> NEAL SOSS, chief economist of the investment bank First Boston, referring to the painful effects of radical changes in the economy, quoted in *Fortune,* December 13, 1993

Gone the heroic workman, a WPA mural in living flesh, ruddy in the glow of the blast furnace; now she's likely to be a middle-aged mom, sitting in front of a screen, who attends night school to study statistical process control.

> THOMAS A. STEWART, *Fortune,* December 13, 1993

We've always thought of "industrials" as meaning more than manufacturing. Now technological innovation and services of all types are major propellants of the United States economy.

> PAUL STEIGER, managing editor of the *Wall Street Journal,* on the replacement of Texaco, Bethlehem Steel, Woolworth, and Westinghouse in the Dow Jones industrial index with Hewlett-Packard, Travellers Group, Johnson & Johnson, and Wal-Mart, quoted in the *Financial Times,* March 13, 1997

Payroll Perspective on Big Employers

	1983	1994
GM	691,000	692,000
PepsiCo	154,000	471,000
UPS	124,200	320,000
Wal-Mart	62,000	600,000
GE	340,000	221,000
IBM	369,545	243,039
Sears	450,000	360,000
U.S. government	5,037,926	4,619,548

Fortune, December 25, 1995

The biggest issue facing the American worker today is not unemployment, but unemployability.

EARNEST DEAVENPORT, CEO of Eastman Chemical, in a speech, November 14, 1996

Any economy in which more individuals escape entrapment in sterile, bureaucratic corporate slots or menial roles and expand their potential can be argued to be morally superior.

GEORGE POSTE of the pharmaceutical firm Smith-Kline Beecham, in a speech, January 14, 1997

The past has ceased to be a predictor for the future.

WILLIAM BRAZILL, president of the forecasting firm Perception International, quoted in the *Wall Street Journal*, May 9, 1997

Most people assume that the jobs of the future will be related to the technologies of the future. They imagine that we will become a society of telecommuting nerds.

Historically, however, the opposite has happened: job growth tends to be greatest in the occupation that new technology affects the least. We have become supremely efficient at growing food; that is why there are so few farmers.

PROFESSOR PAUL KRUGMAN of MIT, quoted in the *New York Times*, August 31, 1997

Small manufacturers accounted for 24 percent of all employment in that sector back in 1972.

Given the rapid rate of contraction among businesses of all sizes, U.S. employers have to create 10 new jobs in order to produce one net new job.

Small Business Advocate, cited in *Inc.*, March 1995

Understanding the impact of the cold-war victory on the United States is the key to understanding every major economic trend now in operation in the United States.

WILLIAM WOLMAN and ANNE COLMOSCA, *The Judas Economy: The Triumph of Capitalism and the Betrayal of Work* (Addison-Wesley, 1997)

Almost 40 percent of the GDP growth is tied to the info-technology business.

JOHN K. SKEEN, of the investment firm Montgomery Securities, quoted in the *New York Times*, September 28, 1997

For more than a century, the world's wealthiest human being has been associated with oil—starting with John D. Rockefeller in the late nineteenth century and ending with the Sultan of Brunei in the late twentieth century. But today, for the first time in history, the world's wealthiest person [Bill Gates, cofounder and CEO of Microsoft] is a knowledge worker.

PROFESSOR LESTER C. THUROW of MIT, *Harvard Business Review*, September–October 1997

The people in the *Social Register* don't run America. They did up through Roosevelt. Now, it's just a nostalgia piece.

DIGBY BALTZELL, the sociologist (and coiner of the term WASP for White Anglo-Saxon Protestant), quoted in the *Wall Street Journal*, May 7, 1996

Because a major portion of the economy is now directly or indirectly dependent on the high-tech industries, we have a built-in motor that generates the perception that technology is moving ahead rapidly.

JED BUCHWALD of MIT, quoted in the *New York Times*, October 5, 1997

The future of technology is about shifting to what people like to do, and that's entertainment. Eventually, robots will make everything. The trend is over time. When Henry Ford was around, a large percentage of the population was involved in manufacturing. Now it's much smaller. I'm telling you: all the money and the energy in this country will eventually be devoted to doing things with your mind and your time.

MARVIN MINSKY, artificial intelligence expert, *New Yorker*, October 20 and 27, 1997

There has been a fundamental psychological change in America where the consumers and buyers are basically expecting premium products and premium services at lower prices. You cannot raise prices, the only thing that you can do is cut costs.

> SUNG WON SOHN, chief economist of the banking firm Norwest Corporation, quoted in the *New York Times,* January 2, 1998

The economy is fundamentally different than it was 25 years ago. Yet you don't have the universal acceptance that this is a different period.

> RICHARD BERNSTEIN of the investment firm Merrill Lynch, quoted in the *New York Times,* January 6, 1998

13.19   UNCONVENTIONAL ECONOMIC INDICATORS

Since the start of the Hoover Administration in 1929, small stocks have risen 22.8 percent a year, on average, during the nine terms of Democratic Presidents and just 1.9 percent during the eight Republican terms. The trend continues even when the Depression years are eliminated. Since 1937, small stocks have risen 17.2 percent a year on average, under Democratic Presidents, compared with 10.2 percent annually under Republican Presidents.

By contrast, large stocks have performed better during Republican administrations than during Democratic ones.

> CAROLE GOULD, *New York Times,* September 15, 1996

Expensive cars, chauffeurs, expensive houses, exotic holidays, pedigree dogs and breast implants.

> *The Economist,* August 3, 1996

Big Mac index.

> A measure of purchasing-power parities based on cost of a Big Mac in different countries, created by the *Economist*

These days, a Big Mac in Tokyo costs 280 yen. At today's exchange rate that makes its dollar cost $2.26, well below the price of a Big Mac in mid-Manhattan, which can run $2.89. So far as the Big Mac is a scorecard, the yen has fallen far enough.

> *New York Times,* February 20, 1997

How long [in minutes] the average wage earner has to work to buy a Big Mac.

Longest time		Shortest time	
Nairobi	193	Chicago, Houston, Tokyo	9
Caracas	117	Los Angeles	10
Moscow	104	Hong Kong	11
Jakarta	103	Toronto, New York	12
Budapest	91	Luxembourg	13
Bombay	85	Montreal, Sydney, Zurich	14
Manila	77	Athens, Geneva	15
Shanghai	75	Frankfurt	16
Mexico City	71	Vienna	17
Prague	56	Berlin	18
		Amsterdam, Dublin, London	19
		Copenhagen, Kuala Lumpur, Taipei	20

> Union Bank of Switzerland study, cited in the *Financial Times,* September 1, 1997

Salsa index.

> Created by writer Rebecca Morris to measure status of U.S.-Mexican trade, based on sales of salsa in the United States

The price of logs has tripled in the last several years because of the demand for log houses.

> MICHAEL LIPKIN, designer in Aspen, Colorado, where rustic homes had become fashionable, quoted in the *Wall Street Journal,* September 30, 1996

How thick is the Sunday *New York Times*?

3"—The economy is ticking along.

4"—[Finnish paper] mills should increase capacity.

> *The Economist,* September 12, 1987

Years ago, Fed economists tracked corrugated-box sales (a lot of stuff is packed in boxes). More recently, [Federal Reserve Board chairman] Mr. Greenspan's command of obscure statistics has ranged from scrap-metal prices (often rising in good times) to railroad carloadings (they also move stuff).

> *Wall Street Journal,* October 22, 1996

Supplier deliveries is a favorite inflation indicator of Fed chairman Alan Greenspan and is getting into the danger zone it was in in 1994 when the Fed tightened aggressively.

> JONATHAN BASILE, economist at the banking firm HSBC in New York, the *Financial Times,* September 3, 1997

A new economic theorem is developing. It states that any economic indicator will invariably turn down once the Chancellor [Norman Lamont, Chairman of the Exchequer in the U.K.] identifies it as an economic indicator.

> SIR DAVID LEES, chairman of the British engineering firm GMK, quoted in *Fortune,* December 14, 1992

Early in the century, when skirts were unappealingly long, the Dow Jones industrials meandered disinterestedly below 100. Then, in the 1920s, the era of the short-skirted flappers, the Dow floated merrily upward to over 300. With the Great Crash, however, both the market and hemlines plunged back down again. As skirts fluttered up to knee-level in the 1940s and 1950s, the market showed periodic signs of renewed liveliness. But it wasn't until miniskirts and hot pants came along in the 1960s that the market really got into high gear, soaring above 1000. More recently, with minis but a memory, the market has plodded along a generally dispirited course.

> *Financial World,* March 1, 1979

[C]andy: we eat more of it in a recession.

> ALISON ROGERS, *Fortune,* November 29, 1993

The Superbowl index. (Ninety-six percent of the time an NFC team beats an AFC team, the stock market has a good year.)

> Public Broadcasting System program *Wall Street Week,* January 31, 1997

From Kuala Lumpur to Moscow, the company acts like an advanced scout for the global revolution, somehow able to detect the emergence of disposable income before other firms see it.

> WILLIAM GREIDER, *One World Ready or Not: The Manic Logic of Global Capitalism* (Simon & Schuster, 1997)

Where Nike produces, economies soar. So far every country that Nike has produced sneakers in has seen high, long-term economic growth.

> Study by Robert Fleming, British brokerage firm. Nike criteria include political stability, staff quality, infrastructure, government openness, duties and quotas; Vietnam qualifies but India doesn't. Cited in the *Financial Times,* April 2, 1997

PR Puff Pitch Index. It would measure career trends based on the story pitches I get from the public relations representatives of career-related firms.

> • Hewitt Associates, a benefits consulting firm, says the strong economy and tight labor market has resulted in the first pay increase for salaried employees since 1990 . . .
>
> • Manpower, the temporary help firm, discovered that 28 percent of the 16,000 businesses surveyed in its most recent quarterly Employment Outlook Survey plan staff additions in the upcoming fourth quarter. The firm notes that the final quarter survey hasn't reflected such strong demand since 1978 . . .
>
> HAL LANCASTER, *Wall Street Journal Interactive Edition,* August 30, 1997

In my [Miami, Florida] building alone we can track what's going on in Latin America by the number of shopping bags. If the Brazilians are here buying like crazy, the economy must be good. If the Venezuelans are not here, they can't get their money out.

> RUTH SHACK of Dade Community Foundation, quoted in Rosabeth Moss Kanter, *World Class: Thriving Locally in the Global Economy* (Simon & Schuster, 1995)

Ignore economic irrelevancies like interest rates, the Dow Jones industrial average, and housing starts. The martini just went up four ounces [to 10 ounces]. The recovery is official.

> WILLIAM GRIMES, *New York Times,* October 29, 1997

14.1 AMERICAN BUSINESS EDUCATION

"Whom are you?" he asked, for he had attended business college.

GEORGE ADE, humorist, *Chicago Record,* March 16, 1898

Business education will, by appealing to the lower motives of securing business prosperity through economy, thrift, and health, do more to root out tobacco using, gambling, idleness, and spendthrift habits than all your preaching, however eloquent.

W. C. STEVENSON, "The Advent of the Commercial High School," *NEA Proceedings,* 1899

By design, the "B-School" trains a senior officer class, the nonplaying captains of industry. . . . This elite, in my opinion, is missing some pretty fundamental requirements for success: humility; respect for people on the firing line; deep understanding of the nature of the business and the kind of people who can enjoy themselves making it prosper; respect from way down the line; a demonstrated record of guts, industry, loyalty down, judgment, fairness, and honesty under pressure.

ROBERT TOWNSEND, *Up the Organization* (Knopf, 1970)

I've taught economics at the secondary level, and found that's already too late to teach certain economic principles.

MARILYN KOURILSKY, founder of Kinder-Economy and Mini-Society, economics courses for elementary school students as young as first grade, quoted in the *Wall Street Journal,* January 4, 1985

One of the things we try to combat is the student's real desire for formulas—a wish for a fact or reinterpretation that must be the key, the answer. They're a little uncomfortable with the great boom and buzzing confusion of how complex things are, and it has always struck me that one of the most valuable things you can learn from history is what you cannot learn from history. It's good to be reminded that there are no keys, no formulas.

RICHARD S. TEDLOW of Harvard Business School, *Harvard Business Review,* January–February 1986

No matter what you do, people are going to leave school with a pet formula or two that they really think will help them know all the answers. From a professional manager's point of view, one of the chief tasks is to knock that thought out of them their first year at work or at least during the first five years.

ALONZO L. McDONALD, CEO of Avenir Group, quoted in *Harvard Business Review,* January–February 1986

American schools teach international business as a subject. At Insead [a business school in France], it's integrated throughout the curriculum. At Insead it's the reason for being. The fact that the United States is no longer the sole driving engine of the world economy has created more need for international focus.

DANIEL MUZYKA, a native of Boston who teaches at the French business school Insead, quoted in the *New York Times,* June 30, 1991

When I go to the United States, I'm amazed at how little the people who teach mainstream business courses know about what's going on outside the United States.

PROFESSOR KAMRAN KASHANI of Switzerland's Lausanne School (known as I.M.D.), quoted in the *New York Times,* June 30, 1991

It's like a cat with nine lives, every time you start a funeral the corpse jumps up.

CHARLES W. HICKMAN of the American Assembly of Collegiate Schools of Business, on the steady rise in number of MBA students in spite of predictions that it will fall, quoted in *Business Week,* October 24, 1994

MBA degrees are union cards for yuppies.

Many American schools treat international as an elective, and that is a statement about what they think is necessary and what they think is a luxury.

PETER ROBINSON, *Snapshots from Hell: The Making of an MBA* (Warner, 1995)

Our business is no different from any other. You've got entrenched players, and once the environment starts to change, that creates opportunities for other players.

There is a big opportunity out there right now. We're at the front end of a major period of shakeout. Some business schools, as in any individual shakeout, are changing faster than others.

> JOSEPH MONROE of Rensselaer Polytechnic Institute, quoted in *Inc.*, August 1996

Existing curricula represent tenure-track faculty.

> ROBERT S. SULLIVAN, dean of the experimental business school IC² Institute, University of Texas, quoted in *Inc.*, August 1996

Copy shamelessly.

> STUART GREENBAUM of Washington University on how to improve the business school's performance, quoted in *Business Week*, September 30, 1996

[I]n some situations the right answer is the best answer, the wrong answer is the second best answer, and no answer is the worst answer.

> SCOTT McNEALY, CEO of the computer firm Sun Microsystems, on what he had *not* learned in his MBA studies, quoted in Randall Stross, *Steve Jobs and the NeXT Big Thing* (Atheneum, 1993)

Having received harsh comments from its graduating class in one *Business Week* survey, a leading school was said to have written a letter to its next *Business Week* class [*Business Week* revisits schools every other year] pointing out to them that their evaluations would have direct repercussions on the economic value of their degrees.

> ROBERT H. FRANK and PHILIP J. COOK, *The Winner-Take-All Society* (The Free Press, 1995)

They expect it [ethics] to be a "don't steal" remedial course for jerks like Ivan Boesky.

> PROFESSOR DAVID MESSICH of Northwestern University, quoted in *Fortune*, January 24, 1994

It's interesting that hard skills are considered better [in business school] than soft. But when people go into management, it's the soft skills that dominate almost everything they do. They are the ones that make the difference in career success.

> PROFESSOR C. THOMAS HOWARD of the University of Denver, quoted in the *New York Times*, February 23, 1997

I asked [senior corporate executives on dean's advisory board] what they most wanted to see in an MBA graduate these days. The answer was someone who is articulate, persuasive, and can read a balance sheet—in that order.

> DAVID PINCUS of the University of Arkansas, Fayetteville, quoted in the *New York Times*, February 23, 1997

Academic achievement is not a valid yardstick to use in measuring managerial potential. Indeed, if academic achievement is equated with success in business, the well-educated manager is a myth.

[M]uch management education is, in fact, miseducation because it arrests or distorts the ability of managerial aspirants to grow as they gain experience.

[M]any highly educated men do not build successful managerial careers [because] they are not able to learn from their own firsthand experience what they need to know to gain the willing cooperation of other people.

> PROFESSOR J. STERLING LEVINSON of Harvard Business School, "Myth of the Well-Educated Executive," *Harvard Business Review*, January–February 1971

Business schools should practice what they preach—they need to be much more customer focused. They're still in their universities looking out; they should be in our shoes looking in.

> JOE GALARNEAU, of the telecommunications company AT&T, quoted in the *Economist*, February 8, 1992

We're looking for action-based learning, not just grinding through case studies.

> "Head of management development at one of Europe's biggest multinationals," quoted in the *Economist*, February 8, 1992

When I hear somebody's got an MBA, I have a feeling of dread, because normally they come to me with an overpompous sense of their own importance. And no way are you going to prick that bubble, with the result that one day there will be a cave-in in their department. So they learn painful lessons at my expense!

> ROBERT KUOK, Chinese businessman, quoted in *Forbes*, July 28, 1997

MBAs, like sea turtles, are hatched by the multitudes from business schools around the world only to perish moments later. As they flop frantically from the beaches to the relative safety of the sea, many are gobbled up and picked off by predators and competitors. The few that survive seem to live long, endless lives.

PROFESSOR KAREN STEPHENSON, anthropologist, of the University of California, in a speech to business school students, September 24, 1992

MBAs are poor decision makers.

F. KENNETH IVERSON, CEO of the steel company Nucor, cited by William J. White, of the electronics company Bell & Howell, in a speech, October 19, 1992

In the '80s, MBAs got really bad representations. They only had two years' experience and not much life maturity coming into big positions.

MAURY HANIGAN, consultant, quoted in the *Wall Street Journal*, March 5, 1996

A model airplane and a runway; a poem; a family album; a video "Don't Start School Without Him." [A list of the answers received by the Stern School of Business at New York University in response to the application question, "Describe yourself to classmates using any method to convey your message."]

Cited in the *Wall Street Journal*, May 9, 1996

[Business schools] are all addicted to left brain number crunching, but we won't need our financial MBAs 20 years from now. Managers of the future must be systems thinkers who see patterns and cooperators who do not just think in a linear way.

PROFESSOR THOMAS GLADWIN of New York University, quoted in the *Financial Times*, October 9, 1997

The MBA's popularity is easy to explain. The typical members of Harvard Business School's class of 1974 now look set to retire with a net worth of $8 million, and the chances are good that their successors will look down on them as paupers.

JOHN MICKLETHWAIT and ADRIAN WOOLDRIDGE, *The Witch Doctors* (Times Books, 1996)

We're in the business of producing sophisticated financial engineers.

PROFESSOR ANDREW LO, Sloan School at MIT, quoted in *Worth*, October 1995

Probably the most valuable course I took as an MBA was Interpersonal Dynamics. The second most valuable was finance, which explained net present value. I'm not sure there was anything else.

At Stanford I took a course in sales force management that tried to teach me how to manage a sales force of 400 people, but I could not take a course in how to sell.

TRIP HAWKINS, founder and CEO of the home computer firm The 3DO Company, interviewed in Rama Dev Jager, *In the Company of Giants* (McGraw-Hill, 1997)

You're useless in business with just an academic background. You're also useless if you spend too much time in the military. You really ought to have backgrounds in both.

KENNETH OLSEN, founder of Digital Equipment Corporation, interviewed in Rama Dev Jager, *In the Company of Giants* (McGraw-Hill, 1997)

Someone asked me if we couldn't just take existing case studies and rename the protagonists. But it would be entirely false to try to introduce more women into the curriculum by simply changing the names.

MYRA M. HART of Harvard Business School, on program to add more case material with women in top management into curriculum, quoted in the *New York Times*, November 14, 1997

The biggest change I've seen in business-school students is that their aspiration has gone from being chairman of General Motors when they grow up to being Bill Gates. The desire for ownership, for having an economic stake, is just stunning.

B. JOSEPH WHITE, dean of the University of Michigan Business School in Ann Arbor, quoted in the *Wall Street Journal*, November 25, 1997

14.2 BRITISH BUSINESS EDUCATION

In the Middle Ages, the rich tried to buy immortality by building cathedrals. These days they set up business schools instead.

The Economist, July 20, 1996

Having a big business institute in the midst of Oxford is a distinctly discomforting arrangement.

> ALEXANDER MURRAY, medieval historian who led resistance to founding of business school at Oxford University, quoted in the *Wall Street Journal,* November 8, 1996

Business professors often pretend they're "really" economists or psychologists who happen to teach business; economists and psychologists seldom pretend that they're "really" management theorists.

[T]here seems to be something in the water at business schools that prevents people from writing in English.

> JOHN MICKLETHWAIT and ADRIAN WOOLDRIDGE, journalists, quoted in the *Wall Street Journal,* November 8, 1996

According to the survey [by Imperial College Management School] 57 percent of alumni believed that employers did not take full advantage of their skills on graduation and 43 percent believe that their employers still do not fully exploit their skills.

On average, managers change employers two or three years after graduation.

> *Financial Times,* September 1, 1997

Only a handful of Britain's most successful business people have MBAs. But a perusal of some of Britain's shareholder millionaires reveals that U.S. business schools outrank European in producing the rich and powerful.

> *Financial Times,* January 13, 1997

It will be the most intellectually rigorous business school in Europe. That's what the Oxford positioning dictates.

> JOHN KAY, first director of Oxford's School of Management Studies, quoted in the *Financial Times,* April 1, 1997

A real major issue for us is to be recognized in the States for what we are and what we are not. We are not an ersatz American business school. If I wanted to go to a U.S. business school, I'd go to the United States.

> BOB GAILLERS, chairman of Warwick Business School, which funds itself substantially through research sponsored by industry, quoted in the *Financial Times,* May 5, 1997

I speak as a boy from the Canadian prairies. If you're sitting in the middle of the Canadian or American prairies then it is very difficult to internationalize. If you're in the middle of London it's much easier.

> GEORGE BAIN, retiring principal of London Business School, quoted in the *Financial Times,* October 9, 1997

14.3 INDIAN BUSINESS EDUCATION

The problem was that until this decade we [graduates of India's management schools] had precious little to manage.

> ANAND MAHINDRA, Harvard-educated deputy managing director of Mahindra & Mahindra, quoted in the *Economist,* March 9, 1996

14.4 JAPANESE BUSINESS EDUCATION

In our universities there were 400 in the class; people slept and picked up notes from the guy in the row in front to study for the exam. Then you could pass.

> YASUSHI OKAMOTO, Japanese MBA student at Dartmouth, quoted in *Fortune,* October 8, 1990

It's as difficult for them [Japanese students] to speak as for Americans to keep quiet. Traditionally our culture penalizes arrogance, and eloquence is a vice.

> MASARU YOSHIMORI, professor of comparative management at Tuck International University in Japan, quoted in *Fortune,* October 8, 1990

Americans are so noisy about business. We don't want U.S. blah blah. We're very reluctant to use a U.S. textbook.

> FATHER ROBERT BALLON, Belgian director of international management seminars at Sophia University, Tokyo, quoted in *Fortune,* October 8, 1990

We're introducing a completely new concept of education. It was unheard of for Chinese students to ask questions or challenge the teacher. But we need highly educated, proactive employees because our customers are highly educated. The employees must also be able to handle a lot of stress because our business requires being constantly in contact with customers.

> MICHELLE HARDWICK of the Shangri-La Hotel Management Training Center, *Asia, Inc.,* February 1996

14.5 BUSINESS EDUCATION— ALTERNATIVES TO BUSINESS SCHOOL

If Thomas Edison had gone to business school, we would all be reading by larger candles.

> MARK H. McCORMACK, *What They Don't Teach You at Harvard Business School* (Bantam Doubleday Dell, 1988)

I think maybe the best education, the best foundation for business is probably reading Shakespeare rather than reading some MBA program out of some great business school. I think I'd rather have an English major than an economics major.

> MICHAEL D. EISNER, CEO of Walt Disney, in an interview on the Academy of Achievement web site, June 17, 1994

Most of what I learned about how to do business I learned from Shakespeare, not Harvard Business School.

> Investment banker LEON D. BLACK, former colleague of Michael Milken at the investment bank Drexel Burnham Lambert, quoted in *Business Week,* July 29, 1996

I learned about people in the funeral business. It's a service business. You service people in an emotional time— you learn about their needs, their feelings.

> The late STEVEN ROSS, CEO of the entertainment conglomerate Warner Communications, quoted by Connie Bruck, *New Yorker,* January 8, 1990

I've learned more from the one restaurant that didn't work than from all the ones that were successful.

> WOLFGANG PUCK, mega-chef, in a speech, quoted in *Inc.,* September 1996

I heard my father make deals all the time and for 24 years I listened attentively when my husband talked about his business.

> LOIDA LEWIS, Filipino-born lawyer, author, and CEO of TLC Beatrice International Holdings (the company

formed in the leveraged buy-out of Beatrice Foods by her late husband Reginald Lewis), on how she learned to run the business, the largest minority-owned company in the United States, quoted in *Asia, Inc.,* March 1997

Business is the most asexual, monastic pursuit for so many people. It should be as full of life as anything else. This would all work better in CD-ROM. People could go as far as they wanted.

> HARRIET RUBIN, business editor at Doubleday, quoted in *Inc.,* November 1994

It was Cornflake University—I learned from business articles I read over breakfast. I clipped articles. I wanted to know what mistakes were made by CEOs of growing companies. So I read articles to find the relevant answers, to get ideas to think about.

> JIRKA RYSAVY, Czech-born entrepreneur who came to the United States in the mid-1980s and CEO of the corporate supply firm Corporate Express, quoted in *Inc.,* December 1995

I'm 30 years old and a manager at a leading technology company. I make in the 90s with enough money in the bank to buy a house, the company pays for my education and I am two payments away from being totally debt-free. Why should I spend two years unpaid at a $20,000-a-year school just to mimic the experience I am already achieving.

> PALMYRA PAWLIK, part-time graduate student in business and technology, Santa Clara University, quoted in the *Wall Street Journal,* February 11, 1997

An MBA for a year could be $30,000 in tuition. That's quite expensive for developing one person. But for $60,000 a company can . . . develop a whole customized curriculum and deliver it to about 60 people.

> MICHAEL KIM of the consulting firm Towers Perrin, on a growing trend toward corporate universities, quoted in the *Financial Times,* September 22, 1997

There is no English word for entrepreneur.

> GEOFFREY WANSELL, *Tycoon: The Life of James Goldsmith* (Atheneum, 1983)

Contrary to popular belief, the United States does not have a monopoly on entrepreneurial drive. We have found four characteristics of an economy that are predictors of high firm gestation rates: economic activity that's become specialized, prevalence of established business within the same economic system, higher-than-average household wealth, and higher-than-average population growth.

> PROFESSOR PAUL REYNOLDS of Marquette University, quoted in *Inc.*, October 1994

I think it's unfortunate that to some degree the word "entrepreneur" has taken on the connotation of a gambler. I don't see it that way at all. Many times action is not the most risky path. The most risky path is inaction.

> FRED SMITH, founder of Federal Express, quoted in Robert Sobel and David B. Sicilia, *The Entrepreneurs—An American Adventure* (Houghton Mifflin, 1986)

[I]t's of no importance what field an entrepreneur operates in. When I went to Olivetti, I knew absolutely nothing about electronics. Even if I know very little about the food industry, I can say as I take over Buitoni that I've eaten plenty of pasta.

> CARLO DE BENEDETTI, Italian businessman, quoted in the *Wall Street Journal*, February 7, 1985

Fear is a very, very important factor in entrepreneurial success.

> HOWARD "TED" GREEN, age 42, chairman of the high-tech firm Hybritech, quoted in *Time*, January 7, 1985

You have to do a lot of things that are boring. I had to recruit my own staff, fill out W-2s, incorporate and read all the paperwork. It takes a lot of hours.

> JOHN STYLES, founder of Ambulatory Hospitals of America, quoted in *U.S. News & World Report*, October 21, 1985

The highs are getting customer calls saying they're really pleased and seeing all the families at the Christmas party whom you've gainfully employed.

> STANLEY MINTZ, founder of the robot makers Intelledex, quoted in *U.S. News & World Report*, October 21, 1985

I can't say I had a happy childhood. I had no contact with the world outside, and when you have nothing to compare with, you aren't aware you should be unhappy. . . . The other kids used to laugh at me as they used to make fun of my homemade clothes. I decided I would show them, and I did.

I believe in miracles. I believe my success is a miracle. . . . I don't commit too much to anything. I can't afford to. I always feel a little insecure. In fact, I think there is no such thing as security. There is no such thing as permanent success.

> JOHN H. JOHNSON, publisher of *Ebony*, quoted in Robert Sobel and David B. Sicilia, *The Entrepreneurs—An American Adventure* (Houghton Mifflin, 1986)

Entrepreneurs are men who build big organizations and have intense unresolved rivalries with their fathers.

> HARRY LEVINSON, clinical psychologist and president of the consulting firm Levinson Institute, quoted in *U.S. News & World Report*, January 26, 1987

The ones who succeed are those who don't jump off the bridge until they know the parachute works.

> JOHN WELSH of Southern Methodist University, quoted in *U.S. News & World Report*, January 26, 1987

Most of the guys who have failed are the ones who stopped listening and got carried away with their own ego. All of a sudden they become folk heroes and started to believe their own public relations.

> WILLIAM HAMBRECHT, cofounder of the investment bank Hambrecht & Quist, quoted in *Time*, January 23, 1984

Pushing a new enterprise past all the barriers to success takes learnable skills, to be sure, but it also takes a tenacious inner passion bordering on monomania. This combination is what I call leadership.

> KYE ANDERSON, chairman, CEO, and president of Medical Graphics Corporation, *Harvard Business Review,* May–June 1992

In periods of major political, social, and environmental change, the number of problems requiring judgment increases, and the demand for entrepreneurship rises.

> MARK CASSON, economics professor at University of Reading, England, *Fortune Encyclopedia of Economics,* 1993

It's astounding how often I have encountered massive problems that were due solely to the fact that financial staffers were unqualified to handle their responsibilities at a fast-growing company.

> ROBERT FALCONI, CFO of Planning Systems, a research and development firm in McLean, Virginia, on entrepreneurial firms that try to get by with their bootstrap era financial personnel, *Inc.,* January 1994

I think I was too stupid to know that it was impossible. So I did it.

> NEIL HIRSCH, who founded Telerate Systems at the age of 21, quoted in *Forbes,* April 8, 1985

Running your own business means you are controlling your own destiny.

> DAVID BIRCH, MIT research director, quoted in *Time,* April 24, 1989

We didn't want to be sitting on rocking chairs when we were 80 years old, never having tried it on our own.

> JEFF ASCHEKENES, president of Tweeds, catalogue company, who had formerly worked for J. Crew, quoted in *Time,* July 17, 1989

Entrepreneurs are gamblers, but the smart ones gamble on themselves.

> JAMES LEVOY SORENSON, founder of Sorenson development, medical research, and manufacturing company, worth $375 million in 1986, *Forbes,* October 27, 1986

I've learned I'm a great team player, as long as I'm captain of the team!

> PORTIA ISAACSON, Texan who launched five successful businesses, quoted by Thomas R. Norton, president and CEO, American Management Association,

in a speech, Commonwealth Club of California, San Francisco, October 5, 1987

[A]t any given moment more people are trying to start a business than are getting married or having children. In fact, evidence suggests that one out of every two adults in the country has tried to start a new business.

> PAUL REYNOLDS, Coleman Chairholder in Entrepreneurial Studies, Marquette University, *Inc.,* October 1994

Your family has to understand the work hours and craziness associated with a start-up.

> MARK BIESTMAN, who left Oracle to help start Netscape, quoted in the *Wall Street Journal,* January 23, 1996

Everyone—headhunters, people I work with, people I used to work with, friends, family—called to ask if I was going through a midlife crisis.

> NATHAN MORTON, when he decided to leave his job as a top executive at Home Depot to run a chain of computer warehouse stores—now called CompUSA, quoted in the *New York Times,* February 28, 1993

I never met a rich pessimist.

> ALLEN BREED, chairman and CEO of Breed Technologies, *Inc.,* December 1995

As you get bigger, you have to tone down your entrepreneurial instincts. But you have to do it in a way that doesn't put out the fire.

> PHILIP H. KNIGHT, CEO of Nike

I did this mainly to finance a hobby and to keep my wife happy.

> JOHN KUNNERT, founder of World Class White Tails Inc., Fremont, Nebraska, which sells fiberglass replicas of his collection of antlers, *Wall Street Journal,* December 13, 1996 (He kept his day job as a manufacturers' representative selling fishing tackle and marine supplies; his wife had objected to the expense of his hobby.)

— Water sold for $10 a gallon.
— 4 packs of batteries for $25.
— Plumber charged $850 for a half-hour's work.

— Department store Robinson May will skip finance charges for two years if customers replace their broken China and crystal there.

> Report by RONALD GROVER about entrepreneurial activity in Los Angeles after earthquake, quoted in *Business Week,* February 7, 1994

Everything is always impossible before it works. That is what entrepreneurs are all about—doing what people have told them is impossible.

> HUNT GREENE, Minneapolis venture capitalist, *Fortune,* May 27, 1996

What do sex and entrepreneurship have in common? All the technical manuals in the world can't prepare you for the actual experience of doing it.

> *Inc.,* January 1996

The challenge in a start-up is that you always have to spread your wings pretty far to see what will work.

> MICHAEL DELL, CEO of Dell Computer, interviewed in Rama Dev Jager, *In the Company of Giants* (McGraw-Hill, 1997)

I would rather be like the Wright brothers and fly 150 feet than sit and wait for the Concorde to arrive.

> WAYNE N. SCHELLE, CEO of American Personal Communications and cellular phone entrepreneur, *Business Week,* July 29, 1996

After Apple hit, Steve Jobs [founder of Apple] began wearing Armani and having lunch with Jerry Brown. He even got an apartment on Central Park. I don't finance guys who have lunch with Jerry Brown and have apartments 3,000 miles away. I want a guy who doesn't even know who the president is, someone driven to a single agenda, to 15-hour days and six-day weeks.

> DON VALENTINE, Silicon Valley venture capitalist, *Worth,* December 1996

I pick the jockeys, and the jockeys pick the horses and ride 'em.

> ROSS PEROT, after deciding to invest in NeXT Inc. without pausing to check business plans and crunch numbers, quoted in Randall E. Stross, *Steve Jobs and the NeXT Big Thing* (Maxwell Macmillan, 1993)

Capitalists are a self-nominating group. To join them is a matter of seizing an opportunity, mobilizing one's savings, borrowing from relatives, friends, and banks, working hard and intelligently, and testing one's acumen and luck. If fortune smiles, you too may become as rich as Colonel Sanders of Kentucky Fried Chicken fame. [Colonel Sanders sold the rights to his trademark relatively early and didn't get all that rich.]

> ROBERT LEKACHMAN and BORIN VAN LOON, *Capitalism for Beginners* (Pantheon, 1981)

Recognize a failure early and go on to the next idea.

One well-publicized success will cover up a multitude of blunders.

Find a vacuum and fill it.

> BILL HEINECKE, Thai-based American entrepreneur, quoted in *Asia, Inc.,* September 1996

I'm not a good shot, but I shoot often.

> TEDDY ROOSEVELT, asked by a reporter about his marksmanship

The people who start these [growth companies] are heroes in my book. In my youth, leaders like them were celebrated in biographies and Horatio Alger novels. Today, there's no comparable celebration of business leaders in our popular culture. . . . Our popular culture saves its adulation for people ranging from Michael Jordan to Hootie & the Blowfish. They may be terrific individuals, but how many jobs did they create?

> PETER LYNCH, ex-manager of Fidelity Magellan Fund, *Wall Street Journal,* September 20, 1996. (Horatio Alger's most recent published novel *Silas Snobden's Office Boy* originally appeared as a serial in *Argosy* from 1889 to 1890. Mr. Lynch was born in 1944.)

It's like the atmosphere generated by Hollywood in the 1930s. The founders of these new companies are the stars of the 1980s.

> THOMAS UNTERBERG, chairman of the brokerage firm L. F. Rothschild, quoted in *Time,* January 23, 1984

We went through our files recently and looked at the history of companies formed in the last four years. It's amazing how many were [formed by] senior corporate officers—ex-IBM and ex-Citibank.

> JOSEPH W. DUNCAN, chief economist at the business information firm Dun & Bradstreet, quoted in *Business Week,* November 21, 1994

The Jews, the Irish, the Pakistanis, the Koreans, and the Chinese have embraced entrepreneurship, whether through home-based businesses, produce stands, or pushcarts. Entry-level enterprises led to Macy's and Gimbel's. The national economy is founded on entrepreneurial endeavors that create wealth in the communities, not by empowerment-zone tax breaks for those who have already secured their wealth.

> TONY BROWN, *Black Lies, White Lies* (Morrow, 1995)

It seemed like the right time to take off your clothes and jump in the frying pan.

> DAVID BONDERMAN, owner of Continental Airlines, on why he struck out on his own, quoted in *Business Week,* May 6, 1996

If you screw up, you've got plenty of time to recover.

> DAVID WISE, on starting a business right out of school and not going into a corporation, quoted in *Fortune,* August 31, 1994

With partners, make sure you get along and you both know which one of you is boss.

> COURTLAND L. LOGUE, Texas entrepreneur, quoted in *Fortune,* July 10, 1996

The secret: crying your way to the top.

> MINDY GOLDBERG, Epoch Films, on relieving the stress of running your own business, quoted in *Forbes,* May 25, 1992

To me one of the most exciting things in the world is being poor. Survival is such an exciting challenge.

> THOMAS MONAGHAN, founder of Domino's Pizza

I want to make a lot of money.

> KAI ZHU, 20-year-old physics major hoping to hone his moneymaking ability by moving into a new dormitory founded to "embody the spirit of entrepreneurship," quoted in the *New York Times,* November 17, 1996

I can smell the Ferrari now.

> ROBERT WELCH, the president of the computer-memory company Zitel before it went public, *Time,* January 23, 1984

I've worked with hundreds of entrepreneurs, and I've never met one who said, "I want to get rich" who did. The successful ones say, "I want to find a way to do animation faster," or "I'm really interested in adhesion."

> PROFESSOR JON GOODMAN of the University of Southern California, quoted in *Fortune,* February 20, 1995

So far, I like it fine. Most entrepreneurs don't last very long in big companies. But I'm not normal. Like my psychiatrist said, "We are all different. We are all like snowflakes."

> TED TURNER, vice chairman of Time Warner, adapting to postmerger life, quoted in the *New York Times,* November 24, 1996

For an American, [getting fired] is a normal part of business. For a Chinese, it is totally humiliating. I said, "Never again. I'm going into business for myself."

> GALINDA WANG, Taiwan-born fashion designer and founder of La Classic Inc., quoted in *New York Newsday,* cited in *Asia, Inc.,* November 1996

If this guy, a passive investor, is already so involved in the company down to the last detail, I can't run this.

> BERNARD MARCUS, CEO of Home Depot, explaining why a $2 million investment from Ross Perot fell through in a venture started before he started Home Depot, quoted in *Fortune,* May 31, 1993

The hardest thing for an entrepreneur to do is to ask for help, to admit you don't know what you're doing.

> CHERYL WOMACK, founder and CEO of the insurance firm VCW, quoted in *Fortune,* November 29, 1993

Is your company so small you have to do everything for yourself? Wait until you're so big you can't. That's worse.

> MICHAEL BLOOMBERG, CEO of the business news firm Bloomberg, *Bloomberg by Bloomberg* (Wiley, 1997)

I'd grown used to five-star hotels, limousines, and the Concorde, but I knew it wouldn't kill me to change my own light bulbs and lick my own stamps.

> KEN VEIT, owner and operator of the retail cartoon art store Cartoon Corner, *Harvard Business Review,* November–December 1992

[M]any felons appear to be natural entrepreneurs. Prof. Sonfield, Hofstra University management professor, along with Rochester Institute of Technology Professor Robert Barbato, administered a widely used entrepreneurial aptitude test to 41 prison inmates. The inmates' scores were comparable to actual entrepreneurs in high-growth companies, and much higher than the scores of entrepreneurs in low-growth firms. The inmates did lag in one test category: planning for the future.

> JOHN R. EMSHWILLER, *Wall Street Journal,* July 3, 1997

I tell all my friends that it's an easy business to get into. All you have to know is "coffee doughnuts have a nice day." That's it. Something else: the coffee has to be good and you can't forget to smile.

> FAHIM SALEH, one of the many Afghan refugees who sell coffee and bagels from carts in Manhattan, quoted in the *New York Times,* September 18, 1997

I worked for an entrepreneur who built a fantastic corporate headquarters building. Floor-to-ceiling glass walls overlooking a panoramic view of the Rocky Mountains. No expense was spared to construct a monument to his success. He'd stepped on lots of people's backs on his way up though. One was a man who was fired but ended up forming a competing company. The man quietly obtained a piece of land in front of my boss's headquarters. Then he built a taller, bigger, more beautiful building right across the highway, totally blocking my boss's mountain view. My boss never got over that retaliation. Every time he looked out his office window he had to see his rival.

> "A corporate controller," quoted in D.A. Benson, *How to Think Like a CEO* (Warner Books, 1996)

I don't think any entrepreneur would say that what they did was an incredible risk. I think most could tell you many reasons why it was obvious to do what they did. When you have nothing, you have nothing to lose; you haven't that far to fall.

> SANDRA L. KURTZIG, founder and CEO of the software firm ASK, interviewed in Rama Dev Jager, *In the Company of Giants* (McGraw-Hill, 1997)

You don't start a business because you want to make money. You start a business because you need to compete.

> T. J. RODGERS, CEO of Cypress Semiconductor, quoted in *Slate,* October 29, 1997

A lot of [people asked when I left Bausch & Lomb] "how could someone who spent 28 years in a big company become an entrepreneur?" [The] question should be, "how could someone as entrepreneurial as me have survived in a corporation for 28 years?"

> DIANE HARRIS, quoted in the *Wall Street Journal,* November 11, 1997

15.1 ENTREPRENEURSHIP— GROWING PAINS

The early 1980s were not scary. Then we were the challengers and had nothing to lose. The hardest time was in 1988, when I decided we had to spend $250 million to ramp up production.

> KAY KOPLOVITZ, chief executive of the cable TV station USA Network, quoted in the *New York Times,* September 15, 1991

These days growing my company feels like what happens when you play one of my kid's video games. You work like crazy to get to the next level, only to have the game become infinitely more complicated as a result.

> JIM ANSARA, founder and CEO of Shawmut Design and Construction, quoted in *Inc.,* January 1995

It's ridiculous to bring in managers if you're not willing to delegate.

> DENNIS PENCE, CEO of the catalogue company Coldwater Creek, quoted in *Inc. 500,* special issue, 1995

The most overrated thing since childbirth is starting your own business.

> Graffito cited by KATHLEEN BROWN, former California treasurer and gubernatorial candidate, *Inc.,* August 1996

When you're a start-up, you spend all your time worrying about very basic things like, "Do I have any cash flow?" I feel like I'm using my skills and my brain in a slightly more orderly world.

> JEAN HAMMOND, founder of the computer-technology firm Axon Network, which chose to be acquired by 3Com Corporation rather than go public, quoted in the *Wall Street Journal,* October 9, 1996

Central planning didn't work for Stalin or Mao, and it won't work for an entrepreneur either.

> MICHAEL BLOOMBERG, CEO of the business information firm Bloomberg, *Bloomberg on Bloomberg* (Wiley, 1997)

Big banks often respond to an entrepreneur and his or her special needs with edicts. If you've built a good relationship with a smaller bank, maintain it. You never know when you'll need that extra level of support.

> MICHAEL McCARTHY, CEO of the construction firm McCarthy Co., quoted in *Inc.,* November 1995

All entrepreneurs want an exit strategy.

> PAUL VERROCHI, founder of the ambulance firm American Medical Response (AMR), quoted in *Inc.,* December 1995

Three capital errors to avoid:

1. Don't take your financing projections too seriously. [Assume you'll need more than you think, and create flexible plans.]
2. Don't expect logic or simplicity in the capital structure that evolves at your company.
3. Don't take rejections from banks or investors too seriously.

> JILL ANDRESKY FRASER, *Inc.,* February 1996

It's my experience that as your business grows, it becomes easier to be talked out of your common sense. You turn to automation at a certain stage of revenue growth, and the abstract logic of standard cost analysis takes over.

> PAT LANCASTER, CEO of the packaging firm Lantech, quoted in *Inc.* technology issue, 1996

15.2 ENTREPRENEURSHIP— THE DOWNSIDE

It was playground politics. Their lawyer said, "You're little. We're big. You lose."

> DONA McKENZIE, a graphic designer who was stiffed for $22,000 of a $50,000 contract because one of the firm's top executives didn't like the navy blue covers of the brochures she designed, quoted in the *Wall Street Journal,* September 3, 1997

If you have capital, you may not see the stream of paperwork that's generated by a regulation or a clause in the tax code.

> STEVE MARIOTTI, founder of the National Foundation for Teaching Entrepreneurship, quoted in *Inc.,* May 1994

[W]hen your numbers are good, you don't really need a formal [business] plan. When your numbers are stinko, a business plan doesn't fool anyone.

> MARY BAECHLER, CEO of the baby-buggy manufacturer Racing Strollers, quoted in *Inc.,* February 1996

The good news is people quit dying. The bad news is people quit dying.

> KATHIE KADZIAVSKAS, founder of the crime-scene cleaner Crime Scene Steam and Clean, on a seven-

week period in which she had no work, quoted in the *Wall Street Journal,* August 29, 1996

It's hard having a partner who doesn't think the chef should be allowed to drink a bottle of wine in his own restaurant.

> DAVID BOULEY, superstar chef whose partner kept a tight hold on the finances, quoted in the *New York Times Magazine,* August 17, 1997

15.3 ENTREPRENEURS AND CAPITAL

Raising money has become a disease. Entrepreneurs are wasting lots of brainpower scheming to raise money.

> MICHAEL LUTZ, CEO of the communications software firm Gammalink, quoted by Amar Bhide, "Bootstrap Finance: The Art of Startups," *Harvard Business Review,* September–October 1990

If we had money, we would have made more mistakes. This way I wrote all the checks. I knew where the money was going.

> TOM DAVIS of medical and research equipment firm Modular Instruments, quoted by Amar Bhide, "Bootstrap Finance: The Art of Startups," *Harvard Business Review,* September–October 1990

[W]hen I hear managers attribute their companies' poor performance to Wall Street's short-term, deal-making orientation, I hear the rhetoric of dependency. I hear the voices of once-strong, committee executives who find it painful to admit that they may have lost their vision and resolve.

It didn't bother me that people were making money off our stock, but it did seem easy compared with the many years of hard work it had taken us to build the company.

> SAFI U. QURESHY, CEO of the computer firm AST Research, quoted in *Harvard Business Review,* May–June 1991

Let me tell you how many times I have been into my home-equity line over the last 10 years.

> JOHN B. COOPER, founder of the computer-services consulting firm Rockridge Consulting, *Wall Street Journal,* February 13, 1996

You know, if they had caught you, they could have put you under the jail, not in it.

> Lawyer for *Hustler* magazine publisher Larry Flynt, on finding out that Flynt had funded *Hustler's* start-up with employee withholding taxes, quoted in Larry Flynt, *An Unseemly Man* (Dove, 1996)

As long as you put your ass on the line and commit personnel assets, they'll [bankers] give you money.

You can write a plan that makes your business look fabulous and gets you money, but you can still go broke.

> JAKE HOLMES, owner of the Stowe Canoe Company, quoted in *Inc.,* August 1996

15.4 SALESMANSHIP

The key principle in selling is honesty. Once you know how to fake that, you've got it made.

> HARVEY BREIT, *New York Times Book Review,* June 10, 1956

They could sell 10-pound bags of horse manure at those parties, there's so much pressure.

> DENNIS HAGGERTY of Eagle Affiliates, a Tupperware competitor, referring to Tupperware sales parties, quoted in the *Wall Street Journal,* January 2, 1985

Salesmen and saleswomen are taught how to sell right now. They are excellent at extracting money in immediate exchange for merchandise. But if the process requires finding the answer to a question or ordering a different model, something happens. Or, to be more accurate, nothing happens.

> SYLVIA ROSE, marketing trainer and consultant, quoted in the *New York Times,* August 25, 1996

Good salespeople must have at least two basic qualities: empathy and ego drive.

[Reasons why standardized tests fail to identify top sales people]

1. Tests look for interest, not ability. But psychologically, interest does not equal aptitude.
2. Tests are eminently "fakeable" . . .
3. Tests favor conformity, not individual creativity . . .
4. Tests try to isolate fractional traits rather than to reveal the whole dynamics of the person.

> DAVID MAYER and HERBERT M. GREENBERG, *Harvard Business Review,* July–August, 1964; reprinted January–February 1992

Nothing can teach you how to be motivated or have instincts or go after orders, but training can give you a lot of tools.

> TOM ASHCROFT of Booklet Binding Inc., quoted in *Inc.,* February 1996

Indifference has no place in a salesman's world; his work precludes it.

> EARL SHORRIS, *A Nation of Salesmen* (Norton, 1994)

When managers don't sell, they get funny ideas about selling. They think it's complicated, mysterious. A kind of sales mystique develops in the company. Then a salesperson comes back and says that he or she can't sell your product at full price, that the market is demanding a steep discount, or a special deal. The managers don't know how to respond. They don't trust themselves.

> NORM BRODSKY, columnist and veteran of six start-ups, *Inc.,* February 1996

Do the dogs have their head in the dish? [Slang for "Are the customers buying?"]

> *Wired,* September 1996

I take great pride in the fact that I was a peddler.

> JOHN R. WALTER, president of the telecommunications firm AT&T, on his days as a salesman for the printer R. R. Donnelly, where his commissions were higher than the chairman's compensation, quoted in the *Wall Street Journal,* December 23, 1996

The art business is people looking for a nice painting that will go above the fireplace. I don't sell customers what they want. I want to prove that an art dealer doesn't have to follow what the art market wants.

> LUCIA CHEN, owner of the New World Art Center in New York, quoted in *Asia, Inc.,* May 1997

Honesty is for the most part less profitable than dishonesty.

PLATO, *The Republic*

Glass, china, and reputation are easily crack'd and never well mended.

BEN FRANKLIN

He who wishes to be rich in a day will be hanged in a year.

LEONARDO DA VINCI, *Notebooks*

Money, and not morality, is the principle of commerce and commercial nations.

THOMAS JEFFERSON, letter to John Langdon, March 5, 1784

These capitalists generally act harmoniously and in concert, to fleece the people.

ABRAHAM LINCOLN, speech to Illinois legislature, January 1837

Business success, whether for the individual or for the Nation, is a good thing only so far as it is accompanied by and develops a high standard of conduct—honor, integrity, civic courage . . . This Government stands for manhood first and for business only as an adjunct of manhood.

THEODORE ROOSEVELT, in his fifth annual message to Congress, December 5, 1905

I hate that old maxim "Business is business," for I understand by it that business is not moral. The man who says, "I am not in business for my health," means that he is not in business for his moral health, and I am an enemy of every business of this kind. But if business is regarded as an object for serving and obtaining private profit by means of service, then I am with that business.

U.S. PRESIDENT WOODROW WILSON, in a speech, *New York Times*, April 25, 1911

We have always known that heedless self-interest was bad morals. We now know it's bad economics. And bad for society.

FRANKLIN ROOSEVELT, second inaugural address, 1937

Business ethics is one of those phrases used by all with a different meaning for each user—and, indeed, a different meaning at different times when used by the same person.

ROBERT W. AUSTIN, *Harvard Business Review*, September–October 1961

A distinction between business and non-business success is relevant. In a market situation, the question is simple: "Will it sell?" A non-profit institution asks: "Is it good?"

Frustrated ambition is the wet nurse of crime.

The insistent spur of American culture is the promise of success for all . . . In a competitive system, you are seduced into cutting corners just as closely as your nearest competitor. The business philosophy of pragmatism—whatever works is good—has always endangered ethics by defining good in terms of the long-term profit and loss statement.

RICHARD M. HUBER, *The American Idea of Success* (McGraw-Hill, 1971)

Optimism is not unethical. But in business, misrepresentation under the guise of optimism is a crime. Information is valuable, but it's ethical only as long as you have the right to have it. Profit is valued, as long as you've earned it. Loyalty is appreciated, as long as it isn't misplaced . . . The Iraqis following Saddam Hussein could be said to have been loyal.

A. THOMAS YOUNG, president of the defense firm Martin Marietta, in a speech, May 5, 1992

[E]thical management is a process of anticipating both the law and the market—and for sound business reasons.

PROFESSOR ANDREW STARK of the University of Toronto, in a review of several books and papers on ethics, *Harvard Business Review*, May–June 1993

Ethics pays.

JOHN SHAD, former chairman of the Securities and Exchange Commission, *Harvard Business Review*, May–June 1993

If we define success as making zillions of dollars while staying within the narrow definitions of the law, then it is indeed difficult to be successful in business without failing as a force for social change. Similarly, if being successful as a force for social change means that we must single-handedly save the world, then we will surely fail both as a business and as a force for social change.

> PROFESSOR FRED L. FRY of Bradley University, quoted in *Inc.,* October 1994

Is it possible that at certain periods in our economic stream those who are responsible for the pricing of financial instruments don't give a damn regarding the accounting numbers?

> PROFESSOR ABRAHAM J. BRILOFF of Baruch College, prominent accounting gadfly, in a 1996 report on America Online profits

It ought to be fairly easy to choose between "right" and "wrong" by relying on moral principles. But big business activity often demands that we select from alternatives that are neither wholly "right" nor wholly "wrong."

> PRESTON TOWNLEY, CEO of the big business association Conference Board, in a speech, November 3, 1991

Once you give up your ethics, the rest is a piece of cake.

> Oily oilman J. R. EWING, character on TV show *Dallas,* quoted by Preston Townley, CEO of the Conference Board, November 3, 1991

Employers often look into the looking glass and upon seeing smudges on their faces smash the glass rather than wash their faces.

> Unnamed Conference Board founder, cited by Preston Townley, CEO of the Conference Board, November 3, 1991

I believe a culture that values integrity, combined with management that tries to address potential causes of unethical behavior, is perhaps the best means of ensuring integrity in business. Without these things, the most stringent regulatory regime in the world is never going to serve the public's interest fully.

> DEAN O'HARE, CEO of the insurance firm Chubb, in a speech, October 20, 1995

Virtue may not always be its own reward. But if you're in business for the long haul, it usually pays some nice dividends.

> RICHARD MUNRO, CEO of Time Inc., in a speech, November 16, 1987

Only the little people pay taxes.

> LEONA HELMSLEY, former hotel owner

Ethics is being unafraid to give your parrot to the town gossip.

> ANONYMOUS

Conscience is the inner voice which warns us that someone may be looking.

> H. L. MENCKEN, "Sententiae," *A Book of Burlesques* (1920)

Society cannot exist apart from basic agreement concerning right and wrong—including the Golden Rule, the importance of moderation, and acceptance of the inequality of results. The Golden Rule—"Do unto others as you would have them do unto you"— is a good starting point, because it is a value common to all of the great religious and ethical traditions, and it applies to all people regardless of their station in life.

> CHARLES S. SANFORD JR., CEO of the investment bank Bankers Trust, in a speech, October 1993

We have high standards in every way. In addition to placing high value on ethics, we stress intellectual honesty in all our decisions. Intellectual honesty is more than what's legislated; it is inherent in the best people, those who take a broader view of their action than simply "What's in it for me?"

> CHARLES S. SANFORD JR., CEO of Bankers Trust, in an orientation speech to new recruits, 1995

What Bankers Trust can do for Sony and IBM is get in the middle and rip them off—make a little money.

Funny business, you know? Lure people into that calm and then just totally f--- 'em.

> Bankers Trust personnel, quoted by *Business Week* in article restrained prior to publication and then published October 1995

Businessmen spent more time in jail for price-fixing in 1978 than in all the 89 years since the passage of the Sherman Antitrust Act.

> NICK GALLUCCIO, "The Boss in the Slammer," *Forbes,* February 5, 1979

Beware of organizations that have the power to police themselves.

> WILLIAM G. CHRISTIE of the Owen Graduate School of Management, Vanderbilt University, co-author of study that led to government investigation of NAS-DAQ, quoted in the *New York Times,* August 25, 1996

Ethics is not a word normally associated with arms makers.

> *The Economist,* July 22, 1995

You wouldn't rat on your boss for taking home a pack of Post-its, but you would for taking home a computer. You wouldn't rat on him for having one dinner you knew didn't have any business angle, but you would if it was a pattern.

> Ethics officer for a *Fortune 500* company, quoted in *Fortune,* October 2, 1995

Values are where the hard stuff and the soft stuff come together.

> ROBERT HAAS, CEO of the clothing company Levi Strauss, *Harvard Business Review,* September–October 1990

The scandal is not what's illegal. The scandal is what's legal.

> MICHAEL KINSLEY, journalist

It's hard to know where ethics stops and insanity begins.

> MICHAEL KINSLEY (writing about journalistic ethics but the point applies in business, too), *Washington Monthly,* April 1984

Profits alone are not the answer.

[Ethics] requires not only harvesting the fruit we can pluck today . . . not only investing in the small trees and environmental hybrids that won't yield a thing in this quarter and the next . . . but also caring for the soil that allows us to produce such a rich harvest in the first place.

> WILLARD BUTCHER, CEO of Chase Manhattan Bank, in a speech, May 15, 1987 (Almost a decade later

Chase merged with Chemical Bank after fund managers began to insist that it do something to raise the value of its shares.)

Grant Tinker: Why do we air Howard Stern?

Bob Walsh: Howard Stern is the difference between profit and loss at WNBC.

Grant Tinker: Look, if that's the only way to make money, we shouldn't be in business.

[Exchange between the chairman of NBC and the head of the radio division in the mid-eighties, leading to cancellation of the Stern program.]

> Quoted in Ken Auletta, "The Power of Shame: Bill Bennett Takes on Gangsta Rap," *New Yorker,* June 12, 1995

" . . . You're selling bonds, aren't you, old sport?"

"Trying to."

"Well, this would interest you. It wouldn't take up much of your time and you might pick up a nice bit of money. It happens to be a rather confidential sort of thing."

I realize how that under different circumstances that conversation might have been one of the crises of my life. But, because the offer was obviously and tactlessly for a service to be rendered, I had no choice but to cut him off there.

"I've got my hands full," I said. "I'm much obliged but I couldn't take on any more work."

> Exchange between Jay Gatsby and Nick Carraway, in F. Scott Fitzgerald, *The Great Gatsby* (Scribner, 1925)

The new generation that is running things threw all the old rules out the window. They key word is greed. All they care about is money, not honor.

> ANTHONY ACCETTURO, member of the Lucchese crime family, turned government witness, quoted in *Fortune,* April 18, 1994

Much of the litigation in our courts centers on determining what words apply to an action, situation, or object. Were the payments "sales incentives" or bribes and kickbacks? Was it a lie or a "strategic misrepresentation"? Was it a robbery or an "unauthorized withdrawal"? Was it murder or self-defense?

> WILLIAM LUTZ, *The New Doublespeak* (HarperCollins, 1996)

When Mr. [Kenneth] Starr [Whitewater special prosecutor] himself was defending tobacco companies some years ago, and signing briefs arguing that nicotine might not be addictive, he seemed to understand that the quest for the truth must be balanced against the rights of defendants.

The Economist, June 6, 1998

[Reasons executives stumble in gray ethical areas]

One—An inability to grasp the fact that "perceptions" are reality. . . . the real facts themselves are often immaterial!

Two—The lack of a developed philosophical base to support their own role and that of their company in the largest public sense.

Three—Bad counsel. Advisors that dogmatically contend that candor and straight talk create personal jeopardy and liability.

> JOHN F. BUDD JR., vice chairman of the PR firm Carl Byoir & Associates, in a speech, March 29, 1989

At Texaco . . . we have had a set of guiding principles in place since the company was founded in 1902. These principles state in no uncertain terms that we expect the highest standards of moral and ethical conduct throughout the company and that these standards will be enforced.

> JAMES W. KINNEAR, retired CEO of the oil company Texaco, in a speech, April 19, 1995

You know, there is no point in even keeping the restricted version anymore. All it could do is get us in trouble. That's the way I feel. I would not keep anything.

> ROBERT ULRICH, retired treasurer for Texaco, referring to a key document to be destroyed in bias lawsuit by black employees, secretly recorded by another executive, quoted in the *New York Times,* November 4, 1996

In civil cases like the Texaco bias suit, we trust litigants to hand over relevant evidence. The temptation to destroy harmful documents can be great because the chance of detection is often low, but we count on honor to insure compliance and avoid injustice. In an ideal world, honor would suffice. In this world, it must be encouraged by making disobedience painfully expensive.

> STEPHEN GILLERS, professor of law at New York University, letter to the *New York Times,* November 7, 1996

Texaco is a corporation. Corporations cannot express emotion. But the top executives are the corporation, and these executives weren't shocked. Texaco's lawyer says that the words constitute "a clear violation of Texaco policy." These guys are the policy makers. They reportedly discussed destroying documents relating to the lawsuit. But didn't they in fact shred corporate policy?

> WILLIAM COMISKEY, letter to the *New York Times,* November 7, 1996

When did I make my greatest hiring mistakes? When I put intelligence and energy ahead of morality.

> W. MICHAEL BLUMENTHAL, former chairman of Bendix Corporation and U.S. Secretary of Defense

If you want to know what a man is really like, take notice how he acts when he loses money.

> New England proverb

[T]he present debate [between academics and business people] is riven with crass oversimplifications. Actions are divided into two kinds: selfish ones deemed bad and unselfish ones deemed good. Left out altogether are the truly atrocious deeds which have more often been committed through self-righteous commitment to ill-conceived moral codes than deliberate selfishness and greed.

> SAMUEL BRITTAN, *Financial Times,* December 19, 1996

Ethics in a corporation is like water—it flows downhill.

> PROFESSOR THOMAS DONALDSON of the Wharton School at the University of Pennsylvania, quoted in Associated Press, April 5, 1997

Money must not be used in a moral vacuum, but should be used to serve and uphold the highest of moral purposes. Otherwise the market economy, which today has no adversary, will eventually become its own adversary.

> JACQUES ATTALI, president of the European Bank for Reconstruction and Development, an institution created by industrial nations to invest in the former

Soviet bloc, in a speech, February 3, 1992 (Attali resigned when it was discovered that EBRD's expenses for decorating and management perks exceeded its loans.)

[Business] is not a game. Business involves real peoples' lives, and deeply affects the human welfare of communities and nations. I think the media do us all a tragic disservice when they treat business as sport, and business people do us an equally tragic disservice when they approach their work as "gamesmanship." In my observation, much unethical practice springs from this misconception.

I do believe the community eventually catches up to the bad guys.

> DAVID GRIER of the Royal Bank of Canada, in a speech, September 19, 1989

Ethics and competitiveness are inseparable. We compete as a society. No society anywhere will compete very long or successfully with people stabbing each other in the back. There is no escaping this fact: the greater the measure of mutual trust and confidence in the ethics of a society, the greater its economic strength.

> JOHN AKERS, chairman of IBM, quoted by David Grier in the September 19, 1989 speech. (John Akers was CEO of IBM when it nearly collapsed)

How do you get people to share your values? You don't. You find people who share them and eject those who don't.

> JIM COLLINS, co-author of *Built to Last* (HarperCollins, 1984), quoted in *Fortune,* November 27, 1995

Common sense dictates many of the decisions I make both large and small. However, there's a problem with common sense. What I may think is pure, unadulterated common sense, someone else may not. So if we, business leaders, rely on the common sense of our co-workers to act in an ethical manner, it simply won't happen as we imagine and even expect it to.

Evil people will do whatever they want one way or the other. That bad people do bad things is uncontrollable. Ethics means making sure good people don't do bad things, intentionally or unintentionally.

When Oliver Cromwell reorganized his army, he said he wanted honest leaders. "When leaders are honest," he said, "honest men follow." And I bet every one of them could probably look themselves in the mirror and

smile. [History doesn't record whether they smiled just before they executed Charles I, or massacred the Irish and confiscated their property and transferred it to British ownership.]

> STEPHEN BUTLER, CEO of the accounting-consulting firm KPMG Peat Marwick, in a speech, February 28, 1997

Once you raise the bar and urge business as a whole to raise its standards, you paint a bull's eye on your back. The press will watch you for signs of hypocrisy. [The Body Shop and Ben and Jerry's are two prominent examples of companies that have been gleefully savaged in the press for violating their trumpeted principles.]

> CRAIG COX, editor of *Business Ethics,* quoted in Anne Murphy, "The Seven (Almost) Deadly Sins of High-Minded Entrepreneurs," *Inc.,* July 1994

Just because you have a high-minded statement of principles or send a certain percentage of your profits to save the rain forests doesn't mean you have the internal controls to prevent ethics problems.

> ED PETRIE, executive director of the Ethics Officers Association, quoted in the *New York Times,* July 6, 1997

If one worker's rights are abused then I can no longer claim to be doing my best.

> BRUCE J. KLATSKY, chief executive of Phillips-Van Heusen Corporation, a shirt company, and board member of Human Rights Watch, quoted in the *Wall Street Journal,* February 24, 1997. (He was stung by reports that the company's factories were paying sub-poverty wages in Guatemala.)

As an American company, you now have no choice but to import from low-wage countries. If you don't do it, you won't survive. A shirt is not a high-tech product.

> *Wall Street Journal,* February 24, 1997

You don't teach ethics, you learn it.

> DIANA WINSTANLEY of the Imperial College Management School, London, quoted in the *Financial Times,* October 9, 1997

16.1 BANKRUPTCY

Solvency is entirely a matter of temperament and not of income.

> LOGAN PEARSALL SMITH, *Afterthoughts* (1931)

I don't recommend [bankruptcy]. But go through it, and, if you are successful, you can look back with a lot of satisfaction.

> JOHN ZIEGLER, head of the conglomerate Willcox & Gibbs Co., quoted in *Forbes,* July 28, 1986

I haven't worked 16 hours a day in a bank just to pay for their [third-world corporate and government elite] lifestyles. The term forgiveness [of debt] does not exist in my vocabulary.

> WALTER SEIPP, chairman of the West German bank Commerzbank, quoted in *Time,* October 10, 1988

Once bankruptcy was a dirty word; now it can be a strategy.

> GERALD BUCCINO, a turnaround consultant, quoted in the *Wall Street Journal,* February 13, 1996

The city itself went bankrupt in 1979, and so have many of its leading citizens, from the founder of the Piggly Wiggly grocery chain to rock & roll legend Jerry Lee Lewis. . . . Friends and neighbors tell each other "bankruptcy works," says David Monypeny, Jerry Lee Lewis' manager. . . . The Memphis Yellow Pages features more than a dozen large lawyers' ads offering to wipe out debt for no down payment; a Honda dealer (its slogan: "The bankruptcy specialists") runs TV commercials promising to sell you a car no matter what your credit history.

> KIM CLARK, *Fortune,* August 4, 1997

Farmers used to have a sense of ethics. They'd commit suicide rather than slide out of debt.

> BRUCE HANSON, Iowa farmer who cut back on his farming and started another business to cope with debt resulting from rising grain prices when corn futures were all hedged against falling prices (the situation pitted farmers against their grain elevator operators and divided the community), quoted in the *Wall Street Journal,* July 2, 1996

I detest bankruptcy. To me it signifies failure—personal failure, corporate failure.

> GEORGE STEINBRENNER III, owner of the New York Yankees (his American Ship Building Company almost went bankrupt in 1992), quoted in the *New York Times,* October 25, 1992

My experience is that the largest percentage of bankruptcies are due not to poor business management but to outside conditions beyond the owners' control.

> JAMES A. GOODMAN, chief bankruptcy judge, U.S. District of Maine, quoted in *Inc.,* October 1996 (He gives as an example, rapid rises in the price of oil which have ripple effects for snowmobile manufacturers and dealers, greenhouse operators, and so on.)

If we practice bailing out lenders whenever they get into trouble, then lenders everywhere will come to count on that and they will continue to make loans they should not make.

> PROFESSOR RICHARD COOPER of Harvard University, in the wake of the 1997 South Korean banking crisis, quoted in the *New York Times,* December 4, 1997

You'd be surprised what you can recover by tugging at a borrower's conscience.

> JOHN FORLINES, CEO of the small, highly profitable, Bank of Granite in North Dakota, quoted in the *Economist,* January 3, 1998

16.2 ETHICAL CRISIS MANAGEMENT

[Steps to follow in the event of accusations of wrongdoing, such as malfeasance, discrimination, environmental degradation, or product danger.]

- Express complete contrition if the company is clearly and totally to blame. Forswear the past and vow to move forward as reformed leaders running a reformed company.
- Express indignant and outraged denial if—and only if—the facts will clear the company's name and such facts can be produced.
- Acknowledge an uncertain situation if one really exists and commit to an honest and thorough investigation and follow-up.
- Maintain absolute silence only to stop certain destruction of the organization, or if public health and safety requires.

> PROFESSOR GERALD C. MEYERS of the University of Michigan, former chairman of American Motors, and his daughter SUSAN MEYERS, freelance writer, *New York Times,* January 12, 1997 (Authors contended that Texaco minimized original discrimination charges and overcompensated later.)

16.3 GLOBAL ETHICS

Insider trading doesn't have much of a stigma [in Germany]. Tax evasion is a gentleman's sport.

Business Week, March 23, 1987

In a recent poll, 46 percent of those [Germans] surveyed agreed with the statement that "those who don't cheat on taxes deserve only pity . . ."

Wall Street Journal, August 22, 1997

In our view, corruption is when you open the safe, take out the money, and put it in your pocket. When you receive a "commission" for projects, you get a debate about whether that is corruption. To me it's corruption, but as the older people see it, when you're in power you have the right to receive this money, as long as it's not contrary to the public interest.

SARWONO, secretary-general, Golkar, Indonesia, quoted in the *New Yorker,* June 13, 1988

Despite the all-pervasive scandals of the 1980s, there is a tendency in Europe to regard the study of business ethics as faddish.

Financial Times, July 3, 1992

It's arrogant to think you can make a difference in another country's culture. But it's equally arrogant to imagine you can't find responsible businesspeople everywhere.

ARNOLD HIATT, former CEO of the shoe company Stride Rite, interviewed in *Harvard Business Review,* March–April 1992

The most important reason why there appears to be so much more white-collar crime in the United States is that there are so many more laws regulating business in the United States to be broken. Moreover, regulations governing business tend to be more strictly enforced in the United States than in other capitalist nations. In addition, thanks to more aggressive journalism, as well as to government disclosure requirements, business misdeeds are more likely to be exposed in the United States.

DAVID VOGEL, *California Management Review,* September 22, 1992

In Japan today, if you have the word "Inc." attached to your name, you can commit crimes with little risk and only minor penalties.

Japanese journalist quoted anonymously in James Sterngold, "Japan's Rigged Casino," *New York Times Magazine,* April 26, 1992

[Aristotle] Onassis installed a luxurious private bathroom adjoining his office. The lavatory door was really a one-way mirror, allowing Onassis to observe unsuspecting visitors. During a business meeting one afternoon, Onassis excused himself and entered the bathroom. While seated, he was horrified to see his reflection staring back at him on the mirrored door. A workman making repairs earlier in the day had replaced the mirror the wrong way . . . reflecting badly not only upon the workmanship but also upon Onassis's ethical standards.

A. THOMAS YOUNG, president of the aerospace corporation Martin Marietta, in a speech, May 5, 1992

The ethics of the global conglomerates are those of the marketplace: give as little as possible and take as much as is politically acceptable.

ROBERT LEKACHMAN and BORIN VAN LOON, *Capitalism for Beginners* (Pantheon, 1981)

We said right from the start, as long as we work to our norms and values in that country we should stay.

Heineken NV spokesman shrugging off threats of a boycott before public opinion forced the brewer to pull out of a joint venture with the Burmese military, quoted in *Asia, Inc.,* September 1996

It's no longer just a question of having the relevant government permits.

Manager of a big mining company, on the ethical challenges to multinational corporations, quoted in the *Economist,* July 20, 1996

We want to engage, not enrage.

Shell slogan in wake of battle with Greenpeace over where to dispose of an old drilling platform, cited in the *Economist,* July 20, 1996

The richer a country is, the less corrupt it is seen to be. Consider the corruption ranking of 54 countries done by Germany's Göttingen University and Transparency

International, a Berlin-based nonprofit group dedicated to fighting corruption. The rankings are based on business people's perceptions of corruption as reported in polls. While necessarily subjective, the rankings represent views that have informed substantial commitments of investment funds. And they show that the 20 countries judged least corrupt all had gross national products per capita in 1994 of more than $10,000, with 13 over $20,000. The 20 deemed most corrupt all had GNP per capita of less than $10,000; 12 were under $1,000.

> URBAN C. LEHNER, Asian edition of the *Wall Street Journal,* October 22, 1996

The Securities and Exchange Commission wants to send a message to companies, particularly foreign ones: If you pay bribes, either disclose the practice or make sure that they do not distort your financial statements. [This was written after the SEC had filed suit against the Italian company Montedison for misrepresenting bribes to Italian officials as loans and overstating its real estate assets.]

> FLOYD NORRIS, *New York Times,* November 22, 1996

In country after country, it is the people who are demanding action on this issue. They know corruption diverts resources from the poor to the rich, increases the cost of running businesses, distorts public expenditures, and deters foreign investors.

> JAMES D. WOLFENSOHN, president of the World Bank, quoted in the *New York Times,* November 28, 1996

In a 1995 report, Mickey Kantor, then the United States trade representative, said American companies lost $45 billion of overseas contracts the previous year because of the bribery ban.

> *New York Times,* November 28, 1996

Corruption by the numbers [Survey of businesspeople by the Berlin-based corruption watchdog group Transparency International]

Most corrupt nations to do business in 1996:

1. Nigeria, 2. Pakistan, 3. Kenya, 4. Bangladesh, 5. China.

Least corrupt:

1. New Zealand, 2. Denmark, 3. Sweden, 4. Finland, 5. Canada, . . . 15. United States

> *New York Times,* November 28, 1996

I carried the history of pirates up through today and found out that pirates were Joe Kennedy and Sam Bronfman [*sic*]. Even in my lifetime, these were considered pirates. I said, there is nothing wrong with that; these countries are changing. You just want to be on the right side of it.

> MICHAEL D. DINGMAN, American financier whose activities in Czech Republic have drawn accusations of asset stripping and complaints from investors, quoted in *Fortune,* December 23, 1996

[A]necdotal evidence clearly indicates that [U.S. exports lost from] bribery and corruption, is a multibillion-dollar problem. . . . [F]rom April 1994 to May 1995, the U.S. government learned of almost 100 cases in which foreign bribes undercut U.S. firms' ability to win contracts valued at $45 billion. . . . [I]t also hurts the economy where the corruption is taking place, by denying it the benefits of trade agreements. And bribery and corruption interfere with trade negotiations—corrupt officials do not want their cozy relationships disturbed by trade liberalization, so they influence governments to resist it in negotiations.

> MICKEY KANTOR, U.S. Commerce Secretary, in a speech, March 6, 1996

Let's not mince words: we need to deal with the cancer of corruption.

> JAMES D. WOLFENSOHN, president of the World Bank, quoted in the *Financial Times,* September 16, 1997

[T]axpayers should be encouraged to maintain records to indicate the name of the recipient of the bribe and the date, method, and amount of the payment, and this information should be available on request of the tax authorities.

> Guideline issued by the fiscal affairs committee of the Organization for Economic Cooperation and Development in the event that taxpayers cannot avoid paying bribes in the conduct of business, cited in the *International Herald Tribune,* April 12, 1997

Be in countries where there is a good legal system and a respect for property rights.

> CHARLES TARGET of the Hong Kong–based investment management company Bowen Asia, quoted in *Asia, Inc.,* March 1997

Corruption can also work your way.

> Said with a laugh by ELIZABETH HASKELL, formerly
> of Baltimore, owner of Betsy's Place, a small hotel
> in Tblisi, Georgia, quoted in the *New York Times,*
> July 5, 1997

European industry is essentially saying, "If this is a way for us to stop bribery without losing business, then we will support it." But the Germans especially feel that they cannot afford to be virtuous on their own.

> PETER EIGEN, president of the Berlin-based corrup-
> tion watchdog group Transparency International,
> on an anti-corruption treaty being drafted for the
> OECD, quoted in the *Wall Street Journal,* September
> 23, 1997

We were viewed as naive Americans who knew very little about how things really worked in the rest of the world.

> THOMAS WHITE, State Department official and chief
> U.S. negotiator on anti-corruption treaty, recalling
> the first time the subject of the treaty was broached,
> quoted in the *Wall Street Journal,* September 23, 1997

16.4 MONEY LAUNDERING

[D]irty money is like water: it follows the path of least resistance.

> CHARLES H. MORLEY, "The Impact of Money Laun-
> dering on State Security," *Money Laundering, Asset
> Forfeiture and International Financial Crimes* (1994)

[Money laundering] sustains every criminal activity engaged in for profit, which is to say all crimes but crimes of passion or vengeance.

> SCOTT SULTZER, "Money Laundering: The Scope of
> the Problem and Attempts to Combat It," *Tennessee
> Legal Review,* 1995

No one says they intend to go into money laundering. You just get drawn into it.

> KENNETH W. RIJOCK, lawyer and ex-con, quoted in
> *Business Week,* May 30, 1994

A phase is the transition period during which assets move from a higher to a lower level of risk.

> FRANKLIN JUARDO, Harvard-educated Colombian
> economist and confessed money launderer for the

Cali cartel (Juardo had a five-phase strategy to clean drug money), *Harper's,* February 1997

At the end of the day, is it really going to be convenient for a criminal to have hundreds and hundreds of cars? He might as well have hundreds and hundreds of dollar bills.

> ROBERT CAPLEHORN, general counsel, Mondex
> International Ltd., London company that licenses
> electronic cash technology to banks and corpora-
> tions, quoted in the *Wall Street Journal,* March 17,
> 1997 (He believes that electronic cash will not be
> much of a help to money launderers because it
> eventually has to be spent.)

If we assume a conservative figure of $50 billion for all illicit drugs sold in the United States, the amount of illicit currency produced by those sales weighs almost 13 million pounds.

> MARY LEE WARREN, U.S. Deputy Assistant Attorney
> General, quoted in the *Washington Post,* March 9,
> 1997

16.5 PRIVACY

Before the reluctant Blockbuster computer technician refused to continue, the MTV people persuaded him to cross-index Senator Ted Kennedy and O. J. Simpson to see what tapes they had rented in common. [Only one: "Grumpy Old Men"]

> *Wall Street Journal,* February 21, 1997

We lost some damn good programmers—pedophiles. Some of our best computer operatives were sex offenders.

> DEEWAYNE BECKHAM, assistant plant manager,
> Records Conversion Facility, Huntsville Prison,
> Texas, after the state legislature (reacting to news
> reports that a convicted rapist had written detailed
> sexual fantasies to a woman based on information
> from a consumer questionnaire processed at the
> prison) banned sex offenders from computer-related
> work (187 of 430 inmates were affected), quoted in
> the *New York Times,* June 12, 1997

Is the government going to sacrifice the money that can be made for a little bit of privacy?

> ANGELA PUGH, supervisor of Geographic Informa-
> tion Systems, Ferguson Prison, on the news that

computer work might be banned from prisons,
quoted in the *New York Times,* June 12, 1997

If you belong to a frequent buyer club at the bookstore, they probably keep a record of the books you buy. But no one follows you around the store and keeps track of what you looked at and how long you looked at it before you bought.

> CHRISTINE VARNEY, member of the Federal Trade Commission, quoted in the *New York Times,* June 22, 1997

When you're ordering something the old-fashioned way, [t]he merchant doesn't bother to ask what you want done with the record of your purchase, and you probably don't give it a second thought. On the Net, the customer ordering the tie is more suspicious, bless him. "Is my credit card number safe?" he asks. [Answer: It's at least as safe as with any restaurant waiter in America.] "What about my data? What are you going to do with them?" Good question. The challenge is to make it easy for him to get an answer.

> ESTHER DYSON, president of the high-tech investment firm EDventure Holdings, quoted in the *Wall Street Journal,* June 17, 1997

The amount of information available at the push of a button has just revolutionized the whole private investigation industry. Everything you want to know is for sale. It's a question of how much risk you want to take and what your personal morals are.

> JASON ROWE, private investigator who works for plaintiffs suing large corporations, quoted in the *New York Times,* September 15, 1997

You can beat the system. Just don't own any property, don't stay in one place, keep your yap shut, don't have credit, don't drive a car, don't keep a job, don't pay your taxes, and never, never apply for a social security number.

> AL COSTA, computer-adept private eye in California, quoted in *Inc. Technology,* Summer 1995

The melding of databases raised profound privacy questions. Big Brother is not necessarily a government surveillance scheme. It can just as readily be a private business.

> DON HAINES, legislative council for the American Civil Liberties Union, quoted in the *Wall Street Journal,* September 3, 1996

"Saks got a copy of my credit report in five minutes with nothing but information they got from me! Why can't I get a copy with the same information?"

"They are a business, sir," she said smugly.

"Have you ever heard of Harvard Law School?" I screamed. "They are a business . . ."

> LYNN M. LOPUCK of Harvard Law School, adviser to National Bankruptcy Review Commission's Data Study Project, who was denied a charge account at Saks, quoted in the *New York Times,* September 20, 1997

16.6 PRIVACY AT WORK

These days, snooping can be done by random urinalysis tests for drugs . . . random blood tests for both drugs and the AIDS virus . . . lie detector tests . . . electronic eavesdropping . . . and pulmonary function tests for smoking. What these tests have in common is that most often they are not being used to diagnose any specific job-performance problem. They are being used broadside, to check up indiscriminately on how people live their lives outside of work.

> JOHN A. MURPHY, president of the Philip Morris Companies, in a speech, May 3, 1988

[The AMA report, published March 1992] demonstrates what the ACLU has been saying for years. That the vast majority of American employees do not abuse drugs and that indiscriminate drug tests of everyone—innocent and guilty alike—are not only an invasion of privacy of hundreds of innocent workers, but also a colossal waste of company money.

> IRA GLASSER, executive director of the ACLU, quoted in the *New York Times,* April 12, 1992

If future competitiveness depends on treating people as an important part of the institution, the least respectful thing I can imagine doing to a human being [is asking him to urinate in a cup].

> TOM PETERS, management guru, testifying to the California Legislature, quoted in the *New York Times,* November 28, 1993

There's no such thing as confidentiality in a corporate setting.

Given the competitive pressures we all face, we need employees who will bust their fannies for us. They're not going to do that if they think you and I are sitting there waiting to bust them for something they may or may not be doing off the job.

> CRAIG CORNISH of the American Bar Association's workplace privacy committee, quoted in the *Wall Street Journal,* June 20, 1996

Don't want your employer to know that you took a surreptitious trip to the pornography site "Genital Hospital" on your lunch hour? Too bad. You probably left an electronic cookie crumb on your hard drive.

> JOHN M. BRODER, *New York Times,* June 22, 1997

You'd be surprised at how many people look at the sticker and walk away.

> CINDY FRANKLIN, president of Background Bureau Inc., which puts its logo on client doors to warn job applicants that their backgrounds will be checked, *Wall Street Journal,* February 4, 1997

16.7 THE TOBACCO INDUSTRY UNDER OATH

I believe that nicotine is not addictive.

> THOMAS E. SANDEFUR JR., Brown & Williamson, 1994 Congressional hearings, quoted in the *New York Times,* September 7, 1997

Cigarettes and nicotine clearly do not meet the classic definition of addiction.

> JAMES W. JOHNSTON, former chairman of R. J. Reynolds Tobacco, quoted in the *New York Times,* September 7, 1997

If you are bitten by a deer tick that carries Lyme disease, you get Lyme disease. In smoking-related illnesses, those connections have not been established.

> JAMES W. JOHNSTON, elaborating on the logic of his earlier statement, in interview in the *New York Times,* September 7, 1997

Perjury is one of the most difficult crimes to prove. You can prove the moon is blue, but they may have believed it when they said the moon is green.

> JOSEPH DiGENOVA, former federal prosecutor, quoted in the *New York Times,* September 7, 1997

I have always believed that smoking plays a part in causing lung cancer. What that role is, I don't know, but I do believe it.

> STEVEN F. GOLDSTONE, chairman RJR Nabisco Holding Corporation, in a deposition, the day after Philip Morris CEO Geoffrey Bible said that about 100,000 Americans "might have" died from smoking-related diseases, quoted in the *New York Times,* August 23, 1997

If [cigarettes] are behaviorally addictive or habit forming, they are much more like . . . Gummi Bears. I love Gummi Bears . . . and I want Gummi Bears, and I eat Gummi Bears, and I don't like it when I don't eat my Gummi Bears, but I'm certainly not addicted to them.

> JAMES MORGAN, president of the tobacco firm Philip Morris, in a sworn videotaped deposition, quoted in *Time,* May 12, 1997

16.8 TRANSPARENCY

Sunlight is the best disinfectant.

> JUSTICE LOUIS D. BRANDEIS

Greater transparency is desirable in its own right, but it is also consistent with movement in the direction of less regulation, less administrative guidance and greater competition.

> E. GERALD CORRIGAN of the investment bank Goldman, Sachs and former president of the Federal Reserve Bank of New York, in a speech, September 24, 1995

Most governments, including my own, have maintained a veil of secrecy over official foreign exchange transactions. This can mean that markets have incomplete, and sometimes quite misleading, information about the government's foreign exchange reserves and the scale of intervention that has been taken. I want to announce the end of all that.

> GORDON BROWN, Chancellor of the Exchequer in the U.K., quoted in the *Financial Times,* September 22, 1997

Q: What was the single most important lesson you learned during the peso crisis?

A: Disclosure was fundamental. We didn't try to hide or mislead the markets.

> GUILLERMO ORTIZ, Mexico's Minister of Finance, discussing lessons (based on Mexico's troubles in 1994) for Asians in the 1997 currency crisis, quoted in the *Wall Street Journal,* October 29, 1997

[I]n the end it is cheaper to give the market all the information it needs to price risk correctly rather than trying to hide the bad news and have it overshoot.

Wall Street Journal, editorial, October 8, 1997

16.9 WHISTLEBLOWING

I'm a disgruntled employee. Is this where I call to get revenge?

> Anonymous caller, quoted by Bob Krueger, director of enforcement for Business Software Alliance, reporting unauthorized software copying at his company, *New York Times,* December 15, 1996

17.1 BUSINESS CONDITIONS

Favorite countries for business, chosen by the European Council of American Chambers of Commerce according to factors like politics and economic conditions; quality of life matters, including health care and culture; business infrastructure; and labor conditions.

Most favorable: Ireland, the Netherlands, Sweden, Switzerland, and Israel.

Least favorable: Bulgaria, Poland, Slovakia, Romania, and Greece.

Germany rates low in labor category, because of pay rates, benefits, and union presence.

Belgium near the bottom in many categories, including politics, labor conditions, business regulations, and taxes.

> Reported in the European edition of the *Wall Street Journal*, October 22, 1996

17.2 CAPITAL

The problem in Europe is that, while major companies are shedding jobs, there is little business formation to create new ones. The United States is blessed with four elements missing in Europe: entrepreneurs, commercial banks looking for loans, large pools of venture capital, and outstanding capital markets. In the last $4^1/2$ years, 3,000 U.S. companies have come public through initial public offerings raising more than $150 billion. This compares with fewer than 150 companies coming public in Europe in the last $6^1/2$ years. I don't know if 3,000 companies have come public in Europe since Charlemagne, and he became king of the Franks in 768.

> PETER LYNCH, vice chairman of Fidelity Management and Research Co. and former portfolio manager for Fidelity Magellan Fund, quoted in the *Wall Street Journal*, September 20, 1996

U.S. pension funds had assets totaling more than $3.5 trillion (59.1% of GDP) in 1993, while U.K. pension funds totaled more than $717 billion (79.4% of GDP). In Italy, however, they amounted to a mere $11.6 billion (1.2% of GDP), while French and German funds totaled $41.1 billion (3.4% of GDP) and $106 billion (5.8% of

GDP), respectively. Moreover, while 80 percent of U.K. pension assets were invested in equity at the end of 1994, Italy had only 9 percent of its meager total invested in equity. France had 13 percent and Germany only 11 percent of pension funds invested in equity.

> *Wall Street Journal*, editorial, September 5, 1996

It's not the Americanization in the 1950s and '60s, when we all drank Coca-Cola. What we associate with America now is they've done lots of things we had in mind but we didn't do, and we need to do them now.

> MARTIN W. HUFNER, chief economist at Bayerische Vereinsbank in Munich, quoted in *Business Week*, October 7, 1996

Europeans [investment bankers] get into too much thought, too much planning, too much strategy. Therefore, we build up teams selling too many old-fashioned products.

> RICHARD WATKINS, chief executive, Latinvest Securities (London), quoted in the *Wall Street Journal*, January 5, 1996

Investors are going to have to concentrate much more on credit stories if they want to maintain the portfolio returns they are used to. To put it crudely, that means there's going to be a growing appetite for junk bonds in Europe.

> "One banker," quoted in the *Financial Times*, May 27, 1997

17.3 COMPETITIVENESS AND THE HEAVY HAND OF THE STATE

Many of the continent's biggest companies were suckled at the state's teat. From Renault to Elf Aquitaine, most of France's biggest firms are headed by ex-civil servants; many of Germany's biggest companies, including Volkswagen, are part-owned by local governments.

In the end . . . the real commercial victims of the failure of structural reform in Europe are not the region's existing companies, but those that are never born.

> *The Economist*, August 2, 1997

For the moment, the more Europe advances on free trade, the more its governments move to intervene for the domestic economy. It's a paradox.

> PETER PRAET, chief economist of Belgium's General Bank, on Europe's protectionism, quoted in the *Wall Street Journal*, April 1, 1996

17.4   ENTREPRENEURSHIP

These people [European entrepreneurs] have all done what they've done *in spite of*. *In spite of* no intelligent politics on the national or European level, *in spite of* no intelligent forms of risk capital. But they couldn't care about the *in spite of*s.

> HEINRICH VON LIECHTENSTEIN, executive director of European Foundation for Entrepreneurship Research in Brussels, quoted in *Inc.*, April 1996

Entrepreneurs should be able to spend 80 percent of their time getting customers. But if you have to spend 50 percent of your time doing administrative work for the government, you have only about 40 percent left to sell.

> KENNETH IVERSON, managing director of Unimerco A/S, Danish tool-grinding company, quoted in *Inc.*, April 1996

17.5   THE ENVIRONMENT

To see where Europe is headed, look at Germany. Germany is the European equivalent of California: the continent's biggest, richest country with the largest amount of waste and the strongest environmental lobby.

Some companies have decided that the best way to comply with tough German rules is to do what many car manufacturers did in the United States years ago when California created demanding emission standards: produce everything to the world's toughest standards.

> FRANCIS CAIRNCROSS, environmental editor of the *Economist, Harvard Business Review*, March–April, 1992

17.6   THE FUTURE

The greatest threat to Europe's economic health is not our social burden but our limited ability to move quickly enough into new value-added businesses.

> HERBERT A. HENZLER, chairman of McKinsey & Co. and professor of international management, Munich

University, *Harvard Business Review*, July–August 1992

Throughout Europe, to a greater or lesser extent, we have rampant dissatisfaction because politicians are elected on promises they can't deliver because the market is global.

We are going to have unelected bureaucrats, distant from any public accountability, running a bank board that will essentially set everything in economic terms in Europe. The results could be explosive.

> JONATHAN EYAL, director of studies at the United Services Institute, a London think tank, quoted in the *New York Times*, November 17, 1996

Open societies are based on the recognition that human understanding is imperfect and all constructs and institutions are flawed to a greater or lesser degree. But the [European] Union has been shaped by bureaucrats, particularly French bureaucrats, and they are not known for their humility. They, better than most, recognize the deficiencies of institutions, which is why they are anxious to impose rigid conditions and a rigid timetable— so that the institutions should move forward, however deficient they are.

The bureaucratic method of building an integrated Europe has exhausted its potential.

> GEORGE SOROS, "Can Europe Work?" *Foreign Affairs*, September–October 1996

The past is Europe's greatest advantage. When price is no object, tradition bestows not only a brand, but also the skills that guarantee the highest quality. [For example, a saddle factory is operating in the rue du Faubourg-Saint-Hôtel, one of the poshest streets in Paris, where it has done business for 159 years, and where a saddle costs FF14,600.]

> *The Economist*, November 23, 1996

Competition in telecommunications is today more urgent than European monetary union.

> BRUNO LAMBROGHINI of the computer company Olivetti, quoted in *Business Week*, September 26, 1994

It is troubling to anyone who cares about European prosperity that today, in general, Europe is investing capital goods, including information technology, at only about half the rate you see in the United States and Asia. That doesn't augur very well for their future.

RICHARD THOMAN, CFO of IBM, quoted in the *Financial Times,* January 27, 1997

We may never catch up . . . If we keep going this way we can bury ourselves.

GERHARD SCHULMEYER, chief executive of the computer firm Siemens Nixdorf Information, quoted in the *Financial Times,* March 14, 1997

Continental Europeans by and large continue to resist the new economy, treating globalization as some sort of capitalist plot. Critics range from the Vatican, which is suspicious of capitalism anyway, to politicians, who (especially in Italy) control the media, government bureaucracy, banks, and top industries. This is a highly centralized system that is deeply threatened by the new economy that America has embraced. It should not be surprising that one of the founding engineers at Netscape, Ari Luotenen, had to leave Europe for America to pursue his research on a Web browser.

MARIO CALVO-PLATERO and MAURO CALAMANDREI, journalists, *New York Times Magazine,* June 8, 1997

We have learned in Europe the same lesson you all have, there's no hiding from the global economy.

JÜRGEN E. SCHREMPP, chairman of Daimler-Benz, in a speech, January 6, 1997

Don't worry. It is only a Revolution. [Title of research paper by Jan Mantel, senior fund manager for Merrill Lynch, predicting that monetary union will spur cross-border investment in Europe, where pension funds invest 70–90 percent of assets in home markets.]

Financial Times, September 23, 1997

Summer is now a hot time, in every sense of the word.

PAOLO VIBERTI, logistics specialist of the auto firm Fiat, referring to the new policy of keeping his factory open in August, reflecting trend away from summer shutdowns in Europe, quoted in the *Economist,* August 15, 1997

17.7   JOBS

[Laws distorting labor market in Europe]

Italy—19 percent value-added tax on house sales; private employment agencies are illegal.

Spain—Andalucia provides six months on dole after a few weeks of employment, producing net immigration despite 34 percent unemployment rate.

The Economist, October 5, 1996

Job creation requires three things: (1) the economy must grow fast enough so that companies want more workers; (2) hiring must be profitable—if labor costs are too high, firms won't hire even if demand is strong; and (3) people must be willing to work. On all counts, the U.S. economy outperforms the European.

ROBERT J. SAMUELSON, *Newsweek,* July 29, 1996

17.8   MODERN CONVENIENCES

Would we buy a refrigerator with the freezer in the "wrong" place if the price were right?

This being Europe, the question is heresy. Discounting and aggressive pricing to build volume are out of the question as long as "national" preferences, real or imagined, can be used as an excuse to keep unit prices in the stratosphere.

ANDREW BLANK, Friolzheim, Germany, in letter to editor, *Fortune,* October 18, 1993

[British Telecom has] a 10-year head start [on other European telecommunications monopolies]. They had Mrs. Thatcher to kick them early.

CARL-FRIEDRICH MEISSNER, Deutsche Telekom board member, quoted in *Business Week,* March 27, 1996

Europeans are just like Americans: They'll fly more if the price is good. Some people said that Americans are different because they speak the same language and have relatives scattered much farther away, but we've shown that Europeans respond to lower fares the same way Americans do.

STELIOS HAJI-IOANNOU, Greek-born British resident, owner of easyJet, European discount airline, quoted in the *Wall Street Journal,* December 9, 1996

17.9   A SINGLE CURRENCY

Would the United States be better off if each state had its own currency?

Rhetorical question posed by proponents of a single European currency, quoted in *Fortune,* September 18, 1995

European monetary union [Emu] could herald a huge upheaval for the operators of the seven-million or so mechanisms around Europe that rely on coins to make them work. The costs in altering existing mechanisms, spare parts, and training activity could be Ecu [European currency units] 15 billion ($17.8 billion), the industry estimates.

> PETER MARSH, *Financial Times,* January 28, 1997

With all the time and energy that has gone into creating a single European central bank you would think the potential members would have a good idea of how the institution would work. They do not.

> STEPHANIE FLANDERS, *Financial Times,* January 20, 1997

Traders' anguish. [Common among European currency traders; fear of losing job as a result of Emu.]

> *Financial Times,* January 7, 1997

You cannot motivate your traders and ask them to work harder one day, then come back the next day and say: "By the way, we have just set up a working group to decide how many of you have to go." So it is easier to hide behind a mask and pretend everything is fine.

> Trader on calm prevailing at European banks, quoted in the *Financial Times,* January 7, 1997

The way our markets and trading technology are changing, people are likely to lose their jobs anyway. How much of that can be attributed to Emu is hard to quantify.

> Independent observer, quoted in the *Financial Times,* January 7, 1997

The technology is very easy. We added 16 new currencies when the Soviet Union fell, without any big disruption, and this will be no harder.

> HANS VAN DER VELDE, European region of Visa, for which Emu will probably be a boon, quoted in the *Financial Times,* March 4, 1997

Some observers in Europe have expressed a desire to gain a dominant role for the Euro as a matter of prestige. I think this view confuses cause and effect. Prestige alone will not create a successful economic outcome. Successful economic outcomes create prestige.

> LAWRENCE SUMMERS, Deputy U.S. Treasury Secretary, quoted in the *Financial Times,* May 1, 1997

[I]f Emu works for Europe, it works for us.

> LAWRENCE SUMMERS, U.S. Deputy Treasury Secretary, quoted in the *Financial Times,* October 22, 1997

The trading and economics profession in the currencies field as we know it will not change in a revolutionary way after January 1, 1999.

> MICHAEL SCARLATOS, foreign exchange strategist for Bankers Trust, London, quoted in the *Financial Times,* May 20, 1997

There's that whiff of panic in the air. People suddenly realize they've got to have everything ready to go.

> GRAHAM BISHOP, of the investment firm Salomon Smith Barney, quoted in the *International Herald Tribune,* December 15, 1997

The elimination of national currencies will make it much easier for consumers to compare prices across borders, a fact that executives say will force the prices of their goods down towards the lowest levels prevailing in Europe.

> TOM BUERKLE, *International Herald Tribune,* December 15, 1997

The people are opposed to it [currency unification]. And who is being stupid in all of this, in my opinion, is the business community in Europe. They're not going to benefit from the Euro, they're going to be harmed by it.

> MILTON FRIEDMAN, Nobel Prize–winning economist, interviewed in *Forbes,* December 29, 1997

I find it amazing that the British are still debating whether Emu is a political project. On the continent to say that Emu is political is simply a truism, a tautology.

> Senior European diplomat, quoted in the *Economist,* January 3, 1998

17.10   TRADE WITH LATIN AMERICA

It can all be summed up quite simply: We are stomping all over their backyard just as they have done over ours for the past 50 years.

> PETER GUILFORD, EU trade spokesman, on Europe's efforts to trade with Latin America, quoted in the *Wall Street Journal,* September 13, 1997

We've suddenly discovered Latin America [and Latin America] is throwing the bloody door open to us.

> MICHAEL VALDES SCOTT, head of Britain's Latin American Trade Advisory Group, quoted in the *Wall Street Journal,* September 13, 1997

18.1 FRANCE

The French complain of everything, and always.

NAPOLÉON, *Maxims* (1804–1815)

Everything is on such a clear financial basis in France. It is the simplest country to live in. No one makes things complicated by becoming your friend for any obscure reason. If you want people to like you, you have only to spend a little money.

ERNEST HEMINGWAY

No one can bring together a country that has 265 kinds of cheese.

CHARLES DE GAULLE, after a 1953 electoral setback, quoted in the *Economist,* June 27, 1992

. . . 60 years ago half the French lived in rural areas. In 1945 farms still accounted for over a third of the working population. Although its farms now provide less than 4 percent of the country's wealth, France still sees itself as an agricultural nation. [This accounts for the power of the French farm lobby in international free trade negotiations.]

The Economist, November 28, 1992

When the place [Euro Disneyland] opens, it will be perfect. And they know how to make people smile—even the French.

MARGO VIGNOLA of the investment bank Salomon Brothers, quoted in the *New York Times,* February 17, 1991

An American company can invest in France, mess it up, and not go bust. A French firm risks the company when it enters America.

ROBERT MADGE, founder of the Internet company Madge Networks, quoted in the *Economist,* December 19, 1995

The Japanese can do a lot of things better than we, but they cannot rob us of our cultural background.

PATRICK LE QUÉMENT of the auto firm Renault, quoted in *Fortune,* January 11, 1993

This car will replace dogs. You just want to take it home and pet it.

PATRICK LE QUÉMENT of the auto firm Renault, commenting on the Twingo, a "high-fashion" car, quoted in *Fortune,* January 11, 1993

People [in Europe] will direct all their anger and resentment over unemployment at the single currency. There may well be a political revolt—particularly in France, notorious for such rebellions—and it would likely take a nationalistic, anti-European direction.

GEORGE SOROS, "Can Europe Work?" *Foreign Affairs,* September–October 1996

We are for a revolution, but a French one.

JEAN-MARIE LE PEN, leader of the National Front, an ultranationalistic, xenophobic political party, quoted in the *New York Times,* November 17, 1996

We're [France] somewhere between the United States and Germany on transparency, probably closer to U.S. practices and certainly less able than German businesses to hide systematic abuses. We're going toward the U.S. model, but it's going to take several years more.

ALAIN MINC, investment adviser to many major corporations in France and business commentator, quoted in the *International Herald Tribune,* October 10, 1996

The French government wants to move more rapidly too, but the trouble is that in France there are so many vested interests that resist the kind of restructuring which is taking place in other parts of Europe.

ROBERT HORMATS, vice chairman of Goldman, Sachs, quoted in the *International Herald Tribune,* October 16, 1996

I don't want to call it xenophobia, but you are seeing a fortress-France mentality.

CHARLES ARMITAGE of the investment bank Lehman Brothers, London, after suspension of sale of Thomson SA, consumer and defense electronic company, to South Korean corporation, quoted in the *Wall Street Journal,* December 5, 1996

Part of France's civilization is at stake here. The situation in France is very tense. Some French blame it on Europe and ultimately on us. But Germany must not forget that it cannot move anything in Europe without or even against France.

> KARL LAMERS, foreign policy spokesman for the Christian Democratic Party, on strains in alliance after the signing of the monetary union pact, quoted in the *Wall Street Journal,* December 16, 1996

The challenge will be to marry dreams with monetary-union criteria. He's [Lionel Jospin, Socialist prime minister-elect] going to have to appear idealistic in a hyper-realistic situation.

> ALAIN DUHAMEL, political analyst, quoted in the *Wall Street Journal,* June 2, 1997

[T]here is something appealing about the French struggle to maintain their lifestyle and to resist the constraints, and one-size-fits-all sterility, of the golden straitjacket. It's Don Quixote versus the bond market.

> THOMAS L. FRIEDMAN, on French attempts to avoid fiscal constraints imposed by the financial markets, *New York Times,* June 5, 1997

I will not be the minister of privatization.

> JEAN-CLAUDE GAYSSOT, member of the Communist Party, upon being named minister of transportation in June, referring to previous government's plans to privatize Air France, quoted in the *Wall Street Journal,* September 3, 1997

"Global market forces" don't vote.

> TONY JUDT, director of the Remarque Institute, New York University, giving one lesson of the 1997 French election, quoted in the *New York Times,* June 5, 1997

Being a leader in not working won't create employment.

> BERNARD GIROUD, a venture capitalist with Schroeder Partners in Paris, commenting on the new government's plan to combat unemployment by cutting the workweek from 39 hours to 35, quoted in *Business Week,* June 16, 1997

This is a pragmatic Socialism which realizes it can't swim against the currents of the global economy.

> PASCAL PERRINEAU, head of French political think tank Centre d'Etude de la Vie Politique Française,

on backtracking following 1997 elections, quoted in the *Wall Street Journal,* September 3, 1997

There are a handful of very successful French companies. But they tend to be those which are far more open. What you don't see is the long tail of depressed companies which are not reaching their full potential and are increasingly doomed.

> MICHAEL JOHNSON, journalist turned corporate manager, who became disillusioned with France when he went to work for a French company. Author of *French Resistance* (Cassell, 1997), quoted in the *Financial Times,* April 11, 1997

To make Anglo-Saxon investors come, you have to speak their language. Options that create shareholder value must take precedence over those that preserve management, tradition, or culture.

> GÉRARD MESTRALLET, chairman of the French holding company Cie de Suez, quoted in the *Wall Street Journal,* April 8, 1996

On the French banking market, those out to make maximum profits are in a minority. That's the fundamental problem of the French banking system. We are dragged down by others who don't operate in the same way. The real structural reform of the French banking system wouldn't be to merge banks; it would be to transform mutual banks and savings and loans into real capitalists.

> MICHEL PEBEREAU, chairman of Banque Nationale de Paris, quoted in the *Wall Street Journal,* April 11, 1996

[The merger of Chemical Banking Corp. and Chase Manhattan Corp.] wouldn't have happened in France. We're in a medieval situation with everyone trying to defend his turf.

> JEAN PEYRELEVADE, chairman of the bank Crédit Lyonnais, quoted in the *Wall Street Journal,* April 11, 1996

Our financial power is vanishing. No French bank was a candidate to acquire Barings, S. G. Warburg, or Kleinwort Benson, and after losing the foreign battle, we're going to lose the domestic one, too. There will be no more French banks; there will be banks in France.

> CHARLES DE CROISSET, chairman of Crédit Commercial de France, quoted in the *Wall Street Journal,* April 11, 1996

As with football clubs, people want to know if you are in the first or second division.

> Investment banker, on conflicting league table of deals with French buyer or target, some showing an American company in first place, supplanting French banks for the first time, quoted in the *Financial Times,* January 15, 1997

18.2   GERMANY

It's truly a new era in Germany. The real significance is that thousands of banks all over central Europe will now issue credit cards because Deutsche Bank no longer opposes them.

> MICHAEL LAFFERTY, editor of *Cards International,* a credit-card industry newsletter based in London, quoted in the *New York Times,* April 13, 1991

We [Europeans] have been so accustomed to teaching engineering to the world that we've lost our receptiveness to learning.

Statistics have indicated that East German living standards were number one in the Communist bloc and Czechoslovakia's were number two. East Germany was actually number one in falsifying statistics.

> CARL H. HAHN, former CEO of Volkswagen, interviewed in *Harvard Business Review,* July–August 1991

The former East German government used to employ 2.2 million people. The new bureaucracy will eliminate at least 1 million of those jobs. East German manufacturing employment used to hover around 3.2 million workers. That number will drop to between 800,000 and 1.4 million.

Although they were thoughtless industrial polluters, the Communists were at least frugal and efficient recyclers of tires, metal, glass, and paper. But as Western lifestyles have taken hold, eastern Germans have been astounded by the volume of plastic, Styrofoam, and disposable diapers that are already piling up in and taxing garbage facilities.

If Western German environmental laws were applied tomorrow, about 70 percent of Eastern German industry would have to be shut down immediately.

> HERBERT HENZLER, chairman of McKinsey & Co.'s German office and lecturer on international manage-
> ment, Munich University, *Harvard Business Review,* January–February 1992

I typically don't receive a phone call at the end of the quarter to discuss results. You don't need to remake the world in 120 days.

I've got to carry a larger reserve for obsolescence and spare parts than I would if I had the same business and it was American owned.

> GEORGE GELFER, president of the U.S. unit of Francotyp-Postalia (a German postal-equipment maker), on his German bosses, quoted in the *Wall Street Journal,* June 4, 1996

I didn't want Berlin to be the capital again. And why are they building so much? We can't fill the buildings we have already.

> BÄRBEL, young blond mother on a bicycle, quoted in the *New Republic,* November 4, 1996

All the German banks recognize that structural changes need to take place. There's simply too much capacity.

> NEIL CROWDER of the investment bank Goldman, Sachs, London, quoted in the *Wall Street Journal,* July 11, 1996

The East German economy is not competitive. Wages are too high, productivity is too low.

> HEINER FLASSBECK, Deutsche Institut für Wirtschaftsforschung, a leading government economic institute, quoted in the *Financial Times,* January 8, 1997

Our biggest export is jobs.

> HANS-OLAF HENKEL, Federation of German Industry, quoted in the *Wall Street Journal,* February 18, 1997

This is the third generation since the war, and we are so lazy and spoiled today, used to a high standard where you get more and more . . . but if you ask them to start something on a Friday afternoon, they wave bye-bye very nicely and leave. . . . Most employees feel they are equal to their bosses.

> DR. STEPHANIE WAHL, a social scientist at a think tank in Bonn, the Institute for Economics and Society, quoted in William Greider, *One World, Ready or Not: The Manic Logic of Global Capitalism* (Simon & Schuster, 1997)

Simple work has become too expensive for Germany. There are so many jobs you can't find anymore. There's nobody to bring your milk or your bread every day.

> HANNO BERNETT, of an association for young entrepreneurs, quoted in William Greider, *One World, Ready or Not: The Manic Logic of Global Capitalism* (Simon & Schuster, 1997)

You always end up with the oldest, least efficient worker. The only ones I can get rid of are the young, well-educated. I can understand it from a social point, but it's ruinous to the company. You are forced to slim down in the wrong way.

> LEO BENZ of telecommunications equipment manufacturer Zettler, on Germany's employment laws, quoted in *Business Week,* January 20, 1986

There are limits to flexibility. We want no part of the hire-and-fire American system where millions of people go without social protection, nor of the British scene where over half the workforce is casual labor and the unemployment rate is still higher than ours.

> HEINER GEISSLER, a parliamentary leader of the ruling Christian Democrats, quoted in the *Economist,* January 27, 1996 (His information on Britain was inaccurate.)

Out of VW's 243,256 employees, 57 percent are in Germany. These workers get six weeks paid holiday every year. They work a 30-hour week. The German autoworker is the highest paid in the world. The average German autoworker earns $39 an hour in wages and benefits. In the United States the average autoworker earns about $25; in Japan, $27.

> *Forbes,* April 7, 1997

Last year, 139,862 eastern Berliners commuted to the western half; only 32,600 commuted in the other direction.

> GREG STEINMETZ, *Wall Street Journal,* July 7, 1997

A sizable part of our workforce is no longer ashamed to say, "I don't like work."

> ERWIN SCHEUCH, sociologist, Cologne University, commenting on an auto strike in which workers demanded a 35-hour workweek, quoted in *U.S. News & World Report,* June 11, 1984

U.S. firms that establish themselves here are shocked by the termination rules. The possibility of firing someone quickly without cause is impossible.

> BERNARD MAHLOW of the recruiting firm Korn/Ferry International in Frankfurt, quoted in the *Wall Street Journal,* March 22, 1996

These are no longer the methods of a democratic state.

> JÜRGEN SARRAZIN, chairman Dresdner Bank AG, on raids by German tax authorities who suspect they had been complicit in helping clients evade taxes, quoted in the *Wall Street Journal,* December 4, 1996

The people who are losing jobs in manufacturing are not finding jobs elsewhere.

> THOMAS MAYER, economist for Goldman, Sachs, quoted in the *Wall Street Journal,* January 10, 1997

The transition to a more Anglo-Saxon banking system, where banks act largely as financial intermediaries, is hard for institutions that traditionally owned large stakes in companies and have been heavy lenders to industry. As a result, the increase in investment banking activity means German banks have large conflicts of interest to resolve.

> ANDREW FISHER, *Financial Times,* September 3, 1997

The *Mittelstand* will in fact become increasingly important. If Germany is to have new jobs, these will come from smaller companies. The bigger companies are not creating jobs.

> PROFESSOR BRUN-HAGEN HENNERKES of the University of Stuttgart, quoted in the *Financial Times,* September 19, 1997

Levity will be welcomed [in Germany] to the extent it contributes to the *Arbeitsklima* (working environment) and supports the highly task-oriented German company. But German managers are less likely to use humor tactically, a means of deflecting criticism, challenging authority, or defusing tension. International managers communicating in German should be direct.

> JEAN-LOUIS BARSOUX of the business school Insead and co-author of *Managing Across Cultures* (Prentice-Hall, 1997), quoted in the *Financial Times,* February 17, 1997

Ten out of ten for ingenuity. One out of ten for credibility.

> JOHN LLEWELLYN of the investment bank Lehman Brothers in London, on German government plan to use Bundesbank gold and currency reserves to plug holes in budget, quoted in the *Financial Times Weekend,* May 11/18, 1997

18.2.1 Germany and the European Community

The beer-purity regulations have the same symbolic value for the German consumer as the D-mark.

> HERBERT FRANKENHAUSER, president of the German Institute for Pure Beer, in a letter to Chancellor Helmut Kohl about the conflict between EC beer standards and Germany's own standards, which have been in force for hundreds of years, quoted in the *Economist,* December 26, 1992

Every time we draft four paragraphs in a directive the Germans add another 20. And they call us bureaucrats.

> European commissioner, quoted in the *Economist,* December 26, 1992

Once upon a time, Germany was a country of modest unemployment, fiscal restraint, and low inflation, but with partners that mostly lacked one, or all, of these virtues, that uniqueness no longer exists.

> MARTIN WOLF, *Financial Times,* September 9, 1997

18.3 GREAT BRITAIN

A lot of companies are quite arrogant when it comes to their customers. I'm talking about retailers who have middle-class lives and never come into contact with the people who buy products.

> MONICA LUCAS, cofounder of Pragma Consulting, quoted in the *Financial Times,* January 20, 1997

The Chancellor of the Exchequer is a man whose duties make him more or less of a taxing machine. He is [sic] with a certain amount of misery which it is [his] duty to distribute as fairly as he can.

> ROBERT LOWE, Viscount Sherbrooke, liberal politician, in a speech, April 1870

In England the rich own the poor and the men own the women.

> TOM STOPPARD, playwright, *Travesties* (Grove, 1974)

When business conditions got tough in recent years, we did not take meat cleavers to our product. . . . We did not reduce the quality of the wine.

> SIR COLIN MARSHALL, chairman of British Airways, *Harvard Business Review,* November–December 1995

The Thatcher government responded somewhat slowly and belatedly to the problems created by rising unemployment. And the recession of the late 1980s hurt entrepreneurial businesses along with more-established companies. The initiatives did not provide sufficient employment and opportunities for those who were pushed out of work by recession, retrenchment, and rationalizations. It's no wonder, then, that Thatcher herself joined the ranks of the un-, I mean, self-employed in 1990.

> CHARLES DELLHEIM, author of *The Disenchanted Isle: Mrs. Thatcher's Capitalist Revolution* (Norton, 1995), *Inc.,* July 1996

[The City of London] will become the financial rustbelt of Europe.

> GRAHAM BISHOP of the investment bank Salomon Brothers, on the consequences to London's status as a financial center if Britain doesn't join the European currency union, quoted in the *Economist,* August 3, 1996

The new British worker has shaken the image of the militant 1970s.

> JOHN ELDER, general manager of Newport Wafer-Fab Ltd., Welsh silicon wafer company owned by Hong Kong's QPL International and France's SGS Thompson, quoted in *Business Week,* February 21, 1996

British ways were not necessarily the ways of the world.

> TONY GILL, chairman of Lucas Industries, on lessons learned from collapse of British car industry, for which his company had made components.

The United States is a selling culture; it's prestigious to be a good salesman. But in the United Kingdom, selling is vulgar. People don't mind buying, but they don't want to be sold.

[I]n the U.K., ads are designed to make you smile, charm you, create rapport, and then sell.

> BARRY DAY, director of creative communications for Interpublic Group and founding judge of British Television Advertising Awards, quoted in the *New York Times,* November 7, 1996

Money does not concern me in the least.

> English executive, spurning advances of KKR banker trying to sell the firm's approach to leverage, quoted in George Anders, *Merchants of Debt* (Basic, 1992)

It is not an accident that unemployment in the U.K. is at a long-time low. It is a lot easier to operate in the U.K. The workforce is a lot more flexible.

> ROBERT PALMER, CEO of Digital Equipment Company, on the advantages of doing business in the U.K. instead of France or Germany, quoted in the *Financial Times,* January 27, 1997

There might have been offers for one-million dollar jobs before, but a million pounds is different; it's a lot of money.

> Bond market expert at London branch of a New York bank, after headhunters advertised three such jobs in one issue of the *Financial Times,* quoted in *Financial Times,* January 31, 1997

The domestic appliance industry is dominated by the multinational companies which all know what their rivals are doing and which have no interest in upsetting the status quo. In principle, today's washing machines are very much the same as when they were invented. The whole area of domestic appliances is ripe for technological innovation and new product.

> JAMES DYSON, founder of Dyson Appliances, inventor of a revolutionary vacuum cleaner that has reached £100 million in sales after four years, quoted in the *Financial Times,* January 28, 1997

The successful conduct of economic policy is possible only if there is, and is seen to be, full agreement between the prime minister and the chancellor of the exchequer.

> NIGEL LAWSON, Chancellor of the Exchequer, in resignation letter to Margaret Thatcher, quoted in the *Economist,* October 26, 1989

The regions of England are not regions of Europe, and nor are Scotland, Wales, or Northern Ireland. They are parts of the Enterprise Centre of Europe—the United Kingdom—and that is crucial to their economic success.

Our approach to regional policy reflects the United Kingdom's new regional industrial landscape as we enter the next century. Self-confident and successful regions within a pro-enterprise economic framework provided by Government at national level. Government is an active partner in regional economic life, but with the drive and ownership of business support activity coming from the business community itself. A nation entering the twenty-first century with strength in depth throughout its regional economies.

> IAN LANG, president of the British Board of Trade, in a speech to the British Chambers of Commerce, July 2, 1996

The British are just half a cycle behind the United States, but way ahead of the rest of Europe.

> Anonymous fund manager, quoted by Alan Friedman, *International Herald Tribune,* October 16, 1996

At the very moment the public is rejecting Thatcherism, New Labor is embracing it.

> TONY BENN (formerly Sir Anthony Wedgewood-Benn), left-wing Labor MP, talking about impending election of Tony Blair as Prime Minister, quoted in *Business Week,* international edition, April 14, 1997

I don't talk about the British car industry. I talk about the car industry in Britain.

> TONY WOODLEY, chief auto negotiator for Britain's Transport & General Workers' Union, quoted in *Business Week,* international edition, April 14, 1997

It is no longer true to speak about the British motor industry, but the motor industry in Britain.

> DAVID LEGGETT of the motor industry consulting firm CSM Europe, quoted in the *Financial Times,* May 21, 1997

Britain has become a live experiment for the global motor industry. You have the best of the Americans, Europeans, and Japanese manufacturing here. It really is the place where you can see it all happen.

> IAN GIBSON, chief executive, Nissan U.K., quoted in the *Financial Times,* May 21, 1997

I want Britain to be a nation of entrepreneurs, a nation where talent and ability flourish.

> PRIME MINISTER TONY BLAIR in a speech to parliament laying out his legislative priorities, quoted in the *Financial Times*, May 15, 1997

The increased productivity of Japanese car manufacturers . . . is laudable, but tells only a small part of the story.

Of far greater importance, bearing in mind the size of the grants they received, is whether they are making profits. Indeed, are they profitable enough for their parent companies to keep them in Britain? Are they repaying by way of taxes the huge sums invested by the government?

> BRIAN GALE, Guernsey, Channel Islands, in a letter to the editor, *Financial Times*, September 3, 1997

This is the generation that claims education, skills, and technology as the instruments of economic prosperity and personal fulfillment, not old battles between state and market.

> PRIME MINISTER TONY BLAIR, in a press conference at 10 Downing Street, quoted in the *Financial Times*, May 30, 1997

There are tons of smart people who, for whatever reason, aren't going to come to Seattle. Going to Europe gives us a way to hire people who bring new talents and new perspectives to our work that we couldn't get any other way.

> NATHAN MYHRVOLD, Microsoft's chief technology officer, on the decision to build a new $80 million research center in Cambridge, quoted in the *New York Times*, June 18, 1997

In the U.K. basic information on the free-market economy was simply not taught. Worse, the schools conveyed a sense that there was something not quite nice about the entrepreneurial spirit.

> JOHN MOORE, minister for 10 years in Margaret Thatcher's government and responsible for privatization program for three years, *Harvard Business Review*, March–April 1992

"But John," he said with a shocked voice, "we don't want all *those* kind of people owning shares, do we?"

> "Head of a large brokerage house" in reaction to government program to sell shares of British Telecom (the model privatization) to the "ordinary public,"

quoted by John Moore, minister for 10 years in Margaret Thatcher's government and responsible for privatization program for three years, *Harvard Business Review*, March–April 1992

[B]efore privatization, the British Gas Corporation had a monopoly on the sale of gas kitchen appliances and their retail outlets were not even listed in the telephone directory.

> JOHN MOORE, minister for 10 years in Margaret Thatcher's government and responsible for privatization program for three years, *Harvard Business Review*, March–April 1992

Whenever I think about the budgetary problems, I think about the problems of Errol Flynn . . . reconciling net income with gross habits.

> MALCOLM RIFKIND, British cabinet minister, *Film Yearbook* (1986)

Imagine the British, transplanted from hell to heaven. Before long they would gather each evening in their celestial paradise to reminisce about the good old days.

> SIEGFRIED SASSOON, British poet most famous for his Great War poems, in the context of the temptations Prime Minister Tony Blair will face to revert to old-Labour solutions when British economy turns down, instead of persisting with reform, *Financial Times*, October 2, 1997

It would be folly for them to neglect a section of the population which is set to grow from 6 percent to nearer 10 percent of the total workforce in the next century.

> GILLIAN SHEPHARD, British education and employment secretary, on need to address the employment needs of minorities, quoted in the *Financial Times*, January 30, 1997

Britain has one of the largest arms industries in Europe. We have a duty to the 400,000 people who work in our defense industries to continue to have the opportunity to work.

> ROBIN COOK, British foreign secretary, quoted in the *Financial Times*, October 3, 1997

[T]here seems to be no shortage of wonderful bank sites waiting to be turned into restaurants.

> DOMINIC FORD, food and beverage director of the London department store Harvey Nichols, on popu-

larity of converting grand old banks into fancy restaurants, quoted in the *Financial Times Weekend,* February 22–23, 1997

18.3.1 British Advertising

We can't show people who look nice, and we can't even show a sunny day. Basically, the ad can't be appealing, which makes it tough.

> Ad writer for a U.K. tobacco account, quoted in the *Financial Times,* October 9, 1997

One of the reasons we have the most creative advertising in the world is because we've had the toughest rules for so long.

A lot of nonsmokers in the U.K. say they haven't got a clue what our ads are about.

> IAN BIRKS, general manager of corporate affairs for Gallaher Tobacco, quoted in the *Financial Times,* October 9, 1997

18.3.2 Great Britain and the European Community

Every member begins its presidency trying to run the show from its home capital. Most give up after a month or two, when they realize that allowing domestic concerns to dominate does not achieve results. But the British are still trying to do everything from London.

> Member of EC Council of Ministers, speaking about the six-month rotating presidency of the Council, quoted in the *Economist,* November 28, 1992

The peculiarity of the British is their seeming inability to notice what others do or say, if they do not like it. They show a stubborn unwillingness to change course.

> Senior Danish diplomat, quoted in the *Economist,* November 28, 1992

Rolls-Royce without a steering wheel.

> Consensus on British presidency of European Council, cited in the *Economist,* December 5, 1992

I see they're taking away our bank holiday. It's Brussels, I suppose.

> Woman to her hairdresser, referring to a British government proposal to change the date of a national holiday, quoted in the *Economist,* December 26, 1992

18.4 GREECE

It's the right moment to bring new investors into the market. The government is keen to create a class of shareholders and there are several large issues planned this year by utilities and the state banks. Of course, our advertising will set out the risks of entering the market.

> PROFESSOR MANOLIS XANTHAKIS, chairman of the Athens Stock Exchange, on junk mailing, to be enclosed with phone bills, to attract new class of investors for privatization of state companies, quoted in the *Financial Times,* February 23, 1997

18.5 IRELAND

This is one strange notion, that Ireland could have to import talent.

> MICHAEL MULQUEEN, design engineer, on the rebirth of Ireland's economy, which allowed him to remain at home instead of emigrating, quoted in the the *Wall Street Journal,* December 5, 1996

. . . Ireland, where a staggering 40 percent of all packaged software and 60 percent of business application software sold in Europe is produced.

> KATHERINE LUCY, director of software for the Irish Business and Employers Confederation, quoted in the *Financial Times,* October 3, 1997

18.6 IRELAND, NORTHERN

You will never know how many companies who had us on their lists will now not even pick up the phone.

> BARONESS DENTON, U.K. northern Ireland Economic Minister, after four days of Protestant rioting, quoted in the *Wall Street Journal,* July 11, 1996

18.7 THE NETHERLANDS

The larger you are, the more figures you have to publish, and everybody can see where your weaknesses are. I know my competitors are looking up my numbers, because I'm doing the same to them.

If people are on your payroll, it's very difficult to get rid of them. I've had a few cases in which people didn't function well, and I've had to pay them quite a bit. I'm afraid to employ an experienced person.

> WALLY DE JONG, president of Inter Active Holding BV, which makes flue systems for gas-fired boilers, on the problems of doing business in heavily regulated Netherlands, quoted in *Inc.*, April 1996

18.8 NORWAY

The tragic thing is that Norway traditionally has exported raw materials. We now have a chance of building a processing industry on a much larger scale. We've spoiled the opportunity to win back jobs.

> SVEIN HATLEM of the Confederation of Norwegian Industry, on the country's refusal to join the EU, quoted in the *Wall Street Journal*, April 8, 1996

Business people want [Norway] to be at the table when the decisions are made. But the importance of this is hard to measure.

> HANS HECKLAND, group secretary of Rieber & Sons AS, a diversified manufacturer, quoted in the *Wall Street Journal*, April 8, 1996

Norway has become too arrogant. In the long run, we need allies, security-wise and business-wise.

> ANDRES GRIMELUND, president of Rolf Olsen Group, a fish-processing and fish-farming company in Bergen, quoted in the *Wall Street Journal*, April 8, 1996

The only solution is to convince Norges Bank that hospitals and schools are better investment objects than Coca-Cola and Shell.

> ASLAK SIRA MYHRE, leader of the Norwegian Red Electoral Alliance (RV), the country's only Communist Party with an elected parliament member (which applied to manage the investment of 3.5 billion kroner of Norway's oil fund, through its company Red Value Enhancement, investing the money in welfare state and freedom movements in the third world), quoted in AP-Dow Jones, July 9, 1997

We have long known RV wants to administer the truth but managing money in the same way casts doubt on the promises of profitability conveyed by RV's proposal . . . We wish them luck anyway.

> Editorial in *Dagens Naeringsliv*, Oslo business daily, quoted in AP-Dow Jones, July 9, 1997

18.9 PORTUGAL

Foreign interest in privatization in Portugal is close to zero.

> Lisbon banker, commenting on the 25 percent limit on foreign ownership of Portuguese firms, quoted in the *Economist*, November 7, 1992

18.10 SPAIN

These [big red tomatoes] are what New Yorkers like. Swedes like their tomatoes small, green, and packaged in plastic. Whatever they want, I give them. Here, the customer is king.

> MANUEL MALDONADO, city hall official, Eljido, Spain, quoted in the *Wall Street Journal*, February 21, 1997

18.11 SWEDEN

Sometimes a jealous neighbor will call tax officials and say, "Please look into my neighbor, who has just bought a new Mercedes-Benz." They call that "the royal Swedish envy." [Since 1914, the Swedish government has published Taxeringskalender, which lists gross and taxable income for every citizen who qualifies.]

> Swedish tax official, quoted in *Forbes*, February 25, 1985

Personally, I have never been sure that having a limited domestic market in reality does not offer some significant advantages. A small-sized domestic economy, particularly if—like in the case of Sweden's—it is combined with corporations to meet international competition head on—everywhere.

> PETER WALLENBERG, chairman of the Federation of Swedish Industries, in a speech, April 18, 1988

Scandinavian business at its best does not merely sell products. The Scandinavians sell values. In the case of Volvo, safety and durability. In the case of IKEA, participation and egalitarian quality.

> MICHAEL MACCOBY, president of The Maccoby Group, Washington, D.C., quoted in *Harvard Business Review*, September–October 1993

If our people in research and development would rather relocate to the United States or the United Kingdom [because of high taxes] what will we do then?

> LARS RAMQVIST, chief executive of Ericsson, major telecommunications firm, quoted in the *Financial Times*, May 6, 1997

18.12 SWITZERLAND

I look upon Switzerland as an inferior sort of Scotland.

> SYDNEY SMITH, letter to Lord Holland, 1815

In Italy for thirty years under the Borgias they had warfare, terror, murder, bloodshed—they produced Michelangelo, Leonardo da Vinci, and the Renaissance. In Switzerland they had brotherly love, five hundred years of democracy and peace and what did they produce . . .? The cuckoo clock.

> ORSON WELLES, original speech added to the script of *The Third Man*, thriller about black market and intrigue in postwar Vienna, 1949

Swiss culture shuns disagreement.

> PERCY BARNEVIK, chairman and CEO of the Swedish-Swiss industrial firm ABB (Asea Brown Boveri)

Among the OECD countries there is—its agriculture apart—no economy more open to the outside world than Switzerland's . . . Like Hong Kong, Switzerland has traded its way to wealth without needing any trade bloc to help it.

> *The Economist*, November 28, 1992

Another favored brand of money, one which appeals to a specialized and small segment of the market (like the Ferrari in automobiles, or Chivas Regal in Scotch whiskey, or Perrier in the bottled water industry) is the Swiss franc.

> PROFESSOR ROBERT Z. ALIBER of the University of Chicago, *The International Money Game* (Basic, 1983)

Big Swiss companies are simply cash machines. Every few years, the war chest is full. Then they go for an acquisition.

> HANS KAUFMANN of Bank Julius Baer, Zurich, quoted in *Business Week*, June 6, 1994

We should not be *importing* cheese.

> DANIEL STUCKI, dairy farmer, Switzerland, on the rising number of imports, quoted in the *Wall Street Journal*, March 22, 1996

Using Switzerland as a safe-haven, off-shore center in times of crisis eventually could ruin Switzerland.

> HILDE PHAN-HUY of the bank Credit Suisse, on the overvaluing of Swiss currency, quoted in the *Wall Street Journal*, November 18, 1996

Switzerland now has the phenomenon of the working poor.

> MARCO ITEN of the Switzerland National Science Foundation, quoted in the *Wall Street Journal*, February 24, 1997

We have studied the Los Angeles riots very carefully.

> ALFRED ROULEIR, Division Commander in the Swiss Army (which hasn't fired on Swiss civilians since a labor rally in Geneva in 1932), anticipating possible civic unrest due to domestic economic problems, quoted in the *Wall Street Journal*, February 24, 1997

[A developing] country's ambassador to Switzerland calls on a local banker and asks for the names of any fellow citizens with deposits of more than $1 million. He is sure, he says, that drug money and the contents of the country's treasury have been spirited into the bank's vaults. "Sorry," replies the banker. "Our tradition of secrecy is sacred." The next day, the diplomat returns with a letter from his president, but gets the same frosty response. That evening the diplomat spots the banker at a party. The banker sees him and makes for the door. "Stop" says the ambassador. "I don't want any names. I'd like to open an account."

> *The Economist*, February 17, 1996

It's in their blood. They learn this stuff at the dinner table.

> American banker in Switzerland, on the Swiss knack for being discreet, quoted in the *Wall Street Journal*, July 3, 1996

They've got enough clean money without needing dirty money.

> American diplomat in Switzerland, quoted in the *Detroit News*, October 15, 1995

Money we receive because the customer lacks confidence in his own country? It's not a problem. We cannot be responsible for the instability of other countries.

Switzerland's 494 banks manage an estimated $2 trillion in assets, about half of the world's privately managed assets.

CHRISTIAN FREY of Union Bank of Switzerland, quoted in the *Detroit News,* October 15, 1995

I have not found a fig leaf big enough to cover up the negligence of my banking colleagues in the period after the Second World War.

GEORGE KRAYER, chairman of the Swiss Bankers Association, quoted in *Newsweek,* August 4, 1997

You have to understand the mentality of the bankers. It's not a robber mentality. They just lived behind the frontier that separated Switzerland and the rest of Europe. They never took consciousness of the Holocaust—so they could not recognize the legitimate demands of the survivors. But the Swiss are not bad people. They needed an emotional shock, but now what they need are just facts, presented coolly, with deadlines for responding.

GUY METTAN, editor of *Tribune de Genève,* quoted in the *New York Times,* September 25, 1997

This country is more than Heidi.

REGINA SCHINDLER, Heidi expert and biographer of Johanna Spyri, author of *Heidi,* quoted in the *Wall Street Journal,* October 2, 1997

We have paradise here. What we don't have is a brand image.

URS KAMBER, head of Heidiland Tourism office, Sargans, Switzerland, quoted in the *Wall Street Journal,* October 2, 1997

Heidi is part of the Swiss story, but it's a one-sided view of an idealized world. Nowhere in the world is like that anymore.

HEIDI REISZ, marketing director of Switzerland Tourism office, London, quoted in the *Wall Street Journal,* October 2, 1997

19.1 BUSINESS

Belgium is a country invented by the British to annoy the French.

> CHARLES DE GAULLE, quoted in an article about ludicrous European Community economic policies, *Harper's,* June 1995

We are not in business, we are in politics.

> WALTER HALLSTEIN, first president of the European Commission, 1958, quoted in the *Economist,* January 25, 1992

We are in politics, not business.

> WALTER HALLSTEIN, *The Economist,* June 6, 1992

Exacerbation of competition is something that makes people feel insecure. In my opinion, it is at the very root of the feeling in Europe right now. You can feel it in the debate about the sluggish pace of the German economy, the official negotiations to create more jobs. This fact is an indication that globalization is not very well understood.

> RUBENS RICUPERO, Secretary-General of the United Nations Conference on Trade and Development, quoted in the *Wall Street Journal,* April 1, 1996

For the moment, the more Europe advances on free trade, the more its governments move to intervene for the domestic economy. It's a paradox.

> PETER PRAET, chief economist of Belgium's General Bank, quoted in the *Wall Street Journal,* April 1, 1996

19.2 NATIONAL TASTE

Are we to be condemned to eat antiseptic, aseptic, industrialized cheese?

> French newspaper *Le Figaro,* after the European Community contemplated new hygiene standards for cheese (when 90 percent of French cheese was made from unpasteurized milk), cited in the *Economist,* June 27, 1992

It took [the European Commission] 14 years of negotiations to adopt a directive specifying the composition of fruit jams, jellies, marmalades, and chestnut puree, while it spent 11 years working on a directive on mineral water.

> DAVID VOGEL, *Trading Up: Consumer and Environmental Regulation in a Global Economy* (Belknap, 1995)

Ask 800,000 snuffers what they think about frogs legs.

> STIG BERGLIND, spokesperson for the Swedish Embassy to the European Community on the EC's ban on sale of snuff, used by 10 percent of Swedes, which was holding up Sweden's application to join the EC, quoted in *Business Week,* January 17, 1994 (The Swedes thought the ban was based on French disgust rather than on health.)

What could happen on our plates within four years [of European free trade in food]? . . . All that is needed is to look at the astonishing menus our neighbors are preparing for us: Spanish foie gras, made with pork fat; mock snails (from West Germany); ice cream made from vegetable fat (from Holland); chocolate made with animal fats (from Britain); minced meat mixed with soya (from Belgium); sausages made with flour (from Britain, a nation with no culinary traditions); and chocolate made without cocoa butter.

> French publication *Le Point,* February 1989, quoted in David Vogel, *Trading Up: Consumer and Environmental Regulation in a Global Economy* (Belknap, 1995)

In Scandinavia, Philly (Philadelphia cream cheese) is positioned as a bread spread, an alternative to butter and margarine. In the U.K., it's eaten warm. And in Belgium, it's positioned against *fromage blanc,* a huge generic category comparable to the fresh cheeses in Italy.

. . . . When I went back to Europe after eight years in the States, I was amazed at how much cream cheese we were selling—to people who didn't eat bagels or cheesecake!

> JOHN RUFF of Kraft Foods International, in a speech, April 22, 1996

An 18-year-old boy in France has more in common with another 18-year-old boy in Germany than with his own parents. We consider them as one nation.

> FRANK BROWN, advertising sales director of the rock 'n' roll television station MTV Europe, quoted in *Business Week,* April 11, 1994

19.3 POLICIES

The philosophy of picking winners is dying. Industrial policy in Europe now aims to enhance the market, not interfere with it.

> GEORGE PAPACONSTANTINOU of the OECD, quoted in *Fortune,* December 14, 1992

The Community is now saddled, for many commodities, with surpluses some of which have no prospect on saturated world markets.

> 1969 European Commission report on agricultural policy, cited in the *Economist,* December 5, 1992

One scandal that came to light last year concerned the passing off of $160 million of foreign imported beef as Irish, so that it could be exported to Iran while being eligible for the various subsidies granted to farmers as compensation for overproduction. Nonexistent and redundant crops or animals now come under the rubric of European protectionism; even the Queen of England, still one of the wealthiest women in Europe, reportedly receives $400,000 each year for planting or not planting various forms of greenery. And yet it never occurs to anyone to blame the Union for such profligacy.

> NICHOLAS FRASER, *Harper's,* June 1995

The European companies that prosper will be those that re-create the European character and flair that Americans and Japanese never had, adding quality, reliability, and value.

> PATRICK FAURE of the French auto firm Renault, quoted in *Fortune,* January 11, 1993

The enormous complexity of the present support mechanisms has left farmers scouring the pages of the official journal of the European Community instead of responding to market signals.

> FRANZ FISCHLER, European Union farm commissioner, who was attempting to reform the Ecu 40 billion (£28.6 billion) subsidy system, quoted in the *Financial Times,* November 3, 1997

20.1 CEOs

There are magical associations with being CEO. Your visibility as a top executive goes way up. Your standing in the community goes up. All of a sudden you're highly respected. Board invitations come in. You're on everybody's list.

> RICHARD FERRY of the executive-search firm Korn-Ferry International, quoted in *U.S. News & World Report,* April 29, 1985

It's easy to get sucked away from running the company. Politicians come knocking on the door; donations are sought from charities you never heard of; friends you've forgotten about come out of the woodwork; former adversaries become intimates.

> ALLEN MICHELS, CEO of Convergent Technologies, quoted in *Time,* January 23, 1984

One of the most important things a CEO can say is, "This is our philosophy, this is the general direction in which we are going, this is the perspective from which we need to view the issues before us at the moment." Having a historical concept supplies a solid reference point.

> ALONZO L. MCDONALD, CEO of Avenir Group, *Harvard Business Review,* January–February 1986

Twenty years ago the CEO of a major company had almost a fiefdom to rule. He was unassailable. That's no longer true.

> JAMES COTTING, CEO of Navistar International, quoted in *Business Week,* October 23, 1987

Of all newly appointed CEOs, roughly 10 percent are fired, with half of them failing within the first three years.

> PROFESSOR RICHARD F. VANCIL of Harvard Business School, *Fortune,* January 4, 1988

In America, we've traditionally had John Wayne CEOs, the lone individual with all the power in his hands. But the norms in corporate America are changing under pressure from institutional investors and outside directors.

> PROFESSOR JAY LORSCH of Harvard Business School, quoted in the *New York Times,* April 12, 1992

The CEO will look less like an emperor than like a Congressman, trying to represent his various constituents and, to the extent he succeeds, being reelected.

> *Fortune,* January 11, 1993

It's something no one ever tells you. You're on and off airplanes all the time. It's a Texas wrestling match with a new team against you every night.

> WALTER WRISTON, former CEO of Citicorp, quoted in the *New York Times,* April 25, 1993

[A] CEO cannot be king even though, as Mel Brooks used to say, "It's good to be king."

> WILLIAM A. DIMMA, chairman of the chemical company Monsanto Canada, Ltd., in a speech, May 13, 1994

There is no school for CEOs—except for the school of experience.

The CEO's job is like no other in the organization. It is infinite.

> CHARLES M. FARKAS and SUZY WETLAUFER, "The Ways Chief Executive Officers Lead," *Harvard Business Review,* May–June 1996

A CEO who has no frustrations better resign at once. Frustration in running a large organization is a burden the CEO has to bear.

> YOSHIHISA TABUCHI, CEO of the investment firm Nomura Securities, quoted in the *New York Times,* March 10, 1991

A search of wire services that carry company news releases found that the epidemic phrase "resigned to pursue" appeared 242 times in the last 18 months. But "CEO" appeared with the word "fired" just twice—and those were public utilities discussing coal-fired plants.

The corporate world might do well for the morale of employees, shareholders, and customers to consider the example of the [Kansas City] Royals and other teams that still (gasp) fire people.

> DON HUNT and BRIAN EDWARDS, PR professionals, *New York Times,* August 3, 1997

It sounds odd to talk of a railroad president as being popular, as if he was a comedian or a politician.

> President of Norfolk & Western Railroad, quoted in J. T. Lambie, *From Mine to Market: The History of Coal Transportation on the Norfolk and Western Railway* (1954)

Turning CEOs into celebrities is society's reaction to complexity. We want to be intimate because everything is big. As things get even bigger, we try to turn these huge edifices into personalities that we can relate to.

> HEIDI SINCLAIR of the talent agency International Creative Management, quoted in the *Wall Street Journal,* September 3, 1997

It's very easy to confuse the company and let your ego get out of control. You're almost required to internalize the company into your mental fabric so that you and the company become one.

> ERIC SCHMIDT, CEO of the software firm Novell, quoted in the *Wall Street Journal,* September 3, 1997

The new CEOs taking over feel they need to come up with an individual branding. They feel a CEO can't just be nondescript; he can't just do his job but has to be identified with a managerial cause.

> PROFESSOR JEFFREY SONNENFELD of Emory University, quoted in the *Wall Street Journal,* September 3, 1997

Energy is No. 1 [among desirable qualities in a CEO]. Intellectual courage is extremely important too—intellectual courage to go out and do something.

> The late ROBERTO GOIZUETA, CEO of Coca-Cola, quoted in *Fortune,* October 13, 1997

Some CEOs have dismally low personal ethics. They talk about shareholder wealth and they mean *their* shares. They scheme to pull money out personally every way they can. Some are afraid and don't know what to do. As a recruiter I have to fulfill job requirements of my clients and find the best person possible. Bad CEOs will not hire good people who they perceive could replace them.

> A headhunter to CEOs, quoted in D. A. Benson, *How to Think Like a CEO* (Warner, 1996)

CEOs have this obsession to know everything and control everything. I mean, that's stupid.

> ED McCRACKEN, founder and CEO of the computer firm Silicon Graphics, interviewed in Rama Dev Jager, *In the Company of Giants* (McGraw-Hill, 1997)

20.2 CEOs AND ACQUISITIONS

Managerial intellect wilted in competition with managerial adrenaline. The thrill of the chase blinded pursuers to the consequences of the chase.

> WARREN BUFFETT, CEO of the investment firm Berkshire Hathaway, quoted in Professors David B. Jemison, and Sim B. Sitkin, University of Texas, "Acquisitions: The Process Can Be a Problem," *Harvard Business Review,* March–April 1986

Recent success . . . The greater the CEO's confidence in his or her own abilities, the greater the benefit that the CEO believes he or she can bring to an acquired entity, and the higher the premium paid [in a takeover].

Self importance . . . Our measure of self-importance was the ratio of the CEO's pay to that of the second-highest-paid executive in the firm, which we took to be a telling indicator of the CEO's sense of potency and self-esteem. In our study, the higher the salary ratio, the higher the acquisition premium.

Media praise. In our sample, each highly favorable article about the CEO resulted, on average in a 5.4 percent increase in premium paid. In a billion-dollar acquisition, one article would then account for an increase of $54 million.

> MATTHEW L. A. HAYWARD and PROFESSOR DONALD C. HAMBRICK of Columbia University School of Business, "Explaining Premiums Paid for Large Acquisitions: Evidence of CEO Hubris," *Harper's,* October 1995

Many CEOs attain their positions in part because they possess an abundance of animal spirits and ego. If an executive is heavily endowed with these qualities—which, it should be acknowledged, sometimes have their advantages—they won't disappear when he reaches the top. When a CEO is encouraged by his advisers to make deals, he responds much as would a teenage boy who is encouraged by his father to have a normal sex life. It's not a push that he needs.

> WARREN BUFFETT, CEO of the investment firm Berkshire Hathaway, in 1994 letter to shareholders, *Harvard Business Review,* January–February 1996

I'm not blending any cultures. I'm acquiring you . . . Look at your paycheck next month. I bet it says CA at the top left-hand corner.

> CHARLES WANG, CEO of Computer Associates, interviewed in Rama Dev Jager, *In the Company of Giants* (McGraw-Hill, 1997)

20.3 CORPORATE SUCCESSION

Nobody told me before I became president.

> FRED L. HARTLEY, then 67-year-old CEO of the oil company Unocal, upon being asked when he would name his successor, quoted in the *Wall Street Journal,* January 3, 1985

If you rough up the CEO and kick him down the stairs, you can create a situation that scares the hell out of any possible candidate.

> PROFESSOR THOMAS WHISTLER of the University of Chicago School of Business, on the problem of finding a successor for an unsuccessful CEO, quoted in the *Wall Street Journal,* January 3, 1985

A company isn't like an oil well, where all you have to do is hold a pan out and collect the oil. It's like a violin. And I'm not sure my sons have what it takes to play the violin.

> H. J. STERN, 71-year-old president of a small gold-mining firm, quoted in George Anders, *Merchants of Debt* (Basic Books, 1992)

If you're 21, it's nice to know the boss has to get out and make room for others. If you look at the companies where the CEO stayed on till he's 80, those are the people who confuse themselves with their company. That's a fatal mistake.

> WALTER WRISTON, former CEO of Citicorp, quoted in the *New York Times,* April 25, 1993

When most founders go out to hire a CEO or top manager, they look for someone just like themselves. That poses two problems. First, the laws of averages and genetics say that there is no one just like yourself. Second, if you were to find someone just like yourself, what do you think the odds are he's going to want to work for a guy like you?

> PROFESSOR RAJIV TANDON, University of St. Thomas, Minneapolis, quoted in *Inc.,* February 1994

From now on, [choosing my successor] is the most important decision I'll make. It occupies a considerable amount of thought almost every day.

> JACK WELCH, CEO of GE, in 1991, nine years before the likely date of his retirement, quoted in Robert Slater, *The New GE* (Irwin, 1993)

I'm totally healthy. I'm 52 years old. What I need is help, not succession.

> MICHAEL EISNER, CEO of Disney, trying to allay fears after his coronary bypass, quoted in *Business Week,* September 5, 1994

I had a belief, which I still do, that people can stay in a job too long—in part because they may run out of ideas and vitality but more importantly because of the need for vibrancy in an organization. Bringing younger people along and giving them opportunities doesn't work as well if the top-level jobs are filled for a long time.

> ALLAN GILMOUR, former CFO of Ford Motor Company, quoted in *Fortune,* September 8, 1997

It's a little like writing a will. Most CEOs don't want to think about it. They're consumed with the business and don't want to consider their own mortality.

> DENNIS C. CAREY of the executive-search firm Spencer Stuart, quoted in *Business Week,* August 11, 1997

Companies should think twice about spending a lot of time and money on someone who may walk out the door anyway. A healthier attitude may be to consider the world as your bench.

> ROBERT FELTON of the consulting firm McKinsey & Co., quoted in *Business Week,* August 11, 1997

Hiring the chief executive is like getting married; if you do it right, you don't have to do it often.

> JOHN RUTLEDGE, economist and chairman of the merchant bank Rutledge & Co., *Forbes,* September 8, 1997

[The late] Roberto [Goizueta, CEO of Coca-Cola] has filled in behind him so well. He established at least four people who can run the company after he decides not to run it anymore, and behind them are ten people who could fill their jobs.

> HERBERT ALLEN, investment banker and Coca-Cola director, quoted in *Fortune,* October 13, 1997

Roberto Goizueta will clearly be mourned at Coca-Cola, the company he headed, but he might not be missed. Strangely enough, that would be one of the greatest compliments a departed chief executive could receive.

> *The Economist,* October 25, 1997

If you've been chairman and running things, you shouldn't sit there and second guess [successors]. If you're going to get out, get out.

> RICHARD JENRETTE, 67, retired chairman of the Equitable Companies and the investment bank Donaldson, Lufkin & Jenrette, quoted in the *Wall Street Journal,* February 14, 1996

20.4 DEALMAKING

A verbal contract isn't worth the paper it is written on.

> SAM GOLDWYN, movie producer, quoted in Alva Johnson, *The Great Goldwyn* (1937)

My style of dealmaking is quite simple and straightforward. I just keep pushing and pushing to get what I'm after.

> DONALD TRUMP, quoted in *Time,* January 16, 1989

I will tell you a secret: dealmaking beats working. Dealmaking is exciting and fun, and working is grubby . . . That's why you have deals that make no sense.

> PETER DRUCKER, in an interview with Edward Reingold, *Time,* 1990, reprinted in *Time Almanac,* 1991

The natural state of any deal is dead. You got to just keep kicking it and kicking it and kicking it.

> ALLEN BREED, CEO of Breed Technologies, quoted in *Inc.,* December 1995

A deal isn't a deal till you're in the men's room counting the cash.

> NIKOLAI STEVENSON, former sugar broker

When I'm in doubt [about a deal], I chat. One of the best ways is to offer a cleverer man than yourself a joint-venture deal, and if it's poison he'll say it's an awful thing. Then you're seeing the deal through other people's eyes.

> ROBERT KUOK, Chinese businessman, quoted in *Forbes,* July 28, 1997

I negotiated my first deal for [the late Time Warner CEO Steve] Ross on the back stairs of the Campbell Funeral Home, while a funeral was going on in the front.

> FELIX ROHATYN, quoted in the *New Yorker,* January 8, 1990

Sometimes you book people, other times you invent them.

> IRVING "SWIFTY" LAZAR, legendary talent agent, who promised an act a Hollywood nightclub called Johnny Pineapple, then found musicians who could pull it off, *Swifty* (Simon & Schuster, 1995)

I just kept stacking billion-dollar bills on the table until Signet said yes.

> EDWARD CRUTCHFIELD, CEO of the banking firm First Union, after buying the bank Signet for $3.5 billion, quoted in the *Financial Times,* September 24, 1997

I ate oysters; I needed strength.

> SANFORD I. WEILL, chairman of the financial firm Travelers, parent of Smith Barney, on a dinner meeting with the CEO of Salomon Brothers to discuss the merger of that firm with Smith Barney, quoted in the *New York Times,* September 25, 1997

I have to say I was relieved. I'm too young to stay home and watch soap operas.

> D. DWAYNE HOVEN, CEO of the drugstore chain Revco DS Inc., after the collapse of an attempted sale to Rite Aid, from which he stood to gain $5 million, quoted in the *Wall Street Journal,* August 28, 1996

It used to bug the hell out of me when I'd drop out of the bidding for something and then get a call from a reporter asking, "So, Mr. Trump, how does it feel to get beat?"

> DONALD J. TRUMP, *Trump: Surviving at the Top* (Random House, 1990)

A lot of these guys want to do deals just to do them. They want to put scalps up on their walls.

> PAUL RAETHER of the leveraged buyout firm Kohlberg Kravis Roberts, quoted in Bryan Burroughs and John Helyar, *Barbarians at the Gate* (Harper & Row, 1990)

The dealmaker doesn't worry about the aftermath. A manager's whole life is the aftermath.

> RICHARD D'AVENI, Tuck Business School, on why dealmakers make lousy managers

My biggest frustration with bankers and lawyers is that they are all hired guns. They don't have to live with the results.

> SANJAY KUMAR, president of Computer Associates (which estimated it saved $64 million in the past eight years by negotiating its own acquisitions), quoted in the *Wall Street Journal,* March 5, 1996

20.5 EXECUTIVE BATHROOMS

Of the 200 or so CEOs I know personally at major corporations, every single one has an executive bathroom.

Executive washrooms help minimize the risk of a breach of confidence. And they also protect executives from being buttonholed by disgruntled employees.

> ANDY SHERWOOD of the executive recruiting firm Goodrich & Sherwood, quoted in the *New York Times,* December 12, 1993

20.6 EXECUTIVE BOOKS

What you realize very quickly is the reason why these people are at the very top of corporate America. They are very bright, never sleep, run at a fever pitch. You have to grab the tail of the dragon and hope you don't get thrown off.

> HARRIET RUBIN of the publisher Doubleday, about working with chief executives and their books, quoted in the *New York Times,* October 3, 1993

Most of them don't really understand the book business to the extent they do their own. So you end up getting calls from all over the country from a traveling CEO who doesn't understand why this or that bookstore isn't carrying his book.

I enjoy working with them but I'm glad I don't work for them.

> ROBERT WALLACE of the publisher Macmillan, quoted in the *New York Times,* October 3, 1993

20.7 EXECUTIVE GROOMING

Plastic surgery is gradually being accepted in the business community. It's acknowledged that everyone wants to look his best. If the boss says, "I'm going out of the office for a week because I'm having my eyelids done," his staff may twitter but they won't burst out laughing.

> DR. ROBERT GOLDWYN of Harvard Medical School, quoted in the *New York Times,* May 26, 1991

It's important for successful people to appreciate fine quality. It's what sets executives apart, the ability to discern.

> JEAN-LOUIS DUMAS HERMÈS, head of the Paris-based fashion house, quoted in the *New York Times,* June 16, 1991

20.8 EXECUTIVE HEALTH

If I'd known I was gonna live this long, I'd have taken better care of myself.

> EUBIE BLAKE, ragtime pianist, on reaching the age of 100, quoted in the *Observer* (London), February 13, 1983

Our CEO got very excited about wellness a couple of years ago. We all went through stress management programs, got rewarded for stopping smoking, and had to read *Fit or Fat.* But last year wasn't profitable, and now all that has stopped.

> Personnel manager for a major transportation company, quoted in *Business Week,* January, 20, 1986

Slim, trim energetic executives? Bull. I've known as many overweight executives who bordered on being slobs and were as effective as the slim ones. It's just another case of American businessmen focusing on the wrong thing.

> TOM PETERS, management guru, quoted in *Forbes,* September 8, 1986

I get my exercise acting as a pallbearer to my friends who exercise.

> CHAUNCEY DEPEW, chairman of New York Central Railroad at turn of the century, who lived to be 94, quoted in *Forbes,* September 8, 1986

A goodly number of our general managers at Loews do indeed exercise. Now they may think they're better executives than those who don't exercise, but I don't necessarily agree with them.

> PRESTON TISCH, former CEO of the entertainment and real estate firm Loews, quoted in *Forbes,* September 8, 1986

Executives busy with a 12- to 14-hour day of intense transactions, of travel and so forth, don't have much time at home. Their sexual interest may be displaced by other interests. Oftentimes, this leads to tension and fatigue, so people perform less well sexually. And once you have performed inadequately, then the idea continues to haunt you. The next time may be a repeat, and it can create a cycle of thinking whereby one can create one's own failures, failures not physiologically based.

> DR. WILLIAM S. WANAGO of the medical consulting firm Executive Health Examiners, quoted in *Forbes*, September 22, 1986

For exercise, I wind my watch.

> ROBERT MAXWELL, rotund Czech-born English publishing mogul, quoted in *Time*, November 28, 1988

When you don't have any money, the problem is food. When you have money, it's sex. When you have both, it's health.

> J. P. DONLEAVY, *The Ginger Man* (Grove, 1955)

If the CEO carries anything to excess, I'd be concerned. But do you also want to check if he puts on his seat belt when he drives his car?

> ALFRED LERNER, CEO of the banking firm MBNA, quoted in the *Wall Street Journal*, October 28, 1997

[Smoking] is an unacceptable practice.

> E. PENDLETON JAMES, executive recruiter, who contends that smoking has become a factor in the recruitment of senior executives, quoted in the *Wall Street Journal*, October 30, 1997

20.9   EXECUTIVE MENTAL HEALTH

Executives are entering therapy at a rate almost triple what it was 10 years ago. . . . [T]hese high-powered people are starting to see that the emotional bankruptcy of their lives has handicapped them. They will do therapy on the phone if the demands of their jobs preclude them from coming to my office.

I had one patient who would jog in Central Park and conduct his session with me over a portable phone. This was one of his issues in therapy, his total type-A personality.

> ELLEN McGRATH, a New York psychotherapist, quoted in the *New York Times*, March 17, 1991

One much more often encounters what I'd call a unidimensional personality among executives—people who put their work ahead of everything else in their lives. But when one encounters polydimensional people with a whole constellation of activities and involvements that are important to them, they are often quite successful as well as full of energy and enthusiasms.

> DR. GENE ONDRUSEK, clinical psychologist at Scripps Memorial Hospital Center for Executive Health, quoted in the *New York Times*, October 24, 1993

20.10   EXECUTIVE PAY

The madness we see in executive compensation is that we pay star performers too little and poor performers too much.

> ALAN JOHNSON of the consulting firm Sibson & Co., quoted in *Time*, May 7, 1984

[There are] few people able and willing to be in the pressure cooker that these jobs are. You have to pay them top dollar for that. Let some of the critics sit in those chairs for a while, and they'd change their tune.

> DAVID PEASBACK, head of an executive search firm, quoted in *U.S. News & World Report*, April 29, 1985

The nation's shareholders need not fear that they are being swindled by greedy executives. Corporate policies normally make a great deal of sense. Companies are, moreover, adopting compensation plans that benefit shareholders by creating better managerial incentives.

> PROFESSOR KEVIN J. MURPHY of the University of Rochester, "Top Executives Are Worth Every Nickel They Get," *Harvard Business Review*, March–April 1986

It is supposed, according to the old antitrade, antisocial theory, and according to the old practices, too much honored by these writers, that all which the plodding classes gain, produce, or possess, is taken from somebody else. They have no faith in honest exertions, and seem to believe that they are not naturally rewarded.

> "The Progress of Wealth and the Preservation of Order," *The Economist*, July 14, 1849, reprinted in *Harvard Business Review*, March–April 1986

The payoff for failure is almost as much as for succeeding.

> Comment about executive contracts negotiated by superlawyer Joe Bachelder, quoted in *Business Week,* January 24, 1994

We have corporate CEOs who raise their pay 20 percent or more in years when they lay off thousands of people. It's obscene.

> Business philosopher CHARLES HANDY, quoted in *Business Week,* April 25, 1994

The salary of the chief executive of a large corporation is not a market award for achievement. It is frequently in the nature of a warm personal gesture by the individual to himself.

> JOHN KENNETH GALBRAITH, economist

The question is not "Are executives paid too much?" The real question is "Are shareholders getting their money's worth from their executives?"

> ANDREW R. BROWNSTEIN and MORRIS J. PUMMER of the law firm Wachtell, Lipton, Rosen and Katz, reviewing books and other literature on CEO pay, *Harvard Business Review,* May–June 1992

If an executive goes into a company doing as badly as Disney was in the early 1980s and performs as well as [Michael] Eisner, he's an entrepreneur. The fact that he isn't Walt Disney or Bill Gates is a distinction without a difference.

> NELL MINOW of the activist investment fund LENS Inc., quoted in *Business Week,* April 25, 1994

I know there's a floor, but where's the ceiling?

> Bear Stearns shareholder on annual-meeting announcement that top executives averaged $16 million-plus, starting with base salaries of $200,000, quoted in the *Wall Street Journal,* November 1, 1996

We all should be compensated based on competitive issues. If you want a world-class shortstop, you pay. The good news is that many CEOs are getting well compensated for really good performances.

> GEORGE FISHER, CEO of Eastman Kodak, quoted in the *Wall Street Journal,* May 13, 1996

[S]tick Michael Eisner into a football game, and make him return a couple of punts. Let's just see if the guy is really worth big-league money.

> DAVE BARRY, interviewed in *Fortune,* July 7, 1997

If the board gives a CEO a million options, he makes a million dollars every time the stock goes up a point, even if the stock's performance is below the market index.

> ROBERT MONKS of the activist investment firm LENS, quoted in *Fortune,* September 18, 1995

Why not? I had a better year than he did.

> Baseball legend BABE RUTH, when it was pointed out that he had made more money ($80,000) in 1931 than President Hoover ($75,000)

You could call this [an era in which CEO pay had reached 130 times that of average employees, up from 42 in 1980] the Marie Antoinette school of management.

> PROFESSOR GRAEF CRYSTAL of the University of California at Berkeley, quoted in *Fortune,* September 24, 1990

Our findings suggest that shareholders are well served by compensation [board] chairs of high social status, since they are better equipped to resist undue CEO influence.

> From a study of CEO pay by MAURA A. BELLIVEAU of Duke University, CHARLES A. O'REILLY of Stanford University, and JAMES B. WADE of the University of Illinois, cited in *Business Week,* February 3, 1997

Hefty signing bonuses don't guarantee loyalty. *Executive Compensation Reports,* which follows salary trends, compiled a list of 24 high-ranking executives who received sizable recruitment bonuses between 1989 and 1991. Of those, just 11 remain at those jobs.

> *Wall Street Journal,* October 29, 1996

A management decision at the top percolates through the whole corporation. Each worker should be willing to pay a little bit so the most talented person is at the top, affecting everybody. In a huge company those little bits add up to a lot.

> PROFESSOR SHERWIN ROSEN of the University of Chicago, quoted in *Forbes,* May 25, 1996

The corporations, they keep firing the permanent employees and hiring temps and then wondering why their trade secrets keep getting leaked. The *Fortune* 500 average CEO made $3.8 million last year. One guy made $207 million. That's 79 cents for every man, woman, and child in America. I want mine back. I could make three phone calls.

> Comedian WILL DURST, on the PBS TV show *Adam Smith's Money World*, 1996

We have enough stock. It's a matter of gluttony.

> BERNARD MARCUS, CEO of Home Depot, on why everyone at the company except the top two people receives stock options

Figure out what your CEO is earning an hour, then ask yourself if you really want him wasting two days traveling by commercial air to call on a customer who could be reached in hours on a corporate jet.

> *Fortune*, May 30, 1994

Saying you will forfeit your base pay sounds heroic. But it's false bravado, because the economic effect on the executives is exactly the same as it would be if the company just gave them smaller bonuses for not making a target.

> BRIAN FOLEY, executive compensation consultant, quoted in the *New York Times*, September 25, 1997

Incentives are built in to reward executives for taking companies forward. Why should they be rewarded for floundering?

> LEE KOPP, head of the fund management firm Kopp Advisors, protesting company decisions to reprice options when stock prices decline so that the executives made money anyway, quoted in the *Wall Street Journal*, June 11, 1997

If you don't do this kind of thing to keep your people you won't have to worry about dilution—you won't have a stock.

> MICHAEL HOLLAND of the benefits consulting firm Holland & Co., arguing that repricing of options is necessary to hold on to experienced executives who might turn a troubled company around, quoted in the *Wall Street Journal*, June 11, 1997

Compensation experts believe that on January 21, 1997, [the late Coca-Cola CEO Roberto] Goizueta became America's first corporate manager to achieve billionaire status through owning stock in a company he didn't help found or take public.

> ERIN DAVIES, *Fortune*, August 4, 1997

Here is a paradox for the management theorists: any boss who cannot outmaneuver a system designed to keep him under control is probably not worth having.

> *The Economist*, August 16, 1997

[B]eware the manager who proclaims to the world he is a long-termer, beginning today.

> T. BOONE PICKENS JR., chairman of Mesa Petroleum, "Professions of a Short-Termer," *Harvard Business Review*, May–June 1986

God didn't set these huge multipliers

> ROBERT MONKS of the activist investment fund LENS, quoted in *Business Week*, April 24, 1995

You can't pay too much for performance. You can only pay too much for mediocrity.

> ARNOLD S. ROSS, pay consultant, quoted in *Business Week*, April 24, 1995

We were courageous as long as we could afford to be. People just go ballistic on this subject.

> GEOFFREY SMITH, editor of *Financial World*, on why it had stopped carrying Graef Crystal's column on inflated executive pay, quoted in the *Economist*, February 29, 1992

Sure, I'm one of the fat cats. In fact, I'm the fattest cat [at GE], because I'm lucky enough to have this job.

> JOHN F. WELCH, CEO of GE, answering stockholder questions at the company's 1997 annual meeting, quoted in the *Wall Street Journal*, April 14, 1997

[D]o your options motivate you?
Absolutely.

> Exchange between shareholder and Jack Welch of GE, quoted in the *Wall Street Journal*, April 14, 1997

Most people aren't motivated by money. Most are motivated by doing things well, being with a good organization, being proud.

> RAND V. ARASKOG, CEO of the conglomerate ITT, quoted in *Business Week*, May 30, 1994

Getting paid on the size of the company is yesterday's thinking.

> JIM GALLAGHER, ITT spokesman, on report that CEO Rand V. Araskog had maintained his income at the same level after shrinking the company from $25 billion in revenues in 1995 to $6 billion in 1997, quoted in the *New York Times,* September 28, 1997

Am I worth it? No. Is anybody?

> TODD JONES, Detroit Tigers relief pitcher, on his new contract, which pays $2.25 million in 1998 and $2.95 million in 1999, quoted in *Sports Illustrated,* September 15, 1997

Does anyone think Michael Jordan is overpaid, given what he's done for Nike, Gatorade, the Chicago Bulls, the city of Chicago?

> The Motley Fool, online investment columnists DAVID and TOM GARDNER

20.11   EXECUTIVE SECURITY

In the '80s, our business was driven by terrorism, so the vast majority of our customers were governments. But in the '90s, the primary driver has become crime.

Security problems are like any bad event. You research them vividly after they happen.

> BILL O'GARA, CEO of O'Gara, which builds armored limousines, quoted in the *Wall Street Journal,* October 1, 1997

20.12   GOLDEN PARACHUTES AND OTHER CUSHY DEALS

When it [the golden parachute] becomes an emotional decision, they get to be excessive. They tend to be eleventh-hour decisions.

> PETER T. CHINGOS of the accounting-consulting firm at Peat Marwick Mitchell (now KPMG Peat Marwick), quoted in *U.S. New & World Report,* February 28, 1983

I just made a smart deal for myself. This is America. This isn't the Soviet Union. It's the supply-and-demand of the marketplace.

> MICHAEL OVITZ, former president of Disney, on his estimated $125 million Disney severance package,

quoted in Robert Slates, *Ovitz: The Inside Story of Hollywood's Most Controversial Power Broker* (McGraw-Hill, 1997)

Special projects [the assignment frequently given to out-of-favor executives who are understood to be looking for a job]. Often derided as an ignominious, career-stopping demotion, this is actually a ticket to a life of leisurely expense-account lunches, bull sessions with similarly underemployed executives, trips to Europe, and periods of "working at home."

> The late HAROLD GENEEN, chairman of ITT, with Brent Bowers, *The Synergy Myth* (St. Martin's, 1997)

20.13   HUMOR

Solemnity is the shield of idiots.

> MONTESQUIEU, 1799

Humor springs from confidence without conceit—a sense of comfort with yourself and those around you. My CEO learned to laugh at himself and at the sometimes preposterous business of running a business. At the end of the day, after battling the details, you want to be able to look in the mirror and not see an enemy.

> KENNETH J. GURIAN, chairman of ad agency Baxter, Gurian, and Mazzei, quoted in the *Wall Street Journal,* October 7, 1996

I am proud of a couple of things. First, I'm very good at projectile vomiting. Second, I've never had a serious venereal disease.

> HERB KELLEHER, CEO of Southwest Airlines, considered the best CEO in America, quoted in *Fortune,* May 2, 1994

There's a lot of comfort in being with similarly disturbed people.

> ROBERT IVERSON, founder of Kiwi International Airlines, on why he started a business in an industry in which most companies were losing money, quoted in *Inc.,* July 1994

I asked my staff to call the conference organizers for some tips and suggestions on what I should speak about. Well, a couple of days later someone came into my office and said, "We just learned from the NIT [National Industrial Transportation League]. They said you can speak on just about anything and you don't have to be witty or intellectual. Just be yourself."

> A. MAURICE MYERS, CEO of the transportation company Yellow Corp., in a speech, November 18, 1996

When I told my wife, Mary Ann, about it [the Kavaler Award], she said, "What exactly does this award do?" And I said, "Well, it doesn't do anything." And she said, "Then they are giving it to the right person."

> EARNIE DEAVENPORT, CEO of Eastman Chemical, receiving the Kavaler Award, November 14, 1996

When I was first interviewed for a job at Honda, one executive asked me what my future goals were. I responded, "I want to design racing engines. There's an idea I have about valve train design and I want to test it out. If Honda won't let me do that, I don't want to work here." The executive looked stunned at my last comment, but he was not impressed with my goal. He said, "Young people these days do not seem to have very big dreams. I was expecting you to say that your goal was to become president of the company."

> SHOICHIRO IRIMAJIRI, president of Honda of America Manufacturing, in a speech, April 7, 1987

When candidates are running helter-skelter it is time for the rest of us to head for shelter or you may wind up in the smelter.

> HUGH L. CAREY of W. R. Grace & Company, in a speech, June 12, 1992

Cruelty is always simmering just below the surface. Laughs are hard to come by in business these days, and cruelty is . . . fun.

> Broadcasting vice president, quoted in the *New York Times*, April 19, 1992

This one is about two girls who were hiking in the woods. They were crossing a brook when a frog jumped out of the water and said, "Kiss me and I'll turn into an investment banker." One girl promptly picked up the frog and threw him into her knapsack. "Aren't you going to kiss him?" the other girl said. "Are you kidding?" the first one said. "Investment bankers are a dime a dozen. But a talking frog will bring millions."

> C. MICHAEL ARMSTRONG, CEO of Hughes Electronics, in a speech, May 9, 1995

Well, you know down at Frito-Lay we made chips and down in Baltimore [at Westinghouse Electronic Systems] we make chips. And chips are chips.

> MICHAEL H. JORDAN, CEO of Westinghouse Electric, answering a shareholder question about his credentials, quoted in the *Wall Street Journal*, February 28, 1996

20.14 MERGERS AND ACQUISITIONS

Which [division] don't I know well? I'd like to submit myself to an examination on it. You give me 20 minutes with a master spreadsheet on any of our divisions and I'll get a 97 percent.

> PETER GRACE, chief executive of W. R. Grace & Co., when asked whether the shipping and chemical conglomerate can run a company better than its original owner, quoted in *Forbes*, May 5, 1986

To make real changes in cross-border mergers, you have to be factual, quick, and neutral. And you have to move boldly. You must avoid the "investigation trap"—you can't postpone tough decisions by studying them to death. You can't permit a "honeymoon" of small changes over a year or two. A long series of small changes just prolongs the pain. Finally, you have to accept a fair share of mistakes.

> PERCY BARNEVIK, CEO of the Swedish-Swiss heavy industrial firm ABB (Asea Brown Boveri), interviewed in *Harvard Business Review*, March–April 1991

Most acquisitions do not work.

> SAMUEL L. EICHENFELD, CEO of the commercial finance company FINOVA Group, interviewed in Charles B. Wendel, *The New Financiers: Profiles of the Leaders Who Are Reshaping the Financial Services Industry* (Irwin Professional, 1996)

The [railroad] yard is like a coffee cup that's already too filled. It just overflowed.

> RICH CARSWELL, railroad yard manager, Englewood, Texas, on effects of merger of Union Pacific with Southern Pacific, quoted in the *Wall Street Journal*, October 2, 1997

They [Union Pacific management] give us excuses. They have derailments, floods, breakdowns, snow, just stuff you wouldn't think would happen. You would think, if a truck can get through, why can't they?

> ARMANDO SÁNCHEZ of Mill's Pride, a customer of Union Pacific freight operations, whose service suffered after the merger of Union Pacific and Southern Pacific, quoted in the *Wall Street Journal*, October 2, 1997

There's [a] rule that says if you can't run this business, buy another one. There are a lot of companies around that need to be restructured and split up, that never had a justification for being.

> PETER DRUCKER, in an interview with Edward Reingold, *Time*, 1990, reprinted in *Time Almanac*, 1991

So many mergers fail to deliver what they promise that there should be a presumption of failure. The burden of proof should be on showing that anything good is likely to come out of one.

Studies by McKinsey & Co. show that over a given 10-year period only 23 percent of mergers end up recovering costs incurred in the deal. . . .

> WARREN HELLMAN, investment banker, quoted in *Fortune*, January 24, 1994

The empirical evidence is clear. In mergers, tender offers, and proxy fights, stockholders of the attacked companies almost always profit.

> PROFESSOR EUGENE FAMA of the University of Chicago, quoted in *Time*, April 22, 1985

In general takeovers are a good thing. If there is no problem with competition, very few economists are going to say there is anything wrong with the merger.

> PROFESSOR THEODORE KEELER of the University of California, Berkeley, quoted in *Time*, April 22, 1985

One of the things I learned long ago about auctions was that it's not about ego or talent. It's simply about raising your hand for the next bid . . . They won. We lost. Next.

> BARRY DILLER, media mogul, who failed to take over Paramount Communications, to the entertainment conglomerate Viacom after five months, quoted in *Business Week*, February 28, 1994

It [new wave of "strategic" mergers] allows managerial empire building to run amok because managers don't see any cost of making mistakes.

> PROFESSOR MICHAEL JENSEN of Harvard Business School, quoted in *Business Week*, August 8, 1994

Synergies are seldom more than constructs for consultants' reports. (Apples and oranges are both fruits from trees, but are grown in totally different environments with differing skills, tools, time frames, and economics. Buying an apple orchard when one already owns an orange grove probably just adds rotting apples and eliminates time to care for the oranges.)

> MICHAEL BLOOMBERG, *Bloomberg by Bloomberg* (Wiley, 1996)

JP Morgan, an investment bank, has found that the 30 largest takeovers in the past 10 years in Europe produced returns after 3 years that were, on average, 21 percent better than the market at large—although 12 of the 30 performed worse.

> *The Economist*, October 18, 1997

Assets will always find asses.

> HOWARD STRINGER, president CBS Broadcast Group, quoted in *Business Week*, October 17, 1994

Any dope with a checkbook can buy a company. It's what you do afterward that matters.

> HENRY SILVERMAN, founder of the real estate and hotel firm HFS, quoted in *Fortune*, October 27, 1997

It's always easier to implement domestic mergers because you have geography, culture, and accounting systems in common. And there's a sense you can move swiftly and decisively with a lot of confidence.

Acquisitions tend to be easier than mergers because one side is in control. This facilitates faster decision-making: one does not have to make compromises. In mergers you are going to make decisions by committee. You are counting heads to make sure representation is fair and you sometimes don't get the best people in upper management. Ultimately things sort themselves out, but it might take nine months or two years.

> FRED HASSAN, CEO of the pharmaceutical firm Pharmacia & Upjohn, quoted in the *Financial Times*, October 22, 1997

When you are in an industry that is consolidating, the time to do a transaction of this type is when you can.

> EDWARD CRUTCHFIELD, CEO of the bank First Union, after buying CoreStates Financial for $16.3 billion, quoted in the *Wall Street Journal,* November 20, 1997

20.15 NEPOTISM

The fatal fact about nepotism is that the really good people won't go to work for you in the first place or will quit or quit trying for your job when they spot your uncle, brother, nephew, wife, mistress, or son on the payroll.

> ROBERT TOWNSEND, *Up the Organization* (Knopf, 1970)

First, they had to work for somebody else and get the spots knocked off of them. Second, they had to come in and ask us.

> CHARLES W. SMITH II, on conditions for his sons to take over his oil- and chemical-industry firm Allied Supply Company, quoted in *U.S. News & World Report,* July 4, 1983

Family sacrifice is one reason we operate successfully.

> PETER STROH, president, Stroh Brewing Company, quoted in *U.S. News & World Report,* July 4, 1983

You're toast.

> TED TURNER to his son when asked over dinner whether he (the son) would keep his job as a man-
ager in Turner Broadcasting System home-video unit after the TBS merger with Time Warner, quoted in the *Wall Street Journal,* October 9, 1996

20.16 OTHER CHIEFS

The initials are the same [CEO]. The pay is quite different, though.

> STEVE BRASWELL, Chief Ethics Officer, Prudential Insurance Company of America, quoted in the *Wall Street Journal,* July 8, 1996

Pretty soon, a chief will be as common as white bread.

> BILL THERRIEN of Prudential, on proliferation of the word *chief* in corporate titles, quoted in the *Wall Street Journal,* July 8, 1996

Chief listener.

> John Sculley's title on his business card at Apple Computer, quoted in the *Wall Street Journal,* July 8, 1996

Chief learning officer.

> Unofficial title of Anthony Rucci, chief administrative officer of Sears Roebuck, charged with revitalizing the corporation's "dinosaur culture," cited in *Fortune,* October 13, 1997

21.1 GOLF

21.1.1 Golf and Business

[Lee] Iacocca insists he will not wield any power [after retiring as CEO of the auto firm Chrysler] and would rather spend his retirement playing golf. But, as one friend points out, "Iacocca doesn't play golf." [A couple of years later, Iacocca lent his support to a hostile takeover attempt against Chrysler.]

> *The Economist,* March 21, 1992

To me golf is like the restaurant business. You make money at the bottom, like at McDonald's, and you make money at the top, like at Lutèce. But you starve in the middle.

> GERALD BARTON, chairman of the golf-course builders Landmark Land Company, quoted in March 24, 1991

It really screwed up my golf game.

> JOHN FRENCH, lobbyist for Philip Morris, on Florida legislation allowing state to sue tobacco industry for $300 million in annual Medicaid expenses for smoking-related diseases, quoted in *Business Week,* July 4, 1994

When I play golf and finish last, I get a prize. If you give me an award [the worst-performing mutual fund of the year] I want to put it in my boardroom.

> HEIKO THIEME of the mutual fund American Heritage Fund, lamenting that he got no trophy for his honor, quoted in the *Wall Street Journal,* February 21, 1997

21.1.2 Golf and Character

[John D.] Rockefeller's golf was the exact reverse of Mr. Andrew] Carnegie's golf. Carnegie could not stand being beaten and would take the utmost liberties with the score. Rockefeller was strictness itself in counting every stroke.

I remember that one tee at Augusta faced a little swamp. If Rockefeller had the misfortune to drive into this morass, he would stop and put on a pair of rubbers, go into the mud, and hammer at his ball . . . Considering everything, he played a remarkable game, and always in strict conformity to the rules.

> Recounted in FRANK NELSON DOUBLEDAY, founder of Doubleday & Co., *Memoirs of a Publisher.* Quoted in John Brooks, ed., *The Autobiography of American Business* (Doubleday, 1974)

Golf is not, on the whole, a game for realists. By its exactitudes of measurement it invites the attention of perfectionists.

> HEYWOOD HALE BROUN, *Tumultuous Merriment* (1979)

I can tell more about how someone is likely to react in a business situation from one round of golf than I can from a hundred hours of meetings.

> MARK H. McCORMACK, *What They Don't Teach You at Harvard Business School* (Bantam Doubleday Dell, 1988)

Golf has a way of magnifying character flaws—whininess, explosiveness, dishonesty, lack of clarity, self-delusion—that are less detectable in other situations. You can know a guy for 20 years and not realize he's a jerk until you've played a round of golf with him. Would you really want to invest your life's savings with somebody who had just toed his ball into a better lie when he thought you weren't looking?

No. But you might want to retain him as your lawyer.

> DAVID OWEN, *My Usual Game* (Villard, 1995)

Golfers like to joke about the player who cheated so badly that when he had a "hole in one," he wrote down "zero" on his scorecard.

> NORMAN AUGUSTINE, CEO of the aerospace firm Lockheed Martin, in a speech, May 24, 1997

With success comes many things one doesn't like. It's a given. But those who are truly successful learn to handle the uncomfortable moments. You may have to hide your feelings, fake it if you will. With winning you lose a piece of yourself. You are a winner on the field. Let's go learn to be one off it.

> IVOR CHARLES, the most successful left-handed golfer ever, recounting a conversation with his son, quoted in *Business Week,* February 7, 1994

I had won almost 17 straight holes and I was beating him [Vernon Jordan, Washington lawyer and power broker] like a drum, and I hit the ball on the green, and he proceeds to hit the ball in the woods. At which point I hear this noise and clatter, and out comes a ball that miraculously goes into the hole. He beat me on that hole. And of course, he doesn't remember anything but that hole. I can't believe he talked to you about that. I took it very gentlemanly until he started to crow about it, and he's still crowing about it years later. So he's leaning on a very thin reed.

> LOUIS V. GERSTNER, CEO of IBM, quoted in *Fortune*, April 14, 1997

21.1.3 Golf and Ego

I don't play customer golf.

> HAROLD "RED" POWLING, ex-chairman of Ford Motor Company, to former U.S. President George Bush, when refusing to allow Bush another drive after hitting into a sand trap

It's amazing how many people beat you at golf now that you're no longer president.

> FORMER U.S. PRESIDENT GEORGE BUSH

He's a real gentlemen although he's not much of a golfer.

> The late U.S. REPRESENTATIVE THOMAS P. "TIP" O'NEILL, on Dwayne Andreas, CEO of ADM (Archer Daniels Midland), quoted in *Fortune*, October 8, 1996

I'm thinking [when a golfing partner lines up a putt] with every brain wave: Miss.

> SCOTT McNEALY, CEO of the computer firm Sun Microsystems, quoted in Randall E. Stross, *Steve Jobs and the NeXT Big Thing* (Maxwell Macmillan, 1993)

21.1.4 Golf and Ethics

[For Pentagon officials and defense contractors] Three days of golf at a plush spa to the tune of several hundreds of thousands of dollars *seems* wrong and *is* wrong, however legal. It creates the perception of abuse.

> JOHN F. BUDD JR., vice chairman of the PR firm Carl Byoir & Associates, in a speech, March 29, 1989

The income tax has made more liars out of the American people than golf has.

> WILL ROGERS, April 8, 1923

21.1.5 Golf and the Japanese

I could sell refrigerators [to Japanese golfer] if they had a golf logo on them.

American executives golf here to relax. But the Japanese are chomping at the bit to get out there.

> GARY BROWN, golf pro for the Turtle Bay Country Club, Oahu, Hawaii, quoted in the *New York Times*, January 21, 1990

They [the Japanese] don't want to slow down the play. I've played in Japan and we ran from shot to shot.

> WADE NISHIMOTO, golf pro for Maui's Wailea Golf Club, Hawaii, quoted in the *New York Times*, January 21, 1990

Japs [sic] are crazy for golf. Did you know that? If you ever want something from a Jap, first play golf with him. It doesn't hurt if you let him win, either.

> KIRK BAINS, financier, quoted in the *New Yorker*, September 8, 1997

21.1.6 Golf and Power

A strange game. Those that want something playing with those that have something.

> CARDINAL HUGH DANAHER, character in John Gregory Dunne, *True Confessions* (Dutton, 1977)

Augusta National might as well be dubbed the CEO Club. Its members . . . are John Akers (ex-IBM), Robert Allen (AT&T), Harold Powling (ex-Ford Motor), Stephen Bechtel (Bechtel), Edward Brenner (Sears), Warren Buffett (Berkshire Hathaway), Charles Knight (Emerson Electric), Hugh McColl Jr. (NationsBank), Thomas Murphy (Capital Cities/ABC), John Reed (Citicorp), Jack Welch (GE), and Thomas Wyman (S&G Warburg, ex-CBS, ex-Pillsbury), to pick 12.

> *Fortune*, April 18, 1994

21.1.7 Golf and Practical Jokes

You say you saw him on the course, tell him you liked his game, so he bites. But then you tell him you didn't like the way he was handling his golf cart, that he was tearing up the green. Let the guy walk on eggshells for a couple of weeks, thinking his membership's in jeopardy. That's a pretty good one.

> Trader at Bear Stearns & Company who called a co-worker, posing as a member of the board of his

colleagues's country club, quoted in the *New York Times*, April 19, 1992

Say they're going away for the weekend. When they step away from their desk, you take out their clothes and put phone books in to make up for the weight. Or you hide their golf shoes when you know they've got a business foursome.

> Banker, at Bank of New York, quoted in the *New York Times*, April 19, 1992

21.1.8 Golf and Productivity

[Salespeople] generally do have a sense of humor but don't get a lot done. Their problem is that they play a lot of golf, which is right up there with heroin abuse as a killer of our nation's productivity. The only difference is that golf is more expensive. If you had an employee with a heroin habit and one with a golf habit, you'd probably get more actual productive time out of the one with the heroin habit.

> Humorist DAVE BARRY, interviewed in *Fortune*, July 7, 1997

If people are golfers and their handicap doesn't go up, they're not doing their job. We like tennis players around here. It's great exercise, in about an hour.

> ELI BROAD, founder and chairman of the insurance company SunAmerica, quoted in *Fortune*, October 13, 1997

21.1.9 The Grass Ceiling

One man left [First State Bank as a commercial client] because, he told me, he never let his wife handle a dime of their money and he couldn't picture me running a bank. The other two came back eventually too, but I had to play golf with them first.

> RUTH SMITH, president of First State Bank of Kansas City, recalling how when she first took over, the bank lost then reclaimed three major commercial accounts, quoted in *Fortune*, August 31, 1987

We don't want to be allowed in the men's locker room [of an all-male golf club]. We just want to play golf.

> JONINA JACOBS, Detroit restaurateur, quoted in *Business Week*, February, 28, 1994

I was an investment banker. I sat there while an executive asked two associates who worked for me to go out and play golf at his country club—where there were no black members. And I didn't play golf. But I remember thinking, "He doesn't know that. He never asked me if I could play." And a lightbulb went on. I realized these guys were going to be out there together for four or five hours without me, bonding.

. . . They came in the next day; they had been out drinking after the golf game until ten o'clock. I had been working all night. They were tanned and relaxed and laughing together. And I said, "I'm going to learn how to play this game. I'm going to learn golf."

> KEN BACON, of the federal mortgage agency Fannie Mae, quoted in "A Question of Color: A Debate on Race in the Workplace," *Harvard Business Review*, September–October 1997

[My husband] still plays golf, but at a public course. I guess he's the one who had to make the sacrifice, but I'm the one who has to hear about it.

> KATHY DAWSON, who quit her corporate personnel career to start a consulting business, on financial and personal sacrifices the move entailed, quoted in the *Wall Street Journal*, November 26, 1996

21.2 ALTERNATIVES TO GOLF

21.2.1 Dogs

You'd be surprised at how many businessmen are afraid to be tough with their dogs.

> BASHKIM DIBRA, dog trainer, quoted in the *New York Times*, May 5, 1992

21.2.2 Football

In attracting viewers, it isn't just the game that matters; it's also what you have to say. *Monday Night Football* proved that. We sustained our ratings through the worst games ever played.

> The late sports commentator HOWARD COSELL, quoted in *U.S. News & World Report*, September 16, 1985

And it's always good being in a town that has something to cheer about on Super Bowl Sunday. Even so, I'm reminded of a comment by George Will that "Football combines the worst two things about America: it is violence punctuated by committee meetings."

> JAMES A. UNRUH, CEO of the computer company Unisys, in a speech, January 16, 1997

21.2.3 Shooting

Not everybody plays golf or tennis. But everybody can shoot.

> REX OGG, CEO of an Ohio manufacturing company, quoted in the *New York Times,* November 17, 1996

I grew up in Brooklyn, so if I heard a gun I ran the other way. We got these guys away for three whole days [of shooting instruction]. We played poker, smoked cigars; it was big testosterone sharing for three days.

> GENE DONNELLY, partner at the accounting firm Coopers & Lybrand, quoted in the *New York Times,* November 17, 1996

A lot of business and politics in this state gets done around places like this. Sure does. You want to know what's going on in Louisiana, the best way is to spend some time out in the duck marshes, with the people in the clubs.

> Shooting partner of Louisiana Governor Mike Foster, quoted in *Forbes, FYI,* fall 1997

22.1 CURRENT TRENDS

Ten hottest technologies for the next decade:

1. Genetic health treatments
2. Personal computers
3. Multifuel automobiles
4. Next-generation televisions
5. Electronic cash
6. Home health monitors
7. Global positioning systems (including electronic maps and tracking devices for people and their possessions)
8. Smart materials (that identify excessive stresses in machine parts, building materials, and other items)
9. Anti-aging and weight-control products
10. Changes in the ways things are acquired (such as greater reliance on leasing instead of purchase)

> Summarized from DOUGLAS E. OLESON, CEO of the high-tech research and development firm Battelle, in a speech, January 21, 1997

22.2 INNOVATION

Delinquents are very creative people.

> FRANK FARLEY of the University of Wisconsin, quoted in *U.S. News & World Report,* January 26, 1987

Elwood Haynes, of Kokomo, Indiana, is often credited with the invention of the automobile. But no one drove here today in a Haynes. The lesson of history is that innovation is a necessary condition for business success—but not a sufficient condition for business success.

> RANDALL L. TOBIAS, CEO of the pharmaceutical firm Eli Lilly, in a speech, April 15, 1997

Invention is the process by which a new idea is discovered or created. In contrast, innovation occurs when a new idea is adopted.

> EVERETT ROGERS, author of *Diffusions of Innovations,* quoted by Randall L. Tobias, CEO of the pharmaceutical firm Eli Lilly, in a speech, April 1, 1997

R&D [research and development] is not all there is to innovation. And, for that matter, funding is not all there is to R&D.

> RANDALL L. TOBIAS, CEO of the pharmaceutical firm Eli Lilly, in a speech, April 1, 1997

Above all, innovation is not invention. It is a term of economics rather than of technology. The measure of innovation is the impact on the environment . . . [Innovation] allows resources the capacity to create wealth.

> PETER DRUCKER, business writer and guru, quoted by Robert G. McVicker Sr. of Kraft General Foods, in a speech, April 3, 1992

When the engineers see him coming down the halls with a fistful of paper napkins they know their morning is over.

> STEPHEN RUDY of Somnus Medical Technologies, on working with a CEO who is also an inventor, quoted in the *Wall Street Journal,* April 29, 1997

Anyone who's ever developed a product knows that it takes longer than you hope.

> DONNA VAILLANCOURT of the software firm Spectrum Associates, quoted in *Inc.,* March 1994

Technology travels with people. You can't just throw it over the wall and, because it's such a good idea, expect another engineering group to simply pick it up and run with it.

> CHUCK GESCHKE, cofounder of software firm Adobe Systems, on why his previous company Xerox, had failed to translate much basic research into commercial success, interviewed in Rama Dev Jager, *In the Company of Giants* (McGraw-Hill, 1997)

Automatic plant watering/baby's crawling aid/battery-operated gloves and boots/chair relaxation system/dustbuster/golfer's stroke saver/hairstyling appliances/image enhancement for cosmetic makeup/ingestible toothpaste/invisible braces/liquid-cooled garments/rechargeable electric footwear/self-adjusting sunglasses/self-injury inhibitor/sports bra/therapeutic scalp cooler/

vacuum-drying technique/whale-identification method/yacht-race monitor.

> *Spinoffs,* 1994 brochure by Hamilton Standard Space
> Systems International, on "lifesaving, necessary,
> and useful items" that have come out of the U.S.
> space program, reprinted in *Harper's,* November 1994

Fifty percent of the developments we try don't work out. We don't publicize our failures. When something doesn't work don't leave the corpse lying around.

We like the saying "If it's worth doing, it's worth doing poorly." Don't study the idea to death with experts and committees. Get on with it and see if it works.

> F. KENNETH IVERSON, chairman of Nucor Corpora-
> tion, in a speech, February 5, 1996

He [Steve Jobs, cofounder of Apple Computer] was the first to see what the PC was all about. The first to recognize the value of the laser printer, the graphical user interface, and object-oriented software. . . . And now with Pixar, his computer-oriented movie and game company, he's pioneering real digital entertainment. Not bad for 40 years old.

> ANDREW GROVE, CEO of the computer chip firm
> Intel, quoted in *Fortune,* July 10, 1996

You must have a well-thought-through product that will provide benefits. Everything else will come. But you can't sell a $100 bill for $50.

> HENRY BURKHARDT, founder of supercomputer
> company Kendal Square Research, quoted in *Forbes,*
> May 25, 1996

[T]here has been no case in history where the pioneer became the dominant producer, whether you are talking about a business or a science. The most successful innovators are the creative imitators, the Number Two.

Edison didn't invent the light bulb. That's an American myth. . . . Edison invented the electric industry.

> PETER DRUCKER, management writer and guru in an
> interview, *Hot Wired,* April 8, 1996

Ideas are a commodity. Execution of them is not.

> MICHAEL DELL, CEO of Dell Computer, quoted in
> *Fortune,* June 14, 1993

[E]very generation has underestimated the potential for finding new ideas. . . . Possibilities do not add up. They multiply.

> PAUL M. ROMER, senior fellow, Hoover Institution,
> quoted in *Fortune,* October 18, 1993

All my life people have said, "David, I thought of that idea long before you did." It's true I don't have that many original ideas. I just make the ideas happen because I won't let them die.

> DAVID MURDOCK, CEO of the food company Dole,
> quoted in *Forbes,* October 26, 1987

Historically, Americans have been among the world's most innovative people. Yet, virtually every American business school propagates the myth of the mature market. Freshly minted MBAs come out believing that you milk your mature products to provide capital to invest in your growth products. On the other hand mature business people know that every market has growth potential, because they constantly redefine the market either by expanding it geographically or by creating new demand through new products.

> LAWRENCE A. BOSSIDY, CEO of the industrial firm
> Allied-Signal, in a speech, June 21, 1995

I became interested in the use of electricity to reanimate people in 1931, when I saw my first Frankenstein movie as a child.

> EARL BAKKEN, founder of the medical products com-
> pany Medtronic and inventor of the first practical
> pacemaker in his garage, quoted in *Fortune,* May 27,
> 1996

In a 1986 speech on creativity, Bill [Hewlett, cofounder of the computer firm Hewlett-Packard] recalled the time he quoted Thomas Edison to an engineering manager. You've probably heard Edison's famous quip, "There ain't no rules around here. We're trying to accomplish something."

When Bill said that, the manager replied, "Don't say that. Creativity is what screws up my engineering schedule."

> LEWIS E. PLATT, CEO of Hewlett-Packard, in a
> speech, February 28, 1997

[D]espite history's lessons, the watchword in all industry during the last few years has not been innovation. It's been replication.

> CATHLEEN BLACK, president of Hearst Magazines,
> in a speech, March 4, 1997

Try it [Biofoam] with salsa. [Biofoam is a sorghum-based, biodegradable packing material that started out being developed as a snack food.]

> ED ALFKE, CEO of Biofoam, *Inc.,* October 1996

Today in most fields I know, the struggle is about creativity and innovation. There is no script.

> ROBERT B. SHAPIRO, CEO of the chemical firm Monsanto, interviewed in *Harvard Business Review,* January–February 1997

When asked to build competitive advantage, managers typically assess what competitors do, and strive to do it better. Their strategic thinking thus regresses toward the competition. In the end, companies expend tremendous effort but often achieve no more than incremental improvement—imitation, not innovation.

> W. CHAN KIM and RENÉE MAUBORGNE, both of the French business school Insead, *Wall Street Journal,* April 21, 1997

Did Toyoda—the guy who runs the company's name is Toyoda—did he suddenly have the idea one day? Did it bubble up from the bottom? Bubble down from the top? Did it have—you know the Japanese—consensus? . . . I don't know how they did it. They somehow said, "We're going to be the best." And that's how they build cars like the Camry.

> DICK LANDGRAFF of Ford Motor Company, quoted in Mary Walton, *Car* (Norton, 1997)

History shows that change eventually becomes inevitable. The first company to break ranks—or the imaginative new entrant is not always the ultimate victor. But the company that holds out the longest, attempting to ignore reality, is always the loser.

> PETER MARTIN, *Financial Times,* May 15, 1997

22.3 NEW TECHNOLOGY

The entertainment industry is now the driving force for new technology, as defense used to be. Making a dinosaur for *Jurassic Park* is exactly the same as designing a car.

> EDWARD R. McCRACKEN, CEO of the software firm Silicon Graphics, quoted in *Business Week,* March 14, 1994

Genetically engineered food will go the way of the Edsel.

> JEREMY RIFKIN, economist noted for his devotion to "green" causes

It [the typewriter] piles an awful stack of words on one page. It don't muss things or scatter ink blots around.

> MARK TWAIN, in letter to his brother in 1874. (He submitted the first typewritten book manuscript to a publisher in 1876: *Tom Sawyer.*)

When I first started in the [electronics] field 40 years ago, a few hundred dollars' worth of instrumentation was all you needed. Today, you can't work at the frontiers of technology and electronics without equipment costing millions of dollars.

> DAVID PACKARD, cofounder of the computer company Hewlett-Packard, quoted in *U.S. News & World Report,* January 26, 1987

Every time there has been a battle between an expensive, low-end technology and a high-end technology, the low-end technology has won.

> MARC SCHULMAN, president of the consulting firm Technology Strategies, quoted in *Fortune,* June 14, 1993

In 1890 you spent half the time looking after the horse, when along comes the car. All of a sudden, you don't need straw or hay, you just need a canister of gasoline from the drug store. The same sort of step-change will come from the fuel cell.

> NICHOLAS ABSON, journalist turned fuel-cell entrepreneur, *Financial Times,* May 27, 1997

22.4 PREDICTING THE FUTURE OF ONE'S OWN BUSINESS

The surest move ever made.

> The late ROBERTO GOIZUETA, CEO of Coca-Cola, on introducing new-formula New Coke, quoted in *Time,* May 6, 1985

We did not understand the deep emotions of so many of our customers for Coca-Cola. It is not only a function of culture or upbringing or inherited brand loyalty. . . . And you cannot measure it any more than you can measure love, pride, or patriotism.

> DONALD R. KEOUGH, president of Coca-Cola after New Coke flopped in the marketplace, quoted in *Time,* July 22, 1985

Mr. [Bill] Gates's [CEO of Microsoft] own estimate is that by 1990 75–80 percent of IBM-compatible computers will be sold with [IBM's proprietary operating system] OS/2.

> *The Economist,* January 30, 1988.

My biggest fear is that we will be too successful.

> ROBERT FITZPATRICK, chairman of Euro Disneyland, quoted in the *New York Times,* February 17, 1991

PepsiCo will be the largest employer in the world in the year 2000 with 1 million worldwide.

> WAYNE CALLOWAY, CEO of the beverage, snack food, and then restaurant company PepsiCo, quoted in *Fortune,* November 29, 1993 (The one million included employees of the restaurants Pizza Hut, KFC, and Taco Bell. These struggling chains were spun off in January 1997 to allow PepsiCo to concentrate on its rapidly growing line of snack foods.)

We're only a million vehicles apart, so one of us has to go up half a million and the other one has to go down half a million. Stranger things have happened.

> ALEXANDER TROTMAN, CEO of Ford Motor Company, on what it would take to surpass General Motors in sales, quoted in *Fortune,* December 27, 1993

Within the next decade malls all across America will institute some form of legalized gambling.

> MELVIN SIMON, developer of Minneapolis's giant Mall of America, quoted in the *Economist,* January 20, 1996

22.5   VISION

If one does not know to which port one is sailing, no wind is favorable.

> SENECA, the younger. *Epistolae Morales*

The device is inherently of no value to us.

> Western Union's rationale for not buying the patent for Alexander Graham Bell's telephone, 1876

Everything that can be invented has been invented.

> CHARLES H. DUELL, commissioner of the United States Office of Patents, recommending that his office be abolished, 1899

A dwarf standing on the shoulders of a giant may see farther than a giant himself.

> ROBERT BURTON, *Anatomy of Melancholy* (1621)

Heavier-than-air flying machines are impossible.

> LORD KELVIN, president of the British Royal Society, 1895

Babe Ruth made a big mistake when he gave up pitching.

> TRIS SPEAKER, baseball player, 1921

There is no likelihood man can ever tap the power of the atom.

> ROBERT MILLIKAN, Nobel Prize winner for physics, 1923

I think there is a world market for about five computers.

> THOMAS WATSON SR., founder of IBM, 1943

The Edsel is here to stay.

> HENRY FORD II to dealers, 1957

I'm lying in bed counting sheep when all of a sudden it hits me. I conceive a character like Samson, Hercules, and all the strong men I heard tell of rolled into one. Only more so.

> JEROME SIEGEL, creator (along with illustrator Joe Schuster) of Superman, about a sleepless night in 1934, quoted in *Time,* March 14, 1988

A rather immature piece of work.

> United Features rejecting the Superman script in 1934, quoted in *Time,* March 14, 1988 (Siegel and Schuster sold the rights to the character and therefore did not share in the huge profits generated by Superman.)

640K [of computer memory] ought to be enough for anybody.

> BILL GATES, cofounder and CEO of Microsoft, 1981

There is no reason why anyone would want a computer in their home.

> KENNETH OLSEN, founder of the computer firm Digital Equipment Corporation, 1977

We don't like their sound and guitar music is on the way out.

> The record company Decca, rejecting the Beatles, 1962

It requires a certain kind of mind to see the beauty in a hamburger bun. . . . Not if you're a McDonald's man.

Not if you view the bun as an essential material in the art of serving a great many meals fast. Then this plump yeasty mass becomes an object worthy of sober study. . . .

> RAY KROC, driving force behind McDonald's, quoted in David Halberstam, *The Fifties* (Villard, 1993)

The last thing IBM needs right now is a vision.

> LOUIS V. GERSTNER JR. upon becoming CEO of the computer company IBM, quoted in *Fortune,* April 14, 1997

It's time for IBM to perform and then talk, instead of talk and then perform.

> LOUIS GERSTNER JR., CEO of IBM, quoted in *Fortune,* May 31, 1993

You can't see the future through a rearview mirror.

> PETER LYNCH, *Beating the Street* (Simon & Schuster, 1993)

The concept [an overnight mail delivery service] is interesting and well formed but in order to earn better than a C, the idea must be feasible.

> Yale management professor in response to student Fred Smith's paper proposing an overnight mail delivery service. Smith later founded Federal Express.

If your only tool is a hammer, everything looks like a nail.

> NATHAN C. MYHRVOLD, chief of research and development for the software firm Microsoft, quoted in *Fortune,* November 29, 1993

Early visions fueled our meteoric rise, but then the visions began to outgrow the company. They no longer fed us. We had to feed them.

> GERALD H. LANGELER, president of Mentor Graphics, quoted in *Harvard Business Review,* March–April 1992

Hindsight is better than foresight. That's why evolutionary forms such as venerable buildings (e.g., the Santa Fe adobe style or the New England Cape Cod house) always work better than visionary designs such as geodesic domes. They grow from experience rather than somebody's forehead.

> STEWART BRAND, cofounder of Global Business Network, author of the original *Whole Earth Catalogue,* member of the hippie adventurers Merry Pranksters, and business guru, quoted in *Fortune,* October 16, 1995

Small business just pays too much for everything.

> THOMAS STEMBERG, founder of the Staples chain, quoted in the *Wall Street Journal,* September 6, 1996 (He started the company in 1985 after finding out that corporations could buy a box of pens for 85 cents that cost $3.68 retail.)

People who eat white bread have no dreams.

> DIANA VREELAND, former editor of *Vogue,* quoted on National Public Radio, September 6, 1997

Our [original] vision? Meet payroll next week.

> CHARLES WANG, CEO of Computer Associates, interviewed in Rama Dev Jager, *In the Company of Giants* (McGraw-Hill, 1997)

Doomsday books usually hit the bestseller lists when the economy is turning for the better.

> PETER BRIMELOW, *Forbes,* September 21, 1987

[I]n 1997, Michael Ovitz will be on top wherever he is.

> Astrologer SHELLEY VON STRUNCKEL, columnist for the London *Sunday Times,* when asked what would happen to Disney's Eisner-Ovitz management team, quoted in *Fortune,* October 30, 1995

To the people with the Chicken Little theories, I say, take another look at the sky. It's not falling. It's expanding.

> PAUL LAXALT, former U.S. senator, in a speech, August 17, 1996

Today's more fashionable nonsenses are that America's trade deficit will grow ever bigger, and that ever more Americans will find their jobs in dynamic small business. It is likelier that America's trade position will quickly get $100 billion a year better, thus making all other countries' trade positions $100 billion a year worse; and that start-ups in small businesses are about to nose-dive.

> *The Economist,* February 6, 1988

The Americans have need of the telephone, but we do not. We have plenty of messenger boys.

> SIR WILLIAM PREECE, chief engineer of Britain's General Post Office, 1876

I dream for a living.

> STEVEN SPIELBERG, most financially successful movie director in history, quoted in *Fortune,* November 16, 1996

23.1 BEATING THE AVERAGES

Like everyone else in this industry, I have an ego large enough to believe I'm going to be one of the select few that will outperform [the Standard & Poors index].

> GEORGE SAUTER, fund manager, quoted in the *Wall Street Journal,* February 25, 1997

Law Number XXII If stock market experts were so expert, they would be buying stock, not selling advice.

> NORMAN R. AUGUSTINE, CEO of the aerospace company Lockheed Martin, *Augustine's Laws* (Viking, 1986)

When someone hands me their money, the first thing they want is for me to make them a lot more. The first thing I want to do is not lose it.

> SUSAN BYRNE, chief executive of Westwood Equity Fund, quoted in *Forbes,* April 21, 1997

Making things requires factories and workers and other expensive inconveniences. You can't multiply your investment 100 times with that kind of financial burden.

> MICHAEL LEWIS, *Slate,* November 13, 1997

23.2 BETTING WRONG

There are two times in a man's life when he should not speculate: when he can't afford it, and when he can.

> MARK TWAIN

If you are looking for Wall Street analysts who follow radio, you will find them hanging from window ledges all over New York.

> JEFF SMULYAN, chairman of Emmis Broadcasting Corporation, on mergers in radio industry, quoted in the *New York Times,* November 4, 1996

More money has been lost reaching for yield than at the point of a gun.

> RAYMOND F. DEVOE JR., of the investment firm Legg Mason Wood Walker, quoted in *Fortune,* April 18, 1994

The recovery in profitability has been amazing following the reorganization, leaving Barings to conclude that it was not actually terribly difficult to make money in the securities business.

> PETER BARING, chairman of Barings Bank, in 1993 meeting with an official of the Bank of England, quoted in Nick Leeson, *Rogue Trader* (Little Brown, 1996) (The 232-year-old Barings collapsed in February 1995 because of unauthorized trading by Nick Leeson.)

23.3 BIG NAME INVESTORS

I am not a professional security analyst. I would rather call myself an insecurity analyst.

> GEORGE SOROS, *Soros on Soros* (Wiley, 1995)

I don't pay attention to what the stock does. If the business does well, the stock eventually follows.

> WARREN BUFFETT, quoted in *Business Week,* October 3, 1994

This is the cornerstone of our investment philosophy: Never count on making a good sale. Have the purchase price be so attractive that even a mediocre sale gives good results.

> WARREN BUFFETT, letter to his partners, quoted in *Fortune,* February 4, 1996

I never talk to brokers or analysts. Wall Street is the only place that people who ride to work in a Rolls-Royce get advice from those who take the subway.

> WARREN BUFFETT, to the *Los Angeles Times,* quoted in the *New Republic,* February 17, 1996

The Woodstock of Capitalism.

> Weekend-long event for shareholders of Berkshire Hathaway Inc. featuring Warren Buffett, quoted in *Newsweek,* May 19, 1985

We're like a cult. Warren just hasn't told us when to take the poison yet.

> LARRY OBERMAN, Chicago investment banker, who came to hear Warren Buffett speak, quoted in *Newsweek,* May 19, 1985

Just look at him. He runs his company with five people in an office the size of a closet.

> KATHARINE GRAHAM, publisher of the *Washington Post,* on Warren Buffett, quoted in *U.S. News & World Report,* July 21, 1986

I think his jokes are all funny. I think his dietary practices—lots of buyers and Cokes—are excellent.

> BILL GATES, on Warren Buffett, reviewing *Buffett: Making of an American Capitalist,* by Roger Lowenstein (Random House, 1995), *Harvard Business Review,* January–February 1996

People forget about mathematical limitations . . . the experience of a bull market dulls the senses.

> WARREN BUFFETT, admonishing investors not to expect another decade of high returns, quoted in the *Financial Times,* May 6, 1997

If you see a bandwagon, it's too late.

> SIR JAMES GOLDSMITH, quoted in his Reuters obituary, July 19, 1997

23.4 CAVEAT EMPTOR

The personal-computer industry is highly competitive and has been characterized by rapid technological advances. Products are vulnerable to early obsolescence.

> Compaq prospectus, quoted in *Time,* January 23, 1984

The recommendations I am about to give you are fundamental recommendations. As for more speculative recommendations, we'd like to give you those over the phone.

> MATTHEW CZEPLIEWICZ, bank analyst for Credit Suisse First Boston, London, at an investor breakfast, quoted in *Fortune,* July 26, 1993

Fees are sometimes ten times as large when a deal closes as when it doesn't, so you'd have to be a saint not to be affected by the numbers involved.

> FELIX ROHATYN, investment banker at Lazard Frères, quoted by David B. Jemison, Sim B. Sitkin, "Acquisitions: The Process Can Be a Problem," *Harvard Business Review,* March–April, 1986

There are plenty of ethical guys on Wall Street. But having worked there, I assure you that no matter what they

say, the advice from the big securities dealers is influenced by other agendas.

> JOHN D. McCAHILL of the corporate advisory firm Cantwell & Company, quoted in the *New York Times,* June 6, 1993

A lot of securities firms do a tremendously good job, but the fact is that they have huge overhead expenses and they need to generate fees by completing securities offerings.

> LAWRENCE A. GOLDFARB, formerly of the investment bank First Boston Corporation and then president of the advisory firm Geneva Financial, quoted in the *New York Times,* June 6, 1993

The larger question here is whether investment banks' opinions are bought opinions. The answer is clearly yes.

> GUY WYSER-PRATTE, arbitrageur, on investment banks involved in hostile takeovers, quoted in the *New York Times,* October 6, 1996

Luck is a significant factor in the success of any thoroughbred-related activity.

> Prospectus for 1983 public stock offering by Spendthrift Farm Inc.

23.5 CRASHES

October. This is one of the peculiarly dangerous months to speculate in stocks in. The others are July, January, September, April, November, May, March, June, December, August, and February.

> MARK TWAIN, *Pudd'nhead Wilson* (1894)

Stock prices have reached what looks like a permanently high plateau.

It was the psychology of panic. It was mob psychology, and it was not, primarily, that the price level of the market was unsoundly high . . . the fall in the market was very largely due to the psychology by which it went down because it went down.

> PROFESSOR IRVING FISHER, Yale University, weeks before the stock market crash, quoted in John Kenneth Galbraith, *The Great Crash* (Houghton Mifflin, 1955)

Experts calculated that almost half a trillion dollars in value had disappeared from the American economy overnight [in a late-nineteenth-century 500-point crash]—but what had happened to it, one wondered. Where had it gone? One answer was that it hadn't gone anywhere; it wasn't now in some new place . . . Rather, it had in a sense never existed . . .

There is always something dreamlike about the great speculative frenzies, and inevitably, at some point the dreamers awake.

LAWRENCE WESCHLER, *New Yorker,* January 25, 1988

I remember being stunned by the 508-point drop in the Dow Jones industrial average last October 19 [1987], but it was not until the morning of October 20, that I became truly frightened. The market, on that day, ceased to exist.

FELIX G. ROHATYN, investment banker, quoted in *Time*, October 17, 1988

The wealth effect of the crash of 1987 was nil, because not that many people were heavily into stock.

MICHAEL METZ, of the investment firm Oppenheimer Securities, quoted in *Fortune,* December 27, 1993

On that day in 1987, most people heard the news, were confused, and did nothing.

PROFESSOR ROBERT SHILLER of Yale University, quoted in *Fortune,* December 27, 1993

[Before the 1987 crash] People used to brag they had pre-knowledge of takeovers. Now they live in fear that someone will accuse them of knowing something, even if they don't.

JAMES J. CRAMER, *New York Observer,* July 28, 1997

It must be what it felt like in 1929. You have to wonder how many future cab drivers are in the room.

Unidentified president of a global asset management firm, on the 1997 Montgomery Securities annual investor conference, quoted in the *New York Times,* September 28, 1997

Computers will get us to the door sooner, but we still can't all fit through at the same time.

HARRISON ROTH, of Drexel Burnham Lambert and later at Cowen & Company, in 1986 letter to the *New York Times,* quoted in his obituary, *New York Times,* November 5, 1997

23.6   DECLINING MARKETS

There were more sellers than buyers.

J. P. MORGAN SR., asked why the stock market had fallen the previous day

How do you call a stockbroker?

Answer: Waiter!

New York Times, September 19, 1993

Wall Street runs on fear and greed. Last year, fear overcame greed.

GUY MOSZKOWSKI, of the investment firm Sanford C. Bernstein, on why 1994 was a bad year in the market

Financial assets can bob all over the place, but they do not collapse unless there is evidence the fundamentals are eroding.

ERIC H. SORENSEN of the investment firm Salomon Brothers, quoted in the *New York Times,* August 31, 1997

Saying that something is in a correction makes an assumption—that conditions have gone to an extreme, and now we're bringing them back in line.

PROFESSOR ROBERT SOBEL of Hofstra University, quoted in the *Wall Street Journal,* April 21, 1997

We are watching the lemmings fly out the window.

MICHAEL MORITZ, venture capitalist with Sequoia Capital, on the fall of high-tech stocks, quoted in the *Wall Street Journal,* July 12, 1996

Just don't be yourself. Don't be upbeat. People will get the message. Stress long-term, but don't smile, don't laugh, and don't be glib.

JEFF BERKOWITZ, partner of hedge-fund operator James J. Cramer, advising Cramer on how to avoid panicking his TV audience the morning of a 554-point stock market drop, quoted in *Time,* November 10, 1997

It doesn't take much to derail a market that has gone to the moon.

STEPHEN ROACH, chief economist for Morgan Stanley Dean Witter, quoted in *Time,* November 10, 1997

In the synonymy of the bears, *decline, sag, sink,* and *slump* are the mildest; *drop,* more sudden; *tumble,* not shocking; *dive* and *plunge,* precipitous; *plummet,* precipitate; *sell-off,* technical; *correction,* interpretive or euphemistic; *free fall,* alarming; *collapse, sudden,* and *steep,* and *crash,* better lock that window.

> WILLIAM SAFIRE, in the *New York Times Magazine,* November 23, 1997

23.7 DERIVATIVES

Options might be used for gambling, but so can stocks, bonds, commodities, and even Treasury securities. However, they can and are used for completely nonspeculative purposes: hedging, protecting a position, locking in a profit and generally avoiding or reducing rather than assuming risk. This is much too good a tool to be dismissed as a gambling device.

> HARRISON ROTH, of Drexel Burnham Lambert and later at Cowen & Company, in 1986 letter to the *New York Times,* quoted in his obituary, the *New York Times,* November 5, 1997

Human behavior is such that if there's a way to do something with a positive accounting effect, we want to make sure we would do it anyhow. When the accounting goodies on the plate are too attractive, I don't trust them.

> EUGENE H. ROTBERG, former president of the World Bank, referring to techniques such as swaps, quoted in the *Wall Street Journal,* January 16, 1985

We plan to bring back to Japan many of the new products and techniques developed in local markets. Interest-rate swaps are an example.

> YOSHIHISA TABUCHI of Nomura Securities, interviewed in *Harvard Business* Review, July–August 1989

They are like salesmen in any other business. They sell the sizzle as well as the steak, and there is a certain amount of sizzle in this.

> MERTON H. MILLER, Nobel Prize–winning economist, on the options business, quoted in the *New York Times,* January 26, 1992

When you have a product that is customized and complex and difficult for the buyer to figure out what it is worth, you have an enormous opportunity for profit.

> PROFESSOR JOHN FINNERTY, quoted in the *New York Times,* January 26, 1992

If you are the writer of options, you collect fees. And if the market behaves, it's fine. But if the market goes south in a big way, you can get killed.

> PHILLIP M. JOHNSON, chairman of Commodity Futures Trading Commission during Reagan administration, quoted in the *New York Times,* January 26, 1992

Derivatives, like NFL quarterbacks, probably get more credit and more blame than they deserve.

> GERALD CORRIGAN of the investment firm Goldman, Sachs and former president of the New York Federal Reserve, testifying before Congress, quoted in *Business Week,* May 30, 1994

Financial risk management is not just a theoretical nicety; it is a practical necessity. Derivatives instruments don't create surprises. They help minimize them.

> DAVID B. WEINBERGER, managing director of Swiss Bank Corporation and general partner of O'Connor Partners, Chicago, quoted in *Harvard Business Review,* January–February 1995

Employ derivatives to transfer risk, but never succumb to the temptation to trade risk for its own sake.

> ARVIND SODHANI, VP and treasurer of the computer chip firm Intel, which uses derivatives extensively, quoted in *Harvard Business Review,* January–February 1995

A number of people . . . wonder why they should adopt new processes . . . when they think the old ones work just fine. Well, whiskey works just fine as a painkiller—just ask any cowboy in the wild, wild, West. But if I were going to have surgery tomorrow, I know I'd much rather have a shot of Demerol than a shot of Jack Daniels.

> CHARLES S. SANFORD JR., former CEO of Bankers Trust, in a speech, October 1994

I've been trying to explain it [derivatives] to my parents and my wife for nine years and they still don't understand it. I still have to assure my mother that what I do for a living is legal.

> JAMES R. HELVEY III, of the banking firm JP Morgan, November 3, 1994

Derivatives. That's the 11-letter four-letter word.

> RICHARD SYRON, president of the American Stock Exchange, quoted in *Fortune,* March 20, 1995

It is unlikely that the underlying markets would have performed as well as they did . . . without the existence of related derivatives markets that enabled currency positions to be managed, albeit with some difficulty in some instruments.

> Federal Banking Supervisors study of market performance in the wake of the 1992 European currency crisis

They[derivatives]'re just like chainsaws. If you read the instructions, they're very useful, but you shouldn't let minors use them, and you should be careful about using them yourself.

> CHARLES TAYLOR of the international banking organization Group of 30, quoted in *Fortune,* November 29, 1993

IBM stock owners lost a lot of money too. Does that mean you should outlaw trading in IBM?

> Unnamed banker, quoted in *Fortune,* November 29, 1993

We didn't do business with them [investment bankers] right away, but they kept calling and calling. They sounded like reasonable people we could trust.

> JOE A. FLOWERS, 75, comptroller, Escambia County, Florida, who invested nearly half of the county's $101 million savings in derivatives with disastrous results, quoted in the *Wall Street Journal,* March 20, 1995

Everyone selling derivatives is so enamored of the technology that they rush beyond the prior question: what is it for?

> BILL SHARPE, Nobel Prize–winning economist of Stanford University, quoted in the *Economist,* February 10, 1996

This is a person who has gotten us all millions of dollars. I don't know how the hell he does it, but it makes us all look good.

> THOMAS RILEY, supervisor of Robert Citrone, treasurer of Orange County, California, who was later blamed for bankrupting the county and prosecuted, quoted in the *Economist,* February 10, 1996

Act of God bonds.

> Describing instruments intended to relieve firms of the obligation to pay in event of natural disasters, *The Economist,* February 10, 1996

Derivatives can often facilitate investments [in emerging markets] that otherwise may be too costly or simply not possible.

> JOHN McNIVEN, of the investment firm Merrill Lynch, Hong Kong, quoted in the *Financial Times,* November 22, 1996

The only perfect hedge is a Japanese garden.

> EUGENE H. ROTBERG, Washington lawyer who formerly worked for the World Bank, the SEC, and Merrill Lynch, *Fortune,* March 7, 1994

A derivative is like a razor. You can use it to shave yourself. . . . Or you can use it to commit suicide.

> JAMES MORGAN, journalist, quoted in *Grant's Interest Rate Observer,* March 17, 1995

No one ever needed derivatives in order to go broke in a hurry. . . . The instrument is the messenger; the investor is the message.

> PETER L. BERNSTEIN, *Against the Gods* (Wiley, 1996)

[L]ike [Chicago Bulls] basketball player Dennis Rodman's wedding to himself: confusing, misleading, and what's the point?

> WILLIAM REBATS, of First Chicago NBD Corporation, on proposed accounting changes for derivatives, quoted in the *Wall Street Journal,* February 21, 1997

Large banks can no longer avoid being involved in the arcane world of financial derivatives trading if they want to remain internationally competitive.

> *Financial Times,* editorial, March 14, 1997

The worst enemy of derivatives is the bad publicity surrounding some extreme cases. Events like these tend to stick in trustees' minds.

> TONY WHALLEY, of Scottish Widows Investment Management, quoted in the *Financial Times,* May 9, 1997

I compare the current standards [of accounting for derivatives positions] to watching night baseball without the lights. There's a game going on and the scoreboard lights up once in a while, but you have little idea of what's actually going on down on the field.

> EDWARD KANE, economist at Boston College, quoted in *Forbes,* August 11, 1997

Creative-writing professors have always said, "Write about what you know." Good advice, to be sure, but there was one problem. A story about asset-backed derivatives was not especially compelling. The bestseller lists were not exactly brimming with books about options on securitizations of pools of J.C. Penney and Home Depot credit-card debt.

> STEVEN RHODES, hedge-fund trader and author of *The Velocity of Money* (a novel about a group that conspires to use derivatives to induce a stock market crash), quoted in the *New York Times*, August 31, 1997

For plain vanilla OTC [over-the-counter] derivatives, 2 percent of the organizations that had used these products reported being somewhat or very dissatisfied with the sales practices of the dealers they used . . . For MBS [mortgage-backed securities] 7 percent of the end users reported being dissatisfied with the dealers they used; for structured notes, 13 percent of the end users reported being dissatisfied.

> General Accounting Office report on derivative sales practices, cited in the *Wall Street Journal*, October 13, 1997

We're not looking for customers who have not done their homework and are expecting this to be a high-flying investment with big gains.

> ROBERT MCBAIN of Bank of America, on marketing derivatives to entrepreneurs who want to shelter their paper wealth from stock market volatility and inheritance taxes, quoted in *Fortune*, November 10, 1997

Derivatives are the most recent example of a basic theme in the history of finance: Wall Street bilks Main Street.

> FRANK PARTNOY, formerly of the investment firm Morgan Stanley and author of *F.I.A.S.C.O: Blood in the Water on Wall Street* (Norton, 1997)

23.8 FINANCIAL INFORMATION

Unless it produces action, information is overhead.

> THOMAS PETZINGER JR., *Wall Street Journal*, May 9, 1997

Someone once described the information business as exactly the opposite of sex. When it's good, it's still lousy.

> MICHAEL BLOOMBERG, founder and CEO of Bloomberg Inc., quoted in *New York*, November 22, 1993

Water is free but clean water costs. The question is whether you want to drink out of the bucket.

> PATRICK McVEIGH of the news agency Reuters, on competition with cut-rate financial data providers, quoted in the *Financial Times*, March 14, 1997

23.9 FINANCE AND TECHNOLOGY

For most of the twentieth century, the (municipal bond) market operated in an almost serenely simple style. Market historians will disagree as to when, exactly, the market changed. . . . we really have to go back to August and September 1961. That period marked the first recorded use of a computer to tabulate bids on bond issues. . . . by a maverick named William S. Morris. . . . [P]ut together from a Heath kit, the [computer] made all else that came after possible. The thought of putting together, say, a combined multipurpose crossover and net cash refunding with synthetic fixed-rate maturities, or a deal mixing variable rate, fixed, and zero-coupon bonds—well, we leave it to your imagination. Such deals would have been unthinkable in the pre-computer age.

> JOE MYSAK, *Grant's Municipal Bond Observer*, June 30, 1995

The [banking] industry taught people to associate banking with visiting marble halls that were almost like cathedrals. Now we're telling them it's all right to pray at home. But we have to understand that money, our product, has a lot of sociological encrustations which we can't remove simply by changing the way we view our business.

> MARTIN TAYLOR, chief executive of Barclay's Bank, quoted in the *Economist*, October 26, 1996

I have always believed that we have never married technology with business thinking. Both in school and work experience we groom people on the information system side. We tell them that they are the technology experts and that business people are never going to figure out what they are talking about. On the business side we too often say that technology people are in a world of their own and that we just have to push down the strategy that we think we need without getting their input.

> ROBERT H. BOHAUMON, CEO of the consumer financial services firm Travellers Express, interviewed in Charles B. Wendel, *The New Financiers: Profiles of the Leaders Who Are Reshaping the Financial Services Industry* (Irwin, 1996)

Computers will get us to the door sooner, but we still can't all fit through at the same time.

> HARRISON ROTH of Drexel Burnham Lambert and later at Cowen & Company, in 1986 letter to the *New York Times*, quoted in his obituary, *New York Times*, November 5, 1997

Program trading [trading by computer-driven strategy] makes the bull markets more bullish and the bear markets more bearish.

> ROBERT N. GORDON, president of Twenty-First Securities Corp., quoted in *Business Week*, April 7, 1986

23.10   FINANCIAL MARKETS

When the capital development of a country becomes the by-product of a casino, the job is likely to be ill-done.

Speculators may do no harm as bubbles on a steady stream of enterprise. But the position is serious when enterprise becomes the bubble on a steady stream of speculation.

> JOHN MAYNARD KEYNES

It is usually agreed that casinos should, in the public interest, be inaccessible and expensive. And perhaps the same is true of Stock Exchanges.

> JOHN MAYNARD KEYNES, quoted in Professor Warren A. Law of Harvard Business School, "A Corporation Is More Than A Stock," *Harvard Business Review*, May–June 1986

[M]arkets are more complex than theories would suggest. They are made up of human investors who behave, well, like humans.

> NANCY A. NICHOLS, *Harvard Business Review*, March–April 1993

[F]inancial markets cannot possibly discount the future correctly because they do not merely discount the future; they help to shape it.

> GEORGE SOROS, financier, testifying to the U.S. House of Representatives, April 13, 1994

The prevailing wisdom is that markets are always right. I take the opposite position. I assume that markets are always wrong.

> GEORGE SOROS, *Soros on Soros* (Wiley, 1995)

Markets look a lot less efficient from the banks of the Hudson than they do from the banks of the Charles.

> FISCHER BLACK, financial theoretician, quoted in Peter L. Bernstein, *Against the Gods* (Wiley, 1996)

Investing in a market where people believe in efficiency is like playing bridge with someone who has been told it doesn't do any good to look at the cards.

> WARREN BUFFETT, quoted in the *New York Times Magazine*, April 1, 1990

Certain markets are too influenced by people who call themselves speculators, but they might be called gamblers.

> ROY R. NEUBERGER, veteran trader, quoted in *Business Week*, August 15, 1994

. . . The problem with hot money and speculation is that it always hits the weakest the hardest. Speculators can't do a lot of harm to the U.S. economy. But they certainly can hurt Mexico, Malaysia, or Indonesia.

> GUILLERMO ORTIZ, Mexico's Minister of Finance, quoted in the *Wall Street Journal*, October 29, 1997

A string of good trades can sometimes lead to inattention to detail and subsequent losses. The markets usually find a way to take down traders at the height of their hubris.

> VICTOR NIEDERHOFFER, hedge-fund manager, in his book *The Education of a Speculator* (Wiley, 1997), quoted by Barry Reilly (who noted that Niederhoffer's $100 million fund was wiped out during the market plunge the previous week), *Financial Times*, November 5, 1997

23.11 GLOBAL FINANCIAL MARKETS

International finance is a game with two sets of players: the politicians and bureaucrats of national governments, and the presidents and treasurers of giant, large, medium-large, medium, medium-small, and small firms.

> PROFESSOR ROBERT Z. ALIBER, *The International Money Game* (Basic, 1983)

Capital is the world's most cowardly commodity. It cuts and runs at the barest jiggle.

> A vice president of the bank Continental Illinois, *Time,* May 28, 1984

A long time ago, you couldn't have a $600 billion trader fraud. Now you can.

> WILLIAM SMITH, president of Kemper Insurance, quoted in *Marsh & McLennan Viewpoint,* Winter 1996

Ten years ago, there weren't that many people we [the United States] could borrow money from . . . Now there's a global bank-teller window that is open 24 hours a day, and we've been one of the most frequent customers.

> PROFESSOR JEFFREY SACHS of Harvard University, quoted in *Time,* January 30, 1989

The new finance is like a highway. It's more efficient. It gets you to where you are going better. But the accidents are worse.

> LAWRENCE H. SUMMERS, Deputy U.S. Treasury Secretary, on newly deregulated banking markets around the world, quoted in the *Wall Street Journal,* May 7, 1997

A fixed exchange rate regime (for most emerging market economies) is like putting the economy on a knife edge. One slip and the economy comes crashing down.

> FREDERIC MISHKIN, economist at the Federal Reserve Bank, New York, quoted in the *Financial Times,* September 1, 1997

We seem to be in a world in which savings are less and less in demand: used more frugally by companies, and resorted to less often by governments. In the long run, how can such a commodity command a high return?

> TONY JACKSON, *Financial Times,* November 1, 1997

The global stock market gyrations of October 1997 are a further confirmation that the world financial system has become a village. There have been many occasions during the twentieth century when stock market developments in New York or London depressed equity values in east Asia, but last month was the first time that the causality worked in reverse.

> DAVID HALE, *Financial Times,* November 7, 1997

The regulation of domestic banks and stock markets is not up to the challenge of hot money.

Flat-out capital controls are an invitation to corruption and inefficiency.

> ROBERT HORMATS of the investment bank Goldman, Sachs, quoted in the *New York Times,* November 20, 1997

23.12 GOLD AND OTHER COMMODITIES

A gold mine is a hole in the ground with a liar at the top.

> MARK TWAIN

Nobody could ever have conceived of a more absurd waste of human resources than to dig gold in distant corners of the earth for the sole purpose of transporting it and reburying it immediately after in other deep holes, especially excavated to receive it and heavily guarded to protect it.

> PROFESSOR ROBERT TRIFFLIN of Yale University, quoted in the *Financial Times,* March 7, 1997

You don't have to know the industry you're going into. If you can apply yourself, you can always find the experts.

> PETER MUNKE of Barrick Gold, partner in Bre-X in Indonesia, quoted in the *Financial Times,* January 19, 1997

The rising gold price might actively contribute to the industry's demise. If the price goes up 20 percent, there will be no incentive to change this industry at all.

> TOM DALE of Gengold, a South African mining company, quoted in the *Economist,* February 3, 1996

I don't think gold has any validity as a barometer of future inflation.

> STEPHEN ROACH, chief economist of the investment firm Morgan Stanley Dean Witter, quoted in the *Wall Street Journal*, December 5, 1997

John Maynard Keynes called gold a "barbarous relic." Charles de Gaulle said gold could be the cornerstone of a new international system. Both were probably right.

> PROFESSOR ROBERT Z. ALIBER, University of Chicago, *The International Money Game* (Basic, 1983)

The large North American gold miners have found it increasingly difficult to discover gold deposits that are large enough to justify their involvement and capable of providing sufficient production to pay for the management time and big company overheads.

> ELENA CLARICI and ROGER CHAPLIN of the London brokerage firm T. Hoare, quoted in the *Financial Times*, January 8, 1997

23.13 HEDGE FUNDS

My original expression, and the proper one, was "hedged fund." I still regard "hedge fund," which makes a noun serve for an adjective, with distaste.

> ALFRED WINSLOW JONES, founder of the investment firm A. W. Jones and Company, a private investment concern started in 1949, quoted in John Brooks, *The Go-Go Years* (Weybright and Talley, 1973)

As with the old pools [of the 1920s], partnership in a hedge fund . . . certified one's affluence while attesting to one's astuteness.

The hedge funds of 1965 . . . were Wall Street's last bastions of secrecy, mystery, exclusivity, and privilege. They were the parlor cars of the new gravy train.

> JOHN BROOKS, *The Go-Go Years* (Weybright and Talley, 1973)

People think of us as gunslingers, but we really have to keep volatility very low: Wealthy people don't like volatility.

> Hedge-fund operator, quoted in *Business Week*, April 25, 1994

I sure wish I could tell you that the public should be in hedge funds. But I think it's better for most people to have their money [in mutual funds] than with some crazy man who's running around shorting everything in sight.

> JAMES J. CRAMER, hedge-fund manager and market pundit, *Time*, September 1, 1997

If the big emphasis is being placed on operating within a defined investment strategy, that presents problems if you're a creative manager who wants to use bonds or make big sector threats.

> ROBERT JAEGER of the hedge-fund manager Evaluation Associates, quoted in the *Wall Street Journal*, April 21, 1997

23.14 INDIVIDUAL INVESTORS

My lawyers and accountants look into these things and explain them to me in baby talk. If it sounds okay, we go ahead.

> BUDDY HACKETT, comedian, asked why he invested in the notorious 1960s Home Stake oil tax-shelter scheme (along with Barbra Streisand, Andy Williams, Liza Minnelli, and other entertainers, senior corporate executives, and scores of lawyers, doctors, and other professionals), quoted in David McClintick, *Stealing from the Rich*, (William Morrow, 1983)

Show people tend to treat their finances like their dentistry. They assume the man handling it knows what he is doing.

> DICK CAVETT, one of many celebrities who invested in tax shelters then under investigation, *Time*, May 6, 1985

My advice to this [first-time] investor is the same that I give to the young investors in my classes . . . Devote the same earnest attention to investing that $50,000 as you devoted to earning it.

> IVAN F. BOESKY, later convicted of insider trading, quoted in the *Wall Street Journal*, January 2, 1985

When I started out as a broker, our typical customer was a white male who owned his own business, had a margin account, and played the market. He didn't spend his time on airplanes. His wife took care of the kids. Playing the market was exactly that—playing.

> WILLIAM A. SHIEBLER of Putnam Investments, in a speech, September 1995

The fact that people will be full of greed, fear, or folly is predictable. The sequence is not predictable.

> WARREN BUFFETT, quoted in *Channels*, November 1, 1986

Speculative bubbles occur, essentially, when investors are watching what other investors are doing, rather than paying attention to the merits of risk and return.

> PAUL SAMUELSON JR. of the investment firm Pangora Asset Management, quoted in the *Wall Street Journal*, December 4, 1996

Things like physical commodities or real estate can all be valid indicators of a person's wealth, but don't really in our minds give a very good clue as to how sophisticated the person is going to be in examining an unregulated investment pool.

> CRAIG TYLE, senior counsel, Investment Company Institute, commenting on changes in SEC criteria for calculating minimums for investing in hedge funds, which excluded jewelry and art but included gold bars and other commodities, quoted in the *Wall Street Journal*, February 4, 1997

This is the poor man's stock market, replete with speculators and arbitrageurs.

> JOHN HANEGHAN, owner of Forbidden Planet, New York City comic book and novelty store, on comic book collecting, quoted in *New York*, October 25, 1993

The American economy increasingly is split into two classes: people who own stocks and those who wish they did.

> MARIA FIORINI RAMIREZ, CEO of her own global economic consulting company, quoted in the *New York Times*, October 14, 1997

The best thing going for small investors is the stupidity of large investors.

> LOUIS RUKEYSER, host of *Wall Street Week*, heard on New York public radio, November 10, 1997

23.15 INSTITUTIONAL SHAREHOLDERS

I . . . believe [it's possible that] by the end of the century a substantial number of U.S. companies will have an absolute majority of their stock held by passive investors as part of an index fund or by active investors whose stock selection is based on a computer program that will purchase any stock meeting predetermined quantitative criteria.

> ROBERT G. KIRBY, chairman of Capital Guardian & Trust, quoted by Samuel W. Bodman, chairman of the investment firm Cabot Corporation, in a speech, October 20, 1992

We own the American economy now.

> CAROL O'CLEIREANCAIN, New York City Finance Commissioner, trustee of four pension funds, quoted in *Fortune*, January 11, 1993

The larger pension funds can't just walk away when companies aren't performing well. There'd be no market.

> THOMAS FLANIGAN, chief investment officer of Calpers (California Public Employees Retirement System), quoted in *Fortune*, March 8, 1993

We're owned by a bunch of index funds. Who votes for an index fund? Some damn mathematical formula votes your stock.

> ANDREW SIGLER, CEO of the paper company Champion International, quoted in *Forbes*, March 11, 1985

23.16 INVESTING ON THE INTERNET

I didn't anticipate the potential people would see in the idea [using the Internet to launch an IPO]—how this little company stumbled into a method that, taken to its logical extreme, could radically change the way stocks were sold.

Under federal securities laws you can sell almost anything to anybody, provided you disclose who you are and what the risks are.

> ANDY KLEIN, founder of New York City's Spring Street Brewery, quoted in *Inc.*, July 1996

Equity trading is going to be a loss-leader in the future. That is where things are going.

> KEVIN BAGNE of the Empire Financial Group, which offers free trading to investors who keep enough money with the firm, quoted in the *Financial Times*, January 8, 1997

It is unclear how the Internet as it exists today could provide a networking environment which guarantees a level playing field for traders.

> R. PATRICK THOMPSON, president of the New York Mercantile Exchange, on proposals for online commodities trading, quoted in the *Wall Street Journal*, January 5, 1998

23.17   INVESTING, HIGH-TECH

At the beginning of 1992, with Apple's stock trading near $60 per share, it is difficult to conclude that the stock market has imposed any significant penalty on Apple management for its long-term thinking.

> MICHAEL Z. RABIN and JOHN E. McDERMOTT, "Does the Stock Market Penalize Long-term Thinking? The Case of Apple Computer," *Harvard Business Review*, May–June 1992

The high-technology industry is like a land race with only one prize, but that prize is a million acres.

> W. BRIAN ARTHUR, economist at the Santa Fe Institute, quoted in *Forbes*, July 7, 1997

23.18   INVESTING (IPOs, LBOs, HOSTILE TAKEOVERS, LIMITED PARTNERSHIPS, ASSET-BACKED SECURITIES, ETC.)

People want to be sold. They want someone to come in and say, "Dammit, this is what you should do."

> ROBERT LONDON of Montgomery Securities, quoted in the *Wall Street Journal*, January 3, 1985

Young, emerging growth companies have the flexibility and energy to respond to market needs much quicker than the big uglies.

> ROBERT C. CZEPIEL of Robertson Stephens Emerging Growth Fund, quoted in *Business Week*, May 23, 1994

We've found that if you advertise an interest in buying collies, a lot of people will call hoping to sell you their cocker spaniels. A line from a country song expresses our feeling about new ventures, turnarounds, or auction-like sales: "When the phone don't ring, you'll know it's me."

> WARREN BUFFETT, 1995 Berkshire Hathaway annual report

This isn't the Seventh Cavalry coming to the rescue.

> K. RICHARD MUNRO, CEO of Time, Inc., at a forum on corporate takeovers, February 23, 1989

There is some evidence that a management preparing to go private can subtly act to drive down the stock price—for example by overfunding the pension plan to depress quarterly earnings—in order to then buy the stock back at a bargain later on. When management swoops in to buy the company, the invisible hand at work is that of Alex Portnoy, not Adam Smith.

> ROBERT KUTTNER, *New Republic*, January 20, 1986

[F]or the advocates of leveraged debt to claim credit for the rise of a new competitive spirit is like the rooster claiming credit for the sunrise.

> RICHARD MUNRO, CEO of Time, Inc., at a forum on corporate takeovers, February 23, 1989

I remember negotiating an acquisition where the burning issue was whether the seller could provide us with a list of all the leases, including the ones on the typewriters. Now people are making multibillion-dollar decisions on the basis of nothing but public information. It used to take weeks to line up bank commitments. Now it can be done in a few days.

> CHARLES NATHAN of Merrill Lynch, at a forum on corporate takeovers, February 23, 1989

Research is tangible, and there is little way we can prove that it benefits the company immediately. So we can save money by firing the scientists, and when this is all over we can just hire them back.

> JOHN NORELL of Provesta, Phillips Petroleum's biotech subsidiary, on the fate of research and development in a takeover, at a forum on corporate takeovers, February 23, 1989

Watching these deals get done is like watching a herd of drunk drivers take to the highway on New Year's Eve. You cannot tell who will hit whom, but you know it is dangerous.

> THEODORE J. FORSTMANN of the buyout firm Forstmann Little, quoted in the *Wall Street Journal*, October 25, 1988

To buy a shoe-shine store, if it costs $3,000, you need $3,000 . . . But if it's an LBO, not only do you not have to bring it, you don't have to see it, you don't know where you're going to get it, nobody knows where they got it from.

> Comedian JACKIE MASON, "What the Hell Is an LBO?" cited in *Barbarians at the Gate* (Harper & Row, 1990)

The only losers are the bondholders of the acquired company, who see the value of their bonds decline with the company's inevitable credit demotion, brought about by the intense leveraging, or debt-lading, of its capital structure.

> CONNIE BRUCK, *New Yorker,* May 8, 1989

People always call and congratulate us when we buy a company. I say, "Look, don't congratulate us when we buy a company, because any fool can overpay and buy a company, as long as money will last to buy it." I said, "Our job really begins the day we buy the company, and we start working with the management, we start working with where this company is headed."

> HENRY R. KRAVIS, financier, in an interview, February 12, 1991, quoted on Academy of Achievement web site

There's no craziness index [of the IPO market], but it's got to be getting close.

> BARTON BIGGS of the investment firm Morgan Stanley, quoted in *Fortune,* May 27, 1996

When everyone wants to securitize, and everyone is willing to buy, and everyone thinks nothing will go wrong, there gets to be a feeding-frenzy atmosphere, and you have to remain cautious.

> PAUL STEVENSON of the asset-backed group at Moody's, quoted in *Business Week,* September 2, 1996

All new wealth comes from creative engineering types, who are difficult to manage and easy to offend. The mentality of a takeover is aggressive, a pirate mentality that upsets morale. The good people leave.

> G. DAN HUTCHESON of VLSI Research, quoted in *Forbes,* July 7, 1997

This [David Bowie's plan to securitize five years of royalties] is a joke, isn't it? I wouldn't know where to begin to analyze this. It's a little far afield for us.

> ROBERT AUETWAERTEN of the Vanguard Group mutual funds, quoted in the *Wall Street Journal,* December 5, 1996

Buying the lottery is the next best thing to winning the lottery.

> Metropolitan Mortgage & Securities Co. web site, quoted in the *Wall Street Journal,* September 23, 1997. (Metropolitan specializes in investing in cash flows such as private mortgages, tax liens, and personal injury settlements, as well as lottery winnings.)

1-800-WHY WAIT.

> Phone number for firm that buys out future lottery proceeds

There are more wallpaper stories in Silicon Valley than successful IPO stories.

> BOB CONCANNON, executive recruiter with Bridge-Gate Group, alluding to the use of worthless stock certificates as wallpaper, quoted in the *Wall Street Journal,* January 23, 1996

23.19   INVESTING (MEDIA AND ENTERTAINMENT)

I approached several different bankers and tried to sell them the idea of big profits in the motion picture business. They were very glad and wished me good luck and hoped I would succeed, but they did not see their way clear to participate in this lucrative business until one day I met Mr. Otto Kahn, of Kuhn Loeb & Co. I thought that on account of his connection with the Metropolitan Opera House and his interest in theaters and artists I could refer to the possibilities of the picture business and perhaps he would be interested. I talked to him a bit and he told me he was much interested.

> ADOLPH ZUKOR, movie pioneer, quoted in Robert Sobel and David B. Sicilia, *The Entrepreneurs— An American Adventure* (Houghton Mifflin, 1986)

If you look at the [film] industry's history, the Americans have trounced the Europeans by being better funded.

> DAVID PUTTNAM, Oscar-winning film producer, quoted in the *Financial Times,* May 6, 1997

In Hollywood, you're a veteran if you've had a job of more than six weeks' tenure with one company.

> JACK VALENTI, president of the Motion Picture Association of America, quoted in *Variety,* 1985

Outsiders can come to Hollywood, but they can never run it.

> PETER DEKAM, entertainment lawyer, quoted in *Time,* September 4, 1989

They [20th Century Fox] said they had no interest in seeing a picture with the word "star" in it, because that suggested science fiction.

> SIDNEY GANIS, formerly of Lucas Films, quoted in *Forbes,* October 5, 1987

The film industry is like a cat with nine lives. It constantly seems to be able to come up with a new salvation. First there was the VCR . . . now the opening up of European television puts new value on second- and third-run new films. The film industry is probably on life six or seven.

> DAVID PUTTNAM, Oscar-winning producer, quoted in *Forbes,* October 5, 1987

The combination of the popularity of American films overseas (particularly in an Asian market that is rapidly building new cinemas) and the proliferation of new distribution channels around the world should keep demand buoyant for a long time.

> *The Economist,* August 9, 1997

Wall Street brought money to Hollywood by the bucket, but it all ended up at the Beverly Hills Rolls-Royce dealers.

> GEOFFREY HOLMES of the media conglomerate Time Warner, quoted in the *New York Times,* July 12, 1992

We don't have the slightest idea of what people are going to buy.

> RUPERT MURDOCH, owner of 20th Century Fox, quoted in *Business Week,* March 14, 1994

Who the hell wants to hear actors talk?

> HARRY M. WARNER of Warner Bros., 1927

Forget it, Louis. No Civil War picture ever made a nickel.

> IRVING THALBERG, MGM executive to studio owner Louis B. Mayer, on producing *Gone With the Wind*

I wish I could just pack it in. Get into developing middle-income housing.

> SYLVESTER STALLONE, actor, quoted in *Newsweek,* February 6, 1989

The key is not to believe any one film, or two or three, will be so successful you take risks that turn out to be unwarranted.

> VICTOR A. KAUFMAN, chairman of the distributing and production company Savoy, quoted in the *New York Times,* November 28, 1993

Studios care more about rewarding talent than investors.

> DAVID DAVIS of the investment bank Houlihan, Lokey, Howard & Zukin, quoted in the *Economist,* March 30, 1996

The most important thing we've done with this company is to stay away from emotional investments in overpriced media assets.

> MICHAEL EISNER, CEO of Walt Disney, quoted in *Forbes,* January 12, 1987

Investors can do very well here, but they should know in advance that talent agents and studio executives will do everything possible to make sure that their money never leaves town.

> KELLY CRABB, L.A. attorney who represents Japanese companies investing in Hollywood, quoted in *Asia Online,* 1995

The film industry is a complex adaptive system poised between order and chaos. People follow simple rules, and this produces complex results.

> PROFESSOR ART DEVANY of the University of California, Irvine, quoted in the *New Yorker,* March 31, 1997

We basically got out of the "middle-class" picture. ["Middle-class" costs $25 million to $40 million to produce.]

> BILL MECHANIC, chairman of 20th Century Fox, explaining the blockbuster mentality in Hollywood, quoted in the *New Yorker,* March 31, 1997

I think we've blown up everything we can blow up.

> SHERRY LANSING, CEO of Paramount Motion Pictures, on the failure of many high-budget action pictures, quoted in the *New York Times,* September 2, 1997

How do you know what idea is good and what isn't? Suppose a guy comes into your office and says, "I've got this great musical about Jesus Christ." You'd lock him up. . . . Hundreds of millions later, that's [composer] Andrew Lloyd Webber.

> WAYNE ROGERS, actor and agent, quoted in *Forbes*, September 21, 1987

This is amateur sport. The next knock on the door could be Elvis Presley.

> JERRY MOSS, chairman of A&M Records, quoted in *Forbes*, September 21, 1987

I once told [French movie director Jean Luc] Godard that he had something I wanted—freedom. He said: "You have something I want—money."

> DON SIEGEL, director of *Dirty Harry*, quoted in *Film Yearbook*, 1988

The funny thing is, better [TV] shows don't cost that much more than lousy shows.

> WARREN BUFFETT, quoted in *Channels*, November 1986

The market will pay you better to entertain than to educate.

> WARREN BUFFETT, speaking at Berkshire Hathaway annual meeting, 1986

Hollywood is not the big studios anymore. It's a collection of small and medium-sized firms—independent producers who come together and actually make films project by project. Very little filming is actually done by the big studios themselves.

> PROFESSOR MICHAEL STORPER, quoted in *Inc.*, March 1995

Coca-Cola Company discovered that it had inadvertently bought Columbia Pictures Inc. Company executives had thought they were buying Colombia, the South American country. Coca-Cola is asking the movie company for its deposit back.

> *Off the Wall Street Journal*, newspaper parody, 1982

It [television] is generally acknowledged to be the single most influential force in the lives of our people.

> WILLIAM M. BULGER, president of the Massachusetts Senate, in a speech, September 19, 1986

They are talking about 500 TV channels. For God's sake, the consumer can't handle 50.

> MICHAEL OVITZ, then president of Walt Disney, quoted in *Fortune*, March 4, 1996

Four hundred of 'em will be offering Japanese brush painting lessons.

> ROGER AILES, formerly of CNBC, on the widely cited figure of 500 cable TV stations, quoted in *New York*, September 13, 1993

Bruce Springsteen sang about "57 Channels—and Nothin' On," but we all know that 57 channels will soon look like child's play.

> RAYMOND W. SMITH, CEO of the telecomunications company Bell Atlantic, in a speech July 1, 1993

It's like a game of musical chairs. There are only five major studios and 10 people looking for a chair.

> MICHAEL P. SCHULHOF, chairman of Sony Corp. of America, on shortage of programming for 500 cable channels, quoted in *Business Week*, January 10, 1994

News has become an old product.

> REESE SCHONFELD, who helped launch CNN, on all-news TV, quoted in the *New York Times*, June 22, 1997

Emulating TV is the precise strategy that will doom newspapers.

We've lost the readership that is, essentially, only looking for headlines.

> MAXWELL E. P. KING of the *Philadelphia Inquirer*, in a speech, October 22, 1992

The term "publishing business" is an oxymoron.

> T. J. ROGERS, then of the computer firm Applied Materials, and author of *No Excuses Management*, quoted in the *New York Times*, October 3, 1993

In the long run, most horses and all trainers lose more races than they win, and most owners lose money in the sport.

> ANDREW PORTER, *New Yorker*, December 26, 1988

23.20 INVESTING (STOCK MARKET)

We have an old saying in journalism: "If you don't understand something, it must be important."

> DAVE BARRY, on the stock market, *Boston Globe Magazine*, September 28, 1997

Professional investment may be likened to those newspaper competitions in which the competitors have to pick out the six prettiest faces from a hundred photographs, the prize being awarded to the competitor whose choice most nearly corresponds to the average preferences of the competitors as a whole; so that each competitor has to pick, not those faces which he himself finds prettiest, but those which he thinks likeliest to catch the fancy of the other competitors, all of whom are looking at the problem from the same point of view.

> JOHN MAYNARD KEYNES, quoted in Norman G. Fosback, *Stock Market Logic* (Dearborn, 1993)

Although similar to horse races or roulette, the market does have three slight redeeming qualities. First, in a casino you have less than a 50 percent chance of winning, while in the market as a whole the average investment should grow with the American economy, which some people feel will grow, despite minor setbacks, forever. Second, when you invest in Wall Street, your capital is generally allocated to projects you might consider more worthwhile than the pockets of other gamblers and casino owners. Third, people who play the market are probably better able to sustain losses than some of the people hooked on the horses.

> ANDREW TOBIAS, *The Funny Money Game* (Playboy Press, 1971)

When everybody stops expecting a correction, that's just when we get one.

> STEVEN EINHORN, of the investment firm Goldman, Sachs, quoted in *U.S. News & World Report,* March 23, 1987

Who makes the really big money? The inside stockholders of a company do, when the market capitalizes the earnings of that company.

> GEORGE J. W. GOODMAN ("Adam Smith"), *The Money Game* (Random House, 1968)

Betting on the stock market is as ludicrous as betting on the lottery, unless you are so independent financially that you can afford to give the money away.

> ITZHAK PERLMAN, world-renowned violinist, quoted in the *New York Times,* September 22, 1996

[R]ather than asking what tomorrow will bring if the future is like the past, one should be asking how the game is changing, and how, therefore, the future will be different from the past.

> JOHN TRAIN, investment counselor, on the use of technical analysis for picking stocks, *Famous Financial Fiascoes* (Fraser Publications, 1995)

It is becoming clearer and clearer that the markets are moved by psychology as much as economic indicators . . . Once the Jupiter/Neptune conjunction in January has passed, the absurd multiples [of Disney shares] will come into question.

> HENRY WEINGARTEN, founder of Astrologers Fund Inc., quoted in *Worth,* October 1996

One key lesson I learned from astrology is that no one sign is intrinsically better than another, but they each are very different.

> RICHARD JENRETTE, investment banker, quoted in *New York Observer,* August 1997

What's really unusual is people are afraid of the future even though they have the means to do well. Even if you're making a lot of money, you're afraid you're not going to be making a lot of money tomorrow.

> WILLIAM DODGE, chairman of the investment-policy committee at Dean Witter Reynolds, quoted in the *Wall Street Journal,* February 23, 1996

Buying on the dips would be a great strategy if we only knew what point on the dip was the lowest.

> TODD JAYCOX of the firm Ibbotson Associates, quoted in the *Wall Street Journal,* October 28, 1996

The market perceives we are in a perfect environment, with a Goldilocks economy and Goldilocks politics.

> DAVID SHULMAN of the investment firm Salomon Brothers, quoted in the *New York Times,* November 26, 1996

It's not the size of the circle that counts, it's how well you define the parameters.

> WARREN BUFFETT of Berkshire Hathaway, on limiting investment to those areas where the investor is competent, quoted in *Fortune,* November 29, 1993

My psychologist asks me that, too.

> WARREN BUFFETT, on why he sank money into USAir, after describing airlines as the worst industry for investing, quoted in *Fortune,* November 29, 1993

You do not disclose the game that makes money for you.

> JACK A. BARBANEL of the investment firm Gruntal & Co., on program trading, quoted in *Business Week*, April 7, 1986

The track record of the handicappers in the *Racing Form* is like the track record of the best stock pickers in *Barron's* or the *Wall Street Journal*.

> VICTOR NIEDERHOFFER, *The Education of a Speculator* (Wiley, 1997)

A bull market, in its late phase, behaves like a soufflé: its volume exceeds the measure of its ingredients.

> TIM KORANDA, former stockbroker and advertising writer, August 1, 1996

23.21 INVESTMENT BANKING AND BANKERS

Finance is an art. Not yes or no, right or wrong. It is an art form, an understanding of who should be the companies of the future, and how to structure transactions. It's an art form greatly misunderstood.

> MICHAEL MILKEN, leveraged finance expert, junk-bond popularizer, in a speech, cited in *Forbes*, May 5, 1986

Finance is the art of passing currency from hand to hand until it finally disappears.

> The late ROBERT W. SARNOFF, chairman of RCA, quoted by A. W. Clauson, former CEO of Bank of America, in a speech, May 19, 1988

If everyone who has something to sell had to be as meticulous and detailed in his statements about what he is selling as those who offer stock in the market are now, under the "Truth in Securities" law, darn little would be sold, in time to be useful at least.

> DAVID LILIENTHAL, investment banker at Lazard Frères, entry for December 8, 1952, *The Journals of David Lilienthal*, vol. 3 (Harper & Row, 1966)

There's an old saying in this business. The assets go down in the elevator every night.

> BURTON GREENWALD, mutual-fund consultant, quoted in the *Wall Street Journal*, February 3, 1997

Investment banking is applying money to ideas, and ideas to money with a seasoning of imagination. In the world of business and affairs, nothing happens until the two are mixed.

> ROBERT LEHMAN, chairman of the investment firm Lehman Brothers, internal memorandum, February 10, 1966

Increasing amounts of our scarcest resource—brain-power—are being devoted to playing [financial] games.

> WARREN LAW, professor at Harvard Business School, quoted in *U.S. News & World Report*, April 8, 1985

When you cut out the investment bankers, you usually cut out the leaks.

> T. BOONE PICKENS, president of Mesa Petroleum, quoted in *Fortune*, February 16, 1987

There are very few truly original ideas in our business. About all of them are evolutionary—not revolutionary.

> ROBERT G. SCOTT, investment banking chief at Morgan Stanley Group Inc., quoted in the *Wall Street Journal*, August 8, 1996

Corporate America likes women. Find a hooker and you'll find a client.

> DONALD "DONNY" ENGEL of defunct junk-bond specialists Drexel Burnham Lambert, and host of a select private party at Drexel's annual "Predator's Ball," quoted in James L. Stewart's *Den of Thieves* (Touchstone, 1991)

Investment banking is a kind of clubby world. We were invited to the party, but we couldn't get the business.

> MITSUO GOTO, of the investment firm Nomura Wasserstein Perella Securities, quoted in the *New York Times*, March 10, 1991

There is more firepower out there in fewer hands, and the stakes for becoming part of the bulge bracket are higher than ever.

> DAVID ROBINS, head of European investment banking for UBS (United Bank of Switzerland), quoted in the *Financial Times*, January 31, 1997

23.22 INVESTMENT BANKING AND ITS REWARDS

Wall Street wags call UBS (United Bank of Switzerland) "the lumberyard," because it offers "two-by-threes" and "three-by-twos" (a $2 million salary guarantee for three years, or a $3 million pay packet for two).

> *The Economist,* on compensation practices by European investment firms to lure American bankers, September 14, 1996

The late-1980s phenomenon of the big-shot investment banker with his "interior decorator" wife will give way to the late-2080s phenomenon of the big-shot interior decorator with her "investment banker" husband.

> MICHAEL LEWIS, looking back from the year 2096, *New York Times Magazine,* September 29, 1996

I love Wall Street bonuses more than they [investment bankers] do.

> BARBARA CORCORAN, prominent upscale real estate broker in Manhattan, quoted in the *Wall Street Journal,* December 3, 1997

23.23 INVESTMENT BANKING AND RISK

When as a young and unknown man I started to be successful I was referred to as a gambler. My operations increased in scope and volume. Then I was known as a speculator. The sphere of my activities continued to expand and presently I was known as a banker. Actually I had been doing the same thing all the time.

> SIR ERNEST CASSEL, private banker to King Edward VII, quoted in Bernard M. Baruch, *Baruch: My Own Story* (Holt, 1957)

[T]he true speculator is one who observes the future and acts before it occurs. Like a surgeon he must be able to search through a mass of complex and contradictory details to the significant facts. Then, like the surgeon, he must be able to operate coldly, clearly, and skillfully on the basis of the facts before him.

> BERNARD M. BARUCH, *Baruch: My Own Story* (Holt, 1957)

If one thing is guaranteed to rile investment bankers, it is being likened to common gamblers.

> *The Economist,* March 2, 1996

Banking is for little margins and little risk. A financial man takes bigger risks for bigger profits.

> GILBERTE BEAUX, adviser to British businessman James Goldsmith, quoted in Geoffrey Wansell, *Tycoon: The Life of James Goldsmith* (Atheneum, 1987)

When you talk to investors they imagine going to the boss to tell her they've just invested in a hurricane hitting North Carolina. And [the risk is] kind of binary. Either the hurricane doesn't hit and they look like a hero. Or it does hit and they get fired.

> Anonymous investment banker, quoted in the *New York Times,* August 6, 1997

The highest bonuses usually go to the "stars," who may feel compelled to justify their status by taking greater risks in the hope of making higher and higher profits.

A culture in which it is acceptable to lose money once in a while (something which is almost inevitable if markets are efficient) may mitigate pressures to take excessive risks.

> DANIEL DAVIES, economist at the Bank of England, quoted in the *Financial Times,* March 4, 1997

23.24 INVESTMENT STRATEGY

Gin rummy managerial behavior (discard your least promising business at each turn) is not our style.

> WARREN BUFFETT, Berkshire Hathaway annual report, 1994

Never invest in any idea you can't illustrate with a crayon.

> PETER LYNCH, *Beating the Street* (Fireside, 1994)

Just as there's no sense owning Kellogg's if you're bearish on cornflakes, there's no sense owning oil companies unless you're convinced that oil has a profitable future.

> PETER LYNCH, *Worth,* October 1996

23.25 MUNICIPAL BONDS

Many practices [in the municipal bond market] belong more to the nineteenth century than the twentieth.

> PAUL MACO, director of the SEC's municipal securities office, quoted in *Newsweek,* November 20, 1995

Mix politics, money, and big taxpayer subsidies, and you get a muni market rife with corruption and questionable transactions.

> *Fortune,* August 7, 1996

Until "I've Got a Secret" ceases to be the favorite game of those involved in the municipal market, The Dark Continent will remain unlit.

> *Grant's Municipal Bond Observer,* on ethics in the municipal bond industry, September 1, 1996

23.26 PORTFOLIO MANAGERS

Portfolio management had the appeal of sports—that one cleanly wins or loses, the results are measurable in numbers . . . and regardless of whether he was popular with his colleagues or had come from the right ancestry or the right side of the tracks . . . the winner became an instant star, his name known and revered in Wall Street.

> JOHN BROOKS, *The Go-Go Years* (Weybright and Talley, 1973)

Turnover is now becoming more of a concern [at Fidelity]. Clearly, the company has gotten much more bureaucratic, and that doesn't set well with people used to working in an autonomous manner.

> ERIC KOBREN, editor of the independent newsletter *Fidelity Insight,* in wake of departure of prominent fund manager, quoted in the *Wall Street Journal,* December 3, 1996

Portfolio managers are rock-star types these days. The fund companies prop them up for marketing reasons, but there are consequences. Investors often fail to realize that stock picking isn't the province of any individual. There's usually a larger investment team behind the scenes.

> BURTON GREENWALD, mutual-fund consultant in Philadelphia, quoted in the *Wall Street Journal,* August 22, 1997

23.27 QUANTITATIVE ANALYSTS

[T]hey're scarier than gunslingers.

Quants tend to be bachelors who live in apartments as messy as the room they left in grade school. Many of them drink hard after hours, mostly with fellow workers. They mate, if that's the word, mostly in one-night stands.

> Article on quantitative analysts, *Time,* April 11, 1994

It's a whole different breed. If superstar status is distinguished by how much money you make for the firm, it's no longer the publicly visible guy who puts together the transactions. It's the quantitative guys coming up with a creative product that has mass-market appeal.

These guys don't make it in newspaper stories for their four-legged currency swaps. No one wants to read it, no one understands it, and it doesn't have the sex appeal of hostile takeovers and junk-bond financing.

> GARY GOLDSTEIN, president of the Wall Street recruiting firm Whitney Group, quoted in the *New York Times,* April 4, 1993

The weirdest relationship you can think of might show up as mathematically significant to them. They have computers crunching numbers all day long looking for nonchance relationships—looking for needles in the stacks that no one else would even be trying to comprehend.

> ANDREW SCHWAEBER, trader, on quantitative analysts, quoted in *Fortune,* February 5, 1996

What you need humans for is to understand the motivation for trading, to come up with the ideas, to take ideas from the blackboard to the trader.

> PROFESSOR ANDREW LO, Sloan School at MIT, quoted in *Worth,* October 1995

There are only a couple of ways to make money in this business. One is to constantly come up with a better idea. Another is to get information to people faster.

> HELEN PETERS of Security Pacific's "rocket scientists" who devise formulas for pension funds, quoted in *U.S. News & World Report,* May 25, 1987

Rocket scientists are building Wall Street's equivalent of atomic bombs, and every now and then one of these things blows up.

> PROFESSOR JAMES SCOTT of Columbia University, quoted in *U.S. News & World Report,* May 25, 1987

The best way to make money out of deterministic chaos is to write about it.

> RON LIESCHING, head of investment firm Pareto Partners, quoted in the *Economist,* January 13, 1996

23.28 REAL ESTATE

If one were not naturally an optimist, one would never choose to be a developer.

> ROBERT PATTERSON of the accounting and consulting firm Laventhol & Horvath, quoted in *Time,* August 26, 1985

It just seems to be a mania. Each developer thinks he's got a super-outstanding product.

> JOHN AMORY of the real estate firm Coldwell Banker, quoted in *Time,* August 26, 1985

Real estate is not what moves the economy. The economy is what moves the real estate.

> JANE JACOBS, urban economist, quoted in the *Wall Street Journal,* October 8, 1997

23.29 RISK TAKNG AND RISK MANAGEMENT

Everything is sweetened by risk.

> ALEXANDER SMITH, "Of Death and the Fear of Dying," *Dreamthorp,* 1863

By definition, risk-takers often fail. So do morons. In practice it's difficult to sort them out.

> SCOTT ADAMS, *The Dilbert Principle* (Harper Business, 1996)

There's no corporate treasurer who doesn't bet all the time, either by acting or not acting.

> EUGENE H. ROTBERG of the World Bank, quoted in the *Wall Street Journal,* January 16, 1985

Historically, risk takers are people who shatter the illusion of knowledge. They are willing to try something that everyone thinks is outrageous or stupid.

> DANIEL BOORSTIN, historian, quoted in *U.S. News & World Report,* January 26, 1987

We've exchanged free enterprise . . . for frightened enterprise.

> C. J. SILAS, CEO of Philips Petroleum, in a speech, March 29, 1989

Danger is nature's way of eliminating stupid people. Without safety, stupid people die in accidents. Since the dead don't reproduce, our species becomes progressively more intelligent (or at least less stupid).

> LAWRENCE A. BULLIS, in a letter to the editor of the *Arizona Republic,* republished in *Harper's,* November 1994

It was to our interest to spread it around. If you cast your bread on the water, sometimes it comes back as angel food cake.

> JACK MORTON of Bell Labs, recalling the 1952 decision to license the transistor instead of protecting the technology, *The Chip Wars,* (Scribner, 1989)

We were making a living when we were playing with cheaters. We should do even better now.

> ALAN "ACE" GREENBERG, chairman of Bear Stearns, after the arrest of insider-trader Ivan Boesky, quoted in the *Economist,* July 11, 1987

Some products are really outrageous chemicals such as acetone, acetaldehyde, methyl butyrate, ethyl caproate, hexyl acetate, methanol, acrolein, and even that stuff called crotonaldehyde? How dare anybody dose up a product with all those chemicals? . . . Well, that would be a problem because the product I've described is a fresh strawberry, naturally grown, with no man-made ingredients.

> R. F. HERBERT, CEO of E. I. Du Pont, in a speech, February 21, 1989

If human nature felt no temptation to take a chance . . . there might not be much investment merely as a result of cold calculation.

> JOHN MAYNARD KEYNES

When you insure substandard drivers, you get paid more than when you insure standard drivers. Some have done very well doing that and some have gotten killed.

> WARREN BUFFETT, chairman of Berkshire Hathaway, on junk-bond financing, quoted in James Stewart, *Den of Thieves* (Touchstone, 1991)

Part of the assessment our business leaders make on a new piece of business is whether or not we'll get paid. That's why we put risk managers down in the trenches with them.

> JIM COLICA, of the financial firm GE Capital, quoted in *Fortune,* November 10, 1997

The risk management at Kidder is equivalent to the lookout on the *Titanic* . . . If Kidder got hoodwinked on something as simple as government bonds—that's just interest-rate risk and mathematics—you can imagine what's going on in its mortgage desk.

> Trading executive, referring to a 1994 government bond scandal involving the investment firm Kidder-Peabody and Joseph Jett, one of its former traders, quoted in *Business Week,* August 22, 1994

History cannot be reduced to a set of statistics and probabilities.

> ALAN S. GREENSPAN, chairman of the U.S. Federal Reserve, in a speech, October 14, 1992

23.30 SECURITIES ANALYSTS

It's like having someone go through your panty drawer. You have to explain why you wear cotton on Monday and lace on Wednesday.

> LANNIE BERNHARD, president of Nursing Management, on talking to securities analysts, *Inc.,* September 1994

If you haven't gotten a letter from Roberto, you can't call yourself an analyst.

> ROY BURRY of Oppenheimer & Company, on Roberto Goizueta's "zeal" for responding to what analysts write about Coca-Cola, quoted in the *Wall Street Journal,* February 16, 1996

I hate like hell for investors to sell the stock based on wrong information they get from an analyst.

> The late ROBERTO GOIZUETA, CEO of Coca-Cola, quoted in the *Wall Street Journal,* February 16, 1996

I gathered up all of the illicit paper products, opened the bathroom door, and threw them into the hall.

"I make toilet paper and you people buy lousy toilet paper!" I roared. "For God's sake, look at the amount of money your shareholders have made on my stock, and you have this crummy toilet paper! I want to see you buying better toilet paper."

> ALBERT "CHAINSAW AL" DUNLAP, former chairman of Scott Paper, on finding a competitor's toilet paper in Scott dispensers at Brown Brothers Harriman, *Mean Business* (Times Books, 1996)

23.31 STOCKBROKERS OF DUBIOUS INTEGRITY

A broker is a man who takes your fortune and runs it into a shoestring.

> ALEXANDER WOOLLCOTT, American playwright

A stockbroker is someone who takes all your money and invests it until it's gone.

> WOODY ALLEN, quoted in the *Economist,* October 25, 1997

Did you hear the one about the new NASDAQ ad slogan? The stock market for the next hundred years—with 25 years off for good behavior.

> Joke about series of investigations into NASDAQ trading practices, quoted in *Business Week,* November 7, 1994

I've always been amused by the fact that they want to sound like they're members of the House of Lords.

> DENNIS KLEJNA, securities lawyer, on penny-stock brokerage firms, quoted in the *New York Observer,* December 9, 1996

Hanover Sterling; Stratton Oakmont; Barron Chase Equities; Sovereign Equity Management; Norfolk Securities; Cartwright & Walker; A. S. Goldmen. [Names of firms that employed some of the 53 people arrested in connection with fraud on NASDAQ exams for securities licenses.]

> *New York Times,* January 9, 1997

That's a sure sign it's crooked.

> British securities lawyer, commenting on British firms with *Sir* in front of their principals' names, quoted in the *New York Observer,* December 9, 1996

Glossary of Mob Stock-Market Terms

chop stock: Thinly traded with very wide spread

vig: Extra wide spread common with Mob-dominated stocks

house stocks: Stocks sold aggressively to investors by the firms that control them

boxing (as in "boxing a stock"): Controlling the market for shares by collusive trading among brokers

parking: Buying a stock for a customer by "mistake," to raise the price and control the market for it

> *Business Week,* December 16, 1996

To the investor who wants a research report: "When Columbus discovered America, he didn't send a report until he actually saw the land."

To the man who says he has to talk to his wife: "Let's be candid, you don't confer with your wife on day-to-day business decisions."

To the prospect who says it is not the right time, or he is not in the right mood for buying stocks: "If I had a 6-foot blonde today, would you be in the right mood?"

> From book of scripts purportedly used for cold sales calls, seized at First United Equities by the New York State Attorney General's staff, quoted in the *New York Observer,* June 15, 1997

The securities laws were designed to be very pro-investor. President Roosevelt even said when he signed them that they represented a movement from "caveat emptor" to "caveat venditor": seller, beware. But in arbitration, the tendency is to undo that.

> BARRY GUTHARY of the Massachusetts state securities division, quoted in the *New York Times,* December 3, 1989

There's no excuse for not finding out someone's income level.

> SCOTT GALLOWAY of the investment firm Prophet Market Research and Consulting, which studied the levels of help brokers gave to novice investors, quoted in the *Wall Street Journal,* July 8, 1996

Smaller firms are quite hungry and thus more willing to take on problems. If you've got a guy who's a million-dollar producer but a big discipline problem, the smaller firms will often just take him and ask questions later.

> DAN MARCUS, former securities executive who became a headhunter, quoted in the *Wall Street Journal,* March 14, 1996

Con artists see these people [new immigrants who invest in schemes promoted by their compatriots]. It's like a law of nature: If there is something there to eat, there will be something there to eat it.

> MARK GRIFFIN, director of the Utah securities commission, quoted in the *New York Observer,* December 29, 1997

23.32 VENTURE CAPITAL

If you're a fast-growing company, it's like having a company that's losing money. It makes the bank nervous.

> PATRICK C. KELLY, CEO of Physicians Sales and Service, entrepreneurial medical services company, *Inc.,* October 1995

In venturing, lemons ripen early and pearls take longer to cultivate.

> STANLEY PRATT, publisher of *Venture Capital Journal,* quoted in *U.S. News & World Report,* May 18, 1987

[R]isk comes in four parts. There's technical risk: can we split the atom? There's market risk: will the dogs eat the dog food, or the fish jump out of the tank? There's people risk: will the people who founded the company stick around? And there's financing risk: can we get the money?

[T]raining a good venture capitalist is like crashing a few F-16s. It costs about 30 million, straight down the drain.

> L. JOHN DOERR of the Silicon Valley venture-capital firm Kleiner, Perkins, Caufield & Byers, quoted in the *New Yorker,* August 11, 1997

People will look back on this period and say, "Oh my God, why did we fund so many of these companies?"

> ROGER McNAMEE of Integral Capital Partners, quoted in *Forbes,* September 22, 1997

When you're looking for start-up capital, you get fat, not rich. Go into any Marriott in the country, and you'll see venture capitalists having breakfast with entrepreneurs. The entrepreneurs are having bacon and eggs, and the venture capitalists are having granola.

> MITCHELL KERTZMAN, founder of the software firm Powersoft, quoted in *Inc.,* October 1995

What does it say about you if you don't invest most of your money in your own business?

> MAYNARD HOWE, clinical psychologist and entrepreneur, quoted in *Inc.,* November 1995

When you invest in a business, especially in a start-up business, you invest in the people.

> MICHAEL EGAN, investor in Nantucket Allserve Inc., maker of Nantucket Nectars (started by the people who cleaned his yacht), quoted in the *New York Times,* September 17, 1997

Venture capitalists like to get to you early, open a dialogue, then string you along.

> ANDY KLEIN, founder of New York City's Spring Street Brewery, quoted in *Inc.,* July 1996

We consider it a very bad sign when all of the equity of a young entrepreneurial company is owned by its chief executive officer. [When] senior members of the management think and act like owners . . . [t]hey will argue aggressively for strategies they believe to be in the best interest of the company rather than passively following the direction of the company's president.

> ROBERT D. PAVEY, general partner of Morgenthaler Ventures

23.33 U.S. FINANCIAL MARKETS

Wall Street does not exist as a place. It is a cultural phenomenon, not just a piece of real estate. And even as a cultural phenomenon it will disintegrate as you move towards globalization.

> DEAN LEBARON, of the money-management firm Batterymarch, *The Economist,* July 11, 1987

There is no human feeling to the [U.S. securities] markets, and sometimes no discernible evidence of human intelligence either. But they work.

> ROBERT EATON, CEO of Chrysler Corporation, in a speech, March 18, 1996

Siemens, Software AG, and SAP aside, Germany has produced few well-known high-tech firms. By contrast, cruel old American shareholder capitalism has spawned a veritable alphabet—from Apple, Borland, Compaq, and Dell all the way through to WordPerfect, Xerox, Yahoo! and Ziff-Davis.

> *The Economist,* September 28, 1996

People forget that the capital markets aren't just supposed to provide capital but also to deny it to companies that can't make efficient use of it.

> PROFESSOR JOHN POUND of Harvard University, quoted in *Fortune,* January 11, 1993

In France, we would have been valued three or four times less than we were on NASDAQ.

> BERNARD LIANTAUD, CEO of the French high-technology company Business Objects, quoted in *Inc.,* April 1996

Foreign companies . . . want their shares listed in the United States for the same reason that Willie Sutton robbed banks ["that's where the money is"].

> JAMES SUROWIECKI, *Slate,* November 13, 1997

In order to make itself more global in character, the [New York Stock Exchange] has committed itself to trading in decimals rather than fractions over the next few years.

> *Financial Times,* September 24, 1997

The better we can make our capital markets, the better we will improve our standard of living.

> WALTER P. SCHUETZE, chief accountant of the SEC's enforcement division, quoted in the *Wall Street Journal,* October 10, 1997

Americans have experience derived from the breadth and width of their capital markets. They are people with an extraordinary knowledge of underwriting, financial markets, and, above all, capital markets. And they have been able to use this knowledge in a very informative way, which has enabled them to change investment banking from the old-fashioned raising of funds for industry and commerce into the aggressive restructuring of industry.

> TED RYBCZYNSKI, visiting professor, City University in London, quoted in the *Wall Street Journal,* January 5, 1996

23.34 VOLATILITY

Volatility tends to increase when we get what I call an information shock. The last time that happened and caused a down market was in 1990, at the beginning of the gulf war.

> ERIC H. SORENSEN, of the investment firm Salomon Brothers, quoted in the *New York Times,* August 31, 1997

Volatility is a clue that other people are reevaluating, and so investors have a rule of thumb: when in doubt, imitate others.

> PROFESSOR ROBERT J. SHILLER of Yale University, quoted in the *New York Times,* September 16, 1997

Let's say you go shopping and buy for $50 an item that's worth $100. You bring it home and find it has a little ding in it. If you only paid $50 for it, you're not likely to be upset. But if you paid closer to full price, you may be a bit more agitated. That may be a good analogy for our market.

> ABBY JOSEPH COHEN, of the investment firm Goldman, Sachs, *New York Times,* September 16, 1997

Bungee jumping is the sport of the moment for stock market investors. Heart-stopping falls are followed, in short order, by breathtaking rises with very little in the way of substantial economic or policy news to explain them.

> PHILLIP COGGAN, *Financial Times,* September 4, 1997

In trying to soothe the markets, officials often elevate the sense of unease. Investors in uncertain times ask themselves: "Why do they feel the need to reassure us? Are they not just drawing attention to how anxious things really are? Or are they afraid themselves because they are unable to act and cannot persuade leaders abroad to act? Is this talk a substitute for concrete action?"

> ROBERT A. JOHNSON, former chief economist to the U.S. Senate Banking Committee and former managing director for Soros Fund Management, quoted in the *New York Times,* December 29, 1997

24.1 EASTERN EUROPE

It's incredibly easy to believe, because you are speaking to a minister with a relevant-sounding title, that you're actually being given something. Three rooms away another minister is negotiating the same exclusivity with another company.

> CHARLES JONSCHER, founder of Central European Trust, a London-based firm that advises Western firms on Eastern European investment, quoted in the *Economist,* February 8, 1992

In Eastern Europe, we've followed a "buy-small-and-build" strategy.

We would typically encounter tariff barriers that kept us from importing our products into a country, so we started by buying local companies (especially in chocolate) with well-known brand names—but not, by Western European standards, high quality. Then we would upgrade the manufacturing facilities, so that they could produce our higher-quality, Western European products.

> JOHN RUFF of Kraft Foods International, in a speech, April 22, 1996

Central Europe is now an economic tiger on our doorstep. Some earlier investors got their fingers burnt. Others were put off by legal and other problems. But these markets are now ready for another look.

> IAN LANG, British trade secretary, quoted in *Financial Times,* January 15, 1997

24.2 INDIVIDUAL COUNTRIES

24.2.1 Albania

The government turned a blind eye to these schemes because it wanted to get re-elected. The population was happy—they were getting money from heaven—and the government did not want to rock the boat.

> Western financial official, referring to pyramid investment schemes that collapsed and led to widescale civil unrest and destabilized the country, quoted in *Financial Times,* February 19, 1997

These were the funds that should have gone into creating small businesses or paid for stakes in companies being privatized. They should have been captured in savings accounts or gone into new housing.

> Foreign banker, quoted in the *Financial Times,* February 19, 1997

24.2.2 Armenia

Special consideration is being given to complete works of the classics of Marxism-Leninism.

> Official Armenian news agency, on reports that freezing people were burning their own books to stay warm, *The Economist,* January 23, 1993

24.2.3 Azerbaijan

The proven reserves beneath Azerbaijan's portion of the Caspian total 17 billion barrels, the equivalent of the North Sea field. Geologists believe that at least 20 billion to 30 billion barrels more remain to be found. The other oil-rich corner of the Caspian belongs to Kazakhstan, with proven reserves of 10 billion barrels and perhaps three times that not yet found.

> STEPHEN KINZER, *New York Times,* September 21, 1996

There are so many interlocking interests (including warlords, hostile neighboring countries, and geography) in this region, not to mention among outside powers and the oil companies themselves. Our job is to balance them and still protect our own interests. Believe me, we don't underestimate the importance or complexity of it all.

> NATIK ALIYEV, president of the Azerbaijani state oil monopoly, quoted in the *New York Times,* September 21, 1996

24.2.4 Belarus

We have McDonald's, but no freedom of assembly. People have subsistence potatoes and vodka; the streets are clean and well-maintained. [President Aleksandr] Lukashenko doesn't kill massively because he doesn't have to. This is the new face of dictatorship in Europe.

> ANDREI SANNIKOV, former Deputy Foreign Minister, quoted in the *New York Times,* July 12, 1997

24.2.5 Bulgaria

Bulgaria likes to think of itself as European. Now our inflation looks more like the old Latin America, and our debt and poverty levels are more like the Sudan.

> LUBOMIR FILIPOV, central bank governor, quoted in the *Wall Street Journal,* February 28, 1997

24.2.6 Czech Republic

In Czechoslovakia, private business was called "illegal enrichment."

> JIRKA RYSAVY, Czech-born CEO of office-supply company Corporate Express who came to the United States in mid-1980s, referring to life under Communism, quoted in *Inc.,* December 1995

[Kafka] has become a symbol for Prague like the gondola is for Venice.

> Czech diplomat, quoted in the *Wall Street Journal,* October 10, 1996

Low jobless rate is spoiling the Czech workforce.

> *Prague Post* headline, November 1996

In some cases, [the conversion to a market system from Communism is] going to be enormously difficult, like in Russia, where it's a long, long process if they ever succeed. In other cases, like the Czech Republic, where I've spent quite a bit of time, it's more possible because they have a heritage of having had relatively efficient rules before the Nazis took over in 1938 and therefore it's much easier to—for example, develop a legal code and enforcement and contract rules that will work there than it is in a place that has no heritage of them.

> DOUGLAS NORTH of Washington University and 1993 Nobel Prize winner, heard on National Public Radio program *All Things Considered,* October 12, 1993

Foreign investment is often a wake-up call. People realize negative suspicions have an impact on the value of a stake. Now, maybe the government can get a fair price.

> Analyst on Czech government crackdown on white-collar crime in advance of privatization, quoted in the *Financial Times,* May 1, 1997

Foreign capital is losing faith in us.

> VACLAV KLAUS, Prime Minister of the Czech Republic, quoted in the *Economist,* May 31, 1997

A lot of Westerners were seduced by the glamour of the place, especially Prague. Now they're seeing the real economy, which is not so picturesque.

> JAMES OATES, an Eastern Europe analyst at UBS Securities in London, quoted in the *Wall Street Journal,* July 15, 1997

Behind the free-market fairy tale of Prague, another Czech Republic is emerging. It is a place where Communist-era companies . . . are still run by Communist-era managers.

> ROBERT FRANK, *Wall Street Journal,* July 15, 1997

In general, we don't intend to take over big chunks of companies' property. But it's the only way to preserve our property in these companies and not lose all our money.

> RICHARD SALZMANN, president of Komercni Bank AS, Prague, on taking over management of insolvent client companies, quoted in the *Wall Street Journal,* July 5, 1996

In five years, domestic prices may not be much higher than they are now. So more and more beer will go for exports. Exports are the key to making more money from Czech beer.

> Executive at one of the three top breweries in the Czech Republic, a country that drinks more beer per capita than any other, quoted in the *Financial Times,* March 11, 1997

Like most post-Communist countries, there was an ingrained system: never tell the truth and always help your buddies.

> HOWARD I. GOLDEN of the Central European Privatization Fund, quoted in the *New York Times,* December 3, 1997

Jay Gould and Vanderbilt were robber barons, but one generation later they were respected people.

> VACLAV KLAUS, former Czech prime minister, quoted by Howard I. Golden, who complained that the government's capital accumulation policies were benefit-

ing insiders at the expense of ordinary investors, *New York Times*, December 3, 1997 (Klaus later resigned in a political contribution scandal.)

24.2.7 Estonia

The Estonians could probably teach their Western European neighbors a thing or two about reining in big government.

> BASIL ZAVOICO, American who represents the IMF in Tallinn, quoted in the *Wall Street Journal*, December 9, 1996

It is better to be on the safe side and live with lower growth today than have big capital outflows tomorrow.

> PETER LOHMUS, deputy governor of the Bank of Estonia, contemplating measures to slow an economy growing 11 percent a year (substantially as a result of foreign investment), quoted in *Financial Times*, September 17, 1997

If bankers go to heaven, they might find the nameplate "Estonia" hanging from the pearly gates.

> JOHN THORNHILL, *Financial Times*, September 24, 1997

All [Estonians] need to do now is take what has been for one thousand years a geopolitical liability and turn it into an asset. They could be the world's beachhead to Russia.

> DAVID HALE, chief economist of the investment company Zurich Group, quoted in *Forbes*, October 6, 1997

24.2.8 Georgia

The cost of business is high because everything is imported. It's like living in Nantucket.

> ELIZABETH HASKELL, Baltimore-born proprietor of Betsy's Place, popular hotel in Tblisi, quoted in the *New York Times*, July 5, 1997

24.2.9 Hungary

After a period of frustrating inaction and delays on our Hungarian launch, I went for advice to one of my colleagues, a Hungarian who now lives in New York.

"It's the culture," he said. "Over the years they've learned: 'I don't have to do it. First, it may not happen. If it does happen and it's that important, someone else will do it.'"

You need local help . . . You need someone who'll catch you if your ad looks like it was created from an American perspective . . . Or remind you that in Hungary last names come before first.

> CAROLE M. HOWARD of the Reader's Digest Association, Inc., in a speech about launching *Reader's Digest* in Russia and Hungary, January 17, 1992

As long as you can steer clear of the government, you're in good shape to do business in Hungary, and I think I can get 12 to 14 percent annual return for the fund. But if you get involved with trying to privatize a state company, you're in trouble. The ministers are good on expounding on history and truth, but they have virtually no technocratic ability and I don't think they ever got a lot done in their lives.

> PETER RONA, chief executive of the Western investment First Hungary Fund Ltd., quoted in the *New York Times*, May 5, 1992

In Hungarian, the name sounds like "fart"—or worse. [The reason that General Mills snack food "Fingos," meant to be eaten with the "fingers," will not be marketed in Europe.]

> *Fortune*, October 18, 1993

We need to see carpetbaggers make windfall profits and disappear. Now, investors are fitting us into their global networks.

> BELA KADAR, former International Economic Relations Minister, quoted in *Business Week*, November 7, 1994

That's one of the most exciting things we've ever done. We bought it from the Communists in the last week of their regime. They were much easier to deal with than the capitalists who replaced them.

> JOHN F. WELCH JR., CEO of GE, on GE's purchase of Tungsram, a lightbulb company in Hungary, quoted in *Fortune*, May 29, 1995

There's a fight going on between the Ukrainian and Hungarian mafias. It used to be that the Ukrainian pimps controlled the bar, disco, and hotel prostitutes and left the Hungarian pimps with the streets. Now the Ukrainians want a bigger share.

> MS. ZSUZSA KADAR, trade union official active in women's issues, quoted in the *Financial Times,* January 28, 1997

24.2.10   Kazakhstan

Where is there no risk? Qatar is risky, Mexico is risky, California is risky.

> LOIK LE FLOCH-PRIGENT, chairman of Elf Aquitaine, on the French oil company's drilling in Kazakhstan, quoted in the *New York Times,* June 27, 1993

It took two months to get these people [the KGB, on site since the 1940s] out, and I'm not completely convinced they're gone.

> MALAY MUKHERJEE, plant manager for Ispat International Ltd., Kazakhstan's largest steel company, quoted in the *Wall Street Journal,* May 2, 1996

It's bitter to acknowledge that we are poorer today and behind in development. In the coming years, our life, our money, and our pockets will be determined by oil and gas . . . Only a real professional can ensure that we do not lose our chances, do not allow others to deceive us.

> NURSULTAN NAZARBAYEV, president, after dismissing reformist prime minister who was popular with foreign investors, quoted in the *Wall Street Journal,* October 13, 1997

24.2.11   Latvia

When the Soviet Union fell, Russia lost its four major Baltic ports. They want to build a new one, but that would take millions. A small investment in our new commercial port would solve their problem.

> IMANTS CIBULIS, president of Trans Liepaja Agency, who had been negotiating with Russian industrialists on joint projects at the Latvian port, which was once a bastion of the Soviet Navy, quoted in the *Financial Times,* March 4, 1997

24.2.12   Poland

Poland is the Hong Kong of Eastern Europe.

> LUKASZ ZUK, former math teacher, who made a killing in the Warsaw stock market, quoted in *Business Week,* January 17, 1994

The popular notion was of Poland as decrepit and shabby with zero know-how, when in fact the economy was a lot more. The Polish people are intrinsically much stronger in business than outsiders thought.

> IAN HUME of the World Bank's office in Warsaw, quoted in the *New York Times,* June 20, 1993

The politics of the East and the economics of the future pull in opposite directions.

> WALTER RUSSELL MEAD, senior policy analyst for the World Policy Institute at the New School for Social Research, on why Eastern European economies will not achieve the affluence of the West for decades, *Worth,* September 1994

Poland was the first place in the region we could show that you can turn companies around.

> PERCY BARNEVIK, chairman of the Swedish-Swiss industrial firm ABB (Asea Brown Boveri Ltd.), quoted in the *Wall Street Journal,* November 25, 1996

Do you have the proper office equipment? Do you have an attractive secretary? If not, call us.

> Polish television advertisement, cited in the *Economist,* December 12, 1992

"Daddy, are the Russians our friends or our brothers?"
"Son, the Russians are our brothers. You can choose your friends."

> Polish banker, reacting to speech to international financial audience by General Alexander Lebed, former Russian security chief and probable presidential candidate, quoted in the *Financial Times,* April 14, 1997

Polish banks learned about banking; they actually got to know their clients, and they cleaned up their balance sheets.

> CHRISTINE BINDERT, independent investment banker who has monitored Polish banks for the European Union, quoted in the *Wall Street Journal,* April 18, 1997

How do you think I could pretend I was producing a nonalcoholic Absolut vodka?

> MICHAEL KOWALSKI, head of Seagrams, Poland, on the disadvantage spirits producers were at compared to other drink makers who advertised nonalcoholic

versions of their products under identical brand names to circumvent advertising restrictions (the loopholes have now been closed), quoted in the *Financial Times*, February 24, 1997

Don't be fooled by headline news of political infighting. It doesn't affect the economy too much. The direction taken by the changes here is irreversible.

> DARIUSZ OLESCZUCK, Warsaw lawyer, quoted in the *Financial Times*, January 6, 1997

The problem is that five years ago it was easy—we knew that capitalism was better than socialism. Now we know that capitalism is not as good as everyone thought. But this is all we know. People fear the foreign capitalists will introduce foreign ways. They only know privatization as a slogan, but they don't really know what it is.

> DOROTA BARTZEL, editor in chief of the American-financed weekly *Warsaw Voice*, quoted in William Greider, *One World, Ready or Not: The Manic Logic of Global Capitalism* (Simon & Schuster, 1997)

Half of the government is convinced that there's a lot of foreign money out there waiting to buy Poland and the other half is scared that they're right.

> An American bank executive based in Warsaw, quoted in William Greider, *One World, Ready or Not: The Manic Logic of Global Capitalism* (Simon & Schuster, 1997)

24.2.13 Romania

According to one of our proverbs, a poor man cannot afford to buy cheap things. In the same way, we are too poor to afford the sort of economy we have now.

We are applying intensive care treatment to a gravely ill economy.

[To attract foreign investment] It is not enough to make a good offer, it must be a shockingly good offer.

> VICTOR CIORBEA, Prime Minister of Romania, quoted in the *Financial Times*, February 21, 1997

On one day alone this year the Bucharest Stock Exchange registered more transactions than the total number of transactions it had for all last year.

> VICTOR CIORBEA, Prime Minister of Romania, quoted in *Forbes*, September 22, 1997

24.2.14 Russia

24.2.14.1 *Before the Fall of the Soviet Union*

I do not know if it is the character of the Russian people that has created such dictators, or if the dictators themselves have given this character to the nation.

> BARON SIGISMUND VON HARBERSTEIN, ambassador from Emperor Frederick III to Russian court, 1517–1526, quoted by Walter Mead, senior policy analyst for the World Policy Institute at the New School for Social Research, *Worth*, September 1994

Russia in one respect represents an exception to all the countries of the world . . . The exception consists in this, that the people have been systematically, over two generations, brought up without a sense of property and legality.

> COUNT SERGEI WITTE, Russian premier under Czar Nicholas II, 1905, quoted in the *Economist*, December 5, 1992

I can think of no better instrument of counterrevolution.

> JOSEPH STALIN, vetoing expansion of Russia's telephone network, quoted in the *Economist*, February 8, 1992

I cannot forecast to you the action of Russia. It is a riddle wrapped in a mystery inside an enigma.

> SIR WINSTON CHURCHILL, in a radio broadcast, October 1, 1939

Bearing all this in mind, we see that there is no Russian national understanding which would permit the early establishment in Russia of anything resembling the private enterprise system as we know it.

> GEORGE F. KENNAN, *American Diplomacy 1900–1950* (1951)

Banks are kidding themselves if they just run willy-nilly developing ties to the Soviet bloc without attention to the security issue.

> LAWRENCE BRAINARD of Bankers Trust, quoted in *U.S. News & World Report*, October 3, 1988

The Soviet Union is a good debtor, and where does one find good debtors these days?

> Frankfurt financier, quoted in *U.S. News & World Report*, October 3, 1988

Don't leave home.

> YAKOV SMIRNOFF, comedian on motto for the "Soviet Express Card," in light of the fact that few citizens were allowed to travel abroad or keep foreign currency, quoted in *U.S. News & World Report,* October 3, 1988

You buy a used light bulb for a few kopecks and take it to work. Then you unscrew the good light bulb from your office lamp and replace it with the blown-out bulb. You tell your boss you need a new light bulb because yours is out—and you take the original good bulb home after it has been replaced, sell it at a flea market—and start the whole cycle all over again.

> Story circulating around Moscow, summer 1991, quoted by CAROLE M. HOWARD of the Reader's Digest Association, in a speech about launching *Reader's Digest* in Russia and Hungary, January 17, 1992

The average citizen believes that there is little difference between businessmen and the Mafia—both are accumulating wealth at the expense of others.

> CAROLE M. HOWARD of the Reader's Digest Association, in a speech about launching *Reader's Digest* in Russia and Hungary, January 17, 1992

Sorry, comrade, here's the list of where all our output is to be delivered, and you aren't on it.

> Russia under the old regime

24.2.14.2 *After the Fall*

Without hard work and discipline, we will achieve nothing. We cannot live as they live in the West and work as we work in Russia.

> PRIME MINISTER VIKTOR CHERNOMYRDIN, in a speech, cited in the *Economist,* January 30, 1993

Two people meet. The first one says, "You want to buy a cart of sugar?" The second one replies, "Yes, fine." They agree on a price . . . Then the first goes to see if he can buy a cart load of sugar, and the second goes to see if he can find some money. [Joke illustrating the difficulty of doing business in Russia following the fall of the Soviet Union.]

> DANIEL YERGIN and THANE GUSTAFSON, *Russia 2010 and What It Means for the World* (Random House, 1993)

The pipeline for money is equivalent to the pipeline for oil and gas in this country. They are both leaky and stuff moves through it slowly.

> MILJENKO HORVAT, head of Citibank's Moscow branch, quoted in the *New York Times,* November 21, 1993

We pile a bunch of rubles in a suitcase and fly them out [because the banks are too slow].

> JIM LEONARD of Occidental Petroleum in Russia, on how he pays employees working in the Arctic and Siberia, quoted in the *New York Times,* November 21, 1993

Not a single reform effort in Russia has ever been completed.

> BORIS YELTSIN, *The Struggle for Russia* (Times Books, 1994)

We aim to be the Evian of Russia.

> JOHN KING, U.S. business partner with Russian water bottler Rodniki and a Russian Orthodox diocese to produce Saint Springs, a bottled mineral water (the first private business deal for the Church since the Revolution), quoted in *Business Week,* August 22, 1994

Russians can get very creative when it comes to not paying taxes, and they have a good chance of getting away with it.

> COLONEL ALEXANDER BORISOV, Moscow Tax Police, quoted in the *Wall Street Journal,* April 18, 1997

Deciding which companies go bankrupt and who gets to buy their assets is a political decision.

> DIRK DAMRAU of Renaissance Capital, Moscow, quoted in *Business Week,* November 11, 1996

[The federal government must tell manufacturers] we will give you protected circumstances for one or two or three years, but you must make your enterprise competitive, because after those two or three years the customs tariffs will be lowered . . . If you do not succeed, you will go bankrupt.

> YURI LUZHKOV, mayor of Moscow, quoted in the *Financial Times,* September 3, 1997

Western programmers can afford to be sloppy because they have so much computer power to work with. Here they had to squeeze the last drop of performance out of every bit and byte of power.

> TONY LOEB of computer firm Sun Microsystems' Moscow office, quoted in *Fortune,* June 10, 1996

This is not the Soviet Union anymore, where we had to pretend that everything Russian was the best.

> OLGA GONCHARIENKO, Russian film student shopping for a Korean television at Moscow's All-Russian Exhibition Center, quoted in *Business Week,* October 7, 1996

I've set the price of bread at 2,000 rubles [37 cents] and prices will go down from there, not up.

> DMITRY AYATSKOV, Yeltsin-backed candidate for governor in Saratov, quoted in the *Wall Street Journal,* September 4, 1997

Most of them [the gubernatorial candidates] aren't reformers. They don't have an ideology; they just want to run things.

> LEONID SMIRNYGEN, Yeltsin aide and strategist for gubernatorial elections, quoted in the *Wall Street Journal,* September 4, 1997

People used to want only to buy things that looked foreign. Now they want Russian.

> SERGEI PLASTININ, a 27-year-old from Wimm-Bill-Dann, Russia's leading manufacturer of fruit juices, quoted in the *Wall Street Journal,* November 29, 1996

The Marlboro Man has nothing to do with Russia. Why should we respond to it?

> Novelist VICTOR PELEVIN, on why Russian advertising should draw on Russian imagery, rather than imitate Western ads, quoted in *Business Week,* January 27, 1997

We have been able to achieve the almost-impossible in Russia: offer first-class service.

> ALEXANDER PLESHAKOV, president of start-up airline Transaero, quoted in *Business Week,* October 10, 1994

We refuse to hire anyone who has had more than five minutes' work experience with Aeroflot.

> SERGEY GRACHEV, marketing director of Transaero, quoted in *Business Week,* October 10, 1994

The new Boris Yeltsin has decided that November 7 will be a day of reconciliation whether the people like it or not.

> ANDREA BOWERS, radio commentator, on Yeltsin's first official act after heart surgery—changing a national holiday from a celebration of the anniversary of the Bolshevik Revolution to a day of reconciliation, heard on National Public Radio, November 10, 1996

When we went to audition children, 90 percent of them sat back in their chairs and started to sing very sad songs. It was astonishing to see. But joy did not come easily to them. In fact, obedience, solemnity, and duty seemed to be all they knew.

> NATASHA LANCE ROGOFF, executive producer and series director of *Ulitsa Sesam,* the Russian version of *Sesame Street,* quoted in the *New York Times,* October 22, 1996

We cannot be enthused about Russia. The laws change almost daily, which makes doing business impossible.

> Member of the Japan-Russia Economic Committee of Keidanren, a powerful association of leading businesses, quoted in *Asia, Inc.,* January 1993

Communism may have been defeated, but the Communists often have not been.

> LADY MARGARET THATCHER, former prime minister of England, quoted in *Fortune,* October 18, 1993

You shouldn't mix up the long-term business opportunities with the occasional shoot-out. These things will happen.

> PERCY BARNEVIK, CEO of the Swedish-Swiss industrial firm ABB (Asea Brown Boveri), reacting to a coup attempt against the administration of Boris Yeltsin, quoted in *Fortune,* November 1, 1993

Every company has talked to the majors there [Russia] and gone away shaking their heads. The [Russian] management tends to be very arrogant. There are manufacturing skills but there is no sense of marketing, and they have grossly inflated ideas of what their franchise is worth.

> KEITH CRANE of PlanEcon, a research company specializing in Eastern Europe, quoted in the *Wall Street Journal,* February 6, 1996

You're always operating in two worlds here. There is the real world of the consumer, that can take much more than you publish, and there is the Soviet world of the bureaucrat, with old values and ideas.

> DERK SAUER, publisher of *Playboy* (Russian-language edition), quoted in the *Wall Street Journal,* February 15, 1996

Most companies have factored political risk into their investments here. They invest gradually and they've built in a way in their deals to get out.

> Western corporate attorney, quoted in the *Wall Street Journal,* February 21, 1996

We have a base of Russian employees and Westerners with experience here. The infrastructure has been built. We don't just want to abandon that.

> EVIND DJUPEDAL, head of Moscow office of the farm commodities company Cargill Enterprises and chief of the local American Chamber of Commerce, quoted in the *Wall Street Journal,* February 21, 1996

Change is embedded in the psychology of the people.

> MARK MOBIUS, emerging-markets guru for the mutual fund company Franklin Templeton, quoted in *Business Week,* September 11, 1995

The government can't regulate more transparency among companies, we can only stimulate them to do audits, protect shareholders' rights. If the companies don't accept the rules of the market, they won't attract investment.

We need to become more like every place else, where it's more lucrative to put money into stocks than bonds.

> VLADIMIR POTANIN, first deputy prime minister for economic policy, quoted in the *Wall Street Journal,* October 3, 1996

It's rigged.

> JIM BUNCH, energy analyst at Renaissance Capital, on plans to tender a 33 percent stake in oil giant AO Yukos, quoted by Dow Jones, November 20, 1996

This has been a speculative market since day one. But now you can actually say these securities have a fundamental value.

> BILL BROWDER of Russian private-equity fund Hermitage Capital Management, in the wake of

consistently low inflation and lower bond yields, quoted in the *Wall Street Journal,* November 22, 1996

There's simply not enough for us to invest in. The risk grows greater as you move down to the second and third tier, but we have no choice.

> MARK MOBIUS, emerging-markets guru for the mutual fund company Franklin Templeton, quoted in the *Wall Street Journal,* November 22, 1996

It's like climbing the Himalayas. You go up and if you're lucky, you can come down.

> JOSEPH ABROMOVICH BAKELEYNIK, Russian-born Harvard MBA, trying to save a decrepit tractor plant in Russia, quoted in *Business Week,* May 2, 1994

Russia is in the process of becoming one of the great markets and economies of the world. Established companies can't afford to stay away.

> DAVID MULFORD, chairman of the investment bank Credit Suisse First Boston Europe, quoted in the *Wall Street Journal,* February 28, 1997

The government is laying down clear and equal rules of behavior. We will ensure that these rules are followed by everyone.

> PRESIDENT BORIS YELTSIN, in a speech, quoted in the *Financial Times,* September 25, 1997

Russia is a different story from other emerging markets. It has several companies worth several billion dollars, and in two or three years it will have a significant number of companies on the New York Stock Exchange.

> DANIELLE DOWNING of the investment bank Salomon Brothers, *Wall Street Journal,* February 28, 1997

What's important to know is who really owns the stock and whether they are on your side. If you're fighting against the side of management, you're probably going to lose.

> Anonymous American fund manager, reflecting the recognition that management of private oil companies made money by milking profits at the expense of ordinary shareholders, quoted in the *New York Times,* October 5, 1997

This is not going to turn into a conventional, cozy little democracy overnight.

> MARK COOKE of the investment firm Brunswick Capital Management, Moscow, quoted in the *New York Times*, October 5, 1997

They [the Russian military] would like to undo everything and reprivatize so they can get a piece for themselves.

> CHARLIE RYAN, investment banker at Moscow's United Financial Group, quoted in *Business Week*, March 4, 1996

[A]fter 1,000 years of Russian history, in which society was founded on the principle of privilege for the chosen few, privatization was never designed to be fair.

> ALLESSANDRA STANLEY, *New York Times*, August 1, 1997

Honest rules of the game presuppose that the seller and the buyer should not be in collusion.

> VLADIMIR GUSINSKY, banking and media tycoon, who lost a bid for a telecommunications company to a consortium that included George Soros, quoted in the *New York Times*, August 16, 1997

There is money and there is money. As far as I am concerned, money has a smell.

> VLADIMIR GUSINSKY, banking and media tycoon, quoted in the *New York Times*, August 16, 1997

This attempt at consumer protection makes the California lemon law look good.

> MARK THIMMING, manager of Trinity Motors, GM dealership in Moscow, reacting to Russian government attempts to regulate the car market, quoted in the *Wall Street Journal*, June 25, 1994

There is no use in killing me, because then who would service you?

> MARK THIMMING, manager of Trinity Motors, GM dealership in Moscow, responding to a show of arms by Russian gangsters who wanted quick service for their cars, quoted in the *Wall Street Journal*, June 25, 1994

You may well find yourselves victims of extortion or that your bank or joint venture is being used for laundering by criminal organizations.

> RICHARD FENNING, of the security firm Control Risk Group, U.K., quoted in the *Financial Times*, February 17, 1997

Government is government. You have to know how to get into the system and work within the system. You've got to get to the guy who makes the decision.

> JOHN ALLEN, generic drug entrepreneur in former USSR, quoted in the *Wall Street Journal*, January 12, 1996

[My relatives and friends] don't even understand that there are restaurants in Moscow. They can't understand that there's a market for that.

> DOMINIQUE BERHOUET, American who has opened eight Moscow restaurants in six years, quoted in the *Wall Street Journal*, October 26, 1996

I truly believe that Russian women became better after *Cosmo*. At least they became more product-conscious.

> ANNEMARIE VAN GAAL, cofounder of Independent Media (which launched Russian editions of *Cosmopolitan*, *Harper's Bazaar*, and *Good Housekeeping*, in partnership with Hearst), quoted in the *Wall Street Journal*, November 11, 1996

We had to write that the labor of a milkmaid is wonderful. We fought for the right for women to drive tractors. Who needs this? We've found out, and our readers have found out, what magazines of good quality are.

> ANASTASIYA KUPRIYANOVA, editor of *Krestyanka* (*Woman Peasant*), which in the face of Western competition now includes articles on sex, domestic violence, and abortion, quoted in the *Wall Street Journal*, November 11, 1996

Russia is one-seventh of the ground on this earth. You could decide not to go to Bolivia, but you can't decide not to go to Russia.

> DOMINIQUE MENU, head representative in Moscow for Banque National, quoted in the *New York Times*, November 21, 1993

[Russia is] the most exciting, biggest potential play in the world. It's crazy.

> BARTON BIGGS of the investment bank Morgan Stanley, quoted in the *Financial Times*, February 19, 1997

In the past, they [the Russian government] would get themselves through the crisis and then relax. This government will not have that opportunity.

> VLADIMIR POTANIN, one of Russia's wealthiest businessmen, on the necessity for sustained economic reform in wake of new crisis, quoted in the *Wall Street Journal*, June 5, 1998

I apply a simple test. When I greet a group of entrepreneurs, I hail them, "Hello, crooks!" If they take it O.K., then they are not hopeless. If they beat their breasts and deny it, then they are incorrigible.

ALEKSANDR I. LEBED, retired general, former chief of security, and presidential candidate, during visit to New York to talk to financiers (after attending Clinton's second inaugural), quoted in the *New York Times*, January 23, 1997

He who doesn't take risks, doesn't drink champagne.

ALEKSANDR I. LEBED, retired general, former chief of security, and presidential candidate, on investing in Russia, quoted in the *New York Times*, January 23, 1997

The highest skyscraper in the world cannot be built next to the Kremlin. We cannot allow anyone spitting from the roof of the skyscraper on the Kremlin.

ALEKSANDR I. LEBED, reacting to Donald Trump's expressed desire to build "something major" in Moscow or perhaps expressing his ideas about the primacy of the state over the private sector in Russia, quoted in the *New York Times*, January 23, 1997

We don't expect to make any money before the next century, but patience is the key.

GEORGE DAVID, president of the aerospace and manufacturing firm United Technologies, quoted in *Fortune*, January 24, 1994

We can't wait for the region to stabilize. We want to create a home market there now.

PERCY BARNEVIK, CEO of the Swedish-Swiss industrial firm ABB (Asea Brown Boveri), quoted in *Fortune*, May 16, 1994

Even after all the liberalization of the last years, it is not money that gives real power but the army, the police, and the secret service.

PAVEL FELGENHAUER, defense analyst for the newspaper *Segodnaya*, quoted in the *Wall Street Journal*, June 4, 1996

You've destroyed how the old economy functioned, and the new one isn't developed yet. So you're left with high taxes, a weak banking system, and high inflation.

MISHA BELKINDAS, economist and adviser to the World Bank, quoted in the *Wall Street Journal*, June 13, 1996

If you want to see where the Russian money is, go to New York, London, or Paris.

Spokesman for the Central Bank of Cyprus, quoted in the *Wall Street Journal*, May 7, 1996

If Russian authorities try to stop business here [Cyprus], the money will flow in one direction only: out of the country. And it won't come back. A lot of money that is raised here is being reinvested in Russia.

SPYROS STAVRINAKIS, an expert on foreign bank supervision at the Central Bank of Cyprus (Cypriot banks are thought to be used for laundering Russian money), quoted in the *Wall Street Journal*, May 7, 1996

A lot of us who are involved deeply with the language and all sorts of things have become relaxed. Be very careful. This is not a game.

RICHARD DANN OPPFELT, trader in Russia, after two Russian counterintelligence agents interviewed him, showing him a video of a North Korean being beaten, quoted in the *Wall Street Journal*, May 15, 1996

Two hunters hire a rickety plane to go hunting bear. The pilot reminds them that the plane can only carry two passengers and one bear. The hunters . . . return with two bears. The pilot protests that the second huge carcass will overload the plane. The hunters say: "That's what you told us last year, and we gave you an extra 100 rubles and you let us load the bear. So here is another 100 rubles' bribe."
 . . . The plane crashes. . . . The hunters . . . ask the . . . pilot, "Where are we?" The pilot . . . replies, "Same place we crashed last year."

Joke told to William Safire by democratic reform leader Gregory Yavlinsky, *New York Times*, February 6, 1997

To sell oil abroad is simple. You bribe someone in government. But to produce and manufacture something—that takes a lot of talent and hard work.

ALEXANDER S. PONIKIN, president of a Moscow-based textile company, quoted in *Business Week*, October 10, 1994

If you have not drunk with a Russian oil and gas man a couple of times, he doesn't know you.

ALEXANDER BLOKHIN of the investment firm United Financial Group, quoted in *Business Week*, February 24, 1997

It's bad enough trying to do business with scientists, but doing business with Russian scientists—that's really something.

> DAVID MUENZER, American businessman in Moscow, after spending hours negotiating with a Russian scientist for rights to a piece of lab equipment with a 50-50 profit split, only to have him back out at the last minute after his demand for $120,000 up front was denied, quoted in *New York,* August 2, 1993

Distrustful of the ruble, Russians hold about $30 billion in cash, much of it under their beds. That constitutes an interest-free loan to the American government far exceeding the value of recent Western loans to Russia, and all Western investment there too.

> *The Economist,* March 22, 1997

Twenty-six tax collectors were killed in Russia last year and 74 were injured in the course of their work; 6 were kidnapped, 41 had their homes burnt down.

> *The Economist,* May 31, 1997

Much of what we took for granted in our free-market system and assumed to be human nature was not nature at all, but culture. The dismantling of the central planning function in an economy does not, as some had supposed, automatically establish a free-market entrepreneurial system.

Certainly, if generations of Russians have been brought up on the Marxist notion that private property is "theft," a breakdown of the Soviet central-planning infrastructure is not going to automatically alter the perceived moral base of its social system.

> ALAN S. GREENSPAN, Federal Reserve chairman, in a speech, June 10, 1997, quoted in the *Wall Street Journal,* June 11, 1997

We have reached the point when it is possible for production to go up. The decline has been stopped.

> BORIS YELTSIN, one year after his reelection as president of Russia, quoted in the *Financial Times,* July 4, 1997

We steal a lot of things from Southeast Asia because in many Asian countries people are easier to bribe.

> Former Soviet KGB Colonel KONSTANTIN PREOBRAZHENSKY, turned freelance intelligence adviser, quoted in *Asia, Inc.,* March 1997

On presenting a suitcase full of used $100 bills to your favorite government official, it is always best to say:

"Here you are, old man. You left this at my office the other day. Thought I'd take the opportunity to return it."

> CHARLES DUBOW, *Forbes FYI,* Fall 1997

At present, the fuel and energy complex is holding the Russian economy together. The question is how long it can go on without investment.

> VICTOR ORLOV, Minister for Natural Resources, quoted in the *New York Times,* September 5, 1997

We used to think that you couldn't do business here like you do in the West. Then it dawned on us that if the laws of physics apply here, the laws of the market must, too.

> MIKHAIL LUBOVICH, 34-year-old chief executive of food company ZAO Soyuzcontract, on the firm's decision to recruit professional management instead of relying on cronies, quoted in the *Wall Street Journal,* September 15, 1997

All successful Russian companies are facing these questions right now. They've accumulated their capital, and now they can't manage what they've built.

> MARINA SHAKALOVA of Management Training International, Moscow, quoted in the *Wall Street Journal,* September 15, 1997

As people understand they need access to capital for a long time to come, the law of the jungle will give way to the conventions of the international marketplace.

> LEONID ROZHETSKIN of the investment bank Renaissance Capital Group, Moscow, quoted in the *New York Times,* September 16, 1997

There's no question that as a whole, the Russian banking system is insolvent.

> Foreign banker in Moscow, quoted in the *Wall Street Journal,* July 12, 1996

The Russians now realize keeping influence by military means is the least desirable option. Body bags don't look too good. They would prefer economics.

> European banker in Central Asia, quoted in the *Wall Street Journal,* October 22, 1997

Conflict resolution must be job one for U.S. policy in the region. It is both the prerequisite for and an accompaniment to energy development.

> STROBE TALBOTT, U.S. Deputy Secretary of State, quoted in the *Wall Street Journal,* October 22, 1997

What do you [Russians] like about Americans?

Optimism	24%
Social mobility	20%
Energy	16%
Easygoing attitude	9%
Sense of purpose	8%
Patriotism	6%

What do you dislike about Americans?

Excessive pragmatism	33%
Nationalistic arrogance	26%
Narrow-mindedness	19%
Consumerism	10%
Aggressiveness	5%

> Center for International Sociological Research, Moscow, cited in the *Economist,* March 22, 1997

24.2.15 Serbia

Sanctions turned a lot of people here into monopolists. And now they are dead set against reform.

> JURIJ BAJEC, a Slovenian economist who advises the government and central bank in Belgrade, quoted in the *Wall Street Journal,* February 6, 1996

24.2.16 Siberia

We tell them the airport is closed.

> Politician in Vladivostok, on tactics Siberians take to avoid official visits from Moscow, quoted in the *Economist,* November 21, 1992

Some of the most significant entities in the Russian economy today were born of criminal origins. We constantly observe the process by which individuals and businesses, which three or four years ago would by most international standards be regarded as criminal or semicriminal, are transforming themselves, often with the assistance of public relations specialists, into paragons of civilized corporate and individual citizenry.

> RICHARD PRIOR of the security firm Kroll Associates, quoted in the *Financial Times,* April 14, 1997

24.2.17 Ukraine

And may God bless privatization in Ukraine.

> Head of Lvov municipal privatization body as closing hammer fell on auction of state-owned enterprises, quoted in the *Economist,* February 27, 1993

Ukraine has entered a qualitatively new phase, which is unprecedented in economic history. I call it hyper-depression.

> DANIEL KAUFMANN, head of World Bank mission to Ukraine, quoted in *Fortune,* October 4, 1993

There is a special mentality here conditioned by Soviet military traditions that makes selling this place to potential foreign investors a hard task.

> ENZO DAMIANI of the European Union's office in Sevastopol, Ukraine, quoted in the *Wall Street Journal,* June 3, 1996

Smaller companies get kicked around like a football until they go away. Unless you are very strong and have lobbying power, you're dead here.

> KLAUS RIFFART of the chemical company Monsanto, quoted in the European edition of the *Wall Street Journal,* November 11, 1996

I can understand competition with other firms. What I can't understand is competing with a government body that is supposed to be regulating you.

> GEORGE PUZIAK, who represented Andrew Communications in Ukraine, quoted in the European edition of the *Wall Street Journal,* November 11, 1996

Many of the people who built the precious [Communist] system remain in the establishment. We have to remake their mentality.

> UKRAINIAN PRESIDENT LEONID KUCHMA, on the reason bureaucratic roadblocks to doing business still exist, quoted in the *Wall Street Journal,* November 4, 1996

Ukraine may be the one country in the world where lower tax rates really would produce more revenue.

> JEFFREY SACHS, director of the Harvard Institute for International Development, quoted in the *New York Times,* November 14, 1996

Shrinkage begets shrinkage, as an ever-smaller tax base is weighed down by the nation's heavy social obligations. Budget deficits make it increasingly difficult to contain inflation. Today, there is just one worker in the official economy to support each pensioner, and payroll taxes—by no means the only tax on enterprises—run an incredible 52 percent.

> PETER PASSELL, *New York Times,* November 14, 1996

I want a real owner in every enterprise. Unfortunately there are no domestic owners who can turn these companies around. The only way out is to create attractive conditions for big Western companies.

> PRIME MINISTER PAVLO LAZARENKO, quoted in *Financial Times,* March 13, 1997

It's criminal what the Ukrainian government is doing to some investors. It's outright theft.

> JOSEPH LEMIRE, Louisiana banker, who had been menaced by gunmen and had bodyguards assigned to him by the U.S. Embassy, quoted in the *Wall Street Journal,* April 23, 1997

24.2.18 Uzbekistan

If the country had an open currency system the foreign capital would be flowing in. But if you have an open exchange market you have to let the people buy whatever they want. [Uzbek officials] have an aversion to the market. They want to interfere with people's choice.

> Western economist, quoted in the *Financial Times,* January 15, 1997

We could have been idealistic and defended our currency, or we could have been pragmatic and defended our industry.

> DR. RUSTAM AZIMOV, chairman of the National Bank of Uzbekistan, on inflationary monetary policy in defiance of the International Monetary Fund, quoted in the *Financial Times,* February 25, 1997

If they want to shrink the money supply, they have to sell something, but it's easier for them to sell dollars than treasury bills.

> Unnamed economist, quoted in the *Financial Times,* February 25, 1997

25.1 BUSINESS LANGUAGE

[Foreigners] Be specific in communications with Americans. Be clear about what you request, and supply all the information that they may need to make a decision.

Americans should be careful in their written and spoken communications with foreigners, especially those whose first language is not English. Keep sentences and terminology simple. In conversations, speak slowly, enunciate carefully, and avoid slang expressions.

> DAVID L. JAMES, *The Executive Guide to Asia-Pacific Communications* (Kodansha, 1995)

25.2 CAPITAL FLOWS

By facilitating the flow of savings to their most productive uses, capital movements increase investment, growth, and prosperity.

> International Monetary Fund ministerial committee report urging executive directors to amend articles of agreement to promote capital liberalization, quoted in the *Financial Times*, September 22, 1997

Now trade is more free and the playing field is more level. Unfortunately, it is not perfectly level. Today's contestants are not of the same class, and free trade is not yet fair trade.

Those who think that manipulated currency devaluations are normal have obviously never run countries, never understood the meaning of poverty, never appreciated the desires of poor countries and poor people to rise above their miserable conditions. All they can see is the money they can make for themselves. That the poor have to pay the price is irrelevant. These manipulators have no conscience.

We welcome foreign investments. We even welcome speculators. But we don't have to welcome share- and financial market manipulators. We need these manipulators as much as travelers in the old days needed highwaymen.

> MAHATHIR BIN MOHAMAD, prime minister of Malaysia, *Wall Street Journal*, September 23, 1997

Even speculators have a role to play, providing they play by the rules.

> *Wall Street Journal*, editorial, September 23, 1997

[F]inancial capital is better situated in the global system than industrial capital; once a plant has been built, moving it is difficult.

> GEORGE SOROS, founder of the Quantum Fund, *Atlantic Monthly*, January 1998

25.3 COMPETITIVENESS

Whenever there is an open competition [for a large construction contract] overseas, an American firm tends to win.

> JOSEPH JACOBS, founder of Jacobs Engineering, quoted in the *Economist*, January 18, 1992

From a standing start, the Europeans are now running neck-and-neck with the Japanese [for Asian infrastructure contracting]. And they're gaining on the Americans.

> Hong Kong–based project financier, quoted in the *Wall Street Journal*, October 2, 1997

I've always been a 100-yen man.

> THOMAS C. GRAHAM, president of U.S. Steel, who wanted a weak dollar to help exports, quoted in *Business Week*, August 22, 1994

[W]hile we may need a balanced budget to discipline our politicians, what we need for export growth is a balanced economy.

> C. MICHAEL ARMSTRONG, CEO of Hughes Electronics, in a speech, May 9, 1995

It's a war here, and we love a war. We're not defenders, we're predators.

> DAVID HANCOCK, president of the Japanese electronics firm Hitachi's U.S. PC unit, quoted in the *Wall Street Journal*, June 5, 1996

People in the United States get very excited that RCA developed the transistor but the commercialization really occurred in Japan. But if we're not smart enough to commercialize it, that's not their problem. That's our problem. You win by moving quicker than your competition, not by trying to build walls.

> PHILIP CONDIT, CEO of the aerospace firm Boeing, interviewed in the *Financial Times,* March 12, 1997

Historically, some countries closed their borders, developed national economies, and then decided to liberalize when a certain style of development was reached. The question is whether those historical precedents are applicable in today's environment.

> DONALD JOHNSON, Secretary General of the Organization for Economic Cooperation and Development (OECD), quoted in *Asia, Inc.,* May 1997

Planting flags around the world, like the British Empire, is not a strategy for success when cost structures, manufacturing systems, and product development effectiveness won't be any better in overseas markets than they are at home. The same competitive problems that beset U.S. companies here will do so in [countries such as] China, Thailand, or Brazil, among others, that every company has targeted [for overseas investment].

> MARYANN N. KELLER of the investment firm Furman Selz, in a speech, April 2, 1997

When foreign airlines lower prices, you have to keep up with them in order to compete. Otherwise, you may find that nobody is on your plane when it's ready to take off.

> MASATO MATSUYAMA of All Nippon Airways after air-fare regulations were relaxed, quoted in the *New York Times,* September 16, 1997

Every country that has caught up has done it by copying.

> PROFESSOR LESTER C. THUROW of the Sloan School of Management at MIT, *Harvard Business Review,* September–October 1997

You have to accept that we are all sinners now.

> Leading tax regulator on OECD task force to curb tax competition between countries, quoted in the *Financial Times,* January 13, 1997

What has happened is that all of the non-tax controls—such as exchange controls—have been removed over time.

> JEFFREY OWEN, head of fiscal affairs at OECD, quoted in the *Financial Times,* January 13, 1997

The events we see rushing toward us make the rough, tumultuous eighties look like a decade at the beach. Ahead of us are Darwinian shakeouts in every major marketplace, with no consolation prizes for the losing companies and nations.

> JOHN F. WELCH JR., CEO of GE, speaking at company's 1989 annual meeting, quoted in "The Return of Karl Marx," *New Yorker,* October 20 & 27, 1997

If there were no overcapacity, we would have less exciting capitalism.

> YASUNO KRIHARA, executive at Sony, quoted in William Greider, *One World, Ready or Not: The Manic Logic of Global Capitalism* (Simon & Schuster, 1997)

Don't get me wrong. I believe in competition, but when you get too much of it and it's just a matter of price, price, price, it's very difficult to keep yourself afloat. For those whose jobs are destroyed in the process, they aren't ever going to get them back. You can't become so efficient that all this stuff is made without any labor content. Because then you have nobody with the money to buy anything.

> PETER SCHAVOR of IBM, quoted in William Greider, *One World, Ready or Not: The Manic Logic of Global Capitalism* (Simon & Schuster, 1997)

25.4 CORPORATIONS AND NATIONAL SOVEREIGNTY

Corporations are frequently more powerful than countries. Indeed, these days, so are some individuals. We live in a capitalistic age. It is not a negative concept that someone's wealth is greater than the GDP of some countries.

Are we above governments? No. We answer to governments. We obey laws in every country in which we operate. However, we do change relations between countries. We function as a lubricant for worldwide economic integration.

> MARC FABER, Hong Kong investment expert, quoted in *Asia, Inc. Online,* 1995

We make visible the invisible hand of global competition.

> PERCY BARNEVIK, CEO of the Swedish-Swiss industrial firm ABB (Asea Brown Boveri)

Fifteen years ago, Asea was a Swedish electrical company with 95 percent of its engineers in Sweden. We could complain about high taxes, about how the high cost of living made it difficult to recruit Germans or Americans to come to Sweden. But what could Asea do about it? Not much. Today I can tell the Swedish authorities that they must create a more competitive environment for R&D or our research there will decline.

> PERCY BARNEVIK, CEO of the Swedish-Swiss industrial firm ABB, quoted in Rosabeth Moss Kanter, *World Class: Thriving Locally in the Global Economy* (Simon & Schuster, 1995)

Region-states are economic units, not political ones, and they are anything but local in focus. . . . their primary linkage is with the global economy.

> KENICHI OHMAE, "Putting Global Logic First," *Harvard Business Review,* January–February 1995

Governments, even when they work together, have already lost control of the finance of the world. Just as wealth is swinging to Asia, capital is swinging away from national jurisdictions. We have assumed since the late nineteenth century that capital was taxable—using funds for the benefit of society. Broadly speaking, that link seems to have been broken.

> WILLIAM REES-MOGG, British member of Parliament and former journalist, quoted in *Asia, Inc. Online,* 1995

In the 1990s, the vast pools of national telecommunications traffic, once a country's patrimony as much as its forests or its mines, have become the subject of fierce multinational bidding.

> GREGORY C. STAPLE, head of the consulting firm TeleGeography Inc., *Business Week,* September 26, 1994

We focus our development on the more well-developed economies—those that are growing and those that are large—and the risks involved in being adventuresome are probably getting too great.

> JAMES CANTALUPO, president of McDonald's International, explaining why countries that have McDonald's have never gone to war against each other, quoted in the *New York Times,* December 8, 1996

I feel these countries want McDonald's as a symbol of something—an economic maturity and that they are open to foreign investments. I don't think there is a country out there we haven't gotten inquiries from. I have a parade of ambassadors and trade representatives in here regularly to tell us about their country and why McDonald's would be good for the country.

> JAMES CANTALUPO, president of McDonald's International, quoted in the *New York Times,* December 8, 1996

Even when people accept, and sometimes prefer, foreign products (why else would McDonald's be one of the best-known American brands worldwide?), they support local sovereignty. The French go wild for American movies but support legislation banning English from billboards.

> *Strategy&Business,* fourth quarter, 1995

Horror stories abound about companies that thought the world had become so homogenized that they could sell standardized products the same way everywhere. But the French don't drink orange juice for breakfast. Middle Easterners prefer toothpaste that tastes spicy. Japanese like herbs in their medicines. And some Mexicans use laundry detergents to wash dishes.

> GEORGE V. GRUNE, CEO of the Readers Digest Association, Inc., in a speech, May 20, 1989

You cannot dig up your infrastructure and take it away if the government decides to nationalize it.

> Official at World Trade Organization talks on telecommunications, quoted in the *Financial Times,* February 18, 1997

25.5 ECONOMIC POLICY

[D]estabilizing influences more often flow from the macro-economy—especially policy—to the financial sector. It is unusual for markets to develop a crisis out of a clear blue economic sky.

> EDDIE GEORGE, governor of the Bank of England, quoted in the *Financial Times,* September 1, 1997

25.6 EMERGING MARKETS INVESTMENT

What are the emerging markets?

They are places where financial institutions and multinational companies see profitable opportunities for investment or speculation in what used to be called the Third World.

> FT Guide to Emerging Markets, *Financial Times,* September 8, 1997

It's important to follow the political situation as well as companies. You have to pay very close attention to political risk.

> JOSEPHINE JIMENEZ of the $1.1 billion Montgomery Emerging Markets Fund, quoted in *Business Week,* September 11, 1995

[O]ne of the lessons people learned in the past 12 months is that all emerging markets are not equal.

> PAUL DURHAM of Bankers Trust, Sydney, quoted in *Business Week,* September 11, 1995

Building a good business in a Third World, developing country—there is no training for that.

> BRIAN L. BOWEN, an accountant and founder of a cellular-phone company in the early 1990s in Uzbekistan, quoted in the *Wall Street Journal,* June 21, 1996

In most places, I'm the first investment person the country has seen.

> MILES MORLAND of the London investment firm Blankeney Management, quoted in the *Wall Street Journal,* November 13, 1996

They say, "This is no business of yours," and throw you out in five minutes.

> MILES MORLAND of the London investment firm Blankeney Management, on what happens when you question businesspeople in developing countries too closely about their numbers, quoted in the *Wall Street Journal,* November 13, 1996

There's a limited number of sneaker makers that the world needs.

> JOYCE CORNELL of mutual fund group Scudder Stevens & Clark, on her reluctance to invest in India and China because of their low literacy rates, quoted in the *Wall Street Journal,* in November 13, 1996

I tried to talk to a [U.S.] pension-fund consultant about Turkey, and his reaction was, "Isn't this the place where they just nominated a Communist for president?" [Actually, it was a Muslim president.]

> KRISTINE LINO of Pangora Asset Management, quoted in the *Wall Street Journal,* December 4, 1996

A survey of local entrepreneurs in 69 countries shows that many states are performing their core functions poorly: they are failing to ensure law and order, protect property, and apply rules and policies predictably. Investors do not consider such states credible, and growth and investment suffer as a consequence.

> Summary of a World Bank Study, World Development Report 1997, "The State in a Changing World."

I am a little worried about such ardor and appetite for putting money in some of those countries. I am not always sure that due diligence and conditionality are up to the intensity of the appetite.

> JACQUES DE LAROSIÈRE, president of European Bank for Reconstruction and Development, quoted in the *Financial Times Weekend,* May 24–25, 1997

There are enough problems in these markets without changing the rules of the game. There are lots of other equity markets around the world to invest in.

> PETER CHURCHOUSE of Morgan Stanley in Hong Kong, on new rules created in the wake of a Malaysian currency crisis, *Wall Street Journal,* August 29, 1997

We need to find a way for investors to take a haircut when this kind of thing happens.

> ROBERT RUBIN, U.S. Treasury Secretary, on the moral hazard of creating bailout funds for Asian markets, quoted in the *New York Times,* September 28, 1997

With the exception of some bankers from Houston, I never hear from anyone who wants to sacrifice taxpayer dollars to go over there [Asia] to bail someone out.

> U.S. REPRESENTATIVE RON PAUL (Republican, Texas), quoted in the *New York Times,* December 4, 1997

25.7 EMPLOYMENT

Despite layoffs and downsizing by big corporations and government, a substantial group of workers hold stable jobs. What seems like higher instability may actually reflect the greater number of jobs that younger workers must hold before finding a permanent one.

> EDDY LEE, chief author of an International Labor Organization report that said 30 percent of the global workforce of roughly 1 billion was either unemployed or underemployed, quoted in the *Wall Street Journal,* November 26, 1996

Travel and tourism will account for 262 million jobs worldwide, 10.5 percent of the total in 1997, says the WTTC [World Travel and Tourism Council]. It projects potential growth of 46.4 percent to 383 million jobs, 10.8 percent of the total, by 2006, if suitable policies are put into place.

> *Financial Times,* January 20, 1997

25.8 FINANCIAL MARKETS RULE

Any country that wishes to have a major international financial center simply cannot impose restraints on international transactions through taxation or the equivalent.

> ALAN S. GREENSPAN, chairman of the U.S. Federal Reserve, in a speech, October 14, 1992

If you impose a strict regime in a free market, other centers that aren't so inhibited will draw away business.

> Senior banker, London, quoted in *Business Week,* August 11, 1997

The very sovereignty of nation-states is being defeated.

> DAVID C. ROCHE, London-based economist, quoted in *Business Week,* November 18, 1994

Who says you have to be elected to influence policy? The market is saying to policy makers, "We're your watchdog."

> NICHOLAS P. SARGEN, managing director of Global Advisors, *Business Week,* November 18, 1994

We are opposed to the issuing of interest-bearing bonds of the United States in time of peace.

> Plank in the 1906 Democratic Party national platform, which also called for the inflationary free coinage of silver

If I'm ever reincarnated, I want to come back as the bond market. Then everybody will be afraid of me and have to do what I say.

> JAMES CARVILLE, adviser to Bill Clinton in 1992, on influence of financial markets over public policy

. . . Lionel, the golden straitjacket comes in only one size, and you're too fat. [The golden straitjacket is a metaphor for policy constraints imposed by the financial markets.]

> THOMAS L. FRIEDMAN, writing to the newly elected French Prime Minister Lionel Jospin in the voice

of Bill Clinton and Tony Blair, the *New York Times,* June 5, 1997

Tell your President he will fall off the list if tax reform doesn't pass.

> JOYCE CORNELL, fund manager for mutual fund company Scudder Stevens & Clark, to Philippine official, quoted in the *Wall Street Journal,* November 13, 1996

The herd [traders] only recognizes its own rules. But the rules of the herd are pretty consistent—they stipulate what savings rate your country should have, what level of interest rates, what deficit-to-GDP ratio, and what level of current account deficit . . . The herd hates surprises.

> THOMAS L. FRIEDMAN, *New York Times,* September 29, 1997

The markets are proving better at forcing change than the authorities.

> Senior Japanese bank regulator, quoted in the *Wall Street Journal,* April 11, 1997

Whatever their personal characteristics, international financial operators like Mr. [George] Soros are much farther down the road to accountability to their constituents than governments are. They have to be, given the speed with which investors can abandon money managers who don't perform

> HOLMAN W. JENKINS JR., *Wall Street Journal,* September 30, 1997

The best defense against currency speculators is to have your fundamentals right.

> RICHARD HU TSU TAU, finance minister of Singapore, quoted in the *Financial Times,* March 4, 1997

I don't want the markets stopping Emu at the last minute. We are not going to have a St. Bartholomew's Day massacre.

> JEAN-CLAUDE JUNCKER, prime minister of Luxembourg, on possibility of speculative attacks that might threaten European currency union, quoted in the *Financial Times,* May 14, 1997

Eventually measures will have to be taken to control macro traders [hedge-fund proprietary traders], who today almost rule the world.

> BARTON BIGGS, chairman of Morgan Stanley Asset Management, quoted in the *Wall Street Journal,* January 5, 1998

25.9 FOREIGN EXCHANGE

In finance, as in comedy, timing is everything. Once a market has scrapped all of its foreign exchange controls, it will be easy for all comers to trade its currency and spreads will shrink. The trick is to make money while some controls are still in place.

> *The Economist,* July 20, 1996

Each national central bank produces its own brand of money. Each of these national monies serves an identical set of functions—as a medium of payment, a store of value, and a unit of account. Each national money is a differentiated product.

Some central banks have changed the brand name of their own product to "dollar" to increase its attractiveness; this name change is sometimes accompanied by changes in packaging. . . . [notably Australia and Jamaica]. But there is only one U.S. dollar; the other central banks are poaching on the established market position of the U.S. producer.

> PROFESSOR ROBERT Z. ALIBER of University of Chicago, *The International Money Game* (Basic, 1983)

The dollar is like a rubber band. The longer it stretches, the harder it snaps back at you.

> RICHARD O'BRIEN of Amex Bank in London, quoted in *Time,* March 5, 1984

When I'm right, my heart starts pounding . . . when I'm wrong, my stomach hurts.

> DAVID GODWIN, chief currency trader for Union Bank of Switzerland, quoted in *U.S. News & World Report,* October 10, 1988

Traders realize they'll be washed up at 35, and they don't care.

> JAMES HOHORST of Manufacturer's Hanover, quoted in *U.S. News & World Report,* October 10, 1988

If Mickey Mouse were President we'd have a stronger dollar.

> DAVID BUCHEN, foreign exchange trader for Citibank, 1995

We care more about action than words. After all, we don't want to overreact.

> ALI, self-taught 21-year-old street trader of dollars for dinars in Baghdad, who bases his trades on news heard over shortwave radio.

If we hear nothing new on the radio, it means negotiations are stalled, which is negative. The dinar will lose 1 percent against the dollar in 24 hours.

> ABU TAGRID, regarding the state of negotiations on oil-for-food sales pact stalled by Iraqi attacks on Kurds in 1996

[The Treasury Secretary's] airplane, President John F. Kennedy's old Air Force One, is equipped with encrypted communications equipment so the Treasury Chief can order currency interventions—the nuclear strikes of the 1990s—from 30,000 feet.

> *New York Times,* September 22, 1996

Most of the traders I talked to didn't merely distrust Clinton; they hated his guts. A fund manager told me, "I hate the fact that the man is going to socialize the medical establishment, that he lies about everything, and that his wife is so powerful and she is pretty certain to be a lesbian, a lesbian in the White House." He said his clients felt the same way. I asked what made him think Hillary Clinton was a lesbian. "Come on!" he said.

> TED C. FISHMAN, former currency trader, on his adventures among Chicago floor traders, "Our Currency in Cyberspace," *Harper's,* December 1994

Financial traders, as everyone knows, are the world's most carnivorous species. So unlike most people, who must take a break from their working day to ingest a little sustenance, the average trader is perfectly capable of devouring his lunch and his clients simultaneously.

> *The Economist,* in an article about the adoption of lunchtime trading in Tokyo, May 31, 1997

Trade and finance are invoiced in dollars because the United States is the largest exporter and importer. After 1999, the European block will be the largest exporter and importer.

> AVINASH PERSAUD, head of currency research for the banking firm JP Morgan, quoted in the *Financial Times,* September 9, 1997

Fixed exchange rates are a little bit like a coiled spring. Compression makes the volatility greater.

Blaming speculators as a response to financial crisis goes back to the Greeks. It's almost always a wrong response. It's wrong because there are deeper causes to which speculative flows are responding and because measures that follow the blaming of speculators are almost always counter-productive in terms of attracting capital. [This comment was made in response to anti-speculative rhetoric by the prime minister of Malaysia in the wake of a collapse of his currency, for which he blamed George Soros and others.]

> LAWRENCE SUMMERS, U.S. Deputy Treasury Secretary, quoted in the *Financial Times,* September 9, 1997

Interfering with the convertibility of capital at a time like this is a recipe for disaster.

> GEORGE SOROS, quoted in the *Financial Times,* September 22, 1997

To stop it [currency trading] means to turn back on globalization.

> THANONG BIDAYA, Thai finance minister, *Financial Times,* September 22, 1997

I would like to suggest that we do away with currency as a commodity.

> MAHATHIR BIN MOHAMAD, prime minister of Malaysia, *Wall Street Journal,* October 2, 1997

25.10 INFORMATION

The businessman in Portland, Oregon, and the businessman in Portland, Maine, need the same information.

> The late BARNEY KILGORE, managing editor of the *Wall Street Journal,* cited in the *Financial Times,* September 9, 1997

[I]n an age of global capital, we think that a business reader in Boston will have many of the same interests as one in Bonn or Beijing.

> RICHARD LAMBERT, editor of the *Financial Times,* September 9, 1997

25.11 MANAGERS

I have no interest in making managers more "global" than they have to be. We can't have people abdicating their nationalities, saying, "I am no longer German, I am international." The world doesn't work like that. If you are selling products and services in Germany, you better be German!

. . . Global managers have exceptionally open minds. They respect how different countries do things, and they have the imagination to appreciate why they do them that way. But they are also incisive, they push the limits of the culture. Global managers don't passively accept it when someone says, "You can't do that in Italy or Spain because of the unions." or "You can't do that in Japan because of the Ministry of Finance." They sort through the debris of cultural excuses and find opportunities to innovate.

Global managers are made, not born.

> PERCY BARNEVIK, CEO of the Swedish-Swiss industrial firm ABB (Asea Brown Boveri), interviewed in *Harvard Business Review,* March–April, 1991

Managerial basics are the same everywhere, in the West and in the Third World. There is a popular misconception among managers that you need merely to push a powerful brand name with a standard product package and advertising in order to conquer global markets, but actually the key to success is a tremendous amount of local passion for the brand and a feeling of local pride and leadership.

> GURCHARAN DAS of Procter & Gamble, *Harvard Business Review,* March–April 1993

I'm Mexican.

> NENNY KARL-ERIK OLSSON, Swedish-born executive of ABB (who has also "been" Venezuelan, Spanish, and South African) one of 500 corporate "missionaries" charged with spreading the ABB way of doing things in 140 countries, quoted in the *Wall Street Journal,* October 2, 1996

If you're buying, you can get away with operating in your own tongue. If you're selling, it certainly helps to speak the customer's language.

> GEORGE BAIN, principal of London Business School, quoted in *Fortune,* January 24, 1994

Language and social things are different. We try to get people to speak the local language. But we also require operating committees in small countries to speak English.

> Gillette executive, quoted by Rosabeth Moss Kanter, *World Class: Thriving Locally in the Global Economy* (Simon & Schuster, 1995)

U.S. managers seem to have a much more difficult time adapting to new cultures. Two generations of economic dominance, combined with a strong domestic market, have contributed to creating a colonial mentality in many U.S. companies.

> DOUG READY, founder and CEO of the International Consortium for Executive Development Research, quoted in *Fortune,* October 16, 1995

Global business makes sense, but it's much more difficult to do it than talk about it. The American manager prides himself or herself on directness, frankness, being in-your-face, being accountable. But that's almost unique in the world.

> A. PAUL FLASH, managing partner of the recruiting firm Korn/Ferry International, quoted in the *Wall Street Journal,* February 4, 1997

I told people, I'm here to accelerate things. If I spoke German, I would slow things to a crawl.

> JEFFREY G. KATZ, chief executive of SwissAir, where managers converse in Swiss German while executive meetings are held in High German or English. He is one of many executives recruited from U.S. carriers to work at European airlines because of their experience with global competition and cost cutting, quoted in the *New York Times,* June 6, 1997

How does a U.S.-based company judge the performance of foreign operations when those operations report their results in foreign currencies? The answer is: poorly.

> ALBERT C. BERSTICKER, CEO of the chemical company Ferro, in a speech, March 27 1997

Instead of paying your executives so much that they can reproduce their American lifestyles, pay them whatever it will cost for them to be able to live at a level comparable with their peers in the country to which they're moving.

> WILLIAM SHERIDAN, director of International Compensation Services of the National Foreign Trade Council, quoted in *Inc.,* March 1996

Large multinationals do appoint people of varying nationalities to their various international subsidiaries. This can be very effective—not least in developing international experience for high flyers.

But, with few exceptions British companies are managed by British managers, American companies by American managers, etc. There is more talk about the modern Euro-manager than actual examples.

> MILES BROADBENT, head of the recruiting firm Miles Partnership, quoted in the *Financial Times,* March 7, 1997

It really is not uncommon now for a hiring decision to be made in New York for a senior position in Hong Kong and for the successful applicant to be working in London.

> TERRY BENSON, CEO of the recruiting firm Michael Paige, quoted in the *Financial Times Weekend,* March 8–9, 1997

We have 22,000 people in 250 different physical locations. How do you get 22,000 people to face in the same direction at the same time?

> MARTIN SORRELL, CEO of the advertising and public relations conglomerate WPP, quoted in the *Financial Times,* March 14, 1997

Our culture is designed around making a hero out of those who translate ideas from one place to another, who help somebody else. . . . If you find a way to get rid of the hierarchical nonsense and allow ideas to flourish, it doesn't matter if you're in Budapest or Beijing.

There are certain people who are extremely comfortable in global environments—the Dutch, for instance, or the Swedes. Pound for pound, Sweden probably has more good managers than any other country.

> JOHN F. WELCH, CEO of GE, quoted in the *Financial Times,* October 1, 1997

Managing globally from the center involves three kinds of important interaction. First, dealing with the corporate functions such as legal, corporate communications, human resources, and finance. They are generally located on the same site.

Second, there is global research and marketing. The interface between those two is critical in our business, and they are also at the same site.

Third, the links with regional management, and that's just three or four people. For us it's the heads of America, Europe/Middle East, and the rest of the world. We consider each of these managers to be a member of the corporate team and they come in at least four times a year. We also have frequent interaction through telephones and mail.

> FRED HASSAN, CEO of the pharmaceutical firm Pharmacia & Upjohn, quoted in the *Financial Times,* October 22, 1997

It is one thing for a chief executive himself to be a global manager. It is quite another to persuade other executives to think and act globally. At ABB we have about 25,000 managers. But not all of these need to be global managers.

> PERCY BARNEVIK, CEO of the Swedish-Swiss heavy industrial firm ABB (Asea Brown Boveri) and the London-based holding company Investor, quoted in the *Financial Times,* October 8, 1997

25.12 MANUFACTURING

It's necessary to produce a British product for the Britons and a Swedish product for the Swedes.

> ULRICH SCHWEITZER of the German appliance company AEG, quoted in *Business Week,* November 2, 1987

The only worldwide appliances to me are small refrigerators, room air conditioners, and microwave ovens.

> ROGER SCHIPKE of GE, quoted in *Business Week,* November 2, 1987

It took Europe 30 years to catch on to mass production and it took Japan 30 years to make it lean. Our Japanese competitors have now been fooling with flexibility for about 15 years. That should not be taken lightly.

> LEN ALLGAIR of General Motors, quoted in the *Economist,* October 17, 1992

Competitive advantage in manufacturing has shifted across continents, led not so much by low wages and capital investment as by evolving management techniques. It is the way a factory is organized that matters most.

> *The Economist,* December 5, 1992

[G]lobal products are often tacky things built to suit the lowest common denominator.

> *The Economist,* March 30, 1996

Our basic mistake [in U.S. manufacturing] was to entrust the design adaptation of the Golf—you knew it as the Rabbit—to "American" thinking. Too much attention to outward appearances, too little to engineering detail.

We made changes in design, so did they [U.S. managers]. . . . if the parts didn't fit, it was the other person's problem.

> CARL H. HAHN, former CEO of Volkswagen, interviewed in *Harvard Business Review,* July–August 1991

There is a greater risk now when you get a number wrong because the numbers are so big. One simple mistake can have huge consequences.

> NIGEL LITCHFIELD, of the Finnish electronics firm Nokia, quoted in the *Wall Street Journal,* March 12, 1996

[I]f we got a big order in the Middle East, we could choose which plant it was supplied from, or take half from Europe and half from South America, according to our capacity at the time. Plus we get cost advantages by using the same specifications for our various plants, and lower prices by buying components in bigger volumes.

> HANS HEDLUN of the Swedish truck maker Scania, on the advantages of going to a single truck design for all markets outside the United States, quoted in the *Financial Times,* January 6, 1997

Wage costs in the Netherlands are 60 percent higher than in Taiwan but because we should get better productivity in Europe, this will not affect overall costs too much.

> ANTONY LO, CEO of the Taiwan-based bicycle company Giant, quoted in the *Financial Times,* October 24, 1997

25.13 MARKETING

We're formulating [recipes] to their [international consumers'] tastes, which we had not been doing before.

> DAVID W. JOHNSON, CEO of Campbell's Soup, quoted in *Business Week,* January 10, 1994

I do not find foreign countries foreign. We decided not to tailor products to any marketplace but to treat all marketplaces the same.

> ALFRED M. ZEIEN, CEO of the razor-blade company Gillette, quoted in the *New York Times,* January 3, 1994

If you want to take on the world, the world better like your product.

> JOHN WAKELY of Shearson Lehman in London, quoted in the *Wall Street Journal,* November 26, 1996

All our clients want common methodologies in the marketplace. They want a common language to talk to one another.

> MARTIN SORRELL, CEO of the advertising and public relations conglomerate WPP, *Financial Times,* March 14, 1997

The world is going two ways. Technology and business are pushing globalization, but at the same time the world is falling apart into smaller communities.

> RICHARD BLOCK, of the advertising agency J. Walter Thompson, on global companies' need to differentiate products according to local tastes, quoted in the *Financial Times,* October 17, 1997

McDonald's serves wine and salads with its burgers in France. For the Indian market, where beef products are taboo, it created a mutton burger: the Maharajah Mac.

> JOHN WILLMAN, *Financial Times,* October 17, 1997

We're not going to take a 55-year-old Frenchman who's been drinking four glasses of wine and coffee in the afternoon and change his habits. But I can take you to France, with its culture, and show you kids walking down the street with Chicago Bulls jackets on and hats on backwards and Nike shoes and drinking Coca-Cola.

> HENRY A. SCHIMBERG, president of Coca-Cola Enterprises, the domestic bottling company spun off from Coca-Cola in 1986, quoted in the *Wall Street Journal,* October 29, 1997

Gin is young and trendy and exciting, except in the U.K., where it's a stuffy old drink that majors and bishops and retired members of the Tory Party drink. Vodka is the party drink of Europe. Bourbon is sexy and imported—the whiskey of the new generation. Tequila is "let's get pissed." And rum—well, Bacardi is the product of its advertising. Bacardi is escape. In Greece and Italy [Scotch] is a hip drink. [Everywhere else] it's my father's drink.

> GOFF MOORE, Leo Burnett worldwide account director for United Distillers, which makes Johnny Walker Red, discussing the difficulties of creating Europe-wide advertising, quoted in the *New Yorker,* April 28 & May 5, 1997

A Mercedes has enormous cachet in Britain, but in Germany it's a taxi.

> DONALD GUNN, Leo Burnett director of creative resources, quoted in the *New Yorker,* April 28 & May 5, 1997

They say Rolls-Royces are for butchers.

> DAVID TANG, Hong Kong businessman, who owns four Bentleys, quoted in *Asia, Inc.,* April 1997

[I] would hurt for me to drive it into a neighborhood where people were having a hard time.

> Disco singer DONNA SUMMER, on why she wouldn't buy a Rolls-Royce (instead she bought a Range Rover), quoted in the *Economist,* February 29, 1992

25.14 MULTINATIONAL BUSINESS SECURITY

The first thing you should know is that you only fly SwissAir now. Even if a terrorist decides to bomb that airline, which of course is unlikely given their neutrality, he'd have a hard time because of the tight security.

> Business traveler, quoted in the *New York Times,* February 24, 1991

Companies used to buy [kidnapping coverage] only for their most senior people. But as companies are working much more in the third world, in places like Russia and Latin America, virtually all their employees, anywhere in the world are being covered. Family members and even guests of employees are covered.

> MACK F. RICE JR., of the insurance brokers Marsh & McLennan, quoted in the *New York Times,* August 30, 1997

In Mexico, Colombia, and Brazil, they clearly prefer locals. In Europe the kidnappings almost always involve wealthy Europeans. They don't think American executives are big enough fish.

> E. C. (MIKE) ACKERMAN, former CIA operative, founder of international security consultants Ackerman Group, quoted in the *New York Times,* August 30, 1997

The guerrillas run your name through a computer to see what you're worth. And they have pretty good financial data.

> E. C. (MIKE) ACKERMAN, former CIA operative, founder of international security consultants Ackerman Group, quoted in the *New York Times,* November 26, 1997

25.15 STRATEGY

A global strategy means fine-tuning an international division of labor, segmenting work, taking advantage of the wage differentials—the different price sensitivities of products, the different contributions products make to overall profitability, and so on. It doesn't mean diminishing the contributions of German engineering and skill.

> CARL H. HAHN, former CEO of Volkswagen, interviewed in *Harvard Business Review,* July–August 1991

New relationships between local markets will create tremendous growth opportunities—but only if we really understand those local markets. It's important that our operations in London, New York, or Paris become part of the local network. This is called *dochakuika,* or becoming deeply rooted. In London, this means everything from helping fund museums to hiring more Oxford and Cambridge graduates than the British Foreign Office.

> YOSHIHISA TABUCHI, former CEO of the investment firm Nomura Securities, interviewed in *Harvard Business Review,* July–August 1989

According to Norway's Trygve Nordbye, chairman of the International Council for Voluntary Agencies (ICVA), 300 million people are hurt by war, earthquake, or famine each year. The 1996 world budget for emergency relief and rehabilitation is $8 billion.

Western companies dominate the market for supplying goods and services to help the devastated. The United States leads with 18 percent, followed by Italy, 12 percent; Croatia and the U.K., 5 percent each; France and Germany, 4 percent. The strong presence at World-Aid 96 of the Benelux countries and Scandinavia (both 4 percent) shows that they are out to increase their share of the aid business.

> ROBERT LACVILLE, *Weekly Mail & Guardian* (South Africa), October 11, 1996

Sometimes you have to let the enemy in your house.

> COR VAN DER KLUGT, president of the Dutch electronics firm Philips, commenting on his deal to share Philips technology with Sony in return for Sony's adopting a Philips standard, quoted in *Fortune,* August 3, 1983

25.16 THE UNITED STATES AND THE GLOBAL ECONOMY

The best course for our nation is not to curse globalization but to shape it, to make it work for America.

> MADELEINE ALBRIGHT, U.S. secretary of state, quoted in the *Financial Times,* September 19, 1997

It is 27 times harder to cope with an operation in Hong Kong than in Duluth.

> ROBERT TOWNSEND, *Up the Organization* (Knopf, 1970)

I'm not going to rest until we're shipping cars to Japan.

> H. ROSS PEROT, then GM's largest individual shareholder and director, quoted in *Forbes,* July 14, 1986

Most business people abroad are better informed than we are simply because they have always had to deal with offshore issues; "offshore," for them, generally denoting the United States and the dollar. So if you're a business person in the U.K. or Japan or Germany, you start right out understanding issues like exchange rates, currency trading, and the difference in commodities.

Globalization is not without risks. America is a regulated society, at least as far as the financial markets are concerned: exchanges, government reporting requirements, and the like. But other countries don't have the same kinds of requirements that we do. So the flow of money builds and whirls around the world, and the control of that flow diminishes. I have asked several leading bankers, do you know how much currency trading occurs on any given day? Or how much is going from here to there? And the answer is no. Nobody in the world knows.

> DONALD B. MARRON, CEO of the investment firm Paine Webber, in a speech, April 30, 1987

I was appalled by what you could get offshore—the prices, the good quality, the tiny stitches, the beautiful buttonholes . . . I could make any shirt pocket I wanted to.

> LIZ CLAIBORNE, fashion designer, quoted in the *New Yorker,* January 18, 1988

Unfortunately in the game of international economics, there is no independent handicapper. The original handicapper was the United States, and when the United States now comes to ask for an adjustment of the handicap, the rest of the world has become so accustomed to the system that it takes the system for granted and accuses the United States of protectionism, unilateralism, or of being retaliatory or practicing economic imperialism, and the adjustment of the handicap has proven in practice to be very, very difficult.

> CLYDE PRESTOWITZ JR., founder and president of the Economic Strategy Institute and former U.S. trade representative, in a speech, April 27, 1992

In order to profit from technological advancement, firms need CEOs who understand process technologies. Large investments in revolutionary technologies will only be made quickly if the man or woman at the top appreciates those technologies. Yet, American CEOs are much less likely to be technologically aware than those in either Japan or Europe. In those countries 70 percent of CEOs have technical backgrounds; in the United States, 30 percent do.

> LESTER C. THUROW, then dean of the Sloan School of Management at MIT, "The New Economics of High-Technology," *Harper's,* March 1992

The car industry used to be a Western Hemisphere business and it's becoming an Eastern Hemisphere business and we don't understand that. It's not going to be answerable to our wonderful Western economic philosophy.

> MARYANN KELLER of the investment firm Furman Selz, quoted in William Greider, *One World, Ready or Not: The Manic Logic of Global Capitalism* (Simon & Schuster, 1997)

We're exporting American culture, and our experience shows the term "global village" is not a hollow phrase.

> JÜRGEN BARTELS, president of the restaurant firm Carlson, quoted in *Business Week,* January 10, 1994

Most U.S. manufacturers only pay lip service to the export market, with the exception of their European subsidiaries.

> AMIN KADRIE, chief operations officer of Alghohim Industries, Kuwait distributor for General Motors, quoted in *Business Week,* February 28, 1994

America has realized that a nation must produce hardware, not just software and services.

> BERTHOLD LEIBINGER, chief executive of the German toolmaking company Trumpf, quoted in *Business Week,* September 26, 1994

Many industries have had to learn the hard way that a market is a market, even if it is half a world away. The population may speak a different language and engage in different customs, but the market itself is fundamentally no different from any other—even if it's on the far side of the international date line. That is why I always say that you are not yet thinking globally if you still see a substantial difference between Singapore and Cincinnati.

> ALBERT C. BERSTICKER, CEO of the chemical firm Ferro Corporation, in a speech, March 27, 1997

The American economy's response to the globalization of markets has been to turn us into a nation of temps.

> HAROLD MEYERSON, labor analyst, quoted in *Atlantic Monthly,* May 1994

When Hollywood recognized that it faced a severe capital shortage, it did not throw up protectionist barriers against foreign money. Instead, it invited Rupert Murdoch into 20th Century Fox, C. Itoh and Toshiba into Time Warner, Sony into Columbia Pictures, and Matsushita into MCA. The result was a $10 billion infusion of new capital—and, equally important, $10 billion less for Japan or anyone else to set up its own Hollywood.

> KENICHI OHMAE, "Putting Global Logic First," *Harvard Business Review,* January–February 1995

It is no secret that Japanese and German automobile makers developed lighter and more fuel-efficient cars in response to new fuel-consumption standards, while the less competitive U.S. car industry fought such standards and hoped they would go away.

> MICHAEL E. PORTER and CLAAS VAN DER LINDE, "Green and Competitive," *Harvard Business Review,* September–October 1995

In the United States we would typically throw these products [esophagus lining, pork tripe, Achilles tendons, and other offal] out. But over there [China and Japan] they end up in the delicatessen end of the market.

> ROD ANDRIESSEN of the Nebraska meat packers IBP, on demand abroad for cuts of meat (which increased by 400 percent over 10 years), quoted in *Fortune,* November 13, 1995

We can copy the Japanese. We can have 14 clerks to sell you a watch. We only have to do three things:

We have to close our borders to foreign competition.

We have to convince American consumers to pay $50 for a melon.

And we have to stop giving owners of American companies a fair return on their investment. That's all. That's how the Japanese have done it.

> ROBERT J. EATON, CEO of Chrysler Corporation, in a speech, March 18, 1996

The answer is to develop our processes to the point where the labor content is so small that any advantage of lower labor costs is more than offset by the shipping costs of moving their products into our marketplace.

With a labor cost under $40 per ton, we are not concerned about the labor cost in Korea, Brazil, or Thailand. It costs close to $40 a ton to ship from those countries to ours.

> F. KENNETH IVERSON, CEO of the steel company Nucor, in a speech, February 5, 1996

We were doing very well as long as the game was played on our court with our rules, our balls, and at our level of proficiency. But here comes somebody who says, "I play the same game, with the same balls, but I have this new racquet and this new technique. And I've been practicing a lot, and I'm a perfectionist. And whereas those guys practice three hours a day and then go to the clubhouse for a drink, we practice twelve hours a day seven days a week. And we learn everything there is to know about the game."

> PROFESSOR MARTIN STARR of Columbia University, quoted in Fred Washofsky, *The Chip War* (Scribner, 1989)

If you don't know how to pronounce someone's name, you don't feel comfortable calling them back.

> SUPON PHORNIRUNLIT, Bangkok-born graphic designer, on barriers to doing business in the United States, *Asia, Inc.,* December 1995

Countries, like companies, have positions in the mind of the buyer. The United States is seen as a country that produces high-quality consumer brands.

> AL RIES, chairman of the marketing strategy firm Trout & Ries, quoted in *Fortune,* August 23, 1993

America doesn't need small. America needs big.

> PRESIDENT BILL CLINTON in a speech broadcast on C-Span, December 15, 1996

[B]igness marks America off from the rest of the world. America is the home of the Big Mac; Britons came up with the Wimpy burger. The Germans are proud of their *Mittelstand.* The signature achievement of Japanese design is the niftily small Walkman. The French think being *grand* matters less than having a nebulous thing called *grandeur.* This is the source of endless tension with Americans, who think bigness qualifies them to run the world.

> *The Economist,* December 21, 1996

Anti-dumping laws have become one of America's leading exports.

> GARY N. HORLICK, attorney for the law firm O'Melveny & Myers, quoted in *Fortune,* January 10, 1994

It is a puzzle that our manufacturing industries . . . need such an assist from the exchange rate to be able to sell competitively.

> MARTIN BAILY of the liberal think tank Brookings Institution, quoted in *Fortune,* April 18, 1994

A lot of companies think that if they can make it here [in the United States] they can make it anywhere, and if they can't make it here, they won't make it anywhere else.

> JAMES B. CARPENTER of the computer firm NEC USA, quoted in the *Wall Street Journal*, February 3, 1997

This is all in hindsight, but we let our labor costs get away from us. We didn't pay attention to foreign competition. We didn't pay attention to the marketplace.

> TOM GRAHAM of U.S. Steel, quoted in the *New Yorker*, February 25, 1991

The challenge facing the United States is, how do we justify our high wages? The answer is to remain innovative, to use American creativity to continue inventing things of greater value, specialty steels instead of basic steels, the next drugs, the new semiconductor chips, the financial services never thought of by anybody before.

> PROFESSOR MICHAEL PORTER of the Harvard Business School, quoted in the *Wall Street Journal*, February 24, 1997

If a customer meets two business people, each with equally good technology, he will still take the one based in America more seriously than the European one.

You are either one of the people in the middle spinning the wheel, or one of those on the outside being spun.

> MICHAEL SKOK, British entrepreneur who started an Internet business in Silicon Valley, quoted in the *Economist*, March 29, 1997

Basically in entertainment we export the English language and the American idiom of political and economic freedom.

> GORDON STULBERG, president of Polygram Pictures, quoted in *Forbes*, September 9, 1987

Music has to be in English to sell all over the world.

> JULIO IGLESIAS, quoted in *Forbes*, September 9, 1987

You don't have 2,000 stores in Japan by being seen as an American company. . . . McDonald's serves meat, bread, and potatoes. They eat meat, bread, and potatoes in most of the world. It's how you package it and the experience you offer that counts.

McDonald's stands for a lot more than just hamburgers and American fast food. Cultural sensitivity is part of it, too. There is no "Euroburger." . . . We have a different chicken sandwich in England than we do in Germany. We are trying not to think as a cookie cutter.

> JOSEPH CANTALUPO, president of McDonald's International, quoted by Thomas L. Friedman, *New York Times*, December 11, 1996

Last year, U.S. poultry companies exported $353 million worth of chicken parts to Hong Kong, almost three-quarters of which were feet. In Russia, Tyson Foods sold nearly $400 million worth of chicken parts, mostly thighs, which are dubbed "Bush legs" after the former President.

> *New York Times Magazine*, June 8, 1997

The U.S. automotive industry, indeed U.S. heavy industry as a whole, has gone from being characterized as "dinosaurs" to being admired around the world for its ability to change.

> JÜRGEN E. SCHREMPP, chairman of Daimler-Benz, in a speech, January 6, 1997

Everyone understands an action movie. If I tell you a joke, you may not get it, but if a bullet goes through the window we all know how to hit the floor, no matter the language.

> LARRY GORDON, producer of the film *Die Hard 2*, quoted in Ken Auletta, "What Won't You Do?" *New Yorker*, May 17, 1993

Our economic well-being, as companies or as individual wage-earners, is tied increasingly to the well-being of the world economy, but the policies that affect the world economy are driven by local political considerations.

When global economics meet local politics, more often than not we act as if interdependence were a fiction, not the reality we know it to be. We respond to short-sighted political pressures to guard parochial economic interests, rather than face up to the troublesome, but vital, job of solving our long-term problems.

> DUANE R. KULLBERG, CEO of the accounting-consulting firm Arthur Andersen, in a speech, December 10, 1987

The United States is just one part of a global marketplace today. There isn't any offshore anymore; it's all onshore.

> WALTER WRISTON, retired chairman of Citicorp, quoted in *U.S. News & World Report,* March 2, 1987

Being global is not just where you do business but how you do business.

> STEPHEN D. HARLAN, then of the accounting-consulting firm KPMG Peat Marwick, in a speech, November 15, 1991

Even underwear has national characteristics.

> JOHN BRYAN, CEO of Sara Lee Corporation, which owns Hanes underwear, reflecting on the problems of making a marketing blitz in Europe, quoted in the *Economist,* November 14, 1992

I think you have to place bets and not predict growth rates.

> JOHN F. WELCH JR., CEO of GE, in a reprint from *Leaders,* 1993

If you misjudge the market, you are wrong in 15 countries rather than only in one.

> European executive on downside of global organization, quoted in *Business Week,* May 23, 1994

Multinational corporations must not start with the assumption that this is a barren field. The trick is not to bet too big.

> PROFESSOR C. K. PARAHALAD of the University of Michigan, quoted in *Business Week,* August 11, 1997

For business purposes, the boundaries that separate one nation from another are no more real than the equator.

> Unnamed former head of now-defunct IBM World Trade Corporation, quoted in Robert Lekachman and Borin Van Loon, *Capitalism for Beginners* (Pantheon, 1981)

Most global corporations have three or four competitors, and you know who they are.

> JOHN F. WELCH JR., CEO of GE, quoted in *Harvard Business Review,* September–October 1989

The consequence of all this is painfully simple: If the whole world operates as one big market, every employee will compete with every person in the world who is capable of doing the same job. There are a lot of them, and many of them are very hungry.

> ANDREW S. GROVE, CEO of the microprocessor firm Intel, quoted in *Fortune,* September 18, 1995

[G]lobalization in the nineteenth century was driven mainly by falling transport costs, whereas now it is being driven by plunging communications costs, which make much deeper international integration possible. Cheap and efficient communications networks allow companies to locate different parts of their production process in different countries while remaining in close contact.

> *The Economist,* September 28, 1996

[If the traditional conservators of freedom were democratic constitutions and the Bill of Rights] the new temples to liberty will be McDonald's and Kentucky Fried Chicken.

> GEORGE STEINER, historian, *International Herald Tribune,* June 2–3, 1990

[A]fter I spoke to a group of engineering students at my alma mater, one of them asked me a simple question: "Which area of the world offers the Coca-Cola Company its greatest growth potential?" Without hesitation, I replied, "Southern California."

They all laughed, thinking I was trying to be funny. So to drive home the point, I shared with them one very interesting fact. The per capita consumption of bottles and cans of Coca-Cola is actually lower in the southern part of California than it is in Hungary, a country which is one of our supposedly "emerging" markets, while the United States is supposedly a "matured" soft drink market.

> The late ROBERTO C. GOIZUETA, CEO of Coca-Cola, in the company's annual report, 1996, quoted in the *Wall Street Journal,* October 20, 1997

Jihad vs. McWorld.

> BENJAMIN R. BARBER, Rutgers University, describing the conflict between American-led changes in consumer preferences and entrenched national tastes and values, quoted in the *New York Times,* November 17, 1996.

We're not going global because we want to or because of any megalomania, but because it's really necessary . . . The costs are so enormous today that you really need to have worldwide revenues to cover them.

> RUPERT MURDOCH, CEO of the media conglomerate News Corporation, quoted in *Worldbusiness,* 1994

We're getting very good at building things. What I would hate to see in India and China is a growth of manufacturing jobs and not very much else.

> FREDERICK GLUCK, managing partner of the consulting firm McKinsey & Co., quoted in *Fortune,* May 30, 1994

Go global or go gray.

> WILLIAM I. CAMPBELL, head of worldwide consumer banking, Citicorp, formerly at Philip Morris, in a speech, quoted in *Fortune,* April 29, 1996

People and institutions, not technologies, are driving globalization. The ability to make a telephone call from Oregon to Vietnam does not require Nike to produce shoes in Vietnam in sweatshop conditions rather than in the country where the company sells its shoes.

> ROBERT WEISSMAN, editor of the *Multinational Monitor,* in a letter to the editor of the *New York Times,* February 6, 1997

We are not merely a German company with foreign interests. One could almost say we are a non-national company.

> JÜERGEN DORMANN, chairman of the drug company Hoechst, quoted in the *New York Times,* February 6, 1997

McDonald's isn't really a product. It may be a ubiquitous American brand, but what you have are hundreds of retail establishments around Europe, many of them decorated in local styles, to suit local tastes, and run and serviced by local people. What's left may come from America, but it's got to become very familiar and wholesome in terms of the local culture, and if it's American food that's an interesting accident.

> FLORENCE WATERMAN, the ad agency Leo Burnett's European account director for McDonald's, quoted in the *New Yorker,* April 28–May 5, 1997

Among many problems for Euro Disney . . . was the fact that European tourists could almost as easily, and sometimes more cheaply, go to sunnier Disney World in Orlando, Florida.

> *Strategy&Business,* publication of Booz Allen & Hamilton, fourth quarter, 1995

You try to shut the door and it [the global economy] comes in through the window. You try to shut the window and it comes in on the cable. You cut the cable, it comes in on the Internet. And it's not only in the room with you. You eat it. It gets inside you.

> RONALD STEEL, historian, quoted by columnist Thomas L. Friedman, *New York Times,* December 11, 1996

[F]ewer than half the population of the world, about 3 billion people, have ever placed a phone call; at the most, 50 percent enjoy daily access to electrical power, and fewer than 11 percent of the world's people have ever owned a car.

> C. MICHAEL ARMSTRONG, CEO of Hughes Electronics, January 15, 1997

BP is probably the most global company in the world. It's interesting to see that in the United States its nationality has begun to disappear. Almost everybody in the United States says BP and not British Petroleum. It's a local kind of company.

> PHILIP CONDIT, CEO of the aerospace firm Boeing, interviewed in the *Financial Times*, March 12, 1997

So I was visiting a businessman in downtown Jakarta the other day and I asked him for directions to my next appointment. His exact instructions were: "Go to the building with the Armani Emporium upstairs—you know, just above the Hard Rock Café—and then turn right at McDonald's." I just looked at him and laughed, "Where am I?"

> THOMAS L. FRIEDMAN, *New York Times*, July 14, 1997

The potential rewards of this expansion will be very large, both in terms of the growth of important markets and as a source of exports. Although there will be transition costs, there is little evidence to justify two of the most common fears, namely downward pressure on unskilled wages in industrial and other developing countries and higher prices for food and energy.

> JOSEPH E. STIGLITZ, chief economist of the World Bank, quoted in the *New York Times*, September 10, 1997

[T]he most fundamental truth about globalization is this: *No one is in charge, you moron!*

> THOMAS L. FRIEDMAN, *New York Times*, September 29, 1997

We do not wish simply to move from a world of ideological confrontation to one of economic competition. We do not want a world without quality. We must be sure that the history we write together is one of cooperation, creativity, change for the good.

We know that globalization is not guided by compassion or solidarity. we know it has two faces: one attractive, the other not. It is our responsibility . . . to make it right, to make it just, not to blame it for our ills.

> EDUARDO FREI, president of Chile, appealing to the U.S. Congress for trade liberalization, quoted in the *Financial Times*, February 28, 1997

Globalization is set to become the biggest political issue of the next century.

> JOHN CASSIDY, "The Return of Karl Marx," *New Yorker*, October 20–27, 1997

People are starting to see the practical implications of global ties. These are not just far-off places having problems. These are your own big corporations that are going to see earnings slow down.

> RICHARD KERSLEY of the investment bank BZW, quoted in the *Wall Street Journal*, October 29, 1997

Globalization was not inevitable. Nor does it merely reflect the march of technology. It marks the successful worldwide spread of the economic liberalization that began nearly 50 years ago in Western Europe with the Marshall Plan. It is now bringing unprecedented opportunities to billions of people throughout the world.

> MARTIN WOLF, *Financial Times*, May 6, 1997

Globalization is a long-lasting competitive advantage. If we build a new gas turbine, in 18 months our competitors also have one. But building a global company is not so easy to copy.

> PERCY BARNEVIK, CEO of the Swedish-Swiss industrial firm ABB and its London-based holding company Investor, quoted in the *Financial Times*, October 8, 1997

27.1 GOVERNMENT

Fear is the foundation of most governments.

> JOHN ADAMS, *Thoughts on Government* (1776)

Our governors, all over the world, are at Sisyphus's work—ever rolling the stone uphill to see it roll back to its proper bed at the bottom.

> ANDREW CARNEGIE, *Triumphant Democracy or Fifty Years' March of the Republic* (1886)

I have said to the people we mean to have less of Government in business as well as more business in Government.

> PRESIDENT WARREN G. HARDING, special address to Congress, April 12, 1921

It is just as important that business keep out of government as that government keep out of business.

> PRESIDENT HERBERT HOOVER, in a speech, October 22, 1928

If the Government is big enough to give you everything you want, it is big enough to take away everything you have.

> PRESIDENT GERALD FORD, quoted in John F. Parker, *If Elected* (1960)

There is no private property without government. [Otherwise] individuals must have possessions the way a dog possesses a bone. But there is private property only if society protects and defends the private right to that possession against other private parties and against the government as well.

> TONY BLAIR, then head of the opposition Labor Party, quoted in the *Financial Times*, January 30, 1997

27.2 PRIVATIZATION

[In] the 1960s rich countries were achieving marvelously greater equalization in almost everything provided by private enterprise, but the underclass became further downtrodden in America's and Europe's inner cities whenever services were instead provided from the public purse. For the first time in history, millionaires and welfare mothers were spending their leisure time in the same way: watching the same television programs, from armchairs in similarly heated rooms, while the consumer durables spread to the living rooms, kitchens, bathrooms, and (in some countries) parking spaces of the few unemployed.

If a middle manager in a private company thinks his boss is making a horlicks of his job, he can set up another firm in competition. If he is in a state firm, he writes a memorandum which says his boss is making a horlicks; and loses all chance of promotion. In Russia he got shot. [A horlicks is a mess, as distinct from Horlick's, which is a chocolate-flavored powder mixed in milk.]

> NORMAN MACRAE, building a case for privatization of everything, *The Economist*, December 21, 1991

Privatization is not a religion. Competition is the religion.

> MAYOR JOHN O. NORQUIST of Milwaukee, Wisconsin, quoted in *Business Week*, May 30, 1994

Indianapolis Mayor Stephen Goldsmith uses a "Yellow Pages test": Only if he can find five or more private services listed in the phone book for a given field is he inclined to open city programs to bidding. [Forty Indianapolis programs, including wastewater treatment and golf-course maintenance, are being managed privately.]

> *Business Week*, May 30, 1994

The wrong way to privatize is to don green eyeshades and try to maximize the government's gain. The right way is to anticipate who might lose and to use some of the gains to win their support. Fifty percent of something is a whole lot better than 100 percent of nothing.

> DAVID R. HOOVER, of the conservative think tank Hoover Institute and the Naval Postgraduate School, *Wall Street Journal*, September 13, 1996

State banks can't take care of people's money.

> PROFESSOR JEFFREY SACHS of Harvard, quoted in the *Wall Street Journal*, May 7, 1997

Governments that want to implement privatization programs must do more than combat explicit opposition.

They must also try to eliminate implicit and systematic resistance to such capitalist mechanisms as free-market private ownership. They need to examine their tax regimes, for example, to make sure they offer incentives and not impediments to investment. They also need to take a hard look at the attitudes and assumptions prevailing in their education systems.

To succeed in countries with socialist traditions, privatization must be part of wholesale cultural revolution. The good news is that privatization itself, by putting equity ownership into the hands of citizens, is one of the most effective ways to promote such a revolution.

> JOHN MOORE, minister for ten years in Margaret Thatcher's government who was responsible for privatization program, 1983–1986, now executive chairman of Credit Suisse Asset Management, *Harvard Business Review*, January–February 1992

In general it is easier to sell off state assets once a supportive environment for private sector development is in place. [Criteria for supportive environment include foundation of law, nondiscretionary policy environment, investment in basic social services and infrastructure, protection for the vulnerable and the environment.]

Experience has shown that the way privatization is managed is terribly important to the end result. The key factors are transparency of process, winning the acquiescence of employees, generating broad-based ownership, and instituting the appropriate regulatory reform.

> Summary, "The State in a Changing World," World Development Report 1997, published by the World Bank

[M]ost newly privatized companies need dominant, experienced shareholders to compensate for weaknesses of managers never before exposed to best business practices. Without the support and prodding of such shareholders, Eastern companies tend to operate very much along the lines learned in the days of central planning, insider contacts, and relentless focus on production.

Old-guard managers simply lack the skills and experience to convert a company from its old Communist predilections to a genuine market orientation.

> KEVIN R. MCDONALD, management consultant and an adviser to Polish government, *Harvard Business Review*, May–June 1993

The most positive effects are from capital privatization, especially if purchased by a foreigner. Why? Because there is new capital investment, access to new markets, and influence on management and the organization of the enterprise.

> JANUSZ DABROWSKI, economist at Gdansk Institute in Warsaw, who conducted a thorough study of 11 privatizations, quoted by Kevin R. McDonald, *Harvard Business Review*, May–June 1993

We have proven that the airport does not have to be the worst part of the journey. And we have proven it can be done profitably.

People confused capitalism with stealing. My system was to explain to our employees that stealing from the customer was a bad thing.

> SIR JOHN EGAN, chief executive BAA PLC, the private operator of Heathrow and some other airports, *Wall Street Journal*, September 24, 1996

Passengers refused to leave a South West Trains service until it took them to their destinations. The train was due to travel from London Waterloo to Exeter about 300 km away. But SWT attempted to end the journey halfway . . . As the weary travelers were advised to travel 150 km out of their way to catch another service, one man jumped back on board and held the doors open with his feet. About 100 people then occupied the train.

> *Financial Times Weekend*, March 15–16, 1997

When you let a wolf into the sheep-pen it is best to know how aggressive the animal is, how long its teeth are, and to give yourself the means to keep it under control.

> ALAIN BOCQUET, a Communist in the French National Assembly, on whether the state would retain overall control of enterprises in the event of privatization, quoted in the *Financial Times*, September 9, 1997

Privatization is the axle of economic policy not just in order to compete in telecommunications—and electricity and resurrect the railways, but also because the funds are necessary to support monetary and fiscal policy.

> FERNANDO MORALES, Guatemalan economic analyst, quoted in the *Financial Times*, February 26, 1997

The fact that the state has been an abysmal administrator is no reason to hand over the people's property to big business.

> CARLOS BARRIOS, from left-leaning Guatemalan Democratic Front, quoted in the *Financial Times,* February 26, 1997

27.3 THE U.S. GOVERNMENT AND BUSINESS

27.3.1 American Government

Americans can always be counted on to do the right thing—after they have exhausted all other remedies.

> WINSTON CHURCHILL

America was never intended to be a nation of the government, by the government, and for the government.

> C. MICHAEL ARMSTRONG, CEO of Hughes Aircraft, in a speech, November 9, 1993

It usually takes a hundred years to make a law, and then, after it has done its work, it usually takes a hundred years to get rid of it.

> HENRY WARD BEECHER, *Proverbs from Plymouth Pulpit* (1887)

If there isn't a law, there will be.

> HAROLD FABER, *New York Times,* March 17, 1968

27.3.2 Corporations and the Government

You get realistic when you lose the kind of money we lost.

> ROGER SMITH, CEO of General Motors, on why the Big 3 automakers were presenting a united front in Washington on issues like free trade (uncharacteristically against it) and higher taxes on fuel to encourage conservation (in favor) [GM had lost $970 million in nine months], quoted in the *Economist,* January 16, 1993

My nightmare isn't Frankenstein. It's the government bureaucrat.

> ALLEN J. BERNSTEIN, president of the restaurant firm Quontum Restaurants, after the business-meal deduction was cut from 80 percent to 50 percent, quoted in *Business Week,* January 10, 1994

As frustrating as the place is for a transplanted company grower, Washington's processes are no worse than those in the business world, only different. For which, it turns out, we should be grateful. Because the things that make Washington so frustratingly difficult also make it relentlessly democratic.

[W]hether because nobody's in charge or everyone is, nothing gets done.

> JOHN ROLLWAGEN, former CEO of the supercomputer firm Cray Research, who spent four months as second in command to Commerce Secretary Ron Brown, *Inc.,* January 1994

What people learn from running a business won't help them formulate economic policy.

A country is not a big corporation. The habits of mind that make a great business leader are not, in general, those that make a great economic analyst; an executive who has made $1 billion is rarely the right person to turn to for advice about a $6 trillion economy.

In a society that respects business success, political leaders will inevitably—and rightly—seek the advice of business leaders on many issues, particularly those that involve money. All we can ask is that both the advisers and the advisees have a proper sense of what business success does and does not teach about economic policy.

> PROFESSOR PAUL KRUGMAN, then of Stanford University, *Harvard Business Review,* January–February 1996

There is nothing the federal government can do better than the private sector except build bombs.

> RONALD E. COMPTON, CEO of Aetna Life and Casualty, pondering the threat of government health care reform, quoted in *Business Week,* January 10, 1994

The greatest contribution business can make is to help it [government] do its job more effectively and more efficiently.

Government has to cast off the presumption that any business proposal represents only the self-interests of business. And business has to move beyond the suspicion that anything government does will be unfair to business.

> DANA G. MEAD, CEO of the automotive and energy firm Tenneco, in a speech, April 16, 1997

27.3.3 Devolution of Federal Power to the States

I do not believe that Washington should do for the people what they can do for themselves through local and private effort.

> SENATOR JOHN F. KENNEDY, campaign address, October 12, 1960

A moron close to a problem usually makes a better decision on how to solve it than a genius a thousand miles away.

> GONZALO SANCHEZ DE LOZADA, former president of Bolivia, quoted in the *Wall Street Journal*, August 28, 1997

[The Constitution] was framed upon the theory that the peoples of the several states must sink or swim together, and that in the long run prosperity and salvation are in union and not division.

> U.S. SUPREME COURT JUSTICE BENJAMIN CARDOZO, 1934

[C]onsider the New Deal. Again, Federal programs proved the answer to problems that were intractable at the level of the states—in this instance, because capital and labor can freely move across state lines. There is a dark side to interstate competition, as the Great Depression made quite clear. No state wants to be the first to adopt Social Security or abolish child labor unless other states will do the same.

> PROFESSOR KATHLEEN M. SULLIVAN of Stanford University Law School, quoted in the *New York Times Magazine,* August 18, 1996

We [the insurance industry] need regulation. But 50 regulatory authorities make about as much sense ultimately as 50 different currencies. Our currency reads *E Pluribus Unum*—"one out of many"—not the other way around.

> DEAN O'HARE, CEO of the insurance company Chubb, in a speech, May 8, 1996

27.3.4 Government-Financed Development

New buildings look good, but often money is better spent on people.

> *The Economist,* July 20, 1996

What kind of deal is 2,000 new jobs for $838 million?

> On a subsidy by the State of Minnesota to Northwest Airlines to keep its hub in Minneapolis, *The Economist,* January 4, 1992

Last year, Amarillo, Texas, decided to undertake an aggressive economic development initiative using a different strategy. Some 1,300 companies around the country were each sent a check for $8 million that the company could cash if it committed to creating 700 new jobs in Amarillo.

> MELVIN L. BURSTEIN and ARTHUR J. ROLNICK of the Federal Reserve Bank of Minneapolis, March 1995

1978—Pennsylvania. $71 million incentive package to Volkswagen for a factory projected to eventually employ 20,000 workers. It never employed more than 6,000, closed within a decade.

1991—Minnesota. $270 million operating loan to Northwest Airlines at a favorable rate of interest for agreement to build (with an additional $400 million of state and local government funding) two repair facilities to employ 2,000 highly skilled workers. The commitment has been reduced to one facility and an airline reservation center, which together would employ fewer than 1,000 workers.

> MELVIN L. BURSTEIN and ARTHUR J. ROLNICK of the Federal Reserve Bank of Minneapolis, March 1995

[C]ities reinvent themselves all the time. New York was a port, then a manufacturing center, and all the while it has managed to maintain its status as the nation's information capital. New Orleans declined into a genteel shabbiness, only to find that shabbiness was actually an asset, at least for the tourist trade. Yet company towns are different. Detroit has never really been able to get past the automobile. Pittsburgh still struggles without steel. And the jury is still out on whether Seattle can build a long-term economy around cappuccino instead of Boeing.

Company towns grow beyond their roots only when the politicians stop giving the company everything it wants.

> *Governing,* September 28, 1996

Too many states are jumping on the bandwagon. If all of these states think they are going to be the next Mecca for the biotech industry, they are crazy. The worst thing we can do is imitate each other.

> WALT POSILLA of the North Carolina Alliance for Competitive Technology, quoted in the *Wall Street Journal*, April 23, 1997

27.3.5 Government Investment in Small Business by the Numbers

A sampling of the Agriculture Department's investments

Product	Company	USDA "investment"
Ethanol windshield-washer fluid	Aquinas Technologies Group, St. Louis	$100,000 loan
Wheat-gluten biodegradable plastic	Midwest Grain Products (Atchison, Kan.)	$818,000 loan
Rapeseed oil for hydraulic fluids, and cosmetics	International Lubricants (Seattle)	$480,000 equity investment
Granite-like composite from waste newspaper and soybean flour	Phenix Composites (Mankato, Minn.)	$1,000,000 loan
Low-grade waste wool for sopping up oil spills	Hobbs Bonded Fibers (Mexia, Tex.)	$700,000 loan

U.S. Agriculture Department data, cited in *Business Week,* June 13, 1994

27.3.6 Government Subsidy to Professional Sports

Professional sports add something to the spirit and vitality of a city. They are a reflection of the city's image of itself. I don't simply believe that; I know it. A winning team can bring a city together, and even a losing team can provide a bond of common misery.

> BILL VEECK, *Thirty Tons a Day* (Viking, 1972)

The NFL has brought cities to their knees by moving teams or by threats of moving that cause cities to give teams things that are totally in defiance of what should be the order of priorities.

> Sportscaster HOWARD COSELL, quoted in *U.S. News & World Report,* September 16, 1985

If a city dipped into its capital budget for an industrial park instead of a stadium, it might generate year-round jobs that require skills and pay high wages. It may well be that sports, from a purely economic vantage point, are not helpful to a city's economy but rather hinder its growth.

There's an ongoing misrepresentation about what it is that stadiums do. I'm not saying they don't provide an important psychological boost to a community. But they don't seem to provide much in the way of an economic boost.

> PROFESSOR ROBERT A. BAADE of Lake Forest (Illinois) College, quoted in the *Economist,* July 20, 1996

27.3.7 Industrial Policy

If given a blank check to select the critical national industries of the future, today's governmental institutions are unfortunately more likely to opt for the interests of pork barreling than natural competitiveness.

> DANIEL BURSTEIN, *Turning the Tables: A Machiavellian Strategy for Dealing with the Japanese* (Simon & Schuster, 1993)

Treating small business preferentially is the same as creating a subsidy for bad jobs.

> STEVEN DAVIS of the University of Chicago, quoted in *Inc.,* March 1994

27.3.8 Lobbyists

A lobbyist is a person that is supposed to help a politician to make up his mind, not only to help him but pay him.

> WILL ROGERS, American humorist, 1929

[Translations of lobbyist-speak]

All we are seeking is a fair shake.
Gimme.

All we are seeking is a level playing field.
Gimme. Gimme.

You know I don't come in here on every niggling thing.
You know I come in here on every niggling thing.

> MARK S. FOWLER, chairman of the Federal Communications Commission, *Wall Street Journal,* January 25, 1985

It's ironic that the tax plan is designed to make the code so simple that lawyers aren't necessary, but it's giving us the best business we've ever had.

> NIELS HOLCH, Gary & Co., Washington lobbying firm, on buildup for 1986 tax reform battle, quoted in the *Wall Street Journal*, February 5, 1985

Their original plan was to hold the fort until they [the tobacco industry] could flood the Third World. They've certainly been successful.

> VICTOR L. CRAWFORD, former tobacco industry lobbyist, quoted in *Business Week*, July 4, 1994

First you do good, then you do well.

> Former government official, on the lobbying opportunities available after leaving the government, quoted in the *New York Times*, December 21, 1997

27.3.9 Political Economics

In general, the art of government consists in taking as much money as possible from one class of the citizens to give to the other.

> VOLTAIRE

[I have] saved America from inflation.

> PRESIDENT HERBERT HOOVER, on the bright side of the Depression

What I remember most about Nixon is how bad it was to be in business when he was president.

> HUGH JOHNSON of the investment firm First Albany, quoted in *Business Week*, May 9, 1994

The President's statements before the election were so broad, he can argue that he's not violating his principles. But there's a perception out there that he's not keeping his campaign promises. These cuts are much deeper than expected.

> U.S. SENATOR CHARLES E. GRASSLEY (Republican, Iowa), on administration's budget proposals, quoted in the *Wall Street Journal*, February 1, 1985

Most people who give money don't want anything. They just want to go backstage and be part of things.

> ROBERT S. STRAUSS, Democratic lawyer, power broker, fixer, ambassador, quoted in *Business Week*, October 12, 1987

It's the economy, stupid.

I'd like to create more millionaires than were created under Mr. Bush and Mr. Reagan.

> BILL CLINTON, 1992 presidential candidate

The rich get the gold mine and the middle class gets the shaft.

> U.S PRESIDENT BILL CLINTON

I sort of innocently asked, well, isn't there a terrible political spin on this? It's my impression that most of the money goes to a handful of big corporations, and if we are ever caught not cutting this while we're biting deeply into the social programs, we're going to have big problems.

> DAVID STOCKMAN, director of the Office of Management and Budget under President Reagan, quoted in William Greider *The Education of David Stockman* (Dutton, 1982)

My morals might be low, but at least I have principles.

> PAULA PARKINSON, former crop-insurance lobbyist who admitted swapping sex for votes with six Republican Congressmen and one Democrat in the early 1980s (including one prominent pro-lifer who gave her $500 for an abortion), quoted in Bill Thomas, *Club Fed—Power, Money, Sex, and Violence on Capitol Hill* (Scribner, 1994)

This is national defense! This is national defense!

> U.S. SENATOR TED STEVENS (Republican, Alaska), exhorting the Senate to vote for ship-industry subsidies, quoted in the *New York Times*, September 25, 1996

This program delivers to the taxpayer higher costs and no additional security benefit. Shouldn't that be a clue that this program is wasteful? The money goes to wealthy companies and powerful unions. It becomes corporate welfare and union welfare. They keep getting more and more money from the Treasury because they have the clout.

> U.S SENATOR CHARLES GRASSLEY (Republican, Iowa), quoted in the *New York Times*, September 25, 1996

We have an underdeveloped democracy and an overdeveloped plutocracy.

> RALPH NADER, quoted in the *Economist*, March 30, 1996

How the hell could you run a business like mine if you didn't have communications with the people who make the big decisions?

> DWAYNE ANDREAS, CEO of Archer Daniels Midland, supermarket to the world, and major financial angel for Bob Dole and other politicians in both major political parties, quoted in *Fortune,* October 8, 1990

Getting someone to do something for you.[A definition of politics]

> CHARLES SANFORD, CEO of Bankers Trust, quoted in the *Economist,* July 11, 1987

Cashing in is simply the last act in the standard four-act Washington epic tragedy. Act One is *idealism.* Our hero gets involved in politics because he or she believes in racial equality, or lower tax rates, or baby seals. Act Two is *pragmatism.* Our hero learns that to achieve important political goals, you must compromise and work within the system. Act Three is *ambition.* Success within the political system—by election or appointment—becomes the goal for its own sake. Act Four is *corruption.* Politics becomes merely instrumental once again, this time for personal enrichment instead of an ideological agenda.

> MICHAEL KINSLEY, *New Republic,* January 28, 1985

In the trade associations, it is the most troglodyte member who will pound the table the hardest and insist the [government] do the least who will set the initial policy. [In] the environmental organizations, the one who is most pure, who wants the most stringent kinds of regulation will set the initial policy.

Those of us who have to make policy and manage this mess almost always start on an issue with a spectrum of opinion that isn't realistic. The first thing to do is lop off the two extremes to get to the area of real disagreement and then forge compromises.

> CONGRESSMAN AL SWIFT, *Atlantic Monthly,* June 30, 1994

The President can't control the business cycle, although he's often held accountable for it.

> ROBERT J. SHAPIRO of the Progressive Policy Institute, Democratic think tank, quoted in *Fortune,* March 4, 1995

The U.S. government has prepared a table titled Risks and Cost-Effectiveness of Selected Regulations. It illustrates the cost of saving one life under various regulations. The following have been taken from that table:

Regulation	Cost of saving one life ($ millions 1990)
Auto passive restraint/seat belt standards	0.1
Aircraft seat cushion flammability standard	0.4
Alcohol and drug control standards	0.4
Auto side door support standards	0.8
Trenching and excavation standards	1.5
Asbestos occupational exposure limit	8.3
Hazardous waste listing for petroleum refining sludge	27.6
Cover/remove uranium mill tailings (inactive sites)	31.7
Asbestos ban	110.7
Diethylstilbestrol (DES) cattle feed ban	124.8
Municipal solid waste landfill standards (proposed)	19,107.0
Atrazine/Alachlor drinking water standard	92,069.7
Hazardous waste listing for wood preserving chemicals	5,700,000.0

> EnviroScan #110, Public Relations Management Ltd.

The Write Cause drafts letters for its members on environmental and animal protection issues. For $45 a year, members are sent two letters per month, printed on personalized stationery, which they simply have to sign, pop into pre-addressed stamped envelopes and mail. The typefaces and stationery colors vary, so letters don't appear to be mass-produced.

> April 1993 issue of *E,* cited by EnviroScan #125, Public Relations Management Ltd.

I'm working on the supposition that good economics can also be good politics. I'll admit that not everyone believes that.

> U.S. TREASURY SECRETARY ROBERT E. RUBIN, quoted in the *New York Times,* September 22, 1996

John F. Kennedy, when he was in Congress, said explicitly that he was testifying in favor of a rise in the minimum wage because he wanted protection for the New

England textile manufacturers from the so-called cheap labor of the South.

> MILTON FRIEDMAN, Nobel Prize–winning economist, interviewed in *Playboy,* February 1973

Economic speeches are like pissing down your leg. It may seem hot to you but it doesn't to anyone else.

> LYNDON JOHNSON, quoted by John Kenneth Galbraith, *Times* [London], March 11, 1997

One of the things the president understood that the people around him didn't always understand was if business people had confidence in the administration, that wasn't just a political event, it was an economic event. Conversely, if they thought he was in a class-warfare mode, that could undermine confidence and could adversely affect the economy.

> U.S. SECRETARY OF THE TREASURY ROBERT RUBIN, in the wake of the big stock market plunge two days before, *Wall Street Journal,* October 29, 1997

27.3.10   Public Sector vs. Private Sector

It costs $54 for [the Defense Department] to process travel vouchers for its personnel. Private travel agencies do the job for about $4 per voucher.

> C. MICHAEL ARMSTRONG, then CEO of Hughes Aircraft, in a speech, November 9, 1993

You didn't need an accountant to tell the difference between the public and private sectors [at a meeting about privatizing welfare]. The corporate executives, who were overwhelmingly male, wore expensive gray suits subtly indented at the waist; their faces were tanned, or at least buffed and peeled to a hearty glow; and they seemed, on average, actually taller than their potential partners in the public sector. The representatives of state and county governments, on the other hand, were in some cases overweight, often bearded, and given to such fashion solecisms as navy suits, heavy gold cufflinks or even . . . a pink checked skirt with a matching pink embroidered sweater. To underscore their evident superiority, the corporate participants tended to sit not at the tables provided but along the wall at the very back of the room, in case their beepers should rouse them to more urgent business outside. And while the public sector bent over its legal pads, none of the corporate people took notes . . .

> BARBARA EHRENREICH, "Spinning the Poor into Gold," *Harper's,* August 1997

27.3.11   Regulation

We must either regulate, or own, or destroy, perishing by the sword we take.

> HENRY DEMAREST LLOYD, journalist, on the case against Standard Oil, quoted in Robert Sobel and David B. Sicilia, *The Entrepreneurs—An American Adventure* (Houghton Mifflin, 1986)

[T]he American Beauty rose can be produced in the splendor and fragrance which bring cheer to its beholder only by sacrificing the early buds which grow up around it. And so it is with economic life. It is merely the working out of a law of nature and a law of God.

> JOHN D. ROCKEFELLER, responding to Lloyd (the previous quote), quoted in Robert Sobel and David B. Sicilia, *The Entrepreneurs—An American Adventure* (Houghton Mifflin, 1986)

One of the most dramatic failures of government has been the case of regulatory agencies. Even the strongest critics of the market and warmest supporters of government will agree that these organizations have become the servants of those they were supposed to protect the government from.

> MILTON FRIEDMAN, Nobel Prize–winning economist, interviewed in *Playboy,* February 1973

Regulators should not be advocates for the people they regulate.

> TONY HOPE, former chairman of National Indian Gaming Commission, quoted in the *Wall Street Journal,* July 22, 1996

It's wink, wink, we can't tell the public.

> Congressional testimony of former Transportation Inspector-General MARY SCHIAVO, of the attitude at the U.S. Department of Transportation about a damning report on the discount airline ValuJet issued May 2, 1996, nine days before a fatal crash in the Everglades, quoted in the *New Republic,* September 23, 1996

I showed up at the airport for a ValuJet flight and instead of asking for a photo ID, they said "Oh no. We just need your dental records."

> DON IMUS, host of radio show *Imus in the Morning,* October 4, 1996 (the same week ValuJet announced a resumption of service at steep discount prices)

It was a set of rules that defined regulation of the railroad industry and has led to the progressive decline and collapse of the railroad industry.

> DOUGLAS NORTH, 1993 Nobel Prize winner in economics, on the 1887 Interstate Commerce Act, on National Public Radio, *All Things Considered,* October 12, 1993

We're forced to compete with our own regulators. They can make life pretty difficult for us if we make trouble.

> Executive at a major Western bank, on competition for check-clearing business with the Federal Reserve Board, quoted in the *Wall Street Journal,* September 12, 1996

We're competing fairly—and we're doing it with one hand tied behind our backs. I have to charge the same price to the Citizen's State Bank of Pembina, North Dakota, that I charge to them [big banks]. Yet my counterparts in the private sector can cut volume deals with other big banks, leaving us with all the junk they can't make money on.

> TED UMHOEFER, check-clearing manager at the Minneapolis Federal Reserve Bank, quoted in the *Wall Street Journal,* September 12, 1996

Victories won on the legislative battlefield are routinely lost in the fog of bureaucratic wars over what the laws mean and how best to implement them.

> PROFESSOR JOHN J. DiIULO of Princeton University, quoted in the *Wall Street Journal,* October 4, 1996

This military ration-control directive subverts the exchange business to the whims or moral dictates of a local military authority. [Memo on new restrictions on beer rations for U.S. troops in Korea, reduced to 8 cases per month from 30, in order to limit a flourishing black market]

> THOMAS A. DOHERTY, head of military sales overseas for Anheuser-Busch, in May 8, 1997, quoted in the *New York Times,* July 5, 1997

We should be able to get at least a 12-pack a day.

> PFC. JOHN MOXLEY, reacting to new directive, quoted in the *New York Times,* July 5, 1997

27.3.12 Regulation—Antitrust

The best of all monopoly profits is a quiet life.

> SIR JOHN HICKS, England, *Econometrica* (1935)

The only consistency I can find [in decisions on mergers] is that the government always wins.

> U.S. SUPREME COURT JUSTICE POTTER STEWART, in a 1966 dissent from a decision to prevent a merger of Los Angeles supermarket chains, cited in the *Wall Street Journal,* February 27, 1997

Unlike other industries, our pace of change is so fast that I don't think it's right to expect the same type of concentration as in the auto industry.

> MICHAEL DELL, CEO of Dell Computer, quoted in the *Wall Street Journal,* February 4, 1997

Is the industry slowing down because of concentration? Is the price going up because of concentration? Is the customer worse served? The answer to all these things is no.

> BERNARD VERGNES, president of Microsoft Europe, quoted in the *Wall Street Journal,* February 4, 1997

[A]s an investor in small companies, I don't care how rich Microsoft is. I care about what my opportunities are. If I had the sense that Microsoft was genuinely holding back the market then I'd care. I don't think they are.

> ESTHER DYSON, president of the high-tech investment company EDventure Holdings, quoted in the *Wall Street Journal,* February 4, 1997

This is called capitalism. We create a product called Windows. Who decides what's in Windows? It's the customers who buy Windows.

> BILL GATES, CEO of Microsoft, reacting to antitrust action against his company, quoted in the *Wall Street Journal,* October 22, 1997

If you asked customers who they would rather have deciding what innovations go into their computer—the government or software companies—the answer would be clear. They'd want the decision left to the marketplace, with competition driving improvements.

> BILL GATES, CEO of Microsoft Corporation, Microsoft web site, November 9, 1997

The old antitrust approach was as much a sociopolitical one as an economic one. That changed when people began to be less concerned about bigness per se, and more interested in what was the effect on the consumer.

> ELEANOR FOX, law professor at New York University, quoted in the *Financial Times,* November 20, 1997

Increasingly the question is: what is the real market in which a business is operating? Is it the whole world, or is it a city block?

> PHILIP RUDOLPH, lawyer with Gibson, Dunn and Crutcher, quoted in the *Financial Times*, November 20, 1997

Where is Teddy Roosevelt when you need him?

> JOHN LEAHY of the European aerospace firm Airbus Industries, on Boeing's sole-supplier agreements with airlines, quoted in the *Wall Street Journal*, April 30, 1997

27.3.13   Cost of Regulation by the Numbers

It's an inexact science, obviously, but common sense tells you there is a limit to how much you can spend. If it costs $100 million for a pollution control regulation to save one life, then to save 10,000 lives it would cost one-third of the gross national product.

> EDWIN DALE of the U.S. Office of Management and Budget, quoted in *U.S. News & World Report*, September 16, 1985

$650,083 [How much a life is worth to the Federal Aviation Administration]

$3,500,000 [How much a life is worth to the Occupational Safety and Health Administration]

> *U.S. News & World Report*, September 16, 1985

The best estimate of the regulatory burden . . . puts the cost of complying with federal rules at $668 billion in 1995, compared with $1.5 trillion in federal spending.

[I]n 1995 federal regulation cost the average American household $7,000 (more than the average income-tax bill, which was $6,000 per household).

> THOMAS HOPKINS of the Rochester Institute of Technology, quoted in the *Economist*, July 27, 1996

27.3.14   (De)Regulation

[N]ow, just over a year since the breakup [of AT&T] took place, what do we have? We have the freedom to buy badly made telephones that we can't get repaired; the freedom to receive 30-page telephone bills that have to be sent over to the National Security agency for decryption; the freedom to hear the operator say wearily: "Thank you for using AT&T." If these are freedoms, give me slavery.

> ALEXANDER COCKBURN, *Wall Street Journal*, January 3, 1985

[D]eregulation has a bright side and a dark side. We should worry more about the dark side.

> YOSHIHISA TABUCHI, former CEO of the investment firm, Nomura Securities, *Harvard Business Review*, July–August 1989

[B]ank directors aren't very much to blame for the industry's problems. The mess for which the government now sanctimoniously holds bankers responsible was largely created by the government itself. The half-hearted attempt during the Reagan years to free the banks from government interference now looks to an outsider more like a kind of sting operation designed to nail the bankers.

> MICHAEL LEWIS, *New Republic*, January 4, 1993

It's a sham. Instead of having regulated monopolies in control, we'll have unregulated monopolies in control.

> JAMES DOYLE, Wisconsin attorney general, on efforts by the postbreakup Baby Bells to eventually sell "new" local services through their own infant carriers, exploiting loopholes in telecom regulations, quoted in the *Wall Street Journal*, July 15, 1996

Electrical power is the biggest American industry ever to be deregulated. It's about twice the size of the long-distance telephone business and dwarfs the gas, airline, trucking, and railroad industries, which were all once regulated.

> KENNETH LAY, CEO of the energy producer Enron, quoted in *Fortune*, September 29, 1997

27.3.15   Regulation—Cost of Compliance

In the United States . . . companies spent $12 billion in 1990 to comply with hazardous-waste regulations, the equivalent to over 6 percent of investment in manufacturing industry.

> *The Economist*, February 29, 1992

In 1993, the last year with published numbers, the U.S. petroleum industry spent more than $10.6 billion on environmental protection. That's a little less than the combined 1995 earnings of the three largest oil companies in the United States, or nearly twice the annual budget of the EPA, or $41 for every man, woman, and child in America.

> KENNETH DERR, CEO of the oil company Chevron, in a speech reprinted in *Speechwriter's Newsletter*, October 15, 1996

According to authoritative groups, reducing fossil fuel use to the levels this administration advocated in Geneva would require adding 60 cents to the price of a gallon of gasoline in the United States and raising the price of residential and commercial fuels by 50 percent.

LEE R. RAYMOND, CEO of the oil company Exxon, in a speech, May 6, 1996.

The few times that someone has looked at what government regulations would really cost companies to comply with, the true costs tend to be twofold, fivefold, sometimes tenfold lower than the predictions that were made.

ADAM FINKEL, director of health standards for the U.S. Occupational Safety and Health Administration (OSHA), quoted in *Consumer Reports,* December 1996

Since 1985, more than 650,000 air bag "deployments" have occurred and, by NHTSA count, 1,136 lives have been saved. But at what price? . . . At $500 a car, the total cost (to the consumer—not the car companies, who pass the cost along) of installing even one air bag in each of the 35 million-plus cars now so equipped is about $18 billion, to date, and the cost per life saved is close to $16 million.

JODIE T. ALLEN, *Slate,* November 7, 1996

The assessments, based on a charge for each carton of produce marketed, can run to a half million dollars or more for a big farm and generate more than $10 million a year for advertising the California produce at issue in this case.

Refers to a New Deal–vintage mandatory government program to promote California fruit (being challenged in Supreme Court on First Amendment grounds), quoted in the *New York Times,* December 3, 1996

If people can't remember to fasten their seat belts, how are they going to remember to turn their airbags back on when they should?

ROBERT A. LUTZ, vice chairman of the Chrysler Corporation, in a speech, April 29, 1997

27.3.16   Regulation—Financial

I sincerely believe that banking establishments are more dangerous than standing armies.

THOMAS JEFFERSON, 1816

You are a den of vipers and thieves. I intend to rout you out.

ANDREW JACKSON, to a group of bankers

The Government has no vision for the evolution of the financial services systems in this country. We are quickly putting together a jerry-built financial structure, which includes flaws that work against the best interest of the public.

C. ROBERT BRENTON, former president of the American Bankers Association, quoted in *Time,* December 3, 1984

The regulators have us so mixed up on what direction banking is moving, it's nearly impossible to make long-range plans. It almost makes a banker want to do nothing.

CHARLES BOYLE, president of Gulf National Bank, on the difficulty of operating with three regulators (the Fed, the Controller of the Currency, and the Treasury Department), quoted in the *Wall Street Journal,* January 27, 1985

Banking systems are the product of their underlying cultures and the business relationships these cultures have developed. At present I see no evidence that suggests that one type of structure is inherently better than another. Therefore, I see no compelling need to seek a one-size-fits-all resolution to the issue of ownership interlocks for competitive equity. Rather, each country can experiment with its own system based on its own unique circumstances, concerns, and historic legacy.

ALAN S. GREENSPAN, chairman of the U.S. Federal Reserve Board, in a speech, October 14, 1992

There is no justification at all for regulating wholesale [financial] markets.

PROFESSOR MERTON MILLER, Nobel Prize–winning economist of the University of Chicago, quoted in the *Economist,* July 22, 1995

We want people to know how much they're actually paying. That may not sound revolutionary, but it is.

LAWRENCE LINDSEY, Federal Reserve Governor, on new Fed rules requiring disclosure of automobile leasing terms, quoted in the *Wall Street Journal,* September 13, 1996

[T]here's the "home run." That's what some dealers call a lease "flip" in which the value of a trade-in car is added to the purchase price. [Example of the kind of shady practice that the new Fed rules are designed to combat]

> *Wall Street Journal,* September 13, 1996

The British . . . created a civil service job in 1803 charging a watchman to stand on the Cliffs of Dover with a spyglass. His job was to ring a bell if he saw Napoleon coming.

The British abolished the job in 1945.

Like the watchman with a spyglass, our outdated geographic restrictions are just now being eliminated. Only Napoleon landed on the shores of the banking industry about 50 years ago. Since then, banks have lost more than half their market share to a variety of less regulated, more nimble, more aggressive and—yes—more hungry nonbank competitors.

> HUGH L. McCOLL JR., CEO of NationsBank, in a speech, October 30, 1996

Regulatory protections designed to benefit 5 percent of retail customers don't do much for the other 95 percent. . . . except add to costs.

> ROBERT K. WILMOUTH, president of the National Future Association (Chicago-based industry self-regulator for the futures market), quoted in the *Wall Street Journal,* April 21, 1997

By international standards, the state of effective regulation here [in the United States] is quite good. Financial institutions are extraordinarily transparent to the regulators . . . It's complicated and expensive to have so many channels, perhaps making operations less efficient. But on balance, it serves the financial system well.

> GEORGE VOJTA, vice chairman of Bankers Trust, interviewed in *ABA Banking Journal,* June 1997

For the first time, we can seriously begin to contemplate a regulatory quantification of what we mean by "soundness."

> ALAN S. GREENSPAN, chairman of the Federal Reserve Board, in a speech, quoted in *ABA Banking Journal,* June 1997

You have to look at the corporation in its entirety to see how well it is managing its overall risk. Do the various risks magnify each other or neutralize each other? At what point does the balance tip?

> BERT ELY, Washington financial consultant, on the difficulty of regulating financial service conglomerates, quoted in the *New York Times,* January 2, 1998

If you're worried about the bank lending too much to the insurance company, that's something the bank regulators have plenty of power to deal with. If you're worried about the insurance company lending too much and putting the insurance claimants at risk, the insurance guys have the powers to deal with that.

> PROFESSOR LAWRENCE J. WHITE of New York University and former member of the Federal Home Loan Bank Board, quoted in the *New York Times,* January 2, 1998

27.3.17 Regulation—A Hollywood View

I can have 300 agents come into this hick town and crawl up into every single orifice you got. I'm going to show you new meaning to the word "violation."

I'm just here doin' God's work.

> STEVEN SEAGAL, actor, as an Environmental Protection Agency agent in the movie *Fire Down Below,* quoted in the *Wall Street Journal,* September 18, 1997

27.3.18 Regulation and Innovation

Mahoney's First Rule of R&D is—if you cite an R&D project in the chairman's letter in the annual report, the project will enjoy perpetual funding whether or not it even sees the light of day in the marketplace.

Mahoney's Second Rule of R&D is that you must keep reminding your research staff in companies like Monsanto that you're in business to sell products. We are all gratified by advancing the frontiers of scientific knowledge, but the only thing that ever gets invoiced is the product.

My Third Rule of R&D is what I would like to discuss with you today: When it comes to technology, there is a profound difference between managing the climate and managing the weather. When we forget what that difference is, as our various national governments so often tend to do, then we place the freedom to innovate in great jeopardy.

> RICHARD J. MAHONEY, CEO of the chemical company Monsanto, in a speech, May 26, 1993

27.3.19 Regulation—Superfund

Say you were driving through a town 10 years ago. Suddenly, 10 years later, you receive a summons for going through a stoplight that's now in the town—even though there was no stoplight there 10 years ago—and you're liable for all the other motorists who drove through the stoplight 10 years ago—even if there wasn't one. That's the liability of Superfund.

> RICHARD J. MAHONEY, CEO of the chemical company Monsanto, in a speech, November 9, 1993

27.3.20 Reinventing Government

Dealing with these contracts is like squeezing a balloon: you squeeze it in one place and it pops out in another.

> U.S. SENATOR CHARLES GRASSLEY (Republican, Iowa), claiming that defense contractors, when pressed to cut costs, respond by raising prices, quoted in *U.S. News & World Report*, April 1, 1985

We do not shoot paper at the enemy.

> VICE ADMIRAL JOSEPH METCALF, explaining why he wanted to get rid of the 20 tons of paper and filing cabinets that weighed down many U.S. Navy ships at the expense of weapons and fuel, quoted in *U.S. News & World Report*, May 18, 1987

In no country does the reform of the bureaucracy come from within. The streamlining of bureaucracy must come from the will of the people themselves and must be carried out by the national leadership.

> MURRAY WEIDENBAUM of Washington University, in a speech, September 16, 1992

As part of his government restructuring efforts, President Clinton has just announced that he wants to combine the Bureau of Alcohol, Tobacco and Firearms with the Bureau of Fisheries and the Interstate Trucking Commission.

They're going to name it the Department of Guys.

> VIRGINIA DEAN of the American Bankers Association, in a speech, September 21, 1995

In the military, you have to do more and more with less and less, and that's a business issue.

> KRIS FUHR of Kraft Foods and former army officer, quoted in the *Wall Street Journal*, February 16, 1997

We've explicitly applied a series of principles you're more likely to find in business school than in public affairs schools.

> STEPHEN GOLDSMITH, mayor of Indianapolis, Indiana, who is known for his efforts to privatize municipal services, quoted in the *New Republic*, June 30, 1997

We want to reinforce the notion that our stamps and products are collectible.

> AZECZALY JAFFER, manager of stamp services, U.S. Postal Service, on new practice of last-day cancellations for sale to collectors, to augment its lucrative business in first-day cancellations, quoted in the *Wall Street Journal*, February 21, 1997

Like most city governments, ours did not think in terms of business units or costs. We used standard government accounting principles that prevented our managers from stealing money, but we did nothing to stop them from wasting it.

When managers in our Department of Public Works analyzed their costs of picking up trash, they discovered that, over four years, they had spent $252,000 on repairs to a garbage truck that sold new for $90,000. The city garage, with a separate budget, maintained the truck and had no reason to care how much money it spent to fix up the same truck. When we loaded in all the costs associated with it we found that the truck was costing Indianapolis taxpayers $39 per mile to operate.

Opportunities for privatization are lost when governments delude themselves into thinking they are efficient by benchmarking their activities only against similar activities performed by other governments [instead of the private sector, too].

> STEPHEN GOLDSMITH, mayor of Indianapolis and pioneer of municipal privatization, *Harvard Business Review*, May–June 1997

27.3.21 Taxes

The art of taxation consists in so plucking the goose as to obtain the largest possible amount of feathers with the smallest possible amount of hissing.

> JEAN-BAPTISTE COLBERT, financial comptroller for Louis XIV

The state is the great fictitious entity by which everyone seeks to live at the expense of everyone else.

> FRÉDÉRIC BASTIAT, nineteenth-century French economic journalist

The hardest thing in the world to understand is income tax.

> ALBERT EINSTEIN

It's a public scandal when members of the *Fortune* 500 pay less in taxes than the people who wax their floors or type their letters.

> ROBERT McINTYRE of Citizens for Tax Justice, quoted in *U.S. News & World Report,* September 9, 1985

The House took a large 25 percent raise. We [senators] took a 3 percent raise, but we kept our right to earn an outside income. In this way the taxpayers don't have to pay.

> SENATOR ALFONSE D'AMATO, quoted in Leonard Lurie, *Senator Pothole* (Birch Lane Press, 1994)

It is as difficult for the king to determine if his officials are stealing some of his money as it is to determine whether the fish in the river are drinking some of the water.

> Ancient Indian sage quoted by Mancur Olson, an economist at the University of Maryland, Asian edition of the *Wall Street Journal,* October 22, 1996

We just debate federal income taxes because that's what we have always debated. They're the most visible.

> C. EUGENE STEURELE, economist at the Urban Institute, quoted in *Business Week,* September 30, 1996

There are, believe it or not, good taxes. A good tax is cheap to administer; a good tax does not distort economic activity; a good tax is fair.

Another sort of good tax corrects an externality—a cost imposed by one set of economic players on another. That is the category that green taxes fall into.

> *The Economist,* November 16, 1996

The last important human activity not subject to taxation is sex. Why this curious exemption? When we are compelled to pay taxes for food, clothing, and shelter, does it make any sense to leave sex tax-free like municipal bonds?

> RUSSELL BAKER, *So This Is Depravity* (Pocket Books, 1983)

Almost without exception, forecasts of the effects of taxes on real behavior have exceeded the actual responses.

> HENRY J. AARON of the liberal think tank Brookings Institution, quoted in *Fortune,* September 6, 1993

Fly the Concorde, take a luxury liner, stay in a four-star hotel, and have a burger for dinner. Everything is deductible except the burger.

> Anonymous restaurateur, commenting on reduction of business-meal deduction from 80 percent to 50 percent, quoted in *Fortune,* January 24, 1994

[A] zero tax rate up to a specific dollar amount, and a 100 percent tax rate—i.e., total confiscation—above that amount. And that amount is whatever my parents leave me.

> JEFF YABLON, Washington tax lawyer, outlining the ideal inheritance-tax formula, quoted in the *Wall Street Journal,* June 11, 1997

When a tax system departs dramatically from the fundamental values of the people it taxes, it cannot sustain public support.

> PROFESSOR MICHAEL J. GRAETZ of Yale Law School, *The Decline and Fall of the Income Tax* (Norton, 1997)

[Dubious tax shelter]

Personal Penny Account: A fund composed entirely of pennies. Since nobody likes pennies, or even wants to count them, this fund is completely tax exempt.

> ROZ CHAST, cartoonist for the *New Yorker,* cartoon printed in *Harvard Business Review,* March–April 1996

27.3.22   Taxes—Capital Gains

[C]apital gains represent risk-taking long-term investment that the government ought to encourage. But if you say that, you can no longer claim the banner of the free market. You have become a central planner, an advocate of "industrial policy," a socialist. You are saying that the market cannot be trusted, that the government knows better than the invisible hand where the nation's investment dollars ought to go.

> MICHAEL KINSLEY, *New Republic,* December 12, 1994

My experience in the financial world has led me to the belief that there is nothing else we could do so easily that would have more beneficial effects on our economy than liquefying $8 trillion in capital that is now frozen out of fear of the tax collector—$1 trillion that is real gain and the $7 trillion that results from inflation, bound up together so neither public sector nor private sector can make proper use of it.

> THEODORE J. FORSTMANN, senior partner of Forstmann Little & Co., on indexing capital gains to inflation, quoted in the *Wall Street Journal,* October 22, 1996

As someone who makes my living catering to these [very wealthy] clients, I find these products [that exploit loopholes to avoid capital gains taxes] useful and successful. But as a citizen, which I am after about 6:30 every evening, I worry that there is a growing perception that these tax techniques are available only to the wealthy few, that the average citizen and investor doesn't have access to them. Nothing does more to undermine our tax system than that.

> ROBERT WILLENS of the investment firm Lehman Brothers, quoted in the *New York Times,* December 1, 1996

27.3.23 Taxes—City and State

The thing generally raised on city land is taxes.

> CHARLES DUDLEY WARNER, "Sixteenth Week," *My Summer in a Garden* (1871)

[T]he European Commission would not tolerate a situation in which a company in Italy trying to sell goods in France had an 8 percent advantage. But if you're in the mail order business in the United States and you're trying to sell goods in Los Angeles, you'd have an 8 1/4 percent advantage if you're based in Nevada, rather than San Francisco.

> BRAD SHERMAN, tax commissioner and chairman of California Board of Equalization, in a speech, July 1, 1993

27.3.24 Taxes—Cost of Compliance

Chrysler's 1991 return . . . was a stack of paper six feet high, prepared by 55 accountants who worked on nothing else that year. The company is perpetually audited by at least nine IRS agents. Chrysler's chief tax counsel estimates that it will be 10 years before all current matters in dispute between Chrysler and the IRS are settled.

> *American Heritage,* May–June 1996

[Eastman Kodak's] tax staff has grown by two-thirds over the past decade, partly because of the tax break al-

lowed under new regulations. The company's annual tax return has doubled in weight to 35 pounds over the same period.

> THOMAS HOPKINS of the Rochester Institute of Technology, quoted in the *Economist,* July 27, 1996

27.3.25 Taxation Costs by the Numbers

Costs of the Federal Tax System to Taxpayers for Every Dollar of Revenues Collected:

Compliance costs	24 cents
Enforcement costs	2 cents
Disincentive to production	33 cents
Disincentive cost of tax uncertainty	2 cents
Evasion and avoidance cost	3 cents
Government cost	1 cents
Total	65 cents

> JAMES L. PAYNE, *Costly Returns* (ICS Press, 1993)

27.3.26 Taxes—The IRS

They should not be hit with outlandish penalties for failing to memorize the tax code.

> U.S. SENATOR NANCY KASSEBAUM (Republican, Kansas) on a $50 penalty against an 84-year-old Kansas City woman who underpaid her income tax by 60 cents, quoted in *U.S. News & World Report,* February 20, 1984

It obviously caused a lot of frustration and anxiety to taxpayers, for which we apologize.

> DAN SEKLECKI, IRS spokesman, saying that because of a computer error, 10,000 companies received letters threatening to seize their property, quoted in *U.S. News & World Report,* February 11, 1985

The IRS has sunk so low in public opinion that a responsible accountant honestly believes he needs a hood [over his head] to protect himself from IRS retaliation.

> RONALD NOLL of the Pennsylvania Society of Public Accountants, quoted in *U.S. News & World Report,* March 25, 1985

The IRS 800 number is the most called 800 number in the country.

> RICK PARKHILL, executive publisher of the interactive phone industry journal *Infotext,* quoted in *Fortune,* March 1, 1992

The IRS probably cannot aspire to taxpayers' affection, but at least it can aspire to their respect.

> LAWRENCE SUMMERS, U.S. Deputy Treasury Secretary, quoted in the *Wall Street Journal,* September 9, 1997

Nothing guarantees more applause and more support than the call to abolish the Internal Revenue Service.

> Memo to Republican legislators circulated by GOP pollster FRANK LUNTZ, quoted in the *Wall Street Journal,* September 9, 1997

Everybody knows someone who's been audited. The stories always read like a Stephen King novel. The ending is always bad.

> FRANK LUNTZ, GOP pollster who urged Republican candidates to go after the IRS, quoted in *Newsweek,* October 6, 1997

27.3.27 IRS by the Numbers

The average income for an IRS agent, including benefits, is $53,309. Each agent, however, collects an average of $904,000 for the government each year. That's an average annual net gain of $850,691 per agent.

> HERBERT BARCHOFF, member of the President's Council of Economic Advisors under President Harry Truman, quoted in the *New York Times,* September 22, 1996

We find that very hard-hitting guys—guys who don't tell their wives or mistresses any of their inner business secrets—have openly told perfect strangers about their two sets of books and how they manipulate their tax returns.

. . . I say, never talk to strangers.

We have seen even the toughest of businessmen wilt when the agents show their badges.

> MARTIN POLLNER, former U.S. Treasury enforcement director, quoted in *Forbes,* August 25, 1986

We are not looking for fear.
We are not looking for love.
We are looking for respect.

> LAWRENCE GIBBS, IRS Commissioner, assuring Congress that there was no need for a taxpayers' bill of rights to govern the conduct of the IRS, quoted in *U.S. News & World Report,* May 4, 1987

27.3.28 Taxes—International

It's incredibly simplistic to suggest you can keep all your money in a no-tax jurisdiction. Governments have lost control of what I call liquid assets, but they have not lost control of fixed assets.

> MICHAEL DOBBS-HIGGINSON, former head of Merrill Lynch Asia, author of *Asia Pacific: A View on Its Role in the New World Disorder, Asia, Inc.,* November 1994

27.3.29 Taxes—Reform

Why does a slight tax increase cost you two hundred dollars and a substantial tax cut save you thirty cents?

> PEG BRACKEN, comic writer

They [friends on Wall Street] are as confused as I am. They don't know the effect.

> DONALD REGAN, then White House Chief of Staff and former CEO of Merrill Lynch, quoted in *U.S. News & World Report,* September 1, 1986

This is unfair. It's like losing a ski race because someone adds a gate at the top of the hill once you're halfway down.

> RICHARD OVERTON of the chemical company Monsanto, on Treasury Department proposal to disallow the "practical capacity" method of inventory valuation for tax purposes in order to implement capitalization provisions of the 1986 Tax Reform Act, quoted in *Forbes,* July 27, 1987

We have a free market in this country, and what it has done is found its way quite clearly around the double taxation of dividends. I think we ought to face that . . . And if you agree with me, I think where we ought to look is to trying to [end] the difference in the way we treat debt . . . and the way we treat equity.

> NICHOLAS BRADY, Treasury Secretary, testifying before the Senate Finance Committee hearings on leveraged buyouts, quoted in the *New Yorker,* May 8, 1988

Now is the time to kill the Taxasaurus monster! Kill the dinosaur, kill him now! If you don't, he's going to eat more jobs. So take this lead pencil and give him lead poisoning. Kill him!

> U.S. SENATOR ALFONSE D'AMATO (Republican, New York), congressional hearings, 1993

Economists have pored over the data from before and after the 1986 reform and have been hard-pressed to find evidence that it had any large effects on the economy whatever—certainly nothing like the major effects that had been forecast by tax reform's supporters and opponents.

> ROB NORTON, "Playing Politics with the Dismal Science," *Fortune,* September 30, 1996

Oh, PUHLEASE. . . . Like, right, cut taxes *and* balance the budget. I made the mistake of believing Ronald Reagan when he came out with that, and he created a $5 trillion debt.

> Airline reservation agent explaining why he was going to vote for Clinton even though he was a lifelong Republican, quoted by Michael Lewis, *New York Times,* November 10, 1996

The war against the IRS may be a citizen uprising, but it's being led by politicians.

> DAVID SHRIBMAN, journalist, *Fortune,* November 24, 1997

[The flat tax is] A snare and a delusion.

> DONALD REGAN, then U.S. Treasury Secretary, quoted in *U.S. News & World Report,* June 25, 1984

28. INDUSTRIES IN TRANSITION

28.1 DEFENSE

The Pentagon, that immense monument to modern man's subservience to the desk.

> BARON OLIVER FRANKS, British philosopher and administrator, quoted in the *Observer* (London), November 30, 1952

This industry is about to go over a cliff.

> MARTIN BOLLINGER of the consulting firm Booz, Allen & Hamilton, quoted in the *Economist,* January 16, 1993

For some defense contractors, antitrust has taken the place of the former Soviet Union as the greatest threat to National Security.

> STEVEN A. NEWBORN of the Federal Trade Commission Competition Bureau, *Business Week,* January 31, 1994

What really sells your product is to have it used in actual fighting.

> JOSE LUIZ WHITAKER RIBEIRO, Brazilian arms manufacturer, whose armored personnel carriers were used in Iraq's war against Iran, quoted in the *Wall Street Journal,* January 4, 1985

In a well-executed arms deal, someone cheats everyone. It's an exercise in pure capitalism—and it's very nasty.

Buyers are all the same to us. There's no politics in the arms business.

> ANTHONY CORDESMAN of high-tech firm Eaton, quoted in *Fortune,* February 16, 1987

Until recently, the closest thing to a risky decision in America's sprawling defense industry was selecting a Washington restaurant in which to entertain a Pentagon contact.

> *The Economist,* November 28, 1992

The "winner" of the competitive bidding process often wins only the right to lose millions of dollars.

> JERROLD T. LUNDQUIST of the consulting firm McKinsey & Co., quoted in *Harvard Business Review,* November–December 1992

[T]he Ministry of Defense's requirements do not necessarily gel with the demands of export markets.

> PETER KENYON, managing director of the privatized Royal Ordnance, who was finding that British arms weren't selling well abroad, quoted in the *Economist,* February 22, 1992

I believe defense will come back. I read history books. Human nature has not changed in 1992.

> NORMAN R. AUGUSTINE, CEO of the aerospace firm Lockheed Martin, quoted in *Fortune,* February 22, 1993

For sovereign nations, the ability to defend themselves is as fundamental as food, air, and sex to humans. If countries don't buy our F-15s, they'll buy British Tornadoes.

> BERNARD SCHWARTZ, chairman of the defense electronics firm Loral, quoted in *Fortune,* February 22, 1993

Should the defense industry be treated in the same fashion as a General Motors, United Airlines, or Wrigley's chewing gum?

> NORMAN R. AUGUSTINE, CEO of the aerospace firm Lockheed Martin, in a speech, August 10, 1993

The U.S. aerospace industry began to shed employees at a rate of one every 30 seconds—and quickly found itself saddled with an excess plant capacity two-thirds greater than that which was needed. Over a million employees lost their jobs, and the combined market value of the four largest aerospace firms tumbled below that of McDonald's. It seemed the stock-purchasing public had a greater appetite for McDonald's hamburgers than for McDonnell's fighters.

By far the most imaginative strategy for dealing with the evolving crisis was offered by Kent Kresa, the CEO of [aerospace firm] Northrop. His strategy was described in *U.S.A. Today* as follows: "CEO Kent Kresa also said that Northrop will continue to sell nonproductive assets. Last year it sold its headquarters in Los Angeles."

> NORMAN R. AUGUSTINE, president of Lockheed Martin Corporation, in a speech, April 21, 1995

Point one. [In response to another character's appeal that he stop selling weapons as a matter of conscience] There is actually only one point actually. *I don't give a fart.* The difference between me and the other charlies is, *I* admit it. If a horde of niggers—yes, I said *niggers,* I meant *niggers*—if these *niggers* shot each other dead with my toys tomorrow and I made a bob out of it, great news by me. Because if *I* don't sell 'em the goods, some *other* charlie will. Government used to understand that. If they've gone soft, tough titty on 'em.

> SIR ANTHONY JOYSTON BRADSHAW, arms dealer character in John Le Carré's, *The Secret Pilgrim* (Knopf, 1990)

There is a big difference between selling subs to Iran and F-15s to Saudi Arabia. If you can't distinguish between the two, you shouldn't be in the foreign affairs business.

> JOEL L. JOHNSON of the Aerospace Industries Association, quoted in *Fortune,* February 22, 1993

Saudi Arabia is a black hole. We have enormous gaps in understanding what is going on there.

> Senior government figure in article headlined "U.S. Takes Hard Look at Saudis with Bombing and Shah in Mind," quoted in the *New York Times,* December 1, 1996

Since the number of jobs peaked at 1.44 million in 1987, companies that do most of the business with the Pentagon have cut payrolls by nearly 600,000—a drop of 40 percent.

> TRICIA WALSH, *Fortune,* October 30, 1995

The Europeans are scared to death of the combinations taking place on this side of the Atlantic [after merger of Boeing and McDonnell-Douglas].

> PHILLIP A. ODEEN, former Pentagon official and CEO of the defense consulting firm BDM International, quoted in the *Wall Street Journal,* December 16, 1996

Consolidation [merging] has become a better business for these companies than building airplanes or electronic systems. The prime contractors have been grazing in those fields for a while and the fields are now barren. They're going to have to go back to selling airplanes.

> JOHN KUTLER, president of investment bank Quarterdeck Investment Partners, quoted in the *New York Times,* July 4, 1997

It's hard for me to understand this argument that less competition is good for the country and good for the taxpayers.

> U.S. SENATOR CHARLES E. GRASSLEY (Republican, Iowa), reacting to Clinton administration approval of merger between the aerospace firms Lockheed Martin and Northrop Grumman, quoted in the *New York Times,* July 4, 1997

The United States continues to be among the most conservative arms exporters in the world. If it were an open market and these were refrigerators, we'd probably have 70 percent of the market.

> JOEL L. JOHNSON of the Aerospace Industries Association, quoted in the *New York Times,* August 16, 1997

Russia has confronted significant difficulties in making lucrative new sales of conventional weapons because most potential cash-paying arms purchasers have been long-standing customers of the United States or major West European suppliers. These nations are not likely to replace their weapons inventories with unfamiliar non-Western armaments when newer versions of existing equipment are readily available.

> Report to the Congressional Research Service, quoted in the *New York Times,* August 16, 1997

Every gun that is made, every warship launched, every rocket fired signifies, in the final sense, a theft from those who hunger and are not fed, those who are cold and are not clothed. This world in arms is not spending money alone. It is spending the sweat of its laborers, the genius of its scientists, the hopes of its children.

> U.S. PRESIDENT DWIGHT D. EISENHOWER, in a speech, April 16, 1953

Payoffs for layoffs.

> U.S. REPRESENTATIVE BERNIE SANDERS (Independent, Vermont), describing Defense Department subsidies for merging military contractors during consolidation, quoted in the *Wall Street Journal,* July 22, 1996

This a triumph of muscular lobbying over common sense.

> STEPHEN MOORE of the libertarian think tank Cato Institute, quoted in the *Wall Street Journal,* July 22, 1996

Our point (in proposing plan) was that we have half-full plants. If we could be permitted to combine these plants we could have full plants and save a lot of money.

> NORMAN R. AUGUSTINE, CEO of the aerospace firm Lockheed Martin, quoted in the *Wall Street Journal*, July 22, 1996

We have a duty to the 400,000 people who work in our defense industries to continue to have the opportunity to work.

> ROBIN COOK, British foreign secretary, quoted in the *Financial Times*, October 3, 1997

European [defense] markets are narrow, segregated, and shrinking. If the Europeans do not restructure their own industry, the Americans will be delighted to do it for them.

> FRANÇOIS HEISBOURG of French defense company Matra-Defense, quoted in the *Financial Times*, November 4, 1997

Our competitors [arms suppliers in the United States, Germany, Britain, and France] generally abide by no rules or ethical standards in their competition.

> OLEG SIDORENKO of the Russian state-owned arms company Rosvooruzhenie, quoted in the *Financial Times*, January 7, 1997

Russia currently appears to be cynically selling arms purely for financial reasons and there is little or no foreign policy input at all.

> A defense expert, quoted in the *Financial Times*, January 7, 1997

The world's arms makers have suffered more than anybody except the world's apparatchiks from the end of the struggles against Communism.

> *The Economist*, November 28, 1995

The problem with [defense to civilian] conversion is that people look at World War II, when tank plants retooled to make autos. Back then there was huge unmet consumer demand. Today there are no markets that don't already have suppliers who know them well. So we have to invent something new or evolve into something new.

> RENSO CAPORALI, CEO of the aerospace firm Grumman, quoted in *Fortune*, February 22, 1992

Military needs are now too specialized to have much of a spin-off benefit. It was clear the civilian sector had a use for the 707. But who wants a Stealth Bomber other than the military?

> LAWRENCE KORB, of the liberal think tank Brookings Institution, quoted in *Fortune*, February 22, 1992

The growth we get from defense is not bad, but it's not as good as the rest of our business.

> PIERRE-YVES SIMONOT of the Anglo-French information technology firm Sema, quoted in the *Financial Times*, April 2, 1997

The Defense Department studied the 97 bases closed in the 1960s and the 1970s and found that the closings eliminated 87,600 civilian jobs over 20 years. It also found that by 1993 new industries located on the former bases were employing 171,100 people.

> PETER SPIEGEL, *Forbes*, September 22, 1997

28.2 ENERGY

[N]ot since John D. Rockefeller sent free kerosene lamps to China has the oil industry done anything really outstanding to create a demand for its product.

> THEODORE LEVITT of the Harvard Business School, "Marketing Myopia," *Harvard Business Review*, September–October 1975

It has become cheaper to look for oil on the floor of the New York Stock Exchange than in the ground.

> T. BOONE PICKENS, president of the oil firm Mesa Petroleum, quoted in *Time*, March 4, 1985

Most firms' exploration expenditures, in my estimation, have achieved such poor rates of return as to constitute a waste of shareholders' assets.

> BERNARD J. PICHI of the investment bank Salomon Brothers, quoted in T. Boone Pickens Jr., "Professions of a Short Termer," *Harvard Business Review*, May–June 1986

The meek shall inherit the earth but not the mineral rights.

> J. PAUL GETTY, quoted in *Business Week*, April 28, 1986

Oil pricing is not economics, it's politics.

> JOHN CASSIDY JR., owner of Contractors' Exchange Inc., *Business Week,* April 28, 1986

When people get wealthy, they tend to think they're better than they really are. Now, they realize their shortcomings.

> FATHER JOSEPH SCHLEY of St. Nicholas Church, Midland, Texas (which went from being one of the richest towns in the United States in 1983 to having 12.2 percent unemployment in 1986), quoted in *Forbes,* October 27, 1986

A new survey by Arthur Andersen of 30 U.S. oil companies shows that since 1987, foreign exploration and development expenditures have increased 83 percent, compared to an increase of just 13 percent here in the United States. Some people call that "capital flight." But when you look at why it is happening [environmental regulation, in his opinion], I think it would be more accurate to call it "capital expulsion."

> KENNETH T. DERR, CEO of the oil firm Chevron Corporation, in a speech, August 7, 1992

If we don't bring environmentalists into the conversation about trade, they'll beat at the door until they knock it down.

> WILLIAM BROCK, former U.S. Trade Representative, quoted in *Fortune,* January 10, 1994

Since the first day of the gasoline lines . . . decades ago, government, at one time or another, has told us where we can drill for oil and gas, how much we can sell, whom we can employ, what minimum wage rates we must pay—and at one point, not too many years ago, even the extent to which we must subsidize our competitors.

As a result, over the years, the government developed an energy policy that encouraged consumption, discouraged production, and relied on imports to fill the gap. And that, in the 1970s and 1980s, is what gave us what came to be called "The Energy Crisis."

> GEORGE S. SPINDLER of the oil firm Amoco, in a speech, October 24, 1995

The wave of conservation and substitution is largely over.

> CHARLES OBER of the brokerage firm T. Rowe Price, quoted in *Fortune,* October 30, 1995

The lesson is that once you switch from bicycle to moped, there is no turning back.

> JAMES BARROW, manager of Vanguard's Windsor II fund, on why development in emerging economies was prompting him to invest heavily in energy stocks, *Fortune,* October 30, 1995

In this country [the United States] since 1970, lead emissions have decreased by 78 percent. Sulfur dioxide emissions have dropped by more than 30 percent and are expected to be cut by some 40 percent more by the year 2000. Carbon monoxide has been cut by one-quarter and is projected to be reduced by an additional 36 percent by the year 2000.

> LEE R. RAYMOND, CEO of the oil company Exxon, in a speech, May 6, 1996

Gasoline is the cheapest liquid you can get next to water, and it's much cheaper than bottled water.

> LLEWELLYN KIND, publisher of *Energy Daily,* quoted in the *New York Times,* October 26, 1997

Oil-price forecasters make sheep seem like independent thinkers. There's no evidence that mineral prices rise over time. Technology always overwhelms depletion.

> MICHAEL C. LYNCH of MIT, quoted in *Business Week,* November 3, 1997

If you go back 10 or 20 years ago, the Seven Sisters [multinational oil companies] were developers and controllers of all technology. Improving access to that technology has changed the playing field.

> ROBERT P. PEEBLER, CEO of seismic software firm Landmark Graphics, quoted in *Business Week,* November 3, 1997

Electricity [in the approaching age of deregulation] will become one of the most brutally competitive markets with all the unfavorable characteristics of commodity chemicals, and none of the positives.

> JEFFREY SKILLING, president of the energy firm Enron, quoted in the *Financial Times,* March 14, 1997

Among the so-called alternative fuels, none measure up to oil in abundance, performance, and affordability. For example, ethanol, which is made mainly from corn, is about as clean as reformulated gasoline, but costs twice as much to produce. That's, in part, because it takes about the same amount of energy to harvest, transport, and process as it yields as a fuel.

We need economically and environmentally attractive alternative [fuel]s, and those that meet these criteria will succeed in a free marketplace. But government should not try to pick winners by subsidizing one alternative over the other or by specifically discriminating against oil-based products.

> LEE R. RAYMOND, chairman of the oil company Exxon, in a speech, May 6, 1996

Because drivers in nine big cities are required to use special gas to cut air pollution, corn-based ethanol refiners get a $500 million tax break—most of which goes to one company, Archer Daniels Midland Co. A competing product, made from natural gas, gets no such benefit.

> *Business Week,* July 3, 1995

Solar energy has moved a long way, but it really has not moved as far as it should in terms of getting costs down to be competitive with energy generation by other means.

> JOHN ROBIS, chief executive of the British insurance firm Guardian Royal Exchange (the first U.K. insurance company to install solar panels on its headquarters in support of anti–global warming measures), quoted in the *Financial Times,* February 25, 1997

Although the sun's energy in its natural state is "free" so is oil. It is the tools of exploitation which cost money.

> PROFESSOR HARRY RUPPE of the Technical University of Munich, who has done research on satellites that would collect solar energy in space and beam it to earth to generate electricity, quoted in the *Financial Times,* September 18, 1997

Don't underestimate the [auto] industry's desire to keep internal combustion.

> JASON MARK of the Union of Concerned Scientists, on auto industry research into new technologies, quoted in the *Wall Street Journal,* January 5, 1998

The problem with all these fossil fuels . . . is that the number of people increased on earth. We are 6 billion now. When the century started, we were a billion and a half. In 30 years, we will be 10 billion, and all of them

need energy. . . . Within the next decade or two, there will be a substantial, inevitable pressure.

> DR. GEORGE OLAH, Nobel Prize–winning physicist and inventor of methanol-powered fuel-cell technology, quoted in the *Wall Street Journal,* January 5, 1998

28.3 MANAGED HEALTH CARE

It's a painful shakeout. Steel has gone through it, farmers, computers. We doctors have always occupied a very favored position. Now it's our turn.

> DR. RICHARD EGDAHL, director of Boston University Medical Center, quoted in *U.S. News & World Report,* January 26, 1987

You almost need a cookbook with all these plans.

You're caught between the watchdogs who make sure you didn't keep the patients in too long and the watchdogs who make sure you treated them properly.

> DR. EDWARD BOYCE, obstetrician and gynecologist, quoted in *U.S. News & World Report,* January 26, 1987

You cannot have unfettered decision making by physicians and control expenditures.

> DR. WILLIAM ROPER, chief of the Health Care Financing Administration, quoted in *Time,* February 1, 1988

Organizing doctors is like trying to herd cats. [Common explanation for why doctors didn't act collectively in response to rise of managed care]

> Cited by DR. PAUL EHRLICH, allergist

It's not managed care, it's stupid care.

> Manhattan internist and cancer specialist, who complained that the cut-rate lab work that health management organizations insisted on frequently came back obviously flawed and had to be repeated at extra cost, quoted in *New York,* August 23, 1993

We can't exactly hang out a shingle saying: "Anesthesia for Sale." We're dependent on the volume of surgery in hospitals.

> DR. JONATHAN ROTH, chairman of the anesthesiology department of Albert Einstein Medical Center, Philadelphia, quoted in the *Wall Street Journal,* March 17, 1995

Technology made this a very attractive specialty, but now we've almost saturated the market.

> DR. MACELLE WILLOCK of the anesthesiology department at Boston University, quoted in the *Wall Street Journal*, March 17, 1995

Doctors' habits don't change until you have a pharmaceuticals company with a financial incentive to change them.

> CARL SEIDEN of the investment firm Sanford C. Bernstein in New York, *Fortune*, June 9, 1997

Mural dyslexia. ["Inability to read the handwriting on the wall," the diagnosis for doctors who failed to anticipate the success of health maintenance organizations and persisted in traditional practices until the bottom fell out]

> Cited by DR. PAUL EHRLICH, allergist

In welfare fraud, a person has to work very hard to rip off the system for $100,000. In health care, a provider or doctor can burp and take $100,000.

> *Wall Street Journal*, January 31, 1997

It's sad. . . . at the first sign of discomfort we get meat-ax regulation.

> UWE REINHARDT, Princeton economist, commenting on government rules to end "drive-by deliveries" by allowing mothers and newborns two days of hospitalization, quoted in the *New York Times*, October 10, 1996

We probably wouldn't approve of the Kevorkian HMO.

> JOSEPH NEWHOUSE, Harvard economist, referring to the doctor famous for crusading to make assisted suicide legal, on role of state in setting medical priorities, quoted in the *New York Times*, October 10, 1996

In managed care, the primary-care doctors suddenly become the masters instead of the slaves.

> DENNIS FUHRMAN, clinic administrator in Fargo, North Dakota, quoted in the *Wall Street Journal*, October 22, 1996

My current work leads me to forecast that the chronic diseases will be reduced, that medical intervention will continue to be very effective, and that the demand for medical care will continue to go up despite whatever the government does to try to constrain it. Most people my age would rather have a new knee than another VCR.

> ROBERT FOGEL, University of Chicago economist and 1993 Nobel Prize winner, on the National Public Radio program *All Things Considered*, October 12, 1993

If I had my way, we'd have doctors more inclined to have conversation with patients than to order a battery of tests.

> DR. C. EVERETT KOOP, former surgeon general of the United States, quoted in *Fortune*, June 14, 1996

Most pharmaceutical companies confused [*sic*] the physician, rather than the payer, as their customer.

> GEORGE POSTE, of the pharmaceutical firm Smith-Kline Beecham, in a speech, January 14, 1997

We have failed to convince the public of our commitment to quality. That's the crisis we face today.

> DANIEL T. McGOWAN, president of HIP Health Insurance Plans, one of three HMOs that called for enforceable national standards, quoted in the *New York Times*, September 25, 1997

A standard joke about managed care is that the ideal patient is perfectly healthy for 20 years, comes in, gets a diagnosis of something incurable, and dies before any money can be spent.

> DR. PERRI KLASS, pediatrician and writer, "Managing Managed Care," *New York Times Magazine*, October 5, 1997

The sicker you make a patient look, the more money you get. Most doctors don't really understand how that system works.

Physicians are angry about the loss of control. I look at big profits being raked off by for-profit HMOs, instead of going to physicians for working hard. We've sort of gone from a profession to a service industry. . . . The insurance companies think it's all widgets and algorithms. If you're a bad widget, we'll get rid of you; if you're a good widget, it doesn't matter which widget, it doesn't matter which widget you are.

> DR. DEBRA SHAPIRO, quoted in the *New York Times Magazine*, October 5, 1997

Number one rule of managed health care: First, do nothing.

> Heard on National Public Radio program *Science Friday,* November 28, 1997

28.4 PETROCHEMICALS

This is the long-term pattern for base commodities—you make money only occasionally, but when you do, it is big money.

> PAUL BEALE of the petrochemical consulting firm PCI Ltd., quoted in the *Economist,* March 14, 1992

28.5 RETAILING

You can compete on price, but it only goes so far.

> DAVID DWORKIN, CEO of the department store chain Carter Hawley Stores Inc. (which put violinists and guitarists in stores and offered amusement park rides for children on the roof of its San Francisco Emporium store), quoted in *Business Week,* January 10, 1994

There is a clear trend of Christmas becoming less important.

> Economist DAVID WYSS, quoted in the *Wall Street Journal,* January 3, 1997

Nobody puts *Merry Christmas* on their shopping bags anymore. Part of the reason is being politically correct, but also nobody wants to tie their shopping bags to that specific date. The buying season is considerably longer.

> ANN PINKERTON of the shopping-bag firm Continental Extrusions, quoted in the *Wall Street Journal,* December 5, 1996

The dichotomy of American retailing continues. The upper-income stores will continue to do well, as will the lower-end stores because they offer value. And the buys in the middle seem to have the problems.

> JEFFREY FEINER of the investment bank Lehmann Brothers, quoted in the *New York Times,* November 29, 1997

It took stores years to learn that Easter had disappeared as a selling holiday. And after three years in a row of weakness, they have to realize that you can't count on Christmas anymore either. In all honesty, it is much more profitable to get sales in October than in December these days.

> PETER SCHAEFFER of the investment firm Dillon Read, quoted in the *New York Times,* December 26, 1997

28.5.1 Retailing by the Numbers

In 1964, the United States had 5.3 square feet of retail space per capita. Today, the country has 19 square feet.

In 1978, apparel's share of consumer spending was $197. In 1996, that figure was $160.

In 1980, apparel's share of consumer spending stood at 5.2 percent. By 1996, that percent had dropped to 4.4.

> *Women's Wear Daily,* October 30, 1997

28.6 TELECOMMUNICATIONS

There are two kinds of [phone] customers: Those who have been victims of toll fraud, and those who will be.

> JAMES SNYDER, of the telecommunications firm MCI, quoted in *Forbes,* August 3, 1996

It took us almost 75 years to introduce color phones.

While the rest of the world was experimenting with just-in-time manufacturing, we were mired in a just-in-case mentality, designing phones built to last 50 years.

And faced with the first flush of competition, many of us were genuinely concerned about those hobgoblins known as "harms to the network." Attach a rubber cup to the mouthpiece of "our" phone and we threatened to cut off "your" service.

> HARRY BENNETT of the telecommunications company AT&T, in a speech, July 24, 1996

Why should I have to live with that monster [12-story cellular phone antenna] across the street from my house—so some rich guy can make a call from his car?

> KEN KENYON, retired U.S. Marine and maintenance man in New Jersey, quoted in the *Wall Street Journal,* July 2, 1996

When people built the first radio systems, you could almost prove that one approach was better just by counting the number of parts it required. Once everything is on an integrated circuit, almost anything can be made to work.

> STEWART PERSONICK of the telecommunications company Bellcore, quoted in *Fortune,* October 13, 1997

Egos and economic self-interest always get in the way [of completing proposed telecommunications alliances]. Mostly egos.

> H. BRIAN THOMPSON, CEO of the telecommunications company LCI, quoted in *Business Week,* September 26, 1994

Father's Day is the third busiest holiday for phone calls behind Mother's Day and Christmas, but first in collect calls, ahead of Mother's Day and Valentine's Day.

> *Atlantic Monthly,* June 1997

Open telecom markets may ultimately save consumers money, but in the short term, the main beneficiaries are some very busy telecom lawyers.

> AMY BARRETT, *Business Week,* November 4, 1996

The forces of evil unleashed by the new telecom act are now obviously running far ahead of the forces of good.

> MARK COOPER of the Consumer Federation of America, in reaction to merger plans of AT&T and SBC, one of the Baby Bells, quoted in the *Wall Street Journal,* May 28, 1997

This reminds me of Humpty Dumpty: All the king's horses and all the king's men are engaged in putting Ma Bell together again. If there was a reason for splitting the company before, those reasons probably still remain valid.

> U.S. REPRESENTATIVE JOHN DINGELL (Democrat, Michigan), one of the principal drafters of the telecom reform that allowed this combination, quoted in the *Wall Street Journal,* May 28, 1997

28.6.1   Telecommunications—Ma Bell Grows Older

The break-up wasn't my idea.

> CHARLES BROWN, chairman of the telephone company AT&T, in response to a reporter's question about the scant consumer benefits from the court-order split of AT&T, quoted in *U.S. News & World Report,* December 24, 1984

[T]he American public suddenly fell in love with [Coca-Cola] all over again. "Hey, that's ours," they said. "Give it back." They cannot get their telephone company back—but they got original formula Coca-Cola back.

> The late ROBERT C. GOIZUETA, CEO of Coca-Cola, quoted in *Forbes,* July 28, 1986

Not in my lifetime.

> HAROLD H. GREENE, Federal District Court judge who broke up Ma Bell in 1984, asked if he expected any thanks

Everybody is walking around on pins and needles wondering if they're going to be next. We're reminded of what's happening every day. We have rows and rows of empty cubicles and desks.

> ELIZABETH UPORSKY of AT&T, quoted in *Time,* February 16, 1987

Speaking as a former monopoly provider, I can say without reservation that the vibrant competition in the U.S. long-distance market has made us into a stronger, more customer-focused company.

> ROBERT E. ALLEN, CEO of AT&T, in a speech, October 3, 1995

We reached a time when the advantage of integration was outweighed by the disadvantage of complexity.

> ROBERT ALLEN, CEO of AT&T, quoted in *Business Week,* November 2, 1995

It was like they'd been trained forever as an army and now they are suddenly trying to be Navy Seals. And their guys say, "What? I don't swim."

> Unnamed "Wall Streeter," quoted in *Fortune,* February 5, 1996

If everything we did was absolutely perfect or correct, maybe we'd be given another name and be called God or something. So, things didn't work out. We move on to something else.

> ROBERT E. ALLEN, CEO of AT&T, on cutting 50,000 jobs due to losses incurred during AT&T's adventure in computers, quoted in the *Wall Street Journal,* February 22, 1996

The only thing Bob Allen and his managers know how to do is turn out the lights.

> MARTIN SINGER, a former marketing manager, quoted in the *Wall Street Journal,* February 22, 1996

If AT&T hadn't stuck with computers and purchased NCR, it would have $10 billion to $12 billion additional financing to play with today to expand in wireless and fight the Bells.

> JACK GRUBMAN of the investment bank Salomon Brothers, quoted in the *Wall Street Journal,* February 22, 1996

I see a man [Robert Allen] who's not afraid to change a large, successful company.

> CRAIG McCAW, founder of McCaw Cellular, acquired by AT&T, quoted in *Fortune,* November 30, 1996

AT&T . . . paid out almost $350 million to business consultants in 1993 alone.

> ROBERT H. FRANK and PHILIP J. COOK, *The Winner-Take-All Society* (The Free Press, 1995)

One has to look at a business like AT&T over a longer period of time than just a year in which the industry is in turmoil.

> ROBERT ALLEN, CEO of AT&T, quoted in *Business Week,* September 2, 1996

I have no plans to retire at this time.

> ROBERT ALLEN, CEO of AT&T, quoted in *Business Week,* October 7, 1996

We are *they.* Nobody's stopping us from doing anything anymore.

> HENRY SCHACHT, CEO of the AT&T technology spin-off Lucent Technologies, *Wall Street Journal,* October 14, 1996

I don't know. But I get a lot of bills from AT&T.

> JOHN R. WALTER, former chairman of the printing firm R. R. Donnelley & Sons, then new president of AT&T, when asked which long-distance company he used at home, quoted in the *Wall Street Journal,* October 23, 1996 (Walter resigned from AT&T on July 17, 1997.)

We believe it [the executive sabbatical] can be a so-called downsizing tool. AT&T expects that a number of people will not return, a situation that would ease the need to downsize.

> BURKE STINSON of AT&T, quoted in the *New York Times,* September 14, 1997

We're determined to find creative ways of using other peoples' money to further our entry into new markets.

> An AT&T executive, on franchising the AT&T brand name, quoted in the *Wall Street Journal,* September 18, 1997

AT&T doesn't want to be known as a long-distance company in the future. It wants to be an all-distance company.

> An AT&T employee, quoted in the *Wall Street Journal,* September 18, 1997

AT&T has turned out to be our worst nightmare as a corporate partner. People usually think—"Big companies—solid, reliable." Well, they change direction more often and are completely ruthless about dropping things.

> TRIP HAWKINS, founder and CEO of the home computer firm 3DO, interviewed in Rama Dev Jager, *In the Company of Giants* (McGraw-Hill, 1997)

28.7 TOBACCO

[Agreement with government] radically changes the way we do business.

> STEVEN GOLDSTONE, CEO of the tobacco and food firm RJR Nabisco, in a memo to employees after deal was signed to pay hundreds of billions of dollars to end litigation against tobacco companies, quoted in *Time,* June 30, 1997

29.1 THE CANNIBAL PRINCIPLE

The Cannibal Principle: The whole point of integrated circuits is to absorb the functions of what previously were discrete electronic components, to incorporate them in a single new chip, and then to give them back for free, or at least for a lot less money than what they cost as individual parts. Thus, semiconductor technology eats everything, and people who oppose it get trampled. I can't think of another technology or industry like it.

> GORDON MOORE, cofounder of the computer chip firm Intel, quoted in *Fortune,* July 10, 1995

A business built on digital technology. . . . absorbs the functions of other businesses and gives them back free to the consumer. The customer pays less and gets more. The digital supplier gains a new revenue stream. And scores of traditional suppliers lose everything. The results: a win-win-lose world.

In this new world, many traditional businesses might as well have bull's-eyes painted on them. They are the targets of someone's cannibal-principle strategy.

It has been said that digital technology eats everything and tramples anyone who tries to oppose it. I believe that understates the case. You don't have to oppose digital technology to be trampled; innocent bystanders will be flattened, too. There is no neutrality in the Digital Revolution. You must become a digital revolutionary or risk losing everything.

> JOHN R. WALTER, former chairman of R. R. Donnelley & Sons and former president of AT&T, quoted in the *New York Times,* November 10, 1996

In the early days of the digital revolution, it was kind of a revolution and therefore all things seemed possible. So everybody had reasons to read *Wired,* because nobody knew what was going on. But, hey, after the revolution comes the provisional government. And quite commonly, the revolution eats its young, baby.

> BRUCE STERLING, writer for *Wired,* quoted in the *New York Times,* August 4, 1997

29.2 COMPUTERS

People usually compare the computer to the head of a human being. I would say that hardware is the bone of the head, the skull. The semiconductor is the brain within the head. The software is the wisdom. And data is the knowledge.

> MASHAYOSHI SON, founder and CEO, Softbank Corp. of Tokyo, interviewed in *Harvard Business Review,* January–February 1992

We weren't really sure what he was doing, typing away at that computer all the time. I guess now we know.

> LEONARA GRUMBLES of Huntsville, Alabama, after the FBI caught her 16-year-old son hacking into NASA's computer system, quoted in *U.S. News & World Report,* July 30, 1984

The era of the supercomputer is over.

> ED McCRACKEN, CEO of the hardware and software firm Silicon Graphics, quoted in the *Economist,* November 28, 1992

A lot of the great computer companies say that marketing services is as important to them as products. But they'll have international product managers, with high status, and no comparable service development manager, who looks after a whole range of services.

> LAURIE YOUNG, marketing consultant, *Financial Times,* January 20, 1997

29.3 COMPUTERS AND THE ENGLISH LANGUAGE

Doonesbury: Excuse me, sir. Do you have any user-friendly sales reps?

Store manager: You mean, consumer-compatible liveware? No, he's off today.

> GARRY TRUDEAU, cartoonist, *Doonesbury,* 1983

Orwell's vaunted theory of language—including the idea that an elite would control thought by promulgating a jargon with fewer words and concepts—well, history sure has put the kibosh on that one. Today the English language has more words than ever, including bazillions of computer terms that only nerds can understand, like cool, uncool, way-cool, and, of course, *kewl.*

> MOE MYERSON, technology company manager, quoted in *Inc. Technology,* 1996

As of today if you don't read English, you miss nearly everything on the web.

> WALTER S. MOSSBERG, *Wall Street Journal,* May 2, 1996

"Virtual" is an adjective we use in the industry when we're talking about something we can't get a fix on. But we do know it can't dance and it's too fat to fly.

> CARL S. LEDBETTER JR., president of AT&T Consumer Products, at Los Angeles Public Issues Forum, May 17, 1995

Solemn and chubby, Buck Mulligan appeared from the tall one . . . portandos a basin of foam . . . in cross a mirror. [Computer translation of Italian translation of "Stately, plump Buck Mulligan came from the stairhead, bearing a bowl of lather on which a mirror and a razor lay crossed"—the opening line of *Ulysses*.]

> Cited in the *Financial Times,* January 6, 1997

The vodka is good but the meat is rotten. [Early computer translation from English to Russian to English of "The spirit is willing but the flesh is weak."]

> Cited in the *Financial Times Weekend,* February 22–23, 1997

The alien Business minister of Canada. [How Web Translator, a software program that translates web sites, translates "the Canadian foreign minister" from French to English. The program admits that "your translations may contain some rough spots."]

> Cited in the *Wall Street Journal,* May 2, 1996

29.4 COMPUTERS AND RESEARCH

The way you do research is to make up lies that are plausible—then invent the technology to make them true.

> ALON KAY, computer scientist at Apple, quoted in *Business Week,* February 14, 1994

In the old days, if you wanted to impeach a witness you had to go back and fumble through endless transcripts. Now it's on a screen somewhere or on a disk and I can search for a particular word—say every time the witness used the word *glove*—and then quickly ask a question about what he said years ago. Right away you see the witness get flustered.

> JOHNNIE L. COCHRAN, trial lawyer, quoted in the *New York Times Magazine,* September 28, 1997

29.5 COMPUTERS AND THE WORLD BY THE NUMBERS

Computers per 100 people in 1995

United States	35
Australia	27
Canada	25
Britain	20
The Netherlands	20
Singapore	18
Germany	17
France	16
Hong Kong	15
Japan	14
Italy	13
Taiwan	9
South Korea	7

Figures from World Economic Forum, cited in the *Economist,* September 28, 1996

[I]t is broadly estimated that only about 20 percent of European households have personal computers, versus about 40 percent in the United States.

> *New York Times,* January 4, 1998

29.6 THE COMPUTER INDUSTRY AND PROFITABILITY

Anybody who runs a successful high-technology company has to be an eternal optimist, has to be able to take big risks. You're constantly betting the future of the company. If you stop, if you lose your courage, you fail.

No fax manufacturer in the world makes money.

> JOHN SCULLEY, then outgoing CEO of the computer firm Apple, quoted in *Fortune,* July 26, 1993

It's important to step back from an industry that is full of people announcing new widgets every day—faster widgets, smaller widgets, more widgets . . . What I'm learning from customers is that there is an excess of technology out there. The real pressure is, how do I use this stuff to achieve something important for my business.

> LOUIS V. GERSTNER JR., CEO of IBM, quoted in *Fortune,* November 15, 1993

Will you people at *Wired* please accept the fact that the computer industry, as an industry, hasn't made a dime? . . . There was a time when IBM had wonderful profits.

IBM earned enough money, but no more money than the rest of the industry lost. Every year since then the industry as a whole did not make a dime. Intel and Microsoft make money, but look at all the people who are losing money all the world over. It is doubtful that the industry has yet broken even.

PETER DRUCKER in an interview in *Wired*, April 1996

An awful lot of manufacturers are in services just to pull through their hardware.

JOHN R. HARRIS of the data processing firm EDS, quoted in the *New York Times*, January 7, 1997

Equipment margins are so low that services are the only way to improve our bottom line.

DEWAINE OSMAN of the computer firm Unisys, quoted in the *New York Times*, January 7, 1997

29.7 CONTENT

Content is a euphemism for a lack of technical knowledge.

GARY ANDREW POOLE, *Forbes ASAP*, August 25, 1997

29.8 CYBER RETAILING

On-line shopping is fundamentally boring.

JOHN McCREA of the hardware and software firm Silicon Graphics, quoted in the *New York Times*, December 21, 1995

The parking is easy, there are no checkout lines, we are open 24 hours a day, and we deliver right to your door.

Sales pitch at Salami.com, Franklin Square, New York, purveyors of Italian delicacies, quoted in *Business Week*, September 23, 1996

I am secretly looking forward to rediscovering the little pleasures of pre-electronic shopping: holding things in my hands, trying them on, and even taking them home with me after I have paid.

The Economist, December 21, 1996

The lines between advertising and marketing and retail transactions are going to disappear. The Internet is going to become a channel of distribution.

RUSSELL COLLINS, president of Fattal & Collins, unit of Grey Advertising Inc., *Business Week*, September 23, 1996

The Internet is the great equalizer.

DARRYL PECK, founder of Cyberian Outpost, computer store that attracts 7,000 customers a day (twice the population of his Connecticut town) and does $1 million of business a month through a web site, *Business Week*, October 21, 1996

It's [the online shopping revolution] the one thing that really scares us.

ANTHONY DEERING, CEO of mall developer Rouse, quoted in *Fortune*, May 29, 1996

The processing cost for an order taken online is probably around $4, a lot less than the $15 for other methods.

Bock Information Group web site, October 1996

What this is really about is not selling old things more efficiently, but setting the stage to sell an entirely new set of products. It allows you to buy things by the sip rather than the gulp.

PAUL SAFFO, director of Institute of the Future, on CyberCoin, a system that allows Internet customers to buy cheap things, quoted in the *Wall Street Journal*, September 30, 1996

A traditional junk mailing is successful if it gets a response rate of 2 percent or 3 percent. On the Internet, you'll get a 100 percent response. And 90 percent of it will be, "Don't you ever do this to me again."

ERIK FAIR, of Apple, *Fortune*, March 7, 1994

FT Guide to shopping on the Internet.

Computer software and hardware were the first goods widely available online and remain the items most commonly purchased over the Internet. Then there are travel-related items, such as aircraft tickets. Many airline and travel agents will let you look at schedules and buy tickets online. Leisure goods is the third main category, with books, music CDs, and video cassettes being particularly hot items. Pornographic materials are . . . among the biggest sellers over the Internet.

Financial Times, April 1, 1997

We had a week in which we had more fraud than legitimate sales. We were literally going out of business.

WILLIAM S. McKIERNAN, chief executive of the online software company Cyber Source, quoted in the *New York Times*, November 17, 1997

29.9 DEFAMATION ON THE INTERNET

This process may not be real evident up there in Wisconsin, but down here in Oklahoma where the summers are both sunny and hot, this effect is quite a problem. [Supposed customer complaint circulated on the Internet that after Miller Beer cans were painted black instead of gold, they warmed up too fast in the sun to be enjoyed]

> *Wall Street Journal,* October 21, 1996

At Miller beer, it was never our intention to have someone take more than 2.5 minutes to enjoy one of our beers.

> Reply from nonexistent Miller public relations representative, quoted in the *Wall Street Journal,* October 21, 1996

[M]enswear magnate Tommy Hilfiger found himself the target of an ugly and entirely false rumor that he had, while appearing on Oprah Winfrey's show, dissed Asians and blacks. "Summed up, he basically said that if he had known so many Chinamen and niggers were going to buy his clothes, he never would have made [them] so nice," wrote the outraged webmistress of the Official Philippine Anti–Tommy Hilfiger Site. [Example of how the Internet can expose businesses to unsubstantiated bad publicity. Hilfiger's e-mail protests that he had never been on *Oprah* "did little to quell suspicions."]

> *New Republic,* May 12, 1997

The law of libel hasn't gone away on the Internet. As soon as a third person has access to a conversation, then the law of libel applies.

> JAMES GOODALE, an attorney at the law firm Debevoise & Plimpton, quoted in the *New York Times,* August 17, 1997

There are no rules of the road. We're having a hard enough time in legitimate journalism deciding what the rules of engagement are, and we're making them up as we go along. This is electronic graffiti.

> JERRY NACHMAN, former editor of the *New York Post,* quoted in the *New York Times,* August 17, 1997

If someone thinks they are being mistreated by us, they won't tell five people—they'll tell 5,000.

> JEFFREY BEZOS, founder of Amazon.com, quoted in the *Wall Street Journal,* May 16, 1996

29.10 ELECTRONIC COMMERCE

Males are more likely to search for productive information online, while females are more likely to make purchases.

> Nielsen Media Research, quoted in the *Financial Times,* March 14, 1997

Three things must exist for electronic commerce to prosper. Ease, ubiquity, and trust. Technology can take care of the first two. But how can consumers be sure that their transactions are secure and private? . . . The question we're grappling with is whether government has a role in creating that trust.

> CHRISTINE VARNEY, member of the Federal Trade Commission, quoted in the *New York Times,* June 22, 1997

We're not going to see mass markets—the equivalent of Cyber Wal-Mart or Cyber Home Depot. The key to understanding electronic commerce over the Internet is to think of it as a lot of little malls, with a lot of little stores. And the challenge is going to be getting the customers to where you are.

> BARBARA REILLY, research director of the consulting firm Gartner Group, quoted in *Forbes,* September 22, 1997

. . . I don't believe that cultural differences are the main reason why new American payments systems [CyberCash, First Virtual Holdings] are making little headway in Europe. The new payments technologies are making little headway anywhere.

> TIM JACKSON, *Financial Times,* May 26, 1997

29.11 GROWTH OF THE INTERNET

At the current rate of growth, the citizens of cyberspace will outnumber all but the largest nations in just two years.

> *The Economist,* June 1995

In one 18-month period, 3 million new pages of multimedia information, entertainment, and advertising were added to the World Wide Web. Imagine one of those suburban shopping strips with nothing but parking lots, malls, fast food, and gas stations stretching from California to the moon.

> JACK DAVIS of Chase Manhattan Bank, in a speech titled "Banking on the Internet," August 1995

[I]n this business, you measure time in dog's years.

> DOUGLAS HUMPHREY, founder of the Internet service Digital Express, *Fortune*, March 7, 1994

It's possible—the Net has been *under*hyped.

> L. JOHN DOERR, of the venture capital firm Kleiner, Perkins, Caufield & Byers, quoted in the *New Yorker*, August 11, 1997

Every day on the Web is a defining moment. For now this [the weekend of Princess Diana's death] is the defining moment.

> JEFF GRALNICK of ABC TV's news division and head of ABCNews.com, on the web site's first million-hit weekend, quoted in the *New York Times*, September 8, 1997

The Internet is like Darwinism on steroids. You evolve or get eliminated.

> RAUL FERNANDEZ, of the web site design firm Proxicom, quoted in the *Wall Street Journal*, September 9, 1997

Trying to assess the true importance and function of the Net now is like asking the Wright brothers at Kitty Hawk if they were aware of the potential of American Airlines Advantage miles.

> BRAN FERREN, head of the Imagineers, Disney's creative think tank, quoted in the *New Yorker*, October 20 & 27, 1997

AOL is like the Internet on training wheels.

> PETER KESSELMAN of Valencia, California, is an Internet user, quoted in the *Wall Street Journal*, January 18, 1996

29.12 HOME ENTERTAINMENT

People will soon get tired of staring at a plywood box every night.

> DARRYL F. ZANUCK, movie producer, on why television wouldn't last, 1946

Why should people go out and pay to see bad movies when they can stay at home and see bad television for nothing?

> SAM GOLDWYN, movie producer, quoted in the *Observer* (London), September 9, 1956

Through the centuries, the focal point of the house has changed several times. Early on, it was the fireplace. People gathered around it to keep warm and cook their meals. Over time, that focal point switched to the kitchen. And then it seemed to switch to the TV. But now, I believe the home's new focal point is becoming the PC.

> ECKHARD PFEIFFER, CEO of the computer firm Compaq, in a speech, January 5, 1996

The probability that PC production rates are likely to surpass combined black-and-white and color television production rates in the next year or two lends support to the claim that PCs connected by the Internet could, in fact, become a significant alternative to televisions.

> ANDREW S. GROVE, CEO of the microprocessor maker Intel, quoted in *Forbes*, September 23, 1996

While new PCs outship new TVs on a worldwide basis, we still have a long way to go before we win this "war for eyeballs." In this war, "He who captures the most eyeballs wins."

> ANDREW S. GROVE, CEO of the microprocessor maker Intel, in a speech at Comdex, November 18, 1996

[H]ow do you marry the Intel chip with the Frito chip?

> THOMAS ROGERS, of NBC, on the problem of bringing together the PC and television, quoted in December 23, 1996

A Microsoft quiz show? Give me a break. They've been blinded by the raw magnitude of the consumer market, and they are overlooking a gold mine in the business market. Couch potatoes are not going to turn off the TV and go down to the den to hunker around the old 486 PC instead.

> JESSE BERST, editorial director of ZD NET Anchordesk, a World Wide Web news service, on Microsoft's plans to expand its Internet offerings, *New York Times*, October 10, 1996

People tell us they buy computers for home-office use. But they actually use them for games.

> ROBERT AMEZCUA of IBM consumer systems operations, quoted in *Fortune*, February 21, 1994

29.13 INDUSTRY CONCENTRATION

Unlike other industries, our pace of change is so fast that I don't think it's right to expect the same type of concentration as in the auto industry.

> MICHAEL DELL, CEO of Dell Computer, quoted in the *Wall Street Journal,* February 4, 1997

Is the industry slowing down because of concentration? Is the price going up because of concentration? Is the customer worse served? The answer to all these things is no.

> BERNARD VERGNES, president of Microsoft Europe, quoted in the *Wall Street Journal,* February 4, 1997

[A]s an investor in small companies, I don't care how rich Microsoft is. I care about what my opportunities are. If I had the sense that Microsoft was genuinely holding back the market, then I'd care. I don't think they are.

> ESTHER DYSON, president of EDventure Holdings, quoted in the *Wall Street Journal,* February 4, 1997

29.14 THE INFORMATION SUPERHIGHWAY

Leave it to specialists to discuss the latest developments [in computers and communications]. The rest of us need perspective, and the most important elements of perspective are history, a vision of perfection, the reasons we haven't achieved it yet, some pitfalls, and some humor.

Look at the very phrase Information Highway. Being on a highway is a mindless experience. You're usually hustling home from work.

> PROFESSOR MARK CRISPIN MILLER, Johns Hopkins University, quoted in *Business Week,* March 14, 1994

What is the Information Superhighway?

Answer: It's just like cable TV, except a lot more expensive.

> Joke from Silicon Alley (New York City's cyber community), told by Cathleen Black, president of Hearst Magazines, in a speech, March 4, 1997

29.15 THE INFORMATION SUPERHIGHWAY AND THE HUMAN CONDITION

The billions of third-world families that finally began to have some purchasing power when the twentieth century ended did not want to watch pretty graphics on the Internet. They wanted to live in nice houses, drive cars, and eat meat.

> PROFESSOR PAUL KRUGMAN of MIT, looking back 100 years from the year 2096, *New York Times,* September 29, 1996

29.16 THE INFORMATION SUPERHIGHWAY, LEGAL AND ACCOUNTING ISSUES

The Internet is one giant copying machine. All copyrighted works can now be digitized, and once on the Net, copying is effortless, costless, widespread, and immediate.

> DAVID NIMMER, Los Angeles lawyer, quoted in the *Economist,* July 27, 1996

As in the regular world, the easier it is for Joe Consumer to track down an illegal distributor [of Internet content], the easier it is for cops to do the same.

> ROBERT WRIGHT, *Slate,* October 1996

Owning the intellectual property is like owning land: you need to keep investing in it again and again to get a payoff; you can't simply sit back and collect rent.

> ESTHER DYSON, president of the high-tech investment firm EDventure Holdings, from her company's newsletter *Release 1.0,* December 1994

At a workshop we were holding for AT&T he [musician Peter Gabriel] was asked, "How do you deal with piracy of your albums?" Gabriel said, "Oh, I treat it as free advertising. I follow it with a rock concert. When they steal my albums in Indonesia, I go there and I perform."

> PETER DRUCKER, in an interview in *HotWired 1.3,* 1996

Does the company own your thoughts 24 hours a day?

> RICHARD A. SAYLES, attorney for a computer programmer, being sued by his former employer for refusing to disclose his thinking about software that the company claims was developed on its time, quoted in the *New York Times,* September 8, 1997

This treaty is so tilted toward us that no other country is going to ratify it if we don't. The longer we delay, the more we make it clear we don't give a damn.

> JACK VALENTI, president of the Motion Picture Association of America, on Internet piracy, quoted in the *Financial Times,* September 17, 1997

The question is not how to protect copyright [on the Internet], but how to use the content to add value to other items that can be sold.

> ESTHER DYSON, president of the high-tech investment firm EDventure Holdings, quoted in the *Wall Street Journal*, October 10, 1997

First, don't assume that today's ambiguous rules will hold forever. Be prepared for future changes.

Second, be aware of new legal boundaries that emerge from court decisions.

Third, keep an eye on new legislation at federal and state levels.

Fourth, work with industry associations to develop voluntary guidelines for technological innovations. A credible argument that an industry is "self-policing" can sometimes convince legislators to go slowly in enacting additional legislation.

Managers who ignore the changing legal domain risk problems for themselves, their enterprise, and their industry.

> DR. H. JEFFERSON SMITH, associate professor at Georgetown School of Business, on Internet policy strategy, quoted in *Computing*, July–August 1996

29.17 THE INFORMATION SUPERHIGHWAY AND THE PEOPLE WHO PAVE IT

We hire the good people first, and we figure out what we're going to do with them later.

> ERIC SCHMIDT of the computer firm Sun Microsystems, quoted in the *Wall Street Journal*, August 9, 1996

You have to kiss a lot of frogs to get a prince.

> ED BOE of the computer firm Compaq, on the dearth of good job candidates, *Wall Street Journal*, August 9, 1996

The competition for these people [embedded software developers] is so intense, that even if I only hire two of them, it's worth it.

> CHRISTOPHER A. LEWIS of the firm Allied-Signal Aerospace, quoted in the *New York Times*, September 29, 1997

They look at their fathers and say, "Dad didn't get the gold watch." So these young people say, "I'm going to

be a craftsman. And this is my craft, the computer and technology. Armed with this I can go anywhere."

> LAWRENCE SHEEN, chairman of the consulting firm Cambridge Assessment Center, high-tech temps, quoted in the *Wall Street Journal*, August 19, 1996

I spent half the day trying to figure out what people needed in computers and the rest of the day trying to convince an engineer it was his idea.

> BETTY HOLBURTON, now in her eighties, who, with five other young women, programmed the world's first general-purpose digital computer, ENIAC (their approach is deemed to have shaped programming ever since), quoted in the *Wall Street Journal*, November 22, 1996

All the guys I knew and loved when they were so young and cute have become the Establishment. Especially Mr. Gates.

> ESTHER DYSON, president of the high-tech investment firm EDventure Holdings and publisher of *1.0* newsletter, *Fortune*, quoted in June 14, 1993

[T]ry to think of everything you know about something as simple as an invoice. Now try to tell an idiot how to prepare one.

To build a crash-proof system, the designer . . . has to think of every single stupid thing a human being could do. Gradually, over months and years, the designer's mind creates a construct of the user as an imbecile. This image is necessary. No crash-proof system can be built unless it is made for an idiot.

> ELLEN ULLMAN, "Out of Time: Reflections on the Programming Life," *Harper's*, June 1995

It was mostly the nerds, weirdos, and outcasts who built this business. None of us had anything to do on a Friday night.

> VERN RABURN, who opened a computer store in L.A. in 1976 and later became head of the Paul Allen Group, which manages the investments of the co-founder of Microsoft, quoted in *Fortune*, June 10, 1996

You don't know how good it feels to have Microsoft come crawling on its knees to buy something from you instead of the other way around.

> SCOTT McNEALY, CEO of the computer firm Sun Microsystems, after licensing Java to Microsoft for its Explorer 3.0 web browser, quoted in *Fortune*, September 30, 1996

I don't have Bill envy. I have a great wife, a nice house, and I'm sure my kid is smarter than his kid.

> SCOTT McNEALY, CEO of the computer firm Sun Microsystems, quoted in *Forbes,* September 8, 1997

I'm more interested in beating Microsoft than I am in beating Bill Gates.

> LARRY ELLISON, CEO of the computer firm Oracle, quoted in *Time,* May 12, 1997

Bill Gates wants people to think he's Edison, when he's really Rockefeller.

> LARRY ELLISON, CEO of the computer firm Oracle, quoted in *Newsweek,* August 4, 1997

We are a full-service agency. I am a shrink, marriage counselor, and financial adviser.

> BO RINALDI, talent agent for computer programmers, quoted in the *New York Times,* September 8, 1997

People in this business tend to be a little weird. It's where their creativity comes from.

> KIYOSHI NISHIKAWA of America Online, Japan, quoted in the *Wall Street Journal,* November 8, 1996

They haven't figured out we're in a post-yuppie world. You have young guys in positions of huge responsibility, and they don't have any compunction about how they treat human beings.

> Former manager at the computer firm Dell, quoted in *Business Week,* March 14, 1994

There are a lot of people running companies in Silicon Valley who haven't had the experience of managing through both up and down markets.

> SANDRA KURTZIG, founder and CEO of the software firm ASK, interviewed in Rama Dev Jager, *In the Company of Giants* (McGraw-Hill, 1997)

You will leave no heritage for your children. Your name will be forgotten. You will fail. You will fail in everything you do.

> ANDREW GROVE, CEO of microprocessor maker Intel, quoted in review of Tim Jordan, *Inside Intel* (E.P. Dutton, 1997), *Slate,* November 16, 1997

Silicon Valley . . . has succeeded because nobody there understands the European notion that people can be "too big for their boots." Great wealth is generally seen as the by-product of cool ideas being put into practice.

> *The Economist,* January 3, 1998

29.18 THE INFORMATION SUPERHIGHWAY AND PERSONAL RELATIONSHIPS

When my husband was home before [he began surfing the Web], he was *home.*

> Washington writer, on influence of Internet on her marriage, quoted in the *Wall Street Journal,* November 20, 1996

Dear Diary:

Walking through Central Park the other morning along the 72nd Street transverse, I found myself keeping stride with a 30-something couple. The woman was dressed in a navy power suit, the man in a designer ensemble.

The woman said to the man, "I just feel like you don't appreciate me, like you don't want to take time for me anymore."

He responded: "I do so appreciate you, and I do so want more time with you. Didn't you get my E-mail?"

> SALLY SROK FRIEDES, Metropolitan Diary, *New York Times,* July 2, 1997

Well, honey, I'll bet your web site is busy tonight. [Janice Holyfield, to her husband Evander, world heavyweight boxing champion, after Mike Tyson bit off a piece of his ear]

> Quoted in *Sports Illustrated,* July 7, 1997

29.19 THE INFORMATION SUPERHIGHWAY AND ITS POTHOLES

As we get further dependent on electronic means to transmit and store information, ease of use means ease of abuse.

> RICHARD HEFFERNAN, a computer security consultant, quoted in the *Wall Street Journal,* November 20, 1995

The electron, in my view, is the ultimate precision-guided weapon.

> JOHN M. DEUTCH, director of the Central Intelligence Agency, referring to potential use of information weapons, in an address to Congress, June 1996, quoted in the *New York Times*, September 30, 1996

We invite our customers into our computer networks. I think our problem is more challenging than the government's.

> COLIN CROOK of Citibank, quoted in the *New York Times*, September 30, 1996

We want to catch the bastards [computer hackers] and show the rest of them that you don't screw with Citibank.

> JIM BAILEY of Citibank, quoted in the *Wall Street Journal*, 1995

Hackers are hippies who got it right.

> STEWART BRAND, cofounder of Global Business Network, author of the original *Whole Earth Catalogue*, member of the Merry Pranksters, prominent hippie adventurers, and prominent business guru, quoted in *Fortune*, October 16, 1995

Most security breaches are to do with misuse of authority, not hacking. Someone who has authority to move a file late at night might move it to the printer. We caught one contractor browsing information that was confidential, although he had authority to access that file in his systems work.

> DR. PAUL DOREY of Barclay's Bank, quoted in the *Financial Times*, April 2, 1997

The Pentagon's own computer systems were attacked about 250,000 times last year, according to the U.S. Defense Department's computer security force. In an estimated 160,000 of these incidents, hackers succeed in penetrating the systems.

> PAUL TAYLOR, *Financial Times*, September 3, 1997

Hackers rarely hack for material gain. Most hacking is done for enjoyment and personal pleasure and it is rarely malicious.

> IMTIAZ MALIK, author of *Computer Hacking: Detection and Protection* (Coronet, 1996), quoted in the *Financial Times*, September 3, 1997

What people vaguely call common sense is actually more intricate than most of the technical expertise we admire.

> MARVIN MINSKY, artificial intelligence guru at MIT

When something becomes abundant, it also becomes cheap. A world awash in information is one in which information has very little market value.

> PROFESSOR PAUL KRUGMAN of MIT, looking back 100 years from the year 2096, *New York Times*, September 29, 1996

We cannot see the future; we do not know what lies around the next bend on the Information Superhighway; we cannot predict where, ultimately, the Computer Revolution will take us. All we know for certain is that, when we finally get there, we won't have enough RAM.

> *David Barry in Cyberspace* (Crown, 1996)

We built it [the Internet] to be Russian-proof, but it turned out to be regulator proof.

> CRAIG I. FIELDS of online gambling company Alliance Gaming and former head of Pentagon agency that helped create the Internet, quoted in the *New York Times*, October 28, 1996

[*Questions to ask about systems to protect information assets*]

How much did the information cost your company?
How much will it cost to replace?
How much financial benefit will be gained if your competitor accesses it?
How much hardship would be caused if it were not readily available to your customer?
How would it benefit a third party?

> RICH OWEN of the computer firm Dell, *Management Review*, May 1, 1996

For those who will be receiving a PC from Santa, remember: a computer is a gift that keeps on taking.

> PETER H. LEWIS, *New York Times*, December 3, 1996

Modern technology is essential to the modern world. The danger is that the instantaneity of its techniques defines its aims. Instant greed. Instant prestige. The instant future. This is why a sense of history has become a condition for our survival.

> JOHN BERGER, artist and critic, quoted in Herbert I. Schiller, *Culture Inc.: The Corporate Takeover of American Expression* (Oxford University Press, 1989)

You'd rather pay your bills over it [the Internet] than receive your paycheck over it.

> PETER A. MILLER of the banking firm JP Morgan, quoted in *Fortune*, March 7, 1994

Interactive technologies pose great opportunities. But we need to realize that if we don't protect personal information on the highway up front, people won't use it.

> JANLORI GOLDMAN, director of the American Civil Liberties Union's Privacy and Technology Project, quoted in *Business Week*, May 18, 1994

America Online's troubles recall what happened to *Look, Life,* and other major magazines in the 1970s. These publications kept lowering subscription prices to keep circulation high in a vain attempt to compete with TV for advertising.

> ROBERT STEIN, former editor of *McCall's*, quoted in the *New York Times*, February 6, 1997

People have enough enthusiasm to design the sites once—but it's not clear that they have the resources to update them regularly. You have better things to do.

> LOUIS MONIER, architect of the Internet search engine Alta Vista, quoted in the *Wall Street Journal*, March 11, 1997

Our eyes get tired quicker on a computer screen. Plus it isn't very practical. People look at a computer screen as work, not pleasure. It doesn't have the portability of print.

> CLAY FELKER, director of the Felker Magazine Center at the University of California at Berkeley and founder of *New York*, quoted in Ken Auletta, *The Highwaymen: Warriors of the Information Superhighway* (Random House, 1997)

If this is the information superhighway, it's going through a lot of bad, bad, neighborhoods.

> DORIAN BERGER, college student who posted his papers on the Internet so they could be read by more people, only to find that students all over the world

wanted him to write papers for them, quoted in the *New York Times,* June 7, 1997

The Coca-Cola Scholars Foundation. Meet alumni. Find out how to apply. Buy a term paper (just kidding, there).

> Coca-Cola Company web site, June 5, 1997

We haven't really figured out how to use the capabilities we already have. If we were reduced to exploiting existing technology, we might get better advances than we do in pushing the envelope for years.

> PROFESSOR MICHAEL BORRUS, quoted in the *Wall Street Journal,* December 10, 1996

When I first lost my sight, one of the best things about the computer was that I could go into the Internet and get access to information—to newspapers, stock quotes, anything. Now I have to spend half my time finding a web site that is accessible.

> CYNTHIA ICE, a computer trouble-shooter for nine years despite her blindness because DOS-based screen readers allowed her to work, and who had to quit after Windows was installed because it was incompatible, quoted in the *Wall Street Journal,* August 14, 1996

29.20 THE INFORMATION SUPERHIGHWAY AND SOCIETY

Life in cyberspace is often conducted in primitive conditions. But at its best, it is more egalitarian than elitist, more decentralized than hierarchical. It serves individuals and communities, not mass audiences.

> MITCHELL KAPOR, CEO of the software firm Lotus Development, cited in *Harper's*, 1994

29.21 THE INFORMATION SUPERHIGHWAY AT WORK

I have traveled the length and breadth of the country, and have talked with the best people in business administration. I can assure you on the highest authority that data processing is a fad and won't last out the year.

> Editor at Prentice-Hall, rejecting a manuscript on new science of data processing, 1957

E-mail is fun, but it's a toy. When the story department used typewriters we read two scripts a day, and now that we're computerized we still read two scripts a day. E-mail encourages people to chatter and say things that don't need to be said.

> TED DODD, a story analyst at the movie company Columbia Pictures, September 6, 1992

The jury is still out.

> BRIAN PAPPAS of the consulting firm Nolan, Norton, on whether PCs were saving corporations any money, quoted in the *Economist,* December 5, 1992

A new computer system spreads confusion, doubt, and stress. The hardware may work, the software may work, but the system won't work if the people who use it don't cooperate.

> TERRY NEILL of Andersen Consulting, quoted in *Fortune,* October 4, 1993

Groupware is a tool that catalyzes organizational change whether you want it or not.

Start with the problem, not the technology.

> DAVID COLEMAN, editor of a software newsletter, quoted in *Fortune,* December 27, 1993

Technology is not the savior; it is the enabler. All too often, organizations start with technology and then do not achieve the business objective.

> JAMES A. UNRUH, CEO of the computer firm Unisys, in a speech, January 16, 1997

For the first time the computer is an enabler of productivity improvement rather than a cause of a lack of productivity.

> WILLIAM WHEELER of the accounting and consulting firm Coopers & Lybrand, quoted in *Fortune,* December 13, 1993

You'd be horrified at my office. I work in mortal chaos. I have to deal with ribbons, tea, cats and dogs, technology, candle making, cooking, ordering manure—all in the same five minutes.

> MARTHA STEWART, lifestyle guru, in *Inc. Technology,* Summer 1995

People are by nature social animals and much of the satisfaction we get from work comes from the daily opportunity to be with colleagues and friends. Cyberspace can be lonely and it will be one more major challenge for HR professionals to help people maintain the human connections so essential to their health and well-being.

> LAWRENCE PERLMAN, CEO of the information and defense electronics firm Ceridian Corporation, in a speech, July 17, 1995

The world is looking for anyone who can lower complexity [of technology].

> TIMOTHY E. SULLIVAN of First Interstate Bank, Phoenix, quoted in *Business Week,* July 31, 1995

When the first computers were put in, no one knew how to use them. User-friendliness is resulting in tremendous efficiency even in the service sector.

> WILLIAM C. DUNKELBERG, chief economist of the National Federation of Independent Business, quoted in *Business Week,* November 21, 1994

We buy a lot of technology not for what it does but so that we can say we have it.

> JERRY BEHRENS of Tzell Travel Specialists, quoted in *Fortune,* September 9, 1996

I don't know how you're supposed to make intelligent decisions without the facts. Computers give me the facts.

> WILLIAM S. DILLARD SR., founder of Dillard Department Stores, quoted in *Fortune,* September 24, 1996

The buffers of space, time, people, and inventory are gone, so you have to have the lubrication of information to get the flow going.

> JOHN ROCHART of the Sloan School of Management at MIT, quoted in *Fortune,* September 24, 1996

If I hadn't been computerized in this last recession, I wouldn't have been competitive. My customers wouldn't have given me an opportunity to stay in business.

> MICHAEL ALLAWOS, owner of California tool-and-die shop, quoted in *Business Week,* November 21, 1994

Internet-related companies create lots of odd job titles, like *infomaniac,* and *employee who is proficient at finding information. Senior firewall developers* build consumer security systems, *web evangelists* promote groups' World

Wide Web sites, and *code connoisseurs* are expert programmers. [italics added]

> *Wall Street Journal*, October 22, 1996

The line between these network computers being used as really effective corporate tools and being used as mind-control tiger cages is a fine one. There will be a real temptation for corporate managers to go too far in the direction of control.

> PAUL SAFFO, director of the research firm Institute for the Future, quoted in the *New York Times*, November 4, 1996

What's a floppy disk? It's a way to steal company secrets.

> SCOTT McNEALY, CEO of the computer firm Sun Microsystems, quoted in the *New York Times*, November 4, 1996

The key question is do you want to take away the individual flexibility and freedom that the personal computer provides?

People do play computer games at work, but they also doodle with pencils. Do you take away their pencils? And the notion of telling workers they can go to this web site, but not that one is silly. That's not the way a modern work force is managed. You've got to trust people.

> BILL GATES, chairman and cofounder of the computer firm Microsoft, quoted in the *New York Times*, November 4, 1996

One analysis of computer logs by Nielsen Media Research Inc. in New York found that employees at International Business Machines Corp., Apple Computer Inc., and AT&T Corp. together visited *Penthouse* magazine's World Wide Web site 12,823 times in a single month earlier this year. Based on an average visit of 13 minutes, that comes to more than 347 eight-hour days.

> *Wall Street Journal*, November 25, 1996

I look at my computer more than I look at my wife. It ought to be a pleasing aesthetic experience.

> RIK MYSELEWSKI, executive editor of *MacUser*, quoted in *Fortune*, October 4, 1993

It used to be, if you wanted information, you had to go up, over, and down through the organization. Now you just tap in. Everybody can know as much about the company as the chairman of the board. That's what broke down the hierarchy. It's not why we bought computers, but that's what they did.

> FREDERICK KOVAC, of the rubber company Goodyear, quoted in *Fortune*, October 4, 1993

For teens, the New [technology] is a toy; for businesses, it's a tool.

> THOMAS PETZINGER JR., *Wall Street Journal*, May 9, 1997

The top 500 companies in the United States will spend close to $100 billion on information technology in 1996. This is equivalent to approximately $6,000 per employee on average.

> DR. HOWARD RUBIN, CEO of Rubin Systems, on the results of a 1996 study

The amount of time you use a computer is almost inversely proportional to how high up you are in a company.

> RICHARD HADDRILL, CEO of Video Lottery Technologies, quoted in *Forbes*, August 25, 1997

It's far more effective to have other people run the computers.

> STANLEY HUBBARD, CEO of Hubbard Broadcasting, quoted in *Forbes*, August 25, 1997

I'm just glad I didn't have the time that day to compose a more personal or risqué message.

> GILMAN MILLER, associate at a Wall Street law firm who sent his girlfriend the message "Just thinking of you" and accidentally posted it to all 1,000 of his colleagues, quoted in the *New York Times*, October 5, 1997

People who come from other disciplines, not just computer scientists, can now create their own forms of communication. Doctors and architects and educators can use more than words—they can use pictures and sound.

> RED BURNS, chairwoman of the Interactive Telecommunications Program at New York University, quoted in the *New York Times Magazine*, September 28, 1997

[T]he main reason so many people have lost jobs, been forced to change jobs, or been able to upgrade their jobs in the last tumultuous decade is not a lowering of U.S. trade barriers. It's technology. A Mexican working at 75 cents an hour didn't take the job of our office receptionist; a microchip did—the one that operates the voice mail device in all our office phones. A Chinese making 75 cents an hour didn't take that auto worker's job; a robot did. A Brazilian making 75 cents an hour didn't take your neighbor's grocery job; a supermarket scanner did.

> THOMAS L. FRIEDMAN, *New York Times,* October 6, 1997

Imagine you're at your desk. Your PC is the equivalent of a mainframe, you have unlimited bandwidth and can time-share into a virtual supercomputer network. What kind of capabilities will that bring to thousands of entrepreneurs around the world?

> FRED BRIGGS of the telecommunications firm MCI (which is building a very-high-speed supercomputing network), quoted in *Fortune,* October 13, 1997

29.22 THE INFORMATION SUPERHIGHWAY AT WORK— REVENGE EFFECTS

When they [people at work] saw I was doing something [on the computer] if anything they would turn and leave rather than say, "Gee, that's neat, what are you doing?" They would say, "That turkey, that technician, all he ever does is talk his buzz words, can't talk to him."

> STANLEY SYNGSTAD, computer embezzler who used a computer to mail $17,000 in "state-rehabilitation warrants" to himself and two friends, quoted in the *Wall Street Journal,* January 14, 1985

[D]isgruntled employee who—until he was passed over for a promotion or raise or [his] family situation suddenly changed dramatically for the worse—was a sterling middle-aged company man. [Profile of likely computer embezzler that matched Stanley Syngstad precisely, compiled by International Resource Development]

> Cited in the *Wall Street Journal,* January 14, 1985

Nowadays, the three big lies are: the check is in the mail, the goods are on the truck, and the computer's down.

> RICHARD GOLDMAN, part-owner of Ricke Knitting Mills, quoted in the *New Yorker,* January 18, 1988

The fax has destroyed any sense of patience or grace that existed . . . People are so crazy now they call to tell you your fax line is busy.

> JOSH BARON, Hollywood publicist, quoted in *Time,* April 24, 1989

People are putting in poorly thought out, stream of consciousness stuff [into corporate groupware], and it takes hours to wade through.

> Manager of a national media company, quoted in *Fortune,* December 27, 1993

[I]n a world where hundreds and thousands of communications enter the office every day, our expectations that we should carefully digest it all can make us feel overwhelmed and terribly inadequate.

> TOM MALONE, director of the research center Sloan School of Management at MIT, quoted in *Fortune,* December 27, 1993

There's already a rancher in Texas who hangs pagers around the necks of his cows while they're out grazing and has them trained to come in from the pasture when he beeps them.

Think of the I-way [information superhighway] as the road that carries that paging signal to the cows to induce them to transport their *content*—the stuff that cows are full of—back to the barn. The milk, not the manure.

> *Fortune,* December 27, 1993

Replacing personnel with computers in a payables department never works as well as top management thinks it will.

> RONALD LODER, president of the consulting firm Loder Drew & Associates, quoted in the *Wall Street Journal,* September 5, 1996

A payables clerk with long experience would have spotted the error [a double payment]. A computer only spots an error if it's programmed specifically to catch the exact mistake.

> RICHARD SHAFFER of the Niagara Mohawk Power Corporation, quoted in the *Wall Street Journal,* September 5, 1996

Laptops, cellular phones, wireless modems, and fax machines may change the work environment for many professions, but they don't alter the thought processes that ultimately lead to breakthroughs. What these tools have done, however, is help extend the working day; in effect they have created a portable assembly line for the 1990s that "allows" white-collar workers to remain on-line in planes, trains, cars, and at home. So much for the liberating technologies of the Information age.

> "Technology and the 24-hour Day," *Harvard Business Review,* September–October 1996

I'm no Luddite, but I do understand the importance of maintaining a balance between information, knowledge, and meaning. This is a value chain. Technology helps only with the first part of the chain. It sometimes interferes with the other two parts.

Remember what Thoreau said about news: If it's important enough, it'll reach you.

> JAMES CHAMPY, chairman of consulting for the data-processing firm Perot Systems, quoted in *Forbes,* September 22, 1997

We didn't drive the computer, the computer drove us.

> TERRY FARRILL of the packaging firm Lantech, which had to de-automate itself, quoted in *Inc. Technology,* 1996

We were lying to the computer all the time. If we had trouble getting deliveries as fast as a customer wanted, we'd tell the computer the order was two weeks older than it was. The computer would reschedule that job, but then all the rest of the orders would get held up.

> PAT LANCASTER, CEO of the packaging firm Lantech, quoted in *Inc. Technology,* 1996

29.23 INTERACTIVE MEDIA— GLITCHES

There is no way on a conceptual basis to pretest products of this kind [interactive television] without actually putting them into the home and allowing the consumer to respond under natural conditions. It's the same problem faced by advertising agencies in trying to pretest television commercials. You can't replicate the effect of the surrounding in the home, the consumer's mood, the competition within the house for your time, the noise level, in a laboratory setting.

> TULLY PRESSER, market research consultant, quoted in Ken Auletta, "The Magic Box," *New Yorker,* April 11, 1994

The problem is that you're running on the theory of the technology before the technology proves itself.

> HOWARD STRINGER, founder of Tele-TV, unsuccessful joint venture of Bell Atlantic, NYNEX, and Pacific Telesis Group, quoted in the *New York Times,* August 28, 1997

Americast and Tele-TV were deterrents to keep the cable industry out of the phone business. When the cable companies decided not to get into that business, the phone companies didn't care anymore.

> MICHAEL J. WOLF of the consulting firm Booz, Allen & Hamilton, quoted in the *New York Times,* August 28, 1997

The good news is that 6 out of 10 times when you pick up the phone, you get a dial tone. The bad news is that four times you don't, which is unacceptable, of course.

> AMOS B. HOSTETTER JR., founder of Continental Cablevision, on testing of interactive phone-cable network technology, quoted in the *Wall Street Journal,* August 29, 1997

29.24 THE INTERNET AND GOVERNMENT POLICY

We're all for the Information Superhighway. We just don't want a superhighway without a cop on it.

> LOUIS J. FREEH, director of the Federal Bureau of Investigation, quoted in *Business Week,* March 21, 1994

Developing countries and those that want to create their own markets will make it [electronic commerce] as onerous as possible.

> DENNIS GLOVER of the accounting and consulting firm Deloitte & Touche, quoted in *Business Week,* December 9, 1996

This is interstate commerce, pure and simple. States should not be allowed to privateer against interstate commerce.

> U.S. REPRESENTATIVE CHRISTOPHER COX (Republican, California), quoted in *Business Week,* December 9, 1996

The system we want to promote is one that would essentially have governments keep hands off the Internet.

> IRA MAGAZINER, head of the government task force on global electronic commerce, quoted in *Forbes*, August 25, 1997

Imagine 30,000 hands in your pocket at the same time.

> U.S. REPRESENTATIVE CHRIS COX (Republican, California), on the possibility of local taxation of electronic commerce transactions, quoted in *Forbes*, August 25, 1997

The Internet will be the business infrastructure of the twenty-first century. To subject it to as many as 30,000 taxing jurisdictions applying different rules of taxation would be a mistake.

> U.S. SENATOR RON WEIDEN (Democrat, Oregon), sponsor of the Internet Tax Freedom Act, quoted in the *New York Times*, November 10, 1997

If there's just a 2 percent drop in sales tax revenue, it means I have to lay off 3 of my 53 police officers.

> MAYOR HARRY SMITH of Greenwood, Mississippi, which relies on sales taxes for 55 percent of its budget and fears long-term threat from electronic commerce, quoted in the *New York Times*, November 10, 1997

29.25 MAKING MONEY FROM THE INTERNET

Right now companies have to devote five man-years to finding out whether the Internet is an opportunity or a rat hole.

> CHRIS JONES of the consulting firm Meckler Media, quoted in *Fortune*, March 7, 1994

The issue is not how much revenue companies are extracting from the Internet but how much efficiency they are gaining from it.

> THOMAS PETZINGER JR., writer, *Wall Street Journal*, May 9, 1997

If you have content, you need a network, and if you have a network, you need content.

> THOMAS NIEHAUS of the consulting firm Simba Information, Inc., quoted in *Fortune*, June 12, 1995

$150,000, new high price for an Internet address—business.com. Up from $15,000 one year before for tv.com.

> *New York Times*, June 5, 1997

Electricity. . . . was invented in the 1870s and '80s, but the economic payoff didn't happen until advances were commercialized and incorporated into manufacturing processes in the early 1900s. And office innovations like typewriters, teletype machines, and the like initially created jobs only for the very few with the literacy skills and training to use them—it took a full generation before those skills were widespread enough to raise the living standards of the working class.

I believe we are on the brink of a similar "breakthrough" era in the application of information-age technologies—and that the growth opportunities and social implications will be equally profound.

> RAYMOND W. SMITH, chairman of the telecommunications firm Bell Atlantic, in a speech, October 17, 1995

It took a century for the American telephone industry to go from zero to about $160 billion in revenues today. The competitive, unregulated personal-computer industry, by contrast, went from zero to nearly $100 billion in revenues in just 20 years

> REED HUNDT, chairman of the Federal Communications Commission, September 18, 1996, quoted in *Slate*, September 24, 1996

To understand the challenge of getting people to pay for Internet content, imagine trying to sell subscriptions to HBO back in the 1950s. People were still fascinated with the sheer miracle of television. They clustered around their primitive sets to watch the damnedest things (Milton Berle for instance). Before people would pay money for premium content, they had to get so bored with TV that they'd say, "Damn it, there's nothing on I want to watch."

Advertising is the other Holy Grail for Internet-content revenue. The TV analogy seems more cheery in this case—at first. Companies selling everything from soap to pickup trucks pump billions a year into television. Before TV, these same companies were big advertisers in other media. Burma Shave, for example, was a strong brand based on cute little roadside signs. The transition to TV transformed consumer marketing, and changed the rules. Poor Burma Shave stuck to its signs and lost its pre-eminent position, and many of the national brands that we know today rose to prominence. But the shift took decades.

> NATHAN MYHRVOLD, group VP at Microsoft, writing in *Slate,* September 24, 1996

[T]raditional economists say that, after a certain point, increases in output begin to taper off, even if you add more resources. That's the "law of diminishing returns." But that doesn't work in the new economy: Add new technology and better information, and output can keep going up and up and up.

> JAMES G. CULLEN of the telecommunications firm Bell Atlantic, in a speech, December 11, 1995

Never in the history of the industrialized world has there been a business that has the advantages of scale of the software industry.

> BILL GURLEY, of the investment firm Deutsche Morgan Grenfell, *The Economist,* June 10, 1996

The question is: Can you balance the future buildup in franchise value down the road with the costs of keeping the lights on?

> GARY CRAFT, of the investment firm Robertson, Stephens on Security First Network Bank, Atlanta, the first bank created for the Internet, quoted in the *Wall Street Journal,* May 28, 1997

A lot of people out there thought the Internet was a one-way ticket to a pot of gold. But the vast majority of companies that are trying to do content on the Web won't become profitable.

> HALSEY MINOR of the web publisher CNETT Inc., quoted in the *Wall Street Journal,* January 14, 1997

Right now there are too many people who are too damned cheap . . . er, we mean . . . too engaged by the novelty of the medium to pay extra for content.

> MICHAEL KINSLEY, on why Microsoft had abandoned its plan to impose a subscription fee, *Slate,* January 10, 1997

Content is not a venture investment. A lot of New Media companies are working for the good of mankind. The venture capitalists don't speak the same language.

> JASON CHERVOKAS, editor of the online newsletter @NY, quoted in *Forbes ASAP,* August 25, 1997

I just don't get this stuff. Wake me up when you can make money.

> Venture capitalist to Tim Nye, Internet service founder, *Forbes ASAP,* August 25, 1997

If toothpaste had the same lowly ratings as the online services, no one would be brushing their teeth.

> NICK DONATIELLO, president the market-research firm Lyssey, quoted in the *New York Times,* September 8, 1997

Columbus didn't have a business plan when he discovered America.

> ANDREW GROVE, CEO of the microprocessor maker Intel, making the point that to "make money, companies must be prepared to lose money," quoted in a postscript to Ken Auletta, "The Magic Box," *New Yorker,* April 11, 1994

Myth . . . Nobody is making money on the Net.

This is like saying there's no future for post offices or interstate highways because no one makes money from them, either. The issue is not how much revenue companies are extracting from the Internet but how much efficiency they are gaining from it.

> THOMAS PETZINGER JR., writer, *Wall Street Journal,* May 9, 1997

29.26 MOORE'S LAW—ITS COROLLARIES AND SUCCESSORS

Moore's Law: Chips double in capacity, in relation to price, every 18 months.

> GORDON MOORE, cofounder of the computer chip firm Intel, 1965

Between 1976 and 1992, disk-drive performance improved at a stunning rate: the physical size of a 100-megabyte (MB) system shrank from 5,400 to 8 cubic inches, and the cost per MB fell from $560 to $5.

> JOSEPH L. BOWER and CLAYTON M. CHRISTIANSEN, "Why Leading Companies Don't Stay at the Top of the Business," *Harvard Business Review,* January–February 1995

I just don't think the average consumer is going to invest $3,000 in a 60MHz, Pentium-based, 8 megabyte machine with a 540 megabyte hard drive, a CD ROM,

Sound Blaster, SVGA monitor, and a set of operating manuals for which a stand of prime timber gave its life just so they can cruise the chat rooms or alt.pet.cats on the Internet.

> CARL S. LEDBETTER JR., president of AT&T Consumer Products, in a speech, May 17, 1995

HP Pavilion 7420 MiniTower with 166 MHz Intel Pentium processor with MMX technology • 32MB RAM • 2.5GB hard drive • 16X CD-ROM drive • 2MB EDO video RAM • Accelerated 3D graphics • Spatializer 3D Surround Sound • Wavetable sound • Stereo speakers • MPEG • 33.6/14.4Kbps modem—$1,699.99+ Panasonic 17″ color monitor—$399.99

> J&R Computer World advertisement in the *New York Times,* June 15, 1997

[A]ll of the calculations it took one year to do working around the clock back at Los Alamos in 1945 could be accomplished today by a community college undergraduate in one afternoon, and he could do that by sharing the computer's time with 30 other people.

> JOSEPH HANKIN, president of Westchester Community College, in a speech, January 12, 1994

Where a calculator on the ENIAC (early computer) is equipped with 18,000 vacuum tubes and weighs 30 tons, computers in the future may have only 1,000 vacuum tubes and perhaps weigh one and a half tons.

> 1949 *Popular Mechanics* article quoted by Lewis E. Platt, CEO of Hewlett-Packard, in a speech, October 18, 1995

If cars had developed at the same pace as microprocessors over the past two decades, a typical car would now cost less than $5 and do 250,000 miles to the gallon.

> *The Economist,* September 28, 1996

Moore's Law must break somewhere. It's not a question of if, but when.

> MARK MELLIAR-SMITH of the computer firm Lucent Technologies, quoted in the *Wall Street Journal,* December 10, 1996

The world is no longer flat. Earth is no longer at the center of the solar system. And Moore's Law, a longstanding axiom of the computer age, is no longer true.

> JOHN MARKOFF, on Intel announcement that a new chip would shorten the cycle from 18 months to 9 or

less, quoted in the *New York Times,* September 17, 1997

We are running the risk of producing more technology than the world can adapt to.

> G. DAN HUTCHESON, president of the computer consulting firm VLSI Research, quoted in the *New York Times,* September 17, 1997

In our compulsion to improve efficiency, we easily forget that intelligent work by humans is not just a matter of processing speed, Notice the constant stream of spelling mistakes and missing words in the E-mail you receive. Good work takes time and patience; humans are not designed for multi-tasking.

> DAVID SHENK, web journalist, quoted in the *New York Times,* September 19, 1997

Heard the one about the semiconductor maker who was so successful it had to move into smaller premises?

> LOUISE KEHOE, *Financial Times,* October 3, 1997

It is as if you were racing along a freeway in the dark. You know there is a brick wall ahead of you but you cannot see it. [It would be] a tragedy to stop too soon.

> CRAIG BARRETT, president of the computer chip firm Intel, on the shrinking computer chip, quoted in the *Financial Times,* October 3, 1997

The cost of capital equipment to build semiconductors will double every four years.

> ARTHUR ROCK, venture capitalist, quoted in the *Financial Times,* October 3, 1997

29.27 PCs AND THE BRAIN

[W]e should not provide universal access [to the Internet]. I'd rather provide universal good education so that people could afford universal access—but could have the individual choice of whether to pay for it and how much to buy.

> ESTHER DYSON, president of the high-tech investment firm EDventure Holdings, *Atlantic Online,* September 11, 1994

Question: Do you think that too much reliance on the computer for mental stimulation and knowledge actually causes the brain to decrease in capacity?

Bill Gates: On the contrary, the computer stimulates your brain in a very positive way. Unlike the TV, which provides a group experience, the computer engages you with an individual experience. Its interactivity lets you pursue your interests.

> BILL GATES, CEO of Microsoft, July 18, 1996

29.28 PCs—THE DOWNSIDES

There is a major disease in this country called wall-stare. When people read a computer manual, they just want to put it down and stare at the wall for as long as possible.

> SANFORD ROSEN, president of the consulting firm Communication Sciences, *Time,* June 18, 1984

A good manual is not a narrative; it is an outline or report. Nobody ever reads a manual cover to cover—only mutants do that.

> CHRIS ESPINOSA of Apple, quoted in *Time,* June 18, 1984

[T]he PC will have to take a lesson from a device that's the gold standard of simplicity—the telephone. Its keypad offers one of the world's few universal interfaces. And getting a dial tone is so simple that I've heard of dogs being trained to dial 911 in an emergency. Compare that with the PC and it's clear how much work the computer industry has ahead of it.

> ECKHARD PFEIFFER, CEO of the computer firm Compaq, in a speech, fall 1996

To err is human, but to really foul things up requires a computer.

> Anonymous

I thought computers were supposed to make life better, not worse.

> KERMIT THE FROG, in the Muppets CD-ROM, *New York Times Book Review,* September 15, 1996

I'm not using these (expletive deleted) computers, and I'm not readin' no e-mail.

> P. J. CARLESIMO, coach of the Portland Trailblazers basketball team, on being given a laptop computer by team owner Paul Allen, the cofounder of Microsoft, *Sports Illustrated,* June 1995

Ultimately the problem of making sound financial investment decisions is not a statistical problem but an economic problem, and although statistical inference and artificial intelligence technology can add tremendous value, they alone will never provide a complete solution for financial market participants—at least not until software becomes self-aware.

> PROFESSOR ANDREW LO of the Sloan School of Management at MIT, *Worth,* January 1996

Imagine if everybody had a computer for $9,000 and you were stuck by a table every time you had to learn anything or read anything. . . . And all of a sudden somebody invented a whole new thing—a newspaper! You know what would happen? Everybody would say, "What an invention! A newspaper! For half a dollar you got the same thing!" Not only that, you can take it with you wherever you want to go. You can't take a computer to the toilet. You can take this wherever you want—wherever you want! The dog: he's about to go—do you put a computer underneath?

> Comedian JACKIE MASON in his one-man show *Love Thy Neighbor*

29.29 PREDICTING THE FUTURE OF MICROSOFT

For all intents and purposes, you can write the obituary on Windows—it's a dead product.

> DAVID GOLD, consultant, on Microsoft's delay in launching Windows, quoted in the *Wall Street Journal,* January 8, 1985

Bill Gates blew it with Windows. They missed their shot.

> DAVID C. COLE, former chairman of Ashton-Tate Inc. who went on to head Ziff Corporation, quoted in the *Wall Street Journal,* January 8, 1985

There were some people in the past who were very focused on duplicating what Microsoft did and were very jealous of what had been achieved. And what they did was to their own detriment . . . When does it go from being pure economics or competition and become an irrational set of reactions? I guess we'll know in 10 or 20 years.

> BILL GATES, CEO of Microsoft, quoted in *Forbes,* September 8, 1997

29.30 THE POWER OF MICROSOFT

It's kind of a gift from heaven.

> WILLIAM POPE, 37, six-year Microsoft employee, on how many employees had grown rich from the company's stock options, quoted in the *New York Times,* June 28, 1992

He [Bill Gates] follows somebody's taillights for a while, then zooms past. Soon there will be no taillights left.

> ANDREW S. GROVE, CEO of the microprocessor maker Intel, quoted in *Business Week,* June 27, 1994

There is no one who is going to control the printing press of the future, which is the Internet. We will have a percentage of the operating system market.

> BILL GATES, CEO of Microsoft, quoted in the *New York Times,* October 9, 1996

Ask him what percentage [of the operating system market].

> JAMES BARKSDALE, CEO of Netscape, quoted in the *New York Times,* October 9, 1996

Why don't you buy 5 percent of the cable industry?

> BRIAN L. ROBERTS, president of Comcast, the nation's fourth largest cable company, to Bill Gates over dinner, quoted in the *New York Times,* June 10, 1997

Software is likely to be the biggest additional expense over the life of the personal computer. This is the reason Bill Gates is the richest man in America.

> PETER H. LEWIS, *New York Times,* December 3, 1996

Proof that Bill Gates is the Devil:

The real name of the Microsoft C.E.O. is William Henry Gates III. Nowadays he is known as Bill Gates (III), where "III" means the order of the third (3rd).

By converting the letters of his current name to their equivalent ASCII values and adding his (III), you get the following:

B − 66 + I − 73 + L − 76 + L − 76 + G − 71 + A − 65 + T − 84 + E − 69 + S − 83 + 3 = 666 !!!

Some might ask, "How did Bill Gates get so powerful?" Coincidence? Or just the beginning of mankind's ultimate and total enslavement???

Before you decide, consider the following:

M S - D O S 6 . 2 1—77+83+45+68+79+83+32+54+46+50+49 = 666

W I N D O W S 9 5—87+73+78+68+79+87+83+57+53+1 = 666

You decide. . . .

> Courtesy of Professor Ian W. Boyd, University College, London, found on the Internet, November 1996

In this case, maybe Bill Gates isn't Big Brother after all.

> ROBERT X. CRINGELY, web site journalist, on Microsoft's $150 million investment in Apple, quoted in the *New York Times,* August 7, 1997

It doesn't serve our economic interest to advocate any particular ideology [an alternative to Microsoft]. We need to be agnostic.

> L. JOHN DOERR of venture-capital firm Kleiner, Perkins, Caufield & Byers, quoted in the *New Yorker,* August 11, 1997

What do you get when you cross Microsoft and Apple? Microsoft.

> Public radio listener joke about Microsoft's investment in Apple, August 14, 1997

If Microsoft made cars . . . we'd all have to switch to Microsoft Gas.

> PO BRONSON, *The First 20 Million Is Always the Hardest* (Random House, 1997)

Java is like the Monkees. They had a few hits and then disappeared . . . Microsoft is the Beatles.

> CHARLES SIMONYI of Microsoft, *Forbes ASAP,* August 25, 1997

If they embrace Microsoft, they risk getting swallowed. If they fight, they risk getting crushed.

> JULIA PITTA, *Forbes,* September 8, 1997

Do we actually sit and say, "Let's try not to get market share."

> STEVE BALLMER, adviser to Bill Gates, quoted in *Newsweek,* June 23, 1997

John D. Rockefeller wanted to dominate oil, but Microsoft wants it all, you name it: cable, media, banking, car dealerships.

> RALPH NADER, on Microsoft, *Newsweek,* October 20, 1997

29.31   SOFTWARE

Being big does not help you become good in the software business.

> FRED GIBBONS of Software Publishing, quoted in *Time,* April 16, 1984

I could be anywhere. All I need is a satellite dish on my roof.

> Head of software firm in Bangalore, India, quoted in *The Economist,* March 23, 1996

Competition, rather than any desire to serve customers well, is driving the fast release of new software.

It is hardly an advantage to have early access to new software if it does not perform properly.

> LOUISE KEHOE, information technology columnist, *Financial Times,* May 21, 1997

Software is the competitive weapon of the new millennium.

> ANN WINBLAD, cofounder of the venture-capital firm Hummer Winblad Venture Partners, quoted in the *New York Times,* September 28, 1997

The bottom line is that software is a young person's industry and an anarchic industry.

> KATHERINE LUCY of the Irish Business and Employers Confederation, quoted in the *Financial Times,* October 3, 1997

29.32   SOFTWARE AND POLITICS

This is the awakening of Silicon Valley as a political force. Once they see they can put some money into politics and it yields fruit, you'll see that Silicon Valley will no longer put its head in the sand.

> THOMAS PROULX, creator of Quicken personal-finance software who led efforts to make suing companies under securities laws more difficult, quoted in the *Wall Street Journal,* March 11, 1996

The chutzpah of some nerd who wrote a program that balances your checkbook deciding he can fix the bugs of the American civil legal system! There's an unbelievable naïveté and arrogance about these rich, yuppie computer people.

> HARVEY ROSENFELD, a California attorney on Thomas Proulx, creator of Quicken personal-finance

software, quoted in the *Wall Street Journal,* March 11, 1996

A sleeping giant has been awakened.

> BROOK BYERS, venture capitalist, on political activism sparked by efforts to make it easier to sue companies under securities law, *Wall Street Journal,* September 13, 1996

[T]he Business Software Alliance, a trade group . . . says the software industry in 1996 generated $102.8 billion in sales, making it the third-largest manufacturing sector in the United States, accounting for 619,000 jobs. [The announcement was made when Bill Gates and other software executives arrived in Washington to make the case for the industry's legislative agenda.]

> *Wall Street Journal,* June 4, 1997

29.33   WEB SITE NAMES

I'll name it Imelda. That seems to be a lightning rod.

> IMELDA MARCOS, wife of the late Philippine dictator Ferdinand Marcos, on what to call her web site, *Wall Street Journal,* February 13, 1997

29.34   YEAR 2000 PROBLEM— MILLENNIUM BOMB

This is a "bet the company" issue, requiring all the resources of the organization to work together.

> MATT HOTLE of the consulting firm Gartner Group, which has a prominent practice in year 2000 issues, quoted in *Forbes,* September 22, 1997

The problem is particularly acute for supermarkets with their reliance on "sell-by" dates. One chain has already disposed of a consignment of corned beef when the computer system read the sell-by date as 1904 rather than 2004.

> ALAN CANE, *Financial Times,* January 10, 1997

Q: For years people have speculated about why HAL the computer [of the movie *2001: A Space Odyssey*] went crazy. One reason I've never seen: Is it possible that HAL was programmed with two-digit year fields? Sure he worked fine in 1997. But when the year 2000 rolled around, he was a system crash waiting to happen.

> JOHN MILLER, Cambridge, Massachusetts

A: Not only did he try to kill the astronauts, he screwed up their payrolls.

> ROGER EBERT, Movie Q&A, *Journal Gazette,* Ft. Wayne, Indiana, May 4, 1997

It would be very prudent for everybody to get a hard copy of records [of bank accounts, pensions, and investments].

> ROBIN GUENIER, head of the British government body Taskforce 2000, quoted in the *Financial Times,* May 22, 1997

Up until now, when there have been serious systems failures such as . . . Domino's Pizza Delivery System . . . the solution typically was to fire the Chief Information Officer . . . However, because of the known impact of the Year 2000 Millennium Bug, I predict new laws and interpretations will be created to motivate and punish today's real culprits for the Year 2000 Bug—that is, management and management's reluctance to do anything about it!

> WARREN S. REID, founder and managing director of the WSR Consulting Group, headquartered in Encino, California, found on Internet, 1996

It's all very well fixing your own problem, but if none of your customers or suppliers have sorted themselves [out] then you go down the toilet anyway.

> MARK O'CONOR, London lawyer, *Wall Street Journal,* May 16, 1997

Back in 1995, a can of corned beef with a sell-by date of 2000 sent a [Marks & Spencer] checkout machine into apoplexy. Many computers recognize the year only by the last two digits, so the M&S checkout machine thought the corned beef had a sell-by date of 1900—and that just didn't compute.

> *Wall Street Journal,* May 16, 1997

Imagine there was a widespread problem in the world that only those with a high degree of fluency in ancient Greek or Latin could solve.

> GEOFFREY WAINWRIGHT, on demand for "classical language" programmers to solve year 2000 problems (for which most of the code in question is written in Cobol), *Financial Times,* September 3, 1997

Back then, we weren't blinded by conventional wisdom.

> BOB BEMER, 77-year-old former IBM programming executive who claims to know how to solve the year 2000 problem by going back to elemental levels of code that only he is old enough to remember, quoted in the *Wall Street Journal,* June 20, 1997

This thing is going to be on the same scale litigation-wise as the environment, the S&L crisis, and asbestos combined.

> STEVEN HOCK, head of the 24-lawyer "year 2000" team at a San Francisco law firm, quoted in *Forbes,* July 28, 1997

There are two kinds of people. Those who aren't working on it and aren't worried, and those who are working on it and are terrified.

> NIGEL MARTIN-JONES of the consulting firm Data Dimensions, quoted in *Newsweek,* June 2, 1997

If you're not changing code by November of this year [1997], you will not get this thing done on time—it's that simple. *We still don't get it.*

> PETER DE JAGER, a speaker to technical conferences on this problem, quoted in *Newsweek,* June 2, 1997

If you are going to have a failure, you will prefer it if the system just stops because then you can fix it and your data is intact. The worst situation is when it *appears* to be working perfectly, but some routine is quietly corrupting all your data with an incorrect calculation.

> PETER DE JAGER, quoted in the *Financial Times,* April 2, 1997

It's a problem that could bring an institution to its knees . . . The company has to test and fix 60 million lines of code in 200 applications . . . Everyday we see something new that we hadn't thought about.

> DAVID LACINO, head of the year 2000 task force at Bank of Boston, quoted in *Newsweek,* June 2, 1997

Potential buyers (of insurance against the millennium bomb) are being asked to pay $65,000 up front for an audit before receiving a quotation. They then go ahead with a full due diligence audit that can cost another $500,000 depending on the size of the company and the complexity of the risk.

> CHRISTOPHER ADAMS, insurance correspondent, quoted in the *Financial Times,* September 3, 1997

If . . . a credit-card company charges interest on every transaction based on how long it has been outstanding—or issues demands for payment based on when it last recorded a payment from a customer . . . [t]he system could start generating negative numbers and treat all customers if they had not paid since 1900 . . .

> GEOFFREY WAINWRIGHT, *Financial Times,* September 3, 1997

Three-quarters of U.K. companies would have legitimate grounds for claiming against their reinsurers if they suffered financial loss from the "millennium bomb."

> Report by the law firm Cameron & McKenna, quoted in the *Financial Times,* September 4, 1997

We have been working with these executive agencies for almost two years now, and I do not see the sense of urgency that should exist in the executive branch. This is mostly a management problem, not a technical one. I see little concern among agency management that service to the taxpayers will suffer.

> STEPHEN HORN of the U.S. House of Representatives subcommittee on Government Management, Information, and Technology, quoted in the *Financial Times,* September 16, 1997

You are going to see some major slowdowns because of these small companies.

> LOU MARCOCCIO, research director of the Year 2000 practice at the consulting firm the Gartner Group, on problems at bigger companies if their small suppliers don't fix their systems, quoted in the *New York Times,* September 25, 1997

Whilst we can address our own year 2000 systems issues, if companies to whom we link electronically do not take the same action, our operation will be impacted.

> WIN BISCHOFF, chairman of the investment bank Schroeders, quoted in the *Financial Times,* February 26, 1997

If your own management and staff, or your correspondents and customers, take any of the following positions, your organization may be at risk.

- *Denial.* "The year 2000 is not an issue for our organization." It is.

- *No resource problems.* "Our organization can handle the year 2000 with its existing resources and within current budgets." Very unlikely.

- *Vendors will address the issue.* "Our outside vendors and service providers won't let us down." Trust is not a substitute for testing.

- *Covered by contract.* "Our lawyers have determined that we are appropriately protected by our legal agreements." The lawyers may get rich, but will you be in business?

> WILLIAM McDONOUGH, president of the Federal Reserve Bank of New York, quoted in the *Economist,* October 4, 1997

The [Unum Life Insurance Company] was puzzled last year when its revenues started to drop. Investigators tracked the problem to a computer program which deleted policies which had been dormant for five years or more. The computer detected dormancy by adding five years to the last date a policy had been activated. When the software scanned policies started in 1995 it came up with 00. Assuming that these policies had last been touched in 1900, the computer dumped them unceremoniously and the company lost more than 500 records.

> ALAN CANE, *Financial Times Weekend,* March 8/9, 1997

If Saddam Hussein wanted to launch an attack on the United States, the first day of the year 2000 would be the time to do it.

> ROBIN GUENIER, head of the British government body Taskforce 2000, quoted in the *Financial Times,* April 2, 1997

Fortunately, weapons systems are, for the most part, much less date-intensive than most business information systems, so there are fewer Year 2000 "fixes" which need to be made in them.

> EMMETT PAIGE JR., U.S. Assistant Secretary of Defense, quoted in the *Financial Times,* April 2, 1997

In South America, parts of Asia, most of Eastern Europe, and even some countries in Western Europe, banks have almost not started at all. Any company operating in these countries faces a heightened risk that the banks they do business with will have a computer failure that will knock the banks out.

> LOU MARCOCCIO of the Gartner Group, management consultants, quoted in the *New York Times,* November 10, 1997

The "year 2000" problem poses a serious threat that could disrupt the United States economy and bring about a yearlong global recession beginning in January 2000. Such a recession could be as severe as the 1973–74 global downturn that was caused by the OPEC oil embargo . . .

> EDWARD YARDEMI, chief economist of the investment bank Deutsche Morgan Grenfell North America, *New York Times,* December 7, 1997

29.35 YEAR 2000 BY THE NUMBERS

[*Estimated costs to fix millennium bug*]

$600 billion—Gartner Group

$400 billion—JP Morgan.

$280 billion—Killen & Associates, California consulting firm

$200 billion—International Data, Connecticut consulting firm

$52 billion—BZW, British investment bank

> *The Economist,* October 4, 1997

30.1 AMERICAN MANAGEMENT

If an American wants an answer he'll pick up the phone. A European will write a memo. The phone call will seem overly aggressive and pushy to the European manager, but the American needs to convey a greater sense of urgency because competition in the United States is so tough.

> KAI LINDHOLST of the international consulting firm Egon Zehnder, quoted in *Time*, October 9, 1989

Our [American managers'] natural strong suit is the energy and creativity of an irreverent, aggressive, impatient, and curious people. It is ours to win with—if we can shift gears from decades of *controlling* things to a decade of liberating—turning people loose to dream, dare, and win.

> JOHN F. WELCH JR., CEO of GE, a 1993 reprint from *Leaders*

I like to buy a company any fool can manage because eventually one will.

> PETER LYNCH, former manager of Fidelity Magellan, quoted in *Fortune*, December 14, 1992

I admire the capacity of American business executives to continually reinvent what they do; it shows they are never satisfied.

> British member of Parliament, quoted in United Airlines's in-flight magazine *Hemispheres*, December 1996

[T]here are two kinds of businesses in the United States: those that are heading for the cliff and know it, and those that are heading for the cliff and don't know it.

> The late MICHAEL WALSH, CEO of the automotive and energy company Tenneco, quoted in *Fortune*, December 13, 1993

Ninety-five percent of American managers today say the right thing. Five percent actually do it.

> JAMES O'TOOLE of the think tank Aspen Institute, quoted in *Fortune*, February 21, 1994

American businessmen have a love affair with the quick fixes we find in the one-minute manager books.

> LAWRENCE A. BOSSIDY, CEO of the industrial firm Allied-Signal, in a speech, February 14, 1994

In the name of efficiency, bring back the two-martini lunch [as a tool for forging business relationships], before those nimble third world competitors get there first.

> *The Economist,* December 13, 1995

[P]eople no more buy management books for their insights into epistemology than they read *Playboy* for the essays by John Updike.

> *The Economist,* May 31, 1997

30.2 EUROPEAN MANAGEMENT

In contrast to their counterparts in the United States or Japan, European CEOs often give the heads of their operating companies an exceptionally long managerial leash. Written guidelines and objectives are few, and reporting lines often seem ambiguous.

> HERBERT A. HENZLER, chairman of McKinsey & Co. in Germany and professor of International Management of Munich University, quoted in *Harvard Business Review,* July–August 1992

Technologies such as electronic mail are just not part and parcel of the way [European companies] operate. It is largely incidental to the way managers work.

> ANDREW GROVE, CEO of the computer chip firm Intel, quoted in the *Financial Times,* January 27, 1997

30.3 FOREIGN MANAGERS AND U.S. WORKERS

You tend to underestimate their [U.S. workers] strengths and overlook your own weaknesses.

> MICHAEL BESSON, French chief executive of the building materials company Certain Tweed, quoted in *Time,* October 9, 1989

Their people would come here and put down our people, our work ethic. I had a little problem with that. I finally slammed my door shut and told my German counterpart that I didn't need him telling us how good he was and how weak we were. We never had any problems after that.

> U.S. executive of a West German–owned U.S. subsidiary, quoted in *Time,* October 9, 1989

50. [Percent of American managers who either resign or are fired within 18 months of a foreign takeover.]

> *Time,* October 9, 1989

30.4 MANAGEMENT

Just as the student now feels technique is more important than content, so the trainee believes managing is an end in itself, an expertise relatively independent of the content of what is being managed.

> WILLIAM H. WHYTE, *The Organization Man* (Simon & Schuster, 1956)

We're controlled by ideas and norms that have outlived their usefulness, that are only ghosts but have as much influence on our behavior as they would if they were alive. The ideas of men like Henry Ford, Frederick Taylor, and Max Weber—these are the ghosts that haunt our halls of management.

> ROBERT H. WATERMAN JR., *Adhocracy* (Norton, 1993)

If there is a meter that measures the work of the manager, and at one end of the gauge are traditional management skills—all the technical information of finance, marketing, and the rest of the curriculum—and at the other end are leadership, goal setting, motivation, and articulation, then today the needle has swung from conducting monthly budget reviews to articulating where the company is going, for what purpose, and how it's going to get there.

> WALTER B. WRISTON, former CEO of Citicorp, interviewed in *Harvard Business Review,* January–February 1990

[S]ome of our leaders were unwilling, or unable, to abandon big-company, big-shot autocracy and embrace the values we were trying to grow. So we defined our management styles, or "types," and how they furthered or blocked our values. And then we acted.

Type I not only delivers on performance commitments, but believes in and furthers GE's small-company values. The trajectory of this group is "onward and upward," and the men and women who comprise it will represent the core of our senior leadership into the next century.

Type II does not meet commitments, nor share our values—nor last long at GE.

Type III believes in the values but sometimes misses commitments. We encourage taking swings, and Type III is typically given another chance.

Type IV. The "calls" on the first two types are easy. Type III takes some judgment; but Type IV is the most difficult. One is always tempted to avoid taking action, because Type IVs deliver short-term results. But Type IVs do so without regard to values and, in fact, often diminish them by grinding people down, squeezing them, stifling them.

> JOHN F. WELCH JR., CEO of GE, writing in 1995 annual report

The job for big companies, the challenge that we all face as bureaucrats, is to create an environment where people can reach their dreams—and they don't have to do it in a garage.

> JOHN F. WELCH JR., CEO of GE, quoted in *Fortune,* May 29, 1995

What you measure is what you get.

[M]anagers should not have to choose between financial and operational measures. [W]e have found that senior executives can provide a clear performance target or focus attention on the critical areas of the business.

> PROFESSOR ROBERT S. KAPLAN of Harvard University and DAVID P. NORTON, president of the consulting firm Nolan, Norton, "The Balanced Scorecard—Measures that Drive Performance," *Harvard Business Review,* January–February 1992

The [balance] scorecard is not a way of formulating strategy. It's a way of understanding and checking what you have to do throughout the organization to make your strategy work.

> DAVID NORTON, president of Renaissance Solutions, and PROFESSOR ROBERT KAPLAN, quoted in *Financial Times,* April 1, 1997

Even as a manager you have to add value. You have to be good at something in the area you're working in. You can't just say, "Well, I am a manager so I will just manage and coordinate these people." People don't require that kind of management anymore.

> VINOD DHAM of the microprocessor firm Intel, quoted in *Fortune,* April 4, 1994

The art of management is about choice.

> G. RICHARD THOMAN, chief financial officer of IBM, quoted in *Business Week,* December 9, 1996

Getting to know the management of a company is like getting married. You never really know the girl until you live with her. Until you've lived with management, you don't really know them to that same degree.

> PHILIP FISHER, "investment philosopher," quoted in *Forbes*, October 19, 1987

However much senior executives may need to cooperate, they also compete with one another.

> "Getting It Done: New Roles for Senior Executives," *Harvard Business Review*, November–December 1995

Our organizations are constructed so that most of our employees are asked to use only 5 percent to 10 percent of their capacity at work. It is only when those same individuals go home that they can use the other 90 percent to 95 percent—to run their households, lead a Boy Scout troop, or build a summer home. We have to be able to recognize and employ that untapped ability that each individual brings to work everyday.

> PERCY BARNEVIK, CEO of the industrial firm ABB (Asea Brown Boveri), quoted in *Harvard Business Review*, May–June 1995

Procrastination is epidemic. The number of people who finish projects three weeks ahead of time you can count on one hand.

> JEFFREY P. KAHN, a New York psychiatrist who counsels executives, quoted in the *Wall Street Journal*, May 7, 1996

A properly trained first-line manager is the first building brick in lean management.

[T]he supervisor is where management's plans and ideas get transferred and implemented on the shop floor.

> BILL JORDAN, co-leader of Britain's National Economic Development Council and head of the 700,000-member Amalgamated Engineering Union, quoted in the *Economist*, February 1, 1992

30.5 MANAGEMENT FADS

We began crawling around in the dark when I bumped into our president. It was atrocious. We would have done better figuring out how to sell more brownie mix.

> JOHN CLEMENS, former Pillsbury executive who became a professor at Hartwick College, recalling encounter session in which participants had to shed shoes, ties, and name tags before the lights went out. Quoted in *Business Week*, January 20, 1986

If employees suspect that managers are going through the latest fad, cynicism will set in.

> PROFESSOR ROBERT SIMONS, Harvard Business School, *Harvard Business Review*, March–April, 1995

Management by trust, empathy, and forgiveness sounds good. It also sounds soft. It is, in practice, tough. Organizations based on trust have, on occasion, to be ruthless.

> CHARLES HANDY, business philosopher and author, *Harvard Business Review*, November–December 1992

[W]e don't believe in this open-book stuff. When we have a good year, we just walk around the plant and hand each person a check for $10,000. Helluva way to motivate people and reduce turnover. I can't remember the last time anyone quit on us.

> Overheard at annual *Inc.* 500 conference workshop on open-book management, cited in *Inc.*, August 1994

Straightforward as it sounds, there are some subtleties and requirements that go with MBWA [management by walking around]. For one thing, not every manager finds it easy and natural to do. And if it's done reluctantly or infrequently, it just won't work. It needs to be frequent, friendly, unfocused, and unscheduled—but far from pointless. And since its principal aim is to seek out people's thoughts and opinions, it requires good listening.

> DAVID PACKARD, cofounder of the computer firm Hewlett-Packard, *The HP Way* (HarperCollins, 1995)

This is nuts.

> HASSAN PIRASTEHFAR of Motorola, who was sent to Advanced Leadership Academy where one activity is to beat drums for your company, quoted in the *Wall Street Journal*, August 13, 1996

To mess the whole project up, it takes just one person to say, I'm not gonna do this touchy-feely, California stuff.

> ARTHUR HULL, founder of the training company Advanced Leadership Academy, quoted in the *Wall Street Journal*, August 13, 1996

A team is like having a baby tiger given to you at Christmas. It does a wonderful job of keeping the mice away for about 12 months, and then it starts to eat your kids.

> Team leader from American President Companies, quoted in *Fortune*, February 19, 1996

In our leadership classes we have what we call talking hearts. Stones in the shape of a heart you hold in your hand. It's about putting your heart in your hand and putting it out on the floor for all to see. When you have it, you have the floor. Everyone gets a voice, you can't interrupt people, and you're thinking and processing where your head and heart are on any given morning. If you had a bad morning, or you can't start the car, or the kids wouldn't get going, you get to say that.

> MARSHA CLARK of the data processing firm EDS, quoted in *Fortune*, October 14, 1996

They [coffee roasters] have been following the latest management theories [just-in-time inventory management]. That may work in car parts but it doesn't work in commodities. They will be rethinking that strategy now [after a sharp rise in coffee prices because supplies ran out].

> LAURENCE EAGLES of the commodity firm GNI in Brazil, quoted in the *Financial Times*, May 19, 1997

Is this spinach? Without a gas grill and steaks, I'm lost.

> MIKE MAJCHRZAK of FCC National Bank, Wilmington, Delaware, at a $7,500 corporate bonding seminar, quoted in the *New York Times*, July 23, 1997

We developed the cooking idea so a team would see that one senior executive alone cannot create a gourmet meal—they have to team up.

> DR. FILOMENA D. WARIHAY, president of Take Charge Consultants, which created *Cooking by the Book*, quoted in the *New York Times*, July 23, 1997

I tend to be spicy and at times I cause tempers to flare.

> FAYE DADZIE of FCC National Bank, describing what she has in common with a jalapeño pepper, quoted in the *New York Times*, July 23, 1997

It's a terrifying event for people—they think they're going to die—but they learn they can do things they thought were impossible.

> HERSH WILSON of Pecos River Learning (which conducts team-building exercises like climbing to the top of a telephone pole and jumping off—while attached to ropes and a harness), quoted in the *New York Times*, July 23, 1997

The only management philosophy that does work is the one that acknowledges that none of them do: Be flexible and strive for consistency [of performance and growth].

> MARK H. McCORMACK, *What They Don't Teach You at Harvard Business School* (Bantam Doubleday Dell, 1988)

People are starting to realize that changing how people work is more important than reengineering. I hope there comes to be some skepticism about the next big thing. The next big thing will get us into trouble.

> PROFESSOR THOMAS DAVENPORT of the University of Texas, quoted in the *Wall Street Journal*, November 26, 1996

I think practical jokes should be practical. They should help you get what you want. The way I see it, it's better to give ulcers than to get them.

> ALAN ABEL, who teaches seminars on practical joking for revenge or self-defense, quoted in the *New York Times*, April 19, 1992

- Leadership is hard
- Communication is important
- Change is different
- People are human
- The future is tomorrow

To the uninitiated, these principles [from the spoof-of-management book *Why I Love Business!* by "Stephen Michael Peter Thomas"] may sound a little obvious, but by the standards of most management books they are refreshing.

[Spoofing management books is hard because] Anything that you can think of as a joke has already been done in all earnestness.

> LUCY KELLAWAY, *Financial Times*, April 1, 1997

[Case in point] By embarking on a quest to discuss the passion of past human wonder, the book takes us on a breathtaking journey from the Pyramids to the Digital Age, before concluding with a "Future Mindset" for achieving long-term business success.

> Publicity material for *Challenging Reality: In Search of the Future Organization*, cited by Lucy Kellaway, *Financial Times*, April 1, 1997

Total Quality Management; empowerment; reengineering the corporation; the human investment model; cycle-time management (it seems a Canadian consultant was trying to patent this one); the four Rs of reframing, restructuring, revitalization, and renewal; the five skills of breakthrough thinking, open-book management . . . Like mushrooms, they look enticing, but their nutritional value can be suspect. Some are even poisonous.

> The late HAROLD GENEEN, chairman of the international conglomerate ITT, *The Synergy Myth,* with Brent Bowers (St. Martin's, 1997)

In high-wage economies . . . the feeling within management is: we've gone through quality, we've gone through service, and what's left is design.

> TOM PETERS, management guru, quoted in the *Economist,* December 2, 1995

30.6   MANAGERS AS A CLASS

If I look back over a period of 30 years' acquaintance with presidents of companies and directors of corporations, I see a succession of amiable gentlemen posed around the square of a card table, chatting pleasantly on a thirteenth green, rolling dice from a leather cup in a country club bar. They could talk intelligently enough about the specific instances of a specific deal (i.e., shoptalk narrowly defined); once the conversation ranged beyond the vicinity of their immediate financial interest, I can remember none of them making other than pleasantly vacant references to their comfort and travel plans. The phrase, "I got it in Palm Beach," could as easily refer to a new putter as to a suntan, an electronics company, a third wife, or a venereal disease.

> LEWIS H. LAPHAM, *Money and Class in America* (Grove, 1988)

It is still unacceptable for senior people to be seen as needy. Help of this kind [counseling for executives to alter counterproductive management behavior] is regarded as something for psychotics—which it is not— or may be something spouses need because the company has moved them around the country so much.

> ALICIA WHITAKER of the toothpaste firm Colgate, quoted in *Fortune,* December 27, 1993

30.7   MANAGING IN BANKRUPTCY

Most people are now aware that you can fly on an airplane that's in Chapter 11. But management still doesn't appreciate what needs to be said, or how quickly it needs to be said.

> DON BERSTEIN, attorney for firm of Davis, Polk, Wardwell, quoted in the *New York Times,* April 7, 1991

In the first 24 hours of a bankruptcy, there's a window of opportunity when you can win or lose your employees' support.

Everyone wants to know if management is capable of solving the problems that led to the crisis. You shouldn't offer false promises, you should offer concrete information.

When it's an outside crisis, like a product liability, employees will band together. With bankruptcy, employees believe it's a self-inflicted wound. They're frustrated and angry.

> HARRIS DIAMOND of the PR firm Sawyer/Miller Group, quoted in the *New York Times,* April 7, 1991

Employees didn't know if they should show up for work [when Braniff Airlines declared bankruptcy], so many of them didn't. The reservation desk went unattended, and the phones went unmanned.

> MIKE SITRICK, an L.A.-based consultant, quoted in the *New York Times,* April 7, 1991

30.8   MANAGING COMPLEXITY

What most managers think of as scientific management is based on a conception of science that few current scientists would defend. [W]hile traditional science focused on analysis, prediction, and control, the new science emphasizes chaos and complexity.

> DAVID J. FREEDMAN of *Discover* magazine in a book review, *Harvard Business Review,* November–December 1992

Management today has to think like a fighter pilot.

> FRED WIERSAMA of the consulting firm CSC Index, quoted in *Fortune,* December 13, 1993

The shop floor can usually get into teams much easier than the office staff can, and that can lead to departments battling each other. . . . Employees need to think of one another as internal customers and remember that they really are on the same team.

> BRUCE HODES, president of training firm CMI, quoted in *Inc.,* November 1995

Complex processes are the work of the devil.

> DR. MICHAEL HAMMER, management guru, quoted in *Business Week,* August 9, 1996

The effort [to integrate systems] is so gargantuan and takes so long that by the time you have finished, everything has changed and the champions of the project have long gone.

> PROFESSOR BRANDT ALLEN of the University of Virginia, quoted in *Fortune,* September 24, 1990

[T]he more you establish parameters and encourage people to take initiatives within those boundaries, the more you multiply your own effectiveness by the effectiveness of other people.

> ROBERT HAAS, CEO of the clothing company Levi Strauss, quoted in *Harvard Business Review,* September–October 1990

I don't think getting the economics right in a business is necessarily the same thing as decentralization. There is a misconception that small is always more beautiful than big. Just fragmenting an organization does not create conditions sufficient for success.

> LOUIS GERSTNER JR., CEO of IBM, quoted in *Fortune,* May 31, 1993

Management today is reactive behavior. You put your hand on a hot stove and yank it off. A cat would know to do as much.

> W. EDWARDS DEMING, management guru, quoted in *Business Week,* January 10, 1994

Companies that have experienced the most growth—if you measure growth by increased shareholder value—tend to devote the greatest attention to developing their human resources.

> JOHN M. HARRIS, CEO of the consulting firm Forum Corporation, in a letter to the editor, *Wall Street Journal,* January 10, 1997

Cost, cost, cost. Service, service, service. People, people, people. The business model is understandable by any three-year-old.

> TOM PETERS, management guru, on management style at Southwest Airlines, quoted in the *New York Times Magazine,* November 9, 1997

30.9 MANAGING IN DIFFICULT CIRCUMSTANCES

It felt like I was in a continuous long-running nightmare—only I wasn't asleep.

> EDWARD VAN DEN AMEELE, press relations manager for Union Carbide, describing the aftermath of a toxic gas leak at a Union Carbide pesticide plant in Bhopal, India, that killed over 2,000 people, quoted in *Fortune,* January 7, 1985

89, percent of *Fortune* 500 CEOs who agreed that "a crisis in business today is as inevitable as death and taxes."

42, percent of companies who have had a crisis in the past that still do not have a plan in place in case of another crisis.

97, percent of CEOs who felt either "very confident" or "somewhat confident" that they could "respond well to a crisis."

Reality is a community affair . . . People who totally isolate themselves during a crisis (say, Nixon in the waning days of his administration) tend to get carried away into hypervigilant positions that have no touch with reality.

> STEVEN FINK, *Crisis Management* (American Management Association, 1986)

There is nothing like running a company that has been in chapter 11. It's better than starting from scratch because you have rude reminders of failure all around you.

> ARNOLD HIATT, CEO of the shoe company Stride Rite, interviewed in *Harvard Business Review,* March–April 1992

[L]ook what the Mattel Company did last month when the American Association of University Women attacked, of all things, the talking Barbie doll for uttering the phrase "math class is tough." Mattel immediately acknowledged that it made a mistake, that it didn't intend to disparage the ability to master mathematics, and that it would offer a swap of a new Barbie for anyone who bought the offending doll.

> FRASER P. SEITEL of the public relations firm Burson Marsteller, in a speech, November 12, 1992

I used to be a fighter pilot. When you have an emergency, the first thing you do is keep flying the plane.

You can't get so engrossed in the engine failure that you crash.

> RENSO CAPORALI, CEO of the aircraft manufacturer Grumman, quoted in *Fortune,* February 22, 1993

When things go bad, cut the pay at the top first. When things go well, reward at the bottom first.

> STEVE ASHTON, CEO of Ashton Photo, *Inc.,* September 1994

Why do major corporations encounter so many crises? . . . General Motors has about the same number of employees as San Francisco has citizens. . . . AT&T is about the same size as Buffalo, New York. . . . Lockheed Martin is the size of Spokane, Washington. Executives must keep in mind that almost any one of thousands of employees can plunge an entire corporation into a crisis through misdeed or oversight, as the recent collapse of the venerable Barings Bank made abundantly clear.

> NORMAN R. AUGUSTINE, CEO of the defense-aerospace company Lockheed Martin, *Harvard Business Review,* November–December 1995

One's objective should be to get it right, get it quick, get it out, and get it over. You see, your problem won't improve with age.

> WARREN BUFFETT, to Norman Augustine, quoted in *Harvard Business Review,* November–December 1995

If you run a public company, you cannot ignore the public.

> JIM BURKE, CEO of the pharmaceutical company Johnson & Johnson, to Norman Augustine, quoted in *Harvard Business Review,* November–December 1995

Next week there can't be any crisis. My schedule is already full.

> HENRY KISSINGER, while U.S. Secretary of State

It is common sense to take a method and try it. If it fails, admit it frankly and try another. But above all, try something.

> U.S. PRESIDENT FRANKLIN DELANO ROOSEVELT

Texaco stumbled in its initial response to the discrimination accusations [by black employees] two years ago by playing down their importance. Then, when Texaco lawyers couldn't deliver and the tapes turned up, Mr.

Bijur [Texaco CEO] jumped to complete contrition, even though he still didn't have the facts.

> GERALD C. MEYERS, former chairman of American Motors and now professor of crisis management at the University of Michigan, and SUSAN MEYERS, *New York Times,* January 12, 1997

If there was enough discrimination at Texaco to merit a $176 million settlement with the employees, then there was enough discrimination to merit a commensurate payment to Texaco stockholders—not from corporate coffers, but from the personal assets of the corporate executives who bilked their investors by failing to hire the best bargains in the labor market.

> PROFESSOR STEVEN E. LANDSBURG of the University of Rochester, quoted in *Slate,* December 6, 1996

For Chrysler, I think a recession would be an opportunity. It would be an opportunity to prove once and for all that the company has long-term business and product plans that treat a downturn almost like another day at the office. In the past, we and the others have planned up to the next recession. Today, we're planning through the next recession.

> ROBERT EATON, CEO of Chrysler, in his 1996 fourth-quarter earnings announcement, quoted in *Speechwriter's Newsletter,* June 1, 1997

Q: Early reporting on [the TWA Paris-bound 747] Flight 800 suggested that it had been downed by terrorists [when the plane crashed off Long Island in 1996]. As terrible as that would have been, did you almost hope for that—as opposed to a mechanical problem?
A: One of the things I've learned is that you don't "hope" for anything. You try to find out the answer.

Q: But that would have been a better result for the company, wouldn't it?
A: I don't know how there can be a "better result" when people die.

> PHILIP CONDIT, CEO of the aerospace company Boeing, interviewed in the *New York Times,* August 17, 1997

What an airline does in the first 30 days after the crash shapes its relationships with the [victims'] families.

> TOM WHALEN, aviation defense attorney, quoted in the *New York Times,* November 23, 1997

The short fuse crisis involving a failing financial institution is . . . the most difficult, and, I might add, the most nerve-racking and demanding problem for any central bank, because the consequences of a wrong decision can be so serious. In the absolute worst case, a decision may have to be made in a matter of hours as to whether the central bank should take overt steps to contain or cushion the situation at hand.

> E. GERALD CORRIGAN of the investment firm Goldman, Sachs and the former president of the Federal Reserve Bank of New York, in a speech, September 24, 1995

There's no leader of a turnaround who's a beloved leader.

It's impossible to run a leveraged corporation like camp.

> LINDA WACHNER, CEO of the intimate apparel firm Warnaco, quoted in *Fortune*, October 18, 1993

It's me or Dr. Kevorkian.

> ALBERT J. "CHAINSAW AL" DUNLAP, turnaround specialist hired by Sunbeam Corp., quoted in the *Wall Street Journal*, September 11, 1996

There's a New Sunbeam Shining. . . . Now There's a Bright Idea.

> New corporate slogan, launched in the wake of layoffs of 6,000 from a workforce of 12,000, the highest-percentage downsizing in history, quoted in the *New York Times*, November 13, 1996

If all the outsider does is cut costs, people will be afraid and turn off. Long term you don't get cultural change through fear.

> PROFESSOR JOHN KOTTER of Harvard Business School, quoted in *Fortune*, November 29, 1993

30.10 MISSION STATEMENTS

To do really cool things in the field of computer communications and make a buck at it.

> Mission statement of the software firm Galacticomm, quoted in *Inc.*, March 1994

A bunch of guys take off their ties and coats, go into a motel room for three days, and put a bunch of words on a piece of paper—and then go back to business as usual.

> JOHN ROCK of Oldsmobile, on what he thinks of mission statements, quoted in *Fortune*, May 16, 1994

30.11 NEGOTIATING STYLE

He that speaks ill of the Mare will buy her.

> BENJAMIN FRANKLIN, *Poor Richard's Almanack*

Anger can be an effective negotiating tool, but only as a calculated act, never as a reaction. . . . a photo of Nikita Khrushchev's historic shoe-pounding incident at the U.N. revealed that he was still wearing both his shoes. A third "for-pounding-only" shoe. That's calculation.

> MARK H. McCORMACK, *What They Don't Teach You at Harvard Business School* (Bantam Doubleday Dell, 1988)

Basically, a threat is an attempt to get something for nothing.

> H. GEORG MCIOSZEK, industrial management consultant, in a speech, October 6, 1992

The harder a guy negotiates with us about equity, the better CEO he is likely to be.

> HENRY KRAVIS, head of the leveraged buyout firm KKR, quoted in George Anders, *Merchants of Debt* (Basic Books, 1992)

30.12 PERKS

[T]he biggest companies, which all offer essentially the same benefits to employees, have discovered they can distinguish themselves from the pack with the right recreation program.

> STEVE EDGERTON of the Xerox Corporation, quoted in *U.S. News & World Report*, August 13, 1984

Entertainment is to the businessman what fertilizer is to the farmer: it increases the yield.

> U.S. SENATOR RUSSELL LONG (Democrat, Louisiana), quoted in *U.S. News & World Report*, July 14, 1986

When you see executives who get too hung up on perquisites like private airplanes or executive dining rooms or private washrooms, you've got to question what they're really focusing on.

> CHUCK AMES of the buyout firm Clayton, Dubilier & Rice, quoted in the *New York Times*, December 12, 1993

Ben & Jerry's Homemade Inc.—3 pints a day (often bartered for baby-sitting, haircuts, and other services).

Anheuser-Busch—vouchers for two cases of beer per month.

Robert Mondavi—a case of wine after each quarter.

Rubbermaid, Inc.—"rubber bucks," redeemable at company store.

Benjamin Moore—paint.

Eli Lilly—Prozac (health plan covers 100 percent of company products and only 80 percent of other drugs).

Great American Backrub—free massage.

Rodale Press—classes including aerobics and yoga, discount rentals of exercise equipment, and compost from company dining room.

> Corporations and the nonfinancial rewards they offer their employees, cited in the *New York Times*, October 6, 1996

* Same group insurance
* Same holidays
* Same vacation
* Same color hard hats
* No reserved parking place
* No company cars
* No executive dining room
* No company airplane
* No company boats
* No mission statements (although we do have a simple vision: to adopt new technology and develop new management styles in the steel industry)
* No job descriptions
* No hunting lodges
* No fishing lodges
* Everyone travels economy class

> F. KENNETH IVERSON, CEO of the steel company Nucor, on the benefits it offers employees, including executives, in a speech, February 5, 1996

The largest American corporations grant their executives the privileges of infants. The company provides expense allowances, medical treatment, trips and entertainments, planes, picnics and outings, cars, club memberships and, above all else, a ferociously protective secretary, who, like a good English nanny, arranges the daily schedule, pays the bills, remembers to send flowers for anniversaries and birthdays, makes dinner reservations and invents excuses that the nice gentleman's creditors or mistress might find plausible. The comforts and conveniences supposedly permit the executives to do a better job; in fact, they encourage the habit of infantilism prevalent at the higher altitudes of corporate privilege.

> LEWIS H. LAPHAM, *Money and Class in America* (Grove, 1988)

Chicken is chicken. It doesn't justify the price.

> JAMES S. POVEC of Softbank Expos and Conferences, on flying business class, quoted in the *Wall Street Journal*, November 22, 1996

They [my successors] got too used to limousines and perks. Look at the new headquarters. Mahogany paneling everywhere. The swish dining rooms. The chauffeured cars. See you in Boca Raton. See you at the Louvre. That attitude has permeated Merrill as well as the rest of Wall Street.

> DONALD REGAN, former chairman of the investment firm Merrill Lynch, quoted in the *New York Times*, February 4, 1990

It's so small in terms of people's thinking—to pick on a trip or attack the use of a helicopter. I hope God will give them a larger perspective and less of a jealous streak.

> DANIEL P. TULLY, president of the investment firm Merrill Lynch, quoted in the *New York Times*, February 4, 1990

30.13 POWER

Power accumulates when people think you have power.

> The late THOMAS K. "TIP" O'NEILL, Speaker of the U.S. House of Representatives

There are only two fools in this world. One is the millionaire who thinks that by hoarding money he can somehow accumulate real power, and the other is the penniless reformer who thinks that if only he can take the money from one class and give it to another, all the world's ills will be cured.

> HENRY FORD, *My Life and Work* (1922)

Animation is one of the few areas Jeffrey [Katzenberg, formerly of Disney] can still control totally. After all, the characters don't talk back and the backgrounds don't ask for more money.

> Movie director STEVEN SPIELBERG, who later teamed up with Katzenberg and record producer David Geffen to form Dreamworks, quoted in *Business Week*, January 31, 1994

31.1 ARROGANT MANAGEMENT

I never thought that because you were the head of a business you were some kind of a damned king. I've been in a lot of people's airplanes that were fixed up like palaces, and for what? . . . An airplane is a tool, and I was very much for that airplane business because I was going all over this country and hardly ever getting home, and the airplane simply got me home more often.

THOMAS J. WATSON JR., former CEO of IBM

The effect of a title is very peculiar. It is almost equivalent to a badge bearing the legend: This man has nothing to do but regard himself as important and all others as inferior.

HENRY FORD, quoted in John A. Byrne, *The Whiz Kids* (Doubleday, 1993)

The fact that the boss has an antique-decorated office 14 football fields long may produce awe in the eyes of some employees, but it isn't going to get them to work until 11:30 P.M.

PROFESSOR JOHN P. KOTTER of Harvard Business School, quoted in *Business Week,* October 23, 1987

God.

How GODDARD LIEBERSON, former president of CBS Records, signed his letters, quoted in Frederic Dannen, *Hit Men* (Times Books, 1990)

I'm the boss. I'm allowed to yell.

IVAN F. BOESKY, quoted in James B. Stewart, *Den of Thieves* (Touchstone, 1991)

The CEO will look less like an emperor than like a congressman, trying to represent his various constituents and, to the extent he succeeds, being reelected.

Fortune, January 11, 1993

My first feelings were anger. I felt betrayed. Then I had a sense of total frustration. I thought: How can you control 50,000 employees? I thought of my neighbor in Princeton, Jim Burke [CEO of Johnson & Johnson], and what happened to him with Tylenol. Then, I don't really know why, I thought of Gorbachev and the call

he got on the meltdown at Chernobyl. This was my Chernobyl. I sat there and thought, "Why me, Lord, why me?"

WILLIAM SCHEYER, CEO of the investment firm Merrill Lynch, after a bond disaster that cost Merrill hundreds of millions of dollars, quoted in *Business Week,* October 23, 1987

[While I was] working for a large multinational [unspecified maker of business machines], we had to relocate a family from a warm [country] to the north of Scotland . . . [T]he employee asked if we could resettle his *koi* carp. I explained . . . it would be difficult to find a house with a pond and he would have to heat the pond. . . . [He]spoke to a friend [a] somewhat senior within the company. . . . who said, "Relocate the [expletive deleted] fish." Special tanks had to be made to hold the fish at a certain temperature while in quarantine. . . . near his new office so he could visit his fish. Contractors were hired to construct, heat, and light the pond at the house. At 12:30 [the day the pond was finished] the fish arrived and were carefully placed by hand, one by one, into the pond. At 1:30, all was complete. At 1:45, a large flock of herons swooped down and ate all the fish!

ANITA SAUNDERS of Rowan Corporate Relocation, quoted on the Employee Relocation Council Home Page, fall 1997

There are CEOs who brag about never having touched a PC. I say to them, "Get your head out of the sand, kid."

CHARLES WANG, CEO of Computer Associates, quoted in *Fortune,* June 14, 1993

There were chief executive officers who kept their headquarters in New York long after the last rational reason for doing so had vanished . . . because of the ineffable experience of being a CEO and having lunch five days a week in Manhattan!

TOM WOLFE, journalist, novelist, essayist, *Esquire,* 1983

Organizations win championships.

JERRY KRAUSE, general manager of the basketball team Chicago Bulls, quoted in *Sports Illustrated,* October 13, 1997

I'd like to see some of those organization guys step out there and play.

> MICHAEL JORDAN, Chicago Bulls star, quoted in *Sports Illustrated,* October 13, 1997

Well, General, I guess now for a while you'll to have to kick people in the ass with the other leg, won't you?

> Former U.S. PRESIDENT HARRY TRUMAN, upon meeting David Sarnoff, head of RCA, whose leg was in a cast, in an elevator (Sarnoff had a reputation for treating his people roughly), quoted in Carl Dreher, *David Sarnoff: An American Success* (Putnam, 1975)

31.2 BAD MANAGEMENT

Insecure managers create complexity. Frightened, nervous managers use thick, convoluted planning books and busy slides filled with everything they've known since childhood.

> JOHN F. WELCH JR., CEO of GE, interviewed in *Harvard Business Review,* September–October 1989

[T]he well-run factory is a bore. It runs like clockwork. The poorly managed factory is a drama of crises.

> RICHARD F. SCHMIDT of the information company Dun & Bradstreet, quoted in *Business Week,* October 13, 1986

When Frank's in a meeting, the whole chemistry changes. People are waiting for his signals. What he really wants is reaction and debate. But what he often gets are people playing the situation, thinking, "What does Frank want?" And once they see which way he is leaning, a couple of people will hop on it and the train is rolling.

> Former colleague of Frank Lorenzo, then CEO of Texas Air, who went on to bankrupt Eastern and Continental Airlines, quoted in *Business Week,* October 23, 1987

[I]n troubled businesses, we observe the top executive has marginal number skills and won't admit it. He may claim that his own understanding is good "enough." This leaves him at the mercy of the skills and diligence of others.

I don't believe you do have to be a financial wizard to run a company today—even in this age of arbs, options, flips, and flops. Even in this age of pricing strategy,

models, fancy projections, and synchronized debt. That's all nice fine-tuning. I just want the CEO to understand basic addition and subtraction and *do it.*

> C. CHARLES BAHR, CEO of Bahr International, in a speech, September 1, 1988

Managers who have no beliefs but only understand methodology and quantification are modern-day eunuchs. They can never engender competence or confidence.

> MAX DE PREE, author of *Leadership Is an Art* (Michigan State University Press, 1988), quoted in *Time,* September 11, 1989

When there's a deep-seated conflict between management and labor, it's because of autocratic management practices. A manager says to himself, "I'm going to help him do his job." You can't make a person do something.

> KEN IVERSON, CEO of the steel company Nucor, quoted in the *New Yorker,* February 25, 1991

Employees are the first to know that competitors are eating the company's lunch. Employees are the first to know that the company is overstaffed, bureaucratic, slow to innovate, and that stock options are going nowhere. But employees can't call in a corporate raider or initiate an LBO, so they take their clues from top managers. "What's good enough for management is good enough for me" becomes the prevalent attitude.

> PROFESSOR ANDRALL E. PEARSON of Harvard Business School, *Harvard Business Review,* May–June 1992

You want to have an organization that is humble and proud, that is confident but not arrogant, is confident but not self-delusional. . . . If we had everybody saying we're not arrogant, my guess is we would be servile.

> HARVEY GOLUB, CEO of the financial services firm American Express, quoted in *Fortune,* October 30, 1995

You can't train anybody to do anything that he or she doesn't fundamentally believe in.

> ROBERT HAAS, CEO of the clothing company Levi Strauss, *Harvard Business Review,* September–October 1990

If any CEO (male or female) has not built depth and quality into the management team so that he or she is not indispensable, then we should all suspect there is a terminal case of the "CEO disease" at work.

> LAWRENCE PERLMAN, CEO of the information and defense electronics firm Ceridian, in a speech, April 28, 1992

Task forces are usually led by, if not composed of, people from outside the organization, so they will not be tainted by existing biases. It frequently happens they are not tainted by any relevant experience, either.

> FRANK C. CARLUCCI, chairman of the investment firm Carlyle Group and a member of 14 corporate boards

[W]hips and chains are no longer an alternative [for corporate management].

> PROFESSOR WARREN BENNIS of the University of Southern California, quoted in *Fortune,* February 21, 1994

We become slaves to demographics, to market research, to focus groups. We produce what the numbers tell us to produce. And gradually, in this dizzying chase, our senses lose feeling and our instincts dim, corroded with safe action.

> BARRY DILLER, media mogul, quoted in *Fortune,* May 1, 1995

Few managers, even those with hard-driving styles, see themselves as abrasive. They work with blinders on, looking only at bottom-line results, when all around them, subordinates and colleagues, complain about and avoid them.

> DR. VAL ARNOLD, an organizational psychologist with consulting firm Personnel Decisions Inc., quoted in the *Wall Street Journal,* June 11, 1996

Bad bosses are often like Ebenezer Scrooge in *A Christmas Carol.* An awful lot of bad things have to happen to them before they see the light.

> JAN YAGER, sociologist, quoted in the *Wall Street Journal,* June 11, 1996

Someone who's willing to lose a lot of money on a consistent basis should be in Las Vegas and not running a major publicly quoted company.

> ALAIN LEVY, CEO of the entertainment company Polygram, quoted in *Business Week,* April 25, 1994

Subordinates read the leader *all* of the time.

> TAMMY TIERNEY, editor of the *Kansas City Business Journal,* quoted in D. A. Benson, *How to Think Like a CEO* (Warner, 1996)

31.3 MANAGEMENT LESSONS DERIVED FROM PERSONAL EXPERIENCE

My dad was a blue-collar worker. He didn't have health insurance or benefits, and I saw firsthand the debilitating effect that had on him and on our family. I decided if I was ever in the position to make a contribution to others in that way, I would.

> HOWARD SCHULTZ, founder and CEO of the coffee bar chain Starbucks, quoted in *Inc.,* January 1993

Our insurance premiums went up slightly when we decided to provide everybody with full coverage. But that was offset by the lower attrition rate. We normally spend 25 hours of classroom training on every new employee. The longer an employee stays with us, the more we save.

> HOWARD SCHULTZ, founder and CEO of the coffee bar chain Starbucks, on the benefits of providing benefits for all employees, quoted in *Inc.,* January 1993

It's [sailing] a far more strict chain of command on board than in business, because it's a more hostile environment at sea. The risks and downside are too great to screw up. Yet there is no blame culture on the boat. We blew a spinnaker and the conversation about why it happened was 30 seconds.

In business it's very different. You spend hours, days, analyzing what went wrong and who's to blame.

> HUMPHREY WALTERS, chief executive of the international training company Mast, quoted in the *Financial Times,* April 11, 1997

31.4 MANAGEMENT LESSONS DERIVED FROM TOPICAL EVENTS

1. Have we examined the success of similar ventures?
2. Have we sought out alternative viewpoints?
3. Have we asked for quantitative estimates of our chances for success?

4. Have we questioned the range of options with which we've been presented?

> Lessons from Jimmy Carter's 1980 decision to try rescuing 53 U.S. hostages from Teheran, assembled by Assistant Professor Philip Rosensweig of Harvard Business School, *Harvard Business Review,* September—October 1993

In today's business world, where change is occurring so furiously, effective leaders keep a very focused eye on the competition and quickly make necessary adjustments to their team to be successful.

> MAUREEN O'BRIEN, management consultant, on lessons from the New York Yankees baseball team's victory in the 1996 World Series (specifically, manager Joe Torre's decision to change pitchers four times in one game), quoted in the *Wall Street Journal,* October 28, 1996

The most critical game of the season is not a time to get yourself ejected. Managers need to have patience and control and stay focused, and not lose it in times of stress.

> DAVID NOER, president of Noer Consulting Group, on Bobby Cox, manager of the baseball team Atlanta Braves, being ejected from the final game of the World Series, quoted in the *Wall Street Journal,* October 28, 1996

Issues like forming a long-term plan and sticking to its essential elements but at the same time being ready to be flexible in the light of changing conditions—all of those lessons apply.

> LAURENCE S. HUNTINGTON, chairman of the money management company Fiduciary Trust International, on management lessons of the 1996 Everest expedition (several of whose members died), quoted in the *New York Times,* June 1, 1997

In the business world so many executives do give up the home for the pursuit of the peak.

> BOB GORDON of Outward Bound, on management lessons of the 1996 Everest expedition (several of whose members died), quoted in the *New York Times,* June 1, 1997

In order to succeed you must be exceedingly driven. But if you're too driven you're likely to die.

> JON KRAKAUER, *Into Thin Air* (Villard, 1997)

1. In any structured environment, conformity to certain conventions is equated with sanity. You can be a monster, a nitwit, or a boob, but if you shave and put on a suit, people think you're absolutely fabulous. This is why in most cases it pays to wear one.

2. On the other hand, it's unwise, once you reach a certain point in your career, to change your act. If you got your title while wearing a taffeta tutu and Ray-Bans, keep wearing them until you retire. Lose your style, and you might lose your edge.

3. You have to shave only if you're working for somebody else.

> STANLEY BING, columnist, on lessons from the trial of mobster Vincenzo "the Chin" Gigante, who spent years evading prosecution by wandering the streets of Greenwich Village in a bathrobe while his lawyers claimed he was mentally ill (Bing wrote this column *after* Gigante was ordered by the judge to shave and put on a suit before he returned to the courtroom, but *before* the verdict—guilty of racketeering but not of murder), quoted in *Fortune,* August 7, 1997

31.5 PERSONAL MANAGEMENT STYLE

Mr. Morgan buys his partners; I grow my own.

> ANDREW CARNEGIE, quoted in Burton J. Hendrick, *Life of Andrew Carnegie* (1932)

I don't believe in just ordering people to do things. You have to sort of grab an oar and row with them. My philosophy is to stay as close as possible to what's happening. If I can't solve something, how the hell can I expect my managers to?

> HAROLD GENEEN, former CEO of the conglomerate ITT, in a 1977 interview, quoted in his obituary in the *New York Times,* November 23, 1997

Acting angry is part of my management style.

> ROBERT FILDES, CEO at the biotech firm Cetus Corporation, quoted in *Business Week,* March 17, 1986

I pray for Milky Way, I pray for Snickers.

> FORREST EDWARD MARS SR., CEO of the candy company Mars, quoted in *Forbes,* October 27, 1986

You just have to be the kind of guy to get people to do things.

> DONALD TRUMP, real estate magnate, quoted in *U.S. News & World Report*, April 27, 1987

I love to step on toes. That's my M.O.

> LAWRENCE RAWL, CEO of the oil company Exxon, quoted in *Fortune*, August 3, 1987

I'm a child of the corporate struggle. I spent many years dealing with people trying to do me in. I determined that any operation I ran would be as nonpolitical as I could make it.

> MICHAEL EISNER, CEO of Walt Disney, quoted in *Time*, April 25, 1988

I'm seen as terribly abrupt and abrasive. If you're very direct, you're admired in American culture.

> JOHN NEVIN, chairman of the rubber company Firestone, quoted in *Time*, October 9, 1989

Nothing is worse than procrastination. When I look at 10 decisions I regret or failed to make, there will be nine of them where I delayed.

> PERCY BARNEVIK, CEO of the Swedish-Swiss heavy manufacturing firm ABB (Asea Brown Boveri), quoted in the *New York Times*, May 6, 1990

Being aggressive is a lot less risky in the end. Are you going to eat lunch, or have your lunch eaten for you?

> WILLIAM T. ESRY, CEO of the telecommunications firm Sprint, quoted in the *New York Times*, August 23, 1992

I think it's healthy to let all the [employee] frustration get aired. It's good if people go home at night and say, "I told that son of a bitch what I thought of him today."

> LAWRENCE A. BOSSIDY, CEO of the heavy manufacturing firm Allied-Signal, quoted in *Harvard Business Review*, March–April 1995

Once you let people in your office, they'll come in and out all day long. I need to think.

> PHILIP H. KNIGHT, CEO of athletic apparel firm Nike

If we're going to run this business on viscera, it's going to be my viscera.

> THOMAS J. WATSON JR., CEO of IBM, in Harry Levinson and Stuart Rosenthal, *CEO* (Basic Books, 1984)

I learn far more by wandering into stores and talking anonymously with a salesperson or stock clerk than I do from reading reports however thorough and well crafted they are.

> ARNOLD HIATT, CEO of shoe company Stride-Rite interviewed in *Harvard Business Review*, March–April 1992

There's a story about Henry Kissinger. Apparently he asked for a report on some country, his assistants handed it in, and he wrote in the margin, "Is this the best you can do?" So they panicked. They went and did it over. And again, he wrote something in the margins. The third time, he wrote another note, and they responded, "Yes, this is the best we can do." Kissinger then said, "Now I'll read it."

> STEVE KERR, "chief learning officer" of GE, on setting "stretch goals," quoted in *Fortune*, November 30, 1995

This is a basic and simple business. People create problems by not trusting their own judgment. By creating a committee. By constantly needing validation. You guys are empowered. You can find 99 percent of the answer in the aisles, where the customers are.

> BERNIE MARCUS, cofounder and CEO of hardware chain Home Depot, quoted in *Fortune*, March 4, 1996

Generally speaking, you like to dance with the girl that brung you, and if you can't, sometimes you have to shoot her.

> DAVID BONDERMAN, owner of Continental Airlines, on why he replaced the head of a subsidiary, quoted in *Business Week*, May 6, 1996

Remember, all glory is fleeting. Don't take yourself too seriously. To me, that's the characteristic of a long-term successful company: humility.

> FRED MUSONE, president of Morton International Automotive Safety Products, quoted in Michael Hammer, *Beyond Reengineering* (Harper, 1996)

When you've got a probationary employee, and you can tell in your gut that the person has the wrong attitude, then fire them on the spot. Every time I go against my gut, I regret it.

> COLLEEN C. BARRETT, number-two executive at Southwest Airlines and highest-ranking woman in

the airline industry, quoted in *Fortune*, November 30, 1995

Got rid of mine (his secretary) years ago. She separated me from the troops.

> GEORGE W. SZTYKIEL, CEO of autoparts company Sparta Motors, quoted in *Fortune*, December 28, 1992

The first thing I do whenever I visit a plant is use the hourly workers' bathroom so I can see how the company's treating them.

> WILLIAM BINNIE, owner of Carlisle Plastics, quoted in *Forbes*, August 31, 1996

I have always believed that if you do not have a crisis, you have to invent one. You need a rallying point to focus every employee.

> ROBERT H. BOHAUMON, CEO of the financial services firm Travellers Express, interviewed in Charles B. Wendel, *The New Financiers: Profiles of the Leaders Who Are Reshaping the Financial Services Industry* (Irwin Professional Publications, 1996)

I bring my board my toughest problems, not my easiest. I don't want a paperwork board, but one that thinks like owners.

> PAUL O'NEILL, CEO of the aluminum company Alcoa, quoted in *Fortune*, January 11, 1993

I haven't spent any time setting goals. I'm spending my time trying to understand our competitive position and how we're serving customers. Out of our competitive strategy will come the right set of financial objectives.

> LOUIS V. GERSTNER JR., CEO of IBM, quoted in *Fortune*, May 31, 1993

Plenty of producers at *60 Minutes* started out as secretaries. I promoted them because they just impressed the hell out of me.

> DON HEWITT, executive producer of the CBS television show *60 Minutes*, quoted in *Forbes*, October 6, 1986

I prefer to beg for forgiveness than for permission.

> KLAUS BESIER, CEO of software company SAP America, on management decisions made without approval from superiors, quoted in *Business Week*, August 8, 1994

Part of my job is to keep a vague sense of unease percolating through the entire company. The minute you say the job is done, you're dead.

> ARTHUR MARTINEZ, head of the Merchandise Group of Sears & Roebuck, quoted in *Business Week*, August 15, 1994

When the company does things well, that's my ego trip. I don't distinguish between myself and the company.

> ALEX TROTMAN, CEO of Ford Motor Company, quoted in *Fortune*, September 18, 1995

There's too much conventionality and too little risk taking when people have to answer to one boss. You and the boss might not get along or you might spend all your time kissing the boss's ass to get ahead. You can't kiss the ass of 24 people. And together, those 24 people are more likely to have the interests of the shareholders at heart than any one person.

> JEFFREY SKILLING, chairman of Enron Capital and Trading, quoted in *Fortune*, August 5, 1996

[I'm learning to use the computer] [b]ecause I don't like anybody knowing anything I don't know. I've always been a work-around manager, and [this] allows you to back check what people tell you.

> HUGH L. McCOLL, CEO of NationsBank, quoted in the *Wall Street Journal*, July 25, 1996

I think consensus is a poor substitute for leadership.

[M]any CEOs are impeccably logical, but they don't lift your heart. They rely too much on the way things should be done. I believe in provocative disruption.

> CHARLOTTE BEERS, CEO of the ad agency Ogilvy & Mather, quoted in *Fortune*, August 5, 1996

One of the main secrets to my success is the "MBA" I require that each one of my managers have before they come to work for me. It stands for Mop-Bucket Attitude, where no one, including me, is above picking up a mop and bucket to make the places look the best they can be.

> GHULAM BOMBAYWALA, CEO of Watermarc Food Management, quoted in *Asia, Inc.*, August 1997

32.1 CHANGING EMPLOYEE NEEDS

Working men and women tend to place items of interest on or around their work spaces to have something within reach to play with while working through a thought or idea . . . Then came the basketball hoop attached to the circular file [trash basket], small dart boards for the desk and stuffed bean-bag frogs.

> JAY FLEISCHER, toy inventor, quoted in the *New York Times*, May 6, 1990

Eighty-two percent of our employees' families are in some other model with large numbers of single parents and dual wage earners, as well as singles, childless couples, and so on. And therefore, 82 percent of our people have needs that were not anticipated, and often cannot be met, by personnel policies and programs created in the era of Ozzie and Harriet.

> RANDALL L. TOBIAS, CEO of the pharmaceutical firm Eli Lilly, in a speech, April 22, 1996

There is a longing for more time with families, yes. But at home, you often deal with very nebulous issues. You don't get the same kind of clear, tangible results for your efforts that work can provide.

> DEBORAH BRIGHT, psychologist and consultant to the American Management Association, quoted in *Fortune*, November 30, 1992

To my mind, flextime is the essence of respect for and trust in people. It says that we both appreciate that our people have busy personal lives and that we trust them to devise, with their supervisor and work group, a schedule that is personally convenient yet fair to others.

> DAVID PACKARD, cofounder of Hewlett-Packard, *The HP Way* (HarperCollins, 1995)

Candidly, you [must] have people understand that there is less likelihood they'll remain with one company over their career.

> BRUCE CARSWELL, of the telecommunications firm GTE, quoted in Michael Hammer, *Beyond Reengineering* (Harper Business, 1996)

32.2 COMMUNICATION

Real communication takes countless hours of eyeball to eyeball, back and forth. It means more listening than talking. It's not pronouncements on video tape, it's not announcements in the newspaper. It is human beings coming to see and accept things through a constant interactive process aimed at consensus.

> JOHN F. WELCH, CEO of GE, interviewed in *Harvard Business Review*, September–October 1989

A picture of a thousand words [the type-heavy slide] is worthless.

> HENRY EHRLICH, *Writing Effective Speeches* (Paragon House, 1992)

Empowerment is meaningless unless people have access to information. The goal of our technology strategy is to make sure that the information is available on the desktop of the person who is doing the job.

> BILL EATON of the jeans manufacturer Levi Strauss, quoted in *Harvard Business Review*, September–October 1990

I have no illusions about how hard it is to communicate clearly and quickly with tens of thousands of people around the world. ABB has about 15,000 middle managers prowling around markets all over the world. If we in the executive committee could connect with all of them or even half of them and get them moving in roughly the same direction, we would be unstoppable.

> PERCY BARNEVIK, CEO of the Swedish-Swiss heavy industrial firm ABB (Asea Brown Boveri), interviewed in *Harvard Business Review*, March–April, 1991

You don't inform. You overinform. . . . There is a strong tendency among European managers to be selective about sharing information.

> PERCY BARNEVIK, CEO of the Swedish-Swiss heavy industrial firm ABB (Asea Brown Boveri), interviewed in *Harvard Business Review*, March–April, 1991

If you can get into the hearts and minds of employers, they will buy the truth. Dialogue is the oxygen of change.

> JIM MACLACHLAN of the accounting and consulting firm Deloitte & Touche, quoted in *Fortune*, June 10, 1996

We believe that there are two successful ways to manage in relationship to employees. That is: tell them everything or tell them nothing. Both ways can really be successful except we happen to believe in telling our employees anything they want to know about the company, unless it happens to be proprietary or it has to be secret for some reason.

> F. KENNETH IVERSON, chairman of the steel company Nucor, February 5, 1996 (Mr. Iverson himself called the author to follow up a call asking for information. This is unique in my experience with corporate America.)

Starbucks has instituted all sorts of mechanisms for its Gen X-ers to communicate with headquarters: e-mail, suggestion cards, regular forums. And it acts quickly on issues that are supposedly important to young kids today, like using recycling bins and improving living conditions in coffee-growing countries.

> JENNIFER REESE, "Starbucks: Inside the Coffee Cult," *Fortune*, December 9, 1996

32.3 CREATIVE AND OTHERWISE EXCEPTIONAL PEOPLE

Engineers can be as temperamental as opera stars—particularly those among them who have vision and never hesitate to deal with imaginative ideas. Their sensibilities have to be respected.

[T]he same temperament that makes some of these men gravitate toward invention and innovation can also make them nonconformists, born revolutionaries, people dissatisfied with the past. Some brilliant engineers may become revolutionaries simply for the thrill of doing things that are radically different. The challenge to management is to channel the efforts of the revolutionary into productive deeds that will advance group objectives.

> JOHN H. DESSAUER, *My Years with Xerox: The Billions Nobody Wanted* (Doubleday, 1971)

The top executives are going to leave. They have their platinum parachutes; they're all set. Now the mid-level people, the real performers, can come to the fore. They're waiting for that opportunity, and we give it to them.

> CHARLES WANG, founder and CEO of Computer Associates International, on his method for realizing value in takeovers of troubled software firms, quoted in *Inc.*, September 1994

I believe in the adage: Hire people smarter than you and get out of their way.

> HOWARD SCHULTZE, CEO of the coffee chain Starbucks, quoted in *Business Week*, October 24, 1994

All new wealth comes from creative engineering types, who are difficult to manage and easy to offend. The mentality of a takeover is aggressive, a pirate mentality that upsets morale. The good people leave.

> G. DAN HUTCHESON, president of VLSI Research, on why it's easy to lose money when taking over a computer firm, quoted in *Forbes*, July 7, 1997

The rise in the dictatorship of the manageriate is lowering the status of scientists, demoralizing them, and shredding their sense of purpose.

> The scientific journal *Nature*, quoted in the *Financial Times*, May 5, 1997

The key point is that technical professionals tend to be cynical and skeptical about management fads and ideas.

> DAVID ROBERTSON, training consultant at Blessing White, a London firm, quoted in the *Financial Times*, May 5, 1997

Creativity is the motherhood and apple pie of modern business dogma. This has led people to think that creativity is a singular, particular ability. It isn't.

> WINSTON FLETCHER, chairman of the British advertising agency Delaney Fletcher Bozell, quoted in the *Financial Times*, April 14, 1997

Creativity often rewards the nonconformist, the iconoclast, the generalist who treats life not as a linear fast track to success, but as a forest of rich discoveries that one can meander through, creating one's own trail . . . The nation's soul will be shaped by those who are less obviously successful but are willing to take risks: artistic, career, or intellectual.

> HO KWON PING, head of Singapore-based Wah Ching International Group, the diversified regional

conglomerate started by his grandfather, quoted in *Asia, Inc.,* August 1997

The price you pay for conformity is lack of creativity.

TIMOTHY PRICE of MCT Communications, quoted in *Business Week,* August 1, 1994

I have always been very interested in creativity. Even when I was working in construction, what I liked was to work with architects. I have always liked very much creators, and in luxury you are in a sense working with artists, those who have the capacity to transform creative ideas in reality.

BERNHARDT ARNAULT, chief executive of luxury products firm LVMH Moët-Hennessy Louis Vuitton S.A., quoted in the *New York Times,* August 17, 1997

32.4 DECISION MAKING

Decide, v.i. To succumb to the preponderance of one set of influences over another set.

AMBROSE BIERCE, *The Devil's Dictionary* (1906)

A decision is what a man makes when he can't get anyone to serve on a committee.

FLETCHER KNEBEL, American novelist

If you want to understand the way I think, it is this. If 80 percent of the people say it's wrong, then you do it. If 80 percent say do it, don't go that way.

DEN FUJITA, who launched McDonald's in Japan in a 50-50 venture partnership with McDonald's Corporation, quoted in the *New York Times,* March 22, 1992 (He is also a best-selling author in Japan; titles include *The Jewish Way of Doing Business, Stupid People Lose Money, How to Blow the Rich Man's Bugle Like the Jews Do, How to Become Number One in Business.)*

Tired people make bad decisions. That's something Ronald Reagan told me.

DICK JENRETTE, cofounder of Donaldson Lufkin Jenrette and former CEO of the insurance firm Equitable, quoted in *Fortune,* July 22, 1996

Management is more art than science. No one can say with certainty which decisions will bring the most profit, any more than they can create instructions over

how to sculpt a masterpiece. You just have to feel it as it goes.

PROFESSOR RICHARD D'AVENI, Amos Tuck School of Business, Dartmouth College, in a speech, quoted in the *Financial Times,* September 1, 1997

Most decisions are seat-of-the-pants judgments. You can create a rationale for anything. In the end, most decisions are based on intuition and faith.

NATHAN MYHRVOLD, of the software firm Microsoft, quoted in Ken Auletta, *The Highwaymen: Warriors of the Information Superhighway* (Random House, 1997)

Committee—a group of men who individually can do nothing but as a group decide that nothing can be done.

FRED ALLEN, American humorist

32.5 DELEGATING

What is worth doing is worth the trouble of asking somebody to do it.

AMBROSE BIERCE, *The Devil's Dictionary* (1906)

Nothing is impossible for the man who doesn't have to do it himself.

A. H. WEILER, privately circulated memo at the *New York Times*

Here's my thoughts on delegation. It's a waste because half the time they won't do it and I have to check on everybody.

JUDITH REGAN, president of the Regan Company (publisher of Rush Limbaugh and Howard Stern), quoted in the *New York Times,* July 13, 1997

[T]he job of the managers we hire is not to be boss.

JOHN WARNOCK, cofounder of the software firm Adobe Systems, interviewed in Rama Dev Jager, *In the Company of Giants* (McGraw-Hill, 1997)

When an executive has the authority and his subordinate has the responsibility, the executive automatically assumes the responsibility when he approves the action taken by the subordinate. The subordinate in effect, then, is only a glorified clerk.

CHARLES "TEX" THORNTON, post–World War II Ford executive, founder of Ford's Whiz Kids who managed by the numbers, quoted in John A. Byrne, *The Whiz Kids* (Doubleday, 1993)

We've been in the business of recruiting executives from bigger companies for years now . . . There are people who can't make it happen without the support structure. I once recruited someone from the second-largest computer company. The first thing he did was create an organization chart with a vice-president of administration. There were only 13 employees.

> BILL JANEWAY, partner in the venture-capital firm Warburg, Pincus Ventures, on recruiting senior managers for emerging growth companies, quoted in *Inc.,* May 1994

32.6 EMPOWERMENT

I don't like the word [empowerment].

I think the word we're really talking about is involvement. . . . We want everyone to have a say. We want ideas from everyone. But somebody's got to run the ship. Now, that doesn't mean somebody runs the ship by directing it. Somebody runs the ship with a total input from everyone. . . . Involvement is less misleading—high involvement, a say in the decision-making, a stake in the institution, a voice.

> JOHN F. WELCH JR., CEO of GE, quoted in *Industry Week,* May 2, 1994

In the New Economy, where there is much high-minded theory about empowerment, creativity, innovation, and quality, the theory is the sky above. Then there is the mud below.

> ALAN M. WEBBER, former editorial director of *Harvard Business Review,* cofounder of the business and management magazine *Fast Company,* quoted in the *Harvard Business Review,* September–October 1994

The Baring family lost its bank because the management overempowered one individual, Nick Leeson.

> JOHN MICKLETHWAIT and ADRIAN WOOLDRIDGE, *The Witch Doctors* (Times Books, 1996)

[Empowered workplaces] are best for people who are very group-oriented—and it helps to be the real rah-rah, sis-boom-bah type.

> PROFESSOR RICHARD FLORIDA of Carnegie Mellon University, quoted in the *Wall Street Journal,* September 8, 1997

They say there are no bosses here but if you screw up, you find one pretty fast.

> RANDY SAVAGE of the industrial firm Eaton Corporation, quoted in the *Wall Street Journal,* September 8, 1997

The admission ticket for this kind of responsibility is accountability—and not everyone necessarily wants accountability.

> ALEXANDER M. CUTLER, president of Eaton, quoted in the *Wall Street Journal,* September 8, 1997

[W]hat manager hasn't had this experience: you're walking around the company and you come upon a group trying to solve a problem. As you walk toward those people, you begin to feel some of the responsibility for solving the problem moving from their shoulders to yours. . . . I now try to keep walking, leaving them with the responsibility until they call for help.

> ASHLEY KORNBLATT, former president of Merlin Metalworks, quoted in *Inc.,* May 1994

If an institution wants to be adaptive, it has to let go of some control and trust that people will work on the right things in the right way.

> ROBERT B. SHAPIRO, CEO of the chemical company Monsanto, interviewed in *Harvard Business Review,* January–February 1997

Pride of achievement is the strongest single motivation. A man will realize this pride of achievement if (1) he is given full authority to accomplish the job and (2) he is held strictly accountable for his results, be they good or bad.

> Memo by BEN MILLS, head of the Lincoln Division of Ford Motor Company in the 1950s, cited in John A. Byrne, *The Whiz Kids* (Doubleday, 1993)

32.7 FIRING

Don't be needlessly cruel in firing someone. Figure out a reason that is true but enables him to preserve ego. It is usually true that his combination of skills is not what's needed, or that the job is being restructured. If you don't feel compelled to destroy his self-regard, he can move on quickly without scars.

> ROBERT TOWNSEND, *Up the Organization* (Knopf, 1970)

You really have to look hard at whether it's worth it to fire someone knowing that you have to spend three to five years in litigation defending your decision.

> PAT GILETTE of Bank of America, quoted in *U.S. News & World Report,* June 4, 1984

Show me a man who enjoys firing people and I'll show you a charlatan or a sadist.

> ANTHONY O'REILLY, CEO of H. J. Heinz, quoted in *Business Week,* October 23, 1987

Too often a layoff is viewed as some sort of virile gesture, a way of saying that senior management is hard-minded and serious.

> FREDERICK REICHOLD of the management consultants Bain & Co., quoted in *Fortune,* June 10, 1996

32.8 LEADERSHIP

Neither a wise man nor a brave man lies down on the tracks of history to wait for the train of the future to run over him.

> U.S. PRESIDENT DWIGHT D. EISENHOWER, in a campaign speech, quoted in *Time,* October 6, 1952

The first responsibility of a leader is to define reality.

> MAX DE PREE, retired CEO of the furniture company Herman Miller Corporation, *Leadership Is an Art* (DTP, 1993)

People need a leader. Sometimes it doesn't matter in which direction you point as long as someone is pointing.

> STEVEN CAPPS of Apple Computer, quoted in the *New York Times,* December 12, 1993

Leadership has become the universal vitamin C pill. Everyone wants megadoses of it.

> DAVID CAMPBELL, psychologist and senior fellow of Center for Creative Leadership, quoted in *U.S. News & World Report,* December 2, 1989

There is a kind of storytelling that is multiple in people with good judgment. Like the way language works, with different sentences vying to be said. Historians like Churchill may have good judgment because they have really rich and diverse ecology of stories, anecdotes,

and sequences of events in their heads. Hitler had terrible judgment. He'd bore people silly, always paring things down to the two choices, both stupid.

> STEWART BRAND, cofounder of the Global Business Network, author of the original *Whole Earth Catalogue,* member of the hippie adventurers Merry Pranksters, and prominent business guru, quoted in *Fortune,* October 16, 1995

Leadership is an intangible quality with no clear definition. That's probably a good thing, because if the people being led knew the definition, they would hunt down their leaders and kill them.

> SCOTT ADAMS, *The Dilbert Principle* (HarperCollins, 1996)

One of the hardest tasks of leadership is understanding that you are not what you are, but what you're perceived to be by others.

> EDWARD L. FLOM, CEO of the Florida Steel Corporation, in a speech, May 6, 1987

By definition, leaders don't operate in isolation. Nor do they command in the literal sense of the word, issuing a one-way stream of unilateral directions. Instead, leadership almost always involves cooperative and collaborative activity that can occur only in a conducive context.

> LIEUTENANT GENERAL WILLIAM G. PAGONIS, leader of the 40,000-person logistics force for the Gulf War, quoted in *Harvard Business Review,* November–December 1992

We are leaders only if we can look through the eyes of our followers, and ask ourselves the questions that our followers would ask and answer them straight and clear.

> JOHN KLAWSON of the agricultural equipment company Deere & Co., in a speech, February 24, 1994

Leadership is all hype. We've had three great leaders in this century—Hitler, Stalin, and Mao.

> PETER DRUCKER, management guru, quoted in *Fortune,* February 21, 1994

If you look at people in leadership positions and do a time analysis of what they do, I submit you find a great deal of the time they are doing somebody else's job rather than shaping the concept and the structure by which the concept can be implemented across the board in a large, complex organization. That's a very time-consuming task—frankly, what I've found is, it's sufficiently exhausting that a lot of people don't want to take it on.

> MICHAEL H. WALSH, late CEO of the automotive and energy firm Tenneco, quoted in *Fortune,* December 14, 1992

The chairman of the board still needs his "attaboys"—perhaps more than anybody—but once you're on the top rung there are no more superiors to pat you on the back. This is the paradox of power. The more you have, the more vulnerable you feel to being exploited.

> JAY B. RORHLICH, Wall Street psychiatrist, interviewed in *Forbes,* April 22, 1985

"Taking the safe road, doing your job, and not making waves" may not get you fired (right away, at least), but it sure won't do much for your career or your company over the long haul. We're not dumb. We know that administrators are easy to find and cheap to keep. Leaders—risk takers: they are in very short supply. And ones with vision are pure gold.

> RAYMOND W. SMITH, president of the telecommunications company Bell Atlantic, in a speech, August 1, 1988

As a leader, you can influence only three things. You can influence people, you can influence your strategy, and you can influence operations. In my judgment, that's all you do.

> LAWRENCE A. BOSSIDY, CEO of the heavy industrial company Allied-Signal, interviewed in *Harvard Business Review,* March–April 1995

Simplicity is an indispensable element of a *leader's* most important functions: projecting a vision—and demanding and rewarding boldness, speed, and passion. The leader's unending responsibility must be to remove every detour, every barrier to ensure that vision is first clear, and then real.

The leader must create an atmosphere in the organization where people feel not only free to, but *obliged* to *demand* clarity and purpose from their leaders. They must insist on the dignity that goes with achieving. They have to feel the rewards that go with winning—in the soul as well as in the wallet.

> JOHN F. WELCH JR., CEO of GE, in a speech, November 1989

The soft stuff is always harder than the hard stuff.

> ROGER ENRICO, vice chairman of PepsiCo, referring to areas like human resources management as opposed to quantitative factors, quoted in *Fortune,* November 27, 1995

The new model is global in scale, an interdependent network. So the new leaders face new tests such as how to lead in this idea-intensive, interdependent-network environment. It requires a wholly different set of skills, based on ideas, people skills, and values.

> JOHN SCULLEY, former CEO of Apple Computer, interviewed in Warren Bennis, *Leaders on Leadership* (Harvard Business Review, 1991)

Passionate leadership won't succeed if contradictory signals are sent. If you pump up your sales force at a meeting and tell them, "The most important goal is to make customers happy," you can't go back the next day and say, "Your quota just got doubled so go out there and sell twice as much." If you send that kind of mixed message, your salespeople will know that all the talk about customer service was just talk and that the real priority is achieving the higher quota.

> BILL GATES, CEO of Microsoft, on Microsoft's web site, September 12, 1996

Tips for Leaders:

- Don't be afraid to admit ignorance.
- Know when to intervene.
- Learn to truly share power.
- Worry about what you take on, not what you give up.
- Get used to learning on the job.

> *Fortune,* February 20, 1995

If you want to change your company's culture, speak the employees' language, not the consultants' language.

> PAUL THEIBERT, speechwriter, quoted in the *Wall Street Journal,* August 1, 1996

Leadership has a price and sometimes it includes my pocketbook.

> JOHN H. DASBURG, CEO of Northwest Airlines, who gave in to union pressure and returned a bonus of $750,000 he was awarded in 1993 after the airline's employees had agreed to wage cuts to prevent the company from filing for bankruptcy, quoted in *Business Week,* April 25, 1994

- YOU MUST HAVE CLEAR GOALS. And you must be able to articulate them clearly.
- GIVE YOURSELF A CLEAR AGENDA. Every morning write down the five most important things for you to accomplish that day.
- LET PEOPLE KNOW WHERE THEY STAND. Everyone knows you do a disservice to a B student when you give him or her an A.
- WHAT'S BROKEN, FIX NOW. Don't put it off.
- NO REPAINTING THE FLAGPOLE. Make sure all the work your people are doing is essential to the organization.
- SET HIGH STANDARDS. Too often we don't ask enough from people.
- LAY THE CONCEPT OUT, BUT LET YOUR PEOPLE EXECUTE IT. Yes, you must have the right people in place.
- NEVER LIE. EVER. Schwarzkopf said there had been a big debate about whether to use disinformation to mislead the Iraqis during the Gulf War.
- WHEN IN CHARGE, TAKE COMMAND. Leaders are often called on to make decisions without adequate information.
- DO WHAT'S RIGHT. The truth of the matter is that you always know the right thing to do. The hard part is doing it.

> GENERAL NORMAN SCHWARZKOPF's rules for leaders, *Inc.*, January 1992

A leader is one who governs without doubt. The manager also governs—he arbitrates and administers—but the manager is not a leader . . . A leader is one who needs us, needs us ardently. He . . . solicits not only our effort in the task at hand but our constant invention, that which transforms us into creators.

> From the notebooks of French writer and flyer
> ANTOINE DE SAINT-EXUPÉRY, cited in *Fortune*,
> July 10, 1995

Suppose somebody says, "Look, Ross, I'm very busy. What's the most important thing you can tell me about leadership?" I'd say, "Just treat people the way you'd want to be treated." Then he'd say, "That's the golden rule." And I'll say, "That's right." He'll say, "Well, wait a minute. Are you saying that, in a rapidly changing world, the principles of leadership are timeless?" "Yup." And he'll say, "How can that be?" And I'll say, "Because human nature doesn't change." It doesn't change.

> H. ROSS PEROT, quoted in *Inc.*, January 1989

Leadership is so much the shibboleth of the American corporation, and so much that is simply awful has been written about it that one could surely fertilize the San Joaquin Valley with the past 10 years of material on leadership.

> JOSEPH F. COATES of the consulting firm J. F. Coates
> & Associates, in a speech, December 7, 1989

Once our American corporations attain a certain size and complexity, the chief executive officer loses touch with the mechanics of the business; except in a general way he no longer understands the commercial sequences that provide him with stock options and a secretary. Like the heirs to American fortunes, the stewards of our more prominent institutions might as well be guests seated on the afterdeck of somebody else's yacht.

> LEWIS H. LAPHAM, *Money and Class in America*
> (Weidenfeld and Nicolson, 1988)

A leader has to be one of two things: He either has to be a brilliant visionary himself, a truly creative strategist, in which case he can do what he likes and get away with it; or else she has to be a true empowerer, who can bring out the best in others. Managers who are neither can be deadly in organizations that need energy and change.

> HENRY MINTZBERG of McGill University, in a foreword to Patricia Pitcher, *The Drama of Leadership*
> (Wiley, 1997)

Leaders have powerful enemies. There's a war going on out there, and it is not for the faint of heart. The good guys do not always win.

> PATRICIA PITCHER, *The Drama of Leadership* (Wiley, 1997)

Tough is passé. Today you're dealing with a variety of head games. That's where the cruelty is.

> PROFESSOR EMERITUS ABRAHAM ZALEZNIK of Harvard Business School, quoted in *Fortune*, October 18, 1993

A lot of people who call themselves leaders just slow things down. They're insecure, or don't believe in delegation, or aren't willing to deal with the arteriosclerosis that's weakening the organization. By the time they get to be CEOs, many leaders lose their appetite for dealing with change.

> MICHAEL WALSH, late CEO of the automotive and energy firm Tenneco, quoted in *Fortune*, December 13, 1993

The MBA who arrives thinking he or she is a leader has the most problems with hubris and arrogance.

> PROFESSOR ROSS WEBBER of the Wharton School of the University of Pennsylvania, quoted in *Fortune,* January 24, 1994

All leaders have to be great storytellers.

> FRED TALBOTT, former gag writer for the TV show *Saturday Night Live* and communications professor at Owen Graduate School of Management, Vanderbilt University, quoted in the *New York Times,* February 23, 1997

IBM probably invested the most money of any organization in this [leadership training], but they taught people about a world that doesn't exist anymore. They shrank their gene pool down to people who were very good at managing for the 1970s—so when the 1990s arrived, IBM had lots of people who were very good at the wrong thing.

> PROFESSOR EDWARD LAWLER of the University of Southern California, quoted in *Fortune,* November 27, 1995

I don't believe leadership can be taught, but it can be learned.

> PROFESSOR MORGAN McCALL, quoted in *Fortune,* November 27, 1995

Among the elements of leadership, 80 percent is experience. Our first line of offense is just to put them [promising executives] in a job.

> WAYNE CALLOWAY, CEO of PepsiCo, quoted in *Fortune,* November 27, 1995

32.9   MANAGING PEOPLE

Most men are individuals no longer so far as their business, its activities, or its moralities are concerned. They are not units but fractions.

> WOODROW WILSON, in a speech, August 31, 1910

Nine Ways to Change People without
Giving Offense and Arousing Resentment:

Rule 1: Begin with praise and honest appreciation. "A barber lathers a man before he shaves him."

Rule 2: Call attention to people's mistakes indirectly.

Rule 3: Talk about your own mistakes before criticizing the other person.

Rule 4: Ask questions instead of giving direct orders.

Rule 5: Let the other man save his face.

Rule 6: Praise the slightest improvement and praise every improvement. Be "hearty" in your approbation and lavish in your praise.

Rule 7: Give a man a fine reputation to live up to.

Rule 8: Use encouragement. Make the fault you want to correct seem easy to correct; make the thing you want the other person to do seem easy to do.

Rule 9: Make the other person happy about doing the thing you suggest.

> ANDREW CARNEGIE

You have to be willing to challenge people and always advance them a little bit sooner than you think you should.

We drill dry holes with people just like we drill dry holes looking for oil and gas.

> JOHN BOOKOUT, CEO of the oil company Shell, quoted in *Fortune,* January 19, 1987

The key to this whole business is sincerity. Once you can fake that, you've got it made.

> MONTE CLARK, former coach of the Detroit Lions football team, on problem of managing today's professional athletes, quoted in *Sports Illustrated,* September 1, 1997

Pay depressed people less in salary until they have emerged from their depressed state and are ready to resume full work duties.

> *Business Insurance* magazine on dealing with the negative impact of depression in the workplace, quoted in *Inc.,* July 1994

Once we promoted a man, a good worker, to be the manager of our machine shop. A few days later he came to see me. He said he was having a tough time managing and wanted me to come out to the shop and tell his people that he was their boss. "If I have to do that," I said, "you don't deserve to be their boss."

> DAVID PACKARD, cofounder of Hewlett-Packard, *The HP Way* (HarperCollins, 1995)

I have the bias people do better when they are happy. The old style of beating on people to get things done does not work.

> GRACE PASTIAK of telephone equipment maker Tellabs Inc., quoted in the *New York Times,* May 5, 1991

Depopulate. Get rid of people. They gum up the works.

> JEFFREY SKILLING, president of energy company Enron, quoted in the *Financial Times,* March 14, 1997

32.10 MEMOS AND MEETINGS

A memorandum is written not to inform the reader but to protect the writer.

> *Wall Street Journal,* September 8, 1977

A meeting is something to be tolerated.

> SID CATO, corporate communications newsletter publisher and former Greyhound corporate officer, quoted in the *New York Times,* May 5, 1991

One of our senior managers . . . had a meeting with his staff to discuss work-life balance. The meeting started at 5 P.M. and ended at 9—and the manager didn't see the irony.

> LEWIS E. PLATT, CEO of Hewlett-Packard, in a speech, October 18, 1995

When you meet business people, they're pretty funny and cynical. They've been through every kind of stupid meeting, seminar, and motivational thing, which they know are ridiculous. But I discovered when I was teaching the writing seminars that people who were funny and smart individually felt they were being subversive when they acted that way at work. I mean, if you attended a four-hour meeting about objectives in paint quality, and nobody ever said a funny thing, wouldn't you conclude everyone else was a corpse?

> DAVE BARRY, humorist, interviewed in *Fortune,* July 7, 1997

32.11 RECRUITING

The first question should be, What is the man? What is his character? What are his habits? and then; if these are believed to be good, what has been his education?

> CHARLES ELLIOTT PERKINS, memo on the selection of employees, Chicago, Burlington & Quincy Railroad, August 15, 1885

Corporations today are more conscious of their image. They're wary not just of who they hire, but who they promote. They think top management should be like Caesar's wife.

> JEREMIAH McAWARD, president of personnel firm McAward Associates, quoted in the *New York Times,* April 14, 1991

If you've got a $2 billion operation in Europe, a guy who can't manage his own financial affairs might not have the kind of judgment necessary for that challenge.

> Executive recruiter on companies' desire to examine potential employees' personal financial information, quoted in the *New York Times,* April 14, 1991

Clients call us now saying, "Get us someone who treats secretaries the same as peers."

> PETER HARRISON, of the recruiting firm Access Management, quoted in the *New York Times,* April 4, 1993

[M]ost companies spend more time picking out an office copier than deciding on a $40,000 employee. And look which one can cause the most damage.

A résumé isn't enough; it's a balance sheet without any liabilities.

> CRAIG ABERLE, CEO of the software firm Microbiz, quoted in *Inc. 500,* special issue 1995

Some [prospective employees] choose 10 ties that are really the worst. If he does that, then we move on to the scarves. If he is bad with the scarves, well, then he is really in a difficult position.

> BERNHARDT ARNAULT, chief executive of luxury products firm LVMH Moët-Hennessy Louis Vuitton S.A., on his test of taste of job candidates, in which they have to pick 10 good ties from a selection of 100, quoted in the *New York Times,* August 17, 1997

Acquisitions are going to be an alternative to normal recruiting that people haven't really considered before. As the economy continues to boom and as talent gets harder and harder to find, it's increasingly important to acquire the talent.

> JAMES O'DONNELL of the accounting-consulting firm Coopers & Lybrand, quoted in the *Wall Street Journal,* October 6, 1997

Recruiting is one of the most important parts of a CEO's job. Especially in a global company, we are dealing with people who have to live in a global culture. When we're hiring somebody, we look internally but ask ourselves: "Would I hire this person if I was hiring from the outside?" If yes, then we hire. If not we'll go outside.

> FRED HASSAN, CEO of the pharmaceutical company Pharmacia & Upjohn, quoted in the *Financial Times,* October 22, 1997

[B]osses tend to attract clusters of people from their own nationality around them. They do this not because they are racists, but because they feel comfortable with people they know best. You get a German cluster or a Swedish cluster.

> PERCY BARNEVIK, CEO of Investor, Swedish holding company based in London, quoted in the *Financial Times,* October 8, 1997

Do you want to spend the rest of your life selling sugared water or do you want a chance to change the world?

> STEVE JOBS of Apple Computer, inviting John Sculley, then president of PepsiCo, to join Apple, quoted in *Fortune,* September 14, 1987

32.12   REVIEWS

Most of the time, it's just a ritual that managers go through. They pull out last year's review, update it and do it quickly.

> WINSTON CONNOR of the Huntsman Chemical Corporation, quoted in the *Wall Street Journal,* November 19, 1996

Most of us don't like to sit down and hear where we're lacking and where we need to improve. It's like sitting down with your mom and dad and they're telling you, "We know what's best."

> Executive quoted in the *Wall Street Journal,* November 16, 1996

Dictionary of Performance Evaluation Comments

A keen analyst: Thoroughly confused
Active socially: Drinks heavily
Alert to company developments: An office gossip
Average: Not too bright
Bridge builder: Likes to compromise
Charismatic: No interest in any opinion but his own

Competent: Is still able to get work done if supervisor helps
Consults with supervisor often: Pain in the ass
Delegates responsibility effectively: Passes the buck well
Demonstrates qualities of leadership: Has a loud voice
Happy: Paid too much
Is unusually loyal: Wanted by no one else
Judgment is usually sound: Lucky
Spends extra hours on the job: Miserable home life
Uses time effectively: Clock watcher
Will go far: Relative of management

> Circulated on Internet, fall 1997

Motorola . . . has Individual Dignity Entitlement Programs, which take place four times a year. Every quarter all employees are asked such questions as: "Do you have a personal career plan, and is it exciting, achievable, and being acted upon?" and "Do you receive candid positive or negative feedback at least every 30 days that is helpful in improving or achieving your career plan?" These kind of questions are so alien that if I possessed a personal career plan I would add a PS to remind me never to apply for a job at Motorola.

> LUCY KELLAWAY, *Financial Times,* May 5, 1997

The classic problem with performance reviews is managers who don't like doing them, so they just write "fine" or "competent" in a perfunctory manner and they're done. Six months later, they want to get rid of the person, but they have just the opposite—a performance review six months ago in which they called the person "fine" and "competent."

> ROBERT J. SAHL of the consulting firm WMS, quoted in *Investor's Business Daily,* November 19, 1997

32.13   SOLVING PROBLEMS

All the pleasure of life is in general ideas. But all the use of life is in specific solutions—which cannot be reached through generalities any more than a picture can be painted by knowing some rules of method. They are reached by insight, tact, and specific knowledge.

> OLIVER WENDELL HOLMES, *The American Law Review* (1872)

It's often the people at the root of the company, on the shop floor, who will provide the best answers.

> HANS BECHERER, CEO of the farm equipment firm Deere & Co., quoted in *Business Week,* January 31, 1994

32.14 THE STRAIGHT STORY

I give you bitter pills in sugar coating. The pills are harmless; the poison is in the sugar. [Meaning, I believe, that telling the painful truth in a straightforward way will be less destructive ultimately than obfuscating.]

> STANISLAW LEC, *Unkempt Thoughts* (St. Martin's, 1962)

You never really hear the truth from your subordinates until after ten in the evening.

> JÜRGEN SCHREMPP, chairman of the car company Daimler-Benz, quoted in the *Economist,* March 16, 1996

Take some secretaries out to lunch. They usually know exactly who has the real power. The organization chart is the last place to find out.

> HOWARD HAAS of the University of Chicago School of Business, quoted in *Fortune,* November 29, 1993

The biggest lie in business life today is that the boss wants honest feedback. CEOs say, "I want the truth," because they know they won't get it.

> STEVEN BERGLAS of Harvard Medical School, clinical psychologist and specialist in executive stress, quoted in *Fortune,* September 8, 1997

32.15 TEAMWORK

When you're an athlete who's competed on a high level, people know you're a team player, willing to do what it takes to reach your goal. You build a certain amount of mental toughness, so even if you fail to guard that big account, you pick yourself up and go at it even harder the next time.

> DOUG McNEELY of the investment bank Donaldson Lufkin & Jenrette and captain of the 1983 Duke University basketball team, quoted in the *New York Times,* October 25, 1992

Talent wins games, but teamwork wins championships.

> MICHAEL JORDAN, basketball player, quoted by Verne G. Istock, CEO of the bank First Chicago-NBD Corporation, in a speech, October 15, 1996

32.16 TOLERATING FAILURE

Failing is good as long as it doesn't become a habit.

> MICHAEL EISNER, CEO of Walt Disney, in a speech, April 19, 1996

Steve Jobs came to us and asked us to support a new product. We spent a couple of years and a couple of million developing software for NeXT, and then we sold a couple of hundred thousand dollars worth. The manager who made that decision, his credibility may be tainted, but we don't terminate someone who makes that kind of mistake. We can't make the correct decision at every juncture in the road.

> JIM GOODNIGHT, president of software developer SAS Institute, quoted in *Inc. 500,* 1996

33.1 COMPARATIVE ADVANTAGE OF NATIONS

Potato chips, computer chips, what's the difference? They're all chips.

> Attributed to MICHAEL BOSKIN, chairman of the President's Council of Economic Advisors in the Bush administration, quoted by Clyde Prestowitz, founder and president of Economic Strategy Institute and former U.S. Trade Representative, in a speech, April 27, 1992

Why do we want the semiconductor industry? We don't want an industrial policy in this country. We don't want to pick winners and losers. If our guys can't hack it, let them go.

> RICHARD DARMAN, President Bush's Deputy Treasury Secretary, at a cabinet-level meeting on trade, cited by Clyde Prestowitz, founder and president of Economic Strategy Institute and former U.S. Trade Representative, in a speech, April 27, 1992

We don't think that we can pick the winners but we do think we can beat the odds.

> State bureaucrat in either Oregon or Washington state, which had worked together to create a Northwest regional industrial policy, quoted in the *Economist,* February 29, 1992

The point of trade is to allow an economy to specialize. If a country is better at making ships than sealing-wax, it makes sense to put more resources into shipbuilding, and to export some of the ships to pay for imports of sealing-wax.

> *The Economist,* January 11, 1992

America will win because our Asians will beat their Asians.

> Wall Street banker, quoted in the *Economist,* January 18, 1992

The main reason for the United States' higher productivity is our government's relative reluctance to protect companies against the rigors of competition.

> FREDERICK W. GLUCK of the consulting firm McKinsey, in a speech, October 21, 1992

If that's what you want [Japanese wine], you might as well drink water.

> SHINYA TASAKI, Tokyo sommelier and winner of the 1995 World Sommelier contest, quoted in the *Wall Street Journal,* August 9, 1996

The software is already developed in America; we'll buy packages and put them together to do it cheaply and quickly.

> KIYOSHI ASAKAWA, of the Japanese securities firm, on preparing for deregulation of financial services, quoted in the *Wall Street Journal,* September 16, 1997

Michael Jordan may be able to mow a lawn faster than any gardener, but it is best for him to pass up lawn care and stick to basketball. Similarly, the United States may well be more productive than other countries in textiles as well as aircraft production, but it would do better to import those cheap shirts from China and ease the way for Boeing to export planes all over the world.

> PROFESSOR ROBERT EISNER of Northwestern University, *New York Times,* October 13, 1997

33.2 CONSUMER BOYCOTTS

Modern multinational commerce makes moral superiority difficult. If Pepsi-Cola is doing business with Burma, then reach for an alternative. Oops, Coca-Cola is on the streets of Nigeria. When one's appetizer is outrage du jour, boycotting lunch is a tough assignment . . .

> MARTIN NOLAN, *Berkshire Eagle,* August 9, 1997

Berkeley is boycotting so many things that soon there may be no gasoline politically correct enough to run the city's vehicles.

> ELAINE HERSCHER, journalist, quoted by Martin Nolan, *Berkshire Eagle,* August 9, 1997

33.3 DEVELOPING COUNTRIES

Nothing contributes so much to the prosperity and happiness of a country as high profits.

> DAVID RICARDO, nineteenth-century economist

Innovating economies expand and develop. Economies that do not add new kinds of goods and services, but continue only to repeat old work, do not expand much nor do they, by definition, develop.

> JANE JACOBS, *The Economy of Cities* (Random House, 1969)

Success doesn't depend on natural resources and location as much as on the degree of stupidity of the policies and institutions of a country. A poor country can get its act together and grow like a bat out of hell.

> PROFESSOR MANCUR OLSON of the University of Maryland, quoted in *Forbes,* May 5, 1986

[Environmentalists] are suspicious of economic growth, because they think it will use up too much of the world's resources. This is turning them against free trade, because free trade means more growth. They are appalled by the thought that the world's population will double in the coming century, because that will eat up resources even faster. The physical earth is becoming more important to them than the people who live on it.

> *The Economist,* December 21, 1991

[Economic] development is the best contraceptive.

> Attributed to KAREN SINGH, former Indian diplomat, cited in the *Atlantic Monthly,* January 1997

[T]he finances enabling the Cook Islands to participate in this meeting would have funded approximately two outer island classrooms and two health clinics.

> GEOFFREY HENRY, prime minister of the Cook Islands and governor of the Asian Development Bank, quoted in *Asia, Inc.,* August 1994

The promotion of democracy and economic and social development is not "wishful thinking"; to the contrary—it is the soul of a policy of updated *Realpolitik.*

> J. BRIAN ATWOOD of the U.S. Agency for International Development, in a speech, January 13, 1994

A recent study at Princeton found "no evidence that environmental quality deteriorates with economic growth." Instead, they found that, after an initial phase of deterioration, economic growth brought environmental improvement. In most cases, the turning point occurs before a country reaches annual per capita income of about $12,000—about the level of Taiwan.

> LEE R. RAYMOND, CEO of the oil firm Exxon, in a speech, May 6, 1996

My concern is not that there are too many sweatshops but that there are too few. Those are precisely the jobs that were the stepping-stone for Singapore and Hong Kong, and those are the jobs that have to come to Africa to get them out of their backbreaking rural poverty.

> PROFESSOR JEFFREY SACHS of Harvard University, on enforcement of U.S. labor standards on suppliers in developing countries, quoted in the *New York Times,* June 22, 1997

A policy of good jobs in principle, but no jobs in practice, might assuage our consciences, but it is no favor to its alleged beneficiaries.

> PROFESSOR PAUL KRUGMAN of MIT, quoted in the *New York Times,* June 22, 1997

In 1950, the developing world produced only 7 percent of the world's carbon dioxide. In 1987, it produced 28 percent. And by 2020, it could produce more than half.

> FRED KRUPP, executive director of the Environmental Defense Fund, in a speech, August 1, 1992

The only way to convince developing countries to change is if you produce something [an alternative energy source] sufficiently simple so they can use it and sufficiently cheap so the cost is less than coal.

> CARLO RUBBIA, Nobel Prize–winning particle physicist, quoted in the *Financial Times,* March 6, 1997

A lot of third world countries aren't interested in a steel mill that produces 1.5 million tons but employs only 350 people. They want 3,500 jobs.

> JOHN CORRENTI, president of the steel company Nucor, quoted in the *Wall Street Journal,* August 27, 1997

You can help people make crops grow. But if you don't have roads to get them out, microcredits to finance them, facilities to store them, and advice on marketing, then improving crop yields is not going to affect the national scene.

We [the World Bank] can make a difference between peace and war. We can make a difference between poverty and a fair life for people. I'm not saying we can solve all the problems, but we can make a difference.

> JAMES D. WOLFENSOHN, president of the World Bank, quoted in the *New York Times,* September 14, 1997

The IFC [International Finance Corporation, part of the World Bank] has this habit of financing someone who is already a dominant player. Look at all the liquor companies being funded under the rubric of "agro industrial." If you're a financial institution, that is where the money is.

> PROFESSOR DEVESH KAPUR of Harvard, quoted in the *Wall Street Journal,* September 23, 1997

I guess it's a fine line between the missionary and the mercenary.

> SHAHBAZ MAVADDAT of the International Finance Corporation, quoted in the *Wall Street Journal,* October 3, 1997

• In the next 20 years, a dozen emerging economies—with over 10 times the population of the United States—will account for a full 40 percent of all export opportunities.

• In the next decade, 300 million Chinese will achieve for the first time a level of income we define as enabling a consumer economy. Think about that: a market of potential consumers in China that is larger than the entire United States population.

• In fact, today there are more Chinese studying English than there are Americans.

> C. MICHAEL ARMSTRONG, CEO of the high-tech firm Hughes Electronics Corporation, in a speech, February 11, 1997

The bad news is that three-quarters of the private flows to developing countries are going to just 12 of them.

> CAIO K. KOCH-WESER, managing director of the World Bank, in a speech, March 22, 1997

33.4 FREE MARKETS

The uniform, constant, and uninterrupted effort of every man to better his own condition, the principle from which national and public as well as private opulence is originally derived, is frequently powerful enough to maintain the natural progress of things towards improvement, in spite both of the extravagance of government, and of the greatest errors of administration.

People of the same trade rarely meet together, even for merriment or diversion, but the conversation ends in a conspiracy against the public, or in some contrivance to raise prices.

> ADAM SMITH, *The Wealth of Nations* (1776)

Adam Smith's flash of genius was his recognition that the prices that emerged from voluntary transactions between buyers and sellers—for short, in a free market—could coordinate the activity of millions of people, each seeking his own interest, in such a way as to make everyone better off. It was a startling idea then, and it remains one today, that economic order can emerge as the unintended consequence of the actions of many people, each seeking his own interest.

> MILTON FRIEDMAN, 1980, quoted in Robert Lekachman and Borin Van Loon, *Capitalism for Beginners* (Pantheon, 1981)

The price system is wonderfully democratic, the least elitist of human arrangements. Led Zeppelin makes more money for its performances than the Guarneri Quartet because more people eagerly buy tickets and records to hear the first group than the second. In free markets, the ringing of cash registers measures better and worse, not your superior taste or mind.

> ROBERT LEKACHMAN and BORIN VAN LOON, *Capitalism for Beginners* (Pantheon, 1981)

For an ideal free market, you want a large number of producers. For an ideal government, you want a saint.

> MILTON FRIEDMAN, interviewed in *Playboy,* February 1973

The customer is leaving regulators with little choice. Some countries are moving toward free and open markets a lot slower than others, but they are all moving.

> MARIANNE G. BYE of the investment bank Lehman Brothers, quoted in *Business Week,* September 26, 1996

Capitalism is a hotel. Its penthouse suites are always filled, but not necessarily with the same people.

> PAUL SAMUELSON, Nobel Prize–winning economist, quoted in *U.S. News & World Report,* July 14, 1986

The higher the mountain, the lower the valley. That is the logic of capitalism.

> AKIRA NAMBARA, general manager of Bank of Japan's Osaka branch, *The Economist,* December 21, 1991

33.5 FREE TRADE

No nation was ever ruined by trade.

> U.S. founding father BENJAMIN FRANKLIN

Trade is a plant which grows wherever there is peace, as soon as there is peace, and as long as there is peace.

> RALPH WALDO EMERSON, "The Young American" in *Nature: Addresses and Lectures* (1849)

Trade, that pride and darling of our ocean, that educator of nations, that benefactor in spite of itself, ends in shameful defaulting, bubble, and bankruptcy, all over the world.

> RALPH WALDO EMERSON, "Works and Days," in *Society and Solitude* (1870)

Trade is a high-stakes poker game, and you have to keep a poker face.

> EVAN GALBRAITH, former U.S. ambassador to France and later chairman of Moët-Hennessy U.S., quoted in *U.S. News & World Report,* February 2, 1987

One thing is for certain. Once you lose a major industry, you never get it back.

> RONALD LEVIN of the U.S. Commerce Department, quoted in the *New Yorker,* January 18, 1988

In the late 1940s, the average tariff in industrialized nations was 60 percent. Today, it is under 5 percent. In 1950, world trade amounted to $70 billion. Today, it is more than $3 trillion.

> WILLIAM C. STEERE JR., CEO of the pharmaceutical firm Pfizer, Inc., in a speech, September 18, 1992

Trade is a process, not an end. The bottom line is to get more good jobs at high wages for more people. Our economy used to take a back seat to foreign policy. That era is over.

> MICKEY KANTOR, then U.S. Trade Representative, quoted in *Fortune,* May 31, 1993

Kantor says he is not interested in theology but in results. That's like someone filling in potholes in a road with no road map.

> PROFESSOR JAGDISH BHAGWATI of Columbia University, *Fortune,* May 31, 1993

Managed trade is the worst thing we could get into. No one is smart enough to do that.

> JOHN J. MURPHY, CEO of the oil-field services firm Dresser Industries, quoted in *Fortune,* May 31, 1993

The United States should adopt a protective tariff of such a character as will help the struggling industries of Europe get on their feet.

> PRESIDENT WARREN HARDING

Free trade is God's diplomacy, and there is no other certain way of uniting people in the bonds of peace.

> RICHARD COBDEN, British industrialist, 1857

No two countries that both have a McDonald's have ever fought a war against each other.

> THOMAS L. FRIEDMAN, *New York Times,* December 8, 1996

We are always willing to be trade partners, but never trade patsies.

> U.S. PRESIDENT RONALD REAGAN, State of the Union Address, quoted in *Time,* February 9, 1987

The lifting of the iron curtain, the destruction of the Berlin wall, and the collapse of Soviet imperial Communism all simultaneously heralded the elimination of the world's greatest barrier to trade.

> EDWARD YARDEMI, chief economist of the investment bank Deutsche Morgan Grenfell, quoted in the *Financial Times,* August 18, 1997

The American middle class was not made by free trade. Historically it grew behind protective tariffs, which favored U.S. producers over U.S. consumers.

> JACK BEATTY, *Atlantic Monthly,* May 1994

My freshman colleagues know what they were elected for, and free trade isn't part of their agenda.

> U.S. REPRESENTATIVE JIM KOLBE (Republican, Arizona), *Business Week,* May 22, 1995

The destiny of the United States is to be part of a free-trade hemisphere.

> U.S. SENATOR RICHARD G. LUGAR (Republican, Indiana), in a 1995 campaign speech for the Republican presidential nomination

We will not convince Americans that expanding trade is good for them by reciting passages from Adam Smith. Conventional wisdom and past policy prescriptions are not enough. We can't just say, "trust us." We will only convince Americans by continuing to stand up and fight for their interests. We will only convince them by insisting on fair deals and shared responsibility with our trading partners.

> MICKEY KANTOR, then U.S. Trade Representative, in a speech, July 27, 1995

Make no mistake about it. Americans have a commercial stake in China. At least 160,000 Americans owe their jobs to U.S. exports to China. These workers have rights, too—the right to job opportunities, the chance to provide a decent living for their families. Just as we should not make apologies for China, neither should we apologize for our economic interest in China.

> MICKEY KANTOR, then U.S. Trade Representative, in a speech, January 31, 1996

No nation can be competitive in (and be a net exporter of) everything.

> MICHAEL E. PORTER, author of *The Competitive Advantage of Nations* (Free Press, 1990)

We live in a globalized economy. Business is now truly an international affair and the economies of the world are interdependent . . . Our national security and our economic security are permanently intertwined.

Future opportunities for our [U.S.] economic growth and job creation will come from the other 96 percent of the world's population. We cannot turn our back to the global economy, even if we wanted to.

> MICKEY KANTOR, then U.S. Trade Representative, in a speech, November 9, 1995

Governments cannot fundamentally alter the inexorable momentum toward the global integration of manufacturing, but they sure can screw things up.

> JULIUS L. KATZ, trade negotiator in the Bush administration, quoted in *Fortune,* January 10, 1994

For most of America's history, foreign policy has reflected an obsession with open markets for American business . . . Business expansion abroad was often seen as an extension of the American frontier, part of the nation's manifest destiny.

> JEFFREY E. GARTEN of Yale University and former Under Secretary of Commerce (1993–95), quoted in *Foreign Affairs,* May–June 1997

You need to create a constituency for free trade. Big business is the only group that can do that effectively.

> ROBERT RUBIN, Secretary of the Treasury, quoted in the *Wall Street Journal,* June 11, 1997

Every time the trade issue rears its head, a pattern repeats itself. The capital girds for an agonizing battle. The insurgents cite American jobs, cheap labor abroad, environmental threats. The free-traders fly to the defensive, citing the virtues of open markets. The vote looks too close to call. The lobbying is furious.

And ultimately, the free-traders always win.

> DAVID SHRIBMAN, *Fortune,* June 9, 1997

In the end there is still an internationalist bent, but it's getting closer and tougher.

> U.S. REPRESENTATIVE JIM KOLBE (Republican, Arizona), quoted in *Fortune,* June 9, 1997

Congress has gone to the brink and never screwed up. Congress depends on the president to keep it from responding to every protectionist impulse.

> SUSAN C. SCHWAB of the University of Maryland and former Assistant Commerce Secretary, dean of School of Public Affairs, quoted in *Fortune,* June 9, 1997

It is wrong to believe Europe could get more prosperous while the rest of the world stays poor.

> ROBIN COOK, then shadow [opposition] foreign secretary of the British Labour Party, interviewed in the *Financial Times,* March 11, 1997

The fear of being swamped by India is misplaced. . . . If the Indian economy depends on Pakistani purchases, India will think three times before becoming unreasonable.

> ZAHID ZAHEER of Pakistan's Overseas Investors' Chamber of Commerce and Industry, quoted in *Asia, Inc.,* August 1997

America is based on the free-enterprise system. If companies can get their shoes from China cheaper, they should do it. I'm just one of the people who fell through the cracks in that industry.

> GEORGE SHOLA, who worked at shoe manufacturer Leslie Stephen Ltd. and whose new job pays $8.70 an hour, compared to his previous wage of $10, quoted in the *Wall Street Journal,* September 4, 1997

33.6 FREE TRADE—DISSENTING OPINIONS

Free trade cannot be a pillar of a conservative foreign policy. It is not a conservative doctrine; it is a *radical* scheme—one cavalierly embraced by most utopians, unilateral disarmists, international altruists, radical anarchists, foreign lobbyists, and yes, a very few decent citizens across the Potomac River.

PROFESSOR ALFRED ECKES of Ohio University, in a speech, November 23, 1991

In the U.S. market, the theory that tariffs and trade restraints necessarily burden the consumer diverges from the real-world result. In the late nineteenth century, when duties on dutiable imports averaged over 40 percent, protection actually coincided with declining consumer prices. In 1890, the price of steel rails fell under $32 per hundred pounds, down from $106 twenty years earlier. And the price of nails fell more than half. Altogether, the consumer price index dropped 29 percent during those years. If protection burdened the late nineteenth century consumer, declining prices erased the evidence.

PROFESSOR ALFRED E. ECKES of Ohio University, in a speech, May 19, 1993

How do we achieve a new nationalist, as opposed to a globalist, economic policy? . . . The essential first step is to defang the transnational of the multinational companies, the money power that increasingly holds U.S. policy and the American in thrall. And how do we go about defanging them? By restricting their operations, placing limits on those who are headquartered in the United States while rejecting any loyalty to America. If they shift their manufacturing operations to low-wage Third World countries, then let them be subject to penalties. In other words, we strike at their profits.

ANTHONY HARRIGAN of the U.S. Business and Industrial Council Education Foundation, in a speech, June 11, 1995

What is the purpose of our trade policy and what do we want our domestic economy to look like? Who gains and who loses, and to what extent, from the increases in exports and the greater increases in imports? Do American workers benefit, or only consumers and investors? What conditions must exist—concerning human rights, workers' rights, or environmental protection—for us to allow other nations' goods to enter our country? Are there other limits to impose? Would our present policies, for instance, prohibit trading with a country like a Nazi Germany if it wanted to sell us low-priced goods that would make profits for our companies and provide low-cost goods for our consumers? Sadly, I don't think they would.

By my estimate, from 1979 to 1994, twice as many high-paying jobs in the United States economy were lost to imports as were gained from exports.

KENNETH LEWIS, retired shipping company CEO and free-trade advocate who nevertheless dissented from the majority report of President Clinton's Commission on U.S.-Pacific Trade and Investment Policy, *New York Times*, July 13, 1997

I don't believe that unfettered free trade inevitably brings growth in anything but short-term transnational profits and long-term environmental destruction. We need a broader model. I call it fair trade. I call it sustainable trade. The label doesn't matter—the content does.

ANITA RODDICK, managing director of the British cosmetics firm The Body Shop, in a speech, October 21, 1993 (The firm was later revealed not to be living up to some of its espoused ideals.)

For years we've had to settle with accepting inferior products made by inmates in far-off countries . . . Why should we go all the way to China to have things made with prison labor when we can do that right here? . . . We have the largest prison population ever, and there are only so many license plates to be made.

MICHAEL MOORE, corporate gadfly and maker of such films as *Roger and Me*, quoted in the *New York Times*, August 31, 1997

If you believe that economic growth is the best measure of human happiness, you will cheer [the expansion of world trade]. But pause for a moment. Over the past 50 "golden" years, the planet has been steadily deforested. Its oceans have become sinks for human waste. Its cities have become overcrowded ant heaps. The atmosphere is laden with noxious fumes. A quarter of the globe's bird species have been rendered extinct. Many of us are better-fed, longer lived, and healthier than past generations. But famine and undernourishment persist.

Cunning lobbyists, smart lawyers, hired scientists are deployed to win their arguments on the narrowest definitions of what would do the most good.

JOE ROGALY, *Financial Times*, November 6, 1997

Why do some people persist in mouthing the mantra "free trade" when foreign countries can and do engage in all sorts of dishonest tactics that interfere with trade, such as devaluation or other manipulation of the value of their money, confiscation (or nationalization) of U.S.

property, refusing to live up to the contracts and agreements they sign, stealing our patents and copyrights, and counterfeiting our money?

> PHYLLIS SCHLAFLY, conservative spokesperson, March 28, 1996

33.7 HUMAN RIGHTS AND GEOPOLITICAL POLICIES THAT AFFECT TRADE

Sanctions were conceived in piety after the First World War as a better alternative to bloodletting. They are still the best nonlethal way to send the message that there can no longer be business as usual. Misuse has given them a bad name. Too often they inflict punishment on a regime without making it mend its ways.

> *The Economist,* June 6, 1992

Sanctions are the ultimate "feel-good" foreign policy.

> C. MICHAEL ARMSTRONG, CEO of the high-tech firm Hughes Electronics, in a speech, January 15, 1997

They have yet to topple a targeted government. They provide an external scapegoat for well-entrenched regimes to compensate for domestic failings. Once launched, they are extremely difficult to terminate.

> Report by National Association of Manufacturers on sanctions, cited in the *Financial Times,* March 5, 1997

Sometimes it seems as if we Americans are like the proverbial policeman chasing the fleeing criminal and pointing a gun to our own head and saying, "Stop or I'll shoot myself."

> PHILIP CONDIT, CEO of the aerospace firm Boeing, on the place of human rights in trade policy, interviewed in the *New York Times,* August 17, 1997

We're an industrial group with the right to do business. We aren't looking to get involved in politics.

> THIERRY DESMAREST, chairman of the French energy firm Total SA, which ran afoul of U.S. sanctions against Iran in pursuit of a $2 billion natural gas exploration deal, quoted in the *Wall Street Journal,* September 30, 1997

To be effective, an embargo must prevent people in the target country from getting goods, or at least substan-

tially increase the cost of getting goods. But competition is a hardy weed that shrugs off governmental attempts to suppress it. Companies in many countries, especially Canada, produce and sell goods that are close substitutes for the U.S. goods that can't be sold to Cuba. Wander around Cuba, and you're likely to see beach umbrellas advertising Labatt's beer, McCain's french fries, and President's Choice cola.

> PROFESSOR DAVID R. HENDERSON at the Naval Postgraduate School, quoted in *Fortune,* October 13, 1997

Linking human rights and the environment to trade is the lazy man's solution to extremely difficult problems, and a recipe for failure all around.

> PROFESSOR JAGDISH BHAGWATI of Columbia University, quoted in the *New York Times,* October 9, 1997

Sanctions can work. Many leading Afrikaners in South Africa admit they were an important factor in their decision to abandon apartheid and negotiate with the African National Congress.

> EDWARD MORTIMER, *Financial Times,* March 12, 1997

33.8 MALTHUS REVISITED

The modern "population explosion" was sparked not because people suddenly started breeding like rabbits, but rather because they finally stopped dying like flies.

> NICHOLAS EBERSTADT of the conservative think tank American Enterprise Institute, in a speech, November 15, 1996

If you don't feed your country, it's civil war. There's no price too high to avoid that.

> DAVID C. NELSON of NatWest Securities, quoted in the *Economist,* May 20, 1996

The primary reason so much food gets tossed is that America has the cheapest food in the world.

> ROBERT HAHN of the conservative think tank American Enterprise Institute, quoted in the *New York Times,* September 21, 1997

11.3 billion pounds of fruit, 15.9 billion pounds of veggies, 8.2 billion pounds of meat, poultry, and fish, and 17.4 billion pounds of fluid milk never made it from refrigerator (or plate) to mouth. Enough flour, sugar, and margarine end up in landfills to supply the nation's youth with Twinkies.

> PETER PASSELL, *New York Times*, September 21, 1997

The world's worst environmental problem is poverty.

> PATRICK LOW of the World Bank, quoted in *Fortune*, January 10, 1994

We are in a constant race with development. Before we even have a chance to convince the wider audience here that environmentally sound development is a viable way to do things, the plans to build roads, factories, or power plants are moving ahead. We have a problem here with unemployment, so any developer who can sell promises of employment will get support. When that happens, we get labeled as against employment and get treated as outsiders.

> AGUS PURNOMO, head of World Wide Fund for Nature, in Indonesia, quoted in the *New York Times*, July 14, 1997

Today there are about 5.8 billion people in the world. About 1.8 billion of them live in conditions of abject poverty—or subsistence life that simply can't be romanticized as some sort of simpler, pre-industrialized lifestyle. These people spend their days trying to get food and firewood so that they can make it to the next day. As many as 80 million people are so severely malnourished that they can neither work nor participate in family life.

We can't expect the rest of the world to abandon their economic aspirations just so we can continue to enjoy clean air and water. That is neither ethically correct nor likely to be permitted by the billions of people in the developing world who expect the quality of their lives to improve.

> ROBERT B. SHAPIRO, CEO of the chemical company Monsanto, interviewed in *Harvard Business Review*, January–February 1997

33.9 THE MARKET

Civilization and profits go hand in hand.

> PRESIDENT CALVIN COOLIDGE, in a speech, November 27, 1920

The great dynamic success of capitalism had given us a powerful weapon in our battle against Communism—*money*.

> RONALD REAGAN, *An American Life* (Simon & Schuster, 1990)

[T]he market is not an invention of capitalism, it is an invention of civilization.

> MIKHAIL GORBACHEV, former Soviet premier, quoted by George Poste of SmithKline Beecham, in a speech, January 14, 1997

Markets of some sort are ubiquitous. Indeed, they are much more evident in third world countries than in capitalist ones. Many people with low incomes in poorer countries earn their livelihoods by activities such as peddling goods on the streets, repairing cars or equipment, or offering transport in old cars, vans, or buses.

> SAMUEL BRITTAN, *Financial Times*, January 30, 1997

In itself, the market is not a panacea for all problems.

> PRESIDENT BORIS YELTSIN of Russia, in a speech to the Federation Council, the upper house of the Russian parliament, quoted in the *Financial Times*, September 25, 1997

The market is now God; economic planning is the Devil Incarnate.

> WILLIAM WOLMAN and ANNE COLMOSCA, *The Judas Economy: The Triumph of Capitalism and the Betrayal of Work* (Addison-Wesley, 1997)

Every society needs some shared values to hold it together. Market values on their own cannot serve that purpose, because they reflect only what one market participant is willing to pay another in a free exchange. Markets reduce everything, including human beings (labor) and nature (land), to commodities.

> GEORGE SOROS, founder of the Quantum Fund, *Atlantic Monthly*, January 1998

33.10 MICROLENDING

Research shows that one loan is seldom enough to drag a borrower out of poverty—the second and third loans tend to achieve that.

> *Financial Times*, January 31, 1997

33.11 NAFTA (NORTH AMERICAN FREE TRADE AGREEMENT)

That sucking sound you hear is the sound of U.S. jobs going to Mexico.

> ROSS PEROT, founder of the data-processing firm EDS and sometime presidential candidate, on the effects of NAFTA, 1993

It makes you wonder what kind of jobs those are.

> DAVID LETTERMAN, TV talk show host, referring to Ross Perot's use of the adjective *sucking*, 1993

Nothing's agreed [on the final terms of NAFTA] until everything's agreed.

> *The Economist,* February 29, 1992

What carried the day for liberal free trade was the case beyond the addition of some tenths of a percent to the national income of the United States. It was the recognition that, in addition to serving our economic interests, liberal trade policy was an application of American principles, and expression of American concern for the well-being of others, and above all that it made a contribution to the stability of the world we live in.

> HERBERT STEIN, "No Need to Be Scared of NAFTA," *Wall Street Journal,* September 28, 1993

In Mexico, even assuming you had all the efficiencies you have here, you might be able to reduce your costs by 8 percent to 9 percent. That's not something you're going to move a whole plant for. Perot's sucking sound is ridiculous.

> JAMES WOGSLAND of the machine manufacturer Caterpillar, quoted in *Fortune,* April 18, 1994

I was amused to learn that [the late] Secretary of Commerce Ron Brown has signed off on the application by the Perot family for a free foreign trade zone permit for their $200 million Alliance Airport project near Fort Worth. Its success would appear to be assured with NAFTA.

> PRESTON TOWNLEY, CEO of the big-business organization The Conference Board, in a speech, September 14, 1993

NAFTA is not a zero-sum game where one country's increased exports come at the expense of another country's jobs. It's an expanding pie. As their trading with one another expands, each country benefits.

> PAUL FREIMAN of Syntex Corporation, cited by Augustine P. Gallego of the San Diego Community College District, in a speech, October 8, 1992

NAFTA will match or exceed in size and wealth any comparable free-trade area in the world, including the European Community.

Typically, there are almost as many forecasts of NAFTA's impact as there are economists.

> JOHN A. GAVIN, U.S. Ambassador to Mexico, 1981–1986, in a speech, February 5, 1993

Appearances aside, NAFTA is a prudent step toward creating a regional trading bloc that would withstand the devolution of Western Europe and Asia into rival blocs. The treaty's free-trade proponents would never admit this, but NAFTA's underlying thrust is toward managed trade and investment.

> JOHN B. JUDIS, "History vs. NAFTA," *New Republic,* October 11, 1993

NAFTA isn't really about economics, it's about foreign policy. Only a few years ago, many experts worried seriously that a Mexico battered by economic hard times would become a radicalized national security nightmare. Instead, we now have a pro-American, pro-market neighbor that's even inching its way toward real democracy.

> PROFESSOR PAUL KRUGMAN of MIT, interviewed on National Public Radio's *All Things Considered,* November 5, 1993

Our exports have grown 22 percent in the first 10 months of the NAFTA—the great sucking sound has become goods going south and jobs going in our country.

> U.S. COMMERCE SECRETARY MICKEY KANTOR, in the online forum of the *Atlantic Monthly,* November 28, 1996

NAFTA created a climate that has emboldened employers [to take a more aggressive stance in labor negotiations, by threatening to close plants].

> KATE BRONFENBRENNER of Cornell who studied the effects of NAFTA, quoted in *Business Week,* January 27, 1997

You look at the pre- and post-NAFTA figures for job displacement and trade flows, and the reality is it's hard to find any break in the trends.

> SHERMAN ROBINSON of the International Food Policy Research Institute, quoted in the *Wall Street Journal*, June 17, 1997

We were on the road to free trade already. All NAFTA has done has been to fill in the potholes.

> JEFFREY SCHOTT of the Institute for International Economics, quoted in the *Wall Street Journal*, June 17, 1997

If we don't seize these new opportunities, our competitors surely will. Already since 1992, in Latin America and Asia alone, our competitors have negotiated 20 trade agreements that do not include the United States.

> U.S. PRESIDENT BILL CLINTON, on extending "fast-track" authority to negotiate trade deals with hemisphere trading partners, quoted in the *New York Times*, August 24, 1997

Overall, U.S. exports since NAFTA are up 33 percent to Canada and 27 percent to Mexico.

> PAULA STERN, president of the consulting firm Stern Group, in a speech, February 15, 1997

[A]ssume that through NAFTA Mexico becomes extremely successful in exporting to the United States and we double our share, [which] would mean that Mexican imports into the United States would have to grow twice as much as exports from all parts of the world . . . It means that our total exports into the United States would represent one percentage point of total GDP in the United States. It is impossible to think that would create massive job dislocation.

Michigan-made components account for three-fourths of the value of small cars and trucks produced in Mexico by Ford Motor Company. Brakes, fuel tanks, electronic components, interior trim—all come from the United States and from Michigan specifically. Production sharing of this sort sustains about 72,000 jobs.

> JAIME JOSE SERRA PUCHE, Mexican Secretary of Commerce and International Promotion, in a speech, December 9, 1992

We want trade, not aid.

> MEXICAN PRESIDENT CARLOS SALINAS DE GORTARI, on whether he expected a transfer of resources from

his richer partners, as had taken place in Europe when the EC was expanded, quoted in the *Economist*, January 16, 1993

No producers in the world have more-privileged trade status in Mexico than the producers of the Midwest.

> DIANE SWONK, chief economist of the banking firm First Chicago NBD, quoted in the *Wall Street Journal*, April 21, 1997

We opposed it [NAFTA], it passed, and now the United States is getting all the benefits. With something like the tomato dispute [raised by a coalition of Florida farmers who wanted to raise tariffs on Mexican tomatoes], we would want to reverse our commitment to NAFTA. And if we can't abrogate it, we can at least enforce it.

> CONGRESSMAN VICTOR QUINTANA of Mexico's Party of Democratic Revolution, quoted in the *Wall Street Journal*, July 2, 1996

American growers who compete with Mexico have been unable to obtain sufficient relief under NAFTA or other trade laws. Farms and jobs are being lost. Five years ago, Florida had 200 independent tomato growers. Today, there are fewer than 100.

> MICHAEL J. STUART, president of the Florida Fruit and Vegetable Association, quoted in the *New York Times*, October 13, 1997

Americans have got to realize, either they import our tomatoes, or import our people.

> CONGRESSMAN VICTOR QUINTANA of Mexico's Party of Democratic Revolution, quoted in the *Wall Street Journal*, July 2, 1996

33.12 NAFTA—THE NEXT GENERATION

Everyone thinks they should be next [to join NAFTA] after Mexico. Chile says it is ready to go. Venezuela says it supplies us with oil and is a "strategic" partner. Panama says it is a "strategic" partner because of the canal. Costa Rica says its economy is very advanced and it is a cute democracy.

> A Washington official, quoted in the *Economist*, January 4, 1992

No fast track—no concrete negotiations.

> JOSE BOTAFOGO GONÇALVES, the Brazilian Foreign
> Ministry's subsecretary-general of commerce, quoted
> in the *Wall Street Journal*, September 18, 1997

While we're complacent, the Europeans are obsessed
with increasing their exports to Latin America.

> JEFFREY GARTEN of Yale University and former
> Under Secretary of Commerce, *Wall Street Journal*,
> September 18, 1997

We cannot sit on the sidelines with a towel over our
heads while others make the trade and investment plays
that will determine the economic standings of the
twenty-first century.

> MADELEINE ALBRIGHT, U.S. Secretary of State, quoted
> in the *Financial Times*, September 19, 1997

In most Latin American nations import tariffs border on
15 percent. Although this is historically low for the region, it is still very high from a global perspective—the
average U.S. import tariff, for example, is approximately
3 percent.

> PROFESSOR SEBASTIAN EDWARDS of UCLA, quoted
> in the *Wall Street Journal*, April 18, 1997

[It] is not an easy thing to explain to American textile
workers, or to their union. But new free-trade agreements, achieved by fast track or whatever other means,
will be more easily reached if those who may lose by
new trade are helped by all of the rest of us who gain.

Insisting on stronger unions and better wages and
working conditions in foreign countries may well help
foreign workers. It will not help U.S. workers. Lessen-
ing the competition from foreign industries that have
relatively lower labor costs will preserve the jobs of
low-wage U.S. workers rather than increase the proportion of high-wage jobs in our economy.

> PROFESSOR EMERITUS ROBERT EISNER of Northwest-
> ern University, quoted in the *New York Times*, Octo-
> ber 13, 1997

Fast track has become a referendum on NAFTA.

> DAN GRISWOLD, trade expert of the libertarian think
> tank Cato Institute, quoted in *Fortune*, October 27,
> 1997

33.13 PROTECTIONISM

Tariff, *n*. A scale of taxes on imports, designed to protect the domestic producer against the greed of his consumer.

> AMBROSE BIERCE, *The Devil's Dictionary* (1906)

Take back your protection; we are now men, and we
can beat the world at the manufacture of steel.

> U.S. Steel tycoon ANDREW CARNEGIE, testifying at
> tariff hearings before the House of Representatives'
> Ways and Means Committee, December 21, 1908

Protectionism is a plague which, once loosed upon the
world, will cripple all our economies.

> YASUHIRO NAKASONE, Prime Minister of Japan,
> quoted in *U.S. News & World Report*, October 21,
> 1985

Those who are bold enough to throw a stone at our
trading partners are really throwing a boomerang at
ourselves.

> BOB MICHEL, Republican leader (when the Republi-
> cans were seemingly permanently in the minority),
> quoted in *U.S. News & World Report*, August 18,
> 1986

Protectionism is insidious because it leaves no trace of
what might have been.

> PROFESSOR PAUL M. ROMER of the University of Cali-
> fornia, Berkeley, quoted in *Fortune*, December 13,
> 1993

We may be the only American company in an industry
targeted by the Japanese to actually regain market share
without the aid of tariff protection or other government
help.

> DAVID T. KEARNS, chairman of the high-tech elec-
> tronics firm Xerox, annual report letter, 1989

407 Caught Smoking Foreign Cigarettes—Includes 2
Politicians, 4 Civil Servants and 9 Bankers. [Headline in
a Korean newspaper, 1984; imported cigarettes were legalized in 1988.]

> Cited in the *Wall Street Journal*, January 14, 1997

If self-interest is the irreversible force behind the markets' opening, self-interest can also be short-sighted—
clinging to small but immediate advantages and ignor-

ing the long-term opportunities of a truly level playing field.

> C. MICHAEL ARMSTRONG, CEO of the high-tech firm Hughes Electronics, in a speech, January 15, 1997

Texas Instruments spent 29 years trying to get the Japan Patent Office to recognize our fundamental patent on the integrated circuit, the basic building block of virtually all modern electronics. We finally prevailed, only to have a Japanese High Court in 1994 rule that our patents didn't cover products that are made today. The court restricted the scope of the patent to the specific example that was used to explain the invention. It's as if we had been granted a patent on a yellow number two pencil only to be told that the patent does not apply if the pencil is painted red.

> JERRY R. JUNKINS, CEO of the electronics firm Texas Instruments, in a speech, September 22, 1995

The 1920–28 period was a perfect test of Buchananomics. What followed was depression and war.

> LAWRENCE H. SUMMERS, Deputy Secretary of the Treasury, quoted in *Fortune*, November 27, 1995

Louisiana taxpayers are, in effect, paying a lawyer in Washington to drive up the price of their gumbo [by restricting imports of crawfish].

> GREG RUSHFORD, publisher of the *Rushford Report*, newsletter on trade policy, quoted in the *New York Times*, August 8, 1997

It is not possible for this nation to be at once politically internationalist and economically isolationist. This is just as insane as asking one Siamese twin to high dive while the other plays the piano.

> ADLAI STEVENSON, then a Democratic presidential candidate, in a campaign speech in New Orleans, 1952

Here are our factories, our workers, our taxes! They tell me I stop competition. But excuse me, you want us to compete freely with those monsters only two years after opening our own factories.

> MAYOR SERGEI RATYUSHNYAK of Ushgorod, Ukraine, who refused Coca-Cola a warehouse permit and allegedly had its salesmen beaten up and drivers threatened, quoted in the *Financial Times Weekend*, March 8–9, 1997

You can always buy something in English; you can't always sell something in English.

> RICHARD CELESTE, former governor of Ohio, quoted in Rosabeth Moss Kanter, *World Class: Thriving Locally in the Global Economy* (Simon & Schuster, 1995)

What everybody wants to do with their excess capacity is export it, but it is still the case that in a lot of Asian countries there are substantial restrictions on imports because those countries want to develop their own domestic auto sectors. So what you have is a permanent situation for excess supply and downward pressure on prices and wages.

> WYNN VAN BUSSMAN, chief corporate economist of the Chrysler Corporation, quoted in William Greider, *One World, Ready or Not: The Manic Logic of Global Capitalism* (Simon & Schuster, 1997)

[H]istorically, the American Right has always been protectionist. . . . Given the size of the United States and the amount of internal trade and the ability to get around protectionism via the Internet, via various other means—I don't think protectionism is a real threat.

> MILTON FRIEDMAN, Nobel Prize–winning economist, interviewed in *Forbes*, December 29, 1997

33.14 PROTECTIONISM BY THE NUMBERS

Worldwide average subsidies for agricultural products:

Wheat	48 percent
Coarse grains	36 percent
Rice	86 percent
Oilseeds	24 percent
Sugar (refined white)	48 percent
Beef (including veal)	35 percent
Pork	22 percent
Poultry	14 percent
Lamb and mutton	45 percent
Wool	10 percent
Eggs	14 percent
All products	43 percent

Organization for Economic Cooperation and Development (OECD), cited in the *Wall Street Journal*, October 28, 1996

[T]he cost to retain a typical job threatened by foreign trade is estimated to be about $170,000, when measured by increased costs to the average consumer. That's equivalent to about six years of wages for each job saved.

> DAVE COULTER, CEO of Bank of America, in a speech, October 17, 1996

33.15 SANCTIONS BY THE NUMBERS

Nuclear proliferation: Nine measures against China, Cuba, Iran, North Korea, Pakistan.

Political stability: Eight measures against Afghanistan, Angola, Bosnia.

Anti-narcotics: Eight measures against Afghanistan, Burma, Colombia, Cuba, Haiti, Nigeria.

Worker rights and prison labor: Seven countries targeted: Cuba, the Maldives, Mauritania, Pakistan, Qatar, Saudi Arabia, United Arab Emirates.

> *Financial Times,* March 5, 1997

33.16 TRADE DEFICITS

The United States is, to an overwhelming extent, the source of its own trade problem.

> EDWARD GUAY, chief economist of the insurance firm Cigna, quoted in *U.S. News & World Report,* September 23, 1985

Our riches are our curse in our attempts to attain a trade balance. If we were less well-off, commercial realities would constrain our trade deficit . . . We are much like a wealthy farm family that annually sells acreage so that it can sustain a lifestyle unwarranted by its current output. Until the plantation is gone, it's all pleasure and no pain. In the end, however, the family will have traded the life of an owner for the life of a tenant farmer.

> WARREN BUFFETT, quoted in the *Washington Post,* May 3, 1987, and reprinted in Janet Lowe, *Warren Buffett Speaks* (Wiley, 1997)

We're faking it. Our living standard isn't being maintained by higher productivity or wages. It's maintained by foreign capital.

> PROFESSOR JEFFREY SACHS of Harvard University, quoted in *Time,* January 30, 1989

The trade deficit is indeed a powerful, albeit misunderstood, term. It reminds me of the story of the high school student who was studying the U.S.-Japan trade situation for his economics class. One evening he turned to his father and said, "Dad, what factors influence the U.S.-Japanese balance of trade?"

His father said, "Well, exchange rate movements, tariffs, comparative advantages, economic recessions or expansions, domestic savings, consumption, government policies . . ."

Cutting him off the boy said, "Look, Dad, if you don't know, just say so."

Today, the U.S. sells roughly as much to Japan as it does to the U.K., Germany, and France combined.

[O]n a per capita basis, the Japanese citizen buys more U.S. products and services than the U.S. citizen buys Japanese products and services: some $550 more for the Japanese compared to $490 for the American.

> TAKAKAZU KURIYAMA, Japanese Ambassador to the United States, in a speech, April 4, 1994

It can be argued that the very concept of a trade balance is an artifact of the past. As long as capital—both human and money—can move toward opportunity, trade will not balance; indeed, one will have little reason to desire such accounting symmetry between nations as between California and New York.

> WALTER B. WRISTON, former CEO of Citicorp, in a speech, January 25, 1993

There is nothing automatically wrong with large trade deficits. As the United States has a full employment economy, the trade deficit is actually a potential inflation safety valve. It is providing the United States with a larger supply of goods at low prices than would be possible if the country depended solely upon domestic manufacturing capacity . . . America's so-called new paradigm economy is a by-product of globalization.

The problem with trade deficits is political, hence the connection between the Asian shocks and fast track. Many Americans perceive the trade deficit to be a source of job losses or slower wage growth, not an inflation brake which permits a stronger and longer expansion in the economy's nontradeable sectors.

> DAVID HALE, Personal View column, *Financial Times*, November 7, 1997

33.17 TRADE BY THE NUMBERS

- In the past decade, the percentage of U.S. GDP tied to trade has doubled.
- Thus far in the 1990s, exports have accounted for a full one-third of all our growth—and every billion dollars in American exports creates an additional 17,000 American jobs.
- At businesses that export, productivity is 30 to 50 percent higher.
- Growth is 3 to 11 percent greater,
- And jobs pay, on the average, 13 percent more.

> C. MICHAEL ARMSTRONG, CEO of the high-tech firm Hughes Electronics Corporation, in a speech, February 11, 1997

33.18 WORLD TRADE ORGANIZATION

Three times the WTO has tried to topple serious global barriers to trade; three times it has failed.

> HELENE COOPER and BHUSHAN BAHREE, *Wall Street Journal*, December 3, 1997

Things never go as far or as fast as we'd like because we've had to take everybody along.

> RENATA RUGGIERO, head of World Trade Organization, quoted in *Wall Street Journal*, December 3, 1996

34.1 THE MIDDLE EAST

In our Western shortsightedness, we think modern history is the 50-year story of the Cold War. That was an interesting, important struggle, but it's only a sideshow compared with the main conflict of the past 1,300 years—the one between Islam and Christianity. We forget that the world contains a billion Muslims who stretch from Morocco on the Atlantic Ocean to the Philippines in the Pacific. Christians number almost 1.9 billion. The two groups have been duking it out since the Middle Ages and will undoubtedly continue to do so for centuries more.

> JIM ROGERS, investor, *Worth,* November 1995

If it is apolitical, well-managed, and focused on the private sector, it will be terrific. But judging by the past, these are huge ifs.

> ANDRE HORAGUIMIAN, director for Middle East and North Africa, IFC (International Finance Corporation, private sector arm of the World Bank), on American proposal for a Middle East Development Bank along lines of the European Bank for Reconstruction and Development, quoted in the *Economist,* November 28, 1995

Economic arrangements cannot be a substitute for political arrangements. And prosperity is going to come from better access to the region's markets and not grandiose projects.

> LEONARD HAUSMAN, director of the Harvard Institute for Social and Economic Policy in the Middle East, quoted in the *Wall Street Journal,* August 9, 1996

34.1.1 Egypt

The government has embarked on a very aggressive privatization program; earnings growth is expected to be very, very good for the next couple of years, and Egyptian stocks look undervalued.

> JEFF CHOWDHRY, manager of the London-managed Foreign and Colonial Emerging Market Middle East Fund, quoted in the *New York Times,* September 14, 1997

34.1.2 Iran

When it comes to calculating budget revenues in hard-currency terms, we do not know which rate of exchange applies to which item, or part item, of revenue.

> Western diplomat, on Iran's balancing of its budget, despite a 35 percent rise, through manipulation of exchange rates, quoted in the *Financial Times,* January 30, 1997

Iran can't modernize its economy without opening itself more to Western business practices and contacts. And if it opens up to the West on that scale, how does it let Dale Carnegie in and keep Madonna out? How does it allow satellite dishes for business and not "Baywatch"?

> THOMAS L. FRIEDMAN, *New York Times,* June 9, 1997

34.1.3 Iraq

This albatross of Iraq has been around our neck since 1990, and I think we've much exaggerated what the ultimate impact will be. Worldwide demand for crude is so strong that in a relatively short period of time we will absorb the Iraqi oil, and it will be no more than another blip.

> ALAN LEVINE of the investment firm Dean Witter Reynolds, quoted in the *Wall Street Journal,* March 19, 1996

34.1.4 Israel

Socialism hasn't worked in Great Britain and it's being abandoned. Socialism hasn't worked in France and it's being abandoned. The same is true in Portugal, Spain, Mexico, Argentina, etc. etc. Even Communist China is privatizing large areas of its economy. No amount of American subsidy for socialism in Israel is going to save the day.

> MURRAY WEIDENBAUM of Washington University, in a speech, September 16, 1992

Megaprojects stir the imagination, and that was necessary in the beginning in order to attract the private sector into the region. But now we need to implement a project, not talk about it.

> ODER ERAN, Israel's deputy director general of economic affairs, quoted in the *Wall Street Journal,* August 9, 1996

I don't remember one quiet year in the last 50 years, but life goes on as normal. One shouldn't mix politics with business.

> ARIEL SHARON, cabinet minister and controversial former general, quoted in the *Wall Street Journal,* October 7, 1996

We have learned from the experiences of other countries that after you privatize a monopoly it is very hard to open the market to competition.

> MRS. TZIPI LIVNI, director general of privatization, on trying to create competition before privatization, quoted in the *Financial Times,* January, 30, 1997

Let's face it: Israel is probably more like Silicon Valley than, say, Iowa or Florida.

> RONI HEFETZ, partner at Walden Israel, an arm of a San Francisco–based venture-capital firm, quoted in *Business Week,* February 3, 1997

In Germany, if you have six engineers with a good idea, they will probably be put into a division or department. But in Israel or Silicon Valley, they will set up their own start-up. It's a mentality that exists . . . in very few other places in the world.

> EFRAIM ARAZI, Israeli chairman of Silicon Valley firm Electronics for Imaging, quoted in *Business Week,* February 3, 1997

No matter how strong the fundamentals are, the peace process still matters. We can't forget that.

> GAD HAKER of the Israeli investment firm Batucha Securities, quoted in the *Financial Times Weekend,* March 15–16, 1997

Many Israelis have emigrated to Silicon Valley to commercially exploit technologies and skills developed working for the military. But the Israeli government is now encouraging would-be entrepreneurs to stay home with tax breaks and R&D grants.

> International Markets report, cited in the *Financial Times,* April 2, 1997

Israel is almost exactly the right size. If a country's too small, there's not enough diversity, and if it's too big, there aren't enough connections between people. There's also an innovative attitude here, a nonconformity in methods which in some senses is undisciplined.

> ED MLAVSKY, president of the Israeli venture-capital group Gemini Capital Fund Management, quoted in the *New York Times,* August 18, 1997

Israelis have a tendency to work fast, to improvise and find solutions. That's the way the state was created here from zero. There's also a lack of business culture here. People don't do things by the book and they're willing to break the rules, which can be an advantage. The lack of a local market has forced people to think globally and create universal products.

> GIL SHWED, founder of Check Point Software Technologies, which creates software based on the military experience of its employees, quoted in the *New York Times,* August 18, 1997

A few years ago, terrorist attacks like the one that happened in Jerusalem would have had a pronounced effect on stocks, particularly those that trade in Israel. The market was less mature, and political risk in stocks was much greater. Now, investors who have invested in the area realize their prospects are more determined by fundamentals within the company and the industry as opposed to the political scene.

> ROBERT GOLDMAN, Israel specialist for the investment firm Josephthal Lyon & Ross, quoted in the *New York Times,* September 14, 1997

34.1.5 Palestine

One of the few advantages in starting from scratch is that you can install one of the most modern computer networks to facilitate transactions. Trading floors are sort of obsolete. We have also had the advantage of learning from other emerging markets, such as Slovenia, or smaller exchanges, such as Canada's Alberta.

> SAFRAN BATAINE, general manager, Palestinian Stock Exchange, Nablus, quoted in the *Financial Times,* February 18, 1997

The Israeli monopolies, especially in cement . . . are preventing the creation of an entrepreneurial class in

Palestine. The effect is twofold: the consumer pays more and the entrepreneur is stuffed by both sides, the Israelis and the Palestinian Authority, acting in collusion.

> KHALED ABDEL SHAFI, economist with United Nations Development Program (UNDP), quoted in the *Financial Times,* May 4, 1997

Politics gives you opportunities. As long as the [Palestinian] situation doesn't deteriorate into all-out chaos and war, the exchange will find its investors.

> JOHN ASANTE of the London investment firm Framlington Emerging Markets, quoted in the *New York Times,* December 7, 1997

34.1.6 Saudi Arabia

Saudi Arabia's problems include . . . government debt that went from zero to $100 billion in a decade . . .

> *Wall Street Journal,* August 8, 1996

The biggest constraint to industrialization is the lack of electrical power.

> ANZAR AHMAD of the Consulting Center for Finance and Investment in Riyadh, quoted in the *Wall Street Journal,* August 20, 1996

Every job filled by a foreigner is considered a temporary job to be filled by a Saudi whenever it is possible.

> DEPUTY LABOR MINISTER YOUSEF TACOUB KENTAB, quoted in the *Wall Street Journal,* September 12, 1996

Under no circumstances do we ever want to mislead a patient or anybody. We were being sensitive to the culture. . . . We did not want to embarrass anybody by asking them to appear in an ad.

> HOLLI BIRRER, spokesperson for Cleveland Clinic, after it was discovered that an ad to attract Saudi patients featured a phony burnoose-clad model and phony copy, quoted in the *Wall Street Journal,* October 7, 1996 (Saudi law didn't require the disclaimer that U.S. law would.)

We tend to think of Saudi Arabia's neighbors as the greatest threat to the kingdom's stability: Yemen, Bahrain, Iran, and Iraq. But it is really other Saudis who are most dangerous. From a safe base in London, Arabian

dissidents hurl bricks at the regime they hate. Meanwhile, Islamic fundamentalists at home cannot forgive the king for embracing anything Western, be it rock music, Coca-Cola, or the invasion of American troops onto sacred Saudi soil during the Gulf War. A third group, the enlightened, modern Muslims, are angry because they want a Western-style democracy.

> JIM ROGERS, *Worth,* November 1995

How can he when a good chunk of government salaries, on which 90 percent of Saudis depend for their living, have not been raised in 15 years?

> Senior banker, on King Fahd's failure to follow through on promises to cut government subsidies, quoted in the *Financial Times,* January, 2, 1997

What will the world do if Saudi Arabia does not maintain 2 million barrels a day of excess capacity. That is what we would like to advertise.

> Senior Saudi oil-ministry official, quoted in the *Wall Street Journal,* October 27, 1997

34.2 AFRICA

I've always thought that underpopulated countries in Africa are vastly underpolluted.

[T]he economic logic behind dumping a load of toxic waste in the lowest wage country is impeccable and we should face up to it.

> LAWRENCE SUMMERS, World Bank's chief economist from 1991 to 1993, memo quoted in Susan George and Fabrizio Sabelli, *Faith and Credit: The World Bank's Secular Empire* (Westview, 1994)

None of these governments have encouraged the development of local savings institutions. They have concentrated on writing 300-page rule books instead.

> MILES MORELAND of international money managers Blankeney Management, quoted in the *Economist,* March 9, 1997

In 1989, under pressure from groups alarmed by the destruction of African elephant herds, President Bush banned the import of ivory. Most of the rest of the world soon followed, and the ivory trade was devastated. The best thinking now is that this was a bad idea, because it destroyed any incentive Africans might have to nurture and protect the elephant herds. A better approach is to make sure that the elephants' human neighbors have a commercial stake—through reasonably regulated hunting and ivory sales—in seeing the herds thrive.

> MICHAEL KINSLEY, *Slate,* August 30, 1996

There is a whole new generation of African leaders coming up. Some have studied abroad. Some have got MBAs. And they are demanding more-open societies.

> HERMAN COHN, former U.S. Assistant Secretary of State for Africa, quoted in the *Wall Street Journal,* December 10, 1996

Most of the 41 countries classified as heavily in debt are in sub-Saharan Africa, including 25 of the 32 countries rated as severely indebted. In 1962, sub-Saharan Africa owed $3 billion. Twenty years later it had reached $142 billion. Today it is about $235 billion—or 76 percent of GNP.

> MICHAEL HOLMAN, FT Guide to: Poor countries' debt, *Financial Times,* September 15, 1997

People who invested in Japan after World War II when it was in ruins were viewed as quite radical, but they made a lot of money. That's the same argument we're making with Africa today.

> CLIFFORD MPARE and JUSTIN BECKETT of the investment firm New Africa Advisers, quoted in *Fortune,* February 19, 1996

If you look at Malaysian companies, they are not investing in Europe or the United States, they are investing in African countries, high-potential countries, where they can transfer their expertise.

> RAPHAEL AUPHAN of the French company Gemplus, which has joint ventures in Kuala Lumpur, quoted in the *International Herald Tribune,* November 4, 1997

34.2.1 Gabon

We believe that when big companies are working in the country, they'll diversify their activities and send a positive signal to other foreign companies.

> MARCEL DOUPAMBY-MATOKA, finance minister of Gabon, quoted in the *Wall Street Journal,* October 3, 1997

34.2.2 Kenya

There is no point in dumping cash [in the form of aid] into countries where there is political oppression. Have you been to Kenya lately?

> MICHAEL MAREN, author of *The Road to Hell: The Ravaging Effects of Foreign Aid and International Charity* (Free Press, 1997), quoted in *Fortune,* November 10, 1997

34.2.3 South Africa

From white and black, rich and poor, I heard the same things; South Africa must improve the living standards of its poorest citizens, but it cannot risk its future with dangerous economic experiments. Whites are resigned to seeing a higher proportion of spending going to black schools; blacks don't expect miracles overnight.

> WALTER RUSSELL MEAD, *Worth,* October 1994

Most of the developed countries would like to see South Africa take off first before they put their money in. But we're prepared to take the risk.

> SAMSUDIN ABU HASSAN, Malaysian investor, quoted in the *Economist,* August 24, 1996

We South Africans tend to think we're the answer to all Africa's problems.

> NICK BINEDELL, director of Witwatersrand University, quoted in the *Economist,* August 24, 1996

For conventional ex-pats, Africa is a period of their lives and then they are gone. But I'm an African, of Africa. South Africa can't grow unless the rest of the continent does.

> GRAEME BELL, director of Standard Bank's Africa division, quoted in the *Economist,* August 12, 1995

I'll try to help you, but for God's sake, man, if you want to do business in Africa, get yourself some black partners.

> VERNON JORDAN, big-time political insider, corporate board member, and Washington lawyer, to McKinsey & Co., which was trying to do business in South Africa, quoted in *Fortune,* November 1, 1993

It has always been my ambition to build the finest hotel in the world.

> SOL KERZNER, South African casino magnate, who spent $280 million to build the resort "Lost City" in

Bophuthatswana, a "black homeland," quoted in the *Economist,* December 5, 1992

I want every black person to feel that he or she has the opportunity to become rich and only has himself to blame if he fails.

> DON MKHWANAZI, black businessman, quoted in the *Economist,* October 25, 1997

I had no idea what a price-earnings ratio was. Not the slightest clue.

> CYRIL RAMAPHOSA, former president of the National Union of Mineworkers, who led a bid for Anglo-American's controlling stake in Johnnic (an industrial group that had been earmarked for black ownership), quoted in the *Financial Times Weekend,* May 24/25, 1997

34.2.4 Tanzania

The Rubicon of reform has been crossed. Government has no business doing business.

> PRESIDENT BENJAMIN WILLIAM MKAPA of Tanzania, which successfully privatized its national brewery, selling a large share to South African investors, quoted in the *Wall Street Journal,* December 10, 1996

34.2.5 Zimbabwe

Zimbabwe is a small country relatively speaking. With a population of about eight million you must be sure a very large proportion of the population is going to use your products or your investment won't reach critical mass.

> RICHARD B. PATTON of Heinz, which had just bought a local company with 75 percent of the soap and vegetable oil market and 50 percent of the margarine market in Zimbabwe, quoted in the *Wall Street Journal,* January 2, 1985

Southern Africa has 10 million people, but if you're selling color televisions you're selling to less than 10 percent of the population. In China you could sell thousands of televisions a month; in Zimbabwe maybe 20 a month.

> A Zimbabwean who was promoting multinational investment in his country, quoted in the *Wall Street Journal,* January 2, 1985

We want to ensure that in the process of privatizing, we do not create greater room for control by those persons who already control the greater part of our economy [referring to 100,000 whites].

> DR. ROBERT MUGABE, president of Zimbabwe, quoted in the *Financial Times,* March 5, 1997

35.1 AMERICANS AND THEIR SAVINGS

Cessation of work is not accompanied by cessation of expenses.

CATO THE ELDER

As long as they [Americans] have an unused credit balance on their Visa card, they think they have money in the bank.

SAMUEL ARMACOST, president of Bank of America, quoted in *U.S. News & World Report,* October 8, 1984

I talk to some of my clients who are down 5 percent this year because of Merck, and you'd think someone had kidnapped their children. When people lose 5 percent while the market is at new highs, they have the sense that money is falling from the sky—and they don't have a bucket.

MIKE STOLPER, a consultant who matches money managers with wealthy investors, quoted in the *New York Times,* September 26, 1993

Very few among them [the middle class] are saving money. Many of them are in debt; and all they can earn for years, is, in many cases, mortgaged to pay such debt . . .

IRA STEWARD, "Poverty," Statistics of Labor (Massachusetts), 1873, quoted in Stuart Ewen, *PR! A Social History of Spin* (Basic Books, 1996)

Between inflation, taxes, and the limitations of corporate compensation systems, [Americans are] not going to have any serious wealth accumulation [by staying with an established corporation], even though they're working themselves to the bone.

DENNIS KRIEGER, executive recruiter, Seider Krieger Associates, quoted in the *Wall Street Journal,* January 23, 1996

The generation that once warned "Don't trust anyone over thirty" is now passing fifty . . . The real question is, Will America grow up before it grows old?

PETER G. PETERSON, chairman of the investment firm The Blackstone Group, who has been warning of the problems the social security system will face as baby boomers retire, quoted in the *Atlantic Monthly,* May 1996

Generation Xers are:

A: Slackers.

B: Savers.

C: More inclined to believe in UFOs than in the future of Social Security.

D: All of the above.

Those who selected "D" may be closest to the truth.

BARBARA WHITAKER, *New York Times,* October 27, 1996

Social security now provides 40 percent of the income for Americans over 65, but its importance drops as incomes rise. Among the poorest fifth of the elderly, it accounts for about 80 percent of income; among the richest fifth, it's only a fifth.

ROBERT J. SAMUELSON, *Business Week,* October 23, 1995

[Important questions raised by proposals to privatize Social Security]

First, will people be free to invest in any sort of asset, as they can through individual retirement accounts? If so, will administrative costs eat up so much of the return, especially on small accounts, that average returns will be low? What will be done in the case of savers who invest unwisely and reach old age with too little to support themselves in retirement?

Second, if choice among investments is limited, who will regulate the investment choices? Who will assure that the elderly can convert their savings into annuities at a fair price?

Third, how large must the tax increases be to make privatization of any kind work and for how long must these tax increases be maintained?

Fourth, how many elderly and disabled people will have to apply for welfare who are spared the necessity to do so by the internal redistribution of the current Social Security system?

HENRY J. AARON, of the liberal think tank Brookings Institution, *Washington Post,* July 21, 1996

Throughout the early decades of this century, Bank of America and its predecessor, the Bank of Italy, ran frequent advertisements exhorting people to save, and warning them—sometimes very strongly—of the consequences of not saving for their retirement years.

One read: "No man ever retired on the money he spent." And another: "Don't let money slip through your fingers." And still another featured a drawing of discouraged and destitute-looking men sitting on park benches under a headline that said: "They didn't save!"

> DAVE COULTER, CEO of BankAmerica, in a speech, September 17, 1996

35.2 AMERICANS AND WEALTH

You Americans are disgusting. You think everything can be solved by money.

> ANATOLY GRIBKOV, former Soviet chief of staff of Warsaw Pact countries, quoted in *Worth*, February 1996

In no other country of the world is the love of property keener or more alert than in the United States, and nowhere else does the majority display less inclination toward doctrines which in any way threaten the way property is owned.

> ALEXIS DE TOCQUEVILLE, *Democracy in America*

It is remarkable how firmly rooted are bourgeois prejudices even in the working class in such a young country.

> FRIEDRICH ENGELS, quoted in Robert Lekachman and Borin Van Loon, *Capitalism for Beginners* (Pantheon, 1981)

The almighty dollar is the only object of worship.

> Anonymous, quoted in *Philadelphia Public Ledger,* December 2, 1836

Let me tell you about the very rich. They are different from you and me.

> F. SCOTT FITZGERALD, "All the Sad Young Men" (1926)

Yes, they have more money.

> ERNEST HEMINGWAY, responding to Fitzgerald, *Esquire,* August 1936

Americans relate all effort, all work, and all of life itself to the dollar. Their talk is on nothing but dollars.

> NANCY MITFORD, *Noblesse Oblige* (Greenwood Publishing Group, 1974)

The economic success of American capitalism has made the average worker into a sober calculating businessman without ideals. All socialist utopias come to nothing on roast beef and apple pie.

> WERNER SOMBART, German economic historian, socialist, and later Nazi sympathizer, in *Why Is There No Socialism in the United States?* (1906), quoted in Robert Lekachman and Borin Van Loon, *Capitalism for Beginners* (Pantheon, 1981)

The simple opposition between the people and big business has disappeared because the people themselves have become so deeply involved in big business.

> WALTER LIPPMANN, in a speech, March 25, 1931, quoted in Ronald Steel, *Walter Lippman and the American Century* (Vintage, 1990)

Americans want action for their money. They are fascinated by its self-reproducing qualities.

> PAULA NELSON, *The Joy of Money* (Stein and Day, 1975)

The notion that Old Money is cleaner than New is patently false: The blood has just had more time to dry.

> RON ROSENBAUM, *New York Observer,* October 21, 1996

Money is the least humiliating of ways that people can feel inferior.

> GORDON WOOD, historian, on why Americans have historically accepted inequality of wealth, quoted in *Forbes,* May 25, 1996

Those who don't like other people should be the most vigorous proponents of prosperity, which is the most effective reducer of birthrates.

> MALCOLM S. "STEVE" FORBES JR., editor in chief and sometime Republican presidential candidate, *Forbes,* June 8, 1996

America is still a place where most people react to seeing a man in a Ferrari by redoubling their own efforts to be able to afford one, rather than by trying to let down his tires.

> *The Economist,* January 3, 1998

35.3 GREED

What kind of society isn't structured on greed?

> MILTON FRIEDMAN, Nobel Prize–winning economist,
> interviewed in *Playboy,* February 1973

[P]lease don't misunderstand me. Greed is essential to the proper functioning of our economic system. Of course, we don't call it greed in polite company. On the supply side we call it hustle or ambition or push and shove. On the demand side, we call it consumerism or, playfully, "shop till you drop." But greed by any name is not something we want to eliminate. It is, after all and for better and worse, the fuel which powers the free enterprise engine.

> WILLIAM A. DIMMA of Royal Lepage, quoted in *Time,*
> November 15, 1989

Greed. Greed. We all have greed. Some days you'd say, "If I could have $5 million, I'd be the happiest person in the world." Then when you've got 5, you'd want 10 and there's nothing wrong with that. I mean, if it's the only thing you live for, then there's something wrong with it. But there's nothing wrong with wanting more.

> WAYNE HUIZENGA, founder of Blockbuster Video,
> *Making of a Blockbuster,* with Gail DeGeorge (Wiley,
> 1996)

My greatest fear is getting bored.

> DAVID GEFFEN, record industry mogul, quoted in
> *Time,* December 12, 1988

Many people have called me greedy because of the way I amassed real estate, companies, helicopters, planes, and yachts during the last several years. But what those critics don't know is that these same assets that excite me in the chase often, once they are acquired, leave me bored.

> DONALD J. TRUMP, *Trump: Surviving at the Top* (Random House, 1990)

Don't get mad. Get everything.

> IVANA TRUMP, cameo in the movie *The First Wives
> Club* (1996)

A luxury once sampled becomes a necessity. Pace yourself.

> ANDREW TOBIAS, *My Vast Fortune* (Random House,
> 1997)

35.4 INHERITED WEALTH AND OTHER UNEARNED INCOME

If you look at the history of great family wealth, very few families have kept their wealth. It's usually wasted by the third generation.

> MICHAEL DOBBS-HIGGINSON, former head of Asian
> operations for the investment bank Merrill Lynch
> and author of *Asia Pacific: A View on Its Role in the
> New World Disorder* (Heinemann, 1994)

Most of us have married rich women.

> CHARLES BIDDLE, formerly of International Flavors
> and Fragrances, explaining why so many individual
> Biddles are so rich, quoted in *Forbes,* October 27,
> 1986

I just don't think people care about old family names anymore. Today money is enough.

> ANNE BIDDLE, then 61, quoted in *Forbes,* October 27,
> 1986

Don't give kids a whole bunch of money. If someone serves them at a restaurant and they don't say thank you, hit them with a shovel.

> H. ROSS PEROT, quoted in *Forbes,* October 26, 1987

My mother gave me everything but an easy act to follow.

> DONALD GRAHAM, on succeeding his mother Katharine at the *Washington Post,* quoted in *Forbes,* May 5,
> 1986

Money you haven't earned is not good for you.

> ROBERT MAXWELL, Czech-born English publishing
> mogul, on why his children wouldn't inherit anything, quoted in *Time,* November 28, 1988 (The
> real reason was that Maxwell, who had built his
> empire on takeovers, debt, excessive leverage, and
> fraud, later killed himself when his crimes began to
> catch up with him and his fortune unraveled; his
> children went on trial for reasons related to his illegal activities.)

People who know how much they're worth generally aren't worth too much.

> NELSON BUNKER HUNT, an heir of oilman H. L.
> Hunt, said this in 1980, quoted in *Time,* November 28, 1988 (In March of 1980, he and a brother

lost most of their money trying to corner the world silver market, and they were eventually assessed $238 million in back taxes and fines.)

All these people who think that food stamps are debilitating and lead to a cycle of poverty, they're the same ones who go out and want to leave a ton of money to their kids.

> WARREN BUFFETT, CEO of the investment firm Berkshire Hathaway, quoted in the *San Diego Union-Tribune*, October 16, 1994

It didn't interest me, from my childhood on, to spend a lot of time in business or making money. . . . My father had the idea that business would be as interesting to me as it was to him. I tried to explain to him a couple of times that it was a little different for him because that was his life and he started from the beginning doing these things.

> PAUL MELLON, philanthropist and heir to the Mellon fortune (made from banking, coal, oil, and other interests), who had given away more than $1 billion through foundations, quoted in *Time*, September 18, 1989

When you inherit money, the world is your best friend.

> GEORGE W. HELME IV of the banking firm Wilmington Trust Company, quoted in the *New York Times*, September 8, 1991

Besides rendering their world unreal, inherited wealth creates a sense of artificial privilege. For many people, this covers over a sense that they aren't really lovable or special in any way.

> MIO FRIEDLAND, psychiatrist, quoted in the *New York Times*, September 8, 1991

You can't take [wealth] with you. As for leaving it all to your kids, is it necessary, is it wise, do you want to drip acid on their heads constantly?

> ROBERT KUOK, Chinese businessman, quoted in *Forbes*, July 28, 1997

Affluent people are clearly torn between giving their children the advantages of wealth and distorting their values.

> JEFFREY MAURER, president of the private banking firm U.S. Trust Company (which has been conducting research since 1993 on the top 1 percent of

wealthiest Americans), quoted in the *Wall Street Journal*, November 22, 1996

35.5 MONEY

Money, like dung, does no good till 'tis spread.

> THOMAS FULLER, M.D., *Gnomologia* (1732)

Money is like manure. If you spread it around, it does a lot of good.

> CLINT MURCHISON, Texas oilman and former owner of the Dallas Cowboys, quoted in the *Wall Street Journal*, January 22, 1985

Anyone who tries to understand the money question goes crazy.

> FRANK VANDERLIP, president of National City Bank (later Citibank) early in the twentieth century

Money is like an arm or a leg—use it or lose it.

> HENRY FORD, interviewed in the *New York Times*, November 8, 1931

In business, the only justice is winning. There is neither clean money nor dirty money. In a capitalistic society, all methods of making money are acceptable.

> DEN FUJITA, who launched McDonald's in Japan as a 50-50 venture partnership with McDonald's Corporation, quoted in the *New York Times*, March 22, 1992 (He is also a best-selling author in Japan; titles include *The Jewish Way of Doing Business, Stupid People Lose Money, How to Blow the Rich Man's Bugle Like the Jews Do, How to Become Number One in Business*.)

What most people don't seem to realize is that there is just as much money to be made out of the wreckage of a civilization as from the upbuilding of one.

> MARGARET MITCHELL, author of *Gone with the Wind* (Scribner, 1936)

Money isn't important, but it's the only way to keep score.

> ANONYMOUS, quoted in Jerry Kramer, *Farewell to Football* (1969)

Money isn't everything, but lack of money isn't anything.

> FRANKLIN P. ADAMS [F.P.A.], quoted in Robert E. Drennan, *The Algonquin Wits* (Citadel Press, 1989)

Money is like a sixth sense without which you cannot make a complete use of the other five.

> W. SOMERSET MAUGHAM, *Of Human Bondage* (1915)

Mammon, *n*. The god of the world's leading religion. His chief temple is in the holy city of New York.

> AMBROSE BIERCE, *The Devil's Dictionary* (1906)

Money is better than poverty, if only for financial reasons.

> WOODY ALLEN, *Without Feathers* (Random House, 1975)

Money couldn't buy friends but you got a better class of enemy.

> SPIKE MILLIGAN, British comedian, *Puckoon* (Viking Penguin, 1976)

The boy with cold hard cash
Is always Mr. Right
'Cause we are living
In a material world
And I am a material girl

> MADONNA, singer, from her song "Material Girl," quoted in the *Financial Times*, September 18, 1997

Since the minting of the first coins on the western coast of what is now Turkey in about 600 B.C., money has been shedding both substance and quality. For 20 centuries, people thought money was money because it had gold or silver in it; in reality, gold and silver were money because they had been used as money for a long, long time.

> JAMES BUCHAN, author of *Frozen Desire: The Meaning of Money*, quoted in the *New York Times*, October 13, 1997

35.6   MONEY AND MOTIVATION

It's generally said and I agree with it, that earning and spending are among the greatest pleasures that men enjoy in this life and it's difficult to say which gives greater pleasure. I myself, who have done nothing for the past 50 years but earn and spend. . . . have had the greatest pleasure and satisfaction from both, and I really think that it is even more pleasurable to spend than to earn.

> GIOVANNI RUCELLAI, Italian *quattrocento* merchant banker whose palace, speckled with his personal insignia of a diamond ring, is now a tourist attraction

Be the business never so painful, you may have it done for money.

> THOMAS FULLER, M.D., *Gnomologia* (1732)

[Andrew] Carnegie exemplifies to me a truth about American money men that many earnest people fail to grasp—which is that the chase and the kill are as much fun as the prize, which you then proceed to give away.

> ALISTAIR COOK, *America* (Random House, 1977)

Something everybody else has and I must get.

> THEODORE DREISER, *Sister Carrie* (Doubleday, 1900)

Of all the possible values of human society, one and one only is the truly sovereign, truly universal, truly sound, truly and completely acceptable goal of man in America. That goal is money, and let there be no sour grapes about it from the losers.

> C. WRIGHT MILLS, *The Power Elite* (Oxford University Press, 1956)

Money, it turned out, was exactly like sex, you thought of nothing else if you didn't have it and thought of other things if you did.

> JAMES BALDWIN, *Nobody Knows My Name* (Dial Press, 1961)

I'm a target every day—why can't I get better pay? [Signs carried by U.S. Secret Service uniformed branch outside the White House]

> Cited in *U.S. News & World Report*, March 23, 1987

I do not love the money. What I do love is the getting of it . . . What other interest can you suggest to me? I do not read. I do not take part in politics. What can I do?

> PHILIP D. ARMOUR (1824–1901), meatpacking magnate and robber baron, quoted in *Forbes*, October 26, 1987

We're not motivated to make more money. We all have too much already. We want to do good work.

> DAVID GEFFEN, record industry mogul, on why he, Steven Spielberg, and Jeffrey Katzenberg decided to form a new entertainment company (Dreamworks), quoted in *Business Week*, October 24, 1994

This is not fun and games. You can have fun when you work, but for me, this is the pursuit of cash. I want to be wealthy.

> ROSS MANDELL, much-investigated stockbroker, quoted in the *Wall Street Journal,* March 14, 1996

I'm not a financial guy—I just make money.

> RICK DEVOS, owner of the Orlando Magic basketball team, quoted in *Sports Illustrated,* March 25, 1996

It's a standing joke among my friends that I don't know how much I make.

> CHARLES M. SCHULTZ, creator of the comic strip *Peanuts,* quoted in *Forbes,* May 25, 1996

To me, the idea of a person as a marionette whose arms and legs start moving whenever you pull the pay string is too simplistic a notion of what motivates people in organizations.

> ROBERT HAAS, CEO of the jeans company Levi Strauss, quoted in *Harvard Business Review,* September–October 1990

[A] player's salary is determined by what coaches see and what I see. What determines his salary is his contribution to winning—not his statistical accomplishments. . . . I've eliminated the statistics of how many points a guy scores. Where did he score them? Did he score them during garbage time? Did he score them when the game was on the line? Did he score them against good opponents?

[O]ne day I said to one of the players, Frank Ramsey, "Ramsey, give them a motivating talk." So he went up to the board and he put down on it, "If you win, $8,000. If you lose, $4,000." And they all broke up.

[T]he biggest motivating force you can have is the championship ring.

> RED AUERBACH, legendary basketball coach, interviewed in *Harvard Business Review,* March–April 1987

I *am* rich.

> CHARLES BARKLEY, basketball player, after being told by members of his family that he shouldn't vote for Republicans because it is a party for rich people

They've taken the fear out of the game.

> DAN JENKINS, sports columnist on the impact of big money on professional golf, quoted in *Forbes,* August 10, 1987

Most rich people just shop.

> ROBERT MAXWELL, Czech-born English publishing mogul (who had built his empire on takeovers, debt, excessive leverage, and fraud and later killed himself when his crimes began to catch up with him), quoted in *Time,* November 28, 1988

The biggest problem the [Professional Golfers Association] Tour faces is to keep the players enthusiastic.

> DEANE BEAMAN, PGA Tour Commissioner, quoted in *Fortune,* August 10, 1987 (Since he had taken charge in 1974, prize money had grown 500 percent.)

2,066,833
Prize money, in dollars, won by Tiger Woods this year, PGA Tour record.

3,000,000
Bonus, in dollars, Titleist gave Woods for finishing atop the money list.

> *Sports Illustrated,* December 8, 1997

I have concentrated all along on building the finest retailing company that we possibly could. Period. Creating a huge personal fortune was never particularly a goal of mine.

> SAM WALTON, founder of the department store chain Wal-Mart, *Sam Walton: Made in America* (Doubleday, 1992)

I was part of that strange race of people, aptly described as spending their lives doing things they detest to make money they don't want to buy things they don't need to impress people they don't like.

> EMILE GAUVREAU, Walter Winchell's editor at the *New York Graphic* from 1924, quoted in Neil Gabler, *Winchell* (Knopf, 1994)

You can do a lot of talking to your employees, and you can buy turkeys at Christmas if that's your hobby, but it isn't going to help you one bit to keep the employee happy. What's going to make the employee happy is what's in the pay envelope at the end of every week when he shakes it. And then the benefit plans.

> THOMAS J. WATSON SR., former CEO of IBM and father of Thomas J. Watson Jr.

He's got them by their limousines.

> A former executive at the international conglomerate ITT, on CEO Harold Geneen's compensation policies

(distinctly more generous than at other corporations), quoted in Robert J. Schoenberg, *Geneen* (Norton, 1985)

We're overpaid by 20 percent on purpose to keep us so frightened we work like rats on a treadmill. [A staffer describing the habituation to an extravagant way of life at the international conglomerate ITT]

Quoted in Robert J. Schoenberg, *Geneen* (Norton, 1985)

People will always work harder if they're getting well paid and if they're afraid of losing a job which they know will be hard to equal. As is well known, if you pay peanuts, you get monkeys.

The late ARMAND HAMMER, chairman of Occidental Petroleum, quoted in *Hammer,* with Neal Lyndon (Putnam, 1987)

To be clever enough to get a great deal of money, one must be stupid enough to want it.

G. K. CHESTERTON

I have never worshiped money and I never worked for money. I worked for pride and accomplishment. Money can become a nuisance. It's a hell of a lot more fun chasin' it than gettin' it. The fun is in the race.

RAY KROC, driving force behind the fast-food chain McDonald's, quoted in David Halberstam, *The Fifties* (Villard, 1993)

Every day I get up and look through the *Forbes* list of the richest people in America. If I'm not there, I go to work.

ROBERT ORBEN, joke writer

I talked to both Bill Gates and Warren Buffett, the two richest men in the country, and they would be inclined to give more if there was a list of who did the giving rather than the having. What difference does it make if you're worth $12 billion or $11 billion? . . . They are fighting every year to be the richest man in the world. Why don't they sign a joint pact to each give away a billion and then move down the *Forbes* list [of the richest people] equally?

TED TURNER, vice chairman of Time Warner, quoted in the *New York Times Magazine,* October 13, 1996

I'd like to be the highest-paid CEO in the world.

RICHARD SCRUSHY, chairman of the HMO chain Healthsource Corporation, quoted in the *Wall Street Journal,* December 4, 1996

Remember, .200 hitters don't win championships. Overpay and get .300 hitters. Just don't hire more of them than you need.

COURTLAND L. LOGUE, Texas entrepreneur, quoted in *Fortune,* July 10, 1996

50,000. Bonus in dollars, Florida coach Steve Spurrier will receive from new five-year, $5 million contract in any year that the Gators win the national title.

16,081. Bonus in dollars, if 80 percent of his players graduate within six years.

Sports Illustrated, October 28, 1996

You need to recognize and reward people without trying to front-end load it too much. The one thing I know through experience—the one absolute thing I know—is that people don't know why they come to work until they don't have to come to work.

H. ROSS PEROT, quoted in *Inc.,* January 1989

People in the village aren't like this, just doing things for money.

HONG XIAOHUI, 18-year-old girl who traveled 1,200 miles to take a job in the Barbie-doll factory, quoted in the *Wall Street Journal,* October 29, 1996

I once asked one of Eisner's key subordinates why Eisner seemed to be interested in amassing so much money. He said he thought that Eisner wanted to amass one of America's great family fortunes, on the order of the Rockefellers, Mellons, and du Ponts.

GRAEF CRYSTAL, *In Search of Excess: The Overcompensation of American Executives* (Norton, 1991)

Somebody said to me, "But the Beatles were antimaterialistic." That's a huge myth. John and I literally used to sit down and say, "Now let's write a swimming pool."

PAUL McCARTNEY, on the TV documentary *The Beatles Anthology,* 1996

They criticize me: "Why's he doing such muck?" To pay for three children in school, for my family and their future.

LORD LAURENCE OLIVIER, actor, quoted in the *Daily Mail* (London), March 28, 1979

A long time ago I said to myself, "Don't ever let yourself be seduced by money. It is nice to have, but it is not that important. Don't ever sell yourself for money, just make some rules for yourself."

> L. M. "BUD" BAKER, chairman of the banking firm Wachovia, interviewed in Charles B. Wendel, *The New Financiers: Profiles of the Leaders Who Are Reshaping the Financial Services Industry* (Irwin, 1996)

The day I'm laid out dead with an apple in my mouth is the day we'll pay commissions. If you pay commissions, you imply that the small customer isn't worth anything.

> BERNARD MARCUS, cofounder and CEO of Home Depot, quoted in *Fortune,* May 31, 1993

To sell oil abroad is simple. You bribe someone in government. But to produce and manufacture something— that takes a lot of talent and work.

> ALEXANDER S. PANIKIN of the Moscow-based textile company Paninter, on why he pays his workers twice the usual $100-a-month salary, quoted in *Business Week,* October 10, 1994

[Money] gives you power and sex. Without money or power, there is very little sex. After all, when a girl says to her friend, "I have a blind date for you," the friend says, "Oh, really? What does he do?" A guy says, "What does she look like?"

> GENE SIMMONS, lead guitarist and singer for the band Kiss, on the relative importance of money, sex, and power, quoted in the *New York Times,* February 23, 1997

I didn't want 99 percent of my wealth tied up with people I didn't like.

> SANDY LERNER, cofounder of the computer firm Cisco Systems, who lost out on billions in stock appreciation because of disagreement with management, quoted in *Fortune,* December 25, 1995

In New York you think of Judas selling out for 30 pieces of silver and want to weep. Poor guy didn't even ask for stock options.

> RUSSELL BAKER, *New York Times,* March 1997

"Salaried employee" does not mean unlimited free overtime.

> "Letter to an ex-boss," *Computerworld,* June 2, 1997

Success on Wall Street isn't an accident. The people who achieve it are very, very bright. But sometimes their goals conceal more substantial issues they haven't addressed. The dream of making a pile of money, for instance, can turn out to be a displacement for something else.

> JAY B. ROHRLICH, Wall Street psychiatrist, quoted in *Forbes,* April 22, 1985

It was not my intention to get rich. My intention was to not be poor.

> SANDY LERNER, cofounder of the computer firm Cisco Systems, quoted in *Forbes,* July 7, 1997

I'm tired of hearing about money, money, money, money, money. I just want to play the game, drink Pepsi, wear Reebok.

> SHAQUILLE O'NEAL, basketball player, after signing a $121 million contract with the Los Angeles Lakers, quoted in *Money Players: Days and Nights Inside the New NBA* (Pocket Books, 1997)

In a survey of 1,000 adults, 46 percent said they would move next door to their in-laws for a 50 percent pay raise.

> *Wall Street Journal,* interactive edition, September 9, 1997

These young kids always believe my goal was to get rich. I say, gang, I was rich 10 years ago, when I was worth a million or two. I can't spend any more than that. My personal goal for the last 10 years has been to grow 100 CEOs like me.

> PATRICK C. KELLY, CEO of Physicians Sales and Service, quoted in *Inc.,* October 1995

People need to choose if the money is worth the risk.

> BILL CECIL, autoworker who made more than $100,000 two years in a row, working seven 12-hour shifts per week, quoted in the *Wall Street Journal,* August 1, 1996

Money is a pure playing field; it's a forum for competition where brains are what anybody brings to the table. For those reasons, it has attracted the best and the brightest who previously didn't enter finance because it was considered crass or vulgar.

> BENJAMIN APPEN of the investment bank D. E. Shaw, quoted in the *Wall Street Journal,* January 5, 1996

People will take a lateral move to get new adventures. These are people who are up all night because they are working on something at home. It's a passion, and more money does not fix the problem.

> LINDA CARLSON, manager in an investment firm, on what motivates people in information technology and software development, quoted in the *New York Times,* October 5, 1997

Show me the money.

> CAMERON CROWE, screenwriter, from the 1996 movie *Jerry Maguire*

35.7 MONEY AND ITS REWARDS

It is the duty of the man of Wealth: First to set an example of modest, unostentatious living, shunning display or extravagance.

> Steel tycoon ANDREW CARNEGIE, "Wealth," *North American Review,* June 1889

The only incurable troubles of the rich are the troubles that money can't cure,
  Which is a kind of trouble that is even more troublesome if you are poor.

> OGDEN NASH, "The Terrible People," *Verses from 1929 On* (Modern Library, 1959)

I wanted to buy the biggest toy on the block.

> JERRY MOORE, Houston shopping center builder, on spending $6.5 million for a 1931 Bugatti, quoted in *Forbes,* July 28, 1986

The only thing I remember about Sid Bass, was that he always wrote with a solid gold pen.

> MARTIN S. GERSTEL, president of Alaza Corporation and former classmate of Sid's at Stanford Business School, quoted in *Business Week,* October 13, 1986

If you're willing to pay for it, they know you're poor: Rich people don't pay for things. Tell them you want it free. Don't be such a loser. Think rich. Call Park Bernet, call the Metropolitan Museum.

> ANDY WARHOL, to a friend complaining about the cost of furniture, quoted in *Forbes,* October 27, 1986

This level of collecting is not about art. It is about the chase, the activity.

The hardest part of my job is screening collectors. They want to buy something they can sell within five years for a lot of money. People trading paintings so quickly is very, very new.

> Art dealer MARY BOONE, on the frenzied art market of the 1980s, quoted in *U.S. News & World Report,* March 9, 1987

I don't think so. I can't think of anything.

> PAUL MELLON, philanthropist and heir to the Mellon fortune, answering the question, "Is there anything in life that gives you more fun than watching one of your horses win?" quoted in *Time,* September 18, 1989

I gulped many times.

> MALCOLM I. GLAZER, chairman of the oil firm Zapata Corp., after paying a record price for a professional sports club, the Tampa Bay Buccaneers football team, quoted in *Business Week,* January 16, 1995

I swallowed hard. This wasn't my original intent. I never thought about owning a team. But by then, I was hooked.

> WAYNE WEAVER, CEO of the shoe manufacturer Nine West, on being asked to invest in the Jacksonville Jaguars football team, quoted in the *New York Times,* January 10, 1997

Owning your own air-force squadron—it's the ultimate high.

> DANIEL LEHNER, American businessman who bought 10 percent of a former Soviet fighter squadron, quoted in *Business Week,* October 7, 1996

I'm a collector of land. I have eight ranches and three plantations. If you have an olive, you want an olive tree. You want a little more. You want the whole tree. Then you want a little this and then a little that.

> TED TURNER, vice chairman of Time Warner, quoted in the *New York Times,* November 24, 1996

Did you know when you pay cash for stuff, you don't have to fill out any forms? You don't have to wait for management approval. You don't have to give out references, your previous address. No paperwork—this is the life.

> OPRAH WINFREY, quoted in *Forbes,* September 21, 1987

We had a small wager, but the outcome did not affect the *Forbes* rankings.

> WARREN BUFFETT, chairman of the investment firm Berkshire Hathaway, after a round of golf with Microsoft CEO Bill Gates, quoted in *Sports Illustrated,* June 16, 1997

Every few seconds it changes—up an eighth, down an eighth—it's like playing a slot machine. I lose $20 million, I gain $20 million.

> TED TURNER, on tracking his portfolio on his desktop PC, quoted in *Newsweek,* June 16, 1997

A lot of people wrote at the beginning of the nineties that the luxury business was dead. The quantity of bullshit that was written during that period!

> YVES CARCELLE, president of the luggage manufacturer Louis Vuitton, quoted in the *New Yorker,* September 22, 1997

Generally speaking, you're born into the book, you marry into the book, or you're proposed by other listees and are required to furnish seconding letters from non-family members currently listed. The application then goes to an advisory committee. A definite number of letters is not required. It's what the letters tell you about the candidate. The question we always ask is "Would you like to have dinner with this person? Would you like to have dinner with this person twice?"

> J. R. WHARTON, Social Register spokesman, quoted in the *Wall Street Journal,* May 7, 1996

In one sense, the businessman justifies to himself why he's spending so much. You're signaling that not only are you successful but, boy, are you busy.

> CLIVE CHAJET, corporate identity consultant, on the fitting of Rolls-Royces with multiple phone lines, faxes, Internet ports, CD-ROM equipment, and computerized navigation systems, quoted in the *New York Times,* October 12, 1997

It costs a fortune to fund projects and for us to be active and publish our paper. There's no other way but to operate within the system.

> CAROLE MARKS, spokeswoman for the Communist Party USA after the party pulled its portfolio from Merrill Lynch in solidarity with striking steel workers at WHX (whose largest shareholder was Merrill Lynch), quoted in the *New York Observer,* August 4, 1997

35.8   MONEY AND SELF-ESTEEM

Greed is all right, by the way. I want you to know that. I think greed is healthy. You can be greedy and still feel good about yourself.

> IVAN BOESKY, arbitrageur, at the University of California, Berkeley, Business School graduation, May 18, 1986 (these remarks, which were preceded by dull platitudes about his rise to fame and wealth, were met with spontaneous applause), quoted in James L. Stewart, *Den of Thieves* (Touchstone, 1991)

35.9   MONEY AND WISDOM

When you earn money like that, the toughest thing in the world is to keep your perspective.

> DEBBIE ZIEGLER, Ginnie Mae trader, age 26, on prevailing Wall Street compensation between $300,000 and $500,000, quoted in *U.S. News & World Report,* February 7, 1983

If you were a jerk before, you'll be a bigger jerk with a billion dollars.

> WARREN BUFFETT, quoted in *Forbes,* April 21, 1997

35.10   PERSONAL PHILANTHROPY

I indulge my messianic fantasies in giving away money that I've already earned. I don't indulge these fantasies in making money. I try to curb my fantasies.

> GEORGE SOROS, *Soros on Soros* (Wiley, 1995)

It takes a certain ruthless ambition to make the world a better place. That is why George Soros and Ross Perot have each in his own way been so successful.

> MICHAEL LEWIS, *New York Times Magazine,* October 13, 1996

It is in the school's hands. I gave it with no strings attached. They used some of it to keep women out of the Citadel.

> TED TURNER, on his gift to his sons' alma mater, a formerly all-male institution, quoted in the *New York Times,* November 24, 1996

My hand shook when I signed the papers because I knew I was taking myself out of the running for the richest man in America.

> TED TURNER, on giving away $200 million to universities and environmental groups, 1996

I've been learning how to give. It's something you have to keep working on, because people like money the way they do their homes and their dogs.

> TED TURNER, after pledging a third of his $3 billion fortune over 10 years to UN-related causes, including land-mine removal, quoted in the *New York Times*, September 20, 1997

I loved the Coca-Cola commercial where all the kids got on the mountaintop and say "We are the world."

> TED TURNER, to Larry King after announcing he would give $1 billion to UN-related endeavors, quoted in the *Financial Times Weekend*, September 20–21, 1997

I never have any regrets about having spent a lot of money trying to make things better.

> GEORGE SOROS, billionaire founder of the Quantum Fund, on problems with his freedom-promoting foundations (ranging from corruption by personnel in Russia to official harassment in Belarus), quoted in the *New York Times*, July 12, 1997

I am not the Salvation Army.

> ROBERT MAXWELL, Czech-born English publishing mogul, quoted in *Time*, November 28, 1988

Giving away money effectively is almost as hard as earning it in the first place.

> BILL GATES, CEO of Microsoft, on why his philanthropies had been rather limited considering the size of his fortune, quoted in the *Economist*, October 25, 1997

I've always believed you do good by doing well. In the past, most of my charitable gifts were to institutions that benefited myself, my quality of life. But I've become more altruistic with age.

> ELIZABETH B. NOYCE, who used her $100 million fortune to capitalize Maine Bank and Trust Company after two Maine banks closed, quoted in *Forbes*, June 22, 1992

There are no pockets in a shroud.

> Irish saying cited by Niall O'Dowd, publisher of the *Village Voice*, to explain $610 million in anonymous gifts by businessman Charles F. Feeny, quoted in *Newsweek*, February 3, 1997

35.11 VALUE

The value of a dollar is social, as it is created by society.

> RALPH WALDO EMERSON, *The Conduct of Life* (1860)

What is a cynic? A man who knows the price of everything, and the value of nothing.

> OSCAR WILDE, *Lady Windermere's Fan* (1892)

Price, *n*. Value, plus a reasonable sum for the wear and tear of conscience in demanding it.

> AMBROSE BIERCE, *The Devil's Dictionary* (1906)

Money is not worth a particular amount. As money it is not worth anything, for it will do nothing for itself.

> HENRY FORD, *My Life and Work* (Doubleday, 1922)

A woman approached Picasso in a restaurant and asked him to scribble something on a napkin and said she would be happy to pay whatever he felt it was worth. Picasso complied and said, "That will be $10,000."
> "But you did that in 30 seconds," the astonished woman replied.
> "No," Picasso said, "It takes 40 years to do that!"

> MARK H. McCORMACK, *What They Don't Teach You at Harvard Business School* (Bantam Doubleday Dell, 1988)

For me, something you don't want to sell you can't put a value on.

> JAMES GOLDSMITH, quoted in Gregory Wansell, *Tycoon: The Life of James Goldsmith* (Atheneum, 1987)

When is $300 billion not a lot of money? . . . It equals 40 years of profit for Exxon. But if it comes from the tobacco industry, well . . . $300 billion is a sum to sniff at.

> DANIEL KADLEC, journalist, *Time*, May 12, 1997

In exchanging art for money, we exchange one abstraction for another.

> DANIEL SPOERRI, artist, quoted in the *New Yorker*, February 18, 1988

We're the ones who turned this useless chemical [the AIDS drug AZT] into useful medicine.

> KATHY BARTLETT of the pharmaceutical company Burroughs Wellcome, makers of AZT, which then cost $8,000 per year, quoted in *Time,* October 2, 1989

Perfectly good Uzbek cotton that had real value—it could be sold on the world market—was made into shirts so ugly and poorly cut that not even Soviet consumers would buy them. Hence all that spinning, weaving, dyeing, cutting, and sewing actually removed value from them.

> EDWARD LUTTWAK, foreign-affairs analyst, quoted in *Slate,* November 13, 1996

People have an amazing sense of perceived value. There's a point, irrespective of how much money they have, where they look at a product and say it's just not worth it.

> KENNETH BARTLEY BOUDRIE, owner of The Bartley Collection (assemble-yourself kits of Chippendale and Queen Anne reproduction furniture), quoted in *Forbes,* July 28, 1986

Embedded in all share prices is a long-term forecast about a company's productivity—that is, its ability to create value in excess of the cost of producing it.

> PROFESSOR ALFRED RAPPAPORT of the Kellogg Graduate School of Management at Northwestern University, *Harvard Business Review,* May–June 1992

Enterprises are paid to create wealth, not control costs.

> PETER F. DRUCKER, "The Information Executives," *Harvard Business Review,* January–February 1995

Yes, a million dollars looks like a lot to some individuals, but in the scope of things, would that amount really have made a difference?

> Spokeswoman for the energy company Petro-Lewis (whose chairman Jerome Lewis took a $1.1 million cash payment in lieu of exercising stock options after declaring a $54 million loss, firing over 1,100 workers, and auctioning off $860 million in assets), quoted in the *Wall Street Journal,* January 22, 1985

I view you like an equity investment.

> RICHARD RAINWATER, founder of the investment firm Rainwater Inc., to Darla Moore, former banker, who became his wife and CEO and who is credited with helping him triple his fortune in three years, quoted in *Fortune,* September 8, 1997 (She fell for him when he uttered this sentence.)

You borrow money at a certain rate and invest it at a higher rate and pocket the difference. It's that simple. [The Goizueta Rule of Investment]

> The late ROBERTO GOIZUETA, CEO of Coca-Cola, quoted in *Fortune,* October 13, 1997

35.12 WORKER INCOME

To quote *The New Yorker*: "The prototypical middle-class American worked for the better part of two decades, during which he or she saw Communism collapse, four presidents occupy the White House, and five San Francisco 49er teams win Super Bowl rings. He or she collected 832 weekly paychecks—the last one for an amount $23 less than the first one."

> DAVE COULTER, CEO of Bank of America, in a speech, December 1, 1995

36.1 ACCOUNTANTS

CEOs don't like to hear a lot of laughter coming from their accounting departments.

> BOB NEWHART, comedian and actor

Would you believe Charles Bronson playing an accountant?

> MINDY ALBUM, secretary to the film producer Dino DeLaurentiis, on why the profession of the main character in the novel *Death Wish* was changed to architect for the movie

Comedians have always had a robust attitude to accountants.

> *The Economist,* October 17, 1992

[*The Hip Accountants' Oath*]

We the hip accountants of America, in order to form a more perfect bank book, do hereby solemnly pledge that the government of the people, by the people, and for the people, is taking too much money from the people. We'd like to keep a little more of that money. Do you mind?

> Comedian MEL BROOKS, from the recording *2000 and One Years* (1961)

[Creative accounting practices] gave rise to the quip, "A balance sheet is very much like a bikini bathing suit. What it reveals is interesting, what it conceals is vital."

> ABRAHAM J. BRILOFF, *Unaccountable Accounting* (Harper & Row, 1972)

Bean counters have always been thought boring; now it seems [in the wake of a rash of cases of prominent frauds at businesses that had been certified shortly before exposure], they are also bad—incompetent and in some cases, corrupt.

> *The Economist,* January 4, 1992

We often have to sell our solutions, tactfully, without saying, "You're wrong."

> BOB McADAMS of the accounting firm Carneiro, Chumney & Co., quoted in *Inc.,* October 1994

Everybody thinks CPAs are boring people, and I think that's true. But the more successful ones are those who don't fit that stereotype.

> JOSEPH DERBA, certified public accountant who used a psychologist to figure out which of his 10 colleagues had personalities lively enough to work with his eccentric clients upon his retirement, quoted in the *Wall Street Journal,* January 24, 1997 (When the inventory showed that he was uniquely colorful, he merged with another firm.)

Accountancy has become one of the most stress-tortured professions in the modern capitalist world.

> JAY NISBERG, accounting industry consultant, quoted in the *Wall Street Journal,* March 10, 1997

[Accounting-consultant firms] are using the audit as a loss leader. Until the firms make the audit an important part of their real service, they will continue to get into trouble.

> MELVYN I. WEISS of the accounting firm Bershad, Hymes & Lerach, quoted in *Business Week,* December 9, 1996

What has to be worked out is how the audit and the tax side [of accounting-consulting firms] can live with making less money.

> GRESHAM BREBACH, head of the consulting firm Knowledge Universe and formerly of Andersen Consulting, quoted in the *Wall Street Journal,* April 23, 1997

Especially in accounting you see a lot of people who are interested only in the technical aspect.

> ERNEST PELLI, accountant for Chemical Bank who was sent to a Dale Carnegie public speaking course "to practice showing interest in other people," quoted in *Fortune,* January 25, 1996

If someone calls [me] with a complicated tax question, in all likelihood they can't handle it anyway. So I'll give them more information than they can possibly understand, because then they've got to come in.

> Tax-preparation firm H&R Block franchise owner, on how the 1997 tax bill would increase his profits, quoted in *Forbes,* September 22, 1997

I kind of view nonclients as clients being held in trust for us by the competition until we get there.

> BARRY R. WALLACH of the accounting firm Arthur Andersen, quoted in the *New York Times,* March 11, 1990

Very often [former employees] will rise into positions of prominence where they'll have the opportunity to be a good friend of the firm. And that might mean the opportunity to do business.

> J. MICHAEL COOK, chairman of the accounting firm Deloitte & Touche, quoted in the *New York Times,* March 11, 1990

It's funny. Even when the accounting firms were pulling back on their own employees' Christmas parties, the alumni parties were still going full swing.

> ROBERT SERIO, a stockbroker at the investment firm Smith Barney who attended a Smith Barney party as a KPMG alumnus, quoted in the *New York Times,* March 11, 1990

Motion-picture accounting is a bag of wind. The way films are amortized is left far too much to the discretion of management, and it's difficult for auditors to challenge their judgment.

> DAVID LONDONER of the investment firm Wertheim Schroeder, quoted in the *New York Times,* July 12, 1992

All the Big Six firms have taken dramatic, aggressive steps to mitigate risk in their client base. A sterling reputation matters more to us more . . . so we no longer have certain clients, and I'm proud of it.

Now, we won't take a client that has fired its previous accounting firm over an accounting dispute because it indicates a greater risk.

> PAT McCONNELL of the accounting firm Coopers & Lybrand, quoted in the *Wall Street Journal,* April 25, 1997

We want to audit the business—not just the financials.

> NICK LAND of the accounting-consulting firm Ernst & Young, U.K., quoted in the *Financial Times,* January 24, 1997

The significance of the accounting profession in the global marketplace is underestimated, particularly in the financial markets of the United States and Europe.

> JIM SCHIRO, "prospective" CEO of the combination of the accounting firms Coopers & Lybrand and Price Waterhouse, quoted in the *Financial Times,* October 3, 1997

36.2 LAWYERS

36.2.1 Business and the Criminal Law

That's usually impossible to prove [that plant managers who fail to correct workplace hazards are murderers], since it involves intent to kill.

> PROFESSOR THEODORE ST. ANTOINE of the University of Michigan, quoted in the *Wall Street Journal,* February 4, 1997

Massachusetts charged the owner of a scrap-metals plant with manslaughter after one worker was pulled into a giant metal-shredder known as the "cyclone" and another was crushed to death by a loading truck. Prosecutors allege in court papers . . . that the owner of the plant . . . ignored warnings to guard the shredder and to fix the truck's failing brakes.

> *Wall Street Journal,* February 26, 1997

36.2.2 Business and the Law

- 47 percent of U.S. manufacturers have withdrawn products from the market.
- 25 percent of them have stopped some form of product research.
- 15 percent have laid off workers in direct response to product deterrence.
- And for all American companies, insurance rates are 20 to 50 times higher than those of their foreign competitors.

This sue-them-all technique has the same effect on small companies as gunboat diplomacy has on small countries: instant capitulation.

> STEPHEN B. MIDDLEBROOK of the insurance firm Aetna Life and Casualty, in a speech, April 28, 1992

To treat accidents as crimes is to transform accidental manslaughter as premeditated murder. It is absolutely certain that Exxon did not run its Valdez oil super-tanker aground off the coast of Alaska with the criminal intention of polluting the water and killing migratory birds. Yet, the Justice Department's criminal indictment assumed that it did.

> PAUL CRAIG ROBERTS of the Center for Strategic and International Studies, in a speech, May 11, 1992

A man had stolen an airplane and transported it across state lines. He was charged under a statute that had been enacted in the early days of the automobile and that criminalized the transportation of "motor vehicles" in interstate commerce. Because it would require guess-work to decide whether Congress intended to include planes as motor vehicles, the Supreme Court [opinion by Oliver Wendell Holmes] reversed the conviction, re-quiring Congress to be clear about what it meant. Con-gress then amended the statute to include airplanes.

> ALAN M. DERSHOWITZ, writing about the conviction of municipal-finance whiz kid Mark S. Ferber (con-victed under a statute whose wording had to be retrofitted to apply), *New York Times*, March 16, 1996

The beverage you are about to enjoy is very hot.

> Warning placed on polystyrene cups in the wake of personal injury lawsuits, cited in the *Economist*, March 30, 1996

Big money doesn't talk. It hires a battery of lawyers.

> ALDOUS HUXLEY

It took about 150 years, starting with a Bill of Rights that reserved to the states and the people all powers not explicitly delegated to the federal government, to pro-duce a Supreme Court willing to rule that growing corn to feed to your own hogs is interstate commerce and can be regulated by Congress.

> DAVID FRIEDMAN, *The Machinery of Freedom* (Open Court Publishing, 1989)

The decade of the '80s will be remembered as the one in which judges forged the idea that employees have a property interest in their jobs.

> PROFESSOR WILLIAM GOULD, Stanford Law School, quoted in the *Economist*, July 18, 1987

These [liability against the tobacco industry] cases are going to make the O. J. Simpson trial look like a 100-yard dash.

> PROFESSOR JOHN F. BANZHAF III, of George Wash-ington University and Action on Smoking and Health (ASH), quoted in *Governing*, December 1, 1995

State College, Pa.—A student at Penn State University has complained that a student she hired to take a test for her breached a contract by failing the exam . . . The woman asked the police to help her get back a $1,200 stereo she said she had given the student as payment.

> *Chronicle of Higher Education*, cited in *Fortune*, July 12, 1993

36.2.3 Expert Witnesses

Without experts, I am out of the game.

> BRUCE KASTER, plaintiff lawyer who specializes in car tire suits, quoted in the *Wall Street Journal*, June 17, 1997

The climate is real tough right now. You can make a liv-ing, no question, but you do not get filthy rich.

> JACK THRASHER, anatomist, who has appeared on behalf of plaintiffs in various chemical-exposure suits, quoted in the *Wall Street Journal*, June 17, 1997

My basic premise is that jurors can understand science if you take the time to explain it to them.

> DAVID BERNICK, litigator, quoted in "Fatal Litigation Part 2," *Fortune*, October 30, 1995

A St. Petersburg–area elementary school teacher with two prior DUI convictions was arrested again last year on charges of driving under the influence and leaving the scene of an accident. But Frank Vasey, a rheumatol-ogist who regularly testifies for breast implant plaintiffs, offered an "expert" opinion that she wasn't drunk. In-stead, he says, she was suffering from "silicone poison-ing"—even though her silicone implants were removed a year before the accident. The local school board bought this novel explanation, and last week the teacher returned to work.

> *Wall Street Journal*, November 22, 1996

36.2.4 Intellectual Property

The people who make decisions about where to locate R&D centers grew up in an era when the Japanese were knocking off cameras. But given both the importance of the Japanese customer and Japan's increasing dominance in so many technologies, the astonishing thing is that more American companies do not see the necessity of doing R&D in Japan.

> JOHN P. STERN of the Tokyo office of the trade group United States Electronics Association, quoted in the *New York Times,* April 28, 1991

. . . Americans were amused in the aftermath of World War II when Japanese businessmen with their cameras were ubiquitously touring U.S. factories. They are no longer amused. Few will let Third World visitors into their plants.

> PROFESSOR LESTER C. THUROW of the Sloan School of Management at MIT, *Harvard Business Review,* September–October 1997

We used to laugh at them [the Japanese who visited Ford plants in the early 1960s]. This is the absolute truth. We used to think that they were not all there.

> DICK MORRISETT of Ford Motor Company, quoted in Mary Walton, *Car* (Norton, 1997)

By going to California, they are trying to be more creative, trying to meet American entrepreneurs and develop alliances with them to make new products. Or maybe they have given up on their own creativity.

> TAKESHI NAKABAYASHI of Japan Development Bank's venture-capital unit, quoted in the *New York Times,* October 9, 1997

The crime of the twenty-first century [selling counterfeit products].

> JIM MOODY, head of the organized crime and drugs section of the FBI, quoted in *Fortune,* May 27, 1996

Most police go into law enforcement to fight the bad guys, and it's hard to get excited over a bunch of hard-working T-shirt counterfeiters.

> VINCENT VOLPI, former police detective and president of Professional Investigating & Consulting Agency, quoted in *Fortune,* May 27, 1996

We refer to some countries in Asia as one-disk markets. More than 99 percent of the software is illegitimate copies.

> ANNE MURPHY, lawyer for Microsoft, quoted in *Fortune,* May 27, 1996

Given the increasing value of intangible assets like know-how in the information age, there has been a significant amount of recent litigation where corporations, which are vitally interested in protecting their trade secrets, are willing to take their assets to court.

> EUGENE DRIKER, lawyer for Dow Chemical in suit against GE for hiring 14 of its employees, quoted in the *Wall Street Journal,* April 2, 1997

We want to be asked permission to use our work.

> JONATHAN TASINI, president of the National Writers Union, which sued Mead Data, the *New York Times,* and other large companies for reproducing articles in electronic form without paying, quoted in *Business Week,* January 10, 1994

If the economy is a bed of hot coals, companies won't have time to fashion protective footwear [patent protection] anymore. They'll have to plunge in barefoot and just move like hell before the heat catches up with them.

> PROFESSOR CONNIE BAGLEY of Stanford University, quoted in *Inc.,* October 1996

[T]hey took our music and gave you Pat Boone instead of Little Richard. The attitude was "Get the publishing rights and give the nigger a Cadillac." In the end it's about ownership.

> SPIKE LEE, who started the advertising agency Spike DDB in 1996 with DDB Needham, quoted in *Forbes,* April 21, 1997

You claim you own Casablanca and that no one else can use that name without their permission. What about Warner Brothers—do you own that, too? You probably have the right to use the name Warner, but what about Brothers? Professionally, we were brothers long before you were.

> GROUCHO MARX, in a letter to Warner Brothers, responding to a warning that the title of a prospective movie, *A Night in Casablanca,* would infringe the title *Casablanca,* cited in the *New York Times,* October 12, 1997

36.2.5 Law by the Numbers

There are 279 lawyers per 100,000 population in the United States, versus 114 in Great Britain, 77 in West Germany, 29 in France, and 11 in Japan.

> RICHARD D. LAMM, former governor of Colorado, in a speech, October 1, 1988

Our nation's tort bill is running in the neighborhood of $100 billion a year, an amount greater than the combined annual profits of America's 200 largest corporations.

> RANDALL L. TOBIAS, CEO of the pharmaceutical firm Eli Lilly, in a speech, April 1, 1997

36.2.6 Law and the Profit Motive

Greed vs. greed makes for the kind of lawsuits that are settled between the lawyers as soon as both sides decide to take what they can get. Principle vs. principle is a holy war, and no holy war has ever been settled out of court.

> BILL VEECK, *Thirty Tons a Day* (Viking, 1972)

That's the nature of our business. Cancer might have a very different price in a small town in Iowa than in Manhattan, New York City.

> LARRY CHARFOOS, lawyer, on differences in settlements for women whose mothers had taken the drug DES, quoted by Michael Kinsley, *New Republic,* June 14, 1980

The notion that [a blue-chip law firm] is not interested in profit is ridiculous. What lawyers really fear is competition.

> JOEL Z. HYATT, pioneer of standardized legal services, quoted in *Business Week,* January 26, 1987

If I'm a plaintiff's lawyer sitting in my office, and you walk in and describe your case to me, the first thing on my mind is, "Will I get a fee for it?" Bear in mind that the individual is most likely to be out of work and probably can't afford my fee. Unless there is the possibility of a substantive recovery, it doesn't pay to take the case.

> MARTIN PAYSON, lawyer, quoted in *Inc.,* April 1994

Wednesday 4/17/91, to Friday 4/19/91
Trip to New York City for *Phil Donahue* show; King offered several quotations to use on air. Conferred with Donahue staff regarding format of show, taping. Taped show. Returned to California. 20 hours, $16,500.

Wednesday 5/29/91
King arrested with transvestite and charged with running over LAPD vice squad officer in Hollywood. Damage control. All forms of media were now whipped into feeding frenzy; I tried to tie King arrest to LAPD harassment of King in beating case. 12.25 hours. $3,981.25

Monday 5/4/92
Appeared on *Oprah*. 3 hours. $975

> From itemized million-dollar-plus bill submitted October 1994 by Steve Lerman, attorney for Rodney King, *Harper's,* April 1995 (L.A. taxpayers were liable for his legal bills because King won his civil suit. The judge disallowed all but $221,000 related to "the purposes of obtaining a favorable result for Mr. King.")

Tort lawyers are capitalists, too, and they are going where the money is. It seems to me that when the monetary damages are smaller, plaintiffs' lawyers will find themselves less zealous in their pursuit of what they call justice.

> DEAN O'HARE, CEO of the insurance firm Chubb, in a speech, October 1995

Back in 1977, we thought that $170,000 was a lot of money.

> RICHARD MITHOFF, lawyer, on settlement of his first case against a maker of silicone breast implants, quoted in Joseph Nocera, "Fatal Litigation Part 1," quoted in *Fortune,* October 16, 1995

I could hear the angels sing and the cash register ring.

> MELVIN BELLI, litigator, after a weeping client who was suing a surgeon for a botched operation removed her blouse and bra on the witness stand on his orders, revealing her disfigured breasts, quoted in Belli's obituary, *The Economist,* July 20, 1996

Law firms are making a living doing nothing more than objecting to class-action suits.

> ALEXANDER MOORE, lawyer representing investors objecting to proposed settlement of a class-action suit, quoted in the *Wall Street Journal,* January 10, 1997

A lawyer starts as an advocate and ends as an adversary [when final bills are due].

> TIM KORANDA, former stockbroker and advertising writer, in a speech, June 10, 1997

I have a hunch that this attempt to prevent us from using the title [*A Night in Casablanca*] is the scheme of some ferret-faced shyster serving an apprenticeship in the [Warner Brothers'] legal department. I know the type—hot out of law school, hungry for success and too ambitious to follow the natural laws of promotion, this bar sinister probably needled Warner's attorneys, most of whom are fine fellows with curly black hair, double-breasted suits etc. in attempting to enjoin us.

> GROUCHO MARX, in a letter to Warner Brothers, responding to a warning that the title of the prospective movie, *A Night in Casablanca,* would infringe the title *Casablanca, New York Times,* October 12, 1997 (The film was made in 1946.)

This just reflects the fact that we are in a business and this is just another opportunity that comes along.

> PAUL RHEINGOLD, lawyer, founder of the Fen-Phen Litigation Group, formed to handle class-action suits over diet pills that were withdrawn from the market because they cause heart-valve problems, quoted in the *Wall Street Journal,* October 24, 1997

Juanita Madole, aviation plaintiff attorney, testified that in the USAir 427 crash [near Pittsburgh in September 1994], over 60 families were called by an attorney's representative posing as a survivor of prior airline crashes and advocating the attorney's work.

> From an article about post-crash policy in the wake of the TWA flight 800 investigation, *New York Times,* November 23, 1997

What we do is determined by who pays us.

> LAWRENCE JOSEPH, *Lawyerland* (Farrar, Straus and Giroux, 1997)

36.2.7 Legal Ethics

We were doing our job. If the Nazis sent you to the concentration camp, there's nothing wrong with you; there's something wrong with the Nazis.

> PETER FISHBEIN of Kaye, Scholer, Fierman, Hays & Handler (the law firm fined $41 million in 1992 to settle allegations that it concealed crucial informa-

tion about Lincoln Savings and Loan, a prominent player in the savings-and-loan crisis of the 1980s), quoted in the *Wall Street Journal,* August 22, 1997

36.2.8 Legal Language

Legal phraseology should be considered red flags: Lawyers can draw from a litany of words, terms, and phrases which are intended to reverse the meaning of everything that comes before or after.

> MARK H. McCORMACK, *What They Don't Teach You at Harvard Business School* (Bantam Doubleday Dell, 1988)

36.2.9 The Legal Mind

A legal mind can think about something that is related to something else without thinking about the thing to which it is related.

> PROFESSOR THOMAS REED POWELL, Harvard Law School

36.2.10 Litigation

Litigation, *n.* A machine which you go into as a pig and come out of as a sausage.

> AMBROSE BIERCE, *The Devil's Dictionary* (1906)

Law is a bottomless pit.

> *The History of John Bull* (1712)

I have always noticed that any time a man can't come and settle with you without bringing his lawyer, why, look out for him.

> WILL ROGERS, *The Autobiography of Will Rogers* (Chicago, 1921)

36.2.11 Securities Laws

Patch, patch, patch. Each statute is a little different, with a curlicue here and a curlicue there. It means that there are a great many questions that are litigated which ought not to be.

The Supreme Court has considered what is a security ten times. That is remarkable. It is also wasteful.

> LOUIS LOSS, professor emeritus at Harvard Law School, quoted in the *New York Times,* September 26, 1993

36.2.12 Tort System Run Amok

Voltaire once said of the Holy Roman Empire that it was neither holy, nor Roman, nor an empire. The same might be said of the civil justice system in the United States: that it is neither civil, nor just, nor a system.

> STEPHEN B. MIDDLEBROOK of the insurance firm Aetna Life and Casualty, in a speech, April 28, 1992

A psychic conducted a series of séances at which John Milton regularly participated, speaking through her. However, when Milton fell silent, she determined that her psychic powers were being blotted out by a dye used in a CAT scan. She sued her doctor for impairing her ability to make a living. The jurors returned an award of $986,000.

> GEORGE S. SPINDLER of the oil firm Amoco, in a speech, October 24, 1995

A friend of mine had a paraplegic case against Exxon at the same time [I had a case on the death of a bull]. I told him, "I'll get more for my dead bull than you'll get for your paraplegic." And I did. [$8.5 million]

> JOHN O'QUINN, Houston lawyer, quoted in Joseph Nocera, "Fatal Litigation Part 1," *Fortune,* October 16, 1995

The mass tort industry derived its strength from raw numbers, not from evidence or science. If plaintiff lawyers could create enough parallel litigation—if they could scare thousands of clients into filing thousands of lawsuits—then the strength or weakness of the actual cases would be rendered nearly irrelevant.

> JOSEPH NOCERA, writer, "Fatal Litigation Part 2," *Fortune,* October 30, 1995

America is in the midst of a new civil war, a war that threatens to undercut the civil basis of our society. The weapons of choice are not bullets and bayonets, but abusive lawsuits brought by an army of trial lawyers subverting our system of civil justice while enriching themselves.

> GEORGE McGOVERN, former U.S. senator and Democratic presidential candidate, quoted in *Worth,* September 1996

[A Chrysler lawyer] has a running file of lawyer jokes. It's 17 pages long, and there are almost two hundred. . . .
    A woman was killed in a car accident. (That's a tragedy—the joke comes later.) A trailer hitch fell off a vehicle and started a chain reaction that ended in the woman's death. Her estate sued Chrysler. The car she was driving was not one of ours. The truck that hit her was not one of ours. The trailer hitch did fall off a Jeep, but the hitch itself was not one of ours. The original factory-installed towing bar had been removed and . . . replaced by a trailer hitch bought at a flea market!
    Here comes the joke . . . A jury hit us with an $8.8 million verdict! It was obviously another case of "find someone to sue." And whoever heard of suing a flea market?

> ROBERT J. EATON, CEO of the auto company Chrysler, in a speech, August 6, 1996

Latrell [Sprewell] has the fortitude and the state of mind and the determination to have brought this suit because he believes he's right, he believes he will be vindicated in the end through the judicial process.

> ROBERT THOMPSON, attorney for a professional basketball player who choked his coach and then sued his team and the league for $30 million, alleging excessive punishment and civil rights violations, quoted by the Associated Press, May 21, 1998

Question: Was that the same nose you broke as a child?

Question: What happened then?
Answer: He told me, he says, "I have to kill you because you can identify me."
Question: Did he kill you?

Question: Mrs. Jones, do you believe you are emotionally stable?
Answer: I used to be.
Question: How many times have you committed suicide?

> Questions and answers taken from U.S. court records, published in *Dear Abby,* syndicated column.

The ratio of overall punitive damage award assessed against Capital Cities–ABC Inc. to the compensatory damage award is approximately 2,857 to one. A ratio of 2,857 to one is certainly suspect.

> U.S. DISTRICT JUDGE CARLTON TILLEY in a ruling, reducing a $5.5 million jury award (for a hidden-camera exposé accusing the grocery chain Food Lion of selling rat-gnawed cheese and rotting meat) to $315,000, *Wall Street Journal,* August 29, 1997

According to the National Association of Manufacturers, the number of tort cases in the United States has tripled in the last 30 years. And that's five times faster than criminal cases.

And what are the costs [of liability to the consumer]? An estimated $130 billion annually. Or, put another way, 30 percent of the price of a step ladder, 33 percent of the price of a general aviation aircraft, 50 percent of the cost of a football helmet, and 95 percent of the price of a childhood vaccine.

> EARNEST W. DEAVENPORT JR., CEO of Eastman Chemical Company, March 11, 1997

Product liability is largely a United States problem for Du Pont. The company has fewer than 20 lawsuits outside the United States, but nearly 5,000 personal injury lawsuits in the United States. In 1995, slightly more than half of the company's sales came from outside the United States; however, 95 percent of Du Pont's legal costs are incurred in the United States.

> Attributed to Du Pont web site, cited by Earnest W. Deavenport Jr., CEO of Eastman Chemical Company, March 11, 1997

Missouri was America's number one plaintiff's venue in 1995. Of the six largest jury verdicts in the country that year four came from Missouri. [Missouri is referred to as the "sue-me state."]

> ELLIOT M. KAPLAN, lawyer, quoted in the *Wall Street Journal*, February 26, 1997

At most they [neighborhood residents] suffered 36 hours of inconvenience.

> BRENT BARRIERE, lawyer for five transportation companies fined $3.5 billion for a 1987 New Orleans rail-yard fire (the damages were 10 times the payout from the 1989 Bhopal toxic gas leak, which killed 3,000 people), quoted in the *New York Times*, September 10, 1997

These scoundrels, they [companies responsible for rail-yard fire mentioned above] took the position that there's nobody back there worth caring about, they're all black, they're all poor, and nobody cares about them. If it was your family out there, would you feel the verdict was outrageous?

> WENDELL GAUTHIER, New Orleans plaintiff attorney for the same case, quoted in the *New York Times*, September 10, 1997

We've learned that any commodity sold in prisons becomes a target for lawsuits.

> THOMAS M. KELLER, lawyer for the plastics firm BIC, after a lawsuit about its lighters, quoted in *Business Week*, February 7, 1994

36.2.13 Tort System—On the Other Hand

If we don't trust juries, we don't trust democracy and we don't trust ourselves.

> NANCY SMITH, plaintiff lawyer, quoted in *Inc.*, April 1994

Joint and several liability is a powerful solution to a pervasive problem: that people sometimes cook their books. By making auditors consider the full costs of their efforts, it encourages them to approach every audit with a healthy sense of terror.

> *The Economist*, December 16, 1995

We're not concerned about whodunit. We're asking who knew or ought to have known.

> HARVEY STROSBERG, lawyer for shareholders of the gold-mining firm Bre-X, suing JP Morgan and other financial advisers to Bre-X (which salted mines in Indonesia and defrauded investors), quoted in the *Financial Times*, October 17, 1997

36.2.14 What People Think of Lawyers

Three Philadelphia lawyers are a match for the devil.

> Early-nineteenth-century popular saying

I don't want a lawyer to tell me what I cannot do; I hire him to tell me how to do what I want to do.

> J. PIERPONT MORGAN, founder of the banking firm JP Morgan

It is most advisable for the businessman to have legal knowledge or sound legal advice.

> "Legal Developments Significant in Business," *Harvard Business Review*, April 1927

A good lawyer, a bad neighbour.

> BENJAMIN FRANKLIN, *Poor Richard's Almanack*

Lawyers and painters can soon change white to black.

> Danish proverb

My advice to the public is never, never, never under any circumstances engage the services of a lawyer who advertises.

> U.S. SUPREME COURT CHIEF JUSTICE WARREN BURGER, in a speech, July 22, 1985

If the legal profession needed a wake-up call, it got it last summer when a prominent local brewing company presented a television advertisement showing a rather portly attorney coming out of a rodeo chute and being lassoed by a cowboy as the crowd cheered.

> PETER M. GERHART, dean of Case Western Reserve Law School, in a speech, January 28, 1994

I used to be a lawyer. Now I call myself a "humor consultant." Whether or not you think the world needs a humor consultant, you have to agree it could use one less lawyer.

> MALCOLM KUSHNER, speaker for hire, quoted in *Inc.,* August 1994

We're aware of the black-hat image tobacco has, so we've been super careful. We know we're under a microscope.

> DAVID K. HARDY, co-chair of the tobacco group at Snook, Hardy & Bacon, quoted in *Business Week,* September 5, 1994

Lawyers make appointments. We knock on doors.

> PHILIP H. STERN, managing director of the private investigators Fairfax Group, quoted in the *Wall Street Journal,* October 24, 1996

A survey conducted . . . showed that . . . more than 22 percent of respondents—one in five—said that they currently have no respect for lawyers. As a point of reference, when asked the same question about accountants, only 3 percent voiced no respect.

> JEFFREY N. HERMAN and SCOTT L. BERMAN of Decision Research, a division of Mercer Management Consulting, quoted in *Marsh & McLennan Companies Viewpoint,* Winter 1996

36.3   MANAGEMENT CONSULTANTS

[Definition of management consulting] Telling a company what it should already know.

> *The Economist,* September 12, 1987

Just as Lenin predicted the outbreak of World War I three years after it happened, management gurus are forever prophesying a future that arrived yesterday.

> JOHN MICKLETHWAITE and ADRIAN WOODRIDGE, *The Witch Doctors: Making Sense of Management Gurus* (Times Books, 1996), quoted in the *Wall Street Journal,* November 8, 1996

A prince who is not himself wise cannot be wisely advised . . . good advice depends on the shrewdness of the prince who seeks it.

> MACHIAVELLI, *The Prince*

The best servants of the people, like the best valets, must whisper unpleasant truths in the master's ears. It is the court fool, not the foolish courtier, whom the king can least afford to lose.

> WALTER LIPPMANN

The world is filled with people who are anxious to act in an advisory capacity.

> CHARLIE BROWN, *Peanuts* cartoon character, surrounded by his baseball team, all of whom are telling him what to do, cited by Professor J. Sterling Levinson of Harvard Business School, *Harvard Business Review,* January–February 1971

The world is also full of people who are seeking advice.

> TIMOTHY J. STURM of the insurance company Chubb & Sons, Inc., responding to Professor J. Sterling Levinson, *Harvard Business Review,* January–February 1971

The insights [I] delivered [as a management consultant] were sometimes impractical. I was probably batting 25 percent to 30 percent on an implementation rate.

> FRANCIS GOUILLART of Gemini Consulting, quoted in *Business Week,* July 25, 1994

The United States has a vast oversupply of consultants. Many of them succeed not on the basis of what they know, but by loudly trumpeting their wondrous, easy-to-swallow potion.

> GEORGE BAILEY of the accounting firm Price Waterhouse, quoted in the *Wall Street Journal,* September 30, 1996

If you initiate a project on your own and it succeeds, well, that's your job. If the program fails, it's your neck.

However, if you hire a consultant and the project succeeds, it's a feather in your cap. If the project fails, you have the consulting firm to blame. After all, they're the experts.

> CHARLES F. YARHAM, president of Industrial Handling, Inc., in a letter to the editor, *Fortune*, November 29, 1993

[*Questions to ask consultants before retaining them*]

1. What specific approach do you use to improve and how does it differ from the approaches of other consultants?
2. What specific examples do you have of savings on prior jobs? Where did they come from? How did you get them?
3. How did you get paid? Do you want the bulk of the fee up front or after the savings start coming in?

> HANK McHALE, CEO of GO/DAN Industries, *Actual Experiences of a CEO* (Irwin, 1995)

A consultant is an individual handsomely paid for telling senior management of problems about which senior management's own employees have told the consultant. The consultant thus offers the advantage of generally having had no firsthand experience in the matters of interest, thereby assuring a clear mind uncluttered by any of the facts.

> NORMAN R. AUGUSTINE, CEO of the aerospace firm Lockheed Martin, *Augustine's Laws* (Viking, 1986)

Most management books should not be tossed aside lightly; they should be hurled against the wall with great force.

> PROFESSOR MICHAEL HAMMER, quoted in *Hemispheres*, United Airlines' in-flight magazine, December 1996

Can anyone remember the last time a McKinsey or Boston Consulting Group report analyzed a corporation and recommended the wholesale firing of top management?

> BRUCE NUSSBAUM of *Business Week*, in the *New York Times Book Review*, January 12, 1997

Many consultants are more interested in the problem than they are in the solution.

> An anonymous former consultant and current CEO of a *Fortune* 500 company, quoted in *Fortune*, October 14, 1996

There are basically three kinds of consultants in the world: minders, grinders, and finders.

> An anonymous former consultant (who describes *grinders* as those who solve one kind of problem very well but can't do anything else, *minders* as those who lead the teams and provide most of the value, and *finders* as rainmakers who talk a good game but get bored), quoted in *Fortune*, October 14, 1996

All of us [consultants] sort of slide in behind whoever is the hero du jour—a Colin Powell or a Thatcher, who can get $75,000 a speech. You pray for a war so Schwarzkopf will boost the market up 15 percent.

> TOM PETERS, management guru, quoted in *Fortune*, October 14, 1996

A consultant is a person who takes your money and annoys your employees while tirelessly searching for the best way to extend the consulting contract.

> SCOTT ADAMS, creator of the cartoon strip *Dilbert*, quoted in the *Economist*, March 22, 1997

Other people's problems are our opportunities and there's a bull market in problems at the moment.

> LOWELL BRYAN of the consulting firm McKinsey & Co., quoted in the *Economist*, March 22, 1997

Consultants have had a ball in Britain, where management has been relatively unprofessional and not very system driven. French executives tend to be dismissive [of consultants], considering them as thickos, trying to sell them gross oversimplifications.

> PETER LAWRENCE of Britain's Loughborough University and co-author of *Management in France* (Cassell, 1997), quoted in the *Financial Times*, April 11, 1997

One thing that the management industry deserves to be flagellated for repeatedly is that it so often sells its ideas as permanent solutions.

> JOHN MICKLETHWAIT and ADRIAN WOOLDRIDGE, *The Witch Doctors* (Times Books, 1996)

It is demoralizing to work with consultants who get paid more than you, never work overtime . . . and do not share the on-call duties. When vacancies go unfilled, that tells me the company is not paying enough for the expertise, which means I am underpaid.

> "Letter to an ex-boss," *Computerworld*, June 2, 1997

37.1 THE MEDIA

On the whole and over time, your company usually gets the publicity it deserves. But it can be a bumpy ride, because news is only "news" if it's different from the last story.

> ROBERT T. GILBERT, PR adviser, quoted in the *Wall Street Journal,* June 17, 1996

I have observed that newspaper publicity is usually followed by a jail sentence.

> NICK THE GREEK, gambling handicapper

Political reporters [during the presidential campaign] didn't understand economics, and they didn't want to try. Their arrogance was amazing. TV was the worst.

> GRETCHEN MORGENSON, publisher and presidential candidate Steve Forbes's former press secretary and editor at *Forbes,* quoted in *Business Week,* November 11, 1996

It's always dangerous to give interviews.

> STEVEN JOBS, at a press conference after he had sold his computer firm NeXT to Apple (at which it was pointed out that he had recently said Apple was dead in the water), quoted in the *Wall Street Journal,* December 23, 1996

It is the *Journal's* policy to engage brains as well as to get the news, for the public is even more fond of entertainment than it is of information.

> WILLIAM RANDOLPH HEARST, in an editorial on the first anniversary of the *New York Journal,* November 2, 1896, on its practice of sensationalizing the news to sell papers, quoted in W. A. Swanberg, *Citizen Hearst* (Scribner, 1961)

The reason they call television a medium is that it's neither rare nor well done.

> FRED ALLEN, American humorist

I suggest that pay-TV entrepreneurs examine introductory offers from sports promoters as cautiously as if they were come-ons from Mephistopheles or a heroin dealer.

> Memo written by a Time Inc. executive on the board of Sterling Manhattan Cable in 1971, responding to a

proposal by Chuck Dolan, for something called the Green Channel, to offer sports and movies on pay TV (this became HBO), quoted in *The World of Time Inc.* (Curtis Prendergast, 1986)

Television is moving rapidly from the sound bite to the sound buck.

> RALPH NADER, heard on National Public Radio, October 7, 1996

I'm quite worried about reading. But I worry more about the quality of our education system than about whether entertainment is a big negative factor in our country's reading habits.

> GERALD M. LEVIN, CEO of the media conglomerate Time Warner, quoted in *Business Week,* March 14, 1996

People need to get out of their homes. Kids need to get away from their parents, the parents away from the kids.

> MICHAEL D. EISNER, CEO of Disney, quoted in *Business Week,* March 14, 1996

On May 9, 1961, then FCC chairman Newton Minow. . . . said, "I invite you to sit down in front of your television set when your station goes on the air. Stay there without a book, magazine, newspaper, or profit and loss sheet to distract you . . . and keep your eyes glued to that set until the station signs off. I can assure you," he said, "that you will observe a vast wasteland."

. . . With my PC and the Internet, I can get my first choice of interactive digital information and entertainment, whenever I want it, no matter where in the world I happen to be. What's more, the PC and the TV are coming together . . . [to produce] what I might call an emerging "vast wonderland."

> ECKHARD PFEIFFER, CEO of Compaq Computers, in a speech, fall 1996

I wouldn't kill to have [the same capability] but I'd maim for it.

> DAN RATHER, CBS anchorman, on MSNBC's ability to provide instant coverage of Princess Diana's death, quoted in the *Wall Street Journal,* September 23, 1997

We in the media, as a rule, are not good with financial matters. Some veteran journalists have not yet turned in their expense accounts for the Civil War.

> DAVE BARRY, *Boston Globe Magazine*, September 28, 1997

In my experience, trouble comes not when you attack a company but when you attack the owner's friends. For example, Warren Buffett [a friend of Microsoft CEO Bill Gates].

> MICHAEL KINSLEY, editor of *Slate*, Microsoft's online magazine, quoted in "Jumping Off a Bridge: Microsoft and Michael Kinsley Enter Cyberspace," *New Yorker*, May 13, 1996

[T]he biggest health crisis since Chernobyl.

> OPRAH WINFREY, talk show host, reacting to the claim of a guest that 100,000 cows died overnight for indeterminate reasons, were ground up and fed to other cows, possibly spreading mad cow disease, of which there has never been a case in the United States, quoted in the *Wall Street Journal*, June 3, 1997

If I lose one consumer of beef, that's part of my market I'll never recover.

> PAUL ENGLER, owner of cattle-feeding operations and ranch, who claims that he lost $6.7 million when the futures market reacted to Oprah the next day, quoted in the *Wall Street Journal*, June 3, 1997. (He sued Winfrey under Texas's False Disparagement of Perishable Food Products law, which was passed after the Alar apple-juice scare, and lost.)

Small and growing companies are only considered newsworthy when they are eccentric, such as a mutual fund that bases its investments on astrology, or otherwise amusing. When it comes to hard news about how economic trends and public policies will affect business, those companies which create the most jobs are overlooked by network reporters.

> *MediaNomics*, newsletter published by Media Research Center, quoted in *Inc.*, November 1995

I got a little publicity. I didn't mean to get it that way.

> JAMES HUDSON, founder and chairman of Hudson Foods Inc., after the recall of 25 million pounds of hamburger because bacteria in it had poisoned consumers, quoted in the *New York Times*, September 5, 1997

37.2 PR

Reputation is commonly measured by the acre.

> THOMAS FULLER, M.D., *Gnomologia* (1732)

The truth of an idea is not a stagnant property inherent in it. Truth happens to an idea. It becomes true, is made true by events.

> WILLIAM JAMES, *Pragmatism: The Meaning of Truth* (1907)

The war taught us the power of propaganda. Now when we have anything to sell the American people, we know how to sell it.

> ROGER BABSON, business consultant, 1921, cited in Stuart Ewen, *PR! A Social History of Spin* (Basic Books, 1996)

Private enterprise has no press agent. Government does.

> MILTON FRIEDMAN, *Economic Myths and Public Opinion*, January 1976

How do you feel this morning, Governor?
Wouldn't you like to know?

> Exchange between reporter and GOVERNOR LELAND STANFORD, who had earlier founded the Southern Pacific Railroad, quoted in S. N. Behrman, *New Yorker*, November 9, 1951

Formerly, a public man needed a private secretary for a barrier between himself and the public. Nowadays he has a press secretary, to keep him properly in the public eye.

> DANIEL J. BOORSTIN, *The Image* (Atheneum, 1961)

There aren't any embarrassing questions—just embarrassing answers.

> CARL ROWAN, *New Yorker*, December 7, 1963

[I]n a society where "communications standards" are defined by the likes of Geraldo and Arsenio and *Hard Copy* and *A Current Affair* and the *National Star*, keeping standards high is no easy task.

> FRASER P. SEITEL, public relations counselor, in a speech, November 12, 1992

Public relations must be the conscience of the organization. We must be the ones who ask management—before we do anything else—the following question: "Is what we're doing here the right thing to do?" Few others will have the nerve to raise such an issue.

> FRASER P. SEITEL, public relations counselor, in a speech, November 10, 1993

We need to make people understand that the cigarette industry is not made up of a bunch of evil people.

> STEVEN PARRISH of Philip Morris, USA, quoted in *Business Week,* July 4, 1994

Cancer is a lifestyle disease.

> CHARLES R. WALL of the Philip Morris Companies, quoted in *Business Week,* August 8, 1994

Corporate America has always had a PR problem. We haven't found a way to dress up certain economic realities so we can take them out in public.

> ROBERT J. EATON, CEO of Chrysler, in a speech, March 18, 1996

With 10,000 locations nationwide, we're a lightning rod for the issue du jour.

> CHUCK EBLING of McDonald's, referring to recurring rumors about McDonald's purported destruction of rain forests to raise beef, quoted in *Fortune,* December 25, 1995

Which of our various special skills in crisis communications, investor relations, employee relations, litigation PR did we develop *before* the need was obvious?

> LUIS MORALES, president of the Public Relations Society of America, in a speech, April 13, 1996

While its [the Tobacco Institute] PR campaigns were a failure with the public, they accomplished something more important: They gave politicians cover for failing to act.

> MATTHEW MYERS, who helped negotiate the 1997 tobacco deal as counsel for the National Center for Tobacco-Free Kids, quoted in the *Wall Street Journal,* June 23, 1997

The Chinese have a saying: "Tall trees experience strong winds."

> ROBERT KUOK, Chinese businessman, quoted in *Forbes,* July 28, 1997

The Carlton Hotel is pleased to present a special package in conjunction with the popular U.S. Holocaust Memorial Museum. Only a limited number of tickets are available each day to experience this haunting and moving museum; the Carlton offers its premier package featuring these exclusive and sought-after tickets. Other components of the "Weekend Museum" package include deluxe accommodations at our newly renovated hotel, a late checkout, and a lavish Sunday brunch, including a sumptuous buffet and an array of delectable desserts. The brunch ambiance is enhanced by piano accompaniment.

The U.S. Holocaust Memorial Museum is dedicated to presenting the history of persecution and murder of 6 million Jews and millions of other victims of Nazi tyranny from 1933 to 1945.

> Press release, 1994, reprinted in *Harper's,* April 1995

I used to think "No comment" would be the best option if a company has problems. Now I realize that executives who speak for themselves have an air of credibility, and if you play your cards right you can use the media as a tool.

> STACIE A. SOULE of General Motors Corporation's Packard electric division, quoted in the *New York Times,* January 21, 1990

[M]uch as they [fast-track executives] might like to, they cannot avoid contact with the media as they climb the corporate ladder.

> PROFESSOR IRV SHENKLER of the Stern School of Business at New York University, quoted in the *New York Times,* January 21, 1990

Managers have to learn that there is no magic pill that will transmute bad behavior into a good image, and that a good portion of their time will be taken up with external communications.

> STEPHEN A. GREYSER of Harvard Business School, quoted in the *New York Times,* January 21, 1990

As the business moguls have become celebrities, they have reacted in a typical way. They've become absolutely crazy about their image.

> DANIEL ROEBUCK, president of the photo agency Onyx, quoted in the *New York Times,* January 14, 1990

God forbid that you don't take Malcolm Forbes's picture. If he sees you standing near him with a camera around your neck, he reminds you to.

> L.A. photographer, quoted in the *New York Times,* January 14, 1990

I think that there are certain angles where [Mike Ovitz] doesn't look good. You know, the way his hair comes down kind of funny on the left side, and the gaps between his teeth. He doesn't have a movie-star smile.

> PETER BORSARI, L.A. photographer, on why former agent and Disney president Michael Ovitz goes nuts when he sees surprise photos of himself in magazines, *New York Times,* January 14, 1990

Reputation grows from the inside out.

> ALAN TOWERS, president of the PR firm Alan Towers Associates, quoted in the *New York Times,* June 16, 1991

You're not getting inside my head.

> LOU GERSTNER, CEO of IBM, to reporter Betsy Morris, quoted in *Fortune,* April 14, 1997

The price of justice is eternal publicity.

> ARNOLD BENNETT, British novelist, quoted in *Slate,* November 1997

38.1 ENVIRONMENTALISM AND ECONOMICS

Bring to the debate whatever economic criteria you wish, but don't pretend that the starting point of an argument on environmental issues must be that the discounted present value of economic benefits outweighs the corresponding cost. After all, the bottom line in the environmental debate is not a matter of net profit but of life itself.

> NICHOLAS DEWAR, letter to the editor, *The Economist,* June 6, 1992

If environmental standards are worth pursuing, they are worth pursuing for their own sake . . . countries that use charges, taxes, and other market-based devices will find they become cleaner more cheaply than those which insist on elaborate regulations.

> *The Economist,* December 5, 1992

Has [environmental protection] cost jobs? OECD officials have found no evidence for that. Spending on pollution control amounts to 1–2 percent of GDP in most rich countries, but that has not cut jobs overall. True, certain industries such as mining have lost jobs, and some companies have moved to less strict third-world countries. But greenery, like any new market, has also created jobs: the market worldwide (which in practice means largely in OECD countries) was worth some $200 billion in 1990.

Some [environmental] regulation has gained support because it protects vested interests. German recycling laws, obliging brewers to use refillable bottles, helps small brewers, with local distribution networks already in place, against incoming foreigners. The rich countries' ban on CFCs is backed by big chemical firms eager to create a market for their substitutes. Britain's National Trust, which conserves a growing proportion of its countryside, also helps to conserve its less-rich-than-they-were land-owning aristocrats in the homes to which they have become accustomed.

> *The Economist,* February 10, 1996

In making our final [power generation] choices, we really need to be clear-eyed, seeing things as they are rather than as we might wish they could be.

> ALAN SCHRIESHEIM, director emeritus of Argonne National Laboratories, in a speech, April 17, 1997

While there may be "good" subsidies in principle, in practice most are wasteful of scarce fiscal resources, miss their intended targets (the poor, for example), and have the undesirable effect of stifling innovation and limiting competitiveness.

> *Environment Matters,* World Bank report on fossil fuel, irrigation water, and pesticides, cited in the *Financial Times,* March 12, 1997

All the cars and light trucks on the road in the United States today contribute less than 2 percent of the world's man-made emissions of greenhouse gases. What's the biggest culprit (by far)? You guessed it, coal-fired power plants, like those we will be encouraging in developing countries.

> ROBERT A. LUTZ of the auto firm Chrysler Corporation, in a speech, April 29, 1997

I used to think that money was the world's most important commodity, but now I realize that it is air.

> RICHARD SANDOR, creator of the world's first interest-rate futures contract, on pollution trading-rights exchange, quoted in the *Economist,* November 28, 1995

There has been too much emphasis on top-down modeling of the expected costs of tackling climate change and not enough emphasis on price signals. Markets have eyes.

> RICHARD SANDOR, quoted in the *Financial Times,* October 21, 1997

By now we have enough experience with emissions trading to predict that it will reduce pollution at a fraction of the cost of regulation.

> PROFESSOR ALAN S. BLINDER, Princeton, former vice chairman of the Federal Reserve Board, quoted in the *New York Times,* October 22, 1997

Since none of the effect is localized, carbon is a perfect pollutant for emissions trading.

It's cheaper to engineer new products for energy efficiency than it is to retrofit old ones. That means we can greatly lower the costs of reducing carbon emissions if we allow our existing transportation fleet, factories, home heating systems, and especially power-generating plants to wear out rather than scrapping them.

> DAN DUDEK of the Environmental Defense Fund, who helped push the sulfur trading program in 1990, quoted in the *New York Times,* October 24, 1997

If foreigners are foolish enough to foul their own air and water in order to produce more cheaply, it is in our selfish interest to take advantage of their cheap products and devote our resources to production that does not damage our environment. Of course, if their fouled air and water flow over or into the United States, that is another matter.

> PROFESSOR ROBERT EISNER of Northwestern University, *New York Times,* October 13, 1997

Price matters. But Americans don't do great with amortization of costs. So it has got to be something that we know works. And the only thing we can think of that we know works is requiring that energy-saving technology be put on the things we drive, the things we use to heat our homes, the things we use to cool our food. We know that works.

> DAN BECKER of the environmental organization Sierra Club, *New York Times,* October 26, 1997

We think of ourselves as Adam Smith with a green thumb.

> JOHN SAWHILL, CEO of the Nature Conservancy, quoted in *Harvard Business Review,* September–October 1995

38.2 ENVIRONMENT AND MANAGEMENT

My concern is that environmental groups are marginalized by being seen as a bunch of people who have nothing better to do than protest. It needs men in gray suits like me to take a stand. I'm already a millionaire but I want a pleasant planet on which to enjoy my money.

> ADRIAN FOSTER-FLETCHER, headhunter and adviser to Friends of the Earth, quoted in the *Financial Times,* May 13, 1997

"Why do industrialists leave their individual human values at the door when they get to work, only to pick them up again when they go home?"

"I don't think they do. But it is difficult to quantify the value of certain activities or virtues when the market is waiting impatiently for your quarterly returns."

> Exchange from seminar to seek common ground between environmentalists and industry, quoted by Peter Coombes of Waste Management International, *Financial Times,* September 3, 1997

None of us today, whether we're running a business, is living in a sustainable way.

If emerging economies have to relive the entire industrial revolution with all its waste, its energy use, and its pollution, I think it's all over.

How do you react to the prospects of the world population doubling over the next few decades? First you may say, Great, 5 billion more customers. That is what economic development is all about. Think about the physical implications of serving that many new customers. And ask yourself the hard questions. How exactly are we going to do that and still live here? That's what sustainability is all about.

> ROBERT B. SHAPIRO, CEO of the chemical company Monsanto, *Harvard Business Review,* January–February 1997

38.3 ENVIRONMENTAL REGULATION

. . . [B]efore your state buys into any more of them [pioneering environmental regulations], take a good look at what the cutting edge has actually cut.

> KENNETH T. DERR, CEO of the oil firm Chevron, in a speech, August 7, 1992

- In the 1950s . . . the environment was a minor issue or a nonissue.
- In the 1960s . . . we had confrontation and accusation.
- In the 1970s . . . there was legislation and regulation.
- In the 1980s . . . government applied command and control solutions to "end of the pipe" treatment, which means "conventional pollution controls."
- The 1990s are focusing on prevention and minimization.
- From year 2000 and beyond . . . the issue will be sustainable development . . . which involves designing national policies . . . as well as products and pro-

cesses to eliminate or reduce impact on the environment.

JOSEPH LING of the industrial firm 3M Corporation, in a speech, January 2, 1993

The first instance of pollution in the Bible occurs when Cain slays Abel and his blood falls on the ground.

U.S. VICE PRESIDENT AL GORE, *Earth in the Balance* (Houghton Mifflin, 1994)

38.4 GREENHOUSE EFFECT

Energy subsidies, net of taxes, cost the world $235 billion in 1985. The effect is to underwrite CO_2 output. In OECD countries, the implicit carbon subsidy worked out at $90 a ton in 1985, the equivalent of $10 a barrel of oil. Removing these subsidies will make their economies work more efficiently—and reduce their output of global-warming gases.

Based on OECD economic study, cited in the *Economist,* March 6, 1993

Proponents of the global warming theory say that higher levels of greenhouse gases—especially carbon dioxide—are causing or will cause global temperatures to rise. But more than 96 percent of the carbon dioxide is naturally produced in the environment, and it has nothing to do with human activity. It and the other greenhouse gases are necessary for life to survive on Earth. Currently, the scientific evidence is inconclusive as to whether human activities are having a significant effect on the global climate.

LEE R. RAYMOND, CEO of the oil company Exxon, in a speech, May 6, 1996

Capital keeps its nose to the wheel. The people who run the world's oil and coal companies know that the march of science, and of political action, may be slowed by disinformation.

ROSS GELBSPAN, *Harper's,* December 1995

If we are all to take responsibility for the future of our planet, then it falls on us to begin to take precautionary action now.

JOHN BROWNE, CEO of the oil firm British Petroleum, breaking ranks with other big oil firms, expressing concern about global warming, quoted in the *Economist,* June 14, 1997

There's no proof of the looming greenhouse crisis. It might be real. It might not be. We'll be able to tell in plenty of time to do something about it if it is real. Stumbling around in the dark and overreacting now won't help. And neither would be shutting down relatively clean factories in the United States and Europe while permitting the whole Third World to put up a dirty, coal-fired industry infrastructure that would look like ours did 50 years ago.

ROBERT J. EATON, CEO of the auto company Chrysler, in a speech, February 26, 1997

We in the timber industry are carbon stewards; we convert trees into building materials and other products that last a very, very long time. Have you ever considered the fact that by producing buildings or furniture we are actually keeping carbon dioxide out of the atmosphere?

CARL JANSEN, timber industry recruiter, "Your Work Is Valuable to Global Environment," *Timber Processing,* September 1994, reprinted in *Harper's,* December 1994

Since 1970, our nation's gross domestic product and its use of electricity have both risen by more than 70 percent. Meanwhile, our nation's rate of CO_2 emissions per dollar of GDP has dropped by more than 40 percent.

GIRARD F. ANDERSON, president and chairman of Tampa Electric Company, in a speech, June 18, 1993

We are convinced that global warming is a serious issue. We reckon that the loss burden due to natural catastrophes will increase because of climate changes and other factors.

IVO KNOEPFEL of the international reinsurance firm, Swiss Re, quoted in the *Financial Times,* September 5, 1997

If climate is changing radically, and perhaps very quickly, how can risks be assessed and priced? Will insurers be forced to withdraw or sharply reduce cover? If that happens, will society allocate the costs? What might be the implications for life and economic activity in regions considered to be high risk? Might entire vulnerable cities such as Miami have to be abandoned?

OLIVER PETERKEN of the reinsurance brokers Willis Faber & Dumas, quoted in the *Financial Times,* September 5, 1997

You're going to let Russia be able to sell credits for plants that have already been closed so that General Motors can emit more pollution here?

> DANIEL BECKER of the Sierra Club, on plan to extend U.S. program of tradeable pollution rights to global marketplace, quoted in the *Wall Street Journal,* October 3, 1997

As the result of a modernization program, New York state's Niagara Mohawk Power Corp. cut its carbon-dioxide emission rights for that amount to an Arizona utility for 20,000 tons of sulfur-dioxide allowances. Then Niagara donated the sulfur-dioxide allowances to local environmental groups, which are retiring them. And $125,000 of the tax benefits Niagara received from the deal are being used to convert a Mexican fishing village to nonpolluting solar power.

> JOHN J. FIALKA, *Wall Street Journal,* October 3, 1996

If you want to see what climate change might be like just look at El Niño. It's the trailer for "Climate change, the movie."

> TOM BURKE, environmental adviser, quoted in the *Financial Times,* October 21, 1997

If we switched from a coal project to a gas project in a country where gas is expensive, just because we were do-gooders and wanted to reduce the global-warming impact, it starts adding 10, 20, or 30 percent to the cost of a kilowatt-hour.

> ROGER F. NAILL of the power plant–building AES Corporation, quoted in the *New York Times,* January 2, 1998

38.5 JUNK SCIENCE

Every year we at the American Council on Science and Health publish a dinner menu featuring a typical American holiday meal. We have our toxicologists analyze every one of the natural foods on that menu—and those toxicologists find a toxin or an animal carcinogen in every course. Carrots contain carotatoxin, a fairly potent nerve poison. Radishes contain goitrogens—chemicals that promote goiter by interfering with the body's use of iodine. Shrimp are a rich source of several minerals, including arsenic. Pepper and nutmeg contain myristicin, a powerful hallucinogen.

> ELIZABETH WHALEN, president of the American Council on Science and Health, in a speech, April 8, 1997

Researchers reported that in a typical population of 100,000, folks were three times as likely to die over the course of a lifetime from being struck by lightning as from succumbing to a health problem traceable to asbestos poisoning in a school building. Seventy-five would die in bicycle accidents, 730 would be killed in plane crashes, and nearly 22,000 would die from smoking-related diseases.

> Data from a 1988 Harvard Energy and Environmental Policy Center symposium on asbestos, cited in *New York,* September 13, 1993

Once you get past the tree-hugging, save-the-whales stuff, you realize that we ignore these problems [deforestation, air pollution et al.] at our peril.

> DR. NORM KAHN of the Central Intelligence Agency's environment center, quoted in the *Wall Street Journal,* November 20, 1997

Many people, politicians and the public alike, believe global warming is a rock-solid certainty. But it's not.

> LEE RAYMOND, CEO of Exxon, quoted in the *New York Times,* December 12, 1997

No one knows precisely what's going on, but it doesn't mean you do nothing. Our position is to continue to provide energy to the world but to do it better.

> JOHN BROWNE, CEO of British Petroleum, quoted in the *New York Times,* December 12, 1997

38.6 RALPH NADER

Let it not be said by a future, forlorn generation that we wasted and lost our great potential because our despair was so deep we didn't even try, or because each of us thought someone else was worrying about our problems.

> RALPH NADER, corporate watchdog, quoted in *Worth,* September 1996

The pleasure of a hot dog means nothing to Ralph. He tastes only the nitrite . . . In this world of sinners, though, not everyone wants to live on raw vegetables and set the thermostat at 60. Intelligent public policy requires trade-offs that the fanatic is ill equipped and indisposed to make.

> MICHAEL KINSLEY, *New Republic,* December 9, 1985

We support him [Nader] overtly, covertly, in every way possible. He is our hero. We have supported him for decades. . . . I would think we give him a huge percentage of what he raises. What moneyed groups could he turn to other than trial lawyers?

> PAT MALONEY, multimillionaire trial lawyer, quoted in *Worth,* September 1996

I can get on the phone and raise $100,000 for Nader in one day.

> HERB HAFIF, multimillionaire trial lawyer, quoted in *Worth,* September 1996

38.7   RECYCLING

Americans consume the equivalent of five Great Pyramids of solid steel every year—105 million tons . . . and about 40 percent of it is recycled steel. Toyotas, tin cans, skyscrapers, bolts, supertankers—eventually, they wind up back in a furnace in a steel mill.

> RICHARD PRESTON, *New Yorker,* February 25, 1991

. . . Foam plastics account for no more than 1 percent of the volume of material in land fills, and the fast-food industry accounts for no more than a third of 1 percent of the same 1 percent. Paper, to which McDonald's switched, takes up about 40 percent of landfills. All plastics, when compacted, take up only 16 percent of landfill space. In other words, the environmentalists attacked the wrong products, in the wrong industry, leading to a "solution" that's worse than the imagined problem.

> FRED BRADLEY, Ferguson, Montana, responding to McDonald's shift from plastic packaging to paper, letter to the editor, *The Economist,* October 17, 1992

Man is messy, but any creature that can create space vehicles can probably cope.

> GEORGE F. WILL, *Suddenly: The American Idea Abroad and at Home, 1986–1990* (Free Press, 1990)

The diversity of plastics is really defeating its ability to be recycled.

> JOHN RUSTON of the Environmental Defense Fund, quoted in the *Economist,* October 18, 1997

39.1 BEING DOWNSIZED

My boss said, "Hey, John, do you have a minute?" As I found out, I had a lot more than a minute.

> JOHN BOEGEHOLD, then age 55, ex-personnel director for Burroughs, where he worked for 29 years, quoted in *U.S. News & World Report,* March 23, 1987

At the minimum, the stress is equivalent to being in an earthquake or getting divorced.

> STEVEN BERGLAS, clinical psychologist in Boston who counsels fired managers, quoted in *U.S. News & World Report,* March 23, 1987

I was just George Bradbury, U.S. citizen, without the financial power of a *Fortune* 500 company behind me.

> Former Pitney Bowes executive who took a buyout in 1985, quoted in *U.S. News & World Report,* March 23, 1987

I went from fast track to derailment.

> J. RALPH HAMMOCK, after his speechwriting job at Exxon was eliminated, quoted in *U.S. News & World Report,* March 23, 1987

I have 28 years of experience. I've made millions for the company and have knowledge that will cost them millions more to duplicate in someone else. Yet they were willing to spend $500,000 for nothing or just to get rid of me.

> KEN VEIT, owner of Cartoon Corner, Scottsdale, Arizona, who was fired as president of the international division of a major insurance company, *Harvard Business Review,* November–December 1992

That's like going to a funeral and reading a statement to the widow that her husband's death, while regrettable, was actuarially necessary to make room on the planet for other people.

> DAVID NOER of the Center for Creative Leadership, advising executives not to concentrate only on economic benefits when justifying downsizing, quoted in *Fortune,* January 10, 1994

When I first heard the downsizing was going to occur, I experienced the same feelings I had when my brother was diagnosed with leukemia.

> JANET MILLS of the chemical firm Marion Merell Dow, quoted in *Fortune,* January 10, 1994

My view of myself as economically secure is shattered. And the world is a scarier place.

> BILL COLLIER, a 33-year IBM employee who founded his own business after being let go, quoted in *Inc.,* January 1994

39.2 DOWNSIZING

Better to make one cut than amputate two inches at a time.

> HOWARD H. STEVENSON and MIHNEA C. MOLDOVEANU, "Power of Predictability," *Harvard Business Review,* July–August 1995

Maintaining employment for the sake of employment isn't paternalistic, it's irresponsible if it jeopardizes the welfare of all employees.

> ROBERT HAAS, chief executive of the jeans manufacturer Levi Strauss, quoted in *Forbes,* August 11, 1986

One popular approach is the chainsaw. Climbing through the corporate tree, though you cannot see the tree for the leaves, you saw off branches and departments to fit a predetermined cost objective. The only problem with that method is that you may saw off the tree's most vital limbs.

> THOMAS A. HORTON, CEO of the American Management Association, in a speech, December 1988

Efficiency without social justice has little staying power in America.

> WILLIAM TAYLOR, *Harvard Business Review,* January–February 1992

There is no excuse for treating employees as if they are disposable pieces of equipment.

> ROBERT B. REICH, U.S. Labor Secretary, quoted in *Fortune,* November 29, 1993

As far as being a paternalistic company, a company that is company from cradle to grave—we never were that. We never *told* people we were that. Nobody owns a job, nobody owns a market, nobody owns a product. Somebody out there can there always take it away from you.

> RONALD E. COMPTON, chairman of the insurance company Aetna Life and Casualty, quoted in the *New York Times*, March 1, 1992

So widespread have layoffs become that employers seem to have let go any residual inhibitions they may have had against reducing their payrolls further.

> JAMES E. CHALLENGER, president of the outplacement firm Challenger, Gray and Christmas, quoted in *Fortune*, October 18, 1993

After getting whacked by the oil embargo, American business decided the best way to compete in the global economy was by driving down labor costs.

Not by innovation, not by Yankee ingenuity, not through labor-management cooperation, not by insisting on international social standards and rights for workers . . . but by squeezing the last possible ounce of productivity out of American workers and then throwing them on the scrap heap of unemployment or old age with reduced pensions and health insurance coverage.

> JOHN J. SWEENEY, president of the labor union AFL-CIO, in a speech, December 6, 1995

Large corporations have a singular problem. When their stocks go up and they are reducing the payroll, that makes the American people unhappy.

> PETER HART, pollster, quoted in the *Wall Street Journal*, April 8, 1996

It is increasingly apparent to me that these are the result of plant closures, job cuts, and other forms of downsizing that are not recipes for lasting productivity enhancement.

Tactics of open-ended downsizing and real wage compression are ultimately recipes for industrial extinction.

The demand side of the global economy is about to enter an era of geometric growth. It would be tragic if newly revitalized U.S. companies squandered the fruits of restructuring by continuing to downsize their capabilities on the supply side. The hollowing strategies of the current productivity-led recovery could be setting just such a trap.

> STEPHEN S. ROACH, chief economist of the investment bank Morgan Stanley, *Financial Times*, May 14, 1996

Psst. You want to make a killing in the stock market? Find out which *Fortune* 500 company intends to fire enough employees to make a splash in tomorrow's *Wall Street Journal*. It's a sure bet that the company's stock will jump, perhaps big (depending upon the number of people axed). Our rule of thumb at my investment company: we'll pay up to $2 more per share for every 10,000 people discarded.

> JAMES J. CRAMER, president of the hedge fund Cramer & Co., *New Republic*, April 29, 1996

Chase Manhattan and Chemical Bank announce a merger that will put 12,000 people out of work—and their stock goes up.

Does a rising tide now sink all boats?

> JOHN J. SWEENEY, president of the labor union AFL-CIO, echoing President John F. Kennedy's famous line, "a rising tide lifts all boats" (which was used to justify income tax cuts), in a speech, December 6, 1995

It seems to me the worst thing many CEOs do is announce huge cuts before the fact, thereby upsetting the entire organization so that no one feels secure. Companies are trying too hard to please Wall Street. CEOs should just make the cuts and stop beating their chests like Superman.

> RICHARD JENRETTE, retired CEO of the Equitable Companies and cofounder of the investment bank Donaldson Lufkin & Jenrette, quoted in *Fortune*, July 22, 1996

It is a criminal sin for a company to make an announcement one morning that they are letting 22 percent—or some such number—of their workforce go. You have got to ask yourself: Where the hell was management? How did they get 22 percent too many people?

> SAMUEL L. EICHENFELD, CEO of the commercial finance company FINOVA Group, interviewed in Charles B. Wendel, *The New Financiers: Profiles of the Leaders Who Are Reshaping the Financial Services Industry* (Irwin, 1996)

[Layoffs] are a major admission that senior management has really screwed up.

> GEARY A. RUMMLER of the consulting firm Rummler-Brach Group, quoted in *Business Week,* January 24, 1994

I believe you can go into any traditionally centralized corporation and cut its headquarters staff by 90 percent in one year. You spin off 30 percent of the staff into free-standing service centers that perform real work—treasury function, legal services—and charge for it. You decentralize 30 percent of the staff—human resources for example—by pushing them into line organizations. Then 30 percent disappears through head-count reductions.

> PERCY BARNEVIK, CEO of the Swedish-Swiss industrial firm ABB (Asea Brown Boveri), interviewed in *Harvard Business Review,* March–April, 1991

[C]onsider the panic over "downsizing" that gripped America in 1996. As economists quickly pointed out, the rate at which Americans were losing jobs in the "90s was not especially high by historical standards. Downsizing suddenly became news because for the first time, white-collar, college-educated workers were being fired in large numbers, even while skilled machinists and other blue-collar workers were in demand.

> PROFESSOR PAUL KRUGMAN of MIT, looking back 100 years from 2096, *New York Times Magazine,* September 30, 1996

Downsizing and layoffs are part of the price of becoming more competitive. The price for not doing it, however, is much higher in both economic and human terms.

> ROBERT J. EATON, CEO of Chrysler Corporation, in a speech, March 18, 1996

Corporations downsized too much. They laid off people with a lot of experience, and they also laid off their bench strength so that they had appropriate staffing for the amount of business they were doing in, say 1991, but hadn't anticipated how much it would grow. Now they need college graduates to replace all those people who were laid off.

> MAURY HANIGAN, CEO of the human-resources firm Hanigan Consulting, quoted in *Fortune,* April 14, 1997

I told my broker, "You buy the stocks. I don't know anything about that."

> PATRICK BUCHANAN, presidential candidate critical of downsizing (particularly by AT&T) and promoter of protectionist trade policies, when confronted on CBS TV show *Face the Nation* with the fact that he owned $15,000 worth of AT&T stock, quoted in *Fortune,* April 29, 1996

If you haven't restructured your company in the past three years, you're in trouble. A company is not a Catholic marriage—forever. It's California style, one year at a time.

> ICHAK ADIZES, management theorist, quoted in *Inc.,* September 1996

Boosting profits through downsizing was easy; all executives had to do was take the heat from layoffs.

> G. WILLIAM DAUPHIANAIS of the accounting and consulting firm Price Waterhouse, quoted in the *Wall Street Journal,* July 5, 1996

The idea that competitiveness lies in "jobless" companies is as wrongheaded as the notion that every job can be saved forever.

> AUGUSTO MATEUS, economic minister of Portugal, quoted in the *Financial Times,* February 25, 1997

[Y]ou can't treat your people like an expense item.

> ANDREW GROVE, cofounder and CEO of the microprocessor firm Intel, on why the company had gone to great lengths to avoid layoffs during a business downturn, interviewed in Rama Dev Jager, *In the Company of Giants* (McGraw-Hill, 1997)

39.3 EUPHEMISMS FOR BEING FIRED

Asked to resign	Dehiring
Axed	Deployment
Canned	Deselected
Career assessment and re-employment	Destaffing
	Discharged
Career transition	Dismissal
Chemistry change	Displacement
Coerced transition	Downsizing
Decruited	Excessed
Degrowing	Executive culling

Force reduction
Fumigation
Indefinite idling
Involuntary separation
Job separation
Let go
Negotiated departure
Outplacement
Personnel surplus
  reduction
Position elimination
Premature retirement
Redeployment
Redirected
Redundancy elimination
Release

Reorganization
Replaced
Requested departure
RIF—Reduction in Force:
  "I was riffed."
Right-sizing
Sacked
Selected out
Selectively separated
Skill mix adjustment
Termination
Transitioned
Vocational relocation
Workforce adjustment
Workforce imbalance
  correction

JAMES H. KENNEDY, publisher of *Executive Recruiters News,* cited in the *New York Times,* May 26, 1996

Balancing.

Word used by IBM in announcing thousands of lay-offs in September 1996

Your job has been suppressed.

Your job description has been revised and you're invited to apply for it.

SCOTT ADAMS, creator of the cartoon strip *Dilbert,* public radio, October 17, 1996

I didn't *lose* the job. They took it from me. I *know* where it is.

HILTON LUCAS, 30-year airline employee, played by Bill Cosby on CBS show *Cosby*

Displaced . . . put into the mobility pool.

The Economist, December 21, 1996

uninstalled . . . excess to requirements . . . correctsized . . . career change opportunity.

Cited by William Lutz, *The New Doublespeak* (Harper Perennial, 1996)

39.4 OUTPLACEMENT

[*Advice on how to fire someone*]

- A 10–15 minute statement of position is better than a 2-hour argument.

- Don't use platitudes and make promises you can't keep.
- Don't be casual or be humorous.
- Don't try to be liked. People who have been fired need someone to dislike.
- Sack people on Monday morning, rather than Friday afternoon. That reduces the trauma of their first un-employed weekend.

WILLIAM MORIN, chairman of the outplacement firm Drake Beam Morin, in the wake of 1987 stock-market crash, quoted in the *Economist,* January 23, 1988

The outplacement geek wants to think of himself as a useful citizen, a kind of midwife, not an accessory after the fact.

G. J. MEYER, *Executive Blues: Down and Out in Corporate America* (Franklin Square, 1995)

Juries walk in there to put employers' feet to the fire. Legal issues often give way to a sense of shared humanity with the plaintiff.

The angry employee, not necessarily the one that is simply hurt or displaced, is usually the one that sues.

RONALD M. GREEN, corporate lawyer, *Fortune,* June 10, 1996

39.5 OUTSOURCING

What we know how to do is make a good pizza. They [Ryder] can make sure everything goes where it needs to go.

ROBERT WADELL of the pizza chain Papa John's International, which pays Ryder Dedicated Logistics to deliver its fresh dough and other ingredients, cited by the consulting firm The Outsourcing Institute

The question isn't why companies are engaging in more outsourcing, but why they haven't done so faster. Goods and services are inevitably less expensive when purchased in the open market. The stumbling block has always been the transaction costs companies have had to bear when going outside. But today's information technology makes it much easier for companies to coordinate with suppliers, building a closer relationship, improving service, and reducing transaction costs.

ALAN S. ALEXANDROFF, Canadian political and trade analyst, on a Canadian Auto Workers strike against

General Motors, *Wall Street Journal,* October 14, 1996

Why should any plant keep spare parts or develop logistics software when there are so many people outside with those skills?

> RONALD A. GLAH of the aluminum company Alcoa, quoted in the *New York Times,* November 6, 1996

Outsourcing is no panacea. It's often called the "make or buy" decision. Well, let me tell you, it can quickly become the make or break decision. It can make or break your human resource management, wreak havoc on your productivity, and ultimately hurt your profitability.

> JOE NEUBAUER, CEO of the food-services firm ARA Services, in a speech, June 4, 1993

[O]utsourcing provided the most criticism of the techniques studied. It was seen as ineffective at everything except cutting costs, where it was only moderately successful.

> VANESSA HOULDER, citing data from *The Use and Effectiveness of Modern Manufacturing Practices in the U.K.,* Institute of Work Psychology, University of Sheffield, *Financial Times,* September 5, 1997

39.6 QUALITY

There will always be a conflict between "good" and "good enough."

> HENRY MARTYN LELAND, turn-of-the-century mechanical engineer who built the original engines for the Oldsmobile, quoted in Robert Sobel and David B. Sicilia, *The Entrepreneurs—An American Adventure* (Houghton Mifflin, 1986)

We had all the quality slogans and logos, but it was physically impossible to build a quality paint job . . . we could not prove by the numbers that the investment in a new paint system could be justified so we could never get the investment approved.

> DONALD LENNOX, controller for a Ford assembly plant during the 1950s, quoted in John A. Byrne, *The Whiz Kids* (Doubleday, 1993)

I have never met a quality guru I didn't like.

> RICHARD BUETOW, director of quality at the electronics company Motorola, quoted in the *Economist,* January 4, 1992

It has always been an Achilles' heel for us—getting production done at a high-quality and competitive cost.

> U.S. SECRETARY OF COMMERCE ROBERT MOSBACHER, quoted in *Time,* November 13, 1989

We used to talk about "commercial quality," which meant that you expected to have a certain amount of defects.

> ROBERT STEMPEL, president of General Motors, quoted in *Time,* November 13, 1989

Our customers are not there to field-test our products.

> STANLEY GAULT, chairman of the household products company Rubbermaid, quoted in *Time,* November 13, 1989

Consumers resent it when a company presumes to judge the quality of its products on their behalf.

> ANDREW GROVE, CEO of the computer chip firm Intel, reflecting on the company's dismissive response to glitches in its early Pentium chips that caused errors in certain types of calculations, quoted in *Fortune,* May 1, 1995

We've talked about quality for years. The difference this time is we're actually doing it.

> JOHN FERNANDEZ of Chrysler Corporation on delaying a major product launch because of unacceptable defect levels, quoted in *Business Week,* August 22, 1994

Early in our quality journey, it was believed that the quality tools were so wonderful that great progress could be achieved simply by training everyone. When this was done in a vacuum, nothing actually changed.

> R. C. FLOYD of an Exxon Chemical Company plant, quoted in *America's Best: Industry Week's Guide to World-Class Manufacturing Plants* (Wiley, 1996)

TQM [total quality management] is a risky venture, and the failure to implement it correctly can leave a company much worse off than it was before it even considered the process.

> JEFF HALEY and PETER CROSS, engineering consultants, *Harvard Business Review,* May–June 1991

We always assumed that fewer defects inherently cost more. We stopped thinking about quality. The consumer became an adversary. Consumer complaints were treated as enemy propaganda. Companies did not stand up for their products, and they in essence said, "Screw you," to the consumer.

> PROFESSOR MARTIN STARR of Columbia University, quoted in Fred Washofsky, *The Chip War* (Scribner, 1989)

In a 1991 survey of more than 300 electronics companies sponsored by the American Electronics Association, 73 percent of the companies reported having a total quality program under way; but of these, 63 percent had failed to improve quality defects by as much as 10 percent.

> ROBERT H. SCHAEFFER and HARVEY A. THOMPSON, management consultants, *Harvard Business Review*, January–February 1992

Isn't this more like dictatorship than partnership?

> Allied-Signal supplier, on Allied's program of compelling its suppliers to go to its Total Quality training, quoted in *Fortune*, November 30, 1992

There's nothing wrong with a Rolls-Royce. It is an extremely finely made car, and I don't think Jesus was opposed to quality.

> RICHARD HARRIS, Bishop of Oxford, quoted in *Fortune*, July 12, 1993

If I were living in a monastery in Tibet, in charge of the Monastery's TQM program, I might consider advocating quality solely on the basis of it being a good thing. However, since I work for a large corporation that is very much in the business of making money, I advocate quality programs and people-centered policies on the basis that they contribute not just attitudes and morale but also very importantly—to improving the bottom line and winning new business.

> LAURIE A. BROEDLING of the aerospace company McDonnell Douglas, in a speech, April 8, 1996

You can make a pizza so cheap nobody will buy it. Have you ever seen a successful company that doesn't have a good product and where people don't like coming to work every day?

> GORDON M. BETHUNE, president of Continental Airlines, quoted in the *New York Times*, November 12, 1996

It is said [that Henry Ford] commissioned a survey of the car scrapyards of America to find out if there were parts of the Model T Ford which never failed. His inspectors came back with reports of almost every kind of breakdown: axles, brakes, pistons—all were liable to go wrong. But they drew attention to one notable exception, the *kingpins* of the scrapped cars invariably had years of life left in them. With ruthless logic Ford concluded that the kingpins on the Model T were too good for their job and ordered that in future they should be made to an inferior specification.

> NICHOLAS HUMPHREY, psychologist, cited in Richard Dawkins, *River Out of Eden* (Basic Books, 1995)

I went to the Far East in 1964 on a fact-finding trip to the two main centers for making cutlery: Hong Kong and Japan. They thought I was a potential customer, but I realized that two types of people would exist in the U.K. in the future. One would be importers, and the other would have a heavily branded product based on quality. I have never looked back.

> JOHN PRICE, head of the family-owned firm Arthur Price, one of the 12 cutlery firms remaining in Sheffield, England, quoted in the *Financial Times*, February 28, 1997

Your company has to be applying total quality management already, including customer satisfaction, management commitment, and employee involvement. The danger is that it gets applied as a panacea, as the latest fad. If you don't believe in TQM, six sigma won't do anything for you.

> ROY DAVIS, of the consulting firm Arthur D. Little, on "six sigma," which seeks to reduce defects to under three per million, quoted in the *Financial Times*, February 24, 1997

At what point in the crash do ribs break? There is no way to know that except to test ribs.

> SHERMAN HENSON, manager of side-impact safety planning for Ford, quoted in Mary Walton, *Car* (Norton, 1997)

The ancient Romans had a tradition: whenever one of their engineers constructed an arch, as the capstone was hoisted into place, the engineer assumed accountability for his work in the most profound way possible: He stood under the arch.

> C. MICHAEL ARMSTRONG, CEO of Hughes Electronics, in a speech, May 9, 1995

39.7 REENGINEERING THE CORPORATION

Revolutions often begin with the intention of only improving the systems they eventually bring down. The American, French, and Russian revolutions all started as efforts to ameliorate the rule of a monarch, not to end it. Reform turns into revolt when the old system proves too rigid to adapt. So, too, the revolution that has destroyed the traditional corporation began with efforts to improve it.

> MICHAEL HAMMER, president of consulting firm Hammer and Company, who coined the term "reengineering," *Beyond Reengineering* (Harper, 1996)

When you have a $7 billion gorilla, you don't go into the cage and quickly change him.

> CHARLES PARRY, then new chairman of the aluminum company Alcoa, interviewed in *Forbes*, February 25, 1985

Our prevailing system of management has destroyed our people. People are born with intrinsic motivation, self-esteem, dignity, curiosity to learn, joy in learning. The forces of destruction begin with toddlers—a prize for the best Halloween costume, grades in school, gold stars, and on up through the university. On the job, people, teams, divisions are ranked—reward for the one at the top, punishment at the bottom. MBO (management by objectives), quotas, incentive pay, business plans, put together separately, division by division, cause further loss, unknown and unknowable.

> W. EDWARDS DEMING, management guru

Our dream for the 1990s is a boundaryless company . . . where we knock down the walls that separate us from each other on the inside and from our key constituencies on the outside.

> JOHN F. WELCH, CEO of GE, in the company's 1990 annual report

I think a lot of senior managers have lost their resolve and their ability to face up to hard work. Change is never easy and there are no special formulas, no quick fixes. You just have to roll up your sleeves and keep working at it without backing down.

> ARDEN C. SIMS, CEO of Global Metallurgical, quoted in *Harvard Business Review*, May–June 1992

There are three forces driving restructuring: first, the need to react to excess capacity; second, the need to lift profitability in the teeth of recession; and third, the availability of more competitive wage rates in the global labor pool.

> PRESTON TOWNLEY, CEO of the corporate association Conference Board, in a speech, September 14, 1993

We've gotten pretty good at teaching the "how-to." But we forget about the "want-to."

> MARK MILLER, executive with Chick-fil-A chain of restaurants in Atlanta, on the failure of various reengineering methods, quoted in *Inc.*, June 1995

I thought it was a no-brainer. We spent a lot of time and money on professionals to teach motivation and leadership. But many people who were good soldiers under the old system just couldn't change.

> PHIL LANG, plant manager for the optical firm Bausch & Lomb, on the firm's embrace of team management, quoted in the *New York Times*, July 18, 1996

How hard will I have to work?
What recognition, financial reward, or other personal satisfaction will I get for my effort?
Are the rewards worth it?

> PROFESSOR PAUL STREBEL of IMD (International Institute for Management Development), Lausanne, Switzerland, on why employees resist change, *Harvard Business Review*, May–June 1996

[I]n the end, restructuring a company is no more and no less than rethinking that company, rethinking what it is and what it does; rethinking who it serves and the ways in which it provides value; rethinking how it can build the future that best meets its needs, and those of its many stakeholders.

> JOHN E. JACOBS of the brewer Anheuser-Busch Companies, in a speech, March 4, 1997

In large organizations, middle managers serve the purpose of relaying information up and down—orders down, numbers up. But with the new information technologies and more efficient forms of work, their purpose dwindles. Industries have incentive to shed "information relayers" and make those who remain do more "value-added work," that is, something customers will actually pay for. Does this sound heartless? Yes. Is it avoidable? Probably not.

> JAMES CHAMPY, chairman of the consulting firm CSC Index, quoted in the *New York Times,* January 7, 1996

From the perspective of American industry, the Reagan period represented the beginning of a renaissance that saved whole sectors of the economy and rescued us from being relegated to nothing more than the world's largest soda dispenser.

Until Reagan fired the illegally striking air traffic controllers, Professional Air Traffic Controllers Organizations (PATCO), American manufacturers meekly toyed with the idea of eliminating the white-collar ranks of middle management, which had exploded in size in the '60s and '70s. After Reagan took the initiative, American industry followed suit.

> JAMES J. CRAMER, president of the hedge fund Cramer & Co., *New Republic,* April 27, 1996

[C]hange is a process, not an event.

> TOM EHRENFELD, *Harvard Business Review,* January–February 1992

We won't pay for progress reports [from suppliers]. We'll pay for results.

> LEONARD GARRAMBONE of the telecommunications company Nynex, quoted in the *New York Times,* October 6, 1996

Suppliers who can't increase prices are more efficient.

> RICHARD L. HOTTINGER of the industrial firm Owens Corning, quoted in the *New York Times,* October 6, 1996

In these days of fierce global competition, demanding customers, and breakneck change, achieving success is a marathon, not a 100-yard dash. The frantic sprints, seen in companies' stock-price upturns after downsizing and other "mean business" tactics, won't stand the test of time.

In the last decade, corporate America has learned the hard way that job cuts, unaccompanied by changes in the work itself, are illusory. The short-term relief most often gives way to a long-term hangover.

> BRIAN FUGERE of Deloitte & Touche Consulting Group, quoted in the *New York Times,* November 24, 1996

To succeed at reengineering, you have to be a missionary, a motivator, and a leg breaker.

> MICHAEL HAMMER, management guru, quoted in *Fortune,* August 1993

You can survive the old way. You can survive the new way. It's the goddamn transition that'll kill you.

> BRUCE RUPPERT of the agricultural chemical firm Agway, quoted in *Fortune,* August 1993

The danger is that people overlearn the methodology [of reengineering] and underlearn the judgment of when to use it and when not to.

> JOHN SMITH of Andersen Consulting's Center for Professional Education, quoted in *Fortune,* October 4, 1993

It's [asking in-house managers to fix corporate problems] like asking fish to describe the ocean.

> DAVID NADLER, chairman of Delta Consulting Group, quoted in *Fortune,* November 29, 1993

Today manufacturing focus means learning how not to make things—how not to make the parts that divert a company from cultivating its skills, parts its suppliers could make more efficiently.

> RAVI VENKATESAN of the manufacturing company Cummins Engine, *Harvard Business Review,* November–December 1992

It's very difficult to change a successful company.

> P. ROY VAGELOS, CEO of the pharmaceutical company Merck, interviewed in *Harvard Business Review,* November–December 1994

It is easy to say, "Break the company up." But the question is into what.

> FRANK METZ, chief financial officer of IBM, quoted in the *Economist,* December 19, 1992

I wasn't smart enough about that [the human element]. I was reflecting my engineering background and was insufficiently appreciative of the human dimensions. I've learned that's critical.

> MICHAEL HAMMER, author of *Reengineering the Corporation* and *Beyond Reengineering,* on the fact that too many companies interpreted the mandate to reengineer as downsizing rather than changing processes to become more productive, quoted in the *Wall Street Journal,* November 26, 1996

The most successful practices at improving quality were found to be total quality management (seeking continuous change to improve quality); team-based working (allowing teams of operators to allocate work between themselves); and manufacturing cells (giving each group of operators the resources to produce a whole product). These were considered to meet their objectives entirely or a lot in about half the cases.

> VANESSA HOULDER, management columnist, citing data from *The Use and Effectiveness of Modern Manufacturing Practices in the U.K.* (Institute of Work Psychology, University of Sheffield), *Financial Times*, September 5, 1997

A company that pulls through a crisis with its human talent mostly in place carries a real promise of a better outcome, both for its capital supplies and for its people. Yet managers who act in accordance with this reality make themselves vulnerable to the law [because shareholders may take action against them].

> ARIE DE GEUS of Shell, *Financial Times*, May 15, 1997

39.8 SURVIVOR ANGST

Loyalty and all that stuff goes out the window.

> Executive of a major Chicago brokerage firm after it laid off 10 percent of its staff, quoted in *Time*, May 1, 1989

To have a job will be the bonus this year.

> DESMOND HEATHWOOD of Boston Co., a division of the investment firm Shearson Lehman, quoted in *Time*, May 1, 1989

It's just a job now, just a job. It used to be fun. When you made deliveries, you were "the Pabst man" or "the Schlitz man," and it made you proud. Now it's dog-eat-dog. The only things that anyone cares about are volume and money.

> JOE, who worked his way up from a truck driver to middle manager at a Milwaukee brewery, quoted in *Time*, September 11, 1989

Every time I go to a party, I get several résumés from guests the next day. It's not always wise to ask people what they do for a living anymore.

> BERNARD BRENNAN, CEO of the retail chain Montgomery Ward, quoted in *Time*, September 11, 1989

40.1 THE EIGHTIES

Doing a deal was, of course, the all-purpose panacea of the eighties.

> CONNIE BRUCK, *New Yorker,* January 8, 1990

The view was that you had to be in every market doing everything with every product, because you didn't want to miss the pot of gold.

> J. TOMILSON "TOM" HILL of the investment firm Shearson Lehman, quoted in the *New Yorker,* July 23, 1990

I'm not Robin Hood.

> CARL ICAHN, on his receipt of greenmail in hostile takeover attempts, quoted in *U.S. News & World Report,* April 8, 1985

The robber barons look like corner muggers in comparison to the amounts that are now being made.

> ANDREW SIGLER, CEO of the paper company Champion International, quoted in *Time,* April 22, 1985

Can you run America with a large proportion of your investors being casino gamblers?

> FRED HARTLEY, chairman of Unocal, quoted in *Harvard Business Review,* May–June 1986

Greenmail, in case you're wondering, is when a company pays a raider a premium for his holdings—if he'll go away. What I think it really is is blackmail in a pinstriped suit.

> LEE IACOCCA, *Talking Straight,* with Sonny Kleinfeld (Bantam, 1988)

"Boone, you're the largest shareholder. Would you be willing to give me two or three years more?"

"Why would you want two or three more years?" I replied.

"Because I think we can get the stock up to $60 or $65 by then."

"Jimmy, why would we want to wait two or three more years to get the price up to $60 or $65 when you have an offer on the table for $70?"

"Boone, I was afraid you were going to say that."

> Exchange between James E. Lee, then chairman of Gulf Oil, and T. Boone Pickens, then president of Mesa Petroleum, in "Professions of a Short Termer," *Harvard Business Review,* May–June 1986

[B]eware the manager who proclaims to the world he is a long-termer, beginning today.

> T. BOONE PICKENS JR., president of Mesa Petroleum, "Professions of a Short Termer," *Harvard Business Review,* May–June 1986

Look at the world Mike Milken [then head of junk-bonds for Drexel Burnham Lambert, subsequently jailed for charges relating to insider trading] has created. It's almost as if he can print his own currency. A deal has problems? Refinance it through another client. The Federal Reserve should have it so good.

[W]e don't know if Mike Milken will go down in history as a great man or as the person who helped leverage our economy to the breaking point.

> "A One-man Revolution," *Forbes,* August 25, 1986

[I]nvestors believed that should an issue run into trouble, Drexel "would fix it up." The view here is that such reliance on one party violated the spirit of a sound market and paved the way for later collapse. More than any specific illegality, that was why the junk market of the '80s was not always healthy.

> ROGER LOWENSTEIN, "Milken's Junk-Bond Legacy Still Up for Grabs," *Wall Street Journal,* September 5, 1996

I heard [the investment bank] Goldman, Sachs has 10 floors of guys working on this, trying to figure out how to stop us. For us, it's me and Al Kingsley—the Lone Ranger and Tonto—and this one sheet of paper. That's all we need to take over USX [the successor to U.S. Steel].

> CARL ICAHN, takeover specialist, then bidding for steel company USX, *U.S. News & World Report,* October 27, 1986

I accept this price.

> J. PIERPONT MORGAN, reacting in 1900 to Andrew Carnegie's penciled message, naming $480 million as the price at which he would sell his steel holdings (thus allowing the creation of the U.S. Steel Trust, which would control the American steel market),

quoted in Ron Chernow, *The House of Morgan* (Atlantic Monthly Press, 1990)

The level of fees has reached a point that is difficult to justify and invites the suspicion that there is too much incentive to do a deal. Fees are sometimes 10 times as large when a deal closes as when it doesn't, so you'd almost have to be a saint not to be affected by the numbers involved.

> FELIX ROHATYN, investment banker, quoted in *Time,* May 14, 1984

Once a business has become as institutionalized as the LBO [leveraged buyout] business now has, it generates its own momentum. Because entire departments with lavishly compensated employees have high overheads to meet, there is a ceaseless pressure to find new LBO candidates.

> CONNIE BRUCK, *New Yorker,* May 8, 1989

I have concluded that it might be easier to buy Greece.

> LEE IACOCCA, chairman of Chrysler Corporation after the automobile firm's $40 billion bid to buy General Motors was rejected, quoted in *Time,* June 13, 1988

The typical takeover target isn't a company in trouble. It's a company with a solid asset base, low debt, consistent profits, and a few bucks in the bank to diversify or get through the next business downturn.

> LEE IACOCCA, quoted by R. F. Mercer, CEO of Goodyear Tire and Rubber, in a speech, March 3, 1987

[T]he four shining icons of the 1980s collapsed within 36 hours in February 1989: junk bonds, Perrier, the [Donald and Ivana] Trumps' marriage, and Michael Tyson.

> WARREN BENNIS, preface to *Leaders on Leadership: Interviews with Top Executives* (Harvard Business Review, 1991)

What is going on on Wall Street [the boom in leveraged buyouts] is the economic equivalent of AIDS.

> ROBERT MERCER, CEO of Goodyear Tire and Rubber, testifying before Congress, May 1987, after paying $90 million in greenmail to Jimmy Goldsmith, *The Economist,* July 11, 1987

The irony is that some of the problems of the takeover "targets" have arisen from their desire to be more so-

cially responsible. The modern business literature tells management to balance the desires of employees, customers, suppliers, public interest groups, and shareholders. . . . It is interesting to note that shareholders are only listed as one among those worthy groups—and they are listed last.

If raiders are opportunists, it is managements and boards of directors who have given them the opportunity.

> MURRAY WEIDENBAUM of Washington University, in a speech, December 3, 1987

Liquid assets draw raiders like stagnant pools draw mosquitoes. Before companies take on the burden of excessive debt, they should consider the words of Miss Piggy, "Never eat more than you can lift."

> A. W. CLAUSEN, former chairman of Bank of America, in a speech on hostile takeovers in the 1980s

There was crime and excess throughout the Beatrice LBO. But the LBO was not about crime and excess. It was about the value-destroying impact of excessive conglomeration and corporate bureaucracy. The breakup of Beatrice was neither pretty nor painless. But the U.S. economy is stronger because Beatrice companies no longer exist.

If the 1980s were not about crime, surely, then, they were about greed.

> WILLIAM TAYLOR, in a review of books on the '80s, *Harvard Business Review,* October 1, 1992

In the '80s, there was no warm and fuzzy, you just had to make the money.

> PETER HARRISON of the recruiting firm Access Management, *New York Times,* April 4, 1993

Hostile takeovers are a little like wars: once they start, it's impossible to tell where they may end. The full effect of what you've set in motion remains to be seen.

> RICHARD MUNRO, CEO of Time Inc., quoted in *Time,* June 19, 1989

Raiders value [companies] on the basis of liquidation value. [This] is the economics of the Chicago stockyards. A cow is not an animal that produces milk and cheese. Rather, it's something to be eviscerated, hacked up, and sold piecemeal. In short you have to kill the cow.

> A. W. CLAUSEN, former CEO of Bank of America, in a speech, May 19, 1988

The best thing that can happen to our strategy is a dramatic depression. There is more opportunity to make money in a depression for people like us who have the capital and the culture and people to build through the cycle.

> TED FOWLER of the investment bank Prudential-Bache, quoted in the *Economist,* July 11, 1987

America's financial markets have an 1880s look about them. A hundred years ago America depended, as it does in 1987, on imported foreign capital, most of which arrived through sales of shares and bonds rather than through bank lending. Ominously the bear markets of the late nineteenth century all therefore sprang from interruptions in the flow of foreign money.

In 1893 and again in 1896, the cash stopped because of fears that America would abandon the gold standard and devalue the dollar. Financial markets really have seen it all before.

> *The Economist,* September 5, 1987

The officer of every corporation should feel in his heart—in his very soul—that he is responsible, not merely to make dividends for the stockholders of his company, but to enhance the general prosperity and the moral sentiment of the United States.

> ADOLPHUS GREEN, founder of Nabisco, quoted in Bryan Burroughs and John Helyar, *Barbarians at the Gate* (Harper & Row, 1991)

Some genius invented the Oreo. We're just living off the inheritance.

> F. ROSS JOHNSON, president of RJR Nabisco, quoted in Bryan Burroughs and John Helyar, *Barbarians at the Gate* (Harper & Row, 1991)

They put handcuffs on them?

> Phrase on Wall Street when executives at the investment firms Goldman, Sachs and Kidder Peabody were being arrested for insider trading, quoted in *Business Week,* March 2, 1987

Let's face it. If a guy's making money for the firm, no one's going to look too hard.

> "Wall Street veteran," quoted in *Business Week,* March 2, 1987

Chinese Walls didn't keep the Mongols out of China, and they haven't kept the miscreants on Wall Street out of the honey pot either. ["Chinese Walls" are internal barriers within financial organizations to separate lines of business that by law may not be linked.]

> U.S. REPRESENTATIVE JOHN DINGELL (Democrat, Michigan), quoted in *Business Week,* March 2, 1987

Without [Michael] Milken, there is no romance.

> Former executive of Drexel Burnham Lambert, after its star employer Milken was accused of insider trading, quoted in *Business Week,* February 16, 1987

Somebody asked me one time, "You like to be called a corporate raider?"

I said, "No, I like to be identified as a large stockholder who sometimes becomes active."

I see a raider as someone who walks into a bank with a gun and demands all of the money. I feel like I'm the guy who made a large deposit just before the bank robber stuck a gun in the teller's face.

> T. BOONE PICKENS, president of Mesa Petroleum, sometimes credited with having started the "shareholder revolution," in a speech, May 2, 1988

Today in the United States, there are revolutionaries armed with economic intelligence, monetary strength, and ruthlessness. This situation presents real challenges to management. Can it prevent the creation of opportunities for takeover groups? Can it supply the vitality, the imagination, and indeed the internal spirit that is necessary to achieve economic progress in this changing world?

> PROFESSOR CHARLES M. WILLIAMS of Harvard Business School, *Harvard Business Review,* July–August 1955

This bubble, like all bubbles, will eventually collapse, leaving the wreckage of ruined companies, lost jobs, reduced oil production, failed banks and savings and loans, and government bailouts.

> FRED HARTLEY, chairman of the oil company Unocal, quoted in *Time,* April 22, 1985

T. Boone Pickens almost never completes an acquisition after acquiring a block of a target's stock and initiating takeover activity. In the past five years, he has not acquired a single company in a hostile takeover but he has cleared more than $1 billion in profits from these attempts.

> BRUCE ATWATER, CEO of the food company General Mills, in a speech, September 1, 1988

This is a lesson to people who want to be millionaires in their thirties: better do it legally.

> RUDOLPH GIULIANI, then U.S. Attorney in New York City and later mayor of the city, on the arrest of alleged inside traders, quoted in *Time*, February 23, 1987

The accusation that [Michael] Milken bilked thrifts with a fraudulent market is based on a temporary collapse in junk-bond prices resulting from the government's attack on the market.

Ponzi schemes can't recover when they collapse, but junk bonds have come roaring back as have the stocks of leveraged companies.

> PAUL CRAIG ROBERTS of the Center for Strategic and International Studies, in a speech, May 11, 1992

We're really not a bunch of big, bad wolves. Mergers and acquisitions have created a great deal of value.

> IRWIN JACOBS, investor who targeted ITT and Disney stocks, quoted in *Time*, April 22, 1985

Are these guys really Robin Hood and his Merry Men, as they claim, or Genghis Khan and the Mongol hordes?

> ROBERT MILLER of Chrysler Corporation, in a speech, quoted in *U.S. News & World Report*, January 26, 1987

40.2 HOSTILE TAKEOVERS

It was more than I would liked to have spent, but I was in a poker game and couldn't see the other players.

> GEORGE KELLER, chairman Standard Oil of California, which paid $13.2 billion to take over Gulf, quoted in *Time*, March 19, 1984

It's like watching your mother getting ravaged by New York thugs.

> GREG KIESELMANN of the brokerage firm Morgan, Olmstead, Kennedy & Garder, after the financier

Saul P. Steinberg made $32 million in greenmail from Disney, quoted in *Time*, June 25, 1984

Clearly, in many cases, the executives are just messing up the company. Management's feeling is: cripple us, poke our eyes out, and maybe they won't like us any more.

> JAY MARSHALL of the investment bank Merrill Lynch, quoted in *Time*, June 25, 1984

40.3 ROARING EIGHTIES HALL OF SHAME

John DeLorean has turned into a modern day Job—his family is gone, his friends are gone, his assets are gone, his pride is gone.

> Los Angeles newspaper advertisement appealing for donations for the former auto magnate's legal fund, quoted in *U.S. News & World Report*, November 19, 1984

Would you buy a used car from me?

> JOHN DELOREAN, on what the government's case against him (for drug smuggling) had done to his reputation, quoted in *U.S. News & World Report*, November 19, 1984

How many criminals can claim 56,000 victims?

> JUDGE RICHARD NIEHAUS, sentencing banker Marvin Warner to three and a half years in prison and fining him $22 million for his role in the 1985 collapse of Cincinnati's Home State Savings, quoted in *U.S. News & World Report*, April 13, 1987

Jovanovich killed the company. He's a dumb Croat coalminer. Had I met him, I would have told him so.

> ROBERT MAXWELL, Czech-born English publishing mogul, about his attempt to take over the American publishing house Harcourt Brace Jovanovich, quoted in *Time*, November 28, 1988 (Maxwell later committed suicide when his excessively leveraged empire unraveled.)

I would like the opportunity to go forward to redeem myself and leave this earth with a good name.

> IVAN BOESKY, arbitrageur and felon (he was convicted of insider trading), quoted in *Fortune*, January 5, 1988

Everyone involved stands discredited to some degree: Wall Street for its greed; managers for their sloth; and raiders for what is perceived as a predatory search for assets and callous disregard for the social costs of their transactions.

> JOHN POUND of the Kennedy School of Government at Harvard and co-chair of the shareholder committee established by Carl Icahn at the steel company USX, *Harvard Business Review,* March–April 1992.

It's a privilege to address this distinguished gathering of unindicted business-school graduates, their unindicted faculty, family, and friends.

> JOSEPH GRUNDFEST of the U.S. Securities and Exchange Commission, quoted in *U.S. News & World Report,* June 1, 1987

We're not Texans.

> New England bankers trying to reassure federal regulators, quoted in L. William Seidman, *Full Faith and Credit* (Times Books, 1993)

40.4 S&L CRISIS

The thing that's scaring me is that everyone else is scared.

> JEFF SHANK, Maryland auto mechanic, who withdrew $14,000 in savings from Old Court Savings and Loan, quoted in *Time,* May 27, 1985

The S & L industry has been playing a giant game of roulette with taxpayers' money. Without tough capital rules, we will be telling these high-flying speculators, "Okay, go back to the casinos."

> U.S. REPRESENTATIVE CHARLES SCHUMER (Democrat, New York), quoted in *Time,* June 26, 1989

It's the reverse toaster theory. Instead of the bank giving you a toaster when you make a deposit, you give them one.

> L. WILLIAM SEIDMAN, chairman of the Federal Deposit Insurance Corporation, on an administration plan to collect fees from bank depositors to rescue the S & L industry, quoted in *Newsweek,* February 6, 1989

The S & Ls were an invitation to gamble with someone else's money—the taxpayers' of the United States. As a lawyer as well as an accountant, if I had been asked to defend these gamblers in court, I might well have used the defense of entrapment (as some did): a honeypot had been officially created that was irresistible to ordinary mortals.

> L. WILLIAM SEIDMAN, former head of the Federal Deposit Insurance Corporation, *Full Faith and Credit* (Times Books, 1993)

No doubt many Americans believe that most of the money has simply been squandered by crooked savings and loan executives on private air fleets, California beach houses, trips to Paris, and blueprints for branches on the moon. As the losses mount, however, the corruption theory starts to leak (it's not easy, even for a Texan, to embezzle $180 billion). The truth is that a lot of the money was lost legally by crazy gamblers—and a big chunk of that found its way into the pockets of the Wall Street bond traders and salesmen who encouraged the S & Ls to gamble like lunatics in the first place.

> MICHAEL LEWIS, *The Money Culture* (Norton, 1991)

You've got a bunch of know-nothings trying to tell business people how to invest money.

> CHARLES KEATING, former head of Lincoln Savings & Loan, after being released from prison because of mistakes made by trial judge Lance Ito, quoted in the *New York Times,* October 12, 1996

And always remember the weak, meek, and ignorant are always good targets.

> Sales document for sales of Lincoln Savings & Loan bonds, quoted in the *New York Times,* October 12, 1996

I had read materials, listened to experts, participated in discussions, and attended monthly meetings in good faith. And so at the age of 61 and after a lifetime laced with volunteer public service, I am disillusioned, my life threatened by an irrational creature of government that may not be checked in time to save me.

> JAMES L. FISHER, former college president of Towson State University and Baltimore Federal Savings & Loan board member, hit with a $32 million lawsuit for gross negligence when the S & L failed in 1988

(unable to afford legal fees of $14,000 a month, he was reduced to spending all his time researching his defense), quoted in the *New Republic*, January 4, 1993

I went to Disneyland for the first time when I was 24 but my kids have gone there every year. We definitely have it better than my parents.

TED MOORE, San Francisco car dealer, *Fortune*, June 9, 1997

40.5 TAKEOVERS, THE AFTERMATH

You have all the Gulf T-shirts and cuff links. It is more than a job. It's part of your life.

CHARLES RHOADS of Gulf Oil, after its merger with Chevron, quoted in *U.S. News & World Report*, July 22, 1985

We lost, so they treated us like conquerors.

Gulf manager on the new Chevron management, quoted in *U.S. News & World Report*, July 22, 1985

41.1 SECRETS OF SUCCESS

I was taught to work as well as play;
My life has been one long, happy holiday—
Full of work and full of play—
And God was good to me every day.

> JOHN D. ROCKEFELLER, original verse quoted in his obituary, quoted in Robert Sobel and David B. Sicilia, *The Entrepreneurs—An American Adventure* (Houghton Mifflin, 1986)

[I]t frequently appears that skill in handling a long-stemmed glass is virtually as important to the modern businessman as knowing how to work his way through a crowded ledger.

> JOHN McCARTER, "Easy on the Vermouth," *Harper's Bazaar,* July 1950

Of all the things I've done, the most vital is coordinating the talents of those who work for us and pointing them toward a certain goal.

> WALT DISNEY, 1954, quoted in Richard Schickel, *The Disney Version* (Simon & Schuster, 1968)

Fake it till you make it.

> MARY KAY ASH, founder of Mary Kay Cosmetics, quoted in Robert Sobel and David B. Sicilia, *The Entrepreneurs—An American Adventure* (Houghton Mifflin, 1986)

I looked for those sharp, scratchy, harsh, almost unpleasant guys who see and tell you about things as they really are.

> THOMAS J. WATSON JR., former chief executive of IBM, quoted in *Fortune,* August 31, 1987

I never hesitated to promote someone I didn't like.

> THOMAS J. WATSON JR., *Fortune,* August 31, 1987

You want to know how to make a small fortune in the wine business? Start with a large one.

> RICHARD L. MAHER, president of the liquor firm Christian Brothers Sales, quoted in *Business Week,* February 2, 1987

I went under my desk so my voice would be smooth and any buzzing of my phone wouldn't be heard, and I just begged.

> STEVE LEWIS, producer of the TV show *Good Morning America,* on how he used to get celebrity guests, quoted in *U.S. News & World Report,* May 25, 1987

Behind every successful man you'll find a woman—who has absolutely nothing to wear.

> Actor JAMES STEWART, quoted in *1990 Film Yearbook*

I've studied a lot of people, and the common fiber for every successful person is the intensity person. . . . The successful person can reach down and get a little extra, and win when the chips are down.

> D. WAYNE LUKAS, owner and trainer of the most successful racing stable ever, quoted in the *New Yorker,* December 26, 1988

Any young person who doesn't take up bridge is making a real mistake. One bridge game is worth 20 cocktail parties.

> WARREN BUFFETT, CEO of the investment firm Berkshire Hathaway, quoted in the *New York Times,* May 20, 1990

Never run out of cash and never turn down an order.

> FINIS F. CONNER, founder of Conner Peripherals, quoted in the *New York Times,* May 27, 1990

Having a couple of good partners is as good as doing your own thing.

> RALPH ROBERTS, chairman of the cable TV firm Comcast, quoted in Ken Auletta, "Diller Peeks into the Future," *New Yorker,* February 22, 1993

I always went into an area that was in last place, with a philosophy, "You can't fall off the floor."

> MICHAEL D. EISNER, CEO of Disney, quoted on the Academy of Achievement web site, June 17, 1994

I go out on a limb more than I did before with business. Now [when] I go into business meetings, I'm thinking, "If you guys had just half of what I have."

> FRANK WHITEHEAD, a Los Angeles entrepreneur who, in 1995, had an operation to lengthen and widen his penis, quoted in the *Wall Street Journal*, June 6, 1996

Dreams do come true. [Slogan for penile enlargements performed at the Men's Institute of Cosmetic Surgery]

> *Wall Street Journal*, June 6, 1996

Anxiety is the secret to my success. It's the difference between an engineer, who generally has a pretty good idea of how to tackle and solve the problem he's working on, and an inventor who wakes up at night in a cold sweat sure that the thing he's trying to do is impossible.

> RAY DOLBY, chairman of the audio electronics firm Dolby Labs, quoted in *Forbes*, August 3, 1996

[I]f you get the right people leading a business, it will improve.

> LAWRENCE BOSSIDY, CEO of the industrial firm Allied-Signal, quoted in *Fortune*, December 13, 1993

Good decisions come from wisdom. Wisdom comes from experience. Experience comes from bad decisions.

> *Forbes*, August 10, 1987

I stand on my head every day.

> JOHN KLUGE, media magnate, about a day when he was in a Cleveland bar during time off from negotiations to buy a radio station, recounted by Lois Wyse, *Company Manners* (McGraw-Hill, 1986)

It's startling to people when you're attractive and also really smart or extraordinarily good at what you do. You have greater impact. People want to meet you. They remember you.

> REBECCA MARK, CEO of the international ventures division Enron Development, which builds pipelines and power plants, quoted in *Fortune*, August 5, 1996

Real winners do not play by the rules—they change them or even make their own.

> NIALL FITZGERALD, chairman of the food and consumer products company Unilever, quoted in the *Financial Times*, February 17, 1997

Most success springs from an obstacle or failure. I became a cartoonist largely because I failed in my goal of becoming a successful executive.

> SCOTT ADAMS, creator of the cartoon *Dilbert*, quoted in *USA Weekend*, August 8–10, 1997

A mentor had advised me, "Find a niche and become the very best at it." I saw the bankruptcy area as a career opportunity because it had no cachet, no protocols, and no women.

> DARLA MOORE, CEO of the investment firm Rainwater Inc. and wife of Richard Rainwater, reflecting on her career at Chemical Bank, quoted in *Fortune*, September 8, 1997

After hard work, the biggest determinant is being in the right place at the right time.

> MICHAEL BLOOMBERG, founder and CEO of the financial news firm Bloomberg, quoted in *Newsweek*, August 4, 1997

If you have the good sense to keep up with your roommates, your own careers could take quite a turn.

> STROBE TALBOTT, Deputy Secretary of State and former housemate of U.S. President Bill Clinton, *Time*, June 9, 1997

It [playing Ping-Pong with her husband each morning] helps me build up my aggressiveness. That's how I get the energy to do all this.

> KIJA KIM, Korean-born founder of Harvard Design and Mapping Company, quoted in *Asia, Inc.*, April 1997

Number one, I want a concept that's been around for a hundred years or more. . . . Because there's nothing more expensive than educating a market. . . . [Second] I want an industry that is antiquated . . . a business in which most companies are out of step with the customer. . . . [third] a niche.

> NORM BRODSKY, founder of six successful businesses, on secrets of success in choosing a start-up, quoted in *Inc.*, April 1996

[*Sayings found in the letters of the late* ROBERTO GOIZUETA, *CEO of Coca-Cola*]

The stars incline you but never force you (from a Havana astrologer)

Traveler, there is no path. Paths are made for walking (Antonio Machado)

If my grandmother had wheels, she would be a bicycle (Goizueta's grandfather)

Wall Street Journal, February 16, 1996

41.2 BEING ON TOP

It's a lot better to be up here gettin' shot at than being down low and getting stepped on.

MEYER BLINDER, founder of the investment company Blinder Robinson, quoted in *Fortune,* January 19, 1987 (He was age 65 and worth an estimated $200 million when he said this. His company was also under investigation by the SEC for misuse of customers' securities.)

It [being on top] can lead to complacency, which blunts the ability to perceive new opportunities. The money tends to put you in a different peer group, creating a sense of isolation and the need to seek others who are equally successful. Some rich people feel only they can understand each other.

JOHN KAO, psychiatrist and teacher at Harvard Business School, quoted in *Time,* January 23, 1984

42.1 CAREERS

Wall Street people abuse their voices . . . So many start out with wonderful voices, and they're ruined in a few years.

> DR. LUCILLE RUBIN, New York speech consultant, quoted in the *New York Times,* June 23, 1991

Some people in this industry don't have the transferable skills necessary to change industries . . . Brokerage and securities executives find new positions up to 25 percent faster than those in other industries.

> GEORGE MAUZE, general manager at Lee Hecht Harrison, career services firm in Manhattan, on results of a survey of securities executives who lost their jobs, quoted in the *New York Times,* July 9, 1997

I'm basically from a middle-class family. I didn't even know Wall Street existed. . . . When I started at Dean Witter, I was scared to death. My God, I thought they were all geniuses.

> LARRY FEINBERG, founder of the securities fund Oracle Partners LP, quoted in *Financial World,* October 21, 1996

On Wall Street, which has long specialized in taking toothsome men of no particular skill and making them rich, those who make the most money are the socially maladjusted Ph.D.'s in physics and mathematicians from Harvard and MIT.

> MICHAEL LEWIS, *Slate,* October 29, 1997

42.2 DIVERSITY

The growth of black-owned firms is the last and most important phase of the civil-rights movement. We are finally seeing the integration of the capital market.

> TRAVERS J. BELL JR., chairman of the first black-owned member firm of the New York Stock Exchange, quoted in the *Wall Street Journal,* January 31, 1985

Investment banking should not be a welfare program.

> NAPOLEON BRONFORD III, black investment banker with the firm Grisby Bronford & Co., on failing

efforts to increase black involvement by true black-owned firms in the municipal-bond business because they are losing out to tiny firms fronting for larger institutions, quoted in *Business Week,* July 4, 1994

You have a minority firm competing against one of the major firms on Wall Street that, in effect, is cloaked in minority status.

> HAROLD E. DALEY JR. of Daley Securities, quoted in *Business Week,* July 4, 1994

In the more than 10 years I've been at Goldman, working with the highest levels of executives, I've dealt with one other black man outside the firm.

> JIDE ZEITLIN of the investment firm Goldman, Sachs and only the second black partner in the firm's history, quoted in *Fortune,* August 4, 1997

If you buy GM at 40 and it goes to 50, whether you are an Oriental, a Korean, or a Buddhist doesn't make any difference.

> GERRY TSAI, Shanghai-born founder of Fidelity Capital Fund, quoted in John Brooks, *The Go-Go Years* (Weybright & Talley, 1973)

Because Indians don't fit into the stereotypical GQ image of the investment banker, we have to work just that little bit harder to prove ourselves.

> SWAPAN BHATTACHARYA of the investment firm Paine Webber, quoted in *Business Week,* July 11, 1994

42.3 HUMOR

The joke goes on until the guy figures it out, breaks down in tears, or has a heart attack. Makes for a hell of a first day.

> Trader, describing practical joke pulled on novice brokers (they are given phony orders by supposedly important clients at a low market price, which is then driven up by 30 or 40 other brokers before the novice can execute the order at the agreed price), quoted in the *New York Times,* April 19, 1992

I don't know why this kind of environment seems to breed irreverence, whether it's the pressure and people needing a release, but this seems to be the hotbed of jokes.

> ROBERT WILLENS SR., of the investment firm Lehman Brothers, quoted in the *New York Times,* July 25, 1993

Wall Street is known for its ability to come up with absolutely the worst jokes about the worst situations on a moment's notice. Before the fire was out in Waco, I must have heard 30 of them in an hour.

> TRINI CASASIN, trader for Deutsche Bank Capital, quoted in the *New York Times,* July 25, 1993

If you're going to be perceived as a great salesman, proving you have information is really important. If someone calls you up and starts a joke, and you can finish it, you have the edge. It proves you're plugged in.

> Trader at a small securities firm, quoted in the *Wall Street Journal,* January 31, 1997

42.4 OLD WALL STREET

[T]he turn of the century was the age of the banker, so much so that the leading bankers of the day had become legendary figures in the public imagination—vast, overshadowing behemoths whose colossal power seemed to reach everywhere.

> DORIS KEARNS GOODWIN, *The Fitzgeralds and the Kennedys* (Simon & Schuster, 1987)

The plan at that time most in favor was to start off with the largest possible capitalization and then sell all the stock and all the bonds that could be sold. Whatever money happened to be left over after all the stock and bond-selling expenses and promoters, charges and all that, went grudgingly into the foundation of the business.

> HENRY FORD, discussing how his build-from-the-ground-up business ethic conflicted with the ways of Wall Street early in his career, *My Life and Work* (Doubleday, 1922)

The prestige houses issued securities but never distributed them; they had scant capital and little tolerance for risk. Trading was dismissed as a grubby activity best consigned to Jews, Catholics, and others banned from the club.

> RON CHERNOW, *Wall Street Journal,* September 30, 1997

The slaves have all been freed, and the West has been won. The railroads are built and every beggar has his flush toilet. But I think you may find, if you come to work for me, that there's still some adventure left. You were born to the great age of the dollar, of the speculator, of high finance! It should take a century to plunder our new land, and don't worry, the banker will be in the vanguard.

> MARCELLUS DE GRASSE, a character based on JP Morgan Sr., in Louis Auchincloss, *The Embezzler,* a novel based on the life of Richard Whitney who was president of the New York Stock Exchange (Whitney's transgressions were blamed by Wall Street for inviting the Roosevelt administration to regulate the financial markets.) (Houghton Mifflin, 1966)

[I believe] the main reason why Wall Street has lost that quality of dramatic personal adventure which was so marked in my youth will be found in the astonishing extension of the range and area of economic interests covered by the market's activities. This change, in turn, reflects the equally astonishing transformation of America from a frontier-pushing people, concerned mainly with subduing a continent, to the prime stabilizing force for the whole of western civilization. One might label this change as a shift from an era of almost unrestrained individualism to one of global responsibility.

> BERNARD M. BARUCH, *Baruch: My Own Story* (Holt, 1957)

For almost a generation, from the 1929 crash to the bull market of the 1950s, young men of talent and ambition grew up thinking of Wall Street as anathema and did not go to work there . . . (Between 1930 and 1951 . . . only eight persons were hired to work on the New York Stock Exchange trading floor.)

> JOHN BROOKS, *The Go-Go Years* (Weybright & Talley, 1973)

42.5 PERSONALITY

Beyond conformity of dress, a lot of unusual people and unusual behavior are tolerated here. Since the test of any idea is whether it will make money, individualistic thinking is rewarded here more than in other environments.

> JAY B. ROHRLICH, Wall Street psychiatrist, interviewed in *Forbes,* April 22, 1985

Our egos, our fears, our concern about jobs, capital, and looking good have nothing to do with predicting interest rates.

> EUGENE ROTBERG, then president of the World Bank, quoted in *Forbes*, May 19, 1986

The scarce resource today is management, knowledge, vision, dealing with change, recognizing what people want and need in the future, and the ability to work together. You won't find these scarce resources listed on a balance sheet. Unfortunately, most people working in financial institutions, credit analysts, don't recognize this.

> MICHAEL MILKEN, leveraged finance expert and junk-bond popularizer, formerly of Drexel Burnham Lambert (now defunct firm), in 1986 speech, quoted in *Forbes*, May 5, 1986

This business beats you up so bad that if you have low self-esteem, you internalize [your mistakes]. Once you internalize it, it eats up your gut and you start thinking it's your fault. People with high self-esteem let it bounce off. They'll just say: "It's too bad. That guy's not going to have a chance to work with me."

> JOHN KELLY, sales manager for the investment bank Merrill Lynch, quoted in *Worth*, May 1994

Any system is subject to someone getting around it.

> MICHAEL CARPENTER, CEO of investment bank Kidder Peabody, referring to a trading scheme that created $350 million in false profits for parent company GE Capital, quoted in *Business Week*, May 2, 1994

42.6 STOCK MARKET MISCELLANY

Suppose you're on pins and needles, sitting with a 10-million-dollar bond position. The phone rings. It's your wife. She says, "I've got a speeding ticket. What should I do?" It's hard to be civil. Some wives don't understand.

> Wall Street trader, on why so many people in his profession have marital problems, quoted in *U.S. News & World Report*, February 7, 1983

Wall Street is not an easy constituency to represent on the Hill.

> Wall Street lobbyist, citing arrogance and wealth, *New Yorker*, May 8, 1988

If you want to make money hold your nose and go to Wall Street.

> WARREN BUFFETT, speaking to business school students, quoted by Michael Lewis, *New Republic*, February 17, 1992

Racetracks [in the late nineteenth century] were supported primarily by the rental fees of bookmakers who in New York formed themselves into an association modeled along the lines of the New York Stock Exchange. The price of a seat was the same for the Turf Association and the Stock Exchange in the 1880s, approximately $7,000.

> PETER REUTER, *Disorganized Crime: The Economics of the Visible Hand* (MIT Press, 1983)

We concluded that while the stock price is one measure of performance, it is far from the only measure, and probably not the most important. We had been fooled into thinking it was telling us what good managers we were—and then what poor ones.

> SAFI U. QURESHY, CEO of AST Research, *Harvard Business Review*, May–June 1991

81,300,000. Collective pay, in dollars, of the top five executives at Bear Stearns, a Wall Street investment firm—topping by $23 million the payroll of the Chicago Bulls, the NBA's highest-paid team.

> *Sports Illustrated*, October 7, 1996

I have a two-hour train ride each day and when I get tired of reading I look out the window and daydream about the next hot industry. But as Mark Twain said, "I seldom see an opportunity until it ceases to be one." So my [New Year's] resolution is to do less reading and more looking out the window.

> NICHOLAS PRATT of the American Stock Exchange, quoted in the *New York Times*, January 5, 1992

I fear the tyranny of a stock market that favors boring financial conglomerates over innovative, enterprising firms.

> RON CHERNOW, *Wall Street Journal*, September 30, 1997

[The stock market is] a summary of people's views about the future.

> GLENN HUBBARD of the Columbia Graduate School of Business, quoted in the *Wall Street Journal*, October 28, 1997

It's become legendary that this ZIP code [Wall Street] is the heart attack capital of New York.

> ELLEN KARASIK of New York University Downtown Hospital, quoted in the *New York Times,* January 2, 1998

The heart attack death rate during business hours for the 5,000 people who work at the [New York Stock] exchange is 60 percent higher than the national rate for men between 18 and 65, according to the National Center for Health Services.

> *New York Times,* January 2, 1998

Wall Street begins in a church and ends in a river.

> H. L. MENCKEN

42.7   TRADING AND SALES

Around here, one is given a great deal of responsibility very quickly. But it's a two-edged sword. They give you plenty of rope to hang yourself, too.

> JOE SCHNEIDER, recent MBA on a six-month stint on a trading desk, quoted in *U.S. News & World Report,* February 7, 1983

I'm a game player. I require this casino environment. It keeps me going.

> BILL FLINTER, 45-year-old stock trader, quoted in *U.S. News & World Report,* February 7, 1983

It could be a dangerous mistake to believe that there is no relation between the symbolic economy of money, stocks, credit, and capital, and the real economy of goods and services. Yet the financial dealers continue to insist: "These assets are for trading, not for operating."

> LEONARD SILK, former *New York Times* economics columnist, quoted by Joseph A. Katarncic, a partner at Katarncic Salmon Steele, in a speech, April 7, 1985

Wall Street is a lot like the garment business. If it's in vogue, we can sell it.

> J. MORTON DAVIS, of D. H. Blair, top performer in aftermarket for initial public offerings in 1984, quoted in *Forbes,* April 22, 1985

Just imagine that a bond is a slice of cake, and you didn't bake the cake, but every time you hand somebody a slice of the cake a tiny little bit comes off, like a little crumb, and you can keep that.

> MRS. SHERMAN McCOY, wife of a bond trader, explaining to their daughter what Daddy does for a living, in Tom Wolfe, *Bonfire of the Vanities* (Farrar Straus & Giroux, 1987)

[To compete, Americans must push] innovation after innovation. Whether you're talking about derivatives, structured credits, or any kind of innovative cross-border finance, the players that first discovered how to do these things were U.S. players.

> LOWELL BRYANT of the consulting firm McKinsey & Co., quoted in the *Wall Street Journal,* January 5, 1996

There is almost an adverse correlation between education and trading success. It's certainly not an IQ game.

> MIKE SNOW, head of Union Bank of Switzerland's treasury department, quoted in *U.S. News & World Report,* October 10, 1988

When you're an athlete who's competed on a high level, people know you're a team player, willing to do what it takes to reach your goal. You build a certain amount of mental toughness, so even if you fail to guard that big account, you pick yourself up and go at it even harder the next time.

> DOUG McNEELY, equity trader at the investment firm Donaldson Lufkin & Jenrette and the 1983 captain of Duke University's basketball team, quoted in the *New York Times,* October 25, 1992

[A good trader is] ready to bite the ass off a bear.

> JOHN GUTFREUND, former CEO of the investment bank Salomon Brothers, quoted in the *Wall Street Journal,* September 30, 1997

Our audience demands sports and they will go elsewhere if we can't give it to them and we will never get it back.

> MICHAEL BLOOMBERG, CEO of Bloomberg News Service, on why he includes sports as part of a package of general news, quoted in the *Financial Times,* May 19, 1997

If you want loyalty, get a dog.

> A "legendary trader," quoted in the *Financial Times,* January 15, 1997

You can tell a worried trader when you look him in the eye.

> HERBERT FREIMAN, head of sales and trading at the investment firm Shearson Lehman, quoted in the *Economist,* July 11, 1987

There seems to be a natural empathy or bonding between our two groups. We're both required to make quick decisions with limited information.

> U.S. ARMY LT. GENERAL PAUL K. VAN RIPER, after a training session in making decisions amid chaos (trading mock crude-oil and stock-index futures on the floor of the New York Mercantile Exchange), quoted in the *Wall Street Journal,* December 16, 1996

In trading, you win a few and lose a few. And we don't like the idea of losing a few.

> U.S. ARMY COLONEL JAMES LASWELL, quoted in the *Wall Street Journal,* December 16, 1996

Wall Street is a very unreal kind of vocational calling because you're completely divorcing yourself from the products and people your stocks represent. A trader can't "believe" in a product or "trust" a CEO. It's actually called "getting religion," and a trader will not allow that to happen. He can't. But the act of walking into that church lifts him out of that calculated indifference. Even if it's just for a moment, that trader is lifted into a world of God's spiritual presence. People out in Kansas probably think traders come in here and pray for their stocks to go up. They don't.

> DR. DANIEL PAUL MATTHEWS, rector of Trinity church, at the top of Wall Street, quoted in the *New York Observer,* December 29, 1997

42.8 WOMEN

Wall Street in 1965 . . . stood out as a last bastion of all-but-unchallenged male supremacy. It thought working women ought to be office drudges or sex objects, or both. One summer about that time, the Street took a collective notion to make a fuss over a young stenographer of exceptional physical endowments. By word of mouth it became known that she was in the habit of emerging from the subway stop at William and Wall at a certain time each day. Huge crowds began collecting to watch her appearance with cheers and whistles . . . and one day when she surfaced there was a real mob and near riot, as if the girl's arrival were some sort of highly charged political event. The girl herself . . . was first flattered, then abashed, and finally horrified. In a sense, this little episode *was* a political event; Wall Street was unconsciously demonstrating exactly what it thought of women and of what they were good for.

> JOHN BROOKS, *The Go-Go Years* (Weybright & Talley, 1973)

I believe women in the financial services industry were better off 10 years ago. The last cuts decimated women, and the top women you see now in securities firms are the same ones who were at the top 20 years ago.

> BARBARA B. ROBERTS, former investment banker and president of the advertising agency FPG International, quoted in the *New York Times,* September 27, 1992

Even Morgan Stanley, which formed a diversity task force in 1992, has only 30 female managing directors out of 350 worldwide.

> TRACY CORRIGAN, *Financial Times Weekend,* January 25–26, 1997

[S]o far, Wall Street has the edge over the City. No one has "my deared" me since I got here, nor mistaken me for a secretary. And the lowest ebb of my experience in the City firms—when I exited a roadshow dinner just minutes before the "dancers" arrived—would be almost unimaginable here (if only because Americans are better at PR).

> TRACY CORRIGAN, after four months at the New York bureau, *Financial Times Weekend,* January 25–26, 1997

Half the women on Wall Street complain about the guys taking clients there [to an upscale strip joint]: They're forming business relationships from which women are excluded.

> JUDITH VLADECK, leading plaintiff lawyer for sex-discrimination, quoted in *New York Daily News,* October 23, 1997

[*Note:* Several years ago, the New York Public Library opened a Library of Science, Industry, and Business, which—sign of the times—occupies the majestic neo-classical building that once held the department store B. Altman. Here are the business quotes that adorn its walls, with the same lack of elaboration that characterizes most quote books.]

If the spirit of business adventure is dulled, this country will cease to hold the foremost position in the world.

ANDREW W. MELLON

Going into business for yourself, becoming an entrepreneur, is the modern-day equivalent of pioneering on the old frontier.

PAULA NELSON

The chief business of the American people is business.

CALVIN COOLIDGE

Life without industry is guilt, industry without art is brutality.

JOHN RUSKIN

The only thing that keeps us alive is our brilliance. The only thing protecting our brilliance is our patents.

EDWIN LAND

Whenever an individual or a business decides that success has been attained, progress stops.

THOMAS WATSON SR.

In business, willingness is just as important as ability.

PAUL G. HOFFMAN

Small business is the biggest business of all.

J. E. MURRAY

The more people who own little businesses of their own, the safer our country will be, and the better off its cities and towns, for the people who have a stake in their country and their community are its best citizens.

JOHN HANCOCK

I view resources on a global scale. It encourages economic integration, generates new capital resources, and fosters the spread of useful technology and management know-how.

ROBERT W. SARNOFF

Next to knowing about your own business, the best thing to know about is the other fellow's business.

JOHN D. ROCKEFELLER

Modern management is a continuous learning experience.

ROBERT D. STUART JR.

Information about money has become almost as important as money itself.

WALTER WRISTON

There's no ceiling on effort.

HARVEY C. GRUEHAUF

Only through curiosity can we discover opportunities and only by gambling can we take advantage of them.

CLARENCE BIRDSEYE

Be everywhere, do everything, and never fail to astonish the customer.

MARGARET GETCHELL

There is no resting place for an enterprise in a competitive economy.

ALFRED P. SLOAN

My motto is first honesty, then industry, then concentration.

ANDREW CARNEGIE

The only thing that we can predict with certainty is change.

JAYNE SPAIN

44.1 ADAPTING FROM THE MILITARY TO CIVILIAN WORK

I think I would have been a fish out of water if I hadn't got some grounding in what business was about. I knew how government worked and how red tape worked, but I had no idea what a balance sheet was.

> DAVE FOSTER of the auto company General Motors and a former navy officer, on getting an MBA prior to mustering out, *Wall Street Journal,* February 16, 1997

I could barely reel off a sentence without using an acronym.

> KRIS FUHR of Kraft Foods and former army officer, quoted in the *Wall Street Journal,* February 16, 1997

44.2 EMPLOYMENT

[L]ow-paid work is not necessarily either a stepping stone to greater things or a sentence to a life of drudgery. And that seems to be as true in sleepy Europe as in thrusting America, supposedly the land of opportunity.

> *The Economist,* July 20, 1996

44.3 FOLLOWING YOUR SPOUSE TO A NEW JOB

When they asked why they left their previous job, and they say they were following their mate, the employer has to wonder, will it happen again.

> JAMES CHALLENGER of the outplacement firm Challenger, Grey & Christmas, quoted in the *Wall Street Journal,* September 17, 1996

There is a feeling of diminishment. People ask me what brought me to Phoenix; I say I'm following my wife's career. You get a look, like, "What kind of weenie are we dealing with today?"

> JON SPERA, corporate training consultant, quoted in the *Wall Street Journal,* September 17, 1996

44.4 FULFILLMENT

The most thorough research has not brought out a single case of a man's mind being twisted or deadened by the work. The kind of mind that does not like repetitive work does not have to stay in it.

> HENRY FORD, *My Life and Work* (Doubleday, 1922)

It's nice to make a product, take it all the way to completion, and have people like it. I get more strokes in one weekend in this business than I got in a year in the corporate world.

> DICK STARK, winemaker and owner of Page Mill Winery, quoted in the *New York Times,* October 7, 1993

You can be a great success in business but if you have unhappy children, you haven't made it.

> JANE HIRSCH, CEO of Copley Pharmaceutical, a division of Hoechst Celanese, quoted in the *New York Times,* October 17, 1993

I wasn't fulfilled.

> ADRIENNE GLASGOW, who had been manager of International Finance at Borden and treasurer of Reeves International by age 35, and who quit her family firm to become a consultant, quoted in *Fortune,* September 18, 1995

Suddenly women know what men have known all along; work takes a lot of time; work isn't always a day at the beach.

> SHARON McGAVIN of the advertising agency Ogilvy and Mather, quoted in *Fortune,* September 18, 1995

The biggest change in the workplace of the future will be the widespread realization that having one idiot boss is a much higher risk than having many idiot clients.

> SCOTT ADAMS, creator of the cartoon strip *Dilbert,* quoted in the *New York Times,* August 31, 1997

The company's recent reorganization has left me with no work to do and no access even to regular management reports. I am but 30, and want still to contribute and achieve.

> STEVE JOBS's resignation letter, quoted in *Time,* September 30, 1985

Most of us love what we do and none of us would trade our right to do it. But we don't like the way business works. We are increasingly sick of the petty politics, the unmanageable workloads. We are tired of working harder and harder with less satisfaction. We want to work more humanely, with more respect, recognition, and flexibility.

> ELIZABETH PERLE McKENNA, *When Work Doesn't Work Anymore* (Delacorte Press, 1997)

You bet, but is this different from how many men feel?

> CAROL TAVRIS, social psychologist, reacting to McKenna's statement in the *New York Times Book Review,* September 7, 1997

This market is so steady, so solid, so consistent. It's like death and taxes, only much more fun.

> WILLIAM BONDLOW, publisher of *Globe Communications Bridal Guide,* quoted in the *New York Times,* June 23, 1991

I hope people will focus on the fact that I've been with the company 22 years, and I hope that people might say, "Isn't it great that she could work so hard and make such a contribution to her company?"

Every time you would miss a child's birthday, or a school concert, or a parent-teacher discussion, you'd feel the tug.

> BRENDA BARNES, who resigned as head of Pepsico's North American beverage business to spend more time with her family, quoted in the *New York Times,* September 25, 1997

In a 1990 *Los Angeles Times* survey of 1,000 families. . . . 57 percent of fathers and 55 percent of mothers reported feeling guilty that they spent too little time with their children.

> ARLIE RUSSELL HOCHSCHILD, *The Time Bind: When Work Becomes Home and Home Becomes Work* (Metropolitan, 1997)

A job is to a woman as a wife is to a man.

> Woman quoted by Grace Baruch, psychologist, in Arlie Russell Hochschild, *The Time Bind: When Work Becomes Home and Home Becomes Work* (Metropolitan, 1997)

44.5 INCENTIVE COMPENSATION

The CEO of General Dynamics must be the laziest man in the world. Look at all the incentive plans they have to give him to go to work.

> GRAEF S. CRYSTAL, the country's most prominent expert on executive compensation (he teaches an executive compensation course known as Greed 259A at the University of California, Berkeley), quoted in the *New York Times,* February 2, 1992

Incentive pay is toxic because it is open to favoritism and manipulation.

> PAT LANCASTER, chairman of the packaging company Lantech, quoted in *Fortune,* November 30, 1995

Do rewards work? The answer depends on what we mean by "work." Research suggests that by and large, rewards succeed at securing one thing only: temporary compliance. When it comes to producing lasting changes in attitudes and behavior, however, rewards, like punishment, are strikingly ineffective. Once the rewards run out, people revert to their old behaviors.

The surest way to destroy cooperation and, therefore, organizational excellence is to force people to compete for rewards or recognition or to rank them against each other.

Promising a reward to someone who appears unmotivated is a bit like offering salt water to a someone who is thirsty. Bribes in the workplace can't work.

> ALFIE KOHN, "Why Incentive Plans Cannot Work," *Harvard Business Review,* September–October 1993

People are a liability. They see us as a temporary stopping-off point. Now we give our drivers money for driving safely, which used to be a given. It's a positive-reinforcement environment; you have to keep throwing out the candy.

> Service-firm owner in North Carolina, quoted in *Inc.,* October 1996

LTIP [long-term incentive plans] were meant to be the cure for the disease of pay that wasn't warranted by performance. The conclusion is that the cure is worse than the disease.

> ANN SIMPSON, joint managing director of Pensions and Investment Research Consultants (PIRC), U.K., quoted in the *Financial Times,* September 19, 1997

I don't feel like an owner. But I do feel like a partner.

> GUILLERMO CASTILLO, Mexican-born farmworker for McKay Nursery Company, which created a stock ownership plan to attract new seasonal workers, quoted in the *New York Times,* June 26, 1997 (Over 30 years, each worker is expected to amass $100,000.)

I've never heard of giving stock to migrants. I think it's fantastic.

> DOUG BLAYLOCK, administrator of the United Farm Workers Union pension plan, quoted in the *New York Times,* June 26, 1997

In many cases, employers are still thinking "a fair day's pay for a fair day's work," while employees are thinking of bonuses, stock ownership, and creative development opportunity.

> Report by TOWERS PERRIN, quoted in the *Financial Times,* October 3, 1997

44.6 MOTIVATION

Business is the crudest science, the coldest art. It teaches endless lessons in performance measurements, quality checks, profit and loss, but next to nothing about why people give their lives to their jobs, and what it means to do so.

> JOHN A. BYRNE, *The Whiz Kids* (Doubleday, 1993)

Why is KITA [kick in the ass] not motivation? If I kick my dog (from the front or the back), he will move. And when I want him to move again, what must I do? I must kick him again. Similarly, I can charge a man's battery, and then recharge it, and recharge it again. But it is only when he has his own generator that we can talk about motivation. He then needs no outside stimulation. He wants to do it.

> PROFESSOR FREDERICK HERZBERG of Case Western Reserve University, *Harvard Business Review,* January–February 1968

Some employees will be yours forever if you pat them on the head twice a week—with sincerity, assuming you think they deserve it.

> CHARLES DWYER, director and senior research analyst at the Management and Behavioral Science Center at the Wharton School of the University of Pennsylvania, quoted in *U.S. News & World Report,* January 23, 1984

What many people don't appreciate is that fear of failure is one of the greatest positive motivators in business. If you aren't afraid to fail, then you probably don't care enough about success.

> MARK H. McCORMACK, *What They Don't Teach You at Harvard Business School* (Bantam Doubleday Dell, 1988)

We've replaced the concept of having a job with the concept of having a mission.

> JOHN MEYERS of Shenandoah Life Insurance Company, quoted in *U.S. News & World Report,* September 2, 1985

I'm not in baseball for fun or ego. This is a business and I operate it like one.

> GEORGE STEINBRENNER, owner of the New York Yankees, quoted in *Time,* July 29, 1985

If you're a mountain climber, you want to climb Mt. Everest. If you're a flavor chemist, you want to make the perfect chocolate.

> PHILLIP J. CARPASSO of the spice company McCormick, quoted in the *Wall Street Journal,* February 5, 1985

Competitive people, the kind of people that it takes to build a world-class organization, want to know what their company is trying to excel at.

People simply work harder and smarter when they believe their jobs are at stake, not just the company's earnings-per-share records.

> PROFESSOR ANDRALL E. PEARSON of Harvard Business School and formerly of PepsiCo and McKinsey & Co, *Harvard Business Review,* May–June 1992

Look, we're like a baseball team. We strike out sometimes. We have bad days. But our goal is to get to the playoffs every year. And we do.

> TERRY SEMEL, president of the film company Warner Brothers, quoted in the *New York Times,* July 5, 1992

Successful people get to the point where they don't feel valuable unless they're leaping tall buildings in a single bound.

> ANN McGEE-COOPER, *You Don't Have to Go Home from Work Exhausted*

I tend to discount immediately what we have accomplished. Once you know you have a drug or it is coming along, you really want to get on with the next big thing. After all, what's more exciting than trying to do something that's never been done before?

> ROY VAGELOS, CEO of the pharmaceutical firm Merck, quoted in *Time*, February 22, 1988

When self-confident people see a good idea, they love it.

> JOHN F. WELCH JR., CEO of GE, quoted in *Fortune*, December 13, 1993

When you ask children what they want to be when they grow up, they don't say, "I want a boring job where the only thing I look forward to is Friday."

> LAWRENCE PERLMAN, CEO of the information and defense electronics firm Ceridian Corporation, quoted in the *Christian Science Monitor*, December 20, 1994

[W]e became aware long ago that among technical people, as among educators and physicians, the desire to be identified with outstanding professional accomplishments often overshadows all other considerations, even monetary demands. Engineers, we knew, had to be given the opportunity to talk about their successes with their peers—which is to say with other engineers and scientists.

> JOHN H. DESSAUER, *My Years with Xerox: The Billions Nobody Wanted* (Doubleday, 1971)

Nothing defines human beings better than their willingness to do irrational things in the pursuit of phenomenally unlikely payoffs. This is the principle behind lotteries, dating, and religion. You can use this quirk of human nature to your advantage and it won't cost you a dime.

> SCOTT ADAMS, *The Dilbert Principle* (HarperCollins, 1996)

There is no greater drive in human existence than ego gratification.

> GEORGE NADOFF, franchise maven who built Boston Chicken, *Inc.*, November 1995

He's decided to build the greatest financial services company in the history of this country and in the history of the world.

> JOSEPH A. CALIFANO, member of Travelers board, on Travelers CEO Sanford I. Weill's intention to merge Salomon Brothers with Smith Barney, quoted in the *New York Times*, September 25, 1997

I love the factory. That's what business is all about. Making things. Not this Wall Street stuff, not this lawyer stuff. None of that adds value. You gotta make something.

> SCOTT McNEALY, CEO of the computer firm Sun Microsystems, quoted in *Fortune*, October 13, 1997

I've always been fearful that I'd end up in an industry like the railroads when they sneered at airplane travel.

> MICHAEL EISNER, CEO of Disney, quoted in the *New Yorker*, October 20 & 27, 1997

44.7 RETIREMENT

I have a belief that if you keep working, you'll last longer, and I just want to keep vertical. I'd hate to spend the rest of my life trying to outwit an 18-inch fish.

> HAROLD GENEEN, CEO of the conglomerate ITT, in a 1984 interview, quoted in his obituary in the *New York Times*, November 23, 1997

Only a very small minority of workers have any interest in continuing to work full time beyond age 65 or age 70. If workers can retire, they will.

> DALLAS SALISBURY, president of Employees Benefits Research Institute, quoted in *U.S. News & World Report*, August 19, 1985

Golf became boring, tennis was no fun, sailing was boring. I decided to go back to work.

> LOU PURMONT, who had retired in 1981 after selling U.S. Filter Company for $20 million and in 1986 at age 56 started American Toxxic Control, quoted in *Forbes*, July 27, 1987

80 percent—rate of increased risk of heart attack after retirement.

> Cited in *Forbes*, July 27, 1987

I could wax for a half-hour on the utter folly of people being forced to retire at the age of 65. I think I have produced better results in the last five years than in any other five-year period. The refinement that comes from contemplating your own mistakes and improving yourself has continued.

> PHILIP FISHER, "investment philosopher," age 80, quoted in *Forbes,* October 19, 1987

If I was a billionaire, I'd work. I intend to die in my chair.

> COLLEEN C. BARRETT, number two executive at Southwest Airlines and the highest-ranking woman in airline industry, quoted in *Fortune,* November 30, 1995

When I lose my fire, I'll go.

> BERNIE MARCUS, cofounder and CEO of Home Depot, quoted in *Fortune,* March 4, 1996

My son came to me last year and wanted to borrow the keys to the car. I didn't even know he drove.

> Retiring executive, explaining to Charles Wang of Computer associates why he was retiring, recounted in interview in Rama Dev Jager, *In the Company of Giants* (McGraw-Hill, 1997)

I no longer owned the business. It owned me.

> MEL ZIEGLER, founder of Banana Republic, who left the company five years after selling it to The Gap because he was tired of the demands of corporate life, quoted in *Inc.,* February 1994

You know you're in trouble when you need a Cray supercomputer to arrange your free time.

> PETER LYNCH, legendary manager of Fidelity Magellan mutual fund, quoted in *Inc.,* February 1994

Now your limo is yellow and your driver speaks Swahili.

> Retired New York City executive, quoted in the *New York Times,* April 25, 1993

You do wonder if the phone will ever ring again, but it's for about 20 minutes.

> WALTER WRISTON, former CEO of Citicorp, quoted in the *New York Times,* April 25, 1993

You stop being on the "A" list; your calls don't get returned. It's not just less fawning—people could care less about you in some cases. The king is dead. Long live the king.

> DAVID MAHONEY, former CEO of Norton Simon, quoted in the *New York Times,* April 25, 1993

44.8 THE WORK ETHIC

Mankind is as lazy as it dares to be.

> RALPH WALDO EMERSON, quoted by Edward Atkinson, *The Industrial Progress of the Nation* (1890)

Work is the curse of the drinking classes.

> OSCAR WILDE

Hard work never killed anybody, but why take a chance?

> EDGAR BERGEN, comedian and ventriloquist, quoted by Harold Geneen, former chairman of ITT, with Brent Bowers, *The Synergy Myth* (St. Martin's, 1997)

On this kid's first day of work [in 1969], we got a good cast going. Then some hydraulic valves blew off the machine. This kid straddled a hot billet of steel—he stood with his legs apart over a piece of red-hot steel coming out of the caster—and he held the broken hydraulic hoses together with his hands. I was terrified he would burn himself. The hoses blew apart again, and he got hydraulic fluid in his eyes. We took him down to wash his eyes out, and he turned to me and said, "This is the best job I ever had!"

> KEN IVERSON, CEO of the steel company Nucor, quoted in the *New Yorker,* February 25, 1991

I feel almost predestined to run General Electric. I know it's like training for the Olympics. You may never make it, but you want to aspire to something.

If I work less than 60 hours a week, I have a twinge of guilt.

> DEBORAH A. COLEMAN of Apple Computers, quoted in *Business Week,* November 10, 1986

Breakfast is the dinner of champions.

> Anonymous executive, heard on National Public Radio

I am sure Michael Eisner [CEO of Disney] works hard, probably harder than a guard or a technician in the Magic Kingdom, though maybe not harder than a chambermaid in the Ramada Inn. Really, though, how hard should you have to work for a billion dollars? In 1974, the average CEO was paid 35 times more than his lowest-ranking employee; now the average compensation at the top is 150 times the wages on the factory floor.

> RICHARD TODD, quoted in *Worth,* December–January 1995

Recently, one guy said, "Well, I don't care if I'm going to limit my potential; I've gone as far as I want to anyway." I said, "No, no, you've got it wrong. You have to keep growing to stay where you are."

> LAWRENCE A. BOSSIDY, CEO of the industrial firm Allied-Signal, interviewed in *Harvard Business Review,* March–April 1995

By working faithfully eight hours a day, you may eventually get to be a boss and work twelve hours a day.

> ROBERT FROST, American poet

If you don't work 12 hours a day, you're behind. If you don't read 100 trade magazines, don't check your e-mail, don't return somebody's call, or don't go to a developer event, you're behind. Either you're committed or you're not.

> ANN WINBLAD, software venture capitalist and former girlfriend of Bill Gates, quoted in *Wired,* September 1996

You can take people like myself who came from a very poor background, with only a high school education, and if you're willing to work yourself nearly to death and risk everything you have, you can succeed.

> SUE SZYMCZECH, founder and CEO of Safeway Sling, makers of nylon and polyester slings used on cranes, quoted in *Inc.,* September 1996

After I got tenure at MIT I got bored and quit. My wife thought I was crazy.

> MICHAEL HAMMER, author of *Reengineering the Corporation* and *Beyond Reengineering,* quoted in the *Wall Street Journal,* November 26, 1996

If a piece of paper is on my desk, I'm not doing my job.

> MATTHEW STEVENSON of Bank of New York–Inter Maritime Bank, Geneva, in a conversation, 1996

Every day I put on this uniform, just like an NBA [National Basketball Association] player.

> THONG LEE, bartender for 16 years at the Seattle Marriott, quoted in *Business Week,* November 11, 1996

You have no idea what it's like to go from dependence to independence,

> RHONDA TAYLOR, one of 14 welfare recipients, some of them homeless, graduating from Marriott International Inc.'s welfare-to-work program, quoted in the *Wall Street Journal,* October 31, 1996

Even if we did not need to work, most people would choose to do so. Few have the inner resources to function well in a life without appointed tasks.

> PROFESSOR RICHARD B. McKENZIE of Clemson University, quoted in *Forbes,* July 13, 1987

European royalty have become dinosaurs. But, in Asia, members of royal families have been very conscious that unless they are able to find some means of maintaining their lifestyle, they will lose out.

> KHOO KAY KIM of the University of Malaya, quoted in *Asia, Inc.,* May 1997

I've got a lot of sympathy for people where a sudden change catches them. But I've always liked bird dogs better than kennel-fed dogs myself—you know, one who'll get out and hunt for food rather than sit on his fanny and yell.

> CHARLES E. WILSON, ex-boss of General Motors and secretary of defense in the Eisenhower administration, in U.S. Senate hearings before the Committee on Armed Services, January 15, 1953

Only after 20 years did my wife tell me that she was hurt when I told her my job was my number one priority and my family was number two. I'm not sure I even remember having said it, but I'm sure I did.

> Top manager, quoted in Arlie Russell Hochschild, *The Time Bind: When Work Becomes Home and Home Becomes Work* (Metropolitan, 1997)

I gave up screwing around a long time ago. I came to the conclusion that sex is a sublimation of the work instinct.

> DAVID LODGE, British novelist, *Small World* (Viking, 1984)

44.9 WORKER ANXIETY

We are suffering, not from the rheumatics of old age, but from the growing pains of over-rapid changes, from the painfulness of readjustment between one economic period and another. The increase of technical efficiency has been taking place faster than we can deal with the problem of labor absorption.

> JOHN MAYNARD KEYNES, 1930

The psychological consequences of a frayed white collar can be ugly.

> RICHARD M. HUBER, *The American Idea of Success* (McGraw-Hill, 1971)

Most people I know would rather work in a barn than in a modern office.

> BILL STUMPF, office furniture designer, anticipating by a decade the backlash against "open-environment," cubicle-based office design, quoted in the *Wall Street Journal,* January 9, 1985

The new culture is to keep your nose clean and your bags packed. The moral that people see around them is, if you fall in love with your company, you're going to get burned.

> PROFESSOR PAUL HIRSCH of the University of Chicago Graduate School of Business, quoted in *Time,* February 16, 1987

The so-called security of a regular paycheck is an illusion anyway. Either you're answering what the market needs or you're not. If you're not, you're doomed, whether you're in an office at IBM or an office in your basement.

> JODY SEVERSON, business consultant, quoted in *Inc.,* January 1994

. . . Anyone who puts job security at the top of his or her list of perks should be working for the government, not in a growing company.

> GEOFFREY JONES, writer, in a letter to the editor, *Inc.,* October 1994

I don't believe any jobs are secure anymore. People in remote locations make decisions that drop the bottom out of the whole job market. That's true no matter what job you have. Somebody somewhere else can kill it . . . I hate it.

> Limousine dispatcher, quoted in Rosabeth Moss Kanter, *World Class: Thriving Locally in the Global Economy* (Simon & Schuster, 1995)

The discontinuities that so many current management practices introduce into people's lives may not drive them mad, but they do encourage them to keep their résumés up to date and their commitments to their employers minimal.

> HOWARD H. STEVENSON and MIHNEA C. MOLDOVEANU, "The Power of Predictability," *Harvard Business Review,* July–August 1995

No. 1, don't set rules that stress people crazily. No. 2, if you do set goals that stretch them or stress them crazily, don't punish failure. No. 3, if you're going to ask them to do what they never have done, give them whatever tools and help you can.

> STEVE KERR of GE, quoted in *Fortune,* November 30, 1995

If employees have reason to believe that they will be dumped on the street if managers don't like their proposals, they will be less likely to step forward in the first place.

> WILLIAM F. O'BRIEN, CEO of Starlight Telecommunications, *Harvard Business Review,* November–December 1995

While the recent outcry over downsizing has underscored the human cost of global competition, worker backlash was never really about the sad tale of the victims. [W]e have argued all along that the potential trigger was the real wage stagnation of the survivors—those who remained on the job in offices and factories in tough competitive times but who have been rewarded at a rate that has far lagged their productivity contribution.

> *U.S. Investment Research,* Morgan Stanley, September 13, 1996

A boss who can guarantee a job for life is like a doctor who promises that you'll never get sick or a preacher who promises you a place in heaven.

> ROBERT J. EATON, CEO of Chrysler Corporation, in a speech, March 18, 1996

The trouble is, you are what you do. If you are unemployed, what are you?

> EDOARDO LEONCARALLO, architect, quoted in *Fortune,* March 8, 1993

Middle management is middle-aged, and we're scared.

> MARGEY HILLMAN, director of multimedia programs for an educational software firm in San Diego, quoted in *Fortune,* October 4, 1993

I don't think change is stressful. I think failure is stressful.

> BOB STEARNS of the computer firm Compaq, quoted in *Fortune,* February 21, 1994

These are people who are scared to death of being bored . . .

Today students frequently arrive at business school already turned off by a new Darwinism at large corporations.

> MAURY HANIGAN, recruitment consultant, quoted in *Fortune,* February 20, 1995

The question is not how insecure temping is but how secure is full-time employment these days? The gap between the two is narrowing.

> RICHARD M. ROGERS, author of *Temping: The Insider's Guide* (Arco, 1996), quoted in the *Wall Street Journal,* February 18, 1997

America doesn't want throwaway workers. People don't have part-time children or part-time mortgages.

> RON CAREY, former president of the International Brotherhood of Teamsters, during 1997 strike, quoted in the *New York Times,* August 24, 1997

The people who bounce back are people who believe "my problem is temporary, related to the particular situation I'm in, and it's not my fault." Pessimists, who generally don't come back, see their failure as permanent, pervasive, their fault.

> MARTIN SELIGMAN, professor of psychology at the University of Pennsylvania, who has done "optimism studies" of workers in 30 industries, *Fortune,* May 1, 1995

Capitalism is getting meaner.

> ALAN BLINDER, former vice chairman of the Federal Reserve Board and Princeton University economist, on job insecurity as factor in keeping wages and inflation down, quoted in the *Wall Street Journal,* December 16, 1996

Homicide is the number three work-related cause of death behind car crashes and machinery accidents. The leading cause of death in the workplace is foul play. Since 1980 41 percent of females who died on the job were murdered.

> *Business Week,* July 11, 1994

The past decade has seen a nearly tenfold increase in the number of workplace homicides nationwide. The incidence of murder now approaches—and for women even exceeds—that of fatal on-the-job accidents.

> DR. MARTIN BLINDER, psychiatrist, quoted in the *Wall Street Journal,* February 10, 1997

INDEX OF NAMES